# Essential Theories of Counseling and Psychotherapy

## EVERYDAY PRACTICE IN OUR DIVERSE WORLD

# Essential Theories of Counseling and Psychotherapy

EVERYDAY PRACTICE IN OUR DIVERSE WORLD

Carlos Zalaquett, Allen Ivey, and
Mary Bradford Ivey

cognella® | ACADEMIC PUBLISHING

Bassim Hamadeh, CEO and Publisher
Alia Bales, Associate Production Editor
Jess Estrella, Senior Graphic Designer
Alexa Lucido, Licensing Associate
Don Kesner, Interior Designer
Natalie Piccotti, Senior Marketing Manager
Kassie Graves, Vice President of Editorial
Jamie Giganti, Director of Academic Publishing

Cover image copyright © iStockphoto LP/ilbusca.

Printed in the United States of America

ISBN: 978-1-5165-1428-1 (pbk) / 978-1-5165-1562-2 (br) / 978-1-5165-4632-9 (al)

# Contents

## Chapter 8: Behavioral Therapy and Counseling: Behavioral Foundations of Change

## Chapter 13: Toward an Integrated Counseling and Psychotherapy....... 425

# Preface

Counseling and psychotherapy work. Our relationship with clients makes a difference and enriches people's lives. Its healing practices will facilitate:

- individuals, couples, families, and groups to enhance their quality of life and well-being
- improve relationships with others
- navigate job-related demands
- reduce symptoms of mental disorders
- deal effectively with stress, which underlies most interpersonal issues
- change personality, enhance self esteem and self-efficacy

Joined with counseling and psychotherapy theory are multicultural and social justice awareness, knowledge, skills, and actions that will enable you to reach clients of all ages who come to you with vast individual differences. You can make a significant difference.

*Essential Theories of Counseling and Psychotherapy: Everyday Practice in Our Diverse World* is a textbook designed to help you start the process of learning about counseling and psychotherapy theories and applying these practices into our diverse world. This book is for use in undergraduate and graduate courses in counselor education, psychology, rehabilitation counseling, human services, mental health, and social work. It discusses the traditional forces of counseling and therapy, such as psychodynamic, behavioral, existential-humanistic, cognitive, and multicultural, as well as new developments in the field, such as motivational interviewing, solution focus, and acceptance and commitment. Also highlighted throughout are the microskills, the building blocks of effective counseling and psychotherapy, the importance of learning more than one theory, and the factors common to all.

This book shows how to apply abstract theory to concrete practice. Through the readings and activities infused in each chapter, students will be able to grasp major theoretical ideas, use research findings, and construct interventions in a culturally and gender-sensitive fashion. Strongly integrated within each chapter is a multicultural approach to counseling and therapy. Each theory is viewed with respect to its past and its progression toward new multicultural frameworks to the helping process.

Our ultimate goal is to empower students and professionals so they can take complex theories into action in our diverse world. We seek to facilitate students' learning of main theories and practices and how original theoretical formulations are combined with newer ones. Reflection and applied exercises, theory application examples, and case demonstrations are used to reinforce student learning.

Throughout this book, we have attempted to show how the integrity of traditional theory can be enhanced through increased multicultural awareness. Learning about counseling and psychotherapy from an awareness of cultural and social issues helps counselors and therapists become more critical and active in learning how to apply theory-based interventions with sensitivity to the diversity of the clients they serve. Neuroscience findings show that these methods change the mind and the brain. Family methods are especially appropriate supplements to the traditional one-on-one counseling. We argue that individual therapy and counseling without awareness of systems and family issues is incomplete. Developmental counseling and therapy offers an integrative paradigm for other theories while also providing specific assessment and treatment skills.

Our emphasis is on worldview, multiple perspectives, and the need for each counselor or therapist to generate his or her own integrative construction of counseling and therapy. Our teaching and learning working with theorists, educators, students, therapists, and social systems moved us from searching for the "best" therapy. We advocate for each theory presented. We believe that each theory has some value for most clients and, thus, find that integrating two or more theories simultaneously in the session can be helpful to clients.

We think of this book as a new reading of traditional material. Each time we work through the writings of such giants as Freud, Horney, Rogers, Frankl, Pearls, and Skinner, we come away more deeply impressed by their wisdom and the value of their contributions. At the same time, more modern theorists such as Beck, Satir, Meichenbaum, Ellis, and the authoritative writings of the family therapists, multiculturalists, and neuroscientists have enriched the basic legacy.

Enjoy the journey. We look forward to your comments and reactions to this book. And, again, we will listen and do our best to engage in a mutual process of reconstructing our views of counseling and psychotherapy.

# Acknowledgments

We acknowledge and thank the many people who have helped this book become a reality. First, we'd like to acknowledge those who contributed to the foundational knowledge on which this book was built. We offer special appreciation and thanks to six scholars who have been central in defining and expanding multicultural/social justice theory and practice: Patricia Arrendondo, Harold Cheatham, Eduardo Duran, Thomas Parham, Paul Pedersen, and Derald Wing Sue. In addition, we are grateful to Aaron Beck, Evelyn Brooks, Donald Cheek, Michael D'Andrea, Judy Daniels, Albert Ellis, Viktor Frankl, Machiko Fukuhara, Peter Geiger, Oscar Gonçalves, Sunny Hansen, Fran Howe, Maurice Howe, Leon Mann, William Matthews, Robert Marx, Donald Meichenbaum, John Norcross, Sandra Rigazio-DiGilio, Koji Tamase, Bruce Taub-Bynum, Beth Sulzer-Azaroff, and Stephen Weinrach.

We are indebted to Rhea Banerjee, Taylor Bigelow, Aubrey Daniels, Kellie Forziat, Angélica Galván, Elizabeth Gilfillan, and Dogukan Ulupinar, doctoral students at The Pennsylvania State University for their chapter reviews. They provided a fresh critique of content and activities and ensured students understanding of content and activities. We are particularly grateful to Kellie Forziat for her efforts to ensure quality of chapters. Finally, we thank Kassie Graves, editor at Cognella Academic Publishing. Her patience and support were endless and are truly appreciated. Leah Sheets, associate editor, provided sustained support during this process. Jeanine Rees, our production editor, was a joy to work with and Marcy Gamber provided helpful editing for each chapter. We look forward to collaborating with them in future books. Dani Skeen and Jessie Estrella served as consultants for color choice on this book and marketing materials, and we appreciate their skillful advice.

# Instructor Manual, Test Bank, and PowerPoint© Slides

This book is supplemented by an instructor manual, test bank, and PowerPoint slides available from the publisher, Cognella Academic Publishing.

# PART I

# Foundational Theories of Counseling and Therapy

F oundational to counseling and psychotherapy are theories that focus on essential underlying dimensions of the helping process. These theories, discussed in Part I, have the following dimensions in common:

1. A belief in multiple approaches to the helping process.

    Each of the chapters presents a specific theoretical and practical orientation and also stresses the need to incorporate ideas from other theories into counseling and clinical practice.

2. An emphasis on multicultural and social justice issues.

    Each theoretical framework gives attention to issues related to client diversity and the social justice issues impacting them. It is important to support older theories as they become more culturally relevant. Advocacy skills complement interventions when needed.

3. An ability to operate as a separate and distinct helping theory.

    Each framework emphasizes usage. In addition, the ideas in each chapter provide a working set of theories and skills where counseling and therapy can be conducted.

4. An emphasis on those underlying processes believed important to all approaches to helping.

The counselor-client relationship is emphasized early and throughout the book, as it is the largest contributor to client change. Also, we believe that the empathic dimensions, listening skills, and developmental concepts are crucial to all forms of helping.

5. A reliance on research.

Evidence-based treatments and relationships inform of what it is known to work for clients. Newer neuroscience advances provide additional support for treatments. Research honoring both the evidence base of developing relationships and working alliance is integrated in each chapter, as well as evidence that our interventions do lead to change. We encourage you to apply what we know works to improve the therapeutic relationship across theories to positively impact their therapeutic outcome.

This information, combined with your clinical experience, your client's characteristics and preferences, and the cultural system provide the basis of evidence-based counseling and therapy.

The chapters in this part focus on six foundational theoretical and practical frameworks. Chapter 1 offers the basics of theory concepts and illustrates their importance. Chapter 2 explores your reasons for becoming a counselor or therapist and your views of the counseling process. Ways to become an intentional therapist and maintain positive lifestyles for stress management and wellness are reviewed. Chapter 3 presents the basis of empathic theory that emphasizes each client as a unique individual who is intimately involved in the family experience. The family, in turn, is the primary place where culture is learned.

All counselors and therapists, whether they work at the individual, family, or multicultural level, use specific interviewing skills, known as microskills and discussed in Chapter 4. However, different cultural groups tend to use the skills differently. In addition, the major historical forces of counseling and therapy can be considered from a skills perspective. Multicultural counseling and therapy (MCT) is discussed in Chapter 5. MCT points out that all theory is generated within a cultural context. This chapter provides information on universal and focused approaches to MCT, cultural identity theory, and some examples of interviewing practice from this frame of reference.

Person's development can be considered a main goal of counseling and psychotherapy. Developmental counseling and therapy (DCT) is presented in Chapter 6 as an integrative model that is helpful in assessing client cognitive and emotional processes, matching interviewing style to client needs, and generating treatment plans.

The concepts presented in these chapters will prepare you to look to the future and integrate the complex precepts of the major traditional theoretical forces in psychotherapy and counseling discussed in the book.

### CHAPTER 1

# Welcome to the World of Theories

## A Worldview of Theories, Research, and Practitioners

---

### CHAPTER GOALS

Counseling and psychotherapy theory, practice, and research have become increasingly more sophisticated and effective. Research has confirmed that the *talk cure* is, overall, an effective treatment, with fewer side effects and lower number of relapses. In cases such as anxiety and depression, it is as effective as, or more effective than, pharmacological treatments (American Psychological Association, 2012; Gratzer & Goldbloom, 2016; Lewis & Lewis, 2016).

The field has begun to integrate multicultural, gender, and social justice issues into the core of our counseling practices. Neuroscience has demonstrated that counseling produces changes in brain circuits similar to those ascribed to pharmacological treatments. Specific interventions have been developed to assist with crises and disasters affecting our daily living. Counseling and psychotherapy are now fully integrated into the fabric of our societies (Chung & Bemak, 2012; Chung et al., 2016; Ivey, Ivey, & Zalaquett, 2018).

Mental health professionals, students-in-training, supervisors, and educators from a variety of disciplines draw from the theories of counseling and psychotherapy presented in this book. They do so to become effective helpers. The ultimate goal of this altruistic group of professionals is to help others cope successfully with challenges, learn to value themselves and others, develop resiliency, achieve cultural sensitivity, establish positive relationships, make meaning of life, achieve happiness, and become good citizens who positively contribute to their diverse society. At the same time, medicine, law, business, and other professions constantly depend on counseling ideas for their work.

## GOALS FOR THIS BOOK AND CHAPTER

This is a book about theories of counseling and psychotherapy. It is also a book about you—the person who will be applying these theories to help others. There are many possible alternatives for helping clients. Between 500 to 1,000 theoretical and therapeutic schools, procedures, and outcome measures are competing for your attention (Prochaska & Norcross, 2018; Meier, 2016). Needless to say, this book cannot consider them all, but experience has revealed that many have something to contribute.

This book will introduce you to the most popular and tested counseling and psychotherapy theories. These theories offer different understandings of how difficulties with daily living, stress, and psychological disorders develop; and how these challenges can be resolved. These conceptual understandings of clients' issues and how they are best resolved lay the foundations of what is called a helper's *theoretical orientation*.

The major task of this book for you is to (a) define your own worldview and competencies, (b) find your own theory or set of theories, and (c) develop your theoretical orientation to counseling and therapeutic practice as you explore the many available in the counseling and mental health fields.

Major goals of this book and chapter are to:

1. Review the importance of theories and their central role in articulating counseling and psychotherapy models and interventions.

2. Recognize the *variety of existing theories* of counseling and psychotherapy and the value of learning many.

3. Give special attention to the *practitioner-scientist model* and consider how research and data relate to the daily practice of counseling and psychotherapy.

4. Emphasize *ethics*, as all our helping interventions rest on a moral base. Effective practice is ethical practice.

5. Highlight how *neuroscience* supports counseling practices. Current biological and neuroscientific research is confirming much of what mental health professionals do.

6. Utilize *evidence-based counseling and psychotherapy to bring theory into practice*. Evidence-based treatments and evidence-based relationship

factors increase counselors' effectiveness. Evidence for effective practice comes from years of research and clinical testing.

*There is nothing so practical as a good theory.*

—**Albert Einstein and Kurt Lewin**

## AN INITIAL REFLECTION

As soon as class started, one of our students asked why most books on theories do not provide an explanation of what theories are good for or what made them so practical. Either by yourself or with a classmate, write down the reasons you believe counseling and psychotherapy theories are important. How are they different from common sense? Why are they practical? Compare your responses with ours, presented below.

Understanding the role of theories will increase your enthusiasm for learning them, identifying their role in the helping process, formulating your own views of helping, and establishing your theoretical orientation.

Theories of counseling and psychotherapy differ from common sense in many ways. Counseling and psychotherapy are formal fields of academic study, research, and practice. From a common sense point of view, counseling is a way to understand everyday experiences and act appropriately. Theories involve the use of qualitative and quantitative research, and statistical analysis; common sense does not. Theories tend to be internally consistent; common sense often relies on contradictory statements (e.g., "Birds of a feather flock together" and "Opposites attract.") Good theories are grounded in facts; common sense is not necessarily consistent with facts.

Furthermore, theories summarize, explain, and organize facts; suggest novel ways to look at events; are parsimonious (use few principles to explain many behaviors or situations); provide operational definitions of key concepts under study; and make specific predictions that are testable. Common sense relies on lay descriptions of key concepts that are used to make basic judgments and predictions. Such judgments and predictions are hard to test because they are commonly stated in vague and inconsistent terms.

Theories of counseling and psychotherapy provide a consistent *map* or framework for understanding what is going on with the client and how we can help them. This is a process known as conceptualizing client issues, establishing goals, formulating a plan to change thoughts and behaviors, and improve action (Halbur & Halbur, 2015).

A brief description of the role of theories is presented in Table 1.1.

**Table 1.1. Role of Theories**

1.  *Theories provide a map, framework, or worldview of our many and differing clients.* This map helps us organize and make sense of human experience, the complex environment we live in, and the myriad of information we receive through virtual communication.

2.  *Counseling theories help understand clients' issues.* A counseling or psychotherapy theory provides a consistent map to summarize, understand, and explain challenges, behaviors, interactions, and situations. Based on this framework, you can make sense of clients' experiential world. Furthermore, you can help clients understand their issues and clarify goals.

3.  *Counseling theories guide action.* Equipped with a consistent framework, you can generate a plan of action to address client issues, proceed accordingly, and make corrections along the way. The idea of action is important as various theories actually have distinct and different action goals.

4.  *Counseling theories have accumulated evidence.* Theories have accumulated a research and/or clinical base large enough to suggest where they are most effective. Theories suggest best ways and procedures to help specific clients resolve their specific issues and challenges.

5.  *Counseling theories produce outcomes.* Application of learned theories and techniques will help clients achieve positive outcomes, as well as find other areas in need of further improvement.

6.  *Theories facilitate professional communication.* Theories allow for the sharing of ideas with other professionals about behaviors and events, the context in which they occur, and the cause for their occurrence.

7.  *Counseling theories cross-pollinate and integrate.* Many theories enrich their own maps with ideas drawn from other theories. They also attempt to integrate different theories into novel formulations.

8.  *Counseling theories will continue to improve and to be evaluated.* Continued formulations and research will expand our understanding of the effectiveness of theories for specific populations and issues.

9.  *Counseling theories learning is life-long.* Your efforts to help people will bring many satisfactions and challenges. You will feel compelled to learn better ways to apply your theories to resolve clients' specific issues, or to learn additional theories with demonstrated positive effects with those issues. Competent professionals typically engage in an ongoing process of learning and quality improvement.

Your theoretical framework provides a means to understand what you are doing. It is also helpful to explain to your client what you are doing and why you are doing it. Furthermore, it helps establish agreed-upon goals and best course of action to reach those goals. For example, a cognitive-behavioral counselor could identify a client's test anxiety as the result of negative thoughts related to fear of failure. The treatment goal would be to remove the negative thoughts to decrease anxiety and improve test performance. The plan of treatment would include techniques to change negative thoughts and improve behavior. There is a rationale behind theoretical action.

# Counseling and Psychotherapy Theories: A Real Multiplicity

Mental health professionals want to help those in need of counseling or psychotherapy. We have written this book to honor these helpers, many of whom are looking for clear, crisp rules and theories to know the "right" answer to really help others. Before we search the rulebook, let us review the following case.

A group of therapists was called in to diagnose the difficulties of an ailing young girl. Kayla was displaced from her home and family due to the impact of one of the largest hurricanes affecting her hometown. Six months later, she was still living apart from her family. Traditional shelter efforts to help her had failed, and she was deteriorating rapidly. "Perhaps counseling or therapy will help," thought the shelter director. Web pages and phone book pages were examined keenly, and four eminent therapists and counselors were called in for their expert advice.

The first therapist, a physician, noted the nonverbals of the girl and commented that Kayla looked very sad and was clearly suffering from depression; the doctor drew out a prescription pad for a popular medication. The second, a counselor in a community mental health clinic, noted that Kayla had lost weight, was refusing to eat, and diagnosed the youngster as having an eating disorder. "Medication isn't needed; rather, we need to teach Kayla social skills and help build self-esteem."

The third therapist, oriented to family, noted that Kayla had just experienced a major separation and was living alone for the first time. "Let's get Kayla's family together and work on the family system." A fourth counselor recognized the trouble immediately upon arriving at the shelter—"The culture of this place is all wrong. The young clients have no say in their own lives. Kayla was raised in an environment where young girls have some say. We need to rework this environment and make it more democratic before any treatment is going to be effective."

The director of the shelter was at first puzzled by the varying diagnoses and their varying prescriptions for treatment (individual talk therapy, medication, family therapy, and cultural change), but on reflection, realized all four professional helpers were right. Through implementing treatment using all dimensions, Kayla's depression was removed; the eating disorder and self-concept issues resolved; a new relationship with other young children facilitated; and the director learned how to allow Kayla and other children to participate more fully in the management of the shelter.

The competing therapists and counselors were surprised to learn that each of them had a useful answer! The shelter's director just smiled and said, "Thank you—I needed you all."

## REFLECTION EXERCISE

What do you think about Kayla's situation?

Which professional helper's technique resonated most with you and why?

What would you have done differently in this case?

Overall, what did you learn from Kayla's case?

> *There is nothing so practical as becoming competent in several theoretical approaches.*
>
> —Allen Ivey

As Kayla's case suggests, there are many counseling and therapy approaches for helping clients. Furthermore, as you define your own approach, you may need to learn additional counseling theories if you are to help major positive changes occur in clients and their families. Also important, will be to recruit the assistance of other professionals when necessary.

The complexity of our ever-changing world brings clients to counseling and therapy seeking answers to a wide array of issues and situations. These are the clients' stories. They share with us tales of their life challenges, their defeats, and, best of all, their triumphs. Our task is to listen and learn with them. If we are effective, their stories become more positive or they learn new ways to live with them. Clients can take their new knowledge into action in their tasks and relationships.

People experience the same event but may provide widely varying narratives of what they saw, heard, and felt. Multiple counseling and psychotherapy theories have been developed to address the diversity of clients' stories. Your task is to learn about these theories and develop an approach effective enough to help a wide variety of clients' stories. This book seeks to outline theories that provide relevant guidance for organizing the complexity of the varied clients you will encounter daily.

# Counseling and Psychotherapy:
# Personal Style, Influence, and Worldview

We are all in the same world, but each of us makes different sense of what we see. Take a moment to reflect on *Relativity* (Figure 1.1.)

---

**Figure 1.1. *Relativity* by M. C. Escher**

**REFLECTION EXERCISE**

*Relativity.* Where is your attention drawn?

Rotate the print—each new perspective offers a new meaning. As you focus on the characters, you may find yourself wondering, "Where are they going? What relation do these people moving in different directions have to each other? Why does the picture make as much sense when viewed upside-down or sideways?"

Discussing the meaning of *Relativity*, the Dutch artist, Escher (1960), focuses on two individuals located on the stairs at the top and center:

> ... two people are moving side by side and in the same direction, and yet one of them is going downstairs and the other upstairs. Contact between them is out of the question, because they live in different worlds and therefore have no knowledge of each other's existence (60, p. 15).

Counseling and therapy operate on the assumption that significant contact between client and counselor is possible. You, as a helper, counselor, or psychotherapist, are called on to show competence, creativity, and artistry in the way you observe and interact with your clients as they walk down life's path. If you can enter your clients' worlds for a time and join them on their journey, you may find a new understanding and respect for how their worlds are different from your own. Sometimes, simply validating your clients' alternative perceptions of reality may be all that is needed. Other clients may want to change direction, to find new perspectives and new ways of acting. In these cases, your task is more difficult because you will need to see their ways of thinking and being, to share yourself and your knowledge, and to work with them to seek new directions for the future.

This book is about joining the client's world and learning to respect ways of thinking and behaving that are different from your own. Counseling and psychotherapeutic theories are systematic ways of thinking that may help you expand both your own way of being and those of the clients you serve.

# Theoretical Orientation's Effect on Therapeutic Response

Your theoretical orientation influences what you say to those you are helping. Imagine that a client comes to you for help and says,

> My eight-year-old isn't doing well in school. It worries me. I never succeeded either. I hated school. My parents sometimes had to beat me to get me out of the door. But the same approach doesn't seem to work with him. Now I'm told by the school counselor that I'm being abusive and that they are going to file a complaint with youth services. They said that my child might be taken away unless I change. I don't want to be here. What are you going to do to help me?

## REFLECTION EXERCISE

How would you respond to this client? What feelings and thoughts are going through your mind as you think about this person? Take a moment to think about yourself, your gut feelings about a case of this type, and then write down your possible response. After you have written your response, compare and contrast your ideas with those presented in this section.

The first task in a case that involves potential and actual child abuse is to protect the child. This is both a legal and ethical issue. No matter what theory or worldview is used, protecting children and adult clients from harm is our first responsibility. Thus, careful assessment of the client's story is essential so that appropriate action may be taken. It is also vital that you consider the accuracy of the story and cultural attitudes toward the maltreatment of others.

Also important is to inform clients about confidentiality of the information provided and to address exceptions to confidentiality, before they start sharing their stories. Usually, clients are informed of their rights and limitations in verbal and written fashions. Furthermore, typically, clients read and sign the written form before or at the beginning of their first session.

Let us assume that your client was a child at risk for more physical abuse. You have listened and acted, and the child is now safe. You have been asked to counsel the accused perpetrator of violence. Following are some ways therapists of major theoretical orientations might approach this issue.

## The Psychodynamic Worldview

The psychodynamic worldview stresses that the past is often a prelude to the future. Research clearly indicates that those who abuse often suffer from abusive childhoods themselves. A psychodynamic counselor believes that clients have some sense of how their present actions relate to their past experience. A possible response from a psychodynamic professional might be:

> You say you were beaten by your own parents and now you find you are doing the same thing with your own child. It will take some time, but our goal is to find out how your past experiences are being reflected in your present behavior with your child. Let's start by you sharing some of your own thoughts and feelings of what happened to you during childhood.

## The Existential-Humanistic Worldview

The existential-humanistic worldview seeks to understand how the client makes sense of the world. Believing firmly in self-actualization, these therapists often listen to clients carefully in the belief that clients will ultimately find their own positive direction in life. Thus, the response of the existential-humanistic therapist might be:

> It sounds as if you are deeply troubled and angry about being here. At the same time, I hear that you desperately want to straighten things out. Am I hearing you accurately?

## The Behavioral Worldview

The behavioral worldview is more oriented to action and short-term treatment. Parent education, relaxation training, and stress management are some treatment techniques and strategies that might be used. The behavioral counselor will focus on antecedents and consequences of violent behavior, as well as short-term observable change, but will keep an eye to the future and work with the client for long-term maintenance of behavioral change. This counselor's response might be:

> There's a lot happening in your life. We'll be doing a lot of things in our time together. What I find most helpful as a beginning step is dealing with your personal frustration and issues of loss of self-control. We'll be working on how you behave to help you work with your child more effectively and to feel better about yourself. We'll start with some stress management techniques and then move on to look at some specifics of behavior.

## The Cognitive Worldview

The cognitive worldview asserts that the way you perceive and think about things is what promotes your feelings and behaviors. Assessment of cognitive patterns and information processing are the focus of treatment. Cognitive restructuring is typically used as treatment, but they combine this with other behavioral techniques such as relaxation. The cognitive counselor will focus on short-term observable change but will keep an eye on the underlying thoughts involved in the abusive situations in order to sustain change. The cognitive counselor's response might be:

> I sense that this situation and its pressure makes you very angry. And it is that very anger that seems to have led to the issues you now face. We'll spend time exploring what makes you angry. We'll be working on how you think and behave to help you change the way you see things and gain control over your violent behavior. We'll begin with a diary of daily events recording when you feel angry and what you do. We will follow this with a discussion of your thoughts during those

instances and ways to restructure any negative thoughts to change your behavior.

## The Family Systems Worldview

Family counselors and therapists remind us that so-called individual issues and difficulties are often developed in a family context. Rather than working with individuals, family therapists argue that it is more effective to work with family systems. For example, the abusive parent in the interview may be currently experiencing abuse from the partner and transferring it to the child. A response from this therapist might be:

> The next time we get together, I'd like you to bring in your child and your partner. Our behavior and our thoughts are generated in a system of relationships. We'll explore how your family interactions, past and present, reflect your present issues. But, for the moment, let us start with developing a family chart or genogram. Knowing about your family of origin can help us look more completely at the context.

## The Multicultural Worldview

The multicultural counseling and therapy (MCT) worldview is integrative and freely uses other orientations to helping, such as those mentioned above. Multicultural counselors tend to see individuals in a family and cultural context. This means that one part of the therapeutic process is to help clients see how their difficulties may be related to societal and social justice issues concerning race or ethnicity, gender, or socioeconomic status. The multicultural worldview stresses that individual and family counseling can only be fully effective if supplemented by direct action in the community. The following might be the response of a counselor using language appropriate to the client:

> We'll need to look at this issue from three levels. First, I'd like to hear your story as you make sense of it. Then, I'd like to introduce some stress management techniques that may help you deal with the immediate concerns. As part of this process, we'll be looking at how gender, race, and class may play a part in your issues. I'd particularly like to know about what the word *community* means to you and the nature of your present support systems.

The MCT worldview may require more than individual action. The client is seen as part of a larger social system where past and present communities are important. Counselors adopting an MCT approach may refer the client to consciousness-raising groups or become involved in community action themselves.

### Postmodernism, Multiple Realities, and Worldviews in Counseling and Therapy

The counseling worldviews, or frames of reference, presented above are only a small portion of ways where clients' concerns and reasons for consultation can be conceptualized. Needless to say, the techniques and methods of each of the theoretical frameworks lead to very different treatment methodologies.

What is the "correct" worldview and treatment? At one time—not so long ago—counseling and therapy theory operated on the assumption that there existed a "best" therapy. Students and professionals were encouraged to select one theory and then defend that position. Not too surprisingly, we have learned that each of the systems has something to contribute.

The position taken in this book is that effective counselors and therapists need to become familiar with the skills, competencies, knowledge base, and action strategies of multiple theories. Some clients respond best to individualistic methods, some to family orientations, and some to a multicultural orientation. Many clients profit from a combination of approaches. It is important that you develop expertise in several approaches so that you can meet the needs of your culturally diverse clientele more effectively.

# Spirituality and Religion

As we encounter the complexity of the postmodern world, more and more clients are seeking the feeling of wholeness and relationship to the transcendent that spirituality and religion make possible. Victor Frankl's logotherapy argues that issues of faith and spirituality arise from the very core of human experience, whether physical or psychological (see chapter 11).

Human beings are storytellers, and a vital part of the narrative is something beyond the individual. (Jones, Hutchins, Jackson, & Zalaquett, 2014) Religious or spiritual awareness is seen as central to individual, family, and community well-being. Inga Van Pelt is a strong advocate for an even more spirit-centered logotherapeutic healing approach (2009, 2010). Unless we touch on that core, she argues, we are missing the most essential part of our humanity (see Figure 1.2.).

From an existential-humanistic perspective, Vontress (1995, pp. 1–2) comments:

> People cannot be segmented into parts, as if the pieces are somehow unrelated to the whole. My research in West Africa has convinced me that the spiritual dimension of human beings impacts the physical, psychological, and social aspects of living. ... Human beings need the respect, direction, love, and affection of parents, elders, departed ones, and spiritual figures.

The authors have found that counseling and psychotherapy students, as well as many of their clients, have meaningful and deep spiritual interests. Surveys of our classes constantly reveal that 60 percent or more students openly say that these issues are important to them and a source of strength. As individuals get in touch with multicultural experiences, they often find that spirituality is closely related. For example, the emphasis on individual decision making in much of Western psychotherapy and counseling can be related to the Judeo-Christian tradition. Yet many would argue that individuals make decisions best when they consider spiritual foundations. The connection of the individual to community in the Afrocentric orientation is reflected in a spirituality of relationship. This being-in-relationship orientation—as found in Christian, Jewish, Islamic, Buddhist, Mormon, Earth-centered, Native American Indian, and other forms of religion and spirituality—is recognized as an important part of counseling and psychotherapy.

Narrative and storytelling are important in this book. Eventually, you will tell your own story of counseling and psychotherapy and share it with your clients. As you work through this book, you may want to consider the role that spirituality and religion may play in your practice. Your stories and your clients' stories, images, and metaphors are an important part of a person-centered and culture-centered practice. Some practical exercises in this book (the community genogram in Chapter 2 and developing cultural and spiritual images in Chapter 8) provide an introduction to possible methods.

**Figure 1.2. The Spiritual Core, or the Intersection among Individual, Family, and Community Spheres**

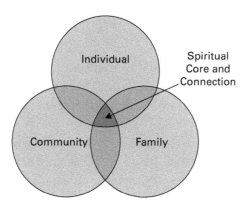

# Research

## The Scientist-Practitioner, the Professional Practice, and the Local Clinical Scientist Models

*No research without action; no action without research.*

**—Kurt Lewin**

Counseling and psychotherapy draw heavily on the concept of the scientist-practitioner, a helping professional who draws on research for more effective practice—and who uses information from clinical work to generate new research questions and plans. The professional practice (a.k.a. practitioner-scientist or practitioner–scientist/researcher model [Houser, 2014, p. 9]) focuses more on actual work with clients, but employs foundational research in their daily practice. The local clinical scientist model uses information from scientific research, academics, and professional experience to articulate communicable conceptualizations of the issues they face within the local context of their practice (Hays-Thomas, 2006). You personally may not be a researcher, but regardless of the model you select, you will be part of the scientific background of the field.

> **REFLECTION EXERCISE**
>
> Each of the models described above fosters applied research and research-informed practice.
> What if we did not seek empirical evaluation of the effects of therapy?
> What would replace research to determine what works for different kinds of mental health disorders?

We need to look at our clinical and counseling practice and search out dimensions of helping that can increase our effectiveness. How can we increase our effect and impact on clients? How can we help maintain the learnings in counseling over time? Two of the important routes toward this direction are evidence-based relationship variables, a set of relationship dimensions with the power to augment the quality of your relationship (Norcross & Wampold, 2011); and evidence-based interventions, such as relapse prevention, a set of techniques designed to help clients keep what they have discovered in therapy (Marlatt & Donovan, 2005). Relapse prevention is discussed in detail in Chapter 8.

## What Research Is Telling Us

Science shows us that counseling and psychotherapy are effective! One of the most effective research method is *meta-analysis* (see Box 1.1.), a complex statistical procedure that computes the average impact or effect size of counseling and therapy.

Meta-analysis combines the results from multiple research studies to answer questions about their effect. Meta-analysis studies have repeatedly confirmed that psychotherapy is an effective, efficacious, and efficient treatment (Lambert, 2013a). It is effective across a broad range of treatments and across a variety of disorders. Overall, 67 percent of those receiving therapy improve significantly, compared to 33 percent of those who do not receive treatment over the same period of time (Lambert, 2013b).

Also, psychotherapy is more effective than many evidence-based medical mental health practices, it is less costly and produces fewer negative effects. Its outcomes or benefits are larger than those observed in many medical treatments. Current studies, meta-analyses and meta-analytical reviews of past studies show that many clients improve to a level of full recovery and maintain this over time (Lambert, 2013a).

You may realize by now that the helping field offers you a bewildering array of competing theories and techniques. At this point, there is no single correct way to begin a theoretical commitment, although some will strongly suggest what you should do. Your task, we suggest, is to examine the field and make your own decision as to how you systematically will organize your counseling and therapy work.

---

**Box 1.1. Establishing Psychotherapy Success**

According to Porzsolt and colleagues (2015), four levels of observation are used to determine the success of an intervention:

1. Efficacy: Achieve therapeutic goals in optimal or ideal conditions.
2. Effectiveness: Achieve therapeutic goals in usual clinical practice.
3. Efficiency: Achieve therapeutic goals at the lowest possible cost.
4. Value of Health Care: Meaning and appreciation of outcomes (Note: outcome can have different meanings, be appreciated differently, and lead to different client and society decisions).

Efficacy can be established using a randomized controlled trial (RCT) completed under ideal study conditions. Effectiveness can be established in a pragmatic controlled trial (PCT) completed under real-life conditions. RCT and PCT cannot be evaluated simultaneously. The first describes what researchers expect to observe in mental health care, while the second describes what they observe in the real-world-setting intervention. To demonstrate client benefit, researchers should first establish efficacy by using an RCT and, second, establish effectiveness by using a PCT.

---

Current research revealed four main therapeutic factors contributing to client improvement in therapy (see Figure 1.3).

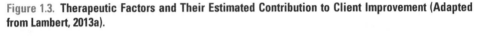

**Figure 1.3. Therapeutic Factors and Their Estimated Contribution to Client Improvement (Adapted from Lambert, 2013a).**

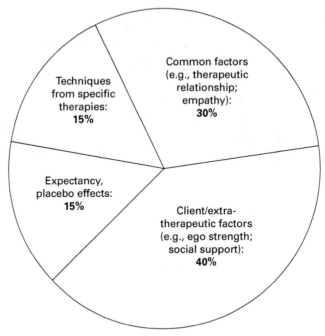

Figure 1.3 clearly suggests that the contributions of the client (expectations and client/extratherapeutic factors) account for the largest amount of therapeutic change. This sobering finding clearly indicates that the client is the hero or heroine of the change process. Does this mean that your counseling and psychotherapy theories are not important? No, counseling theories do matter, as they provide the foundations for the treatments offered and the type of therapeutic relationship established. In fact, theories are included in the current definition of evidence-based practices (EBP) offered by the American Psychological Association (APA): evidence-based practice in psychology is "the integration of the best available research with clinical expertise in the context of patient characteristics, culture and preferences" (APA Task Force on Evidence-Based Practice, 2006, p. 273).

Researchers interested in enhancing counseling outcomes study both the technical procedures (treatments) and the relational aspects (relation) of counseling and therapy. Treatment methods are relational acts, and relational acts are treatment methods (Norcross & Lambert, 2011, p. 5). Relationship and treatment are always interwoven and can be subjected to scientific studies. Current research reveals a number of empirically supported treatments (EST) (e.g., exposure and response prevention treatment for obsessive-compulsive disorder [OCD]) and empirically supported (therapy) relationship (ESR) factors (e.g., empathy). Table 1.2 lists organizations offering current information regarding EBPs for specific disorders.

**Table 1.2. Resources for Evidence-Based Practices**

- Agency for Healthcare Research and Quality's (AHRQ) National Guideline Clearinghouse: https://www.guideline.gov/

- The Campbell Collaboration: https://www.campbellcollaboration.org/

- Child Trends: http://www.childtrends.org/

- The Cochrane: http://www.cochrane.org/

- Effective Child Therapy: Evidence-based Mental Health Treatment for Children and Adolescents: http://effectivechildtherapy.org/

- National Child Traumatic Stress Network: http://www.nctsn.org/resources/topics/treatments-that-work/promising-practices

- The National Guideline Clearinghouse (NGC): https://www.guideline.gov/

- National Implementation Research Network (NIRN): http://nirn.fpg.unc.edu/

- The New Zealand Guidelines Group (NZGG): http://www.health.govt.nz/about-ministry/minis-try-health-websites/new-zealand-guidelines-group

- National Institute for Health and Clinical Excellence (NICE): http://www.nice.org.uk/

- OTseeker: http://otseeker.com/Resources/EvidenceBasedPractice.aspx

- Suicide Prevention Resource Center (SPRC): http://www.sprc.org/resources-programs

- SAMHSA's National Registry of Evidence-based Programs and Practices (NREPP): https://www.samhsa.gov/nrepp

- Social Care Institute for Excellence (SCIE): http://www.scie.org.uk/

- Social Programs That Work, Coalition for Evidence-Based Policy: http://evidencebasedprograms.org/

- Society of Clinical Psychology's Research-Supported Psychological Treatments: http://www.div12.org/psychological-treatments/

The therapy relationship accounts for why clients improve (or fail to improve) more than a particular treatment method (Wampold, 2015). ESRs include (a) elements of the therapy relationship primarily provided by the counselor or therapist; and (b) methods of adapting the therapy to the particular client characteristics. Empathy, your capacity to understand the clients' thoughts, feelings, and difficulties from the client's view, has a demonstrated association with positive therapeutic outcomes. So does the therapeutic alliance; a strong and positive collaborative relationship positively affects outcome. Other factors effective helpers provide are positive regard, congruence/genuineness, feedback, repair of alliance ruptures, self-disclosure, and the management of countertransference (Norcross, 2011), all of which will be discussed in this book.

The field of counseling and psychotherapy is moving away from simple presentation of theories in the realization that presentation and consideration of theory without employment of research data is missing much of what is actually happening in the real world.

The field is moving toward accountability and contracting with clients for specific results from therapy. Again, science and practice become central. It is important to integrate research on your therapeutic action as part of the helping process.

# Neuroscience and the Helping Process

*This is a time of the "mind/brain/body," as we now are aware of the intimate connections and how change in one affects the others.*

**—Allen Ivey, Mary Bradford Ivey, & Carlos Zalaquett**

The counseling relationship changes the brain, facilitating neurogenesis and strengthening the development of new neural networks. Counseling is a planned interpersonal conversation that can also help "rewire" the brain for more effective living.

Neuroscience and neurobiology have shown that the vast majority of what our field has done for years is correct and makes a positive difference for our clients. Empathy is a necessary (and sometimes sufficient) condition for the relationship that can enable client change by itself. Listening is the building block of the relationship. New Japanese brain research using functional magnetic resonance imaging (fMRI) reveals that "listening lights up the brain." Kawamichi and colleagues (2015) found that the Rogerian microskills of attending behavior, paraphrasing, reflecting feelings, and summarizing create the foundation for a strong relationship and the benefits that we see stemming from this alliance.

The centrality of listening and relationship is not new to the counseling field, but at the same time, it is highly reassuring that the humanistic orientation now has fMRI evidence supporting what we have known for years. Listening enables us to bring out client stories and facilitates growth and development.

Counselors activate key brain structures when they listen. The ventral striatum becomes active when encountering abstract positive communication. This has been described metaphorically as a "warm glow." Think of Rogerian positive regard, authenticity, and being with the client as key aspects of listening. The microcounseling approach identified the concrete behaviors of listening in 1966 and originated the term "attending behavior." The importance of culturally appropriate eye contact, body language, vocal tone, and verbal following has since become a basic standard counseling practice and the skills course. "If you are puzzled in the session and don't know what to do, listen!"

These are just a sample of the ways neuroscience informs our theories. Findings from neuroscience studies supporting specific counseling and psychotherapy theories and interventions will be presented in the corresponding chapters.

# Ethics of Counseling and Psychotherapy Theory Application

Effective practice is not only scientific, it is also ethical. Professional helpers are expected to abide by the principles stated in the Code of Ethics of their professions. Codes like the American Counseling Association's (ACA) usually indicate the need of professionals to be aware of best practices and prescribe the use of techniques or interventions grounded in theory or scientific knowledge (for more information, see ACA 2014, sections C.2.f Continuing Education and C.7.a. Scientific Basis for Treatment). Professionals are expected to know their chosen theories well and be competent in their application. A clear theoretical framework will allow helpers to be flexible with that approach and to know when it works and when it does not. They also realize that no one theory can respond to the diversity of issues and individuals requesting their help (Sue & Sue, 2015).

Ethical helpers are culturally competent, honor and respect clients' worldviews, and embrace a multicultural approach to work with their clients (ACA, 2014). They tailor or match their theory application to the racial, ethnic, cultural, and unique characteristics of their clients and the issues affecting them (Ivey et al., 2018; Norcross, 2011). Last but not least, helpers engage in a continued process of reflection regarding their theories and the outcomes of their interventions. Also, they frequently request feedback from clients, in an ongoing process of self-reflection and self-improvement (Miller, Hubble, Chow, & Seidel, 2013; Norcross, 2011). Basic ethical guidelines are summarized in Table 1.3.

**Table 1.3. Basic Ethical Guidelines**

1. Maintain confidentiality. Counseling and psychotherapy depend on trust between counselor and client. As therapist, you are in a powerful relationship; the more trust you build, the more power you have. This book asks you to practice many basic strategies of counseling and therapy. It is essential that you maintain the confidence of your volunteer client, but if you are a student, you do not have legal confidentiality, and your client should be made aware of this.

2. Recognize your limitations. Maintain an egalitarian atmosphere with your volunteer clients. Share with them the task you wish to work through. Inform them that they are free to stop the process at any time. Do not use the interview as a place to delve into the life of another person.

3. Seek consultation. As you practice the exercises presented throughout this text, remain in consultation with your professor, workshop leader, or mentor. Counseling and psychotherapy are private. It is important that you constantly obtain supervision and consultation in your work. You may also find it helpful to discuss your own growth as a helper with other students, without revealing what you have learned about your client.

*(Continued)*

**Table 1.3. Basic Ethical Guidelines *(Continued)***

4. Treat clients the way they want to be treated. This is the Platinum Rule in counseling and therapy. Put yourself in the place of the client. Every person deserves to be treated with respect, dignity, kindness, and honesty.

5. Be aware of individual and cultural differences. This point will be stressed throughout this book. An emphasis on cultural issues can lead at times to stereotyping an individual. At the same time, an overemphasis on individuality may miss background multicultural issues.

6. Give special attention to ethical treatment of children and their rights. Follow the Convention on the Rights of the Child (CRC, UNICEF, 2015) that indicates children are born with the right to survival, food and nutrition, health and shelter, education, and participation. Children are to be heard and protected.

7. Review ethical standards frequently. A selection of relevant associations and standards is presented below:

   - American Association for Marriage and Family Therapy (AAMFT) Code of Ethics: http://www.aamft.org

   - American Counseling Association (ACA) Code of Ethics: http://www.counseling.org

   - American Mental Health Counselors Association (AMHCA) Code of Ethics: http://www.amhca.org

   - American Psychological Association (APA) Ethical Principles of Psychologists and Code of Conduct: http://www.apa.org

   - American School Counselor Association (ASCA): http://www.schoolcounselor.org

   - Commission on Rehabilitation Counselor Certification (CRCC) Code of Professional Ethics for Rehabilitation Counselors: http://www.crccertification.com/pages/crc_ccrc_code_of_ethics/10.php

   - National Association of Social Workers (NASW) Code of Ethics: http://www.naswdc.org

   - National Career Development Association (NCDA): http://www.ncda.org

   - School Social Work Association of America (SSWAA):www.sswaa.org

# The Definition of Helping and Its Context

Helping can be defined as one person giving aid to another or offering a hand. The offering of assistance comes in many forms, as diversified as someone listening to a friend or a professional working in a mental health clinic. For the purposes of this book, however, helping will be defined as a general framework that one person offers another person or group assistance, usually in the form of interviewing, counseling, or psychotherapy.

## Interviewing, Counseling, and Psychotherapy

Throughout this book, the terms helping, interviewing, counseling, and psychotherapy will be used at varying points, sometimes interchangeably, sometimes with specific meanings. *Interviewing* is defined as a method of information gathering and will typically be characteristic of information gathering in a welfare office, employment agency, or placement service, or in career counseling.

*Counseling* is a more intensive process concerned with assisting people without or with less severe pathological issues to achieve their goals or function more effectively. *Psychotherapy* is a longer-term process concerned with reconstruction of the person and larger changes in personality structure. Psychotherapy often is restricted in conception to those with pathological disorders.

The distinctions between these words often become blurred in practice. As an interviewer discovers serious issues, he or she may move with the client into a brief form of psychotherapy. Counseling specialists often have longer series of sessions and go into more depth than psychotherapists. Psychotherapists do interviewing and counseling. Although the definitions suggested here will work for general purposes, completely satisfactory definitions of distinctions are usually considered impossible. Therapy currently is a word that is becoming more popular and may become the generic, common description of both counseling and psychotherapy. Some professionals use the terms interchangeably.

Helpers and their clients enter into the interviewing, counseling, or psychotherapy relationship usually by mutual agreement. In some cases (public schools, prisons, state hospitals), people may be placed in a counseling relationship without their consent with counselors who have been assigned to them. Establishing a mutually beneficial relationship in such situations is, of course, difficult, but still doable.

The many forms of helping span the world in both diversity and scope, and range from UNESCO programs to assist traumatized children internationally to camp counselors to self-help groups such as Alcoholics Anonymous. The functions, skills, training, and backgrounds of the many helpers vary extensively.

You, as a prospective counselor or therapist, may be considering a career in clinical mental health counseling, psychology, school guidance, social work, with the federal government, or with a private business enterprise. You may be interested in working in a community mental health center, a school, a hospital, an alternative street clinic, a personnel office, or a volunteer agency. You may be interested in private practice, or you may wish to donate part of your time to a community agency. You may take only one course in counseling skills, or you may involve yourself in a two-year graduate program leading to a master's degree or a four-year (or longer) graduate program leading to the PhD and follow it with a postdoctoral internship and further study.

## Psychiatrists, Psychologists, Counselors, and Social Workers

The political context of helping cannot be ignored. There is a constant battle for status and power between various professional groups as to who is the most effective helper. An MD psychiatrist with a medical degree and supervised internship often ranks at the top of the pecking order in terms of power with state legislatures and insurance companies. With hospital privileges and the ability to prescribe drugs, the psychiatrist often is found directing the activities of other professionals. The psychiatrist's professional association is the American Psychiatric Association (APA).

Psychologists, represented especially by school, clinical, and counseling psychology, are PhD or PsyD professionals who often have an antagonistic relationship with the medical community. Psychologists point out that they have a more complete education in psychological science and a carefully supervised clinical internship followed by state examinations. The American Psychological Association (APA) is the professional association.

Psychologists now are obtaining hospitalization privileges, and testing has begun to permit them to prescribe medication in a few states. Counseling psychology and clinical psychology, as might be expected, have their own turf battles, as there is considerable overlap in their academic and professional training. In a general sense, counseling psychology focuses slightly more on vocational psychology and normal development, and clinical psychology focuses more on so-called abnormal issues. In actual practice, there are counseling psychologists who are more "clinical" than clinical psychologists and many effective clinical psychologists who do important counseling and preventive work with typical clients and families. School psychology, with its focus on children and adolescents in the schools, has a practice that combines many of the features of both counseling and clinical psychology.

Counselors are usually associated with the American Counseling Association (ACA) and its several divisions. While not as firmly established at the state and national scene as psychiatry and psychology, the ACA has in recent years made large strides toward professional identity and state licensure, despite almost constant strife with the older professional associations. Counselors' academic degrees vary and include the MA, MEd, MSEd, EdD, and PhD. Four important specialties of counselors are clinical mental health counseling, school counseling, rehabilitation counseling, and career counseling. The American Association of Multicultural Counseling and Development and the Counselors for Social Justice have long been active within the framework of the ACA, promoting multicultural and social justice issues in counseling.

Counselors cannot prescribe medication, nor do they have hospital privileges. However, in many cities and towns, particularly in rural areas, counselors find themselves operating in a fashion very similar to psychiatrists and psychologists, as they are the primary mental health professional working with that client. Counselors often develop working relationships with general-practice physicians or internists. School counselors often are the main coordinating mental health professionals making decisions as to the type of treatments are most appropriate.

Clinical social workers with an MSW degree focus their work on clients *and* the client's environment, stressing that community action may be as important as or more important than individual work. Psychiatric nursing enters the field from a different perspective, and many nurses will also have a PhD, EdD, or counseling masters in addition to their specific nursing training. To complicate the delivery of mental health services even more are the wide array of entry-level (AB, BS) and community volunteer groups.

# Finding Your Own Place in the Helping Professions

What does all this mean for you, regardless of your selected field? Each professional program has its strengths and weaknesses, but all are aimed at facilitating client development. Occasionally, you will encounter some form of competition and strife as you work with professionals different from yourself. At times, you will feel that indeed "mental health is a multiplicity." Fortunately, the multiplicity is most often focused for client benefit, and when you are working directly with a client, family, or community, you will find that you will gain respect and trust regardless of your professional background. Increasingly, mental health professionals are becoming aware that no one person or field has all the answers.

## Power Differential

The person seeking help is in a less powerful position than the counselor or therapist. Culturally intentional counselors will always keep this in mind as they offer their services to others and will be sure to evaluate their position as one of power, as well as one of helping.

Humility and wisdom on the part of the therapist are required. We do not yet know precisely how to assist all people to meet all their needs; the issues are simply too complex for the present state of the art and science. Further, the actual time spent between a therapist and a client is minuscule compared with the amount of time the client spends in the rest of the world. Even a series of thirty interviews over thirty weeks is but thirty hours out of a lifetime. It is remarkable that counseling and psychotherapy do make a difference in the lives of clients, considering the time constraint.

# Integrating Skills, Theory, and Practice: Looking Forward

Theory provides the ideas that organize key principles of helping. Skills form the toolbox of counseling and therapy. Practice occurs when you take your skills and theories and apply them directly to clients. If you have a solid foundation of skills and an intellectual understanding of theory, you are well prepared for the practice of therapy and counseling.

Chapter 2 focuses on you as a helper; Chapters 3 through 6 of this book focus on the basic skills of counseling and therapy. These are skills and concepts that are important in many theoretical orientations. For example, regardless of your theoretical orientation, you will find that listening skills are necessary if you are to walk with—that is, to understand—your clients. All theoretical orientations stress listening to clients, and thus you will find that skills such as questioning are useful, regardless of where you commit yourself theoretically. If you are behaviorally oriented, you need listening skills to obtain the behaviors and behavioral sequences of your client. If your orientation is psychodynamic, these same listening skills are necessary for drawing out a dream or the client's early childhood experience.

If you achieve a basic mastery of skills and concepts in the first five chapters, you will come to the later chapters on theories well prepared to develop a beginning understanding of seemingly very different orientations to counseling and therapy. We say *seemingly* because, as you orient yourself to basic helping processes, you will find that you start developing connections between and among different theories. This is the beginning of general theory.

The theories described in this book represent varying worldviews and perspectives and each provides a useful frame of reference for looking at a situation differently. If you take the Escher print in Figure 1.1, turn it on its side, view it upside down, or attempt to see the three-dimensional aspects of the print, you will note that each change of viewpoint offers a richer way of looking at and understanding the print. Similarly, the theories in Part II of this book offer unique ways to frame and understand the reality of therapy. At some point, you will want to commit yourself to an orientation, either to a single primary theory or to an eclectic or general point of view; without some stable basis for work, you and your client will end in chaos.

At times, you will find that we discuss concepts from chapters that you may not have yet read or have just finished reading. This is particularly so in Chapter 5 that provides a vital integrating bridge between skills and theory. These forward and backward references are designed to point out to you how skills and theories are related, how different theories and their techniques are related one to another, and how you use general theory to integrate different points of view.

General theory is about moving systematically and knowledgeably from theory to theory using trans-theoretical skills and concepts. The final chapter of this book focuses on integrated practice, the application of skills and theories for the practical benefit of clients. Skills and theories that are not manifested in direct practice are likely to be lost and forgotten. Underlying the final chapter of this book is Gordon Paul's important axiom, "What treatment, by whom, is most effective for this individual with what specific goal, under which set of circumstances?" (Paul, 1967). To bring Paul's statement up to date, it might be rephrased as

> What treatment, by whom, is most effective for this individual with what specific goal, under which set of circumstances? However, in each phase of the process, *what multicultural conditions apply*?

**You Are Important**

> In Gordon Paul's classic statement, we would emphasize the important word *whom* that refers to you in the helping process. What is to be your selected set of treatments, what are to be your conceptions of the goal of helping, and what circumstances will you find yourself in as you enter the helping field? Furthermore, what is your awareness of client individual and cultural uniqueness? All these dimensions and more constitute the critical construct of intentionality, the deep awareness of yourself and others with a specific commitment to action.

# Developing Your Own Theoretical Orientation

Some in the helping professions are overly zealous in their commitment to their own theoretical frame of reference or worldview in therapy. Commitment and belief are essential if one is to be competent and make a difference in the lives of others, but a single-minded rigidity may make it impossible to help those who may not respond to your first effort at providing assistance. The task is to be flexible in your use of skills and theory and to remain open to new ideas. There are several routes that you may use to develop your own integrated theory of practice in counseling and therapy.

*Eclecticism-Integrationism.* Between a third to one half of currently practicing therapists and counselors describe themselves as eclectics or integratives (Goodyear et al., 2016; Norcross & Rogan, 2013). Eclectics use procedures from many theories; integratives join two or more theories into a consistent approach (Lambert, 2013a). The eclectic recognizes that many theories and methods are of merit and deliberately sets up to select aspects of different theories that may be useful to a varied clientele. The strength of eclecticism lies in flexibility and breadth. At the same time, there are those who criticize this position as overly flexible and lacking systematic thinking in that the counselor or therapist has not taken the time or effort to know one orientation well.

*Single Theoretical Commitment.* The contrasting orientation to eclecticism is represented by the many therapists who may have adopted a strong and studied commitment to a single theory, such as cognitive therapy, behavior modification, psychoanalysis, multicultural, narrative, or structural family therapy (Goodyear et al., 2016). The strengths of this approach are in-depth knowledge of technique and method and an ability to modify the theory to meet individual client needs. Some criticize those committed to a single theory, however, as being rigid and unwilling to change their methods when clients don't respond to the approach.

*General Theory.* George Kelly, the personality theorist, has pointed out that as eclectics become more systematic in their thinking, they are developing their own theory or general theory of helping. They have integrated several different orientations into one unified approach. Ultimately, most reading this text will take some variation of this approach. General theory or metatheory may be described as a larger conceptual view than either eclecticism or adherence to a single theoretical orientation. General theory seeks to connect and organize pieces of theory in a coherent and systematic framework. General theory could be described as a systematic "eclecticism."

However, it is possible to be primarily committed to a single theoretical orientation and still be a general theorist. A general theorist from a behavioral orientation, for example, might work primarily from this point of view but, at the same time, could respect different theories and adapt portions of them in practice. For example, you will find that the cognitive theorist Aaron Beck (Chapter 12) has a clear central theoretical commitment, but he is nonetheless able to draw on concepts of humanistic psychology, behaviorism, and psychodynamic theory at times to enrich his basic orientation.

## REFLECTION EXCERCISE

As a helper, therapist, and counselor, you have different ways to develop your theoretical approach. Which of the options above demonstrates an awareness of the variety of potential client responses, a respect for worldviews other than their own, and an understanding that theories may be combined for the benefit of the client?

Eclectic-integrative, flexible adherence to a single theory, and general theory have the following in common: (1) an awareness that clients respond differently and may need to add the techniques of an alternative orientation to one's own regular method at times; (2) a respect for worldviews and theories different from one's own; and (3) the ability to see how different theories may be systematically related to one another for client benefit.

# Theory into Practice

In each chapter, we present exercises that will allow you to use the theoretical ideas in direct clinical and counseling practice. It is too early to include such exercises here, but it is not too early to include a homework assignment to observe the theories in action. Complete Homework 1.1 to learn how mental health professionals acquire, use, and evaluate their theoretical orientation.

**Homework 1.1. Counseling and Psychotherapy Theories in Practice**

> Individually or in groups of two, interview two mental health professionals about their theoretical orientations. Discuss with each (1) how they chose their theories; (2) what is the role of their chosen theories in their work; (3) how their theories relate to their personal philosophy of life, people, and how people change; (4) if they draw techniques from other theoretical orientations to help clients; and (5) how do they evaluate the effectiveness of their theoretical orientation.

Action in the form of activities and homework will increase your awareness, knowledge, competencies, and repertoire of potential responses. We hope you will actively engage in these actions, as they will help you achieve the main purpose of this book.

The major goal of this book is increasing your flexibility in viewing the world, learning the theories, understanding clients' issues, and maximizing your ability to respond and help others.

# References

American Counseling Association. (2014). *ACA code of ethics*. Alexandria, VA: Author.

American Psychological Association (2012). *Recognition of psychotherapy effectiveness*. Retrieved from http://www.apa.org/about/policy/resolution-psychotherapy.aspx.

APA Task Force on Evidence-Based Practice. (2006). Evidence-based practice in psychology. *American Psychologist, 61*, 271–285. doi:10.1037/0003-066X.61.4.271.

Cambridge Dictionary. (2016). *Common sense*. Retrieved from http://dictionary.cambridge.org/us/dictionary/english/common-sense.

Chung, R., C-Y., & Bemak, F. (2012). *Social justice counseling: The next steps towards multiculturalism*. Thousand Oaks, CA: Sage.

Chung, T., Noronha, A., Carroll, K.M., Potenza, M.N., Hutchison, K., Calhoun, V.D., … Fedelstein, S.W. (2016). Brain mechanisms of change in addiction treatment: Models, methods, and emerging findings. *Current Addiction Reports, 3*, 332–342. doi:10.1007/s40429-016-0113-z.

Escher, M. (1960). *The graphic work of M.C. Escher*. New York, NY: Ballantine.

Goodyear, R., Lichtenberg, J., Hutman, H., Overland, E., Bedi, R., Christiani, K., … Young, C. (2016). A global portrait of counselling psychologists' characteristics, perspectives, and professional behaviors. *Counselling Psychology Quarterly, 29*, 115–138. doi.org/10.1080/09515070.2015.1128396.

Gratzer, D., & Goldbloom, D. (2016). Making evidence-based psychotherapy more accessible in Canada. *Canadian Journal of Psychiatry, 6*, 618–623.

Halbur, D., & Halbur, K.V. (2015). *Developing your theoretical orientation in counseling and psychotherapy* (3rd ed.). Boston, MA: Pearson.

Hays-Thomas, R. (2006). Challenging the scientist-practitioner model: Questions about I-0 education and training. *Industrial Organizational Psychologist, 44*, 47–53.

Houser, R. (2014). *Counseling and educational research: Evaluation and application* (3rd ed.). Thousand Oaks, CA: Sage.

Ivey, A., Ivey, M.B., & Zalaquett, C. (2018). *Intentional interviewing and counseling: Facilitating client development in a multicultural society* (9th ed.). Belmont, CA: Cengage Learning.

Jones, J.W., Hutchins, A.M., Jackson, A.P., & Zalaquett, C.P. (2014). *Letters to friends: Wisdom through storytelling*. Eglin, FL: Windwalker Publications.

Kawamichi, H., Yoshihara, K., Sasaki, A.T., Sugawara, S.K., Tanabe, H.C., Shinohara, R., … Sadato, N. (2015). Perceiving active listening activates the reward system and improves the impression of relevant experiences. *Social Neuroscience, 10*, 16–26. doi:10.1080/17470919.2014.954732.

Lambert, M.J. (2013a). *Bergin and Garfields's handbook of psychotherapy and behavior change*. New York, NY: Wiley.

Lambert, M.J. (2013b). Outcome in psychotherapy: The past and important advances. *Psychotherapy, 50*, 42–51. doi:10.1037/a0030682.

Lewis, G., & Lewis, G. (2016). No evidence that CBT is less effective than antidepressants in moderate to severe depression. *Evidence-Based Mental Health, 19*, 125. doi.org.ezaccess.libraries.psu.edu/10.1136/eb-2016-102381.

Marlatt, A.G., & Donovan, D.M. (2005). *Relapse prevention: Maintenance strategies in the treatment of addictive behaviors* (2nd ed.). New York, NY: Guilford.

Meier, S.T. (2016, October 20). Is it possible to integrate psychotherapy theory on the basis of empirical findings? The disruptive role of method effects. *Journal of Psychotherapy Integration*. Advance online publication. http://dx.doi.org/10.1037/int0000064.

Miller, S.D., Hubble, M.A., Chow, D.L., & Seidel, J.A. (2013). *The outcome of psychotherapy: Yesterday, today, and tomorrow. Psychotherapy, 50,* 88–97. http://dx.doi.org/10.1037/a0031097.

Norcross, J.C. (Ed.). (2011). *Psychotherapy relationships that work: Evidence-based responsiveness* (2nd ed.). New York, NY: Oxford University Press.

Norcross, J.C., & Rogan, J.D. (2013). Psychologists conducting psychotherapy in 2012: Current practices and historical trends among Division 29 members. *Psychotherapy, 50,* 490–495. doi. org/10.1037/a0033512.

Norcross, J.C., & Wampold, B.E. (2011). Evidence-based therapy relationships: Research conclusions and clinical practices. *Psychotherapy, 48,* 98–102. doi: 10.1037/a0022161.

Paul, G. (1967). Strategy of outcome research in psychotherapy. *Journal of Consulting Psychology, 31,* 109–118.

Porzsolt, F., Rocha, N.G., Toledo-Arruda, A.C., Thomaz, T.G., Moraes, C., Bessa-Guerra, T.R., … Weiss, C. (2015). Efficacy and effectiveness trials have different goals, use different tools, and generate different messages. *Pragmatic and Observational Research, 6,* 47–54. doi.org/10.2147/POR.S89946.

Prochaska, J., & Norcross, J. (2018). *Systems of psychotherapy: A transtheoretical analysis* (9th ed.). Stamford, CT: Cengage.

Rosenthal, R. (1990). How are we doing in soft psychology? *American Psychologist, 45,* 775–776.

Sue, D.W., & Sue, D. (2016). *Counseling the culturally diverse: Theory and practice* (7th ed.). Hoboken, NJ: Wiley.

United Nations International Children's Emergency Fund. (2015). *About the convention.* Retrieved from http://www.unicef.org/rightsite/237_202.htm.

Van Pelt, I. (2009). Applying logotherapy in primary care medicine. *The International Forum for Logotherapy, 32* (1), 1.

Van Pelt, I. (2010). Anxiety and depressive disorders in children and adolescents on the rise: How logophilosophy/therapy can influence the threat to mental health. *International Forum for Logotherapy, 33* (2), 79.

Vontress, C. (1995). *The philosophical foundations of the existential/humanistic perspective: A personal statement.* Washington, D.C., George Washington University.

Wampold, B.E. (2015). How important are the common factors in psychotherapy? An update. *World Psychiatry, 14,* 270–277.

# Credits

### CHAPTER 2

# The Culturally Intentional Counselor and Therapist

## Theories, The Helping Process, and You

---

### CHAPTER GOALS

The major task of this chapter is to explore your interests, worldview, and competencies as you begin to form your theoretical orientation to counseling and therapy. Becoming a culturally intentional counselor is the final destination, one that begins with your own reasons and motives to become a mental health practitioner.

### SPECIFIC GOALS OF THIS CHAPTER:

1. Explore your interest in *becoming a mental health professional*. Exploring your reasons for becoming a counselor or therapist will increase your self-awareness, clarify your reasons, and provide a clearer path for your journey.

2. Attend to *your worldviews* and the way they influence your choices of therapies and interventions.

3. Define the concept of *cultural intentionality* as a general, integrated goal for counselors, therapists, and clients.

4. Use the *Therapeutic LifeStyle Changes* (TLC) to improve your brain and life, as well as the lives of others.

5. Bring *theory into practice*. The Community Genogram. In each chapter, we present exercises that will allow you to use the theoretical ideas in direct clinical and counseling practice. This chapter presents the community genogram, a specific way to help you and your clients identify the roots of a personal worldview.

# What Brings You Here?

Counselors, psychotherapists, social workers, marriage and family therapists, school counselors, rehabilitation counselors, and other mental health practitioners and students represent a special group of professionals. Most people minimize the mental distress and psychological suffering experienced by others and avoid contact with those affected by mental disorders (Norcross & Farber, 2005).

What brings you here is a question counselors and therapists often ask of clients during their first meeting, as they want to find out what motivated them to seek help at this time. Barnett (2007) suggests we should ask ourselves the same question. Exploring our reasons for becoming a counselor or therapist will expand our self-awareness and help clarify the reasons for becoming a counselor or therapist. When we ask our students for their reasons to become therapists, they typically assert their desire to help and understand others. This is indeed an altruistic motivation, but there may be more complex motives for your decision, and knowing them will provide a clearer path for your journey. These complex motives may be partly unconscious and may also be influenced by chance events and relationships (Barnett, 2007; Mahrer, 2005). What are the underlying motivations and gratifications for you to become a counselor and therapist?

The following reflection exercise will help you explore what brought you here.

## REFLECTION EXERCISE

What motivated you to become a mental health practitioner?

List your motivating factors. Which ones influenced your decision the most? Which one was the most important of these factors?

Was there an important relation influencing your decision? Were there role models or inspirational relatives, friends, teachers, and practitioners?

Was there one or more significant events in your life that you feel influenced your decision to engage in this career path?

Were you influenced by personal challenges or issues, or the need to resolve those issues?

Did you participate in personal therapy? If you did, did your experience shape your decision?

Are you influenced by the inspirational benefits of what counseling and psychotherapy can offer? If so, what are the benefits you believe helping provides?

Regarding your future work with clients, what aspects do you find most rewarding or fulfilling?

What else do you feel was or is relevant concerning your motivations and reasons for becoming a mental health professional?

Why is it so important to understand your reasons for becoming a counselor or therapist? In the field of mental health, the professionals providing counseling and psychotherapy are the primary agents of change. The client is the primary executor of those changes, but you can greatly advance or detract from their therapeutic success. Your personal attributes and competencies can make a difference. Negative motivation or reasons for entering these types of studies can impair your delivery of good therapy. Even attempting to help others while you are struggling with stressful events may lead to a negative outcome. A stressed-out therapist may not be able to listen carefully to the plight of the client and may not understand the main issues, thus failing to provide effective help.

Your reasons for becoming a counselor or therapist will affect in a positive or negative fashion the way you practice counseling (Farber, Manevich, Metzger, & Saypol, 2005). Understanding your own motivations will help you appreciate what you most want for yourselve from our work (e.g., making sense of clients' behavior or establishing a humane connection with a person in need). This realization of your own personal motives will be a powerful discovery, one that will allow you to find that some of your clients may not want the same. Some clients may prefer help in reducing their symptoms, modifying negative behaviors, or reducing stress. Paradoxically, learning about your motivation to become a counselor will help you become more aware of your "blind spots," defined by Farber et al. (2005) as "our tendency to continue to see the world through our own lens" (p. 1030). Offering only what you value and want, rather than what your client needs or wants, is bound to end in early termination of counseling.

Reevaluating your motives from time to time will help you determine if you are doing well, if you need to rejuvenate your commitment to your profession, or if you need to make changes to improve your job satisfaction. Completing the reflection exercise is an important beginning. Revisit your reasons and motivations from time to time, as they may be fully understood later in your career.

## What Do You Bring with You?

You are the by-product of your past and present relationships and life experiences. Yes, you are here because you want to become a mental health agent of change and want to learn theories and interventions to help others. But you are already a person with a great deal of experiences and knowledge, a person with years of acting in the world and accumulating feedback derived from those actions (Kirkwood, 2012). At the core of your work toward becoming a mental health professional is you. What do you believe are the competencies you bring to counseling and therapy?

Remembering Escher's *Relativity* artwork from Chapter 1, how are you planning to walk along with the client? Furthermore, what do you bring with you that will help you meet that client?

This is another important reflection exercise. Just like the one before, it represents an important first step. One that you should revisit periodically to increase awareness and mastery of relevant competencies, those that you bring with you and those offered by the various theories presented in this book.

## REFLECTION EXERCISE

Take stock!

The following statements will help you explore what you bring with you to the task of becoming a counselor or therapist.

Also, ask a friend or family member what they see as your strengths as a listener, as a helper:

Competencies I bring to counseling and therapy:

My present strengths in self-understanding and emotional awareness:

Ways that I will work with those who are culturally/racially different than me:

Areas where I would like to grow and learn more about myself:

# The Importance of Your View of Helping

Theories provide you with a map for conceptualization and action. Exploration of motives increases your understanding of reasons for engaging in this journey. Reflecting on competencies enhances your ability to walk along with your clients. Now you are ready to explore how you see counseling and psychotherapy.

Whether you have engaged in counseling or not, you have lived through many helping situations, all of which have given you some sense of what good helping and not-so-good helping are. Reflecting on those experiences will increase awareness of your current views of helping. This is important as you will catch yourself leaning toward those theories that best fit your own views. Over time, it will become important to expand your current views to embrace the complexity and diversity of the experiences your clients will bring with them.

## REFLECTION EXERCISE

What is your story of counseling and psychotherapy at this point?

What has been your past experience with those who may have offered you an empathic and caring relationship?

Where might personal relationships have been damaging?

How have positive relationships made a difference in your life?

Remember that in implementing a theory, you are applying a worldview that may or may not be fully compatible with your own. Even more important, the worldview of a particular theory may be incompatible with your clients' ways of thinking and behaving.

## REFLECTION EXERCISE

Since you will be the one who applies theory to practice, you are the central ingredient in working with the ideas of this book. What will be your approach to helping?

Some of you will focus on a single theory, whereas others will develop competence in several theories simultaneously. Regardless of which method you choose, you will still be implementing your own worldview.

Each individual has a unique life experience, even within the same family, and this recognition has long been central to individually oriented counseling and therapy. But we grow and develop in a family context. Our experience in the family is basic to the ways we view the world. Your family experience has been important in the way you construct and think about reality. It is of great benefit in your development as a helper to think about your own family influences on your worldview. Furthermore, cultural context deeply affects the way you and your family interact with the world. What groups are most important to you and your family? Peer groups and friends, spiritual groups, school and political groups, support groups such as Alcoholics Anonymous, online and virtual groups, and many other groups can be important influences. The word *community* encompasses these concepts, and our community puts us most closely in touch with culture. As a first step toward developing and clarifying your own worldviews, the *community genogram* presented in this chapter can be a useful practice technique.

# Personal Style and Interpersonal Influence

Communication and influence are at the core of talk therapy! *One cannot not communicate*, and the related idea that *one cannot not influence* are known axioms of communication (Watzlawick, Beavin, & Jackson, 1967, pp. 48–71). Your personal style and responses influence what happens next. Let us imagine that a client has come to you for help. After some preliminaries, the client tells the following story:

> I feel so inferior … you know I work in the cafeteria. I go out and wipe tables in these little loose white jackets … with a rag in my hand, going around and wiping tables. I feel so self-conscious and that people are staring at me. Maybe they aren't, but I feel that they are. I hate the job. It's a little better behind the serving line, but still it feels low and unimportant to me.

It is important that you take a moment now and think through what you consider to be the central issues in this situation. Imagine you are the counselor or therapist. Write down what you would say to the client.

## REFLECTION EXERCISE

Before you go any farther, have several other people respond to your client's statement and record what they say. Are their responses the same as yours? Would they lead the client in a different direction from you? Is one response necessarily "the best?"

> Could it be that what you say to another person in a counseling or therapy session says as much about you, or more, than it does about the client?

(At this point, you may have glanced ahead in the chapter to find the "correct" answer. We don't have the correct answer, nor do we believe that there is one most appropriate sentence to say to a person who may be coping with conflict. However, it is highly likely that some responses will be more helpful than others.)

Chances are that you do have a response to the client, one which offers something of yourself, is potentially helpful, and may lead to personal growth. Also, if you can "walk" with clients and understand their different view of the world, you may be able to help them find more useful ways to think about and manage their lives.

## How Your Personal Style Affects Others

How you as a helper, counselor, or therapist respond to the client greatly determines what will happen next. Your answer to the client from the cafeteria determines what will be said next, or whether the client's issue will be treated at a surface or deep level. In fact, your response determines whether the discussion will continue at all. The manner in which we respond and conceptualize the world of others can have a great influence on how clients think and act in the future. Even the simple act of listening and encouraging a person to continue talking, as opposed to ignoring what has been said, can influence a person's life greatly over time.

Counseling and therapy are processes of interpersonal influence. But what will the direction and method of our influence be? Let us examine some alternative responses to the client from the cafeteria; later, we can consider some critical cultural implications of our responses.

1. "You sound like you feel terribly nervous and self-conscious in your job." (This focuses on key emotions of the client and may lead to further discussion of feelings toward the self.)

2. "Could you describe another situation where you have felt this way?" (This helps determine whether or not the feelings are a common thread throughout the client's life, and it provides additional data to clarify the picture.)

3. "Inferiority feelings? Think about those feelings of insecurity and self-consciousness. Then, let your mind flash back to the earliest childhood experience you can think of and tell me about it." (This technique seeks to find the roots of present-day experience in childhood and is oriented to therapeutic change.)

4. "You say you felt insecure. What did you do just before you had this feeling? Give me the whole sequence of events leading up to and following a situation

today where you were wiping the tables." (Searching for specificity of behavioral sequences may lead to action training to work against the client's issue.)

5. "That's an irrational idea. We've talked about that before. It's solely in your head. Now let's get on to working some more on how you think." (This helps in examining how a person thinks about her- or himself. In this case, the counselor and client have obviously worked together on parallel issues before.)

6. "I think I can understand how you feel. I've worked on tables too, and felt terribly self-conscious and embarrassed when I was serving. Is that at all what you feel like?" (Self-disclosure of one's own parallel experiences can facilitate client talk.)

7. "I'd say what you need to do is relax and forget it. Doesn't sound that bad." (Advice and suggestion is one possible lead and is a common reaction given by people to others who need assistance, but, unless the client is ready, even the best advice can be discarded or ignored.)

Which of the above responses was most like yours? Which of the above responses is the correct one? It is difficult to say because each leads the client in a very different—but potentially valuable—direction. There are obviously hundreds of other possible responses that could be developed from an array of personal experiences and counseling theories. Given the right person and the right timing, there are many potentially useful responses.

This book will assist you in becoming a constructive helper, counselor, or psychotherapist. While we argue that there is no one "right" way to help and that you must determine your own personal style and manner of counseling, we also urge you to become aware of what you are doing and how it may influence the direction of another person's life. Helping is a process of interpersonal influence, and the therapist can have great power in the life of the client. The more responses you have in your personal repertoire, the more possibilities you have for being a helping person, and the greater the chances are for the client to grow and develop.

# Worldview and Theory in Counseling and Therapy

Awareness of your views of counseling and expanding your response repertoire for helping is not enough; it is also necessary to examine a larger worldview. Put in simplest terms, how do you think the world works?

If you have not thought about this before, a beginning clue may be in your response to the question above where you identified the central issues about your client who works in the cafeteria. The manner in which you identify these central issues provides a small picture of how you view the world. It is out of this worldview, or personal framework, that you make a decision on how to act. Your worldview and theories determine how you relate to others and probably led to what you said to your client.

To give a more precise idea of how important the concept of worldview is in the helping process, examine some of the central issues identified by others who were given the same excerpt about the cafeteria.

1. "The problem in this case undoubtedly relates to feelings of inferiority and inadequacy. Alfred Adler talks about these terms and how childhood experiences often provide the clue as to why these feelings are present now."

2. "This person is a victim of an economic system where some people have enough money to go to college and play around, drive big cars, etc., while others have to struggle. The issue is not feelings, but an unjust society."

3. "A smock is pretty ugly and it makes people stand out. I think I'd feel that way too. Maybe what we need is a less conspicuous uniform."

4. "Lucky to have a job at all. I couldn't find one. This student has no problem and ought to shut up and be happy about what is happening."

5. "The actions of cleaning and serving aren't important. What is important is how one feels about oneself and what one is doing. This student needs to become aware of the self as a person and not as an object."

Each of the above definitions of the key issues reflects a different worldview and leads to very different actions on the part of the therapist. The first response comes from a psychodynamic approach and could lead to long-term psychotherapy. (The psychodynamic approach examines childhood experiences and feelings to see how they present themselves in adult life.) The second worldview or theory is that of a multiculturally oriented approach and could lead to economic consciousness-raising techniques as the mode of influence.

The third worldview comes from a practical business administration approach and seeks to make environmental changes. The fourth theory denies the feelings and risks leading to an angry exchange. The final view presented is a humanistic worldview that emphasizes emotion and could lead the client to enter an encounter group or seek person-centered counseling.

Careful examination of interview typescripts, films, audiotapes, and videotapes reveals that counselors have their own typical patterns of responding to clients. As a counselor, you can start to identify your pattern of working with people. By examining your definitions of key issues and your typical responses, you can eventually evolve a fairly accurate picture of your typical way of looking at other people and their concerns.

Counseling and psychological theories, such as psychoanalysis, behaviorism, humanistic, cognitive, or narrative, discussed in this book represent theories or worldviews and are means of conceptualizing and thinking about people and the world. These theories also offer a clear set of intervention techniques through which people may be helped. Your task is to use these theories to build your own theory about the world.

# An Overall Goal for Counseling: Culturally Intentional Individuals

Most counseling and psychotherapy theories seem to accept the idea that effective daily living and positive relationships with others are the goals of helping. Specific theories over the years emphasize such things as self-actualization; understanding your unconscious; self-efficacy; personal growth and development; okayness; clarified values; and an increased behavioral repertoire. These are only a sampling of the many alternative descriptions of what helping is about.

Note, however, that the above objectives all focus on individuals and their wishes and desires. The goals of counseling as they have generally been presented in the field have been drawn from middle-class Western Europeans and North American frameworks. At first glance, self-actualization sounds like a wonderful idea with which no one could truly disagree. However, a focus on the self would be considered selfish and even a possible mental disorder if carried to extremes in much of Asian, South Pacific, and African culture. Native American culture has long focuses on the relationship of the individual to the group and to the environment.

The humanistic psychologists Abraham Maslow and Carl Rogers are important figures in the helping establishment, and both are recognized for their interest in culturally diverse groups, yet the placing of the very word *self-actualization* as the top of a hierarchy with relational issues placed below is now considered by many as a male and Western statement, not relevant to all cultures.

One important and highly influential scholar effecting change is the developmental psychologist Carol Gilligan (2016). Although therapy and counseling are not her specialty, she has pointed out clearly that male and female constructions of and beliefs about the nature of reality are very different. Before her writing, much important research and thinking about moral and cognitive development tended to be writing about male moral development.

Gilligan has pointed out the obvious—men and women are different. They tend to have varying patterns of psychosocial development that result in varying patterns of thinking. At the risk of oversimplifying a highly complex issue, men may be said to be "linear," or "if-then," thinkers. The male model of thinking tends to focus on results and achieving a specific goal. Gilligan describes women as "relational" thinkers, individuals who think about possibilities and relationships between possibilities before they take action.

You will find that the linear versus relational orientation is basic to an understanding of counseling and therapy. While relational issues play themselves out very differently among cultures, you will find Gilligan's distinction very helpful in understanding not only male and female clients, but also those of many differing cultural groups.

It should be made clear that Gilligan's comments on this issue were not the first. If one were to review the scholarship and research paradigms suggested by the African American scholar W.E.B. Du Bois, one would discover that many—perhaps most—of the current "discoveries " in multicultural work can be gleaned from his early writings. For example, Du Bois wrote in 1908:

> The family group … harks back to the sheltered harem with the mother emerging at first as nurse and homemaker, while the man remains the sole breadwinner. Thus the Negro woman more than the women of any other group in America is the protagonist in the fight for an economically independent womanhood in modern countries. Her fight has not been willing or for the most part conscious but it has, nevertheless, been curiously effectively in its influence on the working world. (Cited in Stewart, 1990, p. 14)

Many of today's issues in counseling and therapy were first noted by minority authors, but full integration of these ideas into the field often have had to wait until they were endorsed by White mainstream authorities.

# Cultural Intentionality

A common theme underlying most approaches to helping, counseling, and psychotherapy, regardless of culture, is expansion of alternatives for living—the development of intentionality or purpose. Cultural intentionality can be described in the following way:

> *Cultural intentionality is acting with a sense of capability and flexibly deciding from among a range of alternative actions. The culturally intentional individual has more than one action, thought, or behavior to choose from in responding to changing life situations and diverse clients*

The broad construct of intentionality underlies the several descriptions of theoretical goals for counseling that we have discussed. Even more important, the goal of full-functioning intentionality for clients is directly analogous to the book's goal for counselors. Specifically, the goal is preparing counselors who are capable, can generate alternative helping behaviors in any given situation, have several alternative helping modes available to respond to the needs of the client at the moment, and have the ability to employ these responses to assist others to reach long-term goals. Both counselor and client seek intentionality.

Intentional living occurs in a cultural context. Cultural expertise and intentionality imply three major abilities on the part of individuals:

1. *The ability to generate a maximum number of thoughts, words, and behaviors to communicate with self and others within a given culture.*

Common to people who come for assistance on personal issues is immobility, the inability to act intentionally and resolve issues, or the experience of feeling stuck in one place. This immobility is described differently in many helping theories. For example, you will find that Gestalt therapy talks about splits and impasses; Rogerian therapy examines discrepancies between the ideal and real self; psychodynamic theorists discuss polarities and unconscious conflicts; and those committed to transactional analysis talk about crossed transactions, or routinized "games people play." The inability to respond creatively and intentionally is a common issue with which all helping approaches must cope. The task of the helper is to free the client to respond and initiate intentionally.

Families also become stuck. They can recycle ineffective patterns of interaction endlessly. Furthermore, behaviors, thoughts, and feelings learned in the family appear in the individual. You will find that many of your clients behave with you in the same fashion they learned in their family of origin.

There are many alternative ways for helping clients generate new verbal and nonverbal behaviors. Assertiveness training could be used to expand ability to deal with difficult situations and to enable the person to express thoughts and feelings freely. A person-centered helper, such as those who follow Rogerian theory, might focus on discrepancies between real and ideal self through listening to feelings and attitudes about self and work. A psychodynamically oriented individual might look into childhood for the roots of the present impasse. A multiculturally oriented therapist would examine the person's historical, cultural, and social context. Special attention would be given to the fact that different modes of being exist among differing cultural groups. A family therapist prefers to work with the entire family in the belief that the "identified patient" somehow is enacting family wishes. These are only a few of a myriad of possibilities. Any one of them used effectively is capable of freeing clients to generate new behaviors and to be more fully functioning.

Thus, an underlying purpose or overall goal of all counseling and therapy is to increase response capacity and the ability to generate or create new behaviors and thoughts.

## Culture and Intentionality

The discussion thus far has omitted the key word *culture*. The assumption of most helping theories is that they are appropriate regardless of the cultural background of the individual. Too often, helping theory omits such considerations. At this point, let us turn to the second dimension of the overall goal of cultural intentionality:

> *2. The ability to generate a maximum number of thoughts, words, and behaviors to communicate with a variety of diverse groups and individuals. Both clients and counselors need to communicate within their own culture and learn the ability to understand others' cultures as well.*

It has been demonstrated in several research studies that 50 percent of third world or minority individuals do not return for a second counseling interview (cf. Sue & Sue, 2016). In addition, a large number of majority individuals also fail to complete the helping process. When these data are combined with the many individuals who need help and never seek it, a failure of considerable dimensions is apparent. One reason for this major issue is lack of awareness and training given to counselors in issues of cultural awareness. The effective therapist must become aware of the fact that different client populations may use different verbal and nonverbal sentences and cues.

Most counseling theories operating in North America are based on a White, middle-class culture. What is appropriate behavior for a White individual may be unsuitable for an African American or Hispanic person. Individual behavior is partly determined by cultural norms. The expression of emotions as necessary in client-centered and psychodynamic therapy may be totally inappropriate and alien for some Asians and Native Americans (as well as many Whites). Not only the goal but the very process, style, and techniques of helping may be inappropriate.

Fortunately, most theories and approaches stress the importance of reflection on the appropriateness of their methods. This requires the counselor to reflect, analyze, and choose appropriate responses and techniques. The therapist who is skilled and knowledgeable in many theories and who has a concise approach to general theory and its application has a strong beginning for cultural intentionality. Evidence is rapidly accumulating that culture, religious background, socioeconomic status, age, and gender can be as important as the unique personality of the client and the reason for the consultation itself.

## Expanding Cultural Intentionality

Treatment of individuals without awareness of age, race, and gender differences is not only naive, but also unethical according to most current codes of ethics of mental health professions. People from different backgrounds respond and are responded to differently. Well-dressed people obtain more attention and better service in a welfare office or a department store. Physically attractive and tall people are likewise better treated than their shorter or less attractive counterparts. Given standard middle-class North American culture, it is most preferable to be young, male, White, of high socioeconomic status, tall, and physically attractive. Similarly, it is less advantageous to be old, female, non-White, of lower socioeconomic status, short, and unattractive. You may find yourself treating clients differently because they either belong or do not belong to a group to which you personally are attracted or favor.

Traditional helping theories do not typically give enough attention to culture. Generating new behaviors in relating within one's own culture and other cultures is not enough in itself. The third aspect of intentionality requires commitment to action.

> *3. The ability to formulate plans, act on many possibilities existing in a culture, and to reflect on these actions.*

Unfreezing an individual so that he or she is able to generate new behaviors is vital, but the simple generation of new ways of responding and acting creatively is not enough. At some point, the person must become committed to action and decide on an alternative. Not all counseling theories have a clear commitment to action as a goal.

Behavioral approaches to counseling are particularly strong on action. Clear, observable goals are developed with follow-up and evaluation. The cognitive-behavioral therapists often assign specific "homework" assignments so the ideas generated in the interview are taken home and practiced. Most approaches to psychotherapy do not get this specific, but all therapeutic approaches encourage clients to look at their plans and the results of their actions.

As an example of the complexity of establishing culturally appropriate goals, consider the eating disorders of bulimia and anorexia. Generally, these are disorders affecting women in North American culture, although male eating disorders are markedly increasing at this time. Thinness is what is valued by the culture, yet the goal of the therapist is to help the client generate a more positive body image and accept whatever weight he or she has. Through helping the client accept a heavier body image, the counselor is actually working against cultural imperatives. As such, cultural awareness and consciousness-raising often need to be part of the treatment of bulimia and anorexia.

By way of contrast, it should be recalled that some cultures consider a heavy woman more beautiful and consider thinness disgusting. What in one culture represents successful adjustment and adaptation can be a serious negative issue in another. White, middle-class North Americans are considered adjusted if they have accumulated private wealth. They would be considered to be suffering from a serious psychiatric disorder if this wealth were given away to friends and family. In South Pacific Fiji, the custom is that the individual must give away any material good if a friend or family member requests it—and give it away *forever*. The Native American potlatch, in which wealth is given to others in elaborate ceremonies, is another example of the fact that one can gain status and prestige in some cultures by sharing rather than acquiring. In a related fashion on US campuses, some African American students can be expected to send money home when the family needs it, with the result that they have insufficient money to pay college bills. As can be seen, "mental health" depends on a cultural perspective.

Learning about other cultural values systems and goals is a lifelong process. Whether we are talking about Canada, the United States, Australia, or Great Britain, all these societies are now recognized as multicultural. Whereas once the White male Eurocentric model was considered appropriate for all clients, this is no longer true. The effort throughout this book will be to provide examples of culture-specific issues that make the application of therapeutic theory and technique more relevant to individuals and families.

Intentionality is a broad framework that provides an all-encompassing goal for the psychotherapy process while simultaneously providing specific frameworks that may assist both therapist and client in deciding how they want to be and act in their culture. Given such a large range of possibilities, it seems that intentionality is oriented toward total cultural respect, with full awareness that definitions of individual freedom and responsibility to the group vary.

Table 2.1 outlines some possible dimensions of the culturally intentional counselor. What would you personally add to that list?

**Table 2.1. The Culturally Intentional Professional Contrasted with the Ineffective Helper**

| Attributes | Culturally Intentional Counselor or Therapist | Ineffective Counselor or Therapist |
|---|---|---|
| Helping goals | Works collaboratively with the client to establish culturally appropriate, agreed-upon goals. Actively searches for clients' strengths. | Imposes goals on the client based on own theory and personal beliefs. |
| Worldview | Aware of own worldview and how it is similar to and differs from others. Aware of how own worldview was generated within a cultural framework. | May have only one worldview or be able to work within only one framework. |
| Dimensions of helping | Multidimensional: aware that individual counseling and therapy are part of a larger treatment process. | Firm in the belief that one intervention or theory, individual or family, can solve all issues. |
| Research | A local scientist-practitioner fully aware of the need to inform clinical practice with empirical and qualitative research that is culturally aware and relevant within the context of their practice. | Denies the validity and usefulness of research or may miss important dimensions of multicultural research, affecting clients. |

*(Continued)*

**Table 2.1. The Culturally Intentional Professional Contrasted with the Ineffective Helper** *(Continued)*

| | | |
|---|---|---|
| Theoretical orientation | Actively involved in examining self and worldview, constantly learning new theories and methods through in-service training. Able to define a clear theory of helping, which may be a general theory or an eclectic/integrative theory. | Slavishly adopts a single theoretical position with no thought of alternatives, or may be unable to consciously define any system at all. |
| Professional orientation | Believes that professional field does not have all the answers and seeks to work effectively with others. Able to define distinct strengths of own profession. | Certain that professional field has the "best" and/or "only" answers. Unwilling or unable to work with others. |
| Ethical orientation | Fully aware of ethical code of profession and works toward implementing that code with cultural sensitivity. | Either unaware of ethics or deliberately unethical. May impose ethical code in a rigid "right-wrong" level of morality. |
| Wellness orientation | Uses a diversity-sensitive, neuroscience-based focus to wellness and stress management. | Overlooks importance of wellness and self-care. |

It is possible for you to become an effective, culturally intentional counselor, interviewer, or therapist. Helping can be a way of life, but it requires the ability to change, grow, and develop with your clients. Faith in humanity and humility on your part are two basic ingredients for this process. The remainder of this book is concerned with sharing relevant constructs that will serve as a beginning to your increased ability to enrich the lives of others.

# Neuroscience-Based Counselor Wellness

Culturally intentional counselors and therapists spend many hours interacting with clients in need of help. The number of clients seen per week varies, but whether it is five, twenty, or more, each one is suffering, stressed, frustrated, or in pain. Furthermore, for each of these clients, counselors hope to alleviate their suffering, resolve their issues, and increase their resilience and well-being.

Helping those in need is a noble and incredibly rewarding task, but it is also stressful. An effective mental health professional needs to be in sound mind and body to fully attend and assist clients sad about romantic breakups, distressed about a marital conflict, or, in more extreme cases, plagued by suicidal thoughts. Myers, Sweeney, and Witmer (2000) define wellness as "a way of life oriented toward optimal health and well-being, in which body, mind, and spirit are integrated by the individual to live life more fully within the human and natural community" (p. 252). Counselors and therapists are expected to advocate for wellness and optimal health for themselves and for their clients (American Counseling Association, 2014). Counselors, therapists, and students in training who respect their wellness are better able to facilitate wellness in their clients (Council for Accreditation of Counseling and Related Educational Programs, 2015; Meany-Walen, Davis-Gage, & Lindo, 2016).

Lifestyle factors and diet are recognized as essential for wellness and for the treatment of stress and mental disorders (Pratt et al., 2016). Nutrition, exercise, and sleep, for example, affect behavior, mood, and cognitive processes and play an important role in the etiology, progression, and treatment of mental disorders (Rössler, 2016). Furthermore, therapeutic lifestyle changes positively affect your brain and the cognitive functions its supports (Ivey et al., 2018). Use the Therapeutic LifeStyle Changes (TLC) in Table 2.2 to reflect on your own life and the changes you can make to achieve a more vibrant, focused, and intentional lifestyle.

**Table 2.2. Therapeutic LifeStyle Changes**

**HOW HEALTHY IS YOUR LIFESTYLE?** Allen Ivey, Mary Bradford Ivey, and Carlos Zalaquett © 2018

**Circle your response**

**ALIOSTRESS/EUSTRESS/STRESS LEVELS: What is your level of stress?**

| 1 | 2 | 3 | 4 | 5 | 1 2 3 4 5 |
|---|---|---|---|---|---|
| Eustress, life is generally calm and interesting, few major or minor stressors, recover from stress fairly quickly. Pleasant, happy life. | Manageable, stressors can be troublesome, but recover. Some tough stressors from time to time. Life is good. | Often feel stressed, sometimes for days, lose some sleep, old stressful events often with me. However, generally, life is good. | Constant feeling of stress, pressure, sleep difficulties, old events still with me. Can blow up, but manage. Life is OK, but … | Chronic stress, tired, angry, sleep difficulties, feel sad, easy to blow up, fall apart, out of control. Need to change my life. | |

**1. Exercise: How frequently do you exercise (walk, swim, bike, garden, run, rock climb)?**

| 1 | 2 | 3 | 4 | 5 | 1 2 3 4 5 |
|---|---|---|---|---|---|
| 5–7 days weekly | 4–5 days weekly | 2–3 times weekly | Occasionally | Couch potato | |

**2. Nutrition: What is your typical diet?**

| 1 | 2 | 3 | 4 (S.A.D) | 5 | 1 2 3 4 5 |
|---|---|---|---|---|---|
| Vegan, vegetarian, fish | Low fat, lean meat, fruit, vegetables | Mediterranean, Paleo | Std. Amer. Diet | Fast food, fries, sugar | |

*(Continued)*

**Table 2.2. Therapeutic LifeStyle Changes** *(Continued)*

**3. Sleep: How many hours nightly, including how restful is your sleep?**

| 1 | 2 | 3 | 4 | 5 | 1 | 2 | 3 | 4 | 5 |
|---|---|---|---|---|---|---|---|---|---|
| 7–9 hours | 7 hours | Sleep challenges | Many meds | Serious difficulty | | | | | |

**4. Social relations: How connected are you to others—close relationships, family, friends, groups?**

| 1 | 2 | 3 | 4 | 5 | 1 | 2 | 3 | 4 | 5 |
|---|---|---|---|---|---|---|---|---|---|
| Well connected | Connected | Friends, some groups | Somewhat social | Alone, angry, sad | | | | | |

**4a. Intimacy, sex life: How satisfied are you with your sex life?**

| 1 | 2 | 3 | 4 | 5 | 1 | 2 | 3 | 4 | 5 |
|---|---|---|---|---|---|---|---|---|---|
| Highly | Moderately | Somewhat | Dissatisfied | Do not care | | | | | |

**5. Cognitive challenge: How actively do you involve yourself in mind-expanding cognitive challenges?**

| 1 | 2 | 3 | 4 | 5 | 1 | 2 | 3 | 4 | 5 |
|---|---|---|---|---|---|---|---|---|---|
| Joy in constantly learning, searching for the new | Involved, active | Moderately interested, read some books, puzzles | Some, no more than 3 hours | None | | | | | |

**6. Cultural health and cultural identity: Awareness of cultural issues influencing you, including sense of cultural identity.**

| 1 | 2 | 3 | 4 | 5 | 1 | 2 | 3 | 4 | 5 |
|---|---|---|---|---|---|---|---|---|---|
| Empathy for self and others. Sees self-in-rela-tion, race/ethnicity, etc., awareness, life vision | At least two of the preceding plus life vision | One of the preceding, some life vision | Slightly aware of issues | Oppressive, no real life vision | | | | | |

**7. Meditation, yoga, etc.: How often you engage in this practice?**

| 1 | 2 | 3 | 4 | 5 | 1 | 2 | 3 | 4 | 5 |
|---|---|---|---|---|---|---|---|---|---|
| Daily | 3–4 times weekly | Aware, occasional | Absent | Hyper, cannot do | | | | | |

*(Continued)*

**Table 2.2.  Therapeutic LifeStyle Changes** *(Continued)*

**8. Drugs, alcohol: Use of alcohol or other drugs?**

| 1 | 2 | 3 | 4 | 5 | | 1 2 3 4 5 |
|---|---|---|---|---|---|---|
| None | Moderate | Has become part of life | Becomes a focus | Addicted | | |

**9. Medication and supplements: How aware are you of possible issues plus appropriate contact with physicians?**

| 1 | 2 | 3 | 4 | 5 | | 1 2 3 4 5 |
|---|---|---|---|---|---|---|
| Regular contact with physician, follows directions | Frequent contact | Occasionally, some difficulty following directions | Seldom | Never | | |

**10. Positive thinking/optimism/happiness: Do you have resilient positive attitudes and a good level of happiness?**

| 1 | 2 | 3 | 4 | 5 | | 1 2 3 4 5 |
|---|---|---|---|---|---|---|
| Resilient, positive, optimistic | Most of the time | Usually, not always | Seldom | Infrequent | | |

**11. Belief, values: How engaged are you with living a meaningful life?**

| 1 | 2 | 3 | 4 | 5 | | 1 2 3 4 5 |
|---|---|---|---|---|---|---|
| A life center | Involved | Occasional involvement | Never | Not interested | | |

**11a. Spirituality, religiosity: Do you participate in spiritual or religious activities?**

| 1 | 2 | 3 | 4 | 5 | | 1 2 3 4 5 |
|---|---|---|---|---|---|---|
| Daily | Every 2–4 days | Once a week | Holidays only | Do not believe | | |

**12. Nature/green/garden: How often do you engage in outside/nature activities?**

| 1 | 2 | 3 | 4 | 5 | | 1 2 3 4 5 |
|---|---|---|---|---|---|---|
| Get outdoors often | Frequently | Sometimes | Seldom | Almost never | | |

**13. Smoking: Do you smoke? If yes, how much?**

| 1 | 2 | 3 | 4 | 5 | | 1 2 3 4 5 |
|---|---|---|---|---|---|---|
| Never | Never, but exposed to secondary | Stopped smoking | Tries to stop | Still smoking | | |

*(Continued)*

**Table 2.2. Therapeutic LifeStyle Changes** *(Continued)*

**14. Screen time (TV, cell, iPad, computer): Amount of time in front of a screen?**

| 1 | 2 | 3 | 4 | 5 | | 1 2 3 4 5 |
|---|---|---|---|---|---|---|
| None | 2 hours or less daily | 4 hours | 6 or more | Never off-line | | |

**15. Relaxation and having fun: How frequently are you involved in leisure or relaxation activities?**

| 1 | 2 | 3 | 4 | 5 | | 1 2 3 4 5 |
|---|---|---|---|---|---|---|
| Something every day | 5–6 hours weekly | 3–4 hours | Limited and stressed | Workaholic and/or stressed out | | |

**16. Education: What level of education have you completed?**

| 1 | 2 | 3 | 4 | 5 | | 1 2 3 4 5 |
|---|---|---|---|---|---|---|
| College, serious hobby | College | Comm. College | High school/ GED | Dropout | | |

**17. Money and privilege: What is your financial situation? Do you benefit from privilege because of race or other factors?**

| 1 | 2 | 3 | 4 | 5 | | 1 2 3 4 5 |
|---|---|---|---|---|---|---|
| Have it all, privileged | Comfortable | Making it | On edge, but Ok | Poor, oppressed | | |

**18. Helping others/community involvement/social justice action: How frequently do you help others or your community?**

| 1 | 2 | 3 | 4 | 5 | | 1 2 3 4 5 |
|---|---|---|---|---|---|---|
| Daily action | Weekly action | Often involved | No time | Destructive | | |

**19. Art, music, dance, literature: How frequently do you release your artistic abilities?**

| 1 | 2 | 3 | 4 | 5 | | 1 2 3 4 5 |
|---|---|---|---|---|---|---|
| Daily | Several times weekly | Moderate/ frequently | Occasionally | None | | |

**20. Joy, humor, zest for living, keeping it simple, not overdoing: How happy or how much fun do you have?**

| 1 | 2 | 3 | 4 | 5 | | 1 2 3 4 5 |
|---|---|---|---|---|---|---|
| Life is a blast | Fun most of the time | Moderately happy | Now and then | Never | | |

*(Continued)*

**Table 2.2. Therapeutic LifeStyle Changes** *(Continued)*

## SELF-EVALUATION OF GENERAL LIFESTYLE

**Work: What is the level of your work or retirement activities?**

| 1 | 2 | 3 | 4 | 5 | | 1 2 3 4 5 |
|---|---|---|---|---|---|---|
| Fully employed. Retired, never bored | Partial employment. Retired and active | Temporary work. OK, but sometimes bored | Jobless. Bored, less happy | Given up work. Inactive, depressed | | |

**In control: How much in control of your life are you?**

| 1 | 2 | 3 | 4 | 5 | | 1 2 3 4 5 |
|---|---|---|---|---|---|---|
| In full control of my life | Mostly in control | Somewhat in control | Low control | Out of control | | |

**Health: How healthy are you?**

| 1 | 2 | 3 | 4 | 5 | | 1 2 3 4 5 |
|---|---|---|---|---|---|---|
| Very healthy | Occasional issues | Good, but could be better | Major issue | Very poor | | |

**Stability: How stable is your life currently?**

| 1 | 2 | 3 | 4 | 5 | | 1 2 3 4 5 |
|---|---|---|---|---|---|---|
| Highly stable | Moderately | Some ups and downs | Unstable | Chaotic | | |

**Resilience: Your ability to bounce back from life challenges.**

| 1 | 2 | 3 | 4 | 5 | | 1 2 3 4 5 |
|---|---|---|---|---|---|---|
| Back "at it" soon | Temporarily troubled | Worry a fair amount | Difficult, but do it | Overwhelmed | | |

**Satisfaction: How satisfied are you with your current lifestyle?**

| 1 | 2 | 3 | 4 | 5 | | 1 2 3 4 5 |
|---|---|---|---|---|---|---|
| Highly | Moderately | Somewhat | Dissatisfied | Helpless | | |

**Action: How ready are you to make changes to increase your well-being?**

| 1 | 2 | 3 | 4 | 5 | | 1 2 3 4 5 |
|---|---|---|---|---|---|---|
| Ready to change | Want to change | Thinking about it | Some interest | Not interested | | |

Therapeutic lifestyle changes, presented on Table 2.2, are a key route to identifying and encouraging an engaged lifestyle. Focus on those items with scores between 3 and 5. Select a few and develop a plan for implementation. Take time to implement these changes in your life. You deserve it! Furthermore, your future clients also deserve it. Whether you use the TLCs to be more present and intentional in the session with your clients or to educate your clients about ways to increase their well-being and prevent stress and mental disorders, either way, you are improving quality of life and brain function.

# Theories into Action: The Community Genogram— A Practice Strategy

"It takes a village to raise a child." This well-known African proverb underlies the community genogram. Our original community is where we learn the culture which will remain with us through our lifetime. Communities consist of our family and perhaps extended family, friends and neighbors, schools, work settings, the physical geography of the community territory, church or spiritual connections, and other unique factors. Our personal experiences with community are as unique as our fingerprints.

The community genogram is presented as a practice exercise, as it provides a way for you and the client to learn more directly how cultural factors, implicit and explicit in the community, underlie individual and family development. Together, the family and community genograms provide a solid way to ensure that individual issues are seen in their full contextual background.

Culture, community, families, groups, and individuals are all interconnected. Difficulty or trauma in the community, such as a tornado, a mass shooting, or the loss of jobs through the closure of a manufacturing plant, will deeply affect not only individual lives, but also what occurs in the family and various community groups. In effect, one major community event can change the total culture. In turn, the madness or skill of one individual will affect the total system as well. Witness what occurs when a criminal terrorizes a family or the positive impact of a single individual such as Martin Luther King Jr.

Individual counseling and therapy exist within a social context. If we want to understand any individual, we need to see that person totally. The community genogram was developed by Ivey (1995) as a way to introduce a positive, strength-oriented view of self, showing how we are all selves in relation one to another. The community genogram is also a way to discover the important groups (church, school, peer groups, neighborhood, etc.) that influence the person. If we take a life-span perspective, we can become aware that the nature of community changes and expands as we grow. The family is the center for the child; peer groups for many teens; work for many adults;

and family again for elders (Ivey et al., 2018; Rigazio-DiGilio, Ivey, Grady, & Kunkler-Peck, 2005).

Many individual issues and concerns are related to community, especially when we consider family as central to that community. The community genogram, while focusing on personal, family, and group strengths, also provides an opportunity to understand the context of past or current issues.

The specific steps toward developing a community genogram are presented in Practice Exercise 2.1. We suggest that you first develop your own community genogram and then later use this strategy with your client. As you work with the strategy, note that the visual style of model developed can be changed to meet your or the client's specific needs and experiences. As mentioned at the beginning of this book reading about theory or about an exercise is, at best, an introduction. To realize the potential of the community genogram, it is essential that you actually engage in the process of the practice exercise.

Visual models for a community genogram: Rather than fixing on a single visual framework for a community genogram, Ivey suggests that you work with each client to develop their own model. Many clients like to draw literal maps of their communities, with pictures of family, school, and church drawn in. One useful visual model is that of a star with interacting influences. Others prefer abstract circles and squares drawn with lines of connection.

## The Community Genogram—A Case Example

One client started his community genogram talking about how he had been called negative names in his home community and peer group because he was the only Jewish child. As he talked about this negative recollection, it became apparent that much of his current lack of trust in his partner is related to issues of anti-Semitism. He also noted that his style of dealing with prejudice in the past was withdrawing and avoiding social contact. He was doing the same in his present job and relationship.

The counselor listened carefully to this discussion and realized that the client's issues were very much tied to ethnic prejudice in the community—the individual concern was reframed as a community/systemic issue. Therefore, before continuing the negative stories too far, the counselor suggested a comprehensive community genogram and a search for strengths and positive resources. This is not to deny the issues and concerns—rather, the pause was used to remind the client of personal strengths that would help deal with very real issues.

**Exercise 2.1. The Community Genogram: Identifying Strengths**

This exercise has three goals: 1) to generate a narrative story of the client in community context; 2) to help the client (or you in this case) generate an understanding of how we all develop in community; and 3) to use visual, auditory, or kinesthetic images as sources of strength. These images of strengths can be called on later in the counseling and therapy interview as positive resources to help clients cope with life's difficulties.

In addition, this exercise will help you understand the cultural background of your client, for it is through family and community that we learn our cultural framework. Finally, many of your clients will have had difficult life experiences in their communities. They may be tempted to first focus on the negative as they develop their awareness and stories of how they developed and live in a community setting. While you will need to attend to potentially negative stories, we urge you to focus first on positive strengths.

### Develop a visual representation of the community.

1. Consider a large piece of paper as representing your broad culture and community. Any other community, past or present, may be used.

   We recommend that you select the community in which you were primarily raised, but any other community, past or present, may be used.

2. Place yourself or the client in that community, either at the center or other appropriate place. Represent yourself or the client by a circle, a star, or other significant symbol.

3. Place your own or the client's family or families on the paper, again represented by the symbol most relevant for you. The family can be nuclear or extended or both.

4. Place important and most influential groups on the community genogram, again representing them by circles or other visual symbols. School, family, neighborhood, and spiritual groups are most often selected. For teens, the peer group is often particularly important. For adults, work groups and other special groups tend to become more central.

5. Connect the groups to the focus individual, perhaps drawing more heavy lines to indicate the most influential groups.

*(Continued)*

### Search for images and narratives of strengths.

While you undoubtedly recognize that many individual difficulties and issues arise in a family, community, and cultural context, the community genogram focuses on strengths (Ivey et al., 2018).

The community genogram provides a frame of reference to help the client see self-in-context. The client is asked to generate narratives of key stories from the community where he or she grew up. If relevant, key stories from the present living community may also be important. The emphasis is on positive stories from the community and positive images. The community genogram is kept and used during the entire counseling series of interviews.

The community genogram in its first stages focuses on positive stories and images. The importance of this point cannot be overstated. You will find that once this positive approach has been used first, clients have a foundation for exploring more difficult and troublesome areas of their lives. In addition, you will have a good foundation yourself as a therapist, which helps you understand the community, family, and cultural background of the client.

The specifics of the positive resource search follow:

1.  Focus on one single community group or the family. You or the client may want to start with a negative story or image. Please do not work with the negative until positive strengths are solidly in mind.

2.  Develop a visual, auditory, or kinesthetic image that represents an important positive experience. Allow the image to build in your mind, and note the positive feelings that occur with the image. If you allow yourself or the client to fully experience that positive image, you may experience tears and/or strong bodily feelings. These anchored body experiences represent positive strengths that can be drawn on to help you and your clients deal with difficult issues in therapy and in life.

3.  Tell the story of the image. If it is your story, you may want to write it down in journal form. If you are drawing out the story from a client, listen sensitively.

4.  Develop at least two more positive images from different groups within the community. It is useful to have one positive family image, one spiritual image, and one cultural image. Again, many of us will want to focus on negative issues. Hold to the search for positive resources.

*(Continued)*

**Exercise 2.1. The Community Genogram: Identifying Strengths *(Continued)***

5. Summarize the positive images in your own words and reflect on them. With a client, encourage them to summarize their learning, thoughts, and feelings in their own words. As you or your client thinks back, what occurs? Record the responses, for they can be drawn on in many settings in therapy or in the daily life of the client.

The community genogram can be a very emotional and dramatic strategy. At a minimum, it will help you to understand the special cultural background of your client, and it serves as a reservoir of positive experiences that can be drawn on to help you and the client throughout therapy.

Becoming a counselor and therapist involves several tasks. You must learn therapeutic theories at a cognitive level, but also you must practice them. Each chapter has a number of practical exercises that will give you an opportunity to take theory into direct practice and learn whether or not the theory works for you—that is, if it is applicable to your personal experience and if you wish to consider the issues in more detail.

Reading a text such as this represents a good first step toward becoming a culturally intentional counselor and therapist. But you will learn far more about the theories if you do the exercises seriously. You may also find it useful to return to these exercises during practicum and internship. Repeating the exercises will give you not only a firm foundation but also a base on which you can develop new ideas for practice.

# References

American Counseling Association. (2014). *ACA code of ethics*. Alexandria, VA: Author.

Barnett, M. (2007). What brings you here? An exploration of the unconscious motivations of those who choose to train and work as psychotherapists and counsellors. *Psychodynamic Practice, 13* (3), 257–274. doi.org/10.1080/14753630701455796.

Council for Accreditation of Counseling and Related Educational Programs. (2015). *2016 CACREP standards*. Retrieved from http://www.cacrep.org/wp-content/uploads/2012/10/2016-CACREP-Standards.pdf.

Escher, M. (1960). *The graphic work of M.C. Escher*. New York, NY: Ballantine.

Farber, B.A., Manevich, I., Metzger, J., & Saypol, S. (2005). Choosing psychotherapy as a career: Why did we cross that road? *Journal of Clinical Psychology, 61,* 1009–1031. doi:10.1002/jclp.20174.

Gilligan, C. (2016). *In a different voice*. Cambridge, MA: Harvard University Press.

Ivey, A. (1995). *The community genogram: A strategy to assess culture and community resources*. Paper presented at the American Counseling Association, Denver, Colorado.

Ivey, A., Ivey, M.B., & Zalaquett, C. (2018). *Intentional interviewing and counseling: Facilitating client development in a multicultural society* (9th ed.). Belmont, CA: Cengage Learning.

Kirkwood, C. (2012). The persons in relation perspective: In counselling, psychotherapy and community adult learning. *International Issues in Adult Education*. Rotterdam, the Netherlands: Sense.

Mahrer, A.R. (2005). What inspired me to become a psychotherapist? *Journal of Clinical Psychology, 61*, 957–964. doi:10.1002/jclp.20168.

Meany-Walen, K.K., Davis-Gage, D., & Lindo, N.A. (2016). The impact of wellness-focused supervision on mental health counseling practicum students. *Journal of Counseling & Development, 94*, 464–472. doi:10.1002/jcad.12105.

Myers, J.E., Sweeney, T.J., & Witmer, J.M. (2000). The Wheel of Wellness counseling for wellness: A holistic model for treatment planning. *Journal of Counseling and Development, 78*, 251–266.

Norcross, J.C., & Farber, B.A. (2005). Choosing psychotherapy as a career: Beyond "I want to help people." *Journal of Clinical Psychology, 61*, 939–943. doi:10.1002/jclp.20175.

Pratt, S.I., Jerome, G.J., Schneider, K.L., Craft, L.L., Buman, M.P., Stoutenberg, M., Daumit, G.L., ... Goodrich, D.E. (2016). Increasing US health plan coverage for exercise programming in community mental health settings for people with serious mental illness: A position statement from the Society of Behavior Medicine and the American College of Sports Medicine. *Translational Behavioral Medicine, 6*, 478–481. doi:10.1007/s13142-016-0407-7.

Rigazio-DiGilio, S., Ivey, A., Grady, L., & Kunkler-Peck, K. (2005). *The community genogram*. New York, NY: Teachers College Press.

Rössler, W. (2016). Nutrition, sleep, physical exercise: Impact on mental health. *European Psychiatry, 33*, S12–S12. doi.org/10.1016/j.eurpsy.2016.01.804.

Stewart, J. (1990). Back to basics: The significance of Du Bois's and Frazier's contributions for contemporary research on Black families. In H. Cheatham & J. Stewart, *Black Families* (pp. 3–30). New Brunswick, NJ: Transaction.

Sue, D.W., & Sue, D. (2016). *Counseling the culturally diverse: Theory and practice* (7th ed.). Hoboken, NJ: Wiley.

Watzlawick, P., Beavin, J.H., & Jackson, D.D. (1967). *Pragmatics of human communication: A study of interactional patterns, pathologies, and paradoxes*. New York, NY: Norton.

### CHAPTER 3

# The Empathic Attitude
## Individual, Family, and Culture

## CHAPTER GOALS

Empathy is foundational to counseling and psychotherapy (Meneses & Larking, 2017). Most counseling and psychotherapy theories assert the importance for counselors to experience what they believe the client is experiencing (Ivey, Ivey, & Zalaquett, 2018). Empathic understanding helps mental health professionals recognize and relate to the clients' emotions and thoughts. Estimating the direct contribution of empathy to counseling and psychotherapy positive results is difficult to accomplish, but studies on the role of the therapeutic relationship, a factor common to all therapies that strongly involves empathy, suggest that the relationship accounts for 30 percent of the therapeutic outcome, a significant contribution (Lambert, 2013; Norcross & Lambert, 2011; Yager, 2015).

The approach to empathy in this chapter varies from the traditional. Empathic understanding that focuses only on the person is incomplete, we need to understand that individual in the context of family, culture, and surrounding circumstances. This approach has the capacity to reduce the potential concerns raised about empathic biases (Bloom, 2017) and potential burnout and exhaustion (Konrath & Grynberg, 2016).

Empathy is central to the development of a positive working relationship with clients. The empathic conditions, particularly with the cultural additions, form the necessary and sufficient basis of a helping theory in their own right. Moreover, empathic theory and research are necessary for the practice of all counseling and psychotherapy.

# SPECIFIC GOALS OF THIS CHAPTER:

1. Define and understand *empathy as a broad construct* and explore its personal meaning to you. We approach empathy as it is traditionally defined, discuss the upstream approach, and add multicultural considerations and research evidence.

2. Describe and engage in the *positive asset search*, a systematic set of strategies to enable you to find something valuable in any client, group, or family.

3. Examine your *own cultural and ethnic background* and consider how empathy may be manifested differently among varying groups of individuals.

4. Study the *facilitative conditions*. We offer an adaptation of the traditional facilitative conditions scale with practice exercises to understand the scale and varied cultural responses.

5. Understand how concepts such as *concreteness, immediacy, and genuineness* are useful ways to deepen understanding of individuals and families.

6. Review *empathy, family, and multicultural issues*. This section has three purposes: 1) to help you and your client become more in touch with their own cultural heritage, particularly as manifested in their family of origin; 2) to encourage awareness that other cultures may construct the same event differently from the culture of the helper; and 3) to introduce the important multicultural competencies that are essential to the definition of the effective helper.

7. Use the *perception check* as an important skill. Checking out with the client and finding out how he or she reacts to the interview helps understand how the client uniquely constructs the meaning of the interview and our interventions.

8. Learn about the neuroscientific foundations of empathy, and its role in the counseling process, prevention and wellness.

9. Bring theory into action through practice and rating of your and others' empathic responses.

# Empathy and Empathic Approaches

*Empathy refers to an individual's ability to experience another person's emotions and feelings as they occur and to share that person's perspective on his/her self and the environment.*

**—Juris Draguns**

Empathy is often described as seeing the world through another's eyes, hearing as they might hear, and feeling and experiencing their internal world. The Native Americans have talked about walking in the other person's moccasins. Empathy involves both affective and cognitive components. The affective component includes feeling the emotions with the other person or having a vicarious (e.g., secondhand) experience of the emotional response of the other. The cognitive component involves understanding and grasping the meaning of the other person's experience (Berliner & Masterson, 2015).

Note that empathy is *not* mixing your thoughts and feelings with those of the client. While the empathic attitude understands and accepts the client's experienced emotions and perspective, the counselor and therapist remain separate, true to self and their own beliefs.

Empathy encompasses positive and negative emotions (e.g., happiness and sadness) but most theories focus on distress and negative emotions. The opposite of empathy is indifference, the inability to experience another individual's emotional reaction. Also different from empathy are sympathy and compassion. Sympathy is the cognitive apprehension of another person's suffering, followed by efforts to alleviate that suffering, instead of co-sharing that suffering intrapersonally (Draguns, 2015). Compassion involves caring concerns (feeling with) but not necessarily shared feelings (feeling as) (Lown, 2016, p. 334).

## Acceptance as the Foundation of Empathy

Acceptance may be described as the foundation of empathy. How would you define and experience acceptance? The following images may be helpful (see Reflection Exercise).

> ## REFLECTION EXERCISE
>
> Recall a time when you felt accepted by someone else just as you are or were. Can you imagine the situation? What is happening, and what are you seeing? What is being said? What are the thoughts and feelings that go with the image?
>
> Note: If you do not work well with visual images, use words, poetry, sounds, or bodily feelings.

Counseling and therapy ask you to accept the client. It is easy to accept a small child crying from an emotional hurt on the playground, or a best friend or a survivor of an abusive spousal physical attack. However, it is far less easy to accept the bully on the playground or the perpetrator of family violence. The following Reflection Exercise can help you explore your ability to be accepting.

> ## REFLECTION EXERCISE
>
> How do you imagine yourself if you were to work with a bully or an abuser? Take time to let that image arise. What are you seeing and hearing? Most important, what are you feeling in your own body?

The feelings you experience in your own body may be the best indicator of your degree of acceptance and ability to be empathic. Taking time to learn how your body is reacting to clients in the here and now will give you a better understanding of deeper client feelings. This awareness also can help you avoid mixing your feelings incorrectly with those of the client. It is fairly easy to note warm feelings of compassion in your stomach when you talk with a client you like. However, most of us have difficulty when we work with those who hurt others. For example, your stomach may tighten and your fists unconsciously clench. Note this and move on; seek to enter the challenging client's world.

The bully, the abuser, and even the rapist need empathy and acceptance as much as the child, adolescent, or adult who has survived their attack. It is much easier to work with survivors than it is with perpetrators. Becoming aware of personal internal body reactions is a skill that is well worth developing.

## Empathic Understanding and Prevention: The "Downstream" and the "Upstream" Approach

As counselors and therapists, we have a special responsibility to protect victims and survivors of attacks. One way to meet this responsibility is by working effectively with those who may harm others. Not only might empathic understanding help those who have been hurt, but it can also serve as a basis for prevention work with perpetrators.

The following analogy illustrates this point. In a rural area, there was a swimming hole bordered by a warm sandy beach near a bend in the river. The local people enjoyed swimming and playing on the beach, but one day a drowning child came around the bend, and a strong swimmer pulled him to safety. The next day, the same thing happened again; this time, a woman was saved. Daily thereafter, drowning people came round the river's bend—men, women, and children, and sometimes whole families. The people decided to organize a lifesaving club to rescue victims as they came downstream. One person disagreed and started walking upriver around the bend, saying, "I think we need to go upstream to see who's throwing these people in!" As the story shows, empathy is not just the understanding of another's experience; it can also include action.

In the "downstream," approach you will primarily work with survivors. If you truly embrace the empathic challenge of acceptance, you can move "upstream" as well to work with perpetrators and abusers and prevent victimization. The real challenge of the empathic approach is to accept those who seem unacceptable and work with them to change their behavior, attitudes, and feelings.

# The Broad Construct of Empathy

> The art of psychotherapy may largely consist of judicious and sensitive applications of a given technique, delicate decisions of when to press a point or when to be patient, when to be warm and understanding, and when to be remote.
>
> Hans Strupp

In 1957, Carl Rogers produced a landmark paper, "The Necessary and Sufficient Conditions of Therapeutic Personality Change," that made a strong case that empathy and related constructs are all that is needed to produce change in a client. To help another person grow, Rogers said, requires: an integrated congruent relationship with the client; unconditional positive regard for the client; and the communication of empathy from the counselor to the client. Rogers's theoretical frames will be explored in detail in Chapter 10, but his work in empathy is considered basic to all theories of helping and thus is emphasized here.

Rogers has referred to the following as a good contemporary definition of empathy. The comments below are important, as they take empathy beyond an attitude and suggest specific actions that a counselor can take in the session.

> This is not laying trips on people. … You only listen and say back the other person's thing, step by step, just as that person seems to have it at that moment. You never mix into it any of your own things or ideas, never lay on the other person anything that person didn't express. … To show that you understand exactly, make a sentence or

two which gets exactly at the personal meaning this person wanted to put across. This might be in your own words, usually, but use that person's own words for the touchy main things. (Gendlin & Hendricks, Rap Manual, undated, cited in Rogers, 1980, p. 145)

In the above definition, Rogers is referring to the skills of the empathic attitude, things a counselor or therapist can *do* in the interview to communicate empathy and understanding to another human being. The year 1980 now seems a long time ago, but professionals still agree that Rogers's and Gendlin's thinking is key to competent counseling and therapy. Chapter 10 on listening skills will extend these concepts with a number of specifics that are helpful in communicating with clients.

As can be seen, empathy demands both positive attitudes and positive actions toward the client. Perhaps no larger demand can be made on you as a counselor than to find something positive in the midst of client negativity.

Table 3.1 presents past and present research on the effects of empathy.

---

**Table 3.1. Research Summary on Empathy**

The research studies on empathy and its effects are legion and basic to our field. The following is a summary from early beginnings to powerful recent findings.

A landmark series of studies by Fiedler (1950a, 1950b, 1951) involved defining the ideal therapeutic relationship through systematic study of therapists of the psychoanalytic, Rogerian, and Adlerian persuasions. He found that expert therapists of the several types appeared more similar to each other than they did to inexperienced therapists within their own theoretical orientations. An equally important study was conducted by Barrett-Lennard (1962), who studied level of regard, empathy, congruence, unconditionality of regard, and willingness to be known, as manifested in therapy sessions of inexperienced and experienced counselors. Barrett-Lennard found higher levels of these facilitative conditions among experienced therapists.

These two studies were pivotal in an avalanche of studies of the Rogerian qualitative dimensions during the ensuing years. Classic reviews of this research may be found in Anthony and Carkhuff (1977) and Truax and Mitchell (1971). Studies of the facilitative conditions of empathy, warmth, respect, and so forth have demonstrated these qualities to be closely related to evaluations of effectiveness in counseling and psychotherapy. Further, these dimensions may be more important in some cases than the theoretical orientation of the counselor, for it is obvious that a warm and attentive counselor of any orientation would be preferable to most clients than a cold and distant individual who fails to show interpersonal respect.

Carl Rogers points out that many therapists fall short of offering empathic conditions and that therapy and counseling can be for better or worse. In a classic and foundational research study, Hadley and Strupp (1976) reviewed extensive research indicating possible deterioration as an effect of the psychotherapeutic process, and point out the importance of a solid relationship appropriate to the need level of the client. Strupp (1977, p. 11) catches the essence of Rogers' argument when he says "the art of psychotherapy may largely consist of judicious and sensitive applications of a given technique, delicate decisions of when to press a point or when to be patient, when to be warm and understanding, and when to be remote." Strupp, then, is suggesting that simple application of a few empathic qualities is not enough. These qualities also must be in synchrony with the client, at the moment, in the interviewing process (cf. Strupp, 1981).

*(Continued)*

**Table 3.1. Research Summary on Empathy (Continued)**

More recent reviews such as the project to identify relevant variables of effective therapeutic relationships, co-sponsored by the Divisions of Psychotherapy and Clinical Psychology of the American Psychological Association, identified empathy as the second highest contributor to positive therapy outcome (Norcross, 2011). The first one was the therapeutic alliance (Elliott, Bohart, Watson, & Greenberg, 2011).

As a more specific example, in a study of 1,383 diagnosed alcohol users, empathy had a significant relationship to drinking. At the end of sixteen weeks of treatment, clients who experienced high levels of empathy from their therapists drank less (Moyers, Houck, Rice, Longabaugh, & Miller, 2016).

Other studies have demonstrated that when the therapist's empathic abilities are compromised, ruptures in the alliance emerge and therapeutic dropout may occur (Coutinho, Ribeiro, Fernandes, Sousa, & Safran, 2014). On the other hand, the more empathic the therapist's responses are, the more understood and validated the client feels. It is the therapist's empathic response perceived by the client that is critical for client change and positive therapy outcome (Coutinho, Silva, & Decety, 2014).

These important results substantiate the central role of empathy anticipated by the pioneering Carl Rogers. Research has confirmed empathy as an active ingredient of counseling and psychotherapy.

# Positive Regard

Positive regard is that part of the empathic attitude that meets all clients with a positive and optimistic attitude and emphasizes their strengths. Carl Rogers's positive way of being with clients and hope for them has become legendary. Positive regard means that you as therapist are able to recognize values and strengths in clients different from yourself, even when the client holds attitudes far different from yours. As it is the case with acceptance, the greatest challenge to positive regard occurs when you work with clients or families that seem to be destructive to themselves and others.

Time and time again, you will find Rogers listening to deep client issues and then reflecting the most positive meanings out of complex situations. The following is just one example:

> S: Yes, I realized the position, that I had to get it out, and I did, Tuesday night, and it wasn't that I sat down and I said, "Well, Arnold, let's talk it out, leave us talk it out …" I didn't do that. My feeling of hatred towards him was so intense that I was weak already, really I was so weak—I said something and he misunderstood me. And, then, I misunderstood him and I said, "Arnold, we just don't meet at all, do we Arnold?" Then he said, "Well, let's talk," so we sat down and talked. So he took the initiative, and I started to talk to him for a whole hour and a half. Before it opened up I hated him, I couldn't talk, "Oh, he won't understand," "We don't meet on the same level." To myself, "Let's get away from each other." "I can't stand to be with you, you irritate me …" Then all of a sudden, I said, "Arnold, do you know that I feel sexually inferior to you," and that did it. The very fact

that I could tell him that. Which was, I think that was the very thing, the whole thought to admit, not to admit to myself, because I knew that all the time, but to bring it up so that I could have admitted it to him, which I think was the whole turning point.

R: To be able to admit what you regarded as your deepest weakness.

S: Yes.

R: Just started the ball rolling.

S: This feeling of sexual inadequacy, but now that he knows it—it isn't important any more. It's like I carried a secret with me, and I wanted somebody to share it and Arnold of all people, and finally he knows about it so I feel better. So I don't feel inadequate.

R: The worst is known and accepted. (Rogers, 1951, pp. 86–87)

In the above, it would have been easy to focus on the negative. Rather, Rogers reflects on the more positive dimensions. He is responding to the deeper structure of the surface sentences. He uses the skill of reflection of meaning (see Chapter 10), bringing out the client's main words and ideas for positive reframing. Rogers is "coming from" the worldview of the client.

Helping the client find positive meanings, noting strengths in the client, and reframing challenges as opportunities is not restricted to Rogerian theory. All successful theories of counseling and therapy use some form of positive regard either explicitly or implicitly. In Chapter 4, the concepts are discussed under the idea of the *positive asset search*. There, specific techniques for drawing out strengths will be defined. You will also find that most theories of counseling and therapy use some form of resource exploration, positive asset search, and positive regard. Family therapy, for example, makes extensive use of the *positive reframe* as a way to help families most out of destructive behavior and patterns.

## The Positive Asset Search

The tendency in counseling and therapy is to focus too much on difficulties and client concerns. You will find that if you give serious attention to positive strengths early in the interview, your client will feel empowered and better able to cope with the negative and often can use those strengths to resolve concerns—"what is the client doing right." Exercise 3.1 will help you practice this important competence.

## The Positive Asset Search: Building Empathy on Strengths

Given counseling and psychotherapy's tendency to focus almost solely on negative issues, give special effort to finding strengths that will help clients build resilience. Yes, we need to discuss client issues fully, but we suggest that more time be given to strengths and positive assets.

With a volunteer client, work through the following brief exercise.

1.  Mention that too much counseling and therapy focuses solely on negative and that you wish to begin your session with a strength assessment, and you will need the client's help in this process.

2.  Discuss with the client possible areas of strengths in present-day life or the past. These positive resources may include many things, but important among them are: present and past successes the client has enjoyed, supportive family members or friends, spirituality, a love of nature, sports, or cultural heroes such as Martin Luther King or Gandhi—even a loved grandparent. As part of client history, specifically search out times when the client felt stronger and was doing well—exceptions to the issues. It is these positives that may provide full or partial solutions for many current client concerns.

3.  Draw out a personal narrative or story from the client that concretizes the positive strength. As you listen to the story, note how the client's body may shift to a position of more softness and/or strength. Reinforce that bodily experience through focusing for a moment on how the client feels when discussing a positive resource. Often, the client can locate that strength or resource somewhere in their body, thus making it accessible when later challenges occur. Comment that this resource may be drawn on in the future, both in counseling and in daily life.

4.  As appropriate during later contacts with the client when he or she seems stressed, draw on this positive story and the felt bodily sense that goes with it. Clients grow from strengths, not from weakness.

---

Finally, think about the client. He or she comes in and talks with you about a series of concerns and difficulties. All this talk often "decenters" the client from any feeling of competency. To ground clients and "center" them, spend time on positive strengths. We and our clients will grow and develop from strengths that are already present, as well as the new ideas that counseling and therapy will provide.

## The Technology of Empathy

There is also a technology of empathy, positive regard, and other core conditions of helping. Specific levels of empathy have been identified by Carkhuff (1969a, 1969b, 2008), and his *facilitative conditions* have had almost as much influence on the field as Rogers's original philosophical statement. Table 3.2 presents a seven-level adaptation of Carkhuff's original work.

---

**Table 3.2. Empathy Rating Scale**

Instructions: Before rating a counselor's statement for its degree of empathy, it is imperative that the context of what the client has been saying be considered as well. Therefore, examine what the client has just said before determining how well the counselor is tuned in. Rate each counselor statement on the following seven-point scale for degree of empathy. It is also possible to examine several counselor statements or an entire interview segment and rate that for empathy.

Level 1: The counselor or therapist is overtly destructive to the interviewing process. He or she fails to attend (sharp body shifts, major topic jumps) in a way that sharply disrupts client flow or attacks the client or discounts information.

Level 2: The counselor or therapist may be implicitly and subtly destructive, even though overtly trying to be helpful. The distinction between levels 1 and 2 is a matter of degree and sharpness. The disagreement or lack of attention doesn't seem as unusual here and is seen in the daily life of most people in some form. (Also see level 5.)

Level 3: At first glance, the session appears to be moving normally. However, on deeper analysis, one sees that the counselor or therapist is detracting slightly from what the client has been saying. The paraphrase is close, but sill misses the client's meaning. Much of our daily conversations fit this pattern. As a result of the interaction, the client is not damaged and has been listened to minimally, but counselor responses take away from what the client says or minimizes statements.

Level 4: Considered by many the minimal level for counseling, level 4 responses are interchangeable with what the client is saying. An interchangeable response is best exemplified by an accurate reflection of feeling, paraphrase, or summary that catches the essence of what the client has said. An open question or a self-disclosure that aids client responding is another example of a level 4 response.

Level 5: At this point, counseling becomes truly additive in that the counselor or therapist is adding something beyond an interchangeable response. In addition to an accurate paraphrase or reflection of feeling, the therapist adds a mild interpretation or a probing question or interpretation that not only catches the major meanings of the client, but adds something new to facilitate growth and exploration. Generally speaking, level 5 requires the use of influencing skills or questioning techniques. Ineffective use of skills at this point, however, may return the counselor or therapist to level 2. As one employs the influencing skills, the possibility for error increases.

Level 6: The counselor is truly becoming an intentional person. Attending and influencing skills are used in combination with the many qualities of empathy (concreteness, immediacy, and so on) to provide a more effective and facilitating level of counseling. Patterns of movement synchrony and movement complementarity often are manifested.

*(Continued)*

**Table 3.2. Empathy Rating Scale** *(Continued)*

Level 7: The highest level of counseling is one that relatively few counselors and therapists attain. In addition to solid, effective intentional manifestation of the many microskills and qualities of empathy, the counselor is totally "with" the client, yet apart and distinct. For some, this can be termed a "peak experience" in a relationship. Direct mutual communication is shown at this stage in its full dimensions.

(Circle appropriate number for each below.)

| | |
|---|---|
| Empathy (global impression) | 1 2 3 4 5 6 7 |
| Positive regard | 1 2 3 4 5 6 7 |
| Respect | 1 2 3 4 5 6 7 |
| Warmth | 1 2 3 4 5 6 7 |
| Concreteness | 1 2 3 4 5 6 7 |
| Immediacy | 1 2 3 4 5 6 7 |
| Confrontation | 1 2 3 4 5 6 7 |
| Genuineness | |
|     in relation to self | 1 2 3 4 5 6 7 |
|     in relation to others | 1 2 3 4 5 6 7 |
| Cultural empathy | 1 2 3 4 5 6 7 |

The seven levels provide you with a way to measure your own degree of empathy and acceptance. At some point, you will want to make an audiotape or videotape of yourself and examine your own ability to be positive and empathic. Consider using this seven-level scale to rate yourself as you listen to one of your own interviews. This exercise will be particularly important when you find yourself working with a difficult client or family. Is part of their inability to grow from counseling related to your level of empathic understanding?

Let us imagine you are working with a parent in a family session. The reason the family has come for treatment is that they are concerned over their ten-year-old's lack of achievement. You observe the family to be cold and disconnected with the only apparent value they have in common that of academic success. In the following segment, all four family members are present. Assume that the following short exchange is representative of what you have been hearing repeated in different words for the past ten minutes.

> Parent 1: Billy just isn't measuring up to Esther. He's bright enough, but he just isn't trying hard enough. I think his stomachaches are just a way to get out of work.
>
> Parent 2: Yes, when I was his age, I studied two hours every night. Esther does that even though she's younger than Billy.
>
> Esther: (sits quietly looking down)
>
> Billy: (squirms in his chair and appears sad)

How would you respond to this family? What would you say? And think about your own feelings about a situation such as the one above. What might you like to say if you could? Take just a moment and think that through. It would help if you took time to write your responses down.

What you say to your client often says as much about you as it does about the client. Examine Table 3.2, and locate the point on the empathy scale that best represents what you would say. Also look at what you might feel tempted to say—where does that rank on the empathy scale? If your two self-ratings are markedly different with the actuality of what you would say much higher than what you would like to say, very likely you have not allowed yourself to respond authentically and your anger and/or frustration might show through nonverbally to the client.

In short, true empathy cannot be an act—it needs to be genuine. This does not mean it is impossible to respond positively to people who have negative behaviors and traits. Rather, empathy can be learned and, with patience and understanding, you can learn to accept and help many difficult types of clients.

Classifying responses as to empathic level can be helpful in examining your own interviewing style. Generally speaking, an interview segment of five to ten minutes is required for more accurate measures of empathy.

It is hard to imagine counseling or therapy being conducted without some minimal level of empathy. What does seem apparent from recent theory and research is that the core conditions of helping and empathy are more complex than originally believed. One important aspect of this complexity is increased awareness of cultural factors that may influence one's understanding of another person.

# Multicultural Empathy: Two People but Four "Participants"[1]

Counseling and therapy are usually thought of as a two-person relationship: specifically, a counselor and the client or as a relationship between a family therapist and a family. There is now reason to believe that the concept of relationship in the interview requires a broader understanding. There may be four participants in the interview: the counselor/therapist and her or his cultural/historical background and the client or family and the cultural/historical background.

Some theorists now suggest that the interview is not just a relationship between the two people physically present in the session (c.f. Clement, 1983; Lacan, 2006). The individual client before you brings with him or her a specific cultural and historical background that may affect the session rather powerfully. Needless to say, you as

---

1   Material adapted here from A. Ivey, "The Multicultural Practice of Therapy: Ethics, Empathy, and Dialectics" (1987).

therapist have your own unique cultural background. At times when you think you are reacting to the client, you may simply be acting from your own encapsulated cultural background.

Intergenerational-contextual family therapy theory discusses the same issue from a family frame of reference (see Chapter 12). When you find yourself liking a certain family or responding especially positively or negatively to one family member, it may simply be that this person reminds you of someone in your own family or your own past. As family therapy sessions often move very fast, self-understanding of your own family and cultural background and their potential effect on your interviewing practice is essential.

In short, what appears to be empathy or lack or empathy may simply be an unconsciously learned behavior from your own life experience. It could be argued that there are at least four major presences involved in counseling and therapy and that what sometimes appears to be the therapist talking with the client may actually be two cultural/historical backgrounds talking with each other.

Counseling is far more complex than just counseling an individual. Your cultural history and family background are always present. Some theories of counseling and therapy tend to be ahistorical and give little attention to the power of history, family, and culture on the client. They tend to focus solely on the client/therapist interaction and omit the importance of broader factors. Schneiderman (1983) states that "Those who attempt to erase cultural differences, who wish to create a society where Otherness is nonexistent, come to be alienated. ... The moral condemnation of Otherness is racist; of this there is little doubt" (p. 174).

Empathy requires that you be aware of both individual uniqueness and "Otherness" (family/cultural/historical factors) in your clients. Historically, empathy has focused on uniqueness to the point that these factors have been forgotten. For example, in much of counseling and therapy in the United States and Canada today, the assumption is still that all clients, regardless of culture, may be expected to respond to the same treatment. A quick examination of current individual psychotherapy theories and texts will reveal minimal attention to the critical role of culture in development, therapy, and counseling.

Cultural and historical forces do impinge on the interview, but the counselor and client tend to be unaware of these issues and close off these critical data.

The desired model, then, is for counselor and client to both be aware of and use culture and history in an empathic manner. Empathy can no longer be considered "necessary and sufficient" without specific attention to cultural issues.

The Lacanian/family models provide further additional stimulation for the constructs of empathy. At times, counselors and their clients think they are talking with each other. However, what is happening is that the counselor and the client are relatively passive watchers as the two sets of cultures and histories interact. You personally may recall unusual reactions you have had with some people, only later to discover that you were having a difficult time communicating due to different cultural styles and meanings.

An example of the above might occur when the client is a recently arrived Haitian or Iranian and the counselor is a middle-class individual (who may be White, African American, or Hispanic/Latina/o). The two may be talking to each other, but the degree of understanding may, at times, be so slight that in truth two cultures are talking "by" each other, and the individuals are lost in the process.

Lacan offers a specific model for psychoanalytic theory where the communication goal of the therapist is to reach the cultural/historical background of the client and to seek eventual personality reconstruction. The task of therapy is to generate an increased awareness of how cultural/historical factors are played out in the concrete life of the individual.

Let us now turn to an examination of examples of culture and empathy, particularly as it plays out in the family of origin.

## Examples of Culture and Empathy

How well are you equipped to have empathy with people of different races (White, African American, Native American, Asian), different religious faiths (Jewish, Catholic, born-again Christians, Muslim), sexual preferences (gay, lesbian, bisexual, heterosexual), ages (children, teenagers, older adults), and those who may be challenged by a disability or have experienced special issues, such as divorce, alcohol, or drugs? Furthermore, it is clear that men and women have varying developmental needs and counseling and therapy issues. As a counselor or therapist, you are expected to work effectively with people whose life experience is quite different from your own.

There are several ways to prepare for a deeper understanding of the diverse clientele that we all face. The first involves a commitment to listen to and learn empathically from and with a vast array of people quite different from yourself. If you listen effectively, your client will eventually indicate to you how he or she feels comfortable. But, as research suggests, a warm, empathic skillful counselor is often not enough. As such, you will want to begin a program of lifelong study, considering some key aspects of individual and cultural differences and examine what theories of therapy are likely to be helpful to those whose background may be different from yours.

A true empathic approach will do much to help us all learn more about and improve our beliefs and attitudes. Study and courses in multicultural, cross-cultural, and culture-specific counseling plus experience will provide an important base for the second dimension. Through time, self-study and applying counseling and therapy concepts with different cultural groups, will help our skills improve. We all have a large task before us.

One beginning step toward multicultural counseling that many counselors and therapists find useful is to examine one's own family and ethnic heritage. In a sense, all therapy and counseling is multicultural, for our family/cultural/historical self is always with us.

## Ethnic and Other Group Differences

Readers of this book come from a wide variety of ethnic or racial backgrounds—your background may be Native American, Irish, Cambodian, Italian, British, Jewish, African American, Puerto Rican, or Russian. Very often, you may be "bicultural" and have expertise, knowledge, and experience in more than one culture. The United States used to be referred to as a melting pot where everyone was to blend together. However, like Canada, the United States has moved more to a varied "salad bowl," in which we are all mixed together, but yet the differences between us enhance us all.

In addition, you may be gay or straight, young or old, or any of a variety of groupings that give a person some joint identity with others but a distinctness from mainstream culture.

An ethnic group may be defined as "those who conceive of themselves as alike by virtue of their common ancestry, real or fictitious, and who are so regarded by others" (Shibutani & Kwan, 1965, p. 23). As such, ethnicity is a broader concept than race or religion. We tend to group ourselves according to *we* and *they*—a way individuals and groups develop strength. But ethnicity may also result in persecution and lack of understanding of people different from ourselves. The definition of ethnicity above may be changed slightly to represent any of a variety of groups such as heterosexual women, lesbians, the handicapped, the aged, or any other special group that has some identity within itself.

## Varying Cultural Goals

The goals of the clients you face will vary with their unique ethnic/cultural background. Much of counseling theory and practice is oriented toward helping individuals self-actualize. But self-actualization and the individualism it represents may be inappropriate with clients who come from a "relational" ethnic group, one that believes challenges are best solved together. A traditional Asian family, for example, will often seek to resolve individual concerns in the family in terms of family harmony rather than in one individual meeting his or her "selfish" individual wishes. The goal of effective therapy varies with the culture and background of the client.

The relational, family, or group orientation will often manifest itself strongly in clients who may be rooted closely to African American, Native American, South American/Caribbean, Caribbean Asian, or Italian backgrounds. The family is the repository of the culture. If you were raised in an Italian family, the chances are far greater that you live in the same city (perhaps even on the same block) as your parents or grandparents.

African American families who live in a hostile, racist environment tend to support one another from within and reject with suspicion help offered by outsiders. To be empathic requires an understanding of the unique individual and his or her cultural/ethnic background.

Given this complexity, it is important to remember that techniques that work well with one cultural group may be offensive and rude in another. Attending patterns differ; the use of questions may be considered intrusive; rapport may be more or less important; one theory from this text may be useful, another inappropriate. The desired goals for therapy with a client with a disability, a born-again Christian client, a recently arrived Cambodian, and an Irish American may be very different.

Personal history is also very important in the development of an individual. If your client has experienced childhood sexual abuse, parents who have divorced, poverty, severe discrimination in the form of racism and sexism, the traumas of service in Vietnam, or have Jewish parents who survived the German Holocaust, he or she will respond to your interview uniquely. Developing understanding and empathy toward those who have experiences vastly different from your own is a lifelong task.

## Developing Awareness of Your Own Multicultural History

A useful first step toward cultural empathy is awareness of your own personal background. For some people in the United States, a person with an Irish heritage would be considered virtually identical with an individual who comes from a British American history. However, closer examination reveals that even these two cultural backgrounds result in very different types of individual belief systems.

Table 3.3 presents the work of one counseling student who examined his own family background. One parent came from an Irish heritage and the other from a British one. Due to cultural differences, the parents gave the student differing messages and values. Note particularly the perceived pessimism of his Irish heritage as contrasted to the belief in personal action represented by the British heritage. It is this type of cultural difference that illustrates that intentionality is played out very differently among different cultures. As you read the statements, attempt to recall empathically that this is the way this individual views the world. You do not have to agree with those views; your goal is to understand and not to judge.

## Table 3.3. A Student Looks at His Mixed-Family Heritage

The following discussion was generated by Mark Darling, a student in cross-cultural counseling. Mark comes from a family most would consider typically American. One parent is Irish, the other British American. Mark himself is a third-generation American. Until the course in cross-cultural counseling, Mark saw himself solely as "American." With reading and study, he came to realize that many of his beliefs and values were not just American, but were the result of long-term Irish and British values. He also found that some internal conflicts within himself were not solely his own individual "problems," but were also the result of variant cultural messages he received from his parents.

The analysis below presents a summary of his personal observations plus reading in cross-cultural counseling and family therapy (McGoldrick, Pearce, & Giordano, 1982). It should be obvious that cultural intentionality on the part of the therapist requires empathy to the cultural background of the client, an empathy that can only be built through long study and effort on your part into the specifics of varying cultures. Then, armed with that knowledge, you still face a unique individual before you with unique personal syntheses of cultural background. Given this information, would you say that Mark is predominantly Irish, British, or American?

| Irish American Messages | British American Messages |
|---|---|

### Life Expectations

| | |
|---|---|
| People are basically evil; life is determined by fate. You are the victim or beneficiary of luck; you have no say in the matter. | Good and bad are an individual choice. You are responsible for your fate. Live by the rules and work hard. Therein lies success. |

These two basic attitudes underlie the belief system of an English Irish individual. One of these will probably be dominant, yet both will be present. The combined message could likely be "Win or lose, it's not your choice, but you are responsible for your failures." In this case, the individual would consider success to be luck and failure to be a personal lack of initiative or ability. Thus, the individual comes to feel like a failure with certainty of failing again and no expectation of success.

### Family Relations

| | |
|---|---|
| The family is your source and your strength. Family is identity and your obligation. To leave is to be alone and powerless. | You are an individual, strong and self-reliant. Leave home to make your fortune; establish your own family. Your life is up to you. |

The conflict created by these two attitudes is very important. One possible synthesis of these is "You are old enough to leave now, but you do not have the necessary strength to make it on your own." Hence, the individual will feel a strong desire to set out on his own, but a corresponding inability to leave.

### Gender Roles

| | |
|---|---|
| Women are morally superior to men. Men are morally weak, given to uncontrollable weakness. The mother is the strength of the household. | Women are fragile and must be protected. The father is the strength of the household. |

The conflict here becomes one of role in the household. This may be synthesized as "YOU are expected to be strong and virtuous, but you are incapable by nature of being so." In this way, individuals will feel the need to be something they cannot see themselves as being and may experience a tremendous sense of inadequacy.

### Marriage

| | |
|---|---|
| Marriage is a necessity, and you are bound by it for life. If you have problems in your marriage, they are your due, and you must accept them. | Marriage is a social contract. Both parties are responsible to maintain the agreement. If one is in violation, divorce is acceptable. |

*(Continued)*

---

**Table 3.3. A Student Looks at His Mixed-Family Heritage *(Continued)***

These two messages are very hard to reconcile: "You made a bad contract, and you have the right to a divorce, but divorce is wrong." The practical result may be that the individual will get a divorce yet feel that action to be illegitimate and wrong.

### Language

| | |
|---|---|
| Words are poetry, an expression of emotion. They have beauty but no reality and may always be traded for better ones. Words are dreams through which you create an internal reality. | Language is law, the structure of reality. Words are specific and binding. Language is the means of communicating clearly. Through words you create your external reality. |

In this conflict is the expression of a major source of misunderstanding between English and Irish culture. The English function by contracts, and contractual agreements demand that words be specific and binding. The Irish, on the other hand, see words as defined by the context in which they are used. These messages may be synthesized by the individual as "Your daydreaming is a waste of time. You never do what you say you are going to do. Plan for the future, but it's all idle dreaming." The result can be an individual who is unable to follow through on agreements and is not generally relied upon.

A common tendency today is to stereotype and condemn White males, particularly those of Anglo-Celtic background. But, as may be clearly observed here, British and Irish backgrounds are very different. It is not possible to stereotype any one individual because of color or ethnicity. Mark Darling is a unique person, in some ways bicultural, who works his way through the maze of cultural messages uniquely. As a young male, he does not suffer the issues of sexism, racism, or ageism. Yet, it should also be clear that every client comes from a cultural background with special implications. Understanding variations in ethnicity and religion, race and sex, and many other factors will enrich your understanding in the counseling interview.

If you were counseling this student about a possible divorce, it is likely that his attitude would be shaped by his cultural background of mixed messages. If he identified more strongly with his British roots, the decision to divorce might not be so difficult; but if he believed more strongly in his Irish background, he might not even be there for counseling as divorce would not be a viable option. As many people in the United States and Canada come from bicultural backgrounds, it is most likely that some conflict between the two value systems will appear in counseling. Often, this conflict is an internal struggle without awareness on the part of the client or the counselor. Your task may be to facilitate awareness of the relationship between culture and individual consciousness.

And we must not forget that the student is also North American, influenced by materialism, television, and the enthusiastic free choice emphasized in this culture. In a sense, he is tricultural. Many, perhaps most, of your clients will represent some form of bicultural pattern. When issues of age, sex, religion, disability, and so forth are added as additional cultural groupings, the need for expanding your understanding of special populations should be readily apparent.

Think about your own family. How does it respond to issues such as where children are expected to live after marriage? How much emotional and financial support does your family offer? What is the family attitude toward intellectual achievement? What are the expected roles of men and women? Beliefs about drinking? What are attitudes toward pain? Then, look at yourself and your life. How are your constructs similar and different from your own family? Practice Exercise 3.2 presents a framework within which you can examine your own cultural/ethnic heritage.

In the study of cultural differences, it is important to watch out for stereotypes. Chances are that you as a unique individual have some beliefs in common with your family and some significant differences. This is one simple illustration of the danger of taking general group characteristics, such as those identified above, and assuming everyone in that group is the same. A Jewish individual would not appreciate your expecting him or her to have the same values toward education similar to all other Jewish people, despite the fact that education is a general value in Jewish culture (Herz & Rosen, 1982). The particular person in the counseling interview remains unique, and you cannot expect group differences to predict each person you meet.

Nonetheless, a basic understanding of group differences may help you understand that a gay or lesbian client is likely to suffer from job discrimination and may sometimes have a family that rejects him or her. This is not true of all gay and lesbian clients, but an understanding that this may be an issue can be helpful. Many older people face issues of loneliness, but not all. You may see as inappropriate a young Italian family living with parents if that is different from your cultural background. Similarly, it is possible for an Italian family therapist to view a Jewish, Irish, or British American client as strange and different in that they may not be as close as an Italian family.

With the key ideas of basic empathy and positive regard coupled with an awareness of some key cultural issues, let us now turn to additional dimensions of empathy.

---

**Practice Exercise 3.2  Identifying Yourself as a Multicultural Being**

Nine dimensions of multiculturalism are listed below. Think about yourself in each area. Are you able to speak more than one language? If so, what does this mean to you? What influence does your gender have on your life? With what ethnicities and races do you identify? Are you monocultural, bicultural, or multicultural?

Continue through the following list, examining your cultural uniqueness.

How do family attitudes and behaviors affect the way you think about these issues? How do peer groups and other associations in the community and broader aspects of society affect your thinking and feeling about your unique cultural self? Save this exercise, as you may wish to complete it again later in this book.

Language(s)

Gender

Ethnicity/race

Religion/spirituality

Affectional orientation

*(Continued)*

---

**Practice Exercise 3.2 Identifying Yourself as a Multicultural Being *(Continued)***

Age

Physical issues

Socioeconomic situation

Trauma

# The Family Genogram

You and your clients develop in a family within a culture. The family genogram is one of the most useful diagnostic tools in the field. Once the province of family therapists, individual counselors are increasingly using the genogram to help clients understand themselves better. We are never alone. Our family and community histories are always with us. Family genograms are useful in connection with community genograms. They provide both you and the client with vital data on the cultural context. Often, you will find that what was originally thought of as an "individual issue" is reframed as a concern of the client in family and community context. Practice Exercise 3.3 asks you to develop a genogram with a volunteer client.

We suggest you use a large sheet of newsprint as you work with the client. You will also find that take-home assignments to elaborate and understand one's family of origin are very helpful individual, family, and cultural empathic exercises. Not only you will understand the client more fully, so will the client.

Suggested symbols for multicultural family genograms are presented in Figure 3.1.

---

Figure 3.1. **Symbols used in multicultural family genograms.**

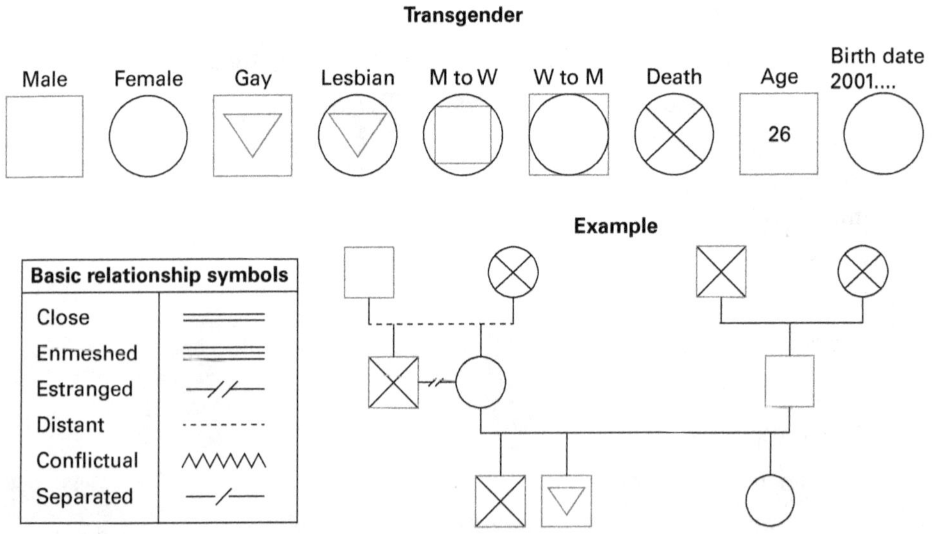

Note that the suggested symbols for a genogram should be adapted to meet the needs and wishes of each unique client, couple, or family.

The symbols used for a genogram should be negotiated with your client. Many clients object to a traditional "X" over those who are deceased, stating that the person "still lives in me." Other clients may prefer a roadmap, a network of rivers, or other symbolic framework to present their families and community heritage. The traditional model of genograms should not be imposed any more than we would want to impose a specific theory or counseling method on an unwilling client.

---

**Practice Exercise 3.3  Family Genogram**

Instructions to complete the family genogram:

1. List the names of family members for at least three generations (four is preferred), with ages and dates of birth and death. List occupations, significant illnesses, and cause of death, as appropriate. Note any issues with alcoholism or drugs.

2. List important cultural/environmental/contextual issues. These may include ethnic identity, religion, economic, and social class considerations. In addition, pay special attention to significant life events such as trauma or environmental issues (e.g., divorce, economic depression, major illness).

3. Basic relationship symbols for a genogram are shown above.

4. As you develop the genogram with a client, use the basic listening sequence to draw out information, thoughts, and feelings. You will find that considerable insight into one's personal life issues may be generated in this way.

After the two of you have created the genogram, ask the client the following questions and note the effect of each question. Change the wording and the sequence to fit the needs and interests of the volunteer.

- What does this genogram mean to you?
- As you view your family genogram, what main theme, concern, or set of issues stands out?
- Who are some significant others, such as friends, neighbors, teachers, or even enemies, who may have affected your own development and your family's?

*(Continued)*

**Table 3.3. Counseling Relationship Social Justice Competencies** *(Continued)*

- How would other members of your family interpret this genogram?

- What impact do your ethnicity, race, religion, and other cultural/environmental/contextual factors have on your own development and your family's?

- As an interviewer working with you on this genogram, I have learned (state your own observations). How do you react to my observations?

Reviewing family and community genograms throughout your sessions with a client will help both you and the client see the total context. Needless to say, you will not have time for a full effort in both areas with all clients, but even a portion of community and family understanding can be very beneficial.

## Toward Multicultural Empathy and Competence

We are indeed individuals, and we also all have our origins in families. These factors impact our empathic understanding, as do the influence of our peer groups and friends, the neighborhood and community, the professional associations, and the overall culture. Throughout this book, we will explore issues relating to all of these areas, although the primary focus will be on the individual developing in a family and multicultural context.

The Multicultural Counseling Competencies Revisions Committee of the Association for Multicultural Counseling and Development has generated a revised set of multicultural and social justice counseling competencies ([MSJCC] Ratts, Singh, Nassar-McMillan, Butler, & McCullough, 2015). The social justice competencies were added due to their interactive relationship with multicultural competences. The revised competencies address the complex multicultural dimensions of the counseling relationship; acknowledges the importance of understanding clients within their social contexts; recognizes the negative consequences of oppression and discrimination on clients' mental health and well-being; and integrates multicultural and social justice competencies within all counseling modalities—individual-couples, families, groups, and institutions.

Table 3.4 outlines some of the challenging goals that may be useful to advance your effectiveness as a helper. The goals, related to the counseling relationship, are briefly discussed here:

1. *Counselor Attitude and Beliefs.* If you are to be empathic with those of different backgrounds, it is essential that you become self-aware. Furthermore, privileged and marginalized counselors need to become aware of how their and their clients' worldviews, values, and group status affect the relationship with

their clients. Chapter 1 focused on this important concept and offered the community genogram, but it is critical that you enhance this brief introduction by further reading and study. Exercise 3.3 in this chapter, exploring your relation to your family of origin, can be a step toward developing sensitivity about yourself as a cultural being. Other exercises in this book will focus on helping you develop this type of awareness.

2. *Counselor Knowledge*. Privileged and marginalized counselors work intentionally to acquire knowledge of how the worldviews, values, and experiences with power, privilege, and oppression affect the counseling relationship. Chapter 1 provided an introduction to these concepts, but further study is necessary. There is a large body of theoretical information available.

3. *Skills*. This book is about theory and practice of counseling and therapy. Thus, the authors have a special responsibility to present a variety of ways to engage in collaborative and constructive conversations with clients from various cultural groups. The goal is to discuss how their worldviews affect their relationship and best ways to understand one another. This book gives extensive attention to new work in multicultural counseling and therapy and feminist theory. We also attempt to provide a more culturally relevant portrayal of empathy, the microskills of listening and attending, and other dimensions.

4. *Action*. Both privileged and marginalized counselors act intentionally to increase their understanding of the way they and the client see the world.

**Figure 3.2. Four Pillars That Influence the Counseling Relationship. (See Table 3.4 for specific competencies)**

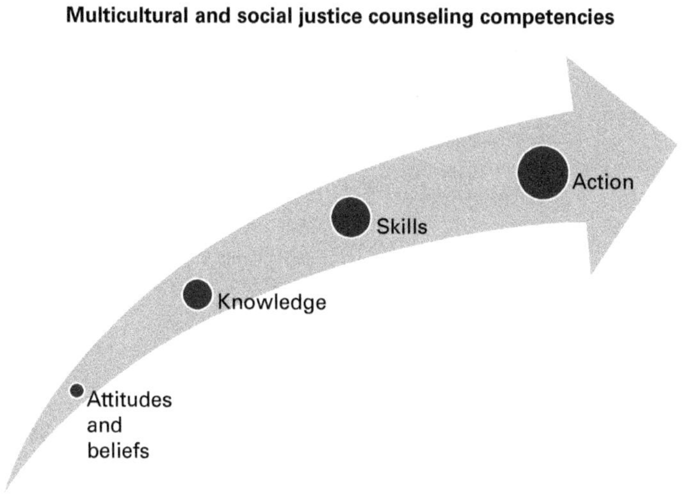

Multicultural and social justice counseling competencies

**Table 3.4. Counseling Relationship Social Justice Competencies**

| 1. Attitudes and Beliefs | 2. Knowledge | 3. Skills | 4. Action |
|---|---|---|---|
| • Acknowledge that the worldviews, values, beliefs, and biases held by privileged and marginalized counselors and clients will positively or negatively influence the counseling relationship.<br><br>• Acknowledge that counselor and client identity development shapes the counseling relationship to varying degrees for privileged and marginalized clients.<br><br>• Acknowledge that the privileged and marginalized status of counselors and clients will influence the counseling relationship to varying degrees.<br><br>• Acknowledge that culture, stereotypes, discrimination, power, privilege, and oppression influence the counseling relationship with privileged and marginalized clients.<br><br>• Acknowledge that the counseling relationship may extend beyond the traditional office setting and into the community. | • Develop knowledge of the worldviews, values, beliefs, and biases held by privileged and marginalized counselors and clients and its influence on the counseling relationship.<br><br>• Develop knowledge of identity development theories and how they influence the counseling relationship with privileged and marginalized clients.<br><br>• Develop knowledge of theories explaining how counselors' and clients' privileged and marginalized statuses influence the counseling relationship.<br><br>• Develop knowledge of how culture, stereotypes, discrimination, power, privilege, and oppression strengthen and hinder the counseling relationship with privileged and marginalized clients.<br><br>• Develop knowledge of when to use individual counseling and when to use systems advocacy with privileged and marginalized clients. | • Acquire assessment skills to determine how the worldviews, values, beliefs, and biases held by privileged and marginalized counselors and clients influence the counseling relationship.<br><br>• Acquire analytical skills to identify how the identity development of counselors and clients influences the counseling relationship.<br><br>• Acquire application skills to apply knowledge of theories explaining how counselors' and clients' privileged and marginalized statuses influence the counseling relationship.<br><br>• Acquire assessment skills regarding how culture, stereotypes, prejudice, discrimination, power, privilege, and oppression influence the counseling relationship with privileged and marginalized clients.<br><br>• Acquire evaluation skills to determine when individual counseling or systems advocacy is needed with privileged and marginalized clients. | • Take action by initiating conversations to determine how the worldviews, values, beliefs, and biases held by privileged and marginalized counselors and clients influence the counseling relationship.<br><br>• Take action by collaborating with clients to identify the ways that privileged and marginalized counselor and client identity development influence the counseling relationship.<br><br>• Take action by exploring how counselor and clients' privileged and marginalized statuses influence the counseling relationship.<br><br>• Take action by inviting conversations about how culture, stereotypes, prejudice, discrimination, power, privilege, and oppression influence the counseling relationship with privileged and marginalized clients.<br><br>• Take action by collaborating with clients to determine whether individual counseling or systems advocacy is needed with privileged and marginalized clients. |

*(Continued)*

**Table 3.4.  Counseling Relationship Social Justice Competencies *(Continued)***

- Acknowledge that cross-cultural communication is key to connecting with privileged and marginalized clients.
- Develop knowledge of cross-cultural communication theories when working with privileged and marginalized clients.
- Acquire cross-cultural communication skills to connect with privileged and marginalized clients.
- Take action by using cross-communication skills to connect with privileged and marginalized clients.

# Additional Aspects of the Empathic Attitude

Empathy asks you to see the world from a perspective different from your own. Understanding and an empathic attitude are not enough; you must communicate to your client the sense of empathy that you feel.

Important constructs that can help communicate your feelings of understanding and empathy for the client include: respect and warmth, concreteness, immediacy and congruence, genuineness, and authenticity. One of the key facilitating conditions is that of confrontation, which will be explored in the following chapter as part of a set of specific skills.

## Respect and Warmth

Cold, distant counselors and therapists may appear professional and competent, but underlying that facade of professionalism may be unconscious hostility and dislike for the client. The intentional counselor likes and respects other people and communicates these feelings to them.

Counselors who lack respect for their clients may call them names behind their backs, devise manipulative games to "help," brag about their effectiveness to other clients and colleagues, offer racist or sexist slurs, or show any of a host of behaviors indicating lack of regard and respect for other human beings. It would be pleasant to be able to say that these behaviors are rare in the counseling profession, but unfortunately they are all too common. The clearest indication of lack of respect occurs in the put-down, where counselors offer negative statements about the client either directly or in subtle form. In addition, there are counselors who do not truly respect themselves; they put themselves down and thus lessen their ability to help others.

Respect is close to positive regard and can be communicated verbally through a language of respect. Virtually all the positive regard, positive asset search, and exploration of resources comments mentioned earlier communicate respect for another person. Enhancing statements might include such things as "You express your opinion well" and "Good insight."

However, the importance of a respectful attitude shows most clearly when you work with a client who has survived trauma, such as a war experience, a rape, or a lifetime of child abuse. Such clients often feel guilty about what happened to them and how they coped with their experience. As a result of the trauma, they may be engaging in alcoholism, drugs, or other undesirable behavior. The counseling axiom "The client is doing the best he or she can at this time" should be recalled. If you listen to and understand any client long enough, their behavior makes sense.

You may start counseling, for example, a man or woman who gambles or is an alcoholic who neglects children, possibly even abusing them. If you listen long enough, you will generally find a family/cultural history that explains the behavior.

*One need not support or respect the behavior to respect the client.* At times like this, it is especially important to sort out negative behaviors, which at times must be stopped forcefully from a positive view of the essence of the human being before you. You will find that antisocial and borderline clients offer a particular challenge to your ability to respect, yet most clients who receive these diagnoses have a history of extremely severe child abuse behind them.

One of the great challenges you may face in your counseling practice is the teenager who is thinking of obtaining an abortion. Whether you are pro-life or pro-choice, the task remains for you to demonstrate your ability to respect the client.

Let us assume that Donna, a client, asks you for your opinion about obtaining an abortion. Recall also that the counselor or therapist is in a position of power and influence in the relationship. How would you respond respectfully so that you maintain your own value stance and simultaneously respect that of the client?

> Donna: (Assume that the teenager has discussed many pros and cons about having an abortion; there is no romantic relationship; having a child would eliminate further education due to finances; and that the client appears somewhat immature.) You've listened to me for quite a while. What do you think I ought to do? I'm so confused.
>
> Helper 1: I see you now leaning toward keeping the baby. I like that; I value life. If I were in your shoes, I suspect I'd be feeling much the same as you. Frankly, I hope you have the baby—yet I think it is your decision. What are your reactions to my thoughts? I think you can handle it.
>
> Helper 2: It's your decision. Let's go back and explore the possibilities again of keeping the baby versus having the abortion.
>
> Helper 3: Well, ultimately it is your decision. I value life—both yours and the unborn baby's. But as we've talked, it doesn't sound as if you are really prepared to take care of a child, and you seem anxious to go to college. You don't sound ready to be a mother. What are you reactions to my thoughts?

Which of these responses are respectful? Depending on one's value stand and theoretical persuasion, the answer can range from all to none. In such situations, counselors do not find easy answers available and perhaps choose not to share their opinions. Whether one should share one's opinion in the interview is open to argument; however, almost all would agree that answering such a question early in the interview would be inappropriate. Later in the session, answering the question may at times be done with care.

Respect is clearly vital to the interviewing and therapy process. It is a different construct from warmth. It is possible to respect another person's point of view but still lack the critical dimension of personal warmth. Together, however, respect and warmth present a powerful combination.

Warmth of counselor response has been demonstrated to be an important factor underlying an empathic relationship. But what is warmth? Warmth may be defined as an emotional attitude toward the client, expressed through nonverbal means. Vocal tone, posture, gestures, facial expression, and the ability to touch when appropriate are how the warmth and support of a counselor is communicated to a client. Smiling has been found to be the best single predictor of warmth ratings in an interview (Bayes, 1972). Furthermore, smiling is consistently associated with positive perceptions of the other person: such as sincere, competent, relaxed, and warm (Senft, Chentsova-Dutton, & Patten, 2016). Warmth, then, appears to be one form of your self-expression in the world. Are you a warm person? How do you communicate your warmth?

Separating warmth, respect, and the earlier concept of positive regard is perhaps not really possible. Yet, one can imagine a person expressing positive feedback, respect, and positive regard to a client in a cold, distant fashion. The lack of warmth can negate the positive message. The communication of warmth through smiling, vocal tone, and other nonverbal means adds power and conviction to counselor comments.

## Concreteness

Returning to Donna, the teenager considering an abortion:

> Donna: And, to top it all off, my parents don't help me. (Vague)
>
> Helper: Could you give me a specific example of how they react? (Concrete)
>
> Donna: Well, they just yell at me a lot. (Less vague)
>
> Helper: Could you share one specific place where they didn't help you? Could you give me a specific example from last week? (Concrete)

> Donna: Well, when they found out I was pregnant, they just yelled and yelled and want me to get rid of it. (More concrete)
>
> Helper: What, specifically, did they say? What did you say? (Concrete)

Clients often begin therapy with vague, ambiguous complaints. A task of the intentional therapist is to clarify and understand vague ideas and concerns expressed by the client. Effective interviews tend to move from vague descriptions of global general issues to highly concrete discussions of what happened or what is happening in the daily life of the client.

Through interviewing leads that focus on concrete client experience, the helper can move from a general opinion to a clear understanding of what actually did happen. Becoming empathic and understanding the other person is easier, obviously, when you understand specific facts. The tone and depth of an interview is often set by the degree of specificity and concreteness employed. Generally speaking, most clients will welcome concreteness, as "objective facts" are less susceptible to personal or cultural distortion. Furthermore, specificity and concreteness will provide a more solid base for client and therapist problem solving.

But sometimes the emotional experience may have been too intense for immediate discussion of concrete specifics. In cases of rape and abuse, the search for concreteness may sometimes wisely be delayed. North Americans in general tend to prefer discussion of concrete specifics of issues, but the concreteness and directness of this approach can put off many Europeans, Asians, or Africans, whose culture may be oriented more toward a subtle approach.

The search for concreteness underlies many—perhaps even most—helping interviews. The client lacks full understanding and often has labeled a situation incorrectly. By asking the open question "Can you give me a specific example?" you can slow down and clarify a confusing interview.

The concept of concreteness will appear again in a different form when a developmental view of therapy is presented in Chapter 6.

## Immediacy

There are two commonly used definitions of this term in counseling and therapy, one focused on time dimensions, the other of the here and now relationship of the interview.

*Immediacy as time orientation:* The English language divides time into past, present, and future tenses. Generally speaking, the most powerful counseling leads are in the present tense and are considered the most immediate. Yet, different theories discussed in this book give different emphases to different time dimensions.

Psychoanalytic theory (at least in the early years of a long-term analysis) operates primarily in the past tense and focuses on past experience. Gestalt therapy and existential helping focus on the now and give special attention to what is happening to the client in the immediate *here and now* world. Behavioral helpers and vocational counselors may delve into the past but are often primarily interested in facilitating client self-expression in the future.

The tense of discussion in the helping interview determines heavily the nature of the client-counselor interaction. Consider the following:

> Client: I'm scared.
>
> Analytic counselor: Free associate to your earliest childhood experience that relates to that feeling.
>
> Existential counselor: You're scared. What are you experiencing right now?
>
> Behavioral counselor: What do you want to do about it?

Which of the above counseling leads is most effective? It will depend on your worldview and your idea of the objective(s) of the therapy interview. Each lead moves the client to more concrete expression but focuses on a very different time sense.

*Immediacy as here and now interpersonal discussion in the interview*: As you move toward a more present-tense orientation in helping, you may find yourself focusing on the here and now experience you and the client are having in the interview. Common to this form of helping is the example question "What's going on with you right now?"

The following examples are taken from an interview conducted by Joann Griswold. You don't need to know the context or the topic of the interview to recognize the power that comes from here-and-now emphasis in the session. The numbers refer to interviewing leads.

> 3. J: Well, look at your smile. (4. S: Today, I feel pretty good.)
>
> 5. J: You feel pretty good today …
>
> 17. J: You're laughing, but I sense from the tone of your voice and the look on your face that underneath it isn't a laughing matter.
>
> 27. J: I sense you can feel the pressure now …
>
> 96. J: You will take care of yourself. The time is now. Is that what I hear you saying?

In each of the above, Joann uses present-tense language that enlivens and enriches the session.

Many of our clients repeat their developmental history in the family in the here and now of the interview. They may respond to you in the here and now as if you were a significant person from their past. When this occurs, you have an important opportunity to relive the past in the present.

Yet, sometimes it is appropriate and desirable to be less immediate and less concrete. If a situation is too threatening and demanding, the counselor can move to the past tense and become vague to remove tension and threat. Consider the client considering an abortion.

> Donna (visibly trembling and about to break into tears): I'm feeling so crummy. Nothing seems to make sense … it all seems so hopeless.
>
> Helper: Last week you seemed to be feeling better … different than now.
>
> Donna: Yeah, I had it together—I thought—but it seems to be falling apart again.
>
> Helper: Let's go back and look at one thing that you did last week that seemed to work with your parents.

The helper's second statement is non-immediate, is primarily in the past tense. The client responds with a similar pattern, showing less immediacy and concreteness. The counselor then focuses the client on the past tense with a positive experience. At this point, it is again feasible to become concrete and specific.

It should be pointed out that retreating from deep emotional client expressions is not always wise. A consistent pattern of avoidance of client emotional expression may be identified in some counselors and therapists. The intentional therapist learns when to become immediate and concrete and when to use these same concepts to take pressure off the client. Furthermore, different theories have differing ways to handle this issue. It is necessary that you examine your own life experience, commitment to counseling, and the several alternative theories to psychotherapy, and generate your own position on this critical issue. Regardless of where you stand on this issue, an awareness of the power of these constructs is mandatory.

## Congruence, Genuineness, and Authenticity

Central concepts of the helping field, congruence, genuineness, and authenticity were introduced by Carl Rogers who stated that the therapist in a counseling relationship should be a

> congruent, integrated person. It means that within the relationship he is freely and deeply himself, with his actual experience represented by his awareness of himself. It is the opposite of presenting a facade either knowingly or unknowingly. (Rogers, 1957, p. 97)

It would seem difficult to fault such a statement, and it is clear that openness and honesty on your part are central to your effectiveness. There are times, however, when complete openness and spontaneity of expression may damage the client. This point was brought home forcefully in 1972 when Lieberman, Yalom, and Miles (1973) studied encounter group casualties. They found that "open," "authentic" group leaders produced more casualties than more conservative types of counselors who developed relationships with their groups.

Two types of authenticity may be considered. The first type is authenticity to yourself. This may be fine, and you may be truthful and open as a model, but your client may not be ready for such behavior. The more important type of authenticity is when you have a genuine, congruent relationship with your client. This means noting where your clients "are at," listening to them, and opening a dialogue of empathy.

Critical work by Strong (1968) is important to consider as you think about authenticity in the interview. He found that three factors—expertness, trustworthiness, and attractiveness—were central dimensions of how well counselors and therapists were perceived by clients. In addition to authenticity, we now must also think of how the client perceives us on these three dimensions. Strong's work shows that if we are to influence a client, we must be seen as worthy of providing influence. For example, with many clients, it has been found that professional degrees hung on the wall, a neat professional office, a professional demeanor, physical attractiveness, and demonstrated ability to win trust are equally important in the success of counseling as the traditional views of authenticity expressed by Rogers.

Given the recognition of Strong's (1968) social influence theory, it is still relevant to consider how genuineness in communication can best appear in the interview. Two concepts of genuineness and authenticity have been suggested: (1) genuineness in relation to self; and (2) genuineness in relation to your client. If you are not authentically the person who fits the image suggested by Strong, degrees on the wall may be more of a hindrance than a help. Ultimately, you must win the trust of the client, and being true to yourself seems an important part of appearing trustworthy.

The following exchange around the abortion issue illustrates some concerns in regard to genuineness:

> Donna: Yes, I can't decide what to do about the bab … I mean abortion, until I know where I stand with Ronnie. He used to treat me nice, especially when we were first dating. He came over and fixed my car and my stereo, he liked to run errands for me. Now if I ask him anything, he makes a big hassle out of it.

> Helper: At this moment, I can sense some confusion. Let me check this out with you. … When someone is nice to me, I get to trust them and feel comfortable. But—then—if they let me down, I get low and lost and really confused. Is my experience at all like yours?

> Donna: I guess I have felt like that. I know I blame him for getting me pregnant and he wouldn't do anything to prevent it. It makes me damn mad!
>
> Helper: Right now, you really are angry with him.

The counselor illustrates genuineness in relationship to self through the skill of self-disclosure. The counselor shares her or his feelings and thoughts in a very real and personal manner. It may be noted that the self-disclosure is relatively vague and nonconcrete. Let us suppose the counselor is thinking of a past event in relation to his or her parents. If that concrete event had been presented, the counselor would still be genuine in relation to self; but the introduction of the parents letting their child down is rather distant from this client's immediate personal experience. This is an example where genuineness in relationship to self actually could disturb the counseling relationship. In this interview, the counselor is genuine not only to self, but also in the relationship. The congruent self-disclosure is helpful to the interviewing process.

Genuine self-disclosure on the part of the counselor produces further genuineness on the part of the client. Intentional counselors tend to produce intentional clients. Let us now turn to an examination of client behavior as it relates to ideas of empathy.

# Neuroscience and Empathy

Neuroscience research offers a refreshing biological view of empathy. Researchers from this area have identified a brain network responsive to emotional and motivational interpersonal experiences (Costa & Costa, 2016). This network responds to our own personal experiences and to the observed experiences of others through involuntary and voluntary processes called "affective empathy" and "cognitive empathy." These processes match the affective and cognitive dimensions of empathy long recognized by counselors and therapists.

With these types of studies, the possibility for interdisciplinary collaboration using imaging research to inform counseling interventions has been born. The neurosciences provide new opportunities to advance our therapeutic work (Ivey et al., 2018). Furthermore, it is possible that neurofeedback training, a neuroscience-based technique used for the regulation of emotional responses, may be used to train professionals' empathic response (Stoeckel et al., 2014).

How does our nervous system help us understand another person's emotional and cognitive state and anticipate their actions to interact appropriately? A neural network involved in affective and motivational processing gets activated when we experience or observe another person's physical or psychological pain. This pain-empathy network involves the anterior insula (AI) and medial and anterior cingulate cortex (MCC, ACC) and can be activated by the involuntary or voluntary system. The involuntary process involved in pain-empathy is known as "experience sharing" or "affective empathy" and the voluntary process as "mentalizing" or "cognitive empathy" (Lown, 2016, p. 334). Neuroimaging studies also demonstrate that helping others activates areas of the brain associated with reward and positive emotions (Decety, Norman, Berntson, & Cacioppo, 2012). Dopamine-related reward-processing areas in the ventral striatum are activated in physicians relieving patients' pain (Jensen et al., 2013).

In sum, witnessing pain or suffering activates neural networks that enable humans to emotionally empathize and cognitively process another person's experience and feel motivated to help; a set of processes central to counseling and psychotherapy (Coutinho, Silva, & Decety, 2014). Figure 3.3 illustrates a neuroscience-based process of counseling.

**Figure 3.3.** **A Neuroscience-Based Counseling Model: The Empathy Action-Oriented Counseling Process**

# Using Multicultural Empathy in the Interview: Checking Out How the Client Responds to You

Your empathic response to one client may represent insensitivity to another. How can you cope with the variety of clients and their many diverse cultures when no formula or theory will provide a totally useful answer—that is, the "correct" response and action? The following three-step model of empathy provides you with a summary framework for balancing the uniqueness of the individual before you with your own general knowledge and with that of counseling and therapy theory:

1.  *Listen* to and observe your client and her or his comments.

2.  *Respond* using the client's main words and constructs. When in doubt, generally use the attending and listening skills. But when culturally and individually appropriate, add your own experience, knowledge, or intuitions.

3.  *Check out* your statement or intervention by asking "How does that sound?" "Is that close?" or some other statement that allows the client to respond to you. You may also do check-out by raising your voice at the end of your response in a questioning tone of voice.

At this point, recycle to the first step and change your style and comments as necessary until you and the client are both comfortable. Empathy is best considered a process wherein counselor and client explore the nature of the client's worldview and beliefs about the concerns together. There is no final standard of "superior" empathy; rather, empathy requires you constantly to attune yourself to the wide variety of individual clients with whom you will work.

Perhaps most important of the three steps in terms of building a solid, empathic relationship is the check-out or perception check. "Have I heard you correctly?" implies empathy, shows respect for the client, is an authentic response, and will provide you with concrete data as to the effectiveness of your comment or intervention. If you responded accurately, the client will often smile and say yes or some other term and continue. If you were off-target, the client will correct you, and you can use your new understanding to proceed with the session.

Experienced counselors and therapists have learned over time to use the check-out frequently throughout the session to avoid misunderstandings and to clarify key issues.

# Theory into Action

Bringing theory into action helps master key concepts and ideas. We find if students can master the basics of the Empathy Rating Scale that they can understand and work with the other facilitative conditions more easily. The following exercises (Practice Exercises 4, 5, and 6) will help you practice empathy.

---

**Practice Exercise 3.4  Empathy Rating Exercise**

Here are some responses at varying levels on the Empathy Rating Scale. Rate each one, and then check your rating with the classifications at the end of the chapter.

1. It sounds as if achievement is very important in this family. Could you two parents talk to each other about achievement so I can understand its importance a bit more?

2. (Angrily) Stop it, I'm sick and tired of you sitting there so complacently while your two beautiful children are suffering in front of your eyes.

3. It's really important to you to have the children achieve. At the same time, I note that Billy and Esther haven't said a word and we've been here fifteen minutes. They look a bit sad and uncomfortable. What types of things happen in your family that work well and involve you all together? What works in this family?

Now, complete the second theory in action exercise (Exercise 3.5).

---

**Practice Exercise 3.5  Empathy Rating Exercise**

Imagine that you are working with a twelve-year-old who has a reputation as a bully. You know through your practice that children who bully other children often are abused themselves in some way at home.

Warren (rapidly and defensively): The teacher said I hit him. I didn't hit him, I hardly touched him … and it was his fault.

First, write your own response to Warren. Then, classify your response and the following sample responses as to empathy level:

4. (Slowly and calmly) So, Warren, you feel that the teacher is after you again and that you didn't do anything. Could you tell me in your own words what you think happened? What happened just before you got in trouble? What did he say? What did you say? What did you do? (The questions are spaced in time to obtain a detailed picture of the incident from Warren's frame of reference.)

*(Continued)*

---

**Practice Exercise 3.5 Empathy Rating Exercise** *(Continued)*

> 5. (Calmly) Warren, we've talked about this before and you've simply got to stop.
>
> 6. (Calmly with warmth) So, Warren, it happened again. The last time it happened I remember you had just had a licking from your dad that morning. Was Dad drinking again?

Turn to the end of the end of the chapter and note the comments there. Finally, complete Practice Exercise 3.6 to sharpen your cultural empathy.

---

**Practice Exercise 3.6 Multicultural Empathy**

> To complete this exercise:
>
> Find a volunteer willing to help you practice cultural empathy.
>
> Select a topic the volunteer would like to talk about. It can be a decision they would like to make, a study-related concern, or a work-related issue.
>
> Practice cultural empathy using the three steps presented in the section above:
>
> 1. Listen to and observe your client and her or his comments.
> 2. Respond using the client's main words and constructs.
> 3. Check out your statement or intervention.
>
> After three to five minutes, stop and debrief with the volunteer. Was this helpful to them? What was missing, and what would they add?
>
> How was your experience? What would you have done differently?

Applying your new learnings to everyday activities is a must. For concept mastery, spend time observing people interacting in the news, movies, or real life, and actively rate their level of empathy.

Also, practice multicultural empathy using the three steps presented in the previous section. The more you practice, the more you will understand how empathy works.

## Responses to Empathy Levels

1. Level 4. Interchangeable response. This response has the advantage of enabling the parents to feel heard. It builds trust, and later the therapist can confront and use higher-level responses. Attempting to use levels 6 and 7 without a prior foundation of trust actually can be destructive.

2. Level 1. Attacking response. (A level-2 response might appear similar but would be more subtle.)

3. Level 6. The counselor has listened accurately but is adding a useful family therapy technique in which positive assets and strengths of the family are noted. If this response is successful, later the family may use this strength to work on their issues.

4. Level 4. An important task of any interview is to get the data out clearly. With young children who tend to be very concrete, specific questions oriented to sequence may be helpful.

5. Level 2. This response may be necessary, but it comes from the frame of reference of the helper and is likely to be seen as controlling.

6. Level 5. This response recognizes Warren the person and reminds Warren that he has a pattern of fighting, particularly when his father has been drinking heavily. It adds something else to the recent fight. Used by itself solely as an interviewing style, this might be destructive to Warren. But used judiciously as part of a set of other responses, it may eventually help Warren see his situation more completely as it is. Effective interviewing, counseling, and therapy require you to use differing levels of empathy, yet the level 4 interchangeable response may be considered the foundation level.

# References

Anthony, W.A., & Carkhuff, R.R. (1977). The functional professional therapeutic agent. In A.S. Gurman & A.M. Razin (Eds.), *Effective psychotherapy: The functional professional therapeutic agent* (pp. 103–119). New York, NY: Pergamon Press.

Barrett-Lennard, G.T. (1962). Dimensions of therapist response as causal factors in therapeutic change. *Psychological Monographs, 76* (43)(Whole No. 562).

Bayes, M. (1972). Behavioral cues of interpersonal warmth. *Journal of Counseling Psychology, 39*, 333–339.

Berliner, R., & Masterson, T.L. (2015). Review of research: Promoting empathy development in the early childhood and elementary classroom. *Childhood Education, 91*, 57–64. doi.org.ezaccess.libraries.psu.edu/10.1080/00094056.2015.1001675.

Bloom, P. (2017). Empathy and its discontents. *Trends in Cognitive Sciences, 21*, 24–31. doi. org/10.1016/j.tics.2016.11.004.

Carkhuff, R. (1969a, b). *Helping and human relations*, Vols. I and II. New York, NY: Holt, Rinehart and Winston.

Carkhuff, R. (2008). *The Art of Helping in the 21st Century* (9th ed.). Amherst, MA: Human Resource Development Press.

Clement, C. (1983). *The lives and legends of Jacques Lacan*. New York, NY: Columbia.

Costa, M.J., & Costa, P. (2016). Nurturing empathy and compassion: What might the neurosciences have to offer? *Medical Education, 50*, 281–282. doi:10.1111/medu.12980.

Coutinho, J., Ribeiro, E., Fernandes, C., Sousa, I., & Safran, J.D. (2014). The development of the therapeutic alliance and the emergence of alliance ruptures. *Anales de Psicología, 30*, 985–994. doi.org/10.6018/analesps.30.3.168911.

Coutinho, J.S., Silva, P.O., & Decety, J. (2014). Neurosciences, empathy, and healthy interpersonal relationships: Recent findings and implications for counseling psychology. *Journal of Counseling Psychology, 61*, 541–548. doi.org/10.1037/cou0000021.

Decety, D., Norman, G.H., Berntson, G.G., & Cacioppo, J.T. (2012). A neurobehavioral evolutionary perspective on the mechanisms underlying empathy. *Progress in Neurobiology, 98*, 38–48.

Draguns, J. (2015). Empathy: Its deep roots and tall branches. *Baltic Journal of Psychology, 16* (l, 2), 28–54.

Elliott, R., Bohart, A.C., Watson, J.C., & Greenberg, L.S. (2011). Empathy. In J.C. Norcross (Ed.), *Psychotherapy relationships that work: Therapist contributions and responsiveness to patients* (2nd ed.) (pp. 132–152). New York, NY: Oxford University Press.

Fiedler, F. (1950a). The concept of an ideal therapeutic relationship. *Journal of Consulting and Clinical Psychology, 14*, 235–245.

Fiedler, F. (1950b). A comparison of therapeutic relationships in psychoanalytic, non-directive and Adlerian therapy. *Journal of Consulting Psychology, 14*, 436–445.

Fiedler, F. (1951). Factor analysis of psychoanalytic, nondirective, and Adlerian therapeutic relationships. *Journal of Consulting and Clinical Psychology, 15*, 32–38.

Gendlin, E., & Hendricks, M. (1978). *Changes*. Rap manual: Mimeographed, undated. Cited in E. Gendlin, *Focusing*. New York, NY: Everest House.

Hadley, S.W., & Strupp, H.H. (1976). Contemporary views of negative effects in psychotherapy: An integrated account. *Archives of General Psychiatry, 33*, 1291–1302.

Herz, F., & Rosen, E. (1982). Jewish families. In M. McGoldrick, J. Pearce, & J. Giordano (Eds.), *Ethnicity and family therapy* (pp. 364–392). New York, NY: Guilford.

Ivey, A., Ivey, M.B., & Zalaquett, C. (2018). *Intentional interviewing and counseling: Facilitating client development in a multicultural society* (9th ed.). Belmont, CA: Cengage Learning.

Jensen, K.B., Petrovic, R., Kerr, C.E., Kirsch, I., Raicek, J., Cheetham, A., Spaeth, R., ... Kaptchuk, T.J. (2013). Sharing pain and relief: Neural correlates of physicians during treatment of patients. *Molecular Psychiatry, 19*, 392–398.

Konrath, S., & Grynberg, D. (2016). The positive (and negative) psychology of empathy. In D.F. Watt & J. Panksepp (Eds.), *Psychology and neurobiology of empathy*. Hauppauge, NY: Nova.

Lacan, J. (2006). *Écrits: The first complete edition in English*. New York, NY: Norton.

Lambert, M. J. (2013). Outcome in psychotherapy: The past and important advances. *Psychotherapy, 50*, 42–51. doi: 10.1037/a0030682.

Lieberman, M. A., Yalom, I. D., & Miles, M. B. (1973). *Encounter groups: First facts*. New York, NY: Basic Books.

Lown, B.A. (2016). A social neuroscience-informed model for teaching and practising compassion in health care. *Medical Education, 50*, 332–342.

McGill, D., & Pearce, J. (1982). British Families. In M. McGoldrick, J. Pearce, & J. Giordano (Eds.), *Ethnicity and family therapy* (pp. 457–482). New York, NY: Guilford.

McGoldrick, M., Pearce, J., & Giordano, J. (Eds.) (1982). *Ethnicity and family therapy*. New York, NY: Guilford.

Meneses, R.W., & Larkin, M. (2017). The experience of empathy: Intuitive, sympathetic, and intellectual aspects of social understanding. *Journal of Humanistic Psychology, 57*, 3–32. doi:10.1177/0022167815581552.

Moyers, T.B., Houck, J., Rice, S.L., Longabaugh, R., & Miller, W.R. (2016). Therapist empathy, combined behavioral intervention, and alcohol outcomes in the COMBINE research project. *Journal of Consulting and Clinical Psychology, 84*, 221–229. doi.org/10.1037/ccp0000074.

Norcross, J. C. (Ed.) (2011). *Psychotherapy relationships that work* (2nd ed.). New York, NY: Oxford University Press.

Norcross, J.C., & Lambert, M.J. (2011). Evidence-based therapy relationships. In J. C. Norcross (Ed.), *Psychotherapy relationships that work: Therapist contributions and responsiveness to patients* (2nd ed.) (pp. 3–24). New York, NY: Oxford University Press.

Pinderhughes, E. (1982). Afro-American families and the victim syndrome. In M. McGoldrick, J. Pearce, & J. Giordano (Eds.), *Ethnicity and family therapy* (pp. 108–122). New York, NY: Guilford.

Ratts, M.J., Singh, A.A., Nassar-McMillan, S., Butler, S.K., & McCullough, J.R. (2015). Multicultural and social justice counseling competencies. Retrieved from http://www.counseling.org/docs/default-source/competencies/multicultural-and-social-justice-counseling-competencies.pdf?sfvrsn=20.

Rogers, C. (1957). The necessary and sufficient conditions of therapeutic personality change. *Journal of Consulting Psychology, 21*, 95–103.

Rogers, C. (1980). *A way of being*. New York, NY: Houghton-Mifflin.

Schneiderman, S. (1983). *Jacques Lacan: The death of an intellectual hero*. Cambridge, MA: Harvard.

Senft, N., Chentsova-Dutton, Y., & Patten, G.A. (2016). All smiles perceived equally: Facial expressions trump target characteristics in impression formation. *Motivation and Emotion, 40*, 577–587. doi:10.1007/s11031-016-9558-6.

Shibutani, T., & Kwan, K. (1965). *Ethnic stratification*. New York, NY: Macmillan.

Stoeckel, L.E., Garrison, K.A., Ghosh, S., Wighton, P., Hanlon, C.M., Gilman, J.M., Greer, S., Turk-Browne, N.B., … Evins, A.E. (2014). Optimising real time fMRI neurofeedback for therapeutic discovery and development. *Neuroimage: Clinical, 5*, 245–255.

Strong, S. (1968). Counseling: An interpersonal influence process. *Journal of Counseling Psychology, 15*, 215–224.

Strupp, H.H. (1977). A reformulation of the dynamics of the therapist's contribution. In A.S. Gurman & A.M. Razin, (eds), Effective psychotherapy: A handbook of research (pp. 3–22). New York, NY: Pergamon.

Strupp, H.H. (1981). Clinical research, practice, and the crisis of confidence. *Journal of Consulting and Clinical Psychology, 49*, 216–219. doi.org/10.1037/0022-006X.49.2.216.

Strupp, H.H., & Hadley, S. (1977). A tripartite model of mental health and therapeutic outcomes: With special reference to negative effects in psychotherapy. *American Psychologist, 32*, 187–196. doi.org/10.1037/0003-066X.32.3.187.

Truax, C.B., & Mitchell, K.M. (1971). Research on certain therapist interpersonal skills in relation to process and outcome. In A.E. Bergin & S.L. Garfield (Eds.), *Handbook of psychotherapy and behavioral change: An empirical analysis* (pp. 299–344). New York, NY: Wiley.

Yager, J. (2015). Updating empathy. *Psychiatry, 78*, 134–140. doi.org/10.1080/00332747.2015.1051439.

# Credits

Tab. 3.2: Maryanne Galvin and Allen E. Ivey, Researching One's Own Interviewing Style: Does Your Theory of Choice Match Your Actual Practice? Copyright © 1981 by John Wiley & Sons, Inc.

### CHAPTER 4

# Conducting an Intentional Interview

## Theory, Skills, and Brief Interventions

Individual and cultural empathy may be considered basic conditions for effective participation in the interview. But what happens more specifically in the session to make it work for you and your client? The microskills of attending and influencing are the identified blocks for building positive therapeutic relationships and effective interventions (Ivey, Ivey, & Zalaquett, 2018). This chapter identifies key microskills critical to the counseling and psychotherapy process and outcome. Furthermore, through the use of microskills, it is possible to examine and improve your own "in-interview" or "in-session" behavior with the specific aim of making a significant difference in the lives of your clients.

## SPECIFIC GOALS OF THIS CHAPTER:

There are two major goals of this chapter

1. Understand the specifics of the microskills approach and how to engage in a five-stage interview, thus enabling a client to make decisions and find solutions in a short series of interviews that can be adapted for multiple cultural and cross-cultural situations.

2. Develop sufficient mastery of the microskills and five-stage interview structure so that you can actually use these concepts in practice with clients—and later apply them to multiple theories of counseling and psychotherapy.

Additional goals of this chapter are

3. Identify the basic *nonverbal factors* exhibited by therapists and clients that affect counseling and therapy.

4. Briefly review current *neuroscience support* of the microskills.

5. Use solution-oriented brief counseling and therapy to help clients find resolutions to at least some of their issues within a relatively short time.

6. Bring *theory into action* through practice exercises to draw out the client's story and engage in a brief solution-oriented process to facilitate goal achievement.

This chapter introduces the use of microskills and structuring an effective interview. This can be considered the foundation of interviewing, counseling, and psychotherapy practice. If you master these concepts, you can use them with many counseling and therapy theories. Furthermore, practice decision-making oriented interventions to find solutions in a shorter period of time. The microskills approach was the first in the nation and the world to employ video recordings to examine and analyze observable specifics of what happens in the interview (Ivey, Normington, Miller, Morrill, & Haase, 1968). These video analyses revealed close correspondence with the work of Frank Parsons, who is recognized as the founder of the counseling movement. The essence of the microskills and decisional tradition could be summarized in the following paraphrase of Frank Parsons's (1909) pioneering work in vocational counseling:

> In counseling and therapy there are three main issues: (1) a clear understanding of how the thoughts, feelings, and actions within a client's story are constructed; (2) a clear understanding of how the client's story was constructed in a social context of family, community, and culture; and (3) exploration of how the story might be changed and reconstrued by emotional and rational understanding and pragmatic action in the real world.

The microskills approach focuses on identifying specific thoughts, feelings, and actions useful in the interview; specific skills for drawing out and elaborating a client's story; and skills and strategies for working with that client to change and reconstruct the story and move on with life more effectively and pragmatically. As you read the story of the microskills and decisional counseling approach, examine it for its possible relevance as a part of your own major narrative on the nature of the helping process.

# The Microskills Approach

Establishing an effective counseling session demands that you have individual, family, and cultural empathy. However, at the same time, it requires effective and specific skills to accomplish change. The process of identification of specific skills of counseling is the Microskills Approach (Daniels & Ivey, 2007; Ivey, Ivey, & Zalaquett, 2016, 2018; Ivey & Daniels, 2016).

Using the microskills approach, we have deconstructed the complex interactions of the counseling session into manageable and learnable dimensions. The microskills are presented in Figure 4.1, the Microskills Hierarchy.

# The Microskills Hierarchy

Microskills are single, identifiable skills of counseling and psychotherapy. These specific skills of interviewing have specific goals and anticipated results in client verbalizations and behaviors. The skills are organized within the framework of the microskills hierarchy (Figure 4.1). The hierarchy assembles aspects of the interview into attending skills and influencing skills. Using the word *hierarchy* can imply that "higher is better" and that arriving at the top is "best." This is not the intention. Rather, the importance

**Fig. 4.1  The Microskills Hierarchy**

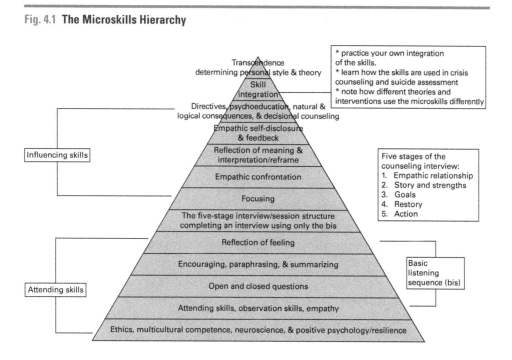

of basic foundation skills of attending behavior and client observation remains critical to all professional helpers, no matter how extensive their experience.

The microskills hierarchy presented in Figure 4.1 summarizes the successive steps of intentional counseling and psychotherapy. The skills rest on a base of ethics, multicultural competence, neuroscience, positive psychology, and resilience. On this foundation rests attending, observation, and empathy, essential to successful use of all the other aspects of questioning, encouraging, paraphrasing, summarizing, and reflecting feelings. Equipped with these skills, you should be able to conduct a whole interview to help your client to achieve resolution of basic concerns. On the other hand, without the attending skills, the upper reaches of the pyramid are meaningless and potentially damaging.

Develop your own style of being with clients, but always with respect for the importance of listening to client stories and issues.

The five-stage structure provides a framework for integrating the microskills into a complete counseling session (see Table 4.8). We encourage you to use the *empathic relationship—story and strength—goals—restory—action* framework to organize and guide the session, and as a checklist for your meetings with clients.

The influencing skills to help clients explore personal and interpersonal conflicts are next in the hierarchy. Focusing will help you and the client to see personal, cultural, and contextual issues related to their concerns. Empathic confrontation will help client growth and change in gentle ways. Interpretation/reframing and reflection of meaning will help clients think about themselves and their situations in new ways. These are followed by an array of influencing skills that offer tested methods for change and building resilience. Here, you will first find the skills of self-disclosure and feedback. Then, strategies of logical consequences, along with some basics of decisional counseling. Specific examples of the best ways to provide information and direction for the client follow. These include stress management, psychoeducation, and the use of therapeutic lifestyle changes to provide more self-direction for clients.

At the apex of the microskills hierarchy is integration of skills, developing your own personal style of counseling and therapy, and transcendence. Competence in skills, strategies, and the five stages are not enough to become a culturally intentional counselor or therapist. In the end, you will have to determine your own approach to the practice of counseling and psychotherapy.

As you develop expertise and mastery, you will find that each client has a totally unique response to you and your natural style. Many clients may work well with you, whereas others may require you to adapt intentionally to them and their individual and multicultural style.

The microskills will prepare you to start building competence in multiple theories of counseling and psychotherapy. Once you have mastered the microskills, you can assemble them into the several types of counseling and therapy methods outlined later in this text.

# The Basic Microskills of Attending and Influencing

## Identifying Nonverbal Skills

Figure 4.2 presents three counselors listening to a client in two different ways. Which of the counseling styles do you prefer, the one on the right or the one on the left?

Before reading further, list on a separate sheet of paper the specific behaviors of the two counseling styles. Be as precise as possible and identify observable aspects of their behavior.

Through examination of the intentional and ineffective examples of counselor eye contact and body language, you have just participated in a basic exercise in microskills training that leads to the central concept of attending behavior. If you are going to interview or counsel another person, it seems obvious that you should look at them and maintain natural eye contact. Further, your body should communicate interest.

By body language and words, the skilled counselor communicates that he or she is attending to the client. In Figure 4.2, you see the counselors on the left displaying a forward trunk lean, a direct eye contact, and a relaxed body style that communicates interest and assurance. The counselors on the right display a tense body position, and closed arms and legs. This second style communicates lack of interest.

Figure 4.2. **Counselor Attending Style**

*(Continued)*

**Figure 4.2.** **Counselor Attending Style** *(Continued)*

It is possible through such analysis to identify highly specific verbal and nonverbal behaviors of the intentional and the ineffective counselor. Table 4.1 presents SURETY, a list of effective aspects of nonverbal communication offered by a nurse practitioner.

## REFLECTION EXERCISE

What is your attending style? Think about the way you sit and feel when listening to a person who is experiencing sadness or expressing concerns. Take the time to let that image arise.

- What are you seeing?
- Most important, what are your thoughts and feelings about your own body position?
- Is your style closer to one of the styles presented in Figure 4.2?

What do you think of the SURETY dimensions of nonverbal communication (Table 4.1)?

- How do they inform your own style?
- What do you think about the use of intuition? Do you use it? How, when, and with what results?
- What do you think about touching the client?

Last but not least, take this reflective exercise further and practice intentionally and with full attention to the dimensions mentioned in this chapter. Get feedback from your volunteers.

---

**Table 4.1. SURETY Effective Nonverbal Communication**

SURETY (Stickley, 2011)
The acronym spelled out:
S - Sit at an angle to the client
U - Uncross legs and arms
R - Relax
E - Eye contact
T - Touch
Y - Your intuition

*Sit at an angle to the client:* Sitting in a slight angle, opposite to a client, creates a nonconfrontational sitting arrangement that facilitates communication. Sitting directly in front may be perceived as confrontational and sitting side by side as impersonal.

*Uncross legs and arms:* Crossed arms and legs may communicate defensiveness, low interest, or superiority. Uncrossed arms and legs communicate that we are open and receptive to what the person is communicating. Important to avoid a slouched position or one that is too open.

*Relax:* Relax in an appropriate position. It will be inappropriate that you appear too relaxed or overly concerned when a client is sharing a very disturbing experience. Leaning toward the client may demonstrate active listening, but it is a position to maintain temporarily as it is difficult to sustain.

*(Continued)*

**Table 4.1. SURETY Effective Nonverbal Communication** *(Continued)*

*Eye contact:* Appropriate eye contact is an effective way to communicate that you are listening. Wandering eyes communicate disinterest. Staring communicates intrusion and insensitivity. Eye contact breaks are expected, as it is to keep eye contact when the client is sharing a distressful event, even if they are looking down, because they may come back and find that you are looking away; this may break trust. Remember that clients from other cultures or with different cultural values may prefer varying styles of eye contact.

*Touch:* This is a concerning area for counselors and psychotherapists, and many admonish to avoid touching at all costs (for an extended discussion on this topic, see Zur & Nordmarken, 2016). Excessive or inappropriate use of touch can be abusive and disrespectful, but sensitive use of touch may communicate compassion, empathy, love, support, and understanding. Cultural sensitivity is essential, as there is no universal agreement about appropriate use of touch. Sensitive use of touch is often very important to distressed children, adolescents, or older people. Appropriate touch may focus on generally accepted "safe" zones of the body, such as the hand, lower arm, or top of the shoulder. A hand on the client's shoulder during a grieving moment may convey support and humane interest.

*Your intuition:* Intuition governs the entire process of nonverbal communication in the SURETY model. Research suggests intuition in nursing is an important part of effective clinical decision making that supports safe patient care (Robert, Tilley, & Petersen, 2014). Nonverbal and verbal communication are in part an art. Intuition should be used when implementing all of the above components to sense how the client responds and increase communication effectiveness. The minimal clues of discomfort should be intuitively noted and responded to.

Microcounseling was the first in the world to use videotape to study what can be actually observed in an interview. Out of this early research, counseling and psychology had a new and clearer awareness of the importance of nonverbal communication. It was once believed that counseling was solely a verbal occupation, but with the arrival of videotape and increased use of videos in interview training, it has become obvious that nonverbal communication is basic in any interviewing, counseling, or therapy session. Thus, eye contact and body language are the physical fundamentals of attending behavior.

A third aspect of attending behavior is vocal tone. Does your voice communicate warmth and interest, or boredom and lack of caring? Even though you may be physically attending, your voice often indicates the quality of your willingness and interest in listening.

Moreover, if you are to attend to someone else, you must also "listen" to them. Listening, however, is not an observable behavior. Intentional therapists not only maintain attentive body postures, they also stay on the topic of the client and seldom change topics abruptly or interrupt. A major mistake of beginning counselors is to change the topic of discussion and ignore or fail to hear what the client has to say. For example:

> Client: I've been downtown this afternoon, and I really got anxious. I wanted to run when I saw a friend even. I broke out in a sweat and felt I couldn't move. I've been in my room until just now.

Nonattending Counselor: Let's see now, you're a sophomore this year?

Attending Counselor: You say you wanted to run when you saw your friend. Could you describe the situation and what was happening in more detail?

It is seldom necessary or desirable to change the client's topic, particularly when the client above is describing what most likely is a panic attack. Attend carefully and the client will tell you all you need to know. However, attending behavior varies from culture to culture and from individual to individual.

Machiko Fukuhara (2012) introduced the microcounseling to Japan and formed the Japanese Association Microcounseling (JAMC). She conceptualized microcounseling as a meta-model for training and an integrated model for practice. Her verbal and physiological studies using galvanic skin response, heart rate, and brain activity to assess the impact of the microskills demonstrated the efficacy of the listening skills with college students and adult clients. Key among her findings was the importance of cultural differences among clients and the use of an intentional approach to embrace those differences in the counseling relationship (Fukuhara, Zalaquett, Ishiyama, Kawamichi, Asazuma, & Backenroth, 2016).

## Attending and Cultural Differences

Attending behavior, then, is a central aspect of all interviewing, counseling, and psychotherapy. It involves four key dimensions, all of which are modified by the individual and the cultural background: eye contact, appropriate body language, vocal tone, and verbal following.

Table 4.2 illustrates some cultural patterns observed among different groups. When using such summaries of cultural patterns, do not assume that one pattern of attending (or influencing) is appropriate for each individual whom you may meet. Data are clear that individual differences among clients may be as important as cultural patterns. Avoid stereotyping and expecting each member of each group to be the same or even similar.

Sue and Sue (2016) present a framework for culture-specific strategies in counseling. They cite research showing that many minority clients terminate counseling early and suggests that more culturally sensitive approaches are needed. They summarize literature demonstrating the vital importance of including spatial, nonverbal, and related dimensions in the helping process. They support this by quoting a saying common among African Americans: "If you really want to know what White folks are thinking or feeling, don't listen to what they say, but how they say it" (p. 267).

Original microskills research and theoretical conceptions were generated from a Eurocentric frame of reference (Ivey et al., 1968; Ivey, 1971). Since that time, however, continuous attempts have been made to correct the original constructions and recognize cultural differences (Ivey & Authier, 1978; Ivey et al., 2016, 2018).

Table 4.2 compares different cultural styles. It is critical to continue to update our counseling theories as the field discovers more multicultural influences. Multicultural perspectives are frequently omitted from theories and models of counseling and therapy, or are included as appendices. It is good to be alert to old, outdated methods that are still used in counseling and psychotherapy theory and practice. Table 4.3 reports findings of microskills research and practice.

**Table 4.2. Nonverbal Attending Patterns of European Americans Compared with Patterns of Other Cultures**

| Nonverbal Dimensions | European Americans | Other Races/Ethnicities/Cultures |
| --- | --- | --- |
| Eye Contact | When listening to a person, direct eye contact is appropriate. When talking, eye contact is often less frequent. | Some African Americans may have patterns directly opposite and demonstrate more eye contact when talking and less when listening. |
| Body Language | Slight forward torso lean facing the person. Handshake is a general sign of welcome. | Certain Eskimo and Inuit groups in the Arctic sit side by side when working on personal issues. A male giving a female a firm handshake may be seen as giving a sexual invitation. |
| Vocal Tone and Speech Rate | A varied vocal tone is favored, with some emotionality show. Speech rate is moderate. | Many Latina/o groups have a more extensive and expressive vocal tone and may consider European-North American styles unemotional and "flat." |
| Physical Space | Conversation distance is ordinarily "arm's length" or more for comfort. | Common in Arab and Middle Eastern cultures is a six- to twelve-inch conversational distance, a point at which the European American becomes uncomfortable. |
| Time | Highly structured, linear view of time. Generally "on time" for appointments. "Time is money." | Several South American countries operate on a more casual view of time and do not plan that specified, previously agreed-upon times for meetings will necessarily hold. |

**Table 4.3. Research on Attending Behavior and Interviewing Skills**

More than five hundred microskills research studies have been conducted (Ivey & Daniels, 2016). The model has been tested nationally and internationally in more than one thousand clinical and teaching programs. Microcounseling was the first systematic video-based counseling model to identify specific observable counseling skills. It was also the first skills training program to emphasize multicultural issues. Some of the most valuable research findings include the following:

1. You can expect results from microskills training. Several critical reviews have found microtraining an effective framework for teaching skills to a wide variety of people, ranging from beginning interviewers and counselors to experienced professionals who need to relate to clients more effectively. Teaching your clients many of the microskills will facilitate their personal growth and ability to communicate with their families or coworkers.

2. Practice is essential. Practice the skills to mastery if the skills are to be maintained and used after training. Use it or lose it! Complete practice exercises and generalize what you learn to real life. Whenever possible, audio or video record your practice sessions.

3. Multicultural differences are real. People from different cultural groups (e.g., ethnicity/race, gender) have different patterns of skill usage. Learn about people different from you, and use skills in a culturally appropriate manner.

4. Different counseling theories have varying patterns of skill usage. Expect person-centered counselors to focus almost exclusively on listening skills, whereas cognitive behaviorists use more influencing skills. Microskills expertise will help you define your own theory and integrate it with your natural style.

5. If you use a specific microskill, then you can expect a client to respond in anticipated ways. You can anticipate how the client will respond to your use of each microskill, but each client is unique. Cultural intentionality prepares you for the unexpected and teaches you to flex with another way of responding or another microskill.

6. Neuroscience and brain research now support clinical and research experience with the microskills approach. Throughout this book, we will provide data from neuroscience and brain research. This research explains and clarifies much of what counseling and psychotherapy have always done and, at the same time, increases the quality and precision of our practice.

# Mirroring Nonverbal Behavior

In a successful, smoothly flowing interview, movement complementarity, or movement symmetry, often occurs between counselor and client. Movement complementarity is represented by a "passing" of movement back and forth between client and counselor. For example, the client pauses in the middle of a sentence, the counselor nods, and the client then finishes the sentence. Movements between counselor and client pass back and forth in a rhythm.

In movement symmetry, counselor and client unconsciously assume the same physical posture; their eye contact is usually direct; and their hands and feet may move in unison as if they were dancing or following a programmed script. Movement symmetry can be achieved in a rudimentary fashion by deliberately assuming the posture and "mirroring" the gestures of the client. This mirroring of nonverbal behavior often brings the therapist to a closer and more complete understanding of the client.

The series of photographs in Figure 4.3 shows a client and counselor discussing an issue of mutual interest. The time for the completion of this series of movements is about one second. Careful examination of helping interviews reveals many examples of movement symmetry, as well as dyssynchronous movement, which often indicates failure to communicate effectively.

This lack of complementarity and symmetry is an important factor in counselor-client communication. For instance, the counselor may say something, and the client's head may jerk noticeably in the opposite direction. Dyssynchronous body movements that occur between counselor and client can indicate that the interview is on the wrong track. A solid knowledge and awareness of body language is necessary to consistently observe dyssynchronous behavior. Furthermore, keen observation of this type of behavior may help counselors and therapists note the presence of what Muran and Safran (2016) call therapeutic alliance ruptures—negative client communications and client-therapist interactions.

Once you become skilled in observing and practicing mirroring, it can be a valuable tool. If you note the general pattern of body language of your client and then deliberately assume the same posture, you will find yourself in better synchrony and harmony with the client. Through mirroring, new understandings and communication can develop. This tool should not be used manipulatively, but rather to develop increased awareness and new levels of insight. Figure 4.3 demonstrates counselor and client symmetrical movement.

**Figure 4.3. Movement Symmetry Between Client and Counselor**

(Continued)

Figure 4.3. **Movement Symmetry Between Client and Counselor** *(Continued)*

*(Continued)*

**Figure 4.3. Movement Symmetry Between Client and Counselor** *(Continued)*

# The Basic Listening Sequence

Attending skills can be organized into a coherent and systematic framework called the basic listening sequence (BLS). Table 4.4 identifies the specific microskills of listening: open and closed questions, encouraging, paraphrasing, reflection of feeling, and summarization. All these skills are intended to bring out the client's story. The aim of listening skills is to discover how the client presents his or her story, with minimal intrusion on the part of the counselor or therapist.

The microskills of listening have been part of counseling and therapy for fifty years. The basic listening sequence was first identified through direct observation by a skilled manager at Digital Computer Corporation. When an employee came up to the manager with a challenge on the production line, the manager engaged in good attending behavior. His responses to the employee included the following listening skills:

> Could you tell me about the issue on the production line? (open question)
>
> The zenos chip? (encouraging)
>
> You say the supply department hasn't given you enough computer chips to keep your group moving smoothly? (paraphrasing)
>
> Sounds like the situation really makes you angry. (reflection of feeling)

The manager then summarized the employee's view of the challenging situation, and only then did he start to move toward action.

Subsequent work has revealed the importance of the basic listening sequence in a multitude of helping settings. Many counseling and therapy theories use the basic listening sequence to draw out information from the client. Although the skills are not always sequenced as clearly as they are in the following example, most therapists and counselors use variations of this basic model as they get to know their client and the client's life concerns.

> Could you tell me about your family and how they react to your fear of going out in public? (*Open question—leads to drawing out how client organizes the issue*)
>
> Protect you? (*Encouraging—leads to exploring client's key words and underlying meanings*)
>
> So, when you find yourself not wanting to go outside, the family goes out for you? (*Paraphrase—client knows she or he is heard*)
>
> Is that right? (*Perception check—helps client know whether or not hearing has been accurate*)
>
> And you seem to be feeling very sad/frightened/inadequate right now. (*Reflection of feeling—leads client to explore emotion*)
>
> So this is what I'm hearing you say … (*Summarization—counselor emphasizes main points of the client's story to enhance understanding of the client's issue in a more organized fashion*)

**Table 4.4. Basic Listening Sequence (BLS)**

| Skill | Description | Function in Interview/ What to Expect |
|---|---|---|
| Open questions | "What": facts<br>"How": process or feelings<br>"Why": reasons<br>"Could": general picture | Used to bring out major data and facilitate conversation. |
| Closed questions | Usually begin with *do, is,* and *are* and can be answered in a few words. | Used to quickly obtain specific data, close off lengthy answers. |
| Encouraging | Repeating back to client a few of the client's main words. | Encourages detailed elaboration of the specific words and their meanings. |
| Paraphrasing | Repeating back the essence of a client's words and thoughts using the client's own main words. | Acts as promoter for discussion; shows understanding; checks on clarity of counselor understanding. |
| Reflection of feeling | Selective attention to emotional content of interview. | Results in clarification of emotion underlying key facts; promotes discussion of feelings. |
| Summarization | Repeating back of client's facts and feelings (and reasons) to client in an organized form. | Useful in beginning interview (intake); periodically used in session to clarify where the interview has come to date and to close the session. |

The basic listening sequence has specific goals. It is vital that we bring out the client's story by using these skills. In doing this, we need to know the *main facts* as described by the client; how the client *feels about those facts*; and how the client *organizes the story*.

In approaching these goals, it is good to take into account multicultural and gender issues. Men tend to ask more questions than women (and they also tend to interrupt more often). Women tend to use the techniques of paraphrase and reflection of feeling more often than men. Then, too, a European American therapist working with a minority client may appear too intrusive if too many direct questions are used. Although it is vital that you draw out the client's story and the key facts, feelings, and organization of the story, the basic listening sequence must be modified in the here and now of the interview.

Whether you are helping a client with a vocational decision, negotiating a divorce, or conducting a psychodynamic dream analysis, you will need to know the facts and how the client feels about those facts and then organize them for further analysis. The basic listening sequence and its accompanying microskills can be very useful when you employ the different therapeutic approaches discussed later. Whether you are a behavioral counselor, a reality therapist, or a family counselor, the basic listening sequence is a critical therapeutic tool.

# Using Listening Skills with Children

The basic listening sequence and all the microskills are helpful in working with young children, with some modification. If you have a highly verbal child, perhaps even as young as five or six, listening skills work very effectively and you can follow the general rules presented here. But most children will need help in expressing information.

Many children will respond to an open question with confusion, looking puzzled, and saying perhaps only a few words. Closed questions, phrased gently, often are useful in helping children express themselves. The danger, of course, is leading the child to a conclusion. The child may be anxious to please you as the counselor and follow your lead too easily. The danger closed questions pose for leading the child is especially critical when a child is being interviewed on issues of child abuse.

Paraphrasing can be especially useful in helping children talk. Effective classroom teachers constantly paraphrase comments of their students. Paraphrasing helps children keep on topic, acts as a reinforcer, and indicates that you have heard them. Each child generates a unique construction, and if you use the key words of the child, you are more likely to learn how that child sees the situation.

O'Brien and Schlechter (2016) offer a novel way to begin interviewing children using a positive framework. After completing the set of questions presented in Table 4.5, they ask children what challenges are getting in their way to use their strengths that the earlier questions have revealed. Similar to our stand regarding the word *problem*, these physicians assert that *challenge* conveys the message of something they can overcome. Complaint or problem, on the other hand, conveys the message that something is broken or wrong. Identifying what can be overcome increases children's motivation and confidence and stimulates a sense of agency and goal-oriented thinking and behaving.

---

**Table 4.5. A Positive Sequence to Assessment and Engagement**

SEQUENCE OF INTERVIEW QUESTIONS
O'Brien & Schlechter (2016)

Assessment Area: PERMA Strengths: positive emotions, engagement, positive relationships, meaning, and accomplishment

- If a friend were to say some good things about you, about what makes you great, what do you think they would say?
- What do you do that is meaningful?
- Are you a good friend?
- What do you feel like you are good at?
- What do you like to do?

*(Continued)*

**Table 4.5. A Positive Sequence to Assessment and Engagement *(Continued)***

Assessment Area: Future vision and goal-directed thinking

- If you were given two weeks to do whatever you wanted to do and be whoever you wanted to be, what would you say?
- If tomorrow could be better than today, what would it look like?

Assessment Area: Current challenges

- You have listed several strengths, and you have the capacity to flourish based on [paraphrase answers from above questions]; is there anything getting in the way of your good qualities?
- What is the particular challenge that you want to work on that brought you in here today?

Beyond these guidelines, your personal ability to establish rapport and trust is essential. A pleasant office, small children's furniture, and suitable pictures and games can be helpful. Warmth and a cheerful smile are important to children. Most children talk more easily while playing games such as checkers or cards, molding clay with their hands, or drawing pictures. Children can readily do two things at once, so you can move easily between the game and your interview goals. Children may be highly emotional about a fight on the playground or continued abuse at home one moment, and in the next giggling with delight as they make a good move in a checkers game against you.

**The Neuroscience of Cognitive and Affective Empathy:** Counseling Impacts Brain Processes

The listening skills, of course, are the basis of empathy—joining each client in her or his view of the world. We know that "attending behavior lights up the brain." Attending, of course, is a precursor for empathic understanding. Active listening behaviors impact the medial prefrontal cortex (mPFC), right and anterior insula, and superior temporal sulcus, STS, and anterior insula (Kawamichi, et al., 2015).

This book focuses on twin tasks of empathy—cognitive empathy and affective empathy. Emotion underlies as the more foundational factor and the counseling relationship and the working alliance are key to change and growth. At the same time, cognitions, our thoughts and meaning making, are our guide to emotional regulations and organizing daily life. This was consistently demonstrated in a metanalysis of 40 fMRI studies (Fan, Duncan, de Greck, & Northoff, 2011).

Not only does counseling change the brain, but our counseling skills and responses from differing theoretical orientations impact different types of brain functioning (Ivey, Ivey, & Zalaquett 2018). Fan and colleagues point out that paraphrasing is oriented primarily to cognitive empathy while reflection of feeling is associated with affective empathy. Summarization, most often, involves both.

Rogerian person-centered counseling tends to focus more on emotion, while behavioral and cognitive behavioral therapy (CBT) on cognition. However, both are aware of and use both (for example, the "E"—emotion in Ellis's REBT). Expect a balanced use of cognitive and emotional skills in Multicultural Counseling and Therapy, Developmental Counseling and Therapy, narrative, family therapy, and others.

Associated with cognitive empathy are the midcingulate cortex and dorsal medial prefrontal cortex. The insula appears to be central in experiencing emotions vicariously (Eres, Decety, Louis, & Molenberghs, 2015). These authors found that higher scores on a test of empathy showed increased fMRI gray matter density in the insula for those oriented to affective empathy. Gray matter density increases in the MCC and DMPFC were associated with those leaning more to cognitive empathy.

As a next definitional step, the brain's default mode network (DFM) and its relation to empathy was explored by Oliveira-Silva and colleagues (2018). This is a separate and complex region that is not consciously involved in daily tasks and goals. It is negatively correlated with attentional networks and what is call the "task positive brain network." This study found similar results to the above in that high cognitive empathy was again associated with the medial prefrontal cortex (mPFC). However, emotional empathy had a negative correlation with the mPFC. Given the vital importance of the prefrontal cortex in emotional regulation, this is not surprising. Furthermore, this illustrates the importance of a cognitive/emotion balance in your counseling and psychotherapy. Emotional warmth needs to be balanced with cognitive understanding and effective goal setting. Figure 4.4 illustrates dramatically how neuroscience is helping us understand and guide our work in the interview.

On the left, DMN regions positively correlated with cognitive empathy (in light gray) and negatively correlated with emotional empathy (in medium gray), as measured by IRI (Interpersonal Reactivity Index). To allow the discrimination of the precise location and extent of each cluster, the overlap between brain regions involved in both positive and negative correlations is shown in dark gray color. For all the correlations, the $p < .05$ (corrected for multiple comparisons). On the top right, the graph shows the positive correlation between the individual cognitive scores of empathy and the DMN components. On the bottom right, the graph shows a negative correlation between the medial prefrontal cortex and individual emotional scores of empathy and the DMN components.

# Influencing Skills and Strategies

Clients can profit and grow even if you use only attending skills. A basic competency to achieve is the ability to conduct a full interview using only basic listening sequence skills. Many clients can often work through issues and concerns very effectively if you avoid giving advice, direction, or suggestions. The early theories of nondirective counseling as presented by Rogers advocated using only listening skills and even went so far as to severely criticize the use of questions.

However, solely using attending and listening skills can make growth slow and arduous. When you become an active participant in the interview, you can influence and speed the change process. Through your knowledge of theory and skills, personal life

**Figure 4.4. Empathy by Default: Correlates in the Brain at Rest By permission of Patrícia Oliveira Silva, Liliana Maia, Joana Coutinho, Brandon Frank, José Miguel Soares, Adriana Sampaio, and Óscar Gonçalves (2018, Empathy by default: Correlates in the brain at rest. Psicothema, 30, 97–103, p. 100).**

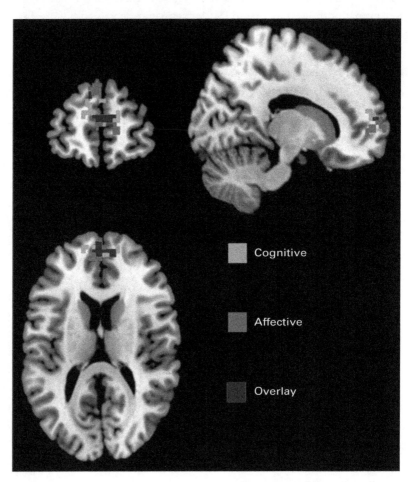

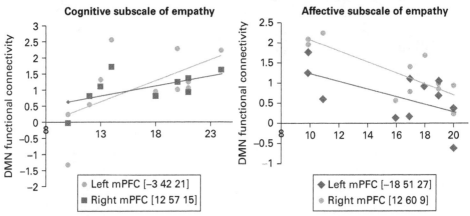

experience, and specific understanding of the unique client and his or her culture, you can share more of yourself and your knowledge to the benefit of your client.

Influencing skills and their functions are summarized in Table 4.6. Influencing skills are complex and often are more effective if used sparingly and in careful concert with listening skills. The *interpretation, or reframe*, may be considered the central influencing skill. It provides clients with a new and alternative way to view their challenges and themselves that can lead to a change in worldview. The frame of reference for a paraphrase or reflection of feeling is the client's way of making sense of the world. The frame of reference for an interpretation (and the remainder of the influencing skills) is primarily that of the therapist.

The reframe is used sparingly by most effective therapists and counselors. Two or three skillful reframes are usually the maximum for a session. Clients can only accommodate so much challenging of their existing frame of reference, and overuse of interpretation will result in a client rejecting your wisdom or perhaps leaving the interview completely.

In the following example, the counselor reframes the client's concept that she should be trying harder as "enabler behavior" that actually may support her husband's drinking issue.

> Client (tearfully): Well, I think that Chuck would be OK and stop drinking if only I did a better job. I really should keep the house better. A lot of our troubles are my fault.
>
> Counselor (interpreting/reframing): You're feeling responsible for his drinking. You've been to AA family groups, and you're taking the enabler role again. The more you rescue Chuck and take responsibility for his actions, the more he will be likely to continue drinking. You can only take care of yourself.

Theoretical orientation plays an important role in the use of interpretations, as it does for most influencing skills (see Table 4.6). The above intervention might be expected from an alcohol counselor working within an AA twelve-step orientation. A counselor working from a family systems orientation might have a somewhat similar approach but might focus more on the family system, saying, "Suzanne, it's the classic system. Chuck gripes at what you do; you try harder, but can never match his expectations. You miss one detail, and then he starts hitting you. After he hits you, you make up, and then the cycle starts again."

For a client in long-term psychoanalytic therapy, the counselor might relate childhood patterns to actions in the present by saying, "Your issue with Chuck goes back to your own father. You're trying to please Chuck as you never were able to please Dad." A behavioral therapist might interpret the same situation in still another way by commenting, "Suzanne, you're always reinforcing Chuck's gripes by trying harder."

Which interpretation or reframe is correct? Most likely all of them. Each theoretical orientation has a useful way of constructing and making sense of the world. The interpretation is one that the client can use to make a difference in her or his own life. Each alternative interpretation of life experience encouraged by the counselor lays the groundwork for the later change in client behavior and illustrates how cognitions can lead to behavior change.

The "directive" is the most actively "influencing" of the influencing skills. Despite extensive belief to the contrary, counselors often tell their clients what to do. Directives are therapist statements that direct a client to do something, say something, or feel in a certain way. The counselor may provide a directive by guiding a client through a fantasy (humanistic counseling), suggesting specific behavioral changes (assertiveness training), or making focused free association suggestions (psychodynamic therapy). Asking a client to complete an action homework assignment is a directive.

A useful, but potentially dangerous, set of influencing skills centers around *advice* and *information giving*. In this mode, the counselor makes suggestions, provides instructional information, and may even say, "If I were you, I would ..." At times, counselors must give advice because they have important information the client needs. Vocational counselors give advice or provide vocational information. Transactional analysts sometimes acquaint their clients with the theoretical basis of the therapy. Reality therapists teach clients skills and knowledge necessary for practical coping in the world.

However, advice and instruction can be overused. Advice must be given carefully and mainly at the request of the client; otherwise, the client will likely say, "Yes, but ..." Anytime the client responds with "Yes, but ..." it is generally time to change your style and move to an attending skill, such as questioning or paraphrasing. For example, you might say, "You feel that suggestion isn't helpful. What might be more useful to you?" With clients like Suzanne in the foregoing example, advice must be given carefully, as people stuck in alcoholic systems have real difficulty in accepting and listening to advice.

*Self-disclosure* occurs when you share your own life experience with the client, as when you say, "I've been there, too. My father was an alcoholic, and I married an alcoholic. It took years for me to realize that I was an enabler myself."

*Feedback* is closely related to self-disclosure in that you share your impressions of the client with the client, as, for example: "We've been talking for a half hour now, and I'm impressed with your ability to hang on through these challenges. You've got a lot of strength in you. I can see it. How do you react to that?" In this example, the counselor uses the perception check after providing feedback. This can be especially helpful in giving back the conversational lead to the client and learning if your influencing skill was helpful or not.

Both feedback and self-disclosure are useful for helping clients know how they are coming across to others. Distinctions between the two skills are obviously somewhat arbitrary, but both can help clients feel more comfortable and more willing to self-disclose. Too much personal feedback and self-disclosure may close off client interchange. For some clients, an open counselor is helpful and reassuring; for others, such an approach can be more intrusive than a barrage of questions.

For instance, self-disclosing your own experience, as did the counselor with the enabler background, can be useful if correctly done in an appropriate context. If the timing or context is wrong, however, self-disclosure can be destructive to the interview. Self-disclosure of your feelings to the client is often considered helpful if you are working from any of several multicultural orientations or in a modern Rogerian theoretical framework. Many therapists who work with complex clients, such as those diagnosed as multiple or borderline personalities, would argue that self-disclosure is inappropriate. Self-disclosure must be employed with some caution with all clients.

Feedback is basic to encounter groups and to other group experiences. With feedback from group members, the client learns how others perceive him or her. Feedback also may be an important skill to use in the family therapy treatment program. In family therapy, the client may need to learn how other family members view his or her behavior.

Employing *logical consequences*, a complex skill, involves leading clients to understand the possible consequences of their actions. For instance, the counselor may say, "Suzanne, as I listen to you, I hear that if you try to meet Chuck's needs, then you are likely to up the ante, and he only demands more. The consequence of your trying harder is that he asks even more of you. How does that sound?"

The structure of a logical consequence statement is basically one of paraphrase and reflection of feeling, with the addition of the logical consequences of continuing the behavior. The logical *if/then* structure underlies this influencing skill. It is important to include a perception check to give the client room to react and lessen the imposition associated with this skill. The influencing skills are presented in Table 4.6.

---

Table 4.6 **Influencing Skills**

| Skill | Description | Function in Interview | Anticipated Client Response |
|---|---|---|---|
| Interpretation/ Reframing | Provides the client with a new perspective, frame of reference, or way of thinking about issues. Interpretations/ reframes may come from your observations; they may be based on varying theoretical orientations to the helping field; or they may link critical ideas together. | Attempts to provide the client with a new way to view the situation. The interpretation provides the client with a clear-cut alternative perception of "reality." This perception may enable a change of view, which in turn may result in changes in thoughts, constructs, or behaviors. | The client may find another perspective or way of thinking about a story, issue, or concern. New perspective could have been generated by a theory used by the interviewer, from linking ideas or information, or by simply looking at the situation afresh. |

*(Continued)*

**Table 4.6 Influencing Skills** *(Continued)*

| | | | |
|---|---|---|---|
| Empathic Self-Disclosure | Self-disclosure is sharing your own personal experience related to what the client has said and often starts with an "I statement." Or sharing your own thoughts and feelings concerning what clients are experiencing in the immediate moment, the here and now. | Emphasizes counselor "I" statements. This skill is closely allied to feedback and may build trust and openness, leading to a more mutual relationship with the client. | Carefully said, clients respond well to self-disclosure, especially at the beginning of a session. They are often pleased to know more about you at that point. Later in the session, sharing your thoughts and feelings about the client can allow them to talk more openly about their issues. Self-disclosure almost always needs to be positive and supportive. |
| Empathic Feedback | Presents clients with clear nonjudgmental information (and sometimes even opinions) on client thoughts, feelings, and behaviors, either in the past or here and now. | Provides concrete data that may help clients realize how others perceive behavior and thinking patterns, thus enabling an alternative self-perception. | Feedback can be supportive or challenging. Supportive feedback searches for positives and strengths, while challenges ask clients to think more carefully about themselves and what they are saying. |
| Natural and Logical Consequences | Explore specific alternatives and the logical positive and negative consequence of each decision possibility with the client. "If you do this …, then …" | Provides an alternative frame of reference for the client. This skill helps clients anticipate the consequences or results of their actions. | Clients will change thoughts, feelings, and behaviors through better anticipation of the consequences of their actions. When you explore the positives and negatives of each possibility, clients will be more involved in the process of making their creative new decision. |
| Directives, Instruction, Psychoeducational Strategies | Clear directions, encouraging clients to do what you suggest, underlies instruction and psychological education. These offer specifics for daily life to help change thoughts, feelings, and behaviors. Providing useful instruction and referral sources can be helpful. Psychoeducational strategies include systematic educational methods such as Therapeutic Lifestyle Changes. With all these, a collaboration approach is essential. | Provides suggestions, instructional ideas, homework, guidance on how to act, think, or behave. Tells the client what action to take. May be a simple suggestion of what to do or may be a sophisticated technique from a specific theory. Used sparingly, may provide client with new and useful information. Specific vocational information is an example of necessary use of this skill. | Clients will make positive progress when they listen to and follow the directives, use the information that you provide for them, and consider your advice and engage in new, more positive thinking, feeling, or behaving. Psychoeducation can lead to major life changes for physical and mental health. |

# Focus and Selective Attention

Beginning helpers often focus on issues instead of the people in front of them. It is generally (but not always) wiser to first focus on the client and later on the issues. The client is sitting there in front of you and is likely the one who will be solving their concerns. A temptation in much of therapeutic practice is to focus on the issue and solve it, perhaps even disregarding the thoughts and feelings of the client.

> Client: Yes, you've got it. I've got to cope with so many things, and it seems endless. I don't know where to turn. I've tried to get Chuck to AA (Alcoholics Anonymous), but he only goes for a session or two and then quits. The school guidance counselor called me in because Joss got into trouble on the playground. They said he was bullying a smaller boy. How can I solve all those problems?

> Counselor: I hear *you* as overwhelmed by it all. Let's start first with *you* and what's happening with *Suzanne*.

Note that the counselor here used two personal pronouns and the client's name. Personalizing counseling and therapy by naming the client is seldom stressed sufficiently in the helping profession. Therapy is for the individual client and the client has a name. By focusing on Suzanne, the counselor indicates an interest in the person and what that person feels and thinks.

Although focus is usually on the client, it can be invaluable to broaden the situation by focusing in a balanced fashion on several additional dimensions. In working with a complex case such as this, it should be clear that focusing just on Suzanne will not be sufficient in the long run. This client needs to work out her relationship with her husband, help her children, and work with a wide variety of pragmatic issues. Thus, while counseling is indeed for the client, the ability to look beyond the client and focus the interview more broadly is critical.

Client-centered Rogerian theory and psychoanalytic theory, of course, see the issue differently. These individualistically oriented systems of helping rarely focus their interviewing leads anywhere else but on the client. Behavioral theory, family theory, feminist and multicultural theory, by way of contrast, find it important to consider a host of situational/contextual variables if the client is to be helped. You will also find that some clients can best be reached by first focusing on the issue, and only later will they focus on themselves and their feelings. An issue in the above paragraph is your own conception of the interview and the purpose of counseling and therapy. Case management—helping the client handle multiple issues in their lives—is increasingly recognized as a valid and important facet of effective professional helping. Increasingly more helpers are emphasizing that their clients live their lives in a social and economic context. At the same time, the conventional wisdom of the field remains that we must focus on the individual client (or family) right there in the clinical session or interview. Table 4.7 illustrates six types of focus analysis.

---

**Table 4.7. Six Types of Focus Analysis in the Session**

**Focus Analysis**

It is important to ensure we have considered most, if not all, of the possible aspects of the client's concern. Focus analysis helps us consider all possible aspects of a client's issues. For example, it would be possible to respond to Suzanne with a variety of foci:

Suzanne: Yes, you've got it. I've got to cope with so many things, and it seems endless. I don't know where to turn. I've tried to get Chuck to AA, but he only goes for a session or two and then quits. The school guidance counselor called me in because Joss got into trouble on the playground. They said he was bullying a smaller boy. How can I solve all those problems?

1. Client focus: "Suzanne, you feel confused and lonely. You're unsure of what you want to do." In this example, there are four personal references to the client. While counseling generally recommends a client focus, this may be culturally inappropriate in some situations. This may be the case with Suzanne, as it places most of the responsibility on her and tends to ignore family and gender factors.

2. Concern/main-theme focus: The presenting concern or main theme of the session could be said to be the general issue of how alcohol affects the client and her family. More specifically, this client seems to be nearing a crisis. Sample responses focusing on the issue and its solution would include: "What can I do to help you find housing so you could move out?" "The situation sounds like an emergency. I'll call the women's shelter right now. You'll be safe there." "Let's talk about how we could help your husband become more involved with AA." Clients often need concrete concerns solved, particularly in times of crisis, and a focus on the individual client could be inappropriate at times.

3. Other-person focus: "Tell me more about your husband." Here, we can predict that the client will start telling us about her husband and his drinking. "What's going on with Joss?" would lead to a focus on the son. Both of these leads may be valuable information, but they do not tell us about the client and her reaction to the situation.

4. Family focus: Family therapy stresses the importance of this dimension. Rather than focus on the identified patient (IP, the concerning family member), family therapy focuses on the family as a whole. Individual therapy and counseling focus on individuals, and family therapy adherents often criticize this view as limited and naive.

5. Interviewer focus: "I grew up in an alcoholic family, too. I can sense some of your issues." Focusing on oneself may be useful as a self-disclosure or feedback technique, and it may help develop mutuality with the client. As rapport develops, such responses may be increasingly helpful. However, they must not be overdone. With people of culturally different backgrounds from your own, such self-disclosure can be helpful at times.

6. Cultural/environmental/contextual focus: "This is a concern facing many women. Society and its limited support systems do not always make it easy." Underlying our client's issues are long histories of interaction with sociopolitical systems. With some clients, this can become an important focus for discussion. Helpers with an African American or feminist orientation often use this focus with real effectiveness to produce change ("Many African Americans feel a sense of rage because of discrimination—it's institutionalized in our society." "You say that you can't speak assertively for yourself. This is a concern that many women have in our culture due to sexist conditioning." Yet most counseling theories often forget the cultural/environmental context and the historical background of the individual. You will find very little of this focus in the major theories of counseling and therapy.

These six dimensions of microskill focus analysis are critical for understanding what is happening in any therapy session. Focus analysis is concerned with the subject or main theme of the client and counselor sentence structure. Counseling is centrally concerned with getting clients to make "I statements" where they discuss themselves and their concerns. Counselors produce "I statements" in their clients by using the personal pronouns *you, your*, etc., and by using their clients' names.

# Confrontation Skill

The Merriam-Webster dictionary defines *confrontation* as "a situation in which people, groups, etc., fight, oppose, or challenge each other in an angry way" (2017). This meaning is sometimes incorrectly infused in the teaching of intentional counseling. At its least effective operation, a confrontation can represent an open or subtle display of hostility from the counselor.

As Ivey, Ivey, and Zalaquett have observed, a confrontation can be more subtle:

> Empathic confrontation is a gentle skill that involves first listening to client stories carefully and respectfully and then encouraging the client to examine self and/or situation more fully. Empathic confrontation is not a direct, harsh challenge or "going against" the client; rather, it represents "going with" the client, seeking clarification and the possibility of a creative New that enables resolution of difficulties. However, with some clients, you will find that rather direct and assertive behavior will be required before they can hear you. (2018, p. 229)

A confrontation is not telling a client that he or she is in error or a bad person. In counseling, the meaning of confrontation, cited above, is central; the dictionary meaning is potentially destructive.

Double messages, incongruities, and discrepancies appear constantly in counseling interviews. A client may present an open right hand and smile while the left hand is closed in a fist. The counselor may be sitting with an open posture while covering the genital area with both hands. The client may say, "I really like my parents," while sitting in a closed posture with arms crossed over the chest. Double messages appear at the verbal level as well. The "Freudian slip" is a classic example of a mixed verbal message. A Freudian slip occurs when someone says one thing but means another. The client may say, "I liked my parents," when intending to say he or she dislikes them. The past tense *liked* could be interpreted as a "death wish." More directly, some clients will say, "I both love and hate my children, and those mixed feelings scare me." Dreams represent a type of mixed and incongruent message as well. The task for the therapist is to identify mixed messages and to search for the underlying meaning or deeper structure.

One of the main tasks of counseling is to assist clients to work through, resolve, or learn to live with incongruities. Incongruities, discrepancies, and mixed or double messages are often at the root of immobility, and the inability to respond creatively. Most counseling theories have as their main focus the resolution of incongruities. Freudians talk about resolving polarities and unconscious conflicts; Gestaltists, about resolving splits; client-centered therapists, about resolving mixed feelings; rational-emotive therapists, about the need to attack incongruent irrational thinking; vocational counselors about the distinction between unreal and real goals ... the list could continue. The importance of naming and resolving incongruities cannot be overstressed. Examples of ways to confront Suzanne, the client in the above examples, include:

> Counselor: You're laughing, but I sense from the tone of your voice and the look on your face that underneath it isn't a laughing matter. (*Confrontation of discrepancy between verbal behavior and nonverbals.*)

> Counselor: On the one hand you say you want to get out of this relationship with Chuck, but on the other hand, you've been saying this for several months and still you are staying. How do you put that together? (*Confrontation of discrepancy between what is said and what is done.*)

The following model sentence is often helpful to the beginning counselor or therapist: "On the one hand, you think (feel, behave) ..., but on the other, you think (feel, behave). ..." This model sentence provides the essence of confrontation statements. It is nonjudgmental and provides an often clarifying picture of the confusing situation faced by the client. You will also find that using your hands as a balance scale (as if weighing the two alternatives) can be very useful in emphasizing the contradiction.

It seems that most schools of psychotherapy pay special attention to incongruities and discrepancies. However, each theory has its own means of coping with these issues and uses vastly different routes toward meeting the common objective of resolving and coping with the inevitable incongruities and double messages we meet throughout life.

There is evidence that the overly confronting therapist can be damaging to client growth (Norcross, 2016). Creating discrepancy, rolling with resistance, and expressing empathy work better than confrontation (Lundahl, Kunz, Brownell, Tollefson, & Burke, 2010; Schumacher, Madson, & Nilsen, 2014). Similarly, there is evidence that the overly cautious therapist may accomplish very little growth. Intentional counseling suggests a careful balance of empathic confrontation with supporting qualities of warmth, positive regard, and respect. It is suggested that the empathic therapist is one who can maintain a balance of "push-pull" and support, employing a wide variety of counseling skills and theories. However, this balance must be authentic to the counselor's true self.

Clients come to counseling for the resolution of their discrepancies and incongruities. While they may not always be consciously aware of the nature of the mixed messages they receive (and they give to others), therapy and counseling are about the resolution of differences. These incongruities may exist within the individual in terms of an unconscious "battle" with one's parents, the inability of an African American person or a woman to cope with excessive discrimination, conflict with a spouse, difficulties in vocational choice, or inability to behave in a satisfactory manner in social situations. These incongruities are shown in verbal and nonverbal messages.

Your task as a counselor or therapist is to "read" these nonverbal and verbal messages, get underneath the surface structure, and determine the nature of the conflict. Incongruities and mixed messages are the "stuff" of counseling and psychotherapy, and in their identification and resolution, you show your ability and caring as a professional helper.

# Different Skill Patterns and Focus for Different Theories

All systems of counseling and therapy use some microskills, particularly the basic listening sequence. If you master the specific skills presented here, you can mix and match these foundational patterns so that mastery of many alternative theories of therapy becomes possible. When you learn new methods of therapy, you then may build on these skills and frame them into a wide variety of techniques and strategies, appropriate to the system you are studying.

Rogerian theory almost exclusively uses attending skills and very few questions. By way of contrast, note that rational-emotive and feminist therapies make extensive use of influencing skills. The microskills are not used solely by counselors and therapists. Professionals in medicine, management, and teaching also benefit from competence in the communication skills. One increasingly important role of the therapist or counselor is that of teaching others the effective interview skills.

Focus of therapy may also vary from theory to theory. A feminist therapist will focus extensively on the cultural/environmental context, while this may receive only limited attention in Gestalt therapy, for example. Virtually all methods of counseling and therapy stress the importance of focusing on the individual in the interview. While it may be helpful to obtain information on family and friends, the task is to work with the person sitting in front of you.

If you gain a mastery of the attending and listening skills, you have a solid foundation on which to build a specific theory at a later point. Improved quality in helping comes from applying the theories and skills in an individually and culturally sensitive manner.

## Decisional Counseling—Pragmatism in Action

As you work in the counseling and therapy field, you will encounter more than a thousand theories and practices (Meier, 2016). A subset of these theories focuses on decision making, and you will find that they use similar—but different—language in their approaches.

We and others (for example, Janis & Mann, 1977) would argue that decisional counseling in its various guises dates back to Benjamin Franklin, who is credited for first outlining pragmatic decision making. You will recognize these ideas as the foundation of brainstorming or other creative problem-solving work you have encountered in the past.

1. Define the issue or concern clearly.
2. Generate alternative possibilities for solution.
3. Weigh the positives and negatives of each alternative in a simple *balance sheet.*
4. Select one alternative for action, and see how it works.

Franklin's system is perhaps the ultimate expression of the pragmatic worldview. His discovery of electricity by flying a kite is a particularly apt example of testing your idea to see if it works.

The decisional model presented here is one of many available in the field. For example, Egan (2013) has an entire theory of helping and the interview based on a three-stage model: 1. Present Scenario: current story—reviewing the issue; 2. Preferred Scenario: possibilities—developing the preferred scenario; and 3. Strategy: getting there—determining how to get there. Each of the three stages is in turn divided into sub-stages, such as storytelling, setting up goals, and brainstorming possible resolutions. D'Zurilla and Nezu (2006) have developed a whole theory of helping titled *Problem-Solving Therapy*; Carkhuff (2009) has long been known for his problem-oriented model; and Brammer and MacDonald (2002) have been particularly influential in orienting beginning professionals to creative problem solving. Hansen (2011) draws from the Minnesota trait and factor model, with an especially appealing gender and culturally sensitive model of decisional counseling termed "Integrated Life Planning." The model presented here was influenced by work with Leon Mann (1982) and a structure for the five-stage interview was developed by Ivey and Matthews (1984). Nonetheless, Benjamin Franklin must be recognized as the originator of all these ideas.

## The Five-Stage Interview Model: Pragmatic Decisional Counseling

The central theoretical and pragmatic point of the five-stage interview decisional model is that *counseling and therapy are not only about decisions, but the interview itself also may be structured using a decision-making framework.* Drawing from social constructivist theory, the five-stage model is also a way to consider how interviews are conducted through many forms of therapy. This later point will be elaborated as we discuss issues about alternative theories throughout this book.

Table 4.8 presents the five-stage interview model in brief form. Note that key counselor leads for each stage are identified. You will find that vocational counseling, employment counseling, family problem solving, issues of conflict between disputing parties, life planning, retirement counseling, financial advisement, management discussions, nutritional counseling, compliance with medical advice, and even legal counsel can be given effectively using this model. In fact, the microskills and accompanying five-stage interview model have been used for all of the above and more.

Note that the model as presented is linear; it is oriented to specific problem solving and moves step by step. The model has been translated into at least fourteen languages and has been proven useful in settings as diverse as alcohol counselors in the Central Arctic, managers with Mercedes-Benz in Germany, and with peer counselors in Hong Kong. But in each setting, adaptations must be made for individuals who exist within that cultural framework. As you work with the five-stage decisional counseling model, please recall the following guidelines for individual and multicultural adaptation:

> *Stage 1: Empathic Relationship: Rapport and structuring.* Microskills are particularly important at this stage. Use individually appropriate attending behavior and the ability to observe client reactions, to adapt the structure and pace of the interview to meet individual and cultural needs. It is through your ability to establish rapport both early in the session and later that that you will establish an empathic bond between you and the client.

> When working with delinquent acting-out youngsters, this stage may take weeks before trust is developed. In Aboriginal Australia, social workers often take more than half of the interview focusing on family and social interconnections before even asking about the issue to be discussed. With many middle-class people in North America, this stage can almost be omitted, as the client starts talking about their issue so quickly. Nonetheless, continual development of rapport and trust is vital.

> *Stage 2: Story and Strengths: Gathering data and identifying assets.* Microskills most associated with this phase of the interview are those of the basic listening sequence. Use the BLS to draw out the client's narrative or story. And remember to use the BLS again to draw out client strengths. Focus analysis can be helpful in enabling clients to see their concerns from varying perspectives. Your ability to summarize the client's story or issue in his or her own words is one important part of empathic understanding.

Focus analysis reminds us that defining the client's issues or challenges is not as easy as it seems. The pragmatic model of Ben Franklin gives insufficient attention to the fact that the way we define and tell the story of an issue often decides how the issue will be resolved. Is the issue "in the client" and thus an issue of internal locus of control, or is it "in the environment," and thus we need to focus on contextual issues? Feminist theory, for example, would point out that environmental contingencies of sexism are vital issues in any work with women. Some rational-emotive theorists, on the other hand, focus on "it is not things, but how we think about things." The approach to problem definition obviously results in a very different way to construct the meaning of a "problem."

Some point out that the very use of the word *problem* starts decisional counseling on the wrong foot. Decisional counseling argues strongly that counseling and therapy are too much about "problems" and is currently suggesting that counselors and therapists use the words *issues* or *concerns*. Lanier (Personal communication, 1999) noted that many African Americans object to the concept of "problem" and respond more readily to "issues" or "concerns." Recent microskill experience reveals that many clients of other racial and ethnic groups prefer the more open and positive language suggested by Lanier.

Decisional counseling argues for the need to identify positive client strengths in each and every session. These strengths may include such things as positive childhood experiences, an accomplishment in sports or the arts, something that the individual is proud of doing, images of grandparents who were supportive, the times things were "going right" with a difficult partner or situation, to the ability to survive a trauma. Positive stories and images help center the client and actually give them strength to delve more deeply into difficult areas of their lives.

*Stage 3: Goals: Determining outcomes collaboratively.* Again, the basic listening sequence and focus analysis are central. However, this time, the listening sequence focuses on helping the client find positive, clear, and reachable goals. Concreteness, as described in Chapter 2, is essential. Too often counselors fail in this area, as clients are often willing to talk endlessly about their issues and avoid talking about what they want to have happen.

You will find that many clients can benefit from an immediate focus on goals. Solution-oriented therapy (O'Hanlon & Weiner-Davis, 2003) gives minimal attention to Stages 1 and 2, choosing to find out what the client wants to have happen. Only if necessary will they recycle back to Stages 1 and 2. They make the excellent point that if the client can achieve what he or she wants, why bother with long stories and definitions of issues and concerns. Solution-oriented therapy, like decisional counseling, focuses on client strengths, what they are already "doing right," and seeks out specific wishes of the client.

You will find that moving directly to goal setting and establishing a story of joint wishes for the interview may help you work more effectively with clients who are culturally different from you. It is difficult to tell a counselor a story of difficulties and challenges if there is a lack of trust due to a history of racism or spiritual oppression.

Finally, you will note that the goals of counseling are sometimes established by the theorist before the client walks in the door. There are some practitioners who believe that every client needs to understand the unconscious, become self-actualized, or to really look at themselves in a gender-fair society. While all of these goals may be laudable, increasingly the field is moving away from this "top-down" approach and involving clients in establishing their own goals.

*Stage 4: Restory: Generating alternative solutions.* Influencing skills and focus analysis become more important at this stage. Any of a variety of skills or theoretical alternatives may be employed to help the client create new ways of thinking about his or her story. You will find that clear discussion of client stories and strengths followed by precise goal setting is often enough in itself for clients to brainstorm their own solutions. Implied in this is the basic confrontational statement, "On the one hand your issue/challenge/concern is …, and on the other hand, your goal is …" Strength images and stories may be brought in to help clients act on their issues.

*Stage 5. Action: Generalization and transferring learning.* Influencing skills are particularly important here as you want to ensure that the client actually does something as a result of the session. Special attention to *relapse prevention* (Marlatt & Donovan, 2005; Marlatt, Larimer, Witkiewitz, 2011) is given in the chapters on cognitive-behavioral methods. Unless you plan for transfer of decisions and actions in the session, much of your good work simply disappears into thin air.

One very useful strategy at the end of the session is to ask the client a simple question—"What stands out for you today from our session?" or "What one thing might you remember from today?" This open question often provides us with surprising results. What we thought was our brilliant intervention may not have even been noticed by the client. Data obtained from this question often tells us what to do next to ensure that the client returns and/or takes action on the decisions reached.

**Table 4.8. The Five-Stage Structure of the Interview**

| Stage | Function and Purpose | Anticipated Client Response | Cultural and Individual Issues |
|---|---|---|---|
| 1. *Empathic relationship.* Initiate the session. Establish rapport and structure. "Hello, what would you like to talk about?" "What might you like to see as a result of our talking today?" | Build a working alliance and allow the client to feel comfortable with the counseling process. Explain what is likely to happen in the session or series of sessions, including informed consent and ethical issues. Discover client reasons for coming. Structuring helps keep the session on task and informs the client what the counselor can and cannot do. | The client feels at ease with an understanding of the key ethical issues and the purpose of the session. The client may also know you more completely as a person and a professional—and has a sense that you are interested in his or her concerns. | With some clients and some cultural groups, rapport and trust may take longer to develop. |
| 2. *Story and strengths.* Gather data. "I'd like to hear your story." "What are your strengths and resources?" Use the BLS to draw out client stories, concerns, challenges, or issues. | Discover and clarify why the client has come to the session and listen to the client's stories and issues. Identify strengths and resources as part of a strength-based approach. | The client shares thoughts, feelings, and behaviors; tells the story in detail; presents strengths and resources. | Some clients do not appreciate a careful exploration of issues. For these clients, problem solving, decisional counseling, or solution-oriented approaches may work better. |
| 3. *Goals.* Set goals mutually. The BLS will help define goals. "What do you want to happen?" "How would you feel emotionally if you achieved this goal?" One possible goal is exploration of possibilities, rather than focusing immediately. | If you don't know where you are going, you may end up somewhere else. In brief counseling (later in this chapter), goal setting is fundamental, and this stage may be part of the first phase of the session. All the same, openness to change and exploration are good places to start. | The client will discuss directions that he or she might want to go, new ways of thinking, desired feeling states, and behaviors that might be changed. The client might also seek to learn how to live more effectively with stressful situations or events that cannot be changed at this point (rape, death, an accident, an illness). A more ideal story might be defined. | Some cultural groups and individuals prefer to start here. They have clear goals as they understand their concerns. Again, brief solution-oriented approaches may work best for them. |

*(Continued)*

**Table 4.8. The Five-Stage Structure of the Interview** *(Continued)*

| | | | |
|---|---|---|---|
| 4. *Restory.* Explore alternatives via the BLS. Confront client incongruities and conflict. "What are we going to do about it?" "Can we generate new ways of thinking, feeling, and behaving?" | Generate at least *three* alternatives that might resolve the client's issues. Creativity is useful here. Seek to find at least three alternatives so that the client has a choice. One choice at times may be to do nothing and accept things as they are. The system of restorying will vary extensively with different theories and approaches. | The client may reexamine individual goals in new ways, solve issues and concerns from at least those alternatives, and start the move toward new stories and actions. | Respect cultural and individual preferences. What may seem as the correct option or decision for you may not seem as appropriate for the client. |
| 5. *Action.* Plan for generalizing session learning to "real life." "Will you use what you decided to do today, tomorrow, or this coming week?" | Generalize new learning and facilitate client changes in thoughts, feelings, and behaviors in daily life. Commit the client to homework and an action plan. As appropriate, plan for termination of sessions. | The client demonstrates changes in behavior, thoughts, and feelings in daily life outside of the interview conversation. Or the client explores new alternatives and reports back discoveries. | The degree of action will also depend on cultural and individual preferences. Progress will be facilitated by considering clients' styles and preferences. |

---

**PRACTICE EXERCISE 4.1. Using the Basic Listening Sequence to Draw Out a Client's Story**

Regardless of whatever theory you select, it is important that you draw out the client's story and the key facts, thoughts, and feelings within that story. Find a volunteer to role-play as a client, and practice your listening skills and ability to draw out the client's story using the basic listening sequence. Audiotape this interview so you can examine and classify what listening skills you are using. Better yet, videotape it as well so you can examine your own and the client's nonverbal behavior.

As a final check, give special attention to how you summarized the client's story at the end of the exercise. How accurately did you catch the story? Did you obtain the key facts and the client's thoughts and feelings?

## Microskills and Brief Solution-Oriented Counseling and Therapy

Counselors and therapists live in an age of accountability with an orientation to results. Many professionals working in mental health agencies, private practice, and schools are increasingly asked to shorten their time with clients and provide clear evidence of their effectiveness. The "rush to results" can mean that the client gets lost in the process, and solution-oriented approaches are sometimes criticized as being inadequate substitutes for real therapy and counseling.

Brief solution-oriented counseling and therapy (SOCT), however, is best considered another important strategy for all professionals. All important authors in the area (De Shazer, 1985; O'Hanlon & Weiner-Davis, 2003; Talmon, 1990, 2012) in different ways focus on positive strategies with a good deal of client respect. They also emphasize that brief (one to five sessions) therapy is not a cure-all. Rather, it is a concrete way to provide the client with very useful answers to specific issues and concerns. And once provided with the solid base of an answer to a concern, the client may move on by him- or herself and resolve other issues.

SOCT is unlikely to be useful to clients who have issues about the meaning of life or want to examine their life history. Clients with these goals may be better served by existential-humanistic or psychodynamic therapy. A client suffering from a severe depression may benefit from some of the short-term solutions offered by SOCT, but cognitive-behavioral or interpersonal psychotherapy methods may provide more benefit for the client. However, each of these systems would benefit by using concepts of brief therapy to help the client realize specific goals in longer-term therapy.

The purpose of this brief section is to show how the microskills approach and the five-stage structure of the interview can be used to clarify SOCT. In addition, through drawing on the community and family genograms of Chapters 2 and 3, SOCT can be made more culturally relevant and sensitive (Kuehl, 1995). However, the very efficiency of SOCT may still be highly inappropriate with some cultural groups whose view of time is different from European American pragmatic norms.

Practice Exercise 4.2 presents the specifics of SOCT from a microskills perspective. Solution-oriented theorists constantly emphasize the importance of strengths, and this practice exercise starts with positive images and stories from the family and community genograms. Microskills theory believes that we can find our greatest strengths as selves-in-relation and that we can draw on our networks of family and community in our search for solutions.

Rapport and structuring will tend to be given relatively short time spans in SOCT. But relationship is vital, for without a caring, empathic relationship, the chances for finding solutions is reduced. Talmon (2012) stresses that we must structure the interview very early in our search for solutions, as we may only have one session, and suggests that a positive attitude on the part of the counselor is essential in communicating that something can be done to help rapidly—even this very day. Thus, as part of the first few minutes of the session, emphasize that something can be done to make a positive difference in the client's life.

While the basic listening sequence remains important, SOCT believes that most counselors and therapists spend too much time listening to concerns and issues. As such, the second phase of the session—gathering data—will be brief and to the point. While feelings will be noted and reacted to sensitively, solution-oriented counselors are more oriented to concrete and specific action. As part of this action plan, the positive asset search and emphasis on client strength will be highlighted constantly in the session.

"What do you want to have happen?" is the essence of the third phase of the five-stage interview structure. This question becomes even more important for SOCT. Goal setting may be considered the centerpiece of effective SOCT. The practice exercise provides several specifics for goal setting with clients.

Stages 4 and 5 of the five-stage structure tend to collapse into one in SOCT. As each solution is brainstormed, the therapist immediately focuses on how the client could take the suggested resolution into the "real world" and daily life. Transfer of training is particularly important with solution-focused counselors and therapists.

Solution-oriented counseling and therapy is keenly aware that resolution of an issue in one to five sessions does not remake the client. Therapy does not seek a final "cure." There is no cure of life. All of us face issues constantly and long-term therapy may help us find meaning or understand our developmental history. But even with the best long-term therapy, specific issues (divorce, death, living with a serious illness) may lead a client back to therapy again and again over time. SOCT offers a useful model to be employed in conjunction with traditional methods. At times we need to examine life in depth, but often many clients will do well with short-term specific efforts at resolving their concerns.

# Theories in Action

## Toward a Culturally Sensitive Brief Counseling and Therapy

The following structured exercise may be used with a volunteer or real client. Regardless, we suggest that you photocopy the following and share it with your client so that he or she knows very specifically what is going to happen and why. This sharing of interview plans moves you toward collaboration and co-construction in the interview and often provides the client with a feeling of safety.

---

**PRACTICE EXERCISE 4.2. SOLUTION-ORIENTED COUNSELING AND THERAPY**

This exercise seeks to integrate the first four chapters of this book. As such, this is the lengthiest written outline of all our practice exercises. You may find it takes you more than an hour to complete, or you may wish to have a second session with your client. It is also an exercise to practice brief interventions.

*(Continued)*

PRACTICE EXERCISE 4.2. **SOLUTION-ORIENTED COUNSELING AND THERAPY** *(Continued)*

### Stage 1.  *Empathic Relationship: Rapport and Structuring*

Spend some time making the client comfortable in your own natural way. Share with them the interview plan in writing, and talk to them about what is to happen.

"What would you like to have happen today?" is a suggested opening question. Note that this implies that "something" is indeed going to happen. Usually, the client will express a concern or issue. Use the Basic Listening Sequence to hear the client's story briefly.

### 2.  *Story and Strengths: Gathering Data, Identifying Assets*

Listen to the client's concern. Briefly return to the original concern and use the Basic Listening Sequence to draw out their issue in slightly more detail. Even at this early stage, ask questions such as the following, which focus on positives and may serve as resources.

Are things any better now?

What's keeping it from getting worse?

Any good things you observe in the situation?

An essential part of this process is clarifying the narrative. Make sure that the concern is presented in a specific concrete fashion with clearly observable behaviors. If thoughts or emotions are the issue, clarity is equally important.

*Positive asset search.* Any or all the ideas of the positive asset search of Chapter 3 may be used here. "What are you already doing right?" is particularly helpful. Many clients have strengths that can be drawn on to help them find solutions. You may need to help them define these strengths through feedback from your observations. The community and family strengths should again be noted.

*Community and family genograms.* Tell the client that before you go further, you'd like to learn more about their family and community situation. Develop with them on-the-spot brief family and community genograms. This can be done in fifteen minutes. Make it clear that you want to avoid negative stories at this time and will focus only on strengths. It is particularly important to generate two to three positive family and community images. These are resources and strengths that can help later.

*(Continued)*

### 3. *Goals: Collaborative Determination of Desired Outcomes*

"What do you want to happen?" is the basic question of the third phase of the five-stage structure. It is even more important in SOCT. Be aware of your client. You may want to introduce this central question even in the first phases of rapport and structuring. Your task as counselor or therapist is to clarify, specify, and concretize goals. Without clear-cut directions and goals, SOCT will not succeed. It may be helpful to write down with your client the specific *achievable* goal(s) you have defined. The goal should be simple. If the issue is large, work only on a part rather than the whole.

From then on, the major focus of your session is on achieving those goals. Use the client's own main words and language for those goals. If their first language is other than English, write those goals in their own language as well.

Last but not least, determine how you are going to measure change. How would you know when the goal is achieved? You can use an ad-hoc scale (on a scale of 1 [least] to 7 [most], how anxious are you now?) or a validated instrument such as the Beck Anxiety Inventory (BAI) (Beck & Steer, 1993) to measure changes in anxiety.

### 4./5. *Restory and Action: Generating and Implementing Solutions*

This combination of two stages focuses on brainstorming possibilities that meet client goals. It will require a good deal of creativity from you and your client. Essentially, your joint task is to create new solutions to old issues *and* act on them—ideally today or tomorrow.

Throughout all of the following, draw on strengths and positive assets noted earlier in the session.

*Brainstorming suggestions.* Some sample questions that may be useful include:

Now, tell me about times when this issue is absent or less strong. What is happening?

What are exceptions to this issue?

- When does the issue not happen?

- What is different about those times?

- How do you get to that more positive result?

- What did you do (they do) to get a more satisfactory ending?

*(Continued)*

From a different vantage point, the following are sometimes helpful:

What do you do for fun? (Breaks set and may provide surprise answers.)

Use humor and surprise in a culturally sensitive fashion. Laughing about the issue may be exceptionally helpful.

How does your family/culture relate to these issues? What supports/answers do they provide?

*Family and multicultural issues.* The family and community genograms often provide new ideas, positive assets, and support at this stage.

Drawing on your image of the elder in your family, how would he/she look at this issue? Imagine the elder is standing at your shoulder. What would he or she say to you right now?

Your community (or group) has many strengths. Where would you go for support with some of these issues?

*Taking it home.* Aim constantly for generalization of new ideas and resolutions to daily life. The more specific the joint solution, the more possibility of something actually happening as a result of this session. You may even want to write a contract for action in both English and your client's own language (if different).

As part of the brainstorming/transfer process, the following may be helpful:

How will your life be different?

Who will be the first to notice change?

-What will he/she do or say?

-How will you respond?

What would you like to happen?

How can we make that happen?

Do not hesitate to mix in other theories and strategies, according to the needs of your client. Relapse prevention, another cognitive-behavioral strategy, may be very useful at this point to ensure generalization.

*Follow-up.* Use the telephone or e-mail to follow up and provide support. Encourage the client to call in and tell you how it is going. Remind the client that he or she can contact you later for another session to work on another part of the issue.

## Limitations and Practical Implications of Decisional and Brief Solution Microskills Counseling and Therapy

The decisional and microskills approach is noted for its precision and clear description of behavior. One of the axioms of the microskills approach is that all interviews must take into account both individual and multicultural differences.

The microskills of attending and listening work and are clear and teachable. They should, however, be used in a culturally and individually appropriate fashion. There is a danger in teaching culturally inappropriate skills to trainees, particularly those skills that are effective and precise in description.

The second author of this book worked with Matthew Rigney, a highly skilled Aboriginal social worker in Australia, in jointly examining the multicultural implications of attending. Matthew was videotaped interviewing a client in the "Aboriginal fashion," which involved limited eye contact and a more self-disclosing and participative style of interviewing. On reviewing the tape, Matthew commented, "You mean it's OK to do counseling in our people's way?" Despite his obvious skill, Matthew had come to believe that only the European Australian style of listening was appropriate. Needless to say, he was encouraged to maintain and sharpen his traditional ways of listening. Matthew Rigney is very much alive in the ideas presented in this chapter and in this book.

And at present, many people in Australia, Canada, and the United States continue to teach and use microskills and decisional counseling in a culturally insensitive manner. Some books still discuss attending without attention to cultural differences. Needless to say, this gap between theory and practice is not solely associated with the microskills approach. Individualistic psychodynamic and client-centered theories are also transported to relational cultures and presented as "the way to conduct interviewing and therapy." Powerful and intrusive Gestalt techniques may be highly effective in North America, but they can be highly inappropriate in other settings. Cognitive-behavioral techniques, like microskills, are often useful in other cultural settings, but require serious cultural modification to ensure that they are appropriate. What it is assertive behavior for US clients may be perceived as aggressive behavior by Chilean clients.

# References

Beck, A.T., & Steer, R.A. (1993). *Beck anxiety inventory manual*. San Antonio, TX: Psychological Corporation.

Brammer, L.M., & MacDonald, M. (2002). *The helping relationship: Process and skills* (8th ed.). New York, NY: Pearson.

Carkhuff, R.R. (2009). *The art of helping* (9th ed.). Amherst, MA: Possibilities Publishing.

D'Zurilla, T., & Nezu, A.M. (2006). *Problem-solving therapy: A positive approach to clinical intervention* (3rd ed.). New York, NY: Springer.

Daniels, T., & Ivey, A. (2007). *Microcounseling* (3rd ed.). Springfield, IL: Charles C. Thomas.

De Shazer, S. (1985). *Keys to solution in brief therapy*. New York, NY: Norton.

Egan, G. (2013). *The skilled helper: A problem-management and opportunity-development approach to helping* (10th ed.). Pacific Grove, CA: Brooks/Cole.

Eres, R., Decety, J., Louis, W.R., & Molenberghs, P. (2015). Individual differences in local gray matter density are associated with differences in affective and cognitive empathy. *NeuroImage, 117,* 305–310. doi. 10.1016/j.neuroimage.2015.05.038.

Fan, Y., Duncan, N.W., de Greck, M., & Northoff, G. (2011). Is there a core neural network in empathy? An fMRI based quantitative meta-analysis. *Neuroscience & Biobehavioral Reviews 35,* 903-911.

Fukuhara, M. (2012). *Perspectives of microcounseling in Japan*. Tokyo, Japan: Kawashima Shoten.

Fukuhara, M., Zalaquett, C., Ishiyama, I., Kawamichi, H., Asazuma, N., & Backenroth, G. (2016). *Microcounseling all over the world: Basis for counseling and psychotherapy*. Symposium conducted at the 31st International Congress of Psychology (ICP), Yokohama, Japan.

Hansen, S.S. (2011). Integrative life planning: A holistic approach. *Journal of Employment Counseling, 48,* 167–169. doi:10.1002/j.2161-1920.2011.tb01105.x.

Ivey, A.E. (1971). *Microcounseling: Innovations in interviewing training*. Springfield, IL: Charles C. Thomas.

Ivey, A.E., & Authier, J. (1978). *Microcounseling*. Springfield, IL: Charles C. Thomas.

Ivey, A.E., & Daniels, T. (2016). Systematic interviewing microskills and neuroscience: Developing bridges between the fields of communication and counseling psychology. International. *Journal of Listening, 30,* 99–119. doi.org/10.1080/10904018.2016.1173815.

Ivey, A.E., Normington, C., Miller, C., Morrill W., & Haase, R. (1968). Microcounseling and attending behavior: An approach to prepracticum counselor training. *Journal of Counseling Psychology 15,* 1-12.

Ivey, A.E., & Matthews, W.J. (1984). A meta-model for structuring the clinical interview. *Journal of Counseling & Development, 63,* 1556–6676. doi.org/10.1002/j.1556-6676.1984.tb02809.x.

Ivey, A., Ivey, M.B., & Zalaquett, C.P. (2016). *Essentials of intentional interviewing: Counseling in a multicultural world* (3rd ed.). Belmont, CA: Cengage Learning.

Ivey, A., Ivey, M.B., & Zalaquett, C.P. (2018). *Intentional interviewing and counseling: Facilitating client development in a multicultural society* (9th ed.). Belmont, CA: Cengage Learning.

Janis, L., & Mann, L. (1977). *Decision making: A psychological analysis of conflict, choice, and commitment*. New York, NY: Free Press.

Kawamichi, H., Yoshihara, K., Sasaki, A.T., Sugawara, S.K., Tanabe, H.C., Shinohara, R., ... Sadato, N. (2015). Perceiving active listening activates the reward system and improves the impression of relevant experiences. *Social Neuroscience, 10*(1), 16–26. http://doi.org/10.1080/17470919.2014.954732.

Kuehl, B. (1995). The solution-oriented genogram: A collaborative approach. *Journal of Marital and Family Therapy, 21,* 239–250.

Lundahl, B.W., Kunz, C., Brownell, C., Tollefson, D., & Burke B.L. (2010). A meta-analysis of motivational interviewing: Twenty-five years of empirical studies. *Research Social Work Practice, 20,* 137–160.

Mann, L. (1982). *Decision making questionnaire*. Unpublished manuscript, Flinders University of South Australia.

Marlatt, G.A., & Donovan, D.M. (2005). *Relapse prevention: Maintenance strategies in the treatment of addictive behaviors*. New Your, NY: Guilford Press.

Marlatt, G., Larimer, M., Witkiewitz, K. (2011). *Harm reduction: Pragmatic strategies for managing high-risk behaviors* (2nd ed.). New York: Guilford Press.

Meier, S.T. (2016, October 20). Is it possible to integrate psychotherapy theory on the basis of empirical findings? The disruptive role of method effects. *Journal of Psychotherapy Integration.* Advance online publication. doi.org/10.1037/int0000064.

Merriam-Webster Dictionary. (2017). Confrontation (n.d.). Retrieved from http://www.learnersdictionary.com/definition/confrontation.

Muran, J.C., & Safran, J.D. (2016). Therapeutic alliance ruptures. In A.E. Wenzel (Ed.), *Sage Encyclopedia of Abnormal & Clinical Psychology*. New York, NY: Sage.

Norcross, J.C. (2016). Dr. John Norcross on what does not work in psychotherapy. PSYCHALIVE. Retrieved from http://www.psychalive.org/dr-john-norcross-work-psychotherapy/.

O'Brien, K.H., & Schlechter, A. (2016). Is talking about what's wrong necessarily right: A positive perspective on the diagnostic interview. *Journal of the American Academy of Child & Adolescent Psychiatry, 55,* 262–264.

O'Hanlon, W., & Weiner-Davis, M. (2003). *In search of solutions.* New York, NY: Norton.

Oliveira-Silva, P., Maia, L., Coutinho, J., Frank, B., Soares, J.M., Sampaio, A., & Gonçalves, Ó. (2018). Empathy by default: Correlates in the brain at rest. *Psicothema, 30,* 97-103, p 100.

Parsons, F. (1909). *Choosing a vocation.* Boston, MA: Houghton Mifflin.

Robert, R.R., Tilley, D.S., & Petersen, S. (2014). A power in clinical nursing practice: Concept analysis on nursing intuition. *Medsurg Nursing, 23,* 343–349.

Schumacher, J.A., Madson, M.B., & Nilsen, P. (2014). Barriers to learning motivational interviewing: A survey of motivational interviewing trainers' perceptions. *Journal of Addictions & Offender Counseling, 35,* 81–96. doi:10.1002/j.2161-1874.2014.00028.x.

Stickley, T. (2011). From SOLER to SURETY for effective non-verbal communication. *Nurse Education in Practice, 11,* 395–398. doi:10.1016/j.nepr.2011.03.021.

Sue, D.W., & Sue, D. (2016). *Counseling the culturally diverse: Theory and practice* (7th ed.). Hoboken, NJ: Wiley.

Talmon, M. (1990). *Single session therapy.* San Francisco, CA: Jossey-Bass.

Talmon, M. (2012). When less is more: Lessons from 25 years of attempting to maximize the effect of each (and often only) therapeutic encounter. *Australian and New Zealand Journal of Family Therapy, 33,* 6–14. doi.org/10.1017/aft.2012.2.

Zur, O., & Nordmarken, N. (2016). *To touch or not to touch: Exploring the myth of prohibition on touch in psychotherapy and counseling.* Retrieved from www.zurinstitute.com/touchintherapy.html.

# Credits

### CHAPTER 5

# Multicultural Counseling and Therapy

## Metatheory Taking Theory Into Practice

### CHAPTER GOALS

Multicultural Counseling and Therapy (MCT) is a theory that recognizes that all counseling and psychotherapy theories and methods are born and exist within a cultural context. MCT has developed a large array of culturally sensitive therapeutic strategies to work with a diverse clientele and advance social justice action. MCT also serves as an integrative framework for counseling and therapy in general.

### SPECIFIC GOALS OF THIS CHAPTER:

1. Understand the multicultural worldview from a universal and culture-specific perspective.

2. Identify and understand central theoretical propositions of Multicultural Counseling and Therapy (MCT).

3. Present some key MCT techniques and strategies that can be integrated into daily clinical practice.

4. Briefly review current health and neuroscience support of the microskills.

5. Examine your own level of cultural identity development and awareness of cultural issues in the helping process.

6. Bring theory into action through a practice exercise to facilitate understanding of your own racial/ethnicity identity development.

*All counseling is multicultural.*

—**Paul Pedersen**

Multicultural Counseling and Therapy (MCT) starts with awareness of differences among and within clients—it is thus very person centered. However, it adds the importance of family and cultural factors affecting the way clients view the world and so is also culture centered (Pedersen & Ivey, 1993; Sue & Sue, 2016). MCT challenges educators, students, practitioners, theoreticians, researchers to rethink the meaning of our interviewing, counseling and psychotherapy.

African American authorities over the years have been highly influential in redefining counseling and therapy as a multicultural endeavor. Donald Cheek commented on the counseling and psychotherapy field in 1976 (p. 23):

> … I am advocating treating one segment of our population quite differently from another. This is implicit in my statement that Blacks do not benefit from many therapeutic approaches to which Whites respond. And I have referred to some of these approaches of counselors and therapists as "White techniques."

The following years produced slowly increasing attention to the generation of culturally appropriate theory. Harold Cheatham comments first on the danger of therapy that is culturally insensitive and then suggests fundamental changes needed for a truly Multicultural Counseling and Therapy (1990, pp. 380–381):

> … the helping professional doubtless will violate the Black client's sense of integrity or "world view." … Blacks are products of their distinct sociocultural and sociohistorical experience. Counseling and therapy are specific, contractual events and thus, may proceed more effectively on the basis of understanding of the client's cultural context.

Cheatham argues that the role of the therapist is not just to work with an individual, but also with the family *and* extended networks that may be important for the client. An African American client who suffers from depression should not be treated just as an individual; his or her cultural context, which may be pervaded by racism that may contribute to that depression, must also be addressed. According to Cheatham, Multicultural Counseling and Therapy will not be effective until the counselor focuses on and intervenes in issues of racism, sexism, and oppressive societal elements.

According to Sue and Sue (2016) counseling and psychotherapy have done great harm to diverse cultural groups by invalidating their life experiences, defining their cultural values or differences as deviant and pathological, denying them culturally appropriate care, and imposing the values of a dominant culture upon them.

*Culture-centered counseling and therapy* could be described as one of the major focuses of the MCT approach (Pedersen & Ivey, 1993; Ivey, Ivey, & Zalaquett, 2018; Sue & Sue, 2016). Traditionally, counseling and therapy have been "person centered" with little attention paid to contextual issues. The culture-centered approach seeks to provide a new balance in which individuals are seen in the context of culture.

Liberation psychology has gained central attention since Freire (1972) used the term *conscientizacào* as a general goal of education—and by extension, counseling and therapy as well. *Conscientizacào* is focused on the liberation of the individual from personal, social, and economic oppression. Many of your clients come to you blaming themselves for their condition. Your task is to liberate these clients from self-blame, to encourage them to see their issues in a social context, and facilitate personal action to better their situation, as well as that of others.

The liberation of client consciousness could be considered as a general rule for all counseling and therapy that is socially aware, whereas some individualistic theories are so focused on "one client" that the larger context of family, community, and cultural oppression may be missed.

The Multicultural Counseling and Therapy (MCT) framework, then, is concerned with counseling and psychotherapy as liberation and social justice—the viewing of self-in-relation to others and to social and cultural context. Interdependence is basic to philosophy and action in MCT. MCT seeks to work *with* the individual and family in an egalitarian fashion. Furthermore, MCT hopes to see client and therapist cooperatively working together in the community and society to alleviate and prevent future concerns and issues. Table 5.1 illustrates one of such areas.

---

**Table 5.1. First, Do No Harm**

Identification and rejection of harmful therapeutic treatments has been promoted by Lilienfeld's (2007) publication of psychological treatments that cause harm and Barlow's (2010) publication of negative effects from psychological treatments.

Wendt, Gone, and Nagata (2015) remind us of the importance of avoiding potentially harmful counseling and psychotherapy. Also, they make us aware of the need to include lack of multicultural counseling among potentially harmful therapeutic interventions.

If our mandate is to do no harm, then monocultural counseling applied to culturally diverse clients may violate our mandate. Cheek (1976) and Sue and Sue (2008, 2016) provide ample support for this potentially negative effect.

Wendt et al. (2015) provide a compelling argument for the integration of potentially harmful therapy and multicultural counseling discourses. Counseling and psychotherapy can be inherently ethnocentric and as such capable of harming minority clients. Studies of harm should be integrated with a multicultural and social justice perspective.

# The Universal Approach to Multicultural Counseling

Fukuyama (1990) argues for a transcultural, universal approach to Multicultural Counseling and Therapy—certain factors are important regardless of culture. Foremost is the fact that historically traditional counseling theory has been unaware of culture. Fukuyama would point out that if you review the theories presented in this book, there is still a tendency for these theories to focus on values of individualism, rationalism, and self-determination.

Henrich, Heine, and Norenzayan (2010) report that the majority of participants in psychology studies are overwhelmingly WEIRD—**W**estern, **e**ducated, and from **i**ndustrialized, **r**ich, and **d**emocratic countries. And the majority are college students participating in studies for class credit. About 96 percent of participants in studies published in six top psychology journals between 2003 and 2007 were WEIRD. This would be acceptable if these participants were representative of society as a whole or of other cultures, but they are not. Results built on samples of contemporary Western undergraduates limit the generalizability of our findings and call for the infusion of a multicultural perspective, a perspective that takes into account both context and content (Suedfeld, 2016).

The universal approach recommended by Fukuyama challenges all counseling and therapy to become aware of multicultural issues and to recall that all counseling and therapy is culturally based. She (1990, p. 9) argues for a counseling curriculum which:

1. Defines culture broadly (including gender, affectional orientation, age, etc., as well as ethnic/racial issues).

2. Teaches the danger of stereotyping.

3. Emphasizes the importance of language as the vehicle of counseling and therapy.

4. Encourages loyalty and pride in one's own culture and family ties.

5. Provides information on the processes of acculturation and oppression.

6. Discusses the importance of gender roles.

7. Facilitates each individual's identity development as a member of a culture.

8. Builds self-esteem and awareness.

9. Facilitates the understanding of one's own worldview and how it relates to family and cultural history.

If you as a counselor or therapist understand your client's concerns and challenges as an "individual concern," you will seek to help that individual find ways of solving her or his issues. Client-centered Rogerian theory, psychodynamic theory, and cognitive-behavioral theory have all tended to focus on the individual, with minimal attention given to contextual issues. Decisional counseling makes an effort in the direction of environmental action, but once again works primarily with individual issues.

The MCT universal approach requires that you consider cultural issues as part of each counseling contact. Rather than focusing solely on the individual, it is important that you start with the multicultural context and environment of each person. Your treatment may require more than individual therapy. Rather, it may require a network of interventions and even community action.

For example, in counseling with a male Puerto Rican who has just lost his job, a common approach is to assess and treat the individual and plan for a new working setting. MCT therapists would do the same, but also would add awareness of the person-in-context. What are the implications of job loss as they relate to cultural issues such as *machismo* and *respeto*? Are issues of real or perceived discrimination present? What is the family context of the individual? Moreover, what was the context of the work setting? Were cultural differences or lack of understanding part of the dismissal?

Fukuyama's universal approach challenges the foundations of traditional counseling and therapy. In this approach, one starts with awareness of culture and then later seeks to understand how individual or family issues grow out of and relate to cultural background.

## The Focused Culture-Specific Approach

Multicultural experts such as Locke (1990) and Sue and Sue (2016) state that it is incumbent upon you to gain cultural expertise in specific groups that you are likely to encounter. If the multicultural approach becomes too general, specific cultural groups will suffer from inefficient and oppressive methods of counseling and therapy. Taking the universal approach can weaken and dilute efforts for change.

Locke argues for what he terms a "focused approach" where it is important "to see people *both* as individuals and members of a culturally different group" (1990, p. 23). This approach obligates us to:

1. Examine our own racial beliefs and attitudes as they relate to culturally different individuals and groups;
2. Discuss racially relevant topics at an institutional level and be willing to work on issues of oppression beyond the individual and family session;
3. View our clients both as individuals and members of groups.

### REFLECTION EXERCISE

Many do not want to face or cope with the multicultural theoretical orientation and its practice implications at all. There are those who still argue that "people are people" and that the discussion about cultural difference is irrelevant and unimportant.

What is your position on this critical issue?

Current descriptions of multiculturalism are inclusive and embrace race, ethnicity, social class, gender, sexual orientation, disability, spirituality, and other cultural dimensions. Multicultural counseling occurs when a counselor and client are from different cultural groups. Sue and Sue (2016) define multiculturalism as "the integration, acceptance, and embracing of cultural differences that include race, gender, sexual orientation, and other sociodemographic identities" (p. 747). Furthermore, they recognize a tripartite identity framework (see Figure 5.1) with the following levels:

1. Individual Level: All individuals are, in some respects, like no other individuals.
2. Group Level: All individuals are, in some respects, like some other individuals.
3. Universal Level: All individuals are, in some respects, like all other individuals.

The tripartite identity model recognizes that the United States is largely founded on values associated with individualism, autonomy, independence, and uniqueness (Level 1). The focus of counseling, psychology, psychiatry, social work, and related disciplines was to find universal principles and laws to explain human behavior (Level 3). They ignored the group level identity for a long time. Multicultural counseling theory brought our attention to group identity (Level 2). Each cultural group may have its own interpretations of reality and perspectives on identity development, the nature of people, origin of disorders, standards for judging normality and abnormality, and therapeutic interventions.

**Figure 5.1 Tripartite Identity Model**

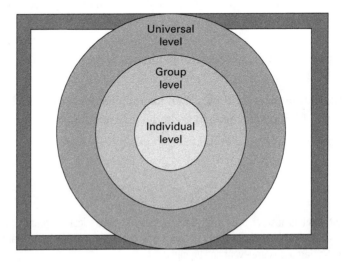

PRACTICE EXERCISE 5.1.  **What Would You Do?**

An African American, older adult female client with a visible disability consults with you because she feels discriminated at work. There are several multicultural dimensions represented in this client. Which one(s) would you address first?

One possible answer is that the most salient and most important issue to the client sitting before you is the one that should be foremost. For example, if a person with a developmental disability is concerned over issues of discrimination or lack of access, this is the issue to approach first. At a later time, racial/ethnic and other cultural issues can be considered.

What do you think about this possible answer? How would you improve it? Please note that even this answer fails to consider the issue of social justice, community action, and societal education.

Think about two or three other complex combinations of cultural dimensions, such as a Hispanic/Latina/o, mobility impaired, and gay client coming to see you because he cannot get his college to provide him access to the school's laboratory. He is frustrated and angry. What issue would you address first?

## REFLECTION EXERCISE

Microaggressions are the everyday slights, put-downs, invalidations, and insults directed to socially devalued group members by well-intentioned people who may be unaware that they have engaged in such biased and harmful behaviors (Sue & Sue, 2016, p. 747).

Examples of racial microaggressions:

- A Black student is complimented by the professor as being articulate and bright. (Hidden message: Most Blacks are inarticulate and lack intelligence.)

- A third-generation Asian American student is complimented by a White classmate for speaking such "good English." (Hidden message: Asian Americans are perpetual aliens in their own country.)

Reflect on what you say or ask to those different from you. Could your well-intended communication send denigrating messages to marginalized classmates, friends, or others?

# Multicultural Counseling and Therapy as Metatheory

The following metatheory of MCT represents only one of many possible paradigms. We have chosen to work with some of the MCT propositions originally proposed by

Sue (1995), who suggested that they needed to be refined with the consequent development of corollaries and basic tenets. As much as possible, we have attempted to ground the propositions and corollaries in the available research and theory of multiculturalism.

> PROPOSITION I—MCT is a metatheory of counseling and psychotherapy. It is a theory about theories, and offers an organizational framework for understanding the numerous helping approaches that humankind has developed. It recognizes that theories of counseling and psychotherapy developed in the Western world and those indigenous helping models intrinsic to other non-Western cultures are neither inherently "right or wrong" or "good and bad." Each theory represents a different worldview.

MCT has evolved from a method of helping members of one cultural group relate to members of different cultural groups into a meta-theoretical perspective, which recognizes the centrality and primary importance of culture as an internalized, subjective perspective constructed in response to contact with persons of contrasting cultural backgrounds. MCT rests on the assumption that all theories of counseling are culture specific and the values, assumptions, and philosophical bases need to be made clear and explicit.

Each theory of counseling and psychotherapy was developed in a particular cultural context, and to the extent that each theory is appropriate to a particular cultural context, it is likely to be biased toward contrasting cultural contexts. Different worldviews lead toward different constructions of client concerns. For example, in traditional Western psychotherapy, psychodynamic approaches may view client issues as originated through unconscious developmental history, while cognitive-behavioral approaches may see the same issues as a result of social learning. These differing worldviews (or stories told by theory authors) result in different modes of conceptualizing and treating clients.

MCT recognizes the utility of Eurocentric theory and practice and would recommend using all traditional and innovative theories drawn from this frame. In addition, MCT points out the importance of seeing the individual-in-context, considering the cultural background of the client, and finding culturally appropriate solutions that may change the way that therapy is conducted. Specifically, the MCT therapist helps the individual see his or her issues in context, draws in group or family members into the treatment, and uses non-Western therapeutic approaches as appropriate to the client. Historically, traditional Western diagnoses and therapy (e.g., *DSM-5*, American Psychiatric Association, 2013) see the "problem" in the client and give limited attention to contextual issues (Zalaquett, Fuerth, Stein, Ivey, & Ivey, 2008).

MCT theory is ultimately concerned with cultural intentionality—freeing individuals, families, groups, and organizations to generate new ways of thinking, feeling, and acting—living with intentionality. This needs to happen both within the client or clients' own cultural framework and with understanding and respect for other worldviews. In that sense, MCT is not in opposition to cognitive-behavioral, psychodynamic, or existential-humanistic approaches. Rather, it seeks to add culture as a main focus, while respecting older traditions.

Moreover, theories of human behavior are defined by their ability to predict future behavior and explain past behavior, MCT qualifies as a theory by predicting failure as resulting from either the overemphasis of cultural differences or of cultural similarities, and success as resulting from a simultaneously combined perspective. When cultural differences are overemphasized, the result is a stereotyped, exclusionary, politicized, and antagonistic perspective. When cultural similarities are overemphasized, the result can be exploitation of less powerful by more powerful groups and the pretense of a melting pot, which disregards essential features of cultural identity.

## Generating New Theory from a MCT Perspective

Practice Exercise 5.1 provides a structure for generating new, more culturally relevant theory and practice. While this example exercise is originally drawn from Afrocentric theory, it can be adapted to other cultural frameworks. Before introducing the background of the exercise, let us examine Afrocentric theory itself.

*The Afrocentric worldview.* The Afrocentric worldview proposes that African American experience in the United States continues African history and culture. Years of slavery and racism have not dimmed the African intergenerational legacy of family relationship and group solidarity. Molefi Kete Asante's (1987) controversial and influential book, *The Afrocentric Idea*, brought this concept to national prominence.

Cheatham (1990) elaborated on the Afrocentric idea:

> Unlike the Western philosophic system, the African tradition has no heavy emphasis on the individual; the individual's being is authenticated only in terms of others. Nobles writes that there is a sense of corporate responsibility and collective destiny as epitomized in the traditional African self-concept: "I am because we are; and because we are, therefore I am." (p. 375)

Further, Cheatham, synthesizing available sources, argues that the philosophic linkages were retained even with transplantation to the United States, that this country's particular physical features facilitated retention of African ethos, and that rigidly enforced isolation of African Americans allowed (perhaps even obligated) retention of their orientation to self-in-connection.

The Afrocentric, or African, worldview is holistic; emotionally vital; interdependent; oriented to collective survival; emphasizing an oral tradition; uses a "being" time orientation; focuses on harmonious blending and cooperation, and is highly respectful of the role of the older adults (White & Parham, 1990, p. 15). As you might anticipate, therapy with African American clients, those of African descent from the Caribbean, and Africans must consider this worldview—and with awareness that each individual client will be affected by that worldview differently (Nobles, 2006).

In contrast, the North American Eurocentric view tends to divide the world into discrete, "knowable" parts; handles emotion somewhat carefully, even to the point of emotional repression; focuses on self-actualization and independence as life goals; emphasizes the clarity and precision of the written word; is oriented to a linear "doing" view of time; stresses individuation and difference rather than collaboration; and is more oriented to youth than to the elderly. Traditional counseling theories support this orientation to a great extent.

Neither frame of reference nor worldview is "right" or "wrong." Rather, each represents a way of constructing the world and making meaning. What may indeed be potentially harmful is to impose an Afrocentric frame on a European American or to impose a Eurocentric frame on an African American. However, both of these clients will at times benefit from exposure to a culturally different frame of reference. Thus, sharing new perspectives and narratives from other cultures may be at times very beneficial to the client.

Moreover, each individual you work with is likely to be some mixture of cultural frames of reference. The African American or Japanese American, for example, is likely to have been influenced by North American culture and may have incorporated many values of the Eurocentric frame. Many women who take a feminist orientation have consciously or unconsciously joined the Afrocentric worldview.

*The Afrocentric worldview related to other cultures.* You will find many families of Chinese or Japanese, and Puerto Rican and Mexican origin whose sons and daughters have a life orientation closer to that of the Afrocentric worldview than to the European American worldview. Sue and Sue (2016) provide an important summary of key issues in multicultural counseling and development. They point out that constructions of the world are very different among Asian, African American, European American, Hispanic/Latina/o, and Native American populations, but that issues of relationship are often more important in non-Eurocentric cultures.

Also, we should recall that each individual is unique and special. There are some African American clients who are more like a farmer from Idaho than their ethnically related brothers and sisters. There are Utah Mormons who adopt a more relational and family-centered orientation than some African Americans. *As always, never stereotype your client.* Start your interview by learning from the client, or your "culturally aware" helping may be more oppressive than if you knew nothing about culture at all.

## REFLECTION EXERCISE

Race is a multidimensional identity. Your race is experienced in accord with how you self-identify and in relation to how you are perceived by others (Vargas & Kingsbury, 2016).

An individual's racial self-classification does not always match how they are perceived racially by others. This phenomenon is referred to as "racial contestation," "racial mismatch," and "racial misclassification."

For example, an individual can self-identify racially as African American, but be perceived by most others as non–African American.

Have you heard of racial contestation cases?

Thinking about those around you, do you notice any instances of racial contestation? What do you think is the experience of those experiencing racial contestation?

Imagine the experience of a Hispanic/Latina school principal who emigrated from Panama and now works in a school with 50 percent African American and 50 percent Hispanic/Latina/o students. She self-identifies as Latina but was seen as Black by many of her colleagues and students because of the dark color of her skin. How would students from each of these two groups relate to her? What communication and trust issues may arise?

# Developing New Theoretical Approaches from an MCT Perspective

The most recent innovation in the microskills discussed in Chapter 4 is a new type of multicultural application—can the microskills approach offer some direction in generating more culturally relevant theory and practice? One route toward this objective has been to start with an examination of a specific African culture and then examine how discoveries here may relate to African Americans, Asian Americans, European Americans, Latina/o Americans, and other groups. Table 5.2. Adapting Therapy to Clients' Cultures will help you increase your skills in this area.

Uchenna Nwachuku (1989, 1990), a Nigerian Igbo, has explored the above question in some detail and has generated the important concrete beginnings for a specifically Afrocentric theory and method of helping (Nwachuku & Ivey, 1991).

---

#### Research on Psychotherapeutic Services for Ethnic Minorities

Sue (1988) reviewed the literature on helping services for ethnic minorities, stating that services for minorities are frequently considered ineffective. We have updated this literature review with similar observations:

1. *There are important differences in the conceptualization of psychological issues and treatments.* Many minority groups conceptualize psychological difficulties as more organic in nature and believe that mental health treatments can be enhanced by sheer will and the avoidance of morbid thoughts (Sue, 1988; Jimenez, Bartels, Cardenas, Dhaliwal, & Alegría, 2012). The surgeon

general asserted that culture counts in the understanding of mental disorders (2001), and the *DSM-5* included the new cultural concept of distress (CCD), which refers to the ways cultural groups experience, understand, and communicate suffering, behavioral disorders, or negative thoughts and emotions (APA, 2013). Thus, understanding cultural differences is important for counseling and psychotherapy. What is a concern for a Caucasian client may not be an issue for an Asian American client (Kohrt et al., 2014).

2. *Many counselors often hold negative stereotypes toward those who are different from them.* Differing worldviews and values associated with multicultural dimensions can introduce both conscious and unconscious biases into a counselor's perception of the client, diagnosis, and treatment option (Sue & Sue, 2016; Zalaquett & Chambers, 2017). Therapists' perceptions of social class and low-income clients frequently elicit predictions of poor therapeutic outcome (Liu, Soleck, Hopps, Dunston, & Pickett, 2004; Kunstman, Plant, & Deska, 2016; Smith, 2005, 2013). Likewise, negative attitudes toward older adults and other multicultural groups may make counseling and psychotherapy a waste of time, energy, and money (Laganà & Shanks, 2002). Afrocentric versus Eurocentric discussions illustrate how very differently the world is viewed by different cultural groups (Leong et al., 1995; Sue & Sue, 2016). If we view these differences as constructions rather than as "reality," we are applying a multicultural understanding and opening ways for understanding, collaboration, and progress.

3. *Despite these issues, research evidence clearly indicates that minority clients do benefit from therapy.* Counseling and psychotherapy help minority clients. Research has confirmed what Griffith and Jones (1979, p. 230) stated: "Unquestionably, race makes a difference in psychotherapy. Still, this is not to say that the skillful and experienced White therapist cannot effectively treat the Black client. Rather the critical requisite is that the White therapist is sensitive to the unique ways in which … race affects the course of treatment." Treatment outcome studies confirm, for example, that depression therapy helps minority, low-income mothers overcome clinical depression (Cicchetti, Toth, & Handley, 2015; Toth et al., 2013), and counseling provided by college counseling centers help minority clients significantly improve on a variety of issues (Lockard, Hayes, Graceffo, & Locke, 2013).

4. *The client-therapist matching is complex.* The examination of cultural matching represent the intersectionality of multiple social identities and

developmental factors (Umaña-Taylor et al., 2014). Multicultural scholars have exposed cultural differences in privilege and power and suggested ways to work with those ethnically and racially different from Caucasians (Arredondo et al., 1996; Sue & Sue, 2016). Furthermore, many propose moving beyond an "us versus them" dichotomy to a more inclusive perspective, and suggest looking at cross-cultural misunderstandings as communication breakdowns that should trigger coordinated efforts to establish shared understandings (Sametband & Strong, 2013).

It seems likely that cultural identity theory may explain some of the complexities associated with counselor and client racial or ethnic matching. If clients are matched with therapists who have similar cultural awareness (and the therapists are competent), a good result may be expected. A culturally sensitive, White therapist may be equally effective *if* the client is at a level of cultural identity development that makes seeing a White counselor a viable alternative. "Ethnicity is important, but what is more important is its meaning" (Sue, 1988, p. 307). Multicultural counselors stress the need for "culturally responsive" counseling and therapy, the need for more prevention work on the part of professionals, and the need for more effective health policies, thus making helping available to those who presently don't have the choice of seeking psychological or counseling assistance.

Mental health professions have developed professional standards and guidelines that recognize the main role of cultural contexts (e.g., Guidelines on Multicultural Education, Training, Research, Practice, and Organizational Change for Psychologists, APA, 2003; Multicultural and Social Justice Counseling Competencies: Guidelines for the Counseling Profession, Ratts, Singh, Nassar-McMillan, Butler, & McCullough, 2016; The Guidelines for Providers of Psychological Services to Ethnic, Linguistic, and Culturally Diverse Populations, APA, 1993).

*Cultural Adaptations to Counseling and Psychotherapy.* A meta-analysis of culturally adapted mental health treatments—evidence-based treatment (EBT) or intervention systematically modified to make them compatible with clients' culture, meaning, and values (Bernal, Jimenez-Chafey, & Domenech Rodriguez, 2009, p. 362)—found that culturally adapted mental health therapies were superior to those that do not explicitly incorporate cultural considerations (Smith, Domenech Rodriguez, & Bernal, 2011). The meta-analysis of 65 studies involving 8,620 participants showed an effect size of $d = 5.46$, indicating that treatments specifically adapted for minority clients were more effective with that clientele than traditional treatments. Furthermore, treatment with a greater number of specific cultural adaptations was more effective.

The authors assert that cultural adaptations should be considered EBPs and recommend the following evidence-based therapeutic adaptations:

- Clients benefit more when counselors and psychotherapists align treatment with clients' cultural backgrounds.

- Counselors and psychotherapists should attend to how client age and acculturation interact with their treatments.

- Conduct psychotherapy in the client's preferred language if possible.

- Culturally adapted treatments should address multiple components, as the more components are incorporated into the cultural adaptations, the more effective the treatment is.

- Culturally adapted treatments are much more beneficial when they are specific to clients of a given race than when they are provided to a group of clients with varied races or ethnicities. The more specific to clients' cultural backgrounds, the more effective the therapy.

- The more culturally focused and specific the treatment, the more effective it will be.

In counseling and therapy practice, the mental health professional should take cultural context into account at all times, recognize and align with client culture, and apply culturally appropriate skills, assessments, and interventions. Multicultural therapy is not only best practice, but ethical practice.

**Table 5.2. Adapting Therapy to Clients' Cultures**

**Guidelines for adapting therapy to clients' cultures:**

- Practice flexibly and respectfully.

- Communicate empathy in a culturally appropriate manner.

- Obtain relevant and effective multicultural competence training.

- Learn about specific cultural norms, study literature about available culture-specific treatment techniques, and consult with expert colleagues.

- Conduct a culturally informed but person-specific functional assessment before implementing treatment.

- Explore client's views of seeking counseling treatment and the nature of the therapeutic relationship.

*(Continued)*

**Table 5.2. Adapting Therapy to Clients' Cultures** *(Continued)*

- Do not dismiss traditional treatments as they may serve as potential resources.

- Review with client services that may be meaningful within their cultural worldview and context.

- Implement appropriate and specific cultural adaptations.

- Avoid interpreting cultural differences as deficits.

- Identify client's culturally related strengths and resources for use in treatment.

- Remain open to what clients bring to counseling.

Adapted from: Asnaani & Hofmann, 2012; Pedersen, Lonner, Draguns, Trimble, & Scharrón-del Río, 2016; Smith, Domenech Rodriguez, & Bernal, 2011; Sommers-Flanagan, 2015.

# The Multiple Contexts and Experiences of MCT

PROPOSITION II - Counselor and client identities are formed and embedded in multiple levels of experiences (individual, group, and universal) and contexts (individual, family, and cultural milieu). The totality and interrelationships of experiences and contexts need to be considered in any treatment.

MCT therapists acknowledge that all individuals possess an individual, group, and universal level of identity (Sue & Sue, 2016). We are all unique (different from one another), share commonalties with our multicultural reference groups (race, culture, ethnicity, religious orientation, gender, sexual orientation, etc.), and all share a universal level of identity in that we are all human beings. These levels of identity are fluid and ever changing so that the salience of one over the other is also changing. An individual client may at one moment focus on individual needs, another moment on an issue related to multicultural reference group identity, and at still another time focus on universal human experience. The effective helping professional validates all levels and strives to relate to that which is most salient and important to the person at the time of contact. Unfortunately, traditional counseling and psychotherapy has had a proclivity to relate at primarily the individual or universal levels, thereby negating multicultural reference group identities.

Basic to MCT theory is the importance of the person-environment interaction. Models like Urie Bronfenbrenner's Ecological Framework for Human Development offer social-ecological models of human development (2005). These ecological systems models describe a child's development within the context of the systems of relationship that form his or her environment. The person's identity is formed and continually influenced by the context. Working effectively with clients requires an understanding of how the individual is embedded in the family; which in turn requires an understanding of how the family is affected by being embedded in a culturally diverse society. The family-culture interface is often best approached through emphasis on community, such as the community genogram of Chapter 2.

Counselors and psychotherapists bring their own family, community, and cultural background to the session. The worldviews associated with their cultural groupings deeply affect the way they conduct therapy. For example, an English-speaking Irish American female, Catholic, upper-middle-class, cancer and rape survivor brings an important store of cultural wisdom to the session. This hypothetical person may practice eclectically from the psychodynamic frame of reference. The worldview of this individual has many perspectives to offer clients, but also has potential limitations with clients whose life experience and worldviews may be different.

MCT therapists presume that the salient cultural feature (individual, multicultural group identification, and universal) will change in a psychodynamic fashion for the client during the interview and that a skilled counselor will be able to accurately track that changing salience from one cultural referent to another. Not all of the client's cultural affiliations will be equally important all of the time.

## The Microskill of Focusing and MCT

In traditional counseling, we are accustomed to make "I" statements and focus on what an individual can do to help him- or herself. We have to realize that this may clash with the worldviews of many minority people whose traditions focus on family. It may be hard for them to separate themselves from others in their family and just think of themselves. Their sense of self is often collective in nature, and their being may be authenticated mainly in terms of others. The counseling significance is that an individually balanced focus is needed between individual, family, and cultural expectations. Some clients will need more of one than another.

In short, a portion of any counseling session must attend to significant others and cultural/environmental/contextual issues. Counseling and therapy have been so focused on the individual that devoting time to asking questions, paraphrasing, and interpreting worldviews as they relate to family and cultural issues will make a significant difference in the way the helper and client conceptualize and consider concerns.

For example, traditional psychology and psychiatry once regarded the Vietnam veteran who had psychiatric distress as a malingerer seeking benefits from the government. We now know this condition as post-traumatic stress disorder (PTSD), a logical result of extreme battle stress. We urge you to change your language to PTS (post-traumatic stress). Why? Cases of PTS have a normal and logical reason for their issues.

What we now recognize as PTS was once considered an individual issue. It took considerable effort on the part of Vietnam veterans to show us that their issues were real and that PTS is for many a reasonable response to an incredibly stressful environment.

Many now would consider it immoral to treat Vietnam veterans as suffering primarily from individual and internal conflicts

Similarly, women suffering from depression, African Americans from high blood pressure, and gays suffering from anxiety need to be treated not just with a focus on their individual issues, but with a supplementary focus on societal sexism, racism, and homophobia. The microskill of focusing is a key reminder that it is essential that we use a culture-centered focus. All behavior occurs in a cultural context and can only be understood within that context.

Another method would be to adapt existing counseling theories to include a multicultural focus. The criticism of the honored words *self-actualization*, *autonomy*, and *independence* by MCT authorities is indeed challenging. MCT would also consider additional concepts like *self-in-relation*, *connectedness and relationship*, and *interdependence*. At issue is how psychodynamic, cognitive-behavioral, and humanistic theories can still be used with new MCT goals and values. Starting with humanistic theory, for example, we would again draw on the microskill of focus. Our clinical experience is that most of the traditional Rogerian skills and values can perhaps even be enhanced if we change the words "You feel ..." to "You feel this in relationship to ... (family and/or cultural background)." The precise phrasing may vary, but we believe that reflective listening skills and the goals of traditional Rogerian theory can remain useful by adding a focus on relational and cultural issues. Often, our clients mention family and cultural issues that we ignore with our constant focus on the individual. Placing the individual in context may be an important new way to honor and enhance individuality even more fully.

Cognitive-behavioral theory is an effective treatment modality with many clients, but it can be considered a theory of pacification if insufficient attention is paid to environmental determinants. For example, we often attack irrational ideas without first looking for possible rational elements when we view the client's statements from a cultural perspective. Very little is done with rational-emotive or cognitive therapy to inform clients of how family and cultural issues affect their being. Is a client irrational in being stressed by environmental issues, such as lack of money, sexual harassment, or some other issue? Focusing specifically on the individual and the irrationality of the context may be a way to reframe cognitive theory and practice. From a more behavioral perspective, stress management programs that focus on meditation, relaxation, and cognitive issues may give insufficient attention to how the client is reacting normally to massive environmental stressors, particularly those of racism, sexism, classism, and homophobia.

## Introspective Developmental Counseling and Life Review

Koji Tamase's (2007; 2014) work is unique in that it combines Eastern and Western frameworks. The famous developmental psychiatrist Eric Erikson's life-span theory (summarized in Table 5.3) has been severely criticized on grounds that he derived his ideas primarily from ideas about White males in northern European and US societies. Nonetheless, it remains a useful framework as modified by Tamase and multicultural theory.

Erikson remains a classic foundation of developmental theory as he defines the developmental task of early childhood (ages two to four) as focused on developing a sense of autonomy. If you think back on the Afrocentric idea or the nature of childhood in Japan and in many South American cultures, the goal of this period is not autonomy, but rather a sense of connectedness to the caregiver. Exaggerated autonomy and separation is considered pathological in many cultures. At the same time, too much dependence on others can occur in any culture.

Drawing on his Japanese and international experience, Tamase avoids labeling any developmental period as being focused on particular tasks—different cultures will focus on different issues and have different crises and issues from those proposed by Erikson. He points out that each individual uniquely finds her or his own life path, but always within a network of relationships. Furthermore, as life experience expands and contracts through accommodation and assimilation processes, each individual makes different meanings.

**Table 5.3. Eric Erikson's Developmental Stages Throughout the Life Span as They Might Be Modified by Multicultural Counseling and Therapy**

| Life Stage, Approximate Age, and Major Developmental Crises Derived from Eurocentric Norms | Key Environmental Systems—Will Vary with the Cultural Experience of the Individual | Developmental Tasks—Will Vary with Family, Community, and Culture | Example of How Life Stages Differ Among Multicultural Groups |
|---|---|---|---|
| Infancy (birth–2) Balancing trust in others vs. mistrust. | Caregiver and family. Families may be traditional, single-parent, blended, grandparents, adoptive, gay or lesbian, rich or poor. Seek out the nature of the early attachment experiences and how they may be unique to the person, the family, and the culture. | Attachment to caregiver, individual, or network. Sensorimotor intelligence. Basic motor coordination. | Caregiver and nuclear family are the focus in European American situations, but may be extended family in many groups. The "holding environment" of Japan may produce closer attachments than in Eurocentric cultures. |
| Early childhood (2–4) Autonomy vs. shame and doubt, or stated more positively, learning one's responsibility to others. | Family, extended family, preschool, playgroup. | How much emphasis is to be placed on individual needs vs. the group? Self-control? Language learning? Attachment to family is basis for developing a beginning sense of self and others. Walking and play activities central. | Autonomy is a Eurocentric construct. In Japan, for example, the child is often encouraged to develop a sense of closeness and dependence on others. Too much autonomy is viewed as selfishness in some cultures. |

(Continued)

**Table 5.3. Eric Erikson's Developmental Stages Throughout the Life Span as They Might Be Modified by Multicultural Counseling and Therapy** *(Continued)*

| | | | |
|---|---|---|---|
| Middle childhood (5–7) Initiative vs. guilt—or responsibly representing one's family and culture. (Initiative exists within a context.) | Family, neighborhood, school. | Gender identity. First stages of moral development. Concrete mental operations. | Boys and girls have been taught since infancy to behave differently, dress differently, and are rewarded for different types of behaviors in virtually all cultures. Initiative may be defined as aggressiveness in some groups. |
| Late childhood (8–12) Industry vs. inferiority— most cultures expect some form of productiv- ity from the child at this stage, yet the focus is on doing. Some cultures would emphasize the importance of "being vs. doing." | Family, neighborhood, school, and peer group. | Basic time of learning social relationships through work and play. Team membership may be as important as building self-esteem and feelings of competence— egocentric learning. Learning of many basic life skills in the culture. Late concrete mental operations: "If …, then" reasoning. Moral development in terms of right vs. wrong. | Children of poverty may not be surrounded by a stimulating environment and may have less chance to learn self-esteem and basic skills that are considered natural to children of a more advantaged background. The word *industry* is related to a "doing orientation" of Eurocentric culture contrasted with Afrocentric and Arabic ideas of "being." |
| Puberty and adolescence (12–18) Identity vs. role confu- sion—role confusion might be translated by feminist theory as a time of developing multiple roles and recognizing that identity can be only defined in relationship to others. | Peer group, school, family, neighborhood, work setting. | Sexual maturation. Formal operational thought. Generation of self-concept and awareness of personal identity in Eurocentric culture as a move toward independent living. In traditional Latina/-o experience, the movement may be to- ward taking one's place in organized society and recognizing relational responsibilities. | Piagetian theorists estimate that between 25% and 40% of the population never reaches full formal operations; about 30% to 40% of adults use formal thinking regularly (Commons & Ross, 2008; Keating, 1979). Gay or lesbian adolescents may have a particularly difficult time at this stage due to cultural expectations. |

*(Continued)*

**Table 5.3.** **Eric Erikson's Developmental Stages Throughout the Life Span as They Might Be Modified by Multicultural Counseling and Therapy** *(Continued)*

| | | | |
|---|---|---|---|
| Young adulthood (20–30) Intimacy vs. isolation—intimacy may be defined in Chinese culture as being part of a larger extended family. Most cultures focus on issues of connection, but in varying ways. | In Eurocentric culture, new family and living mate(s) may become central. Friendship network, may move away from family of origin. Work setting becomes more important. | Finding one's own sense of self in a family relationship of love and commitment. Initial parenting. A new relationship with parents and extended family. Major career decisions and financial decisions. | Adolescent women in US culture work on issues of intimacy during adolescence, perhaps even more so than identity. In some African and Italian cultures, the extended family remains especially important in living and decision-making arrangements. |
| Adulthood (30–65) Generativity vs. stagnation—the definition of generativity in one culture may focus on work, while in another it may be on family. Stagnation may be interpreted by some as a contemplative state of being. | Family and children, friendship network, work setting, community. | Reworking of all the issues above from a new perspective of maturity. Special emphasis on career and family changes. Particularly important are the physical, cognitive, and emotional changes that come with each new decade. | Women's career and life patterns do not easily fit into Erikson's framework. Rather than move systematically through the stages one by one as suggested by Erikson, some women work on many all at once. Maturity may be flexible in the use of all stages, and each culture will define maturity differently. The 30 years of adulthood are more complex than allowed for in the Erikson time frame. |
| Old age (65–death) Ego integrity vs. despair—the concept of *ego* again focuses on the individualistic aspects of Erikson's framework. Is integrity to be defined by an individual or a self-in-relation? | Family, friendship network, community, caring, and health agencies as one faces illness and nears death. | Reworking all previous developmental crises once again. Life review and finding meaning in what one has done. Coping with physical changes and illness. Dealing with the death of family and friends. Financial/living concerns and decisions. | Experts now concede that many are still in middle age at 70. A new and rapidly increasing category is the "old-old" who are 85 and over, many of whom still have good health and enjoy full lives, contrary to cultural stereotypes. Age is valued far more in Native American Indian culture. |

*The basic life stages.* Koji Tamase talks about age-related developmental phases in Introspective Developmental Counseling (IDC), such as birth through preschool, elementary school, adolescence, and present-day life. Tamase's framework offers some advantages over Eriksonian life stages, as he does not impose a set of culturally bound expectations such as "autonomy versus shame and doubt" or "identity versus role confusion." By emphasizing age periods without prior constructions of meaning, Tamase (2007; 2014) seeks to offer a more multiculturally viable life span review process.

It is here that Naikan's (ToDo Institute, 2017) influence shows, especially in IDC. Whereas traditional life review focuses on the individual, IDC demands a focus on self-in-relation and a vastly more complex view of identity development than that proposed by Erikson.

*Making meaning from the past.* Drawing from Naikan therapy values, the goals of IDC are in some ways similar to psychodynamic formulations in that the past is believed to affect the present. However, Tamase attempts to avoid giving theoretical interpretations for the client. Rather, the IDC interviewer simply listens and helps the client review the past. Not too surprisingly, if you listen to past events carefully, clients begin to discover repeating patterns and make their own interpretations. When the interviewer adds the sensorimotor, concrete, formal, and dialectic/systemic (DCT) questions discussed in Chapter 6, IDC turns into a powerful therapeutic tool. Thus, whereas Erikson's work is solely descriptive, Tamase provides room for specific action and treatment.

Tamase has thus far focused his work primarily on the early life stages. As the model expands, additional questions will be raised about later life stages. Early research and clinical practice, however, reveal that the first four phases produce a substantial base of information and insight in about four hours of interviewing

Practice Exercise 5.2 presents a shortened version of IDC. You will find the exercise helpful in thinking about your clients more developmentally and from a multicultural perspective.

---

**PRACTICE EXERCISE 5.2.  Exercise in Developmental Mapping and Storytelling**

This exercise will help you understand how you or your client generated key construct systems and beliefs about the world. The exercise can be quite lengthy, and a review of each life stage could take an hour or more. Or a simple brief story from each stage may help you understand how some life patterns have developed.

Review one life stage or more by asking yourself or your client the following questions. If you wish to work through the framework at a deeper level, add the four-level questioning framework of DCT to your interview. For example, in discussing the family situation in the first question, ask for an image and what is seen/heard/felt; then for a concrete situation; then for patterns; and end with a systematic multicultural examination of the family system.

1. *Key environmental systems.* What was the family situation during this life stage? What important life events or stressors affected your family

*(Continued)*

---

or caregivers during this period? What is the nature of family or extended family in your personal history? Where did you obtain your support at that life stage? The focus here is on the individual and key environmental support systems.

2. *Life stage developmental story.* Tell me one story and/or significant event that stands out for you from this life stage. (Examples might be a birth story, a fragment of a childhood memory, a family story repeated again and again.) As time permits, solicit additional stories from the life stage. The focus here is on the individual recollections, although the recollections are usually in a context.

3. *Multicultural issues.* How did gender, religion, ethnic/racial status, or other multicultural issue affect your development during this period? Tell me a story you recall about the role of men or women, a religious figure, or ethnic/racial figure from that time period. Who were your heroes? Whom did you look up to and respect? The focus here is on the individual and how he or she relates to the community and the multicultural environment.

4. *How does the past relate to the present?* Given the data you've discussed during this time period, how does this relate to your present life experience? Do you see any patterns that relate to how you are now and/or how you relate to others? What do you see as the influence of family and culture on where you are now? The focus here is on balancing the individual with family and multicultural issues.

Interestingly, from developmental questions at the birth-to-preschool period, Tamase finds that clients tend to discuss random, disconnected images and events in fragments. At the elementary school age, concrete stories are obtained, while the adolescent questions bring out a time of self-examination and the beginning of patterns. The final session on one's current life is where clients become quite aware that the present mode of functioning is deeply related to their past developmental history.

## Using Consciousness-Raising Groups to Understand Oppression

A focus group study of native Aboriginal Australians revealed the following concerns. (Aboriginal Educational Foundation, 1992, p.1):

Most have strong criticisms of their schooling.

All are very critical of the employment choices open to them.

Few reported satisfaction with their current employment and training situation.

Many hoped that their children and grandchildren could be spared
similar experiences.

However, if you visited Australia today, the picture has improved, but only marginally.
Those who have been traditionally oppressed face major challenges. One of your tasks
with such clients is to help them become aware that "their problem" is really the system
in which they live day to day. Build awareness and help the cope positively with the
actions that they can take.

This list of concerns would look very familiar to non-majority people throughout
the world. Irish migrant workers in Britain, Inuit and Dene in Canada, and African
Americans, Middle Easterners, and Hispanic/Latinas/-os in the United States might
be expected to view their situation differently but would also have much in common
with Aboriginal Australians. At times, the situation becomes more difficult and thus
the need for you to consider social justice action as a part of effective counseling and
therapy. The social action dimension is all-too-often missing in education, training,
research, and practice.

The Aboriginal Educational Foundation initiated a project aiming to help native
people discuss their issues, their strengths, and their desires for the future. This was
with the goal of empowering families and groups. One of counseling and therapy's
limitations is an almost constant emphasis on individuals. Family or group work may
be more effective than individual counseling in MCT.

The Aboriginal project brought families and groups together to tell their stories in
an intensive two-hour session. The objectives were to draw out their daily life strug-
gles as they related to schooling or study and employment. The task of the leaders was
simply to listen and learn. There was an emphasis on group sharing of experiences in
a safe atmosphere. As the group members discussed their concrete issues, they soon
discovered many commonalties and patterns. The essence of consciousness-raising is
the group discussion of stories. The discussion of such stories helps plan action for the
future.

Feminist theory has a foundation in group consciousness-raising. Women met in
groups to discuss their stories, and out of their concrete naming of common experiences came the beginning of feminist theory and practice. Consciousness-raising can
be conducted with groups, but it can also be an addition to individual counseling and
therapy. Practice Exercise 5.3 provides a beginning specific set of strategies that can be
employed with individuals or groups.

---

**PRACTICE EXERCISE 5.3. Basic Consciousness-Raising**

*Establish a group of at least three participants.* The topic for your session can be as broad as what it means to be male or female; gay, lesbian, bisexual, or heterosexual immigrant; or of some other racial/ethnic or multicultural group. Let us recall that being a White Canadian or White US citizen also represents a multicultural group. You might want the groups to share an experience they may have had with oppression. Eventually, you may wish to help the group talk about liberation and positive action.

*Discuss the general issue.* Begin by asking each member of the group to tell a story that represents what group membership means to them. Allow time for sharing after each story. The group may very likely start to find common patterns in their experiences.

*Divide your time by focusing on three dimensions.* In a consciousness-raising session, one-third of the time may be profitably spent on focusing on personal stories and narratives of oppression or group identity; one-third on group process and reactions of members to each other's stories; and one-third on the cultural/environmental context surrounding the issue. The microskill of focus is particularly helpful here for the leader—think of focusing on individuals, the group, and the cultural/environmental context. Time may be structured formally along these three dimensions, or you may wish to simply balance discussion along the three dimensions from time to time.

*Establish an action commitment.* Ask your participants what one thing they might do differently as a result of this interaction. Something different could be behaving in a new way or it might be cognitive in that the person might think about things differently.

---

The emphasis in Proposition II of MCT is on the complexity of the individual in family and cultural context. The practice exercises provide an introductory framework for considering multiple issues when you are working with a single client. For practical purposes, the following summary may be useful.

1. The client is more than just an individual. If you provide multiple ways to think about an issue, challenge, or concern, this is an important step toward multicultural practice.

2. MCT stresses the importance of making family, multicultural reference group, and contextual factors part of every interview.

3. The microskill of focus, IDC, and consciousness-raising groups are but three examples of specific MCT techniques that can be made part of all counseling and therapy practice.

Research on health disparities and the effects of racism is presented on Table 5.4.

---

**Table 5.4.  Research on Health Inequalities and Racism**

Racial/ethnic disparities in mental and physical health are well documented and persistent (Sawyer, Major, Casad, Townsend, & Mendes, 2012). Drastic differences in disease incidence and mortality among African Americans, Hispanic/Latinas/os, and Whites are observed in the United States. These health inequalities are affected by reduced access to health care, housing, and employment opportunities, as well as lower quality of health care than Whites. Systematic research also documents the negative effect of racial discrimination on physical health and general well-being (Berger & Sarnyai, 2015).

High stress levels caused by exposure to prejudice and discrimination contribute to health disparities. Merely anticipating prejudice leads to psychological and cardiovascular stress responses (Sawyer et al., 2012). Perceived race-based discrimination is positively associated with smoking among African-Americans. Repeated subjection to race-based discrimination is associated with higher blood pressure levels and more frequent diagnoses of hypertension and increase risk of breast cancer in African-American women, and chronic cardiovascular, respiratory, and pain-related health issues in Asian-Americans (Smedley, 2012). Many of the health consequences of racism and discrimination can be passed down from one generation to the next (Goosby & Heidbrink, 2013).

The effects of racial discrimination on stress and disease seem to be mediated by chronically elevated cortisol levels and a dysregulated hypothalamic-pituitary-adrenal (HPA) axis. Racial discrimination converges on the anterior cingulate cortex (ACC). The anterior cingulate cortex (ACC; Broadmann areas A24, 32, 33) is a cortical area that integrates social cues and knowledge related to complex social experiences, such as social exclusion. The ACC is connected to the limbic system and is involved in emotional reactivity. This region of the brain seems to be affected by early life stress and may impair the capacity of the prefrontal cortex (PFC) to regulate emotions during situations involving social rejection (Berger & Sarnyai, 2015). Parts of the PFC are responsible for higher levels of stress related to discrimination and for the continuation of the stress response long after the stressful situation ended. Sustained psychosocial stress decreases gray matter volumes (Berger & Sarnyai, 2015).

# Cultural Identity Development Theory

Cultural identity self-development represents a cognitive/emotional/behavioral progression and expansion through identifiable and measurable levels of consciousness or stages. While theorists vary in the specifics, these stages appear to follow a sequence of: (a) naïveté and embedded awareness of self as a cultural being; (b) encounter with the reality of cultural issues; (c) naming of these cultural issues; (d) reflection on the meaning of self as a cultural being, and (e) some form of internalization and multi-perspective thought about self-in-system. With each level of stage development comes different attitudes toward oneself (self-identity) and others (reference group identity or differences).

PROPOSITION III.—Cultural identity development is a major determinant of both counselor and client attitudes toward the self, attitudes toward others of the same group, attitudes toward others of a different group, and attitudes toward the dominant group. These attitudes, which may be manifested in affective and behavioral dimensions, are strongly influenced not only by cultural variables, but by the dynamics of a dominant-subordinate relationship among culturally different groups. The level or stage of racial/cultural identity will influence how clients and counselors define the issue and will dictate what they believe to be appropriate counseling/therapy goals and processes.

Each client (individual, family, group, organization) has multiple cultural identities that most likely will not progress or expand at the same rate. Different clients have different issues that are most important and salient to them. For example, an individual's identity as a Navajo may be quite high, while awareness of self as a heterosexual or Gulf War veteran may demonstrate less awareness. African American college students may be expected to focus on issues of racial identity, while other issues are often less central to them. The gay or lesbian person will often focus on this sexual identity and place less emphasis on race and ethnicity.

The MCT counselor or therapist is constantly seeking to expand awareness of cultural identity issues both for oneself and for one's clientele. There is no end to cultural identity development. MCT affirms the difference between individual differences and cultural differences. Skin color at birth is a clear and unambiguous example of an individual difference, while the meaning of that skin color to self and others as it has evolved over time is a clear and unambiguous example of a cultural difference. MCT affirms that cultural identities are complex and that culturally learned patterns relate to issues of multiple identities. However, the client takes the lead as to which issue of identity is foremost.

## The Specifics of Cultural Identity Development Theory

The essential idea of cultural identity theory is that individuals have varying levels of consciousness about their ethnic/racial background. It is important that counselors and therapists be able to recognize cultural identity level or awareness. Then, it is considered helpful to be able to match your interviewing style to the level of client awareness. The most highly developed models of cultural identity have been generated by African Americans (Cross, 1995; Helms, 1995, 2007) and Asian Americans (Sue & Sue, 2016; Yoon et al., 2017). Charles Thomas (1971) and William Cross (1995) are regarded as the originators of the model, although the ideas were generated independently in many settings.

Cultural identity theory, however, has come to be used for many other different multicultural groups, including but not limited to Biracial groups (Kerwin & Ponterotto, 1995; Perkins, 2014); students with disabilities (Forber-Pratt & Zape, 2017); Hispanic/Latinas/os (Casas & Pytluk, 1995; Spanierman et al., 2017); Lesbians (Tate & Pearson, 2016); Mapuches (González et al., 2017); and Whites (Helms, 2007; Malott et al., 2015).

A summary of the five-stage model of cultural identity development is presented in Table 5.5. Note that the *movement* of consciousness is from naive lack of awareness to action and awareness of self-in-relation to society. Jackson and Hardiman's (1983) Black Identity Development Theory speaks of the *evolution of consciousness*—the growing awareness of oneself in relationship to others and society.

---

**Table 5.5. Cultural Identity Development Theory**

Stage 1. Naïveté. The individual has little focused awareness of self as a cultural being. This is most clearly represented by children who do not distinguish skin color as an important feature. Helms (1995) points out that many White individuals lack awareness of the meaning that *Whiteness* has in our society. Naive understanding can also be manifested by successful and educated professionals who fully or partially deny that they have been oppressed and discriminated against.

Stage 2. Encounter. Despite lack of contact or efforts to shield oneself from racism, sexism, or other discrimination, the individual encounters experiences in the environment that clearly demonstrate that the earlier naive view was an inadequate cognition structure. For example, the African American goes through a critical transformation and recognizes that discrimination is real and that being African American is different from being White or Asian.

Stage 3. Naming. The act of naming is transformative. When Betty Friedan (1963) named the "problem that has no name" as sexism, she forever changed the way women viewed themselves and their issues. The gay liberation movement named itself gay and thus took on what was previously a negative slur as their own positive identity. At this stage, the individual may feel much anger and may actively or passively refuse to work with those it considers oppressors—most often European White males. In White and majority people seeking to support liberation of consciousness, the naming phase represents a real challenge, as it often leaves the White person without any sense of a positive identity.

Stage 4. Reflection on self as a cultural being. The development of keener awareness of being Asian American, bisexual, or culturally deaf continues. However, at Stage 3, the Black individual may turn more fully away from White culture and become totally immersed in reflecting on African American history and the Black community. The lesbian may move away from confronting men and focus within her own community. At this point, the majority society is less relevant. The developmental task is the establishment of a firm African American, Jewish, or Muslim consciousness in its own right.

Stage 5. Multi-perspective internalization. The individual develops pride in self and awareness of others. This individual makes use of the important dimensions of all stages of development and thus recognizes and accepts the worthwhile dimensions of predominant culture, fights those aspects that represent racism, sexism, homophobia, and oppression, and integrates all the stages in a transcendent consciousness. The individual is able to view the world through multiple frames of reference.

---

Cross (1995) points out that each developmental stage has a special value. Jackson (1976) would argue that all but the first and second stages are valuable places for an African American to spend her or his entire life. Even so, for any individual to be subject to constant oppression, the denial represented by naïveté at times may be necessary for survival and sanity.

While there may seem to be advantages in the fifth level of consciousness, this level involves a multi-perspective division of consciousness that sometimes makes action in a racist society more difficult. Furthermore, this level of critical consciousness may be emotionally and cognitively exhausting at times.

Table 5.6 presents the cultural identity model and women's identity theory and illustrates how both European American and minority women develop consciousness.

**Table 5.6. Cultural Identity Developmental Theory Related to Women**

| Cultural Identity Development Theory | Women's Developmental Identity Theory |
| --- | --- |
| Naïveté | Lacks awareness of system, "buys into the status quo." |
| Encounter | Becomes aware of women's oppression through contact with multiple issues that illustrate the failure of naïveté. |
| Naming | Identifies issue as sexism. Angry with men and takes action to produce change. |
| Reflection on Self | Pride in being a woman. Often separates from men to find self and self-in-relation to other women. |
| Multi-perspective Internalization | Views male/female relationships in cultural/historical perspective. Values aspects of maleness, sees men selectively, able to take parts of women's identity theory interchangeably and accept, act, and reflect as the situation warrants. |

# Identity Development Theory for White American Counselors and Therapists

Joseph Ponterotto developed a theory of identity development for White counselor trainees (Ponterotto, 1988; Ponterotto & Park-Taylor, 2007). His stage model is similar to those described above, particularly that of Jackson. The White counselor trainee often works through the following stages when confronted with multicultural concerns:

> *Stage 1. Preexposure.* The White counselor trainee has not thought about counseling and therapy as multicultural phenomena. He or she may say that "people are just people" and in counseling practice may engage in unconscious racism and sexism or, more positively, try to treat all clients the same.
>
> *Stage 2. Exposure.* When multicultural issues are brought to his or her attention, the White therapist trainee (or experienced

professional) learns information about cultural differences, matters of discrimination and oppression, and that previous educational experiences have been incomplete. The trainee at this stage may become perturbed and confused by the many incongruities that have been presented.

*Stage 3. Zealotry or defensiveness.* Faced with the challenge of multicultural issues, students and professionals may move in one of two directions. Some become angry and active proponents of multiculturalism—even to the point of offending some of their colleagues. Another common response to the incongruities posed by exposure at Stage 2 is a retreat into quiet defensiveness. Criticisms of Eurocentric culture, "the system," and therapeutic theory are taken personally. These students become passive recipients of information and "retreat back into the predictability of the White culture" (Helms, 1984, p. 156).

*Stage 4. Integration.* The counselor acquires a respect and awareness of cultural differences. He or she becomes aware of personal family and cultural history and how this might affect the interview and treatment plan. There is an acceptance that one can't know all dimensions of Multicultural Counseling and Therapy all at once, and plans are made for a lifetime of learning.

While the model above was generated for White European Americans, it does seem to have implications for counselor and therapy trainees of other cultural backgrounds as well. For example, you may be a Lakota Sioux counselor, quite aware of issues for your own culture, and that of Midwestern Euro-Americans, but you may have had limited contact with Mexican Americans and African Americans. You may face some of the same issues of multicultural awareness presented in Ponterotto's model. Where are you in your cultural identity development as a counselor or therapist? Practice Exercise 5.4 outlines an exercise to facilitate your personal awareness as a counselor and therapist.

Another well-known model of White Racial Identity was developed by Janet Helms (1995; 2007). Her model assumes that racism is an important component of White racial identity. Thus, to develop a healthy identity, individuals should abandon racism and adopt a nonracist White identity. Her model includes six racial identity statuses (see Table 5.7).

**Table 5.7. Janet Helms's White Racial Identity Model**

1. Contact: Whites believe that everybody has equal chance of success and are unaware of any aspects of racism and discrimination. Also, they may have limited social or work experiences with People of Color. "I don't pay attention to race … We are all equal …"

2. Disintegration: In this stage, a White person acknowledges his or her Whiteness and ascribed privileges, but becomes conflicted over racial moral dilemmas. He or she may experience dissonance, conflict, guilt, helplessness, or anxiety. "I hate to feel I am privileged by the color of my skin; that is why I don't deal with issues of race …"

3. Reintegration: White persons regress to a basic belief of White superiority and minority inferiority. Negative conditions associated with Black people are thought to result from Blacks' inferior intellectual, moral, and social qualities. "Well, Blacks are given social security and all, but they can't use all that support to get ahead … they are basically lazy …"

4. Pseudoindependence. White persons make conscious and deliberate attempts to understand racial differences and interact with People of Color. They begin to search for a new White identity but still can behave in racist ways. These attempts remain within the intellectual domain and do not yet reach the affective domain.

5. Immersion/Emersion: Whites demonstrate an increasing willingness to redefine their Whiteness and confront their prejudices. They search for accurate information about race and gain a deeper understanding of their own racist socialization. May become involved in social activism to fight racism. There is also an increased experiential and affective understanding that was previously lacking. Affective and experiential upheaval leads to a feeling of rebirth.

6. Autonomy: Whites become knowledgeable about racial differences, value the diversity, are no longer uncomfortable with the experiential reality of race, and establish a nonracist attitude.

These stages are not static. They are fluid as well as context driven.

*Sources:* Castellanos, 2013; Han, West-Olatunji, & Thomas, 2010; Helms, 1995.

# Theories in Action

## Your Racial Identity

The following exercise is designed to help you assess your own level of racial identity. Complete Practice Exercise 5.4 to get a deeper grasp of multicultural and racial identity theory.

**Practice Exercise 5.4. What Has Been Your Personal Journey as a Therapist or Counselor in Terms of Cultural Identity Theory?**

Following are some questions for you to consider as you think about the role of Multicultural Counseling and Therapy in your own practice.

*1. Ethnic/racial identity.* Given the five stages (or the four of Ponterotto or the six of Helms), where are you in your own personal journey as an African American, Hispanic/Latina/o, Japanese American, Arab American, Cuban American, German Canadian, Mexican American, French Canadian, or other ethnic/racial identity?

As time permits, think back on yourself at earlier stages of life where perhaps your identity as an ethnic/racial human being was different from what it is now. How did you think and feel then? What led you to change?

You may find it useful once again to review your community and family genograms. The other practice exercises in this chapter may also be useful, particularly the journey as identified in Introspective Developmental Counseling.

*2. Counselor or therapist identity and multiculturalism.* Trace your personal path in your counseling and therapy training program. Can you identify dimensions of preexposure, exposure, zealotry/defensiveness, and integration in your way of being and thinking?

The most important implication of MCT, as presented in this chapter, is that it stands as a distinct theoretical orientation in itself, with as much or more potential than the traditional therapies discussed in this book. Yet, MCT will continue to be defined by further theory, research, and practice.

# References

Aboriginal Educational Foundation. (1992). *Aboriginals respond to the Royal Commission into Aboriginal Deaths in Custody.* Bedford Park, South Australia: Flinders Press.

American Psychiatric Association. (2013). *Diagnostic and statistical manual of mental disorder* (5th ed.). Washington, DC: Author.

American Psychological Association. (1993). Guidelines for providers of psychological services to ethnic, linguistic, and culturally diverse populations. *American Psychologist, 48,* 45–48.

American Psychological Association. (2003). Guidelines on multicultural education, training, research, practice, and organizational change for psychologists. *American Psychologist, 58,* 377–402.

Arredondo, P., Toporek, R., Brown, S.P., Jones, J., Locke, D.C., Sanchez, J., & Stadler, H. (1996). Operationalization of the multicultural counseling competencies. *Journal of Multicultural Counseling and Development, 24,* 42–78.

Asnaani, A., & Hofmann, S.G. (2012). Collaboration in culturally responsive therapy: Establishing a strong therapeutic alliance across cultural lines. *Journal of Clinical Psychology, 68,* 187–197. http://doi.org/10.1002/jclp.21829.

Barlow, D.H. (2010). Negative effects from psychological treatments. *American Psychologist, 65,* 13–19. doi:10.1037/a0015643.

Berger, M, Sarnyai, Z. (2015). "More than skin deep": Stress neurobiology and mental health conse-quences of racial discrimination. *Stress, 18*, 1–10.

Bernal, G., Jiménez-Chafey, M.I., & Domenech Rodríguez, M.M. (2009). Cultural adaptation of treat-ments: A resource for considering culture in evidence-based practice. *Professional Psychology: Research and Practice, 40*(4), 361-368. doi.org/10.1037/a0016401.

Bronfenbrenner, U. (2005). *Making human beings human: Bioecological perspectives on human develop-ment*. Thousand Oaks, CA: Sage.

Casas, M., & Pytluk, S. (1995). Hispanic identity development: Implications for research and prac-tice. In J. Ponterotto, M. Casas, L. Suzuki, and C. Alexander (Eds.), *Handbook of multicultural counseling*. Thousand Oaks, CA: Sage.

Castellanos, J. (2013). *Identity development*. Retrieved from http://www.socsci.uci.edu/~castellj/ss70c/webpres/2012WhiteIdentity.pdf.

Cheatham, H. (1990). Empowering Black families. In H. Cheatham, & J. Stewart (Eds.), Black fami-lies (pp. 373–393). New Brunswick, N.J.: Transaction.

Cheek, D. (1976). Assertive Black … puzzled White. San Luis Obispo, CA: Impact.

Cicchetti, D., Toth, S.L., & Handley, E.D. (2015). Genetic moderation of interpersonal psychothera-py efficacy for low-income mothers with major depressive disorder: Implications for differential susceptibility. *Developmental Psychopathology, 27*, 19–35. doi:10.1017/S0954579414001278.

Commons, M.L., & Ross, S.N. (2008). What postformal thought is, and why it matters. *World Futures: The Journal of General Evolution 64*(5), 321–329.

Cross, W. (1995). The psychology of Nigrescence: Revising the Cross model. In J. Ponterotto, M. Casas, L. Suzuki, and C. Alexander (Eds.), *Handbook of multicultural counseling*. Thousand Oaks, CA: Sage.

Eisenhart, R.V. (2975). You can't hack it little girl: A discussion of the covert psychological agenda of modern combat training. *Journal of Social Issues, 31*, 13–23.

Erikson, E. (1993). *Childhood and society*. New York, NY: Norton.

Forber-Pratt, A.J., & Zape, M.P. (2017). Disability identity development model: Voices from the ADA-generation. *Disability and Health Journal, 10*, 350–355.

Freire, P. (1972). *Pedagogy of the oppressed*. New York, NY: Herder and Herder.

Friedan, B. (1963). *The feminine mystique*. New York, NY: Dell.

Fukuyama, M.A. (1990). Taking a universal approach to multicultural counseling. *Counselor Education and Supervision, 30*, 6–17. doi:10.1002/j.1556-6978.1990.tb01174.x.

González, R., Lickel, B., Gupta, M., Tropp, L. R., Luengo Kanacri, B. P., Mora, E., De Tezanos-Pinto, P., … Bernardino, M. (2017). Ethnic identity development and acculturation preferences among minority and majority youth: Norms and contact. *Child Development, 88*, 743–760. doi:10.1111/cdev.12788.

Goosby, B.J., & Heidbrink, C. (2013). Transgenerational consequences of racial discrimination for African American health. *Sociology Compass, 7*, 630–643. doi.org/10.1111/soc4.12054.

Griffith, M.S., & Jones, E.E. (1979). Race and psychotherapy: Changing perspectives. In J.M. Masserman (Ed.), Current psychiatric therapies (Vol. 18, pp. 225-235). New York, NY: Grune & Stratton.

Han, H.S., West-Olatunji, C., & Thomas, S. (2010). Use of racial identity development theory to explore cultural competence among early childhood educators. *Journal of Southeastern Regional Association for Teacher Educators, 20*(1), 1–11.

Helms, J.E. (1984). Toward a theoretical explanation of the effects of race on counseling: A Black and White model. *The Counseling Psychologist, 12*, 153–165.

Helms, J. (1995). An update of Helms's White and People of Color identity models. In J. Ponterotto, M. Casas, L. Suzuki, & C. Alexander (Eds.), *Handbook of multicultural counseling*. Thousand Oaks, CA: Sage.

Helms, J.E. (2007). *A race is a nice thing to have: A guide to being a white person or understanding the white persons in your life*. Alexandria, VA: Microtraining Associates.

Henrich, J., Heine S.J., & Norenzayan, A. (2010). The weirdest people in the world? *Behavioral and Brain Sciences, 33*, 61–135. doi:10.1017/S0140525X0999152X.

Ivey, A. (1991). *Developmental strategies for helpers: Individual, family and network interventions*. Pacific Grove, CA: Brooks/Cole.

Ivey, A., Ivey, M.B., & Zalaquett, C.P. (2018). *Intentional interviewing and counseling: Facilitating client development in a multicultural society* (9th ed.). Belmont, CA: Cengage Learning.

Jackson, B.W. (1976). Black identity development. In L.H. Golubchick and B. Persky (Eds.), Urban, social, and educational issues (pp. 158–64). Dubuque, IA: Kendall/Hunt.

Jackson, B.W., & Hardiman, R. (1983). Racial identity development: Implications for managing the multiracial work force. In R.A. Ritvo & A.G. Sargent (Eds.), NTL manager's handbook (pp. 107–119). Arlington, VA: NTL Institute.

Jimenez, D.E., Bartels, S.J., Cardenas, V., Dhaliwal, S.S., & Alegría, M. (2012). Cultural beliefs and mental health treatment preferences of ethnically diverse older adult consumers in primary care. *American Journal of Geriatric Psychiatry, 20*, 533–542. doi:10.1097/JGP.0b013e318227f876.

Keating, D. (1979). Adolescent thinking. In J. Adelson (Ed.), *Handbook of adolescent psychology* (pp. 211–246). New York, NY: Wiley.

Kerwin, C., & Ponterotto, J. (1995). Biracial identity development. In J. Ponterotto, M. Casas, L. Suzuki, and C. Alexander (Eds.), *Handbook of multicultural counseling*. Thousand Oaks, CA: Sage.

Kohrt, B.A., Rasmussen, A., Kaiser, B.N., Haroz, E.E., Maharjan, S.M., Mutamba, B.B., De Jong, J., & Hinton, D.E. (2014). Cultural concepts of distress and psychiatric disorders: Literature review and research recommendations for global mental health epidemiology. *International Journal of Epidemiology, 43*, 365–406. doi.org/10.1093/ije/dyt227.

Kunstman, J.W., Plant, F.A., & Deska, J.C. (2016). White ≠ poor: Whites distance, derogate, and deny low-status ingroup members. *Personality and Social Psychology Bulletin, 42*, 230–243. doi:10.1177/0146167215623270.

Laganà, L., & Shanks, S. (2002). Mutual biases underlying the problematic relationship between older adults and mental health providers: Any solution in sight? *International Journal of Aging and Human Development, 55*, 271–295.

Leong, F., Wagner, N., & Tata, S.P. (1995). Racial and ethnic variations in help-seeking attitudes. In J. Ponterotto, M. Casas, L. Suzuki, & C. Alexander (Eds.), *Handbook of multicultural counseling*. Thousand Oaks, CA: Sage.

Lifton, R.J. (1973). *Home from the war: Learning from Vietnam veterans*. New York, NY: Simon & Schuster.

Lilienfeld, S.O. (2007). Psychological treatments that cause harm. *Perspectives on Psychological Science, 2*, 53–70. doi:10.1111/j.1745-6916.2007.00029.x.

Liu, W.M., Soleck, G., Hopps, J., Dunston, K., & Pickett Jr., T. (2004). A new framework to understand social class in counseling: The social class worldview model and modern classism theory. *Journal of Multicultural Counseling and Development, 32*, 95–122.

Lockard, A. J., Hayes, J.A., Graceffo, J.M., & Locke, B.D. (2013). Effective counseling for racial/ethnic minority clients: Examining changes using a practice research network. *Journal of College Counseling, 16*, 243–257. doi:10.1002/j.2161-1882.2013.00040.x.

Locke, D.C. (1990). A not so provincial view of multicultural counseling. *Counselor Education and Supervision, 30,* 18–25.

Malott, K. M., Paone, T. R., Schaefle, S., Cates, J., & Haizlip, B. (2015). Expanding White racial identity theory: A qualitative investigation of whites engaged in antiracist action. *Journal of Counseling & Development, 93,* 333–343. doi:10.1002/jcad.12031.

Molefi Kete Asante (1987). *The Afrocentric idea.* Philadelphia, PA: Temple University Press.

Nobles, W.W. (2006). *Seeking the Sakhu: Foundational writings for an African psychology.* Chicago, IL: Third World Press.

Nwachuku, U. (1989). *Culture-specific counseling: The Igbo case.* Unpublished doctoral dissertation, University of Massachusetts, Amherst.

Nwachuku, U. (1990). *Translating Multicultural Theory into Direct Action: Culture-Specific Counseling.* Paper Presented at the International Round Table of Counselling. Helsinki, Finland, July.

Nwachuku, U., & Ivey, A. (1991). Culture-specific counseling: An alternative approach. *Journal of Counseling and Development, 70,* 106–51.

Office of the Surgeon General (US); Center for Mental Health Services (US); National Institute of Mental Health (US) (2001). Mental health: Culture, race, and ethnicity: A supplement to mental health: A report of the surgeon general. Rockville, MD: Substance Abuse and Mental Health Services Administration (US). Retrieved from https://www.ncbi.nlm.nih.gov/books/NBK44243/.

Pedersen, P., & Ivey, A. (1993). *Culture-centered counseling.* New York, NY: Greenwood.

Pedersen, P., Lonner, W.J., Draguns, J., Trimble J., & Scharrón-del Río, M.I. (Eds.) (2016). *Counseling across cultures* (7th ed.). Thousand Oaks, CA: Sage.

Perkins, R.M. (2014). Life in duality: Biracial identity development. *Race, Gender & Class, 21*(1), 211–219.

Ponterotto, J.G. (1988). Racial consciousness development among white counselor trainees: A stage model. *Journal of Multicultural Counseling and Development, 16,* 146–156. doi:10.1002/j.2161-1912.1988.tb00405.x.

Ponterotto, J.G., & Park-Taylor, J. (2007). Racial and ethnic identity theory, measurement, and research in counseling psychology: Present status and future directions. *Journal of Counseling Psychology, 54,* 282–294.

Ratts, M.J., Singh, A.A., Nassar-McMillan, S., Butler, S.K., & McCullough, J.R. (2016). Multicultural and social justice counseling competencies: Guidelines for the counseling profession. *Journal of Multicultural Counseling and Development, 44,* 28–48. doi:10.1002/jmcd.12035.

Sametband, I., & Strong, T. (2013). Negotiating cross-cultural misunderstandings in collaborative therapeutic conversations. *International Journal for the Advance of Counselling, 35,* 88–99. doi:10.1007/s10447-012-9169-1.

Sawyer, P., Major, B., Casad, B.J., Townsend, S.S.M., & Mendes, W.B. (2012). Discrimination and the stress response: Psychological and physiological consequences of anticipating prejudice in interracial interaction. *American Journal of Public Health, 102,* 1020–1026.

Smedley, B.D. (2012). The lived experience of race and its health consequences. *American Journal of Public Health, 102,* 933–935. doi.org/10.2105/AJPH.2011.300643.

Smith, L. (2005). Psychotherapy, classism, and the poor: Conspicuous by their absence. *American Psychologist, 60,* 687–696.

Smith, L. (2013). So close and yet so far away: Social class, social exclusion, and mental health practice. *American Journal of Orthopsychiatry, 83,* 11–16.

Smith, T.B., Domenech Rodriguez, M., & Bernal, G. (2011). Culture. *Journal of Clinical Psychology: In Session, 67,* 166–175. doi:10.1002/jclp.20757.

Sommers-Flanagan, J. (2015). Evidence-based relationship practice: Enhancing counselor competence. *Journal of Mental Health Counseling, 37*, 95–108.

Spanierman, L.B., Poteat, V.P., Whittaker, V.A., Schlosser, L.Z., & Arévalo Avalos, M.R. (2017). Allies for life? Lessons from White scholars of multicultural psychology. *The Counseling Psychologist, 45*, 618–650.

Sue, D.W. (1995). Toward a theory of multicultural counseling and therapy. In J. Banks & C. Banks (Eds.), *Handbook of research on multicultural education* (pp. 647–659). New York, NY: Macmillan.

Sue, D.W., & Sue, D. (2008). *Counseling the culturally diverse: Theory and practice* (5th ed.). Hoboken, NJ: Wiley.

Sue, D.W., & Sue, D. (2016). *Counseling the culturally diverse: Theory and practice* (7th ed.). Hoboken, NJ: Wiley.

Sue, S. (1998). In search of cultural competence in psychotherapy and counseling. *American Psychologist, 53*, 440–448.

Suedfeld, P. (2016). On the road from WEIRD to STEM, psychology hits a bump. *Canadian Psychology, 57*, 60–64. doi:http://dx.doi.org.ezaccess.libraries.psu.edu/10.1037/cap0000044.

Tamase, K. (1991). The effects of introspective-developmental counseling. Presentation at the American Association of Counseling and Development. April, Reno, Nevada.

Tamase, K. (2007). The effect of video-modeling in different cognitive-developmental styles based on the Developmental Counseling and Therapy assumption upon participants' verbal responses. *The Japanese Journal of Microcounseling, 2*(1), 5–18.

Tamase, K. (2014). From microcounseling to developmental counseling and therapy. *Tezukayama University Bulletin of Psychology, 3*,1–9.

Tamase, K., & Yoshida, S. (2007). Naikan therapy seen from the viewpoint of Developmental Counseling and Therapy Theory. *Bulletin of Tezukayama University Mental Care Center, 2*, 21–32. (in Japanese).

Tate, C.C., & Pearson, M.D. (2016). Toward an inclusive model of lesbian identity development: Outlining a common and nuanced model for cis and trans women. *Journal of Lesbian Studies, 20*, 97–115. doi:10.1080/10894160.2015.1076237.

Thomas, C. (1971). *Boys no more: A black psychologist's view of community*. Beverly Hills, CA: Glencoe.

ToDo Institute (2018). *Naikan: A method of self-reflection*. Retrieved from http://www.todoinstitute.org/naikan.html.

Toth, S.L., Rogosch, F.A., Oshri, A., Gravener, J., Sturm, R., & Morgan-López, A.A. (2013). The efficacy of interpersonal psychotherapy for depression among economically disadvantaged mothers. *Developmental Psychopathology, 25*, 1065–1078. doi.org/10.1017/S0954579413000370.

Umaña-Taylor, A.J., Quintana S.M., Lee R.M., Cross, W.E., Rivas-Drake, D., Schwartz S.J., … Seaton, E. (2014). Ethnic and racial identity during adolescence and into young adulthood: An integrated conceptualization. *Child Development, 85*, 21–39. doi:10.1111/cdev.12196.

Vargas, N., & Kingsbury, J. (2016). Racial identity contestation: Mapping and measuring racial boundaries. *Sociology Compass, 10*(8), 718–729.

Wendt, D.C., Gone, J.P., & Nagata, D.K. (2015). Potentially harmful therapy and multicultural counseling: Bridging two disciplinary discourses. *Counseling Psychologist, 43*, 334–358. doi:10.1177/0011000014548280.

White, J.L., & Parham, T.A. (1990). *The psychology of Blacks: An African American perspective*. Englewood Cliffs, NJ: Prentice Hall.

Yoon, E., Adams, K., Clawson, A., Chang, H., Surya, S., & Jérémie-Brink, G. (2017). East Asian adolescents' ethnic identity development and cultural integration: A qualitative investigation. *Journal of Counseling Psychology, 64*, 65–79.

Zalaquett, C.P., & Chambers, A.L. (2017). Counseling individuals living in poverty: Introduction to the special issue. *Journal of Multicultural Counseling and Development, 45*, 152–161. doi:10.1002/jmcd.12071).

Zalaquett, C.P., Fuerth, K.M., Stein, C., Ivey, A.E., & Ivey, M.B. (2008). Reframing the DSM-IV-TR from a multicultural/social justice perspective. *Journal of Counseling & Development, 86*, 364–371. doi:10.1002/j.1556-6678.2008.tb00521.x.

# Credits

Fig. 5.1: Derald Wing Sue and David Sue, "Tripartite Identity Model," Counseling the Culturally Diverse: Theory and Practice. Copyright © 2016 by John Wiley & Sons, Inc.

### CHAPTER 6

# Developmental Counseling and Therapy

## Integrating Different Theoretical Perspectives Into A Practical Framework

### CHAPTER GOALS

The major task of this chapter is to offer a metatheory that integrates many of the major theories of counseling and psychotherapy offered in this book. Developmental Counseling and Therapy (DCT) is an integrated theory of counseling and therapy, representative of postmodern thought. Furthermore, DCT embraces a multiple perspective worldview that clearly relates to the multicultural frame of reference. Western psychotherapy and counseling theory seek to discover the unique nature of the self. Postmodern theory argues for multiple selves changing constantly within changing contexts of self, family, and culture.

### SPECIFIC GOALS OF THIS CHAPTER:

1. Outline the central constructs of a developmental metatheory—Developmental Counseling and Therapy (DCT).

2. Present basic DCT practice strategies, including specifics of cognitive-developmental assessment, emotion in the interview, and ways to facilitate client growth.

3. Illustrate how to use the integrative theory of DCT and suggestions for designing a comprehensive treatment plan for depression that allows you to integrate differing counseling theories in a single session.

4. Provide practice exercises that will enable you to help clients work through cognitive/emotional issues from multiple perspectives and examine your own competencies for generating an effective treatment plan.

# The Developmental Counseling and Therapy Integrative Worldview

Developmental counseling and therapy (DCT) is a practical theory with specifics for here and now application. It was developed originally by Allen Ivey (1986) and has been expanded with more specifics by Geiger (2016), Ivey, Ivey, Myers, and Sweeney (2005), and Zalaquett, Chatters, and Ivey (2013).[1]

Psychotherapists who employ this integrated model use developmental theory to assess clients and select appropriate cognitive/emotional style interventions to address client needs.

DCT includes an emphasis on establishing an egalitarian and strength-based psychotherapeutic relationship; therapists work *with* clients, not *on* clients, to foster mutuality in relationship, goals, and treatment plans; they also share equal responsibility for the change process with their clients (Zalaquett et al., 2013).

At the core of DCT is an adaptation and reinterpretation of the thinking of the Swiss epistemologist/psychologist/biologist Jean Piaget (1926/1963). Through observation, Piaget found that children constructed knowledge at four different levels. Piaget's observations have been useful with children but have had only limited use in adolescent and adult clinical and counseling situations, until the adaption for adults by Allen Ivey.

DCT's central assumption is that children, adolescents, and adults metaphorically repeat Piaget's well-known developmental stages of sensorimotor, concrete, formal, and post-formal operations again and again, as they come across different contexts over time (Ivey et al., 2005; Zalaquett, Chatters, & Ivey, 2013). However, while Piaget stressed the importance of moving to higher, more complex forms of thinking, DCT values each style of cognition and emotion. There can be as much value in experiencing the world directly at the sensorimotor level as at the most complex, abstract levels. Piaget's strategies can be used throughout the full life span.

DCT rests on a major adaptation and reinterpretation of the thinking of Piaget. According to DCT, the stages are unrelated to age, and no single stage is better than the others. In terms of DCT, *higher is not better—each perspective is different and clarifies the whole and in turn, the whole is changed by each new perspective.*

DCT translates Piaget's stages to represent four orientations, or levels that must be considered and worked through during the counseling and therapy process. These sensorimotor, concrete, reflective/formal, and dialectic/systemic voices each tap different frames of reference within the whole, and together they provide an organizing framework for the *multiplicity in one*, which is the counseling and therapy field.

---

1 DCT integrates Plato's ancient philosophy, the child development theories of Piaget, and developmentalists (e.g., Erikson, 1963) and the early feminist Gilligan (1982). In addition central to application are multicultural theories (e.g., Sue & Sue, 2016), and neuroscience findings (Ivey & Zalaquett, 2011).

A detailed description of DCT's four major cognitive/emotional orientations is presented in Table 6.4. Figure 6.1 below shows how neuroscience and the brain relate to DCT.

**Figure 6.1. The Neuroscience Foundation of DCT**

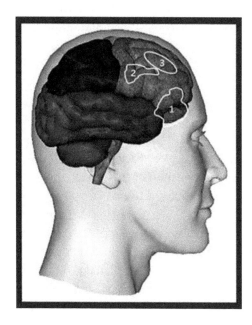

1. Background feelings
   [primarily sensorimotor]

2. Attention to feelings
   [concrete]

3. Reflective awareness
   [formal & dialectic/systemic]

Richard D. Lane, M.D., Ph.D.,
presented here by permission

The neuroanatomy of emotion has been outlined by Chatwal & Lane (2016), Lane (2008), and Lane & Schwartz (1987). They have found that different areas of the prefrontal cortex respond to the four level of DCT (see Figure 6.1). The focus of their model is on emotion, but its parallels to DCT and therapy are obvious. These researchers focus on affective awareness, and this helps us become more aware of the fact that feelings are expressed differently in the brain—and, of course, verbal expressions and nonverbal behavior.

*DCT Level 1 Sensorimotor.* Body sensations and fleeting ideas without much organization represent what Lane terms "background feelings." These sensations typically show as body feelings, although the body or body part may not be mentioned.

At this level, the client may use words representing physical sensation, based on the five senses (for more examples see Noonan, 2010). Examples of body sensations usually experienced as negative: bruised, achy, sore, tense, tight, nauseous, closed in, dizzy, shaky, breathless, pounded, wound up tight, frozen, blocked, cold, dark, numb.

In a more positive sense: light, calm, energized, smooth, warm, cool, relaxed, open, flowing, released, loose, in control, able to let go, joy.

When clients use these words, recall the microskills of reflection of feeling or paraphrasing:

> You have the sensation of distance from your partner and a little bruised. Can you locate those feelings in your body? Tell me more about the sensations—what is your felt body sense? (Note: You can also reach sensations through reflection of feeling or paraphrasing, but sensation is more direct.)
>
> You appear calm today, more so than last week. Where does that feeling of calmness occur in your body? Focus on the specific place, then let it spread throughout and experience deeper calmness.

The *here* and *now* experience is foundational for Level 1. Background feelings and body states underlie conscious experience in the moment. For this reason, the default network plays a large role here. This is the network most active when you act or rest without a specific goal in mind.

*DCT Level 2 Concrete.* This is the foundation of reflection of feeling. The client *names* their feelings and emotions, but they need you to clarify what they mean and their context. You feel_____ because_____, which represents "if____, then _____" caus-ative thought. This is a more cognitive approach to feelings, and words become central rather than body experience. Sensation often will be ignored at this level. Rogerian person-centered therapy and CBT work at this level, as well as in the *reflective/formal*, below.

*DCT Level 3 Reflective/Formal.* Here, our clients are further removed from sensa-tion and have become more abstract in their thinking. Here, we are thinking about feelings, as compared to naming them and experiencing them. The client is often out of touch with the background deeper feelings while intellectualizing. This brings with it advantages, as looking at one's feelings and emotions provides a safe distance to appraise what is going on. The client can begin to see patterns in emotions and in cognitive thought.

When one sees her or his world more in depth, we have more power to change. We also learned about ourselves by observing others. Important for this process are the brain-based mirror neurons. These neurons respond to perceived actions with clear goals, providing the basis for our ability to understand others' actions, as well as ours and the intentions behind (Praszkier, 2016). In addition, rumination and negative thinking occur when higher functions of cortex become less active and operable with increased amygdala activity.

*DCT Level 4 Dialectic/Systemic Style.* Important at this level is the impact of context and social systems on clients' lives. Post-formal thought is in action when you bring multicultural and social justice issues into the counseling session. Social justice action in society exemplifies our commitment to our clients' long-term welfare.

Expect the main area of your counseling and therapy to operate at Levels 2 and 3. We are suggesting, however, that addition of Level 1 sensations and body experience, as well as Level 4, more complex thinking, will make you a more flexible person and therapist able to reach more people at their level of feeling and thinking.

As a holistic framework, DCT depends on multiple seeing and multiple theories (Ivey, 2000; Ivey et al., 2005; Zalaquett et al., 2013). The following summarizes DCT's integrative view of foundational skills:

1.  for effective counseling and therapy, an empathic relationship with a skilled counselor is essential;
2.  most sessions will involve meaning making and decision making;
3.  multicultural factors modify these dimensions and offer additional perspectives.

DCT suggests that it is important for you to be skilled and knowledgeable in these foundational dimensions so that you can meet the needs of a highly diverse clientele. Furthermore, DCT's holistic frame of reference offers a paradigmatic bridge to connect supposedly antagonistic worldviews. For example, DCT finds value in individualistic psychodynamic and cognitive-behavioral approaches and interdependent feminist and multicultural systems. This framework also permits the inclusion, and perhaps even the centrality, of spiritual dimensions of being. Multiple seeing demands multiple realities if we are to maintain a holistic view.

# The Relationship of Multicultural Counseling and Therapy to DCT

Basic to the DCT worldview is that multicultural issues deeply influence the way we think about and construct reality. Counseling and therapy are usually thought of as a two-person relationship—specifically, the relationship between a counselor and the client. There is now reason to believe that the concept of relationship in the interview requires a broader understanding. Some theorists now suggest that the interview is not just a relationship between the two people physically present in the session (Ivey et al., 2018; Sue & Sue, 2016). At times, when you think you are reacting to the client, you may simply be acting from your own encapsulated historical and cultural background (Chung & Bemak, 2012). Figure 6.2 presents the Lacanian Z diagram (1966/1977) of counselor, client, and the cultural social history of each one.

**Figure 6.2. The Influence of Cultural/Historical Background on the Interview**

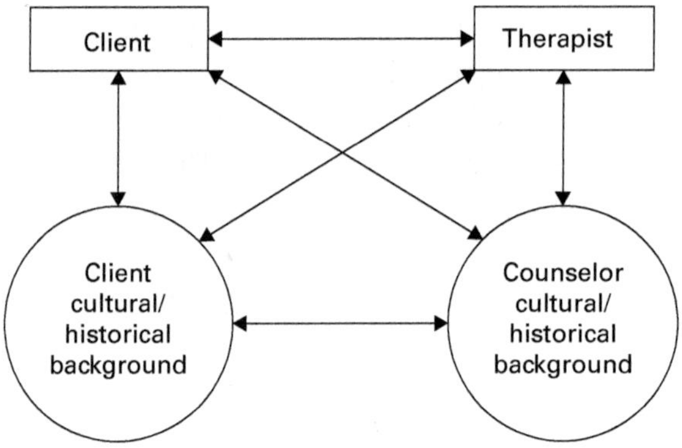

Much traditional counseling and therapy focuses solely on the client and counselor relationship. DCT and multicultural theory would also stress the importance of relationship, but would add that understanding of context—family, groups, community, and culture is essential if we are to work effectively and holistically. The community genogram of Chapter 1 is a DCT strategy.

# Central Constructs of Integrating Skills and Theory: Developmental Counseling and Therapy

Drawing from a holistic worldview that is developmental and focusing on self-in-relation, DCT uses three major theoretical foundations:

1. co-construction of relationships between counselor/therapist and client;
2. a reformulation of Piagetian cognitive stages for use in counseling and therapy;
3. a spherical metatheory integrating the multiple theoretical voices of counseling and therapy.

## Co-construction of Knowledge, Assimilation, and Accommodation

DCT emphasizes that clients and counselors learn together. The word *co-construction* is similar to the self-in-relation concepts of feminist therapy and holistic Afrocentric theory, as the word emphasizes the importance of interdependence of counselor and client—and it is a specific attempt to move toward a less hierarchical, more egalitarian therapist/client relationship.

## The Issue of Therapist Constructions, Ideas, and Even Language Becoming Those of the Client

Traditionally, therapeutic theory starts with the worldview of the theorist, and then the counselor or therapist takes that view and set of techniques and applies them to the client. For example, when a client goes through psychoanalysis, we can anticipate that Freudian worldview will provide an outline for what happens. Through free association, dream analysis, interpretation, and related techniques, the client gradually learns to talk about his or her issues and concerns in Freud's language and eventually often comes to accept the Freudian worldview as truth. Freud's voice has become the client's voice and the language and words applied to one's own thoughts and behaviors.

There is a famous and highly influential film showing a single client, Gloria, being interviewed by Carl Rogers, Fritz Perls, and Albert Ellis (Shostrum, 1966). In a series of classic studies, researchers examined the film in detail. (Meara, Shannon, & Pepinsky, 1979; Meara, Pepinsky, Shannon, & Murray, 1981). Through linguistic analysis, they found that the client, Gloria, tended to assume the language pattern of each different therapist. Gloria used client-centered language with Rogers, Gestalt language with Perls, and a rational emotive language with Ellis.

There is danger in you as therapist superimposing your perceptions or worldview on the client. You are in a powerful position with a vulnerable client, and he or she is likely to take your words very seriously, even to the point of learning your language. In the film, Gloria talks about her difficulties with men and her own father. Each of the three therapists focuses on the *individual* issues that Gloria faces. None of them focuses on how her difficulties may be the result of being a woman in a predominantly male world or on developmental and family issues.

Some reassurance on language and focus of the session, however, is offered by classic research that successful White counselors tend to join their African American clients in language patterns rather than trying to impose their own frames either consciously or unconsciously (Fry, Knopf, & Coe, 1980).

## Co-construction of Knowledge in the Interview

The Fry, Knopf, and Coe study cited above reminds us that not only does the counselor influence the client, but if counselors are flexible, they are also influenced *by the client*. The theory behind a dialectic co-constructivist approach is complex but may be summarized as follows:

1. Client and therapist exist in a unique dialectical relationship. Each has a unique family and cultural developmental history that affects their perceptions and the meanings they make (see Figure 6.1). Who we are depends on our personal experience interacting with others.

2. Thus a new dialectic or interactional system occurs in the therapeutic relationship. Client and counselor act on each other, thereby potentially changing both. Reality is *co-constructed* between counselor and therapist.

3. In turn, counselor and client are each molded by their dialectical relationship with the culture. As in the Gestalt figure of the "young" and "old" woman, what we see and the meanings we make are influenced by our developmental history in a multicultural setting.

4. We are not just culture bearers, we also have the capability to create and change culture. Just as therapist and client can change each other, so can both affect the environment and culture that led to our perceptions. We are part of a "multiplicity in *One*."[2]

The co-constructive process may become a bit clearer when we examine some interpretations of Piagetian theory.

## Basic Schema Theory and Assimilation and Accommodation Processes

Schema[3] theory is basic to Piagetian thinking (Piaget, 1985). Our minds through interaction with the world build structures or theories—*schema*—about this world. Thus, each client you see has created theories or schema about the world as they have developed in relation to others, family, and culture.

From DCT's cognitive/emotional developmental theory, the task of the therapist or counselor is to understand client schema—how these schema were developed in a family and cultural context. And, when necessary, the counselor can help the client generate new, more workable schema or theories for more effective thought, emotion, and behavior.

Assimilation and accommodation are processes identified by Piaget to explain how schema are developed.

> Assimilation and accommodation are different ways to describe a single process. In accommodation, the individual receives (and possibly transforms) a stimulus from the environment; in assimilation, the individual acts on and imposes his or her perspectives on the environment. One aspect is impossible without the other. Like yin and yang, they are inseparable, even though one may be prepotent and primarily operative at a particular time of development. Together these constructions represent the adaptive process of development. (Ivey, 1986, p. 42)

---

2  Modern philosophers relating to these ideas include the founder of the concepts of intentionality, Franz Brentano (1874), and the central existential/humanist and author of *Being and Time* (1927), Martin Heidegger.

3  Varying grammatical forms of schema and schemata (the plural of schema) are used by different authors, including "scheme," "schemes," and "schemas." Here, the word *schema* will be used as both singular and plural.

In *assimilation*, we take our constructions of knowledge and information (schema or theories about the world) and use them to act on the world. For example, Freud and Skinner both had very tightly organized sets of theories/schema that may be used to explain virtually all human behavior. An abused child has assimilated schema/theories about the world that he or she may use throughout life in relationships with others. Assimilated knowledge may be described as what we have internalized over time as the result of our interactions with the world.

One task of counseling and therapy is to help the client find new, more workable schema/theories through *accommodating* to new views of the world. When we encounter a new event or stimulus in our lives, we first try to assimilate it into our existing schema or theories about the world. Sometimes the data from outside doesn't fit, and the person or client simply can't or won't take new information in—this represents rigid assimilated schema/theories. Accommodation occurs when the person either uses new data to modify old schema or builds entirely new schema in his or her mind.

The empathic attitude of Chapter 3 and the microskills of Chapter 4 are oriented to helping the counselor and therapist enter the constructed worldview of the client. Simply listening to and hearing how the client sees, hears, and feels the world may be sufficient for change. In such cases, the therapist has focused on accommodating to and learning from the client. Moreover, when the counselor repeats back to the client what has been said (encourage, paraphrase, reflection of feeling, summary), the client is able to accommodate to this new clarity and change old cognitive structures. Figure 6.3 presents the process of accommodation and assimilation between client and counselor. Rogerian client-centered therapy, for example, may be described as a primarily accommodative theory, as the focus is on the client's constructions of the world.

Some theories and therapists, however, use a primarily assimilative mode—the therapeutic task may be seen as that of encouraging the client to enter the worldview of the therapist. For example, you will find that many clients in psychodynamic therapy tend to talk about their lives using the language of psychoanalysis. DCT would argue for a balance between accommodative and assimilative approaches to human change. There is more than one learner in the counseling and therapy process—see Figure 6.2.

The next section expands on this process and points out that clients (and therapists) bring different levels of previously assimilated ideas to the interview.

## DCT Theory for Adolescent and Adult Cognitions and Emotions

You will find that learning how to recognize client cognitive/emotional-developmental orientation in the here and now of the counseling interview can facilitate your understanding and your choice of appropriate interventions. There are two major issues in assessing cognitive/emotional developmental orientations: 1) identifying the level of the client as they describe their issues and concerns; presenting from orientations

**Figure 6.3. Accommodation and Assimilation Between Client and Counselor**

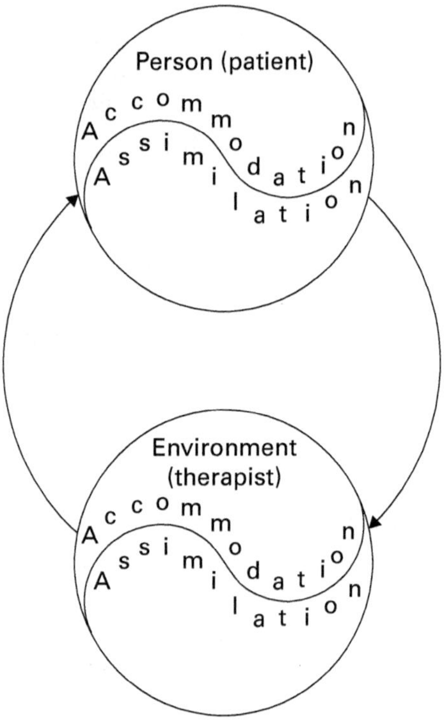

(many clients will be simultaneously concrete and formal, for example); and 2) utilizing these data in the interview and treatment planning.

## Identifying Client Cognitive/Emotional Developmental Level

Piaget talks of four major stages of cognitive development. DCT treats Piagetian thinking as a metaphor and speaks of four major cognitive/emotional-developmental levels or orientations that appear and reappear constantly in our clients. We meet clients who come to us at sensorimotor, concrete, reflective/formal, and dialectic/systemic levels of thinking and emotion.

DCT states that an important task for the counselor or therapist is to enter the world of the client as the client makes sense of that world. Clients make meaning at four major cognitive developmental orientations, which are presented in some detail in Table 6.2.[4] Each orientation involves a different complexity of language and meaning. If you observe your clients carefully, you will find that they do indeed talk about their

---

4    The four levels of client cognitive development are further divided into eight levels. The Standard Cognitive-Developmental Interview and Standard Cognitive-Developmental Classification System may be viewed in Ivey, 1991.

experience at different cognitive-developmental levels. Some clients will be almost totally within one orientation, while others will present several simultaneously. Still others will move from level to level throughout an interview or treatment series.

For example, you may be working with a client going through a divorce. He or she may talk about the divorce from different cognitive and emotional orientations. As you read the following, recall that it is highly likely that clients who present to you at different cognitive/emotional levels are highly likely to need varying types of counseling and therapy.

> Sensorimotor: Tears may be present, the client may talk in a random, confused fashion, but may simultaneously deny feelings of hurt and anger. At times, the client is able to experience the hurt and confusion fully within the body orientation.

> Concrete: The client may talk to you, giving many details and stories around the divorce. Feelings around specific situations may be named, but you may note an absence of self-reflection and considerable blaming and anger toward the spouse.

> Reflective/Formal: Here, the client talks more abstractly. If you listen carefully, you will find that specifics of what happened between the couple are seldom discussed. Rather, the client discusses repeating patterns of interaction. The client is able to reflect on the self and feelings.

> Dialectic/Systemic: The client takes multi-perspectives on the divorce and is even able to see the spouse's frame of reference. The client may see how patterns learned in the family of origin were repeated in the couple's relationship. Multicultural issues of gender, ethnicity, and religion may be part of the awareness.

DCT operates on the assumption that one task of the therapist and counselor is to match language and treatment techniques with the cognitive/emotional level of the client. It does little good to try to get clients who are at the sensorimotor or concrete orientations of cognition and feeling to reflect on patterns or think about how they were involved in the divorce. DCT argues that it is imperative to join the client where he or she is emotionally or cognitively.

You will note in Table 6.1 that each level or orientation has strengths and weaknesses. Full development of human potential suggests the validity of expanding client awareness and potential at each cognitive-development orientation.

**Table 6.1. Four Major Cognitive/Emotional Orientations and Key Counseling Issues at Each Level**

| Cognitive-Developmental Level | Emotional Expression | Counseling Issues | Example Interventions and Goals |
|---|---|---|---|
| *Sensorimotor* | | | |
| (What are the *elements of experience?*) Clients are able to experience life directly in the immediate here and now. They can become enmeshed in sensory experience and in what they directly see, hear, and feel. They may show randomness in their conversation and behavior. They may lack conscious awareness of environmental issues. | Two types of emotion represent the sensori-motor level: (1) emotion is integrated with cognition—"I am my emotions"—with direct access to affective experience; and (2) emotions are split off and unrecognized, as can happen with an adult survivor of child abuse or of an alcoholic family, or a person who is unaware of or denies family/cultural issues. | Counselors and therapists, who are often primarily formal operational, may be weak in skills at this level. They may prefer to talk *about* feelings rather than experience them *directly*. A trainee once said, "I used to think I was good with feelings. Now I know I use formal operational thought and reflect on my feelings rather than experiencing them. I have a lot to learn." | *Interventions:* focus on the here and now and bring the client to awareness—Gestalt exercises, body work, Freire's (1972) use of images to expand consciousness of cultural issues. *Goal:* help client experience the world directly; remove denial and splitting; accept randomness. |
| *Concrete* | | | |
| (What are the *situational descriptions?*) Clients may describe their life events in great detail—"This happened …, then this … and so on." They are concerned with action in the world and with objective, observable events. At the late concrete level, clients will be able to establish cause and effect—if I … then… —thought patterns. | Clients can name emotions but are unable to reflect on them. In the early phases, naming of emotions will be all that can be done. Later, clients will begin to realize that emotions are related to events in a "causal" fashion. The classic counseling response "You feel … because …" is a particularly clear example of late concrete emotions. | Many formal operational counselors often become bored and frustrated with the concrete stories and details of the concrete client. However, Piagetian scholars estimate that from 25–40 percent of North American adults never reach full formal operations (G. Forman, personal communication, 1985). It is important to be able to work with clients at this level. | *Interventions:* focus on action—assertiveness training, decision making on a specific issue, reality therapy, and many behavioral techniques. *Goal:* draw out the specifics of a situation and later cultivate if I … then… thinking. |

*(Continued)*

**Table 6.1. Four Major Cognitive/Emotional Orientations and Key Counseling Issues at Each Level (Continued)**

*Reflective/Formal*

(What is the nature of *self* and repeating *patterns of self, thought, and action?*) Clients are able to move out of the concrete world and deal with abstractions. They like to think about themselves and their personal patterns of feeling and thinking. They can reflect on their feelings (but may not be able to experience them in the here and now of sensorimotor experience). They are able to analyze and look at their issues from more distance.

Clients at this level can reflect on their feelings and examine patterns of feelings and may even be able to examine patterns of patterns. But this ability to reflect on self and feelings may make it difficult to experience emotion in the sensorimotor here and now. Also, despite ability to analyze feelings, the formal client may be unable to act on them.

Much counseling and therapy theory exists primarily at the formal operational level. For example, Rogerian client-centered theory requires one to be able to reflect on feelings, although the microskill of reflection of feelings can be useful at all cognitive levels. Therapists and counselors like to work with formal operational clients, as they tend to be verbal and see patterns. The danger is in a client-therapist relationship that is all talk and no action.

*Interventions:* focus on analysis—Rogerian, psychodynamic, and much of cognitive theory. *Goal:* help clients look at themselves and their life patterns.

*Dialectic / Systemic*

(How did all this develop in a *system* or how is it *integrated?*) Clients are able to reflect on reflections and can work with comfort on systems of operations. Capable of multiple perspectives, they are able to identify how family and cultural pressures affect them and their thinking processes. They may become enmeshed in abstract cognitive processes, with emotion markedly split off from experience.

Clients will see emotions changing with situational context (for example, sadness about death when faced with the immediacy of a loss, but also happiness that a terminally ill parent no longer has to suffer). Emotions are multidimensional and complex. At the same time, this awareness may interfere with ability to experience feelings directly or to act on them.

More and more counselors and therapists are moving beyond reflective/formal thinking to this broader, more contextual and multiculturally aware frame of reference. The dialectic/systemic frame of reference allows one to take a more methatheoretical, integrative approach to the field. When you generate your own theory or metatheory of helping, you are engaged in dialectic/systemic thought.

*Interventions:* consciousness-raising theories—multicultural counseling and therapy, feminist therapy, and much of family therapy. *Goal:* facilitate integrative and multiperspectival thought and awareness of self-in-relation to others and the system.

Clients may be expected to present their issues within several cognitive/emotional-developmental orientations. For example, the client above going through a divorce may start the interview with a dialectic/systemic analysis of issues. Very soon, he or she may be expected to talk in a formal operational fashion about the damage to his self-view. As the counselor, you may note that this person is unable to experience affect at the sensorimotor level, although he or she may reflect on feelings and talk about hurt.

A teenager suffering from bulimia is enmeshed in the sensory world of food and the body, yet may be a very successful gymnast or ballet dancer—very able to act on the world. This same teen may be skilled in formal operations and an excellent student while simultaneously having a very low self-concept. Very often, the family will blame the teenager and deny that the family system in some way affects what is happening.

At the dialectic/systemic level, the teen's family system usually requires assistance. Furthermore, feminist and multicultural theory would remind us that attitudes of society toward food and thinness are an important part of women becoming bulimics. And the gymnastics or ballet teacher may need to be involved—at times they encourage abnormal eating patterns to facilitate performance and physical appearance (McLean et al., 2014; Reas, 2017).

Findings of positron emission tomography show that bulimia is associated with dysregulation in neurotransmitter availability and function. Dysregulation of dopaminergic and serotonergic systems negatively affect food, motivation, executive functions and the regulation of mood, satiety, and impulse control (Schaumberg et al., 2017). Furthermore, structural neuroimaging studies revealed that impulsive eating in bulimia is activated by altered functioning of limbic regions and reduced cognitive control via the prefrontal cortex (Kessler, Hutson, Herman, & Potenza, 2016).

*Cultural identity development theory related to DCT orientations.* The four levels of cognitive/emotional development can be related to Cultural Identity Development theory, discussed in the previous chapter. The embedded consciousness of Stage 1 active and passive acceptance is parallel to many of the cognitions at the sensorimotor level. Stage 2—naming and resistance—and its frequent association with anger and action—has parallels with concrete operational thought. Stage 3, focusing on reflection, has much in common with formal operational thought patterns. Finally, the multi-perspective Stage 4 internalization is integrative while simultaneously demanding multi-perspective thought.

DCT, like multicultural counseling and therapy, holds that a major goal of counseling and therapy is the liberation of consciousness—and acting on that new consciousness.

## The Developmental Sphere: DCT's Metatheoretical Integration of Counseling and Psychotherapy

DCT is metatheoretical in that it provides an integrative framework for combining different theoretical approaches in a single session or treatment series. DCT asks you to be an expert not only in DCT, but also in as many alternative styles of helping as you can master (Ivey, 2000; Ivey et al., 2005; Zalaquett et al., 2013).

Once we have assessed client cognitive-emotional style or orientation, we first need to match and later mismatch interventions to facilitate growth. Generally, clients need to expand their functioning at more than one level or within the orientation. For example, a returning veteran suffering from combat-related stress might need sensorimotor relaxation training to combat tenseness, concrete assertiveness training to cope with a job interview, reflective/formal client-centered work to help self-esteem, and Multicultural Counseling and Therapy to understand the family and cultural issues underlying all of the above issues. Multiple treatment for a single client, even using seemingly antagonistic theories and methods, is basic to the practice of the integrative DCT model.

**Figure 6.4. The Developmental Sphere: A Holistic View of Four DCT Therapeutic Environmental Styles**

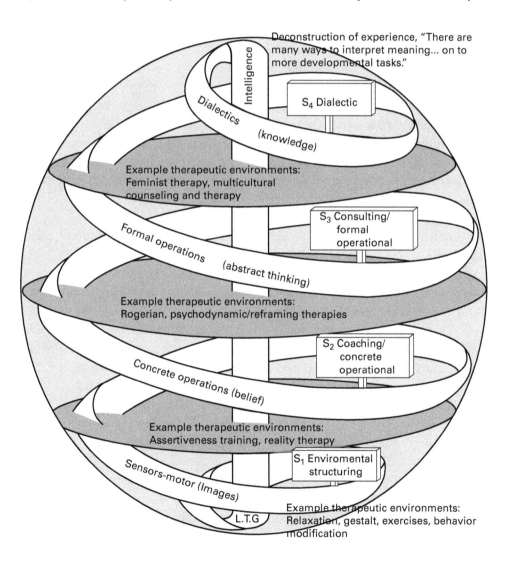

Four basic types of counseling style are identified by DCT and summarized in Figure 6.4. There you will see an integrated spherical model in which client cognitive/emotional-developmental orientations are represented by the spiral. The possible counselor environments are found on four planes, or orientations, with examples of therapeutic interventions. Example interventions from the four environments are also presented in the fourth column of Table 6.1.

Using your imagination, please visualize the sphere as placed at an angle to remind yourself that there is no true hierarchy within the DCT model. Each of us needs balanced learning and development at all four orientations. The list of therapeutic environments is only partial, as there are many other routes toward development. In addition, many techniques and theories are indeed multilevel and multi-orientation. Life is simultaneously a journey, a destination, and a state of being.

The first task is to assess client developmental level and match interventions to the cognitions of the client. *Horizontal development* occurs when we help a client explore further issues at the entering cognitive/emotional-developmental orientation. An African American female, for example, may enter counseling with an Afrocentric therapist at a Level 2 consciousness (concrete resistance and anger). The first task is to help that client expand awareness and competence within that orientation and Cheek's (1976) culturally aware cognitive-behavioral approach (Chapter 8) may be especially appropriate. A reflective/formal operational European American male may enter counseling with doubts about the self and might profit from horizontal development with a client-centered or psychodynamic frame of reference.

*Vertical development*, within the DCT spherical frame, can be either up or down. As all dimensions of consciousness are considered important for holistic development, higher is not better. Both the African American female and European American male client might benefit from imaging, relaxation training, and other sensorimotor techniques at the sensorimotor level. For the African American, the techniques might be useful to help her come in better touch with her hurt feelings around racism. The European American male client might benefit from the same sensorimotor imaging to help him understand the roots of his self-doubt. In turn, both might benefit from further horizontal development inside the sensorimotor orientation on personal and cultural issues. Both might benefit from these exercises in terms of emotional stress.

In short, DCT recommends both horizontal and vertical development on as many cognitive-developmental and emotional issues as feasible for each client. Higher is not better, but DCT argues that helping clients discuss their issues at multiple levels may indeed be more effective. In early research on how developmental issues impact client mental health, Heesacker, Pritchard, Rigazio-DiGilio, and Ivey (1995) found fewer physical and emotional symptoms in individuals who were able to function within multiple orientations, whereas mono-orientation people were more at risk for illness.

# Development Counseling and Therapy in Applied Practice

As a meta-theoretical approach, DCT draws from all the theories and strategies presented in this book. With Multicultural Counseling and Therapy, DCT would argue for an integrated theory and practice of expanding consciousness. Thus acting on that expanded awareness is a major goal of all counseling and therapy—understanding is not enough to produce behavioral, cognitive, and emotional change.

DCT also has generated some additional constructions and techniques of its own that appear to be useful as part of the process of therapy and counseling. We will focus on two dimensions here—developmental questioning strategies and DCT as a way to integrate counseling and therapy treatment plans.

## DCT Questioning Strategies

We all like others to listen to us. When you accommodate to a client through the use of listening skills, not only are you better able to understand their perspective on things, you have given them a rare gift. Through the simple act of listening, clients can see and understand themselves more clearly. If you listen well to a client, that may be enough to promote change.

At the same time, you as counselor or therapist have an immense amount of power. You have seen that research shows that clients tend to take on the language and perhaps even the way of thinking of their therapist. We all selectively attend to what our clients and others say—they are saying so much we can't listen to everything. Some of us focus only on negative things that clients talk about, while others of us focus on the positive. A Rogerian counselor will tend to focus on individual issues, a family therapist on family concerns, and a feminist therapist on issues related to women's role in society. Each therapist, with the best of intentions, inevitably leads the client to certain emphases.

*Not only will clients talk about what you listen to—they will also tend to talk and act at the cognitive-developmental level at which you listen, ask questions, and conduct your interventions.* It is not enough to discover that you have a concrete client. This person is most likely telling you stories with many details. Your interviewing task is dual. First, you need to encourage horizontal development by asking concrete questions and conducting interventions (for example, concrete decision making, assertiveness training). Later, you can mismatch and encourage vertical development at the sensorimotor levels (imaging, body work), reflective/formal operation levels (self-examination of repeating patterns), and dialectic/systemic issues (how the issue may be affected by multicultural, family, or systemic issues).

# Using Specific Questions to Help Clients Talk about Issues at Multiple Levels

Your style of selective listening and focusing, plus the questions you ask, impact how the client presents his or her issues. If a female client talks about difficulties on the job, and you listen and ask questions at the concrete level, the client will give you specific information. If you focus on formal thoughts, the client may examine patterns in the self or situation. Moreover, if you focus on the possible issues of job discrimination or other gender issues, the client may talk to you at the dialectic/systemic level.

DCT has found that using specific questions can help clients explore their issues at each cognitive/emotional orientation in more depth. Practice Exercise 6.1 contains an abbreviated summary of example questions. Experienced practitioners will note that the questions are, for the most part, familiar. DCT has noted that many counselors and therapists of differing theoretical persuasions often use these questions as a natural way to structure their interview. DCT points out that consciousness of the developmental questions can facilitate understanding of naturally occurring events in the session and provide a theoretically useful way to integrate different voices in the therapeutic and counseling process.

---

**PRACTICE EXERCISE 6.1. Developmental Strategies Questioning Sequence (Abbreviated)[5]**

A useful practice exercise is to take a volunteer "client" through the four cognitive/emotional developmental orientations. Begin your exercise by informing your client what you are planning to do, and share the following list of questions with her or him. Once you and your client have selected a topic for discussion, ask the first question and assess the client's cognitive/emotional developmental orientation (or multiple levels) on this specific issue.

Then, work through each of the phases of the DCT questioning sequence slowly, giving your client time to experience each orientation fully. Use particular care at the sensorimotor level to respect your client's privacy.

*Identifying cognitive/emotional developmental orientation*

What occurs for you when you focus on your family ... your difficulty at work ... your divorce ... the harassment on the job?

Obtain a story of about 50 to 100 words. Assess overall functioning of client on varying cognitive-developmental levels.

*(Continued)*

---

5  A more comprehensive eight-level Standard Cognitive-Developmental System is available (Ivey, Rigazio-DiGilio, & Ivey, 1990) and also a research-oriented classification system (Ivey & Rigazio-DiGilio, 1990).

**PRACTICE EXERCISE 6.1. Developmental Strategies Questioning Sequence (Abbreviated)** *(Continued)*

### *Sensorimotor*

Get a single image in your mind involving your family ... difficulty at work ... your divorce ... the harassment.

What are you seeing? Hearing? Feeling? It will be helpful to locate the feeling in the body in a specific place.

### *Concrete*

Could you give me a specific example of the situation/issue/concern?

Describe what happened. Following from applied behavioral analysis, it may be useful to draw out the linear sequence of events through "What happened first, what happened next, and what was the result?" Can you describe/name your feelings in the situation? "You seem to feel ... because ..."

### *Reflective/formal*

Does this happen in other situations? (or) Is this a pattern for you? Do you feel that way in other situations? Have you felt that way before? How do you think about that? As you think back on your feelings in this situation, what do you notice?

### *Dialectic/systemic*

How do you put together/organize all we've been talking about? How might your thoughts and feelings about the concern have taken form in your family of origin? How do you see gender stereotyping ... multicultural issues ... influencing your thoughts and feelings about the concern? How could we describe this from the point of view of some other person or using another framework?

With a sensitive topic, many clients are moved easily to tears by the simple and direct here-and-now orientation of sensorimotor questions. Both of you may be surprised at the strength and easy accessibility of these deeper emotions. If your client is fragile or "on edge," you may want to use safer concrete and formal questioning procedures. Ethics, professional standards, and quality supervision are even more important when working within the sensorimotor orientation.

DCT recommends that you share the purpose of your questions with your client and let them know ahead of time what may happen. If you have shared what will happen with your client in a co-constructive fashion, the surprise will be less, and you can make a joint decision as to where to move next. Your own comfort level with emotion will be important as to how the client copes with the situation. Rather than staying with the immediacy of the emotion, you can say in an empathic fashion, "Tell me what happened when you were feeling that" (concrete) or "Is that way of feeling a pattern for you?" (reflective/formal).

You will find that if you take a client through the standard questions of Practice Exercise 6.1, you and the client will gain new perspectives on the issue. Things seem very different when viewed from sensorimotor, concrete, formal, and dialectic/systemic perspectives. You will find that integrating questions about the family of origin with the standard series is particularly valuable. Table 6.2 offers research supporting the levels described in DCT.

The DCT questioning sequence can be varied, and it is not necessary to follow the standard sequence. Building on the points made clear by Cheek (1976) many years ago, it may be more useful with African American clients to focus first on the dialectic/systemic orientation and follow that later with more individually oriented questions and interventions. Multicultural Therapy and Counseling (Chapter 5) might go so far as to turn the question sequences of DCT "upside down," with a far greater emphasis on cultural and systemic issues. The idea of starting an interview with how individuals are affected by the systems and relationships in their lives is very different from client-centered, cognitive-behavioral, or psychodynamic orientations.

Finally, knowledge of assessment and specific questions from DCT will likely be helpful to you as you work in other theoretical orientations. Therapists of many orientations appear to follow these sequences in their work, although they do not describe what they do from this orientation. For example, the cognitive-behaviorist Aaron Beck (Chapter 9) often asks clients to picture images from earlier in life (sensorimotor). Clients are then encouraged to describe happenings at that time (concrete), and ultimately observe patterns in later life derived from these images. Finally, Beck asks clients to step back from this sequence and reflect on the systems of operations. Through this process, the client obtains a new integration that can lead to new thoughts and behaviors. Beck, however, tends not to discuss multicultural issues as an inherent part of his systematic procedures. Rogers and Perls have been observed to follow similar sequences in their work, but they also maintain an individual focus, much like Beck (Ivey, 1986, pp. 112–116).

**Table 6.2. Research Box: Defining Cognitive-Developmental Level**

Do the constructions of DCT really exist? Can they be identified and measured reliably? Does the claim that multiplicity is a healthy form of being hold validity?

All of these questions were answered in the affirmative in work with in-patient depressed clients (Rigazio-DiGilio & Ivey, 1990). Raters were able to classify patient cognitive-developmental orientations with high reliability (.98, kappa = .87). When answering standard questions from the DCT model, both short- and long-term clients responded consistently with the theory (99 percent). Follow up studies revealed cognitive and behavioral changes after the brief treatment. Mailler (1991) found that instruction in the DCT model was useful with students preparing for the workplace. He used variations of the systematic questioning model to conceptualize a program for burnout prevention, personal growth, and organizational change.

*(Continued)*

**Table 6.2. Research Box: Defining Cognitive-Developmental Level *(Continued)***

Heesacker, Pritchard, Rigazio-DiGilio, and Ivey (1995) conducted a major factor analytic study of DCT constructs with 1700 subjects. The factor structure for the four orientations was again validated. An even more important part of the study found that people who were able to function at multiple levels of understanding had fewer psychological *and physical* troubles than those with single orientations. In effect, an individual capable of functioning with sensorimotor, concrete, and formal styles showed more positive indications of mental and physical health than a person who functioned solely or primarily with a single style.

The following exercise provides a sample of how raters were trained in DCT classification. Use this as an opportunity to test your own ability to rate client statements.

Define the *predominant* cognitive-developmental orientation of the depressed client in each of the following four statements. Expect to find dimensions of other levels, but does the client talk in a *primarily* sensorimotor, concrete, reflective/formal, or dialectic/systemic fashion? The depressed inpatient is talking about the death of his sister. The information is randomized from varying parts of the interview.[6]

1. I'm reacting this time very similarly as I did to my sister's death. I guess everyone saw her as ill but me. I didn't see anything wrong. And when she died, I was completely shocked. I fell apart, just like I'm falling apart now. Everyone else had to take care of things.

2. I feel paralyzed … petrified. I feel like my legs are stiff and still … great weights keeping me stuck … I feel empty … dead inside.

3. What I learned when I was growing up has not prepared me for dealing with loss. My parents did everything to protect me and my sister. … We were never taught to look for problems and try to fix them, or that natural things would occur, and we would have to adjust. This talk is making it clear that I don't know what to do, so I completely pull into myself and become paralyzed.

4. She came home from work and rather than having dinner on the table, she was sitting at the table looking distraught … upset. She said, "We have to talk," and I thought maybe someone died. Then she told me she wanted to leave … she was unhappy for five years. I collapsed. I didn't see it coming. I didn't know what to do. That's why I'm here … she brought me to the hospital, cause I didn't know what to do.

(Rigazio-DiGilio & Ivey, 1990, p. 474)

# Developing an Integrated Assessment and Treatment Plan: Focus on the Many Voices of Depression

Major Depressive Disorder (MDD) is one of the most prevalent mental disorders, characterized by significant role impairment, suicide risk, economic burden, and the largest number of years lived with disability in the United States (Singh & Gottlib, 2014). Whether you are working with children, adolescents, or adults, an understanding of

---

6    Statement 1 is formal, and you may note that the client is reflecting on himself and contrasted his reactions with others (a concrete client would have real difficulty with that cognitive task).

Statement 2 is considered predominantly sensorimotor, although there are concrete elements in which the patient at times names emotions ("I feel paralyzed") as contrasted to experiencing them at a fuller sensorimotor level ("great weights keeping me stuck," "dead inside").

Statement 3 is dialectic/systemic.

Statement 4 is a fairly straightforward example of concrete description.

how to work with depression is essential. Not only is depression a serious clinical disorder, in a more moderate form it is a continuing concern with many clients struggling to function from day to day. If you break through the defenses of an antisocial or borderline personality style, you will usually find severe depression. Depression is often masked in children who act out aggressively or may have been diagnosed with attention deficit disorder. In short, understanding how to diagnose and work with depression is a vital task for any counselor or therapist.

It is not the role of this text to provide an extensive discussion on theories of depression. For examining the depressive process itself, A.T. Beck and E.A.P. Haigh (2014), J. Beck (2012), Ellis (1982), and Seligman (1975, 2011) provide useful clinical insights focusing on cognitive processes. Brown and Harris (1978) and Lewinsohn et al. (2005) provide useful descriptions of environmental factors related to depression. Thapar, Collishaw, Pine, and Thapar (2012) provide an important description of developmental factors related to adolescent depression.

This section will focus on conceptualizing a treatment plan for depression involving dimensions of DCT assessment. DCT suggests that there are multiple narratives or stories in depression or any other client concern. The task of therapy and counseling is to discover, sort out, and work with the multiple voices underlying depression and other client issues. DCT shows how a variety of counseling and therapeutic strategies discussed in this book can be arranged to work with both children and adults in a comprehensive treatment plan.

Nine characteristics of depression as listed in *DSM-5* (APA, 2013) are summarized briefly below. Five or more of the following at a significant level (severe and usually daily) would be required for a clear diagnosis of a major depressive episode. Less severe depression and mood disorders follow the same general framework, but with less intensity. Furthermore, you will find many clients demonstrating one or more of the symptoms of depression while manifesting other clinical characteristics.

1. Depressed mood
2. Diminished interest and pleasure in daily activities
3. Significant weight loss or gain
4. Insomnia or constant sleeping
5. Psychomotor agitation or retardation
6. Fatigue or loss of energy
7. Feelings of worthlessness or excessive guilt
8. Diminished ability to think or concentrate
9. Suicidal ideation.

In this chapter, we talk about depression as a general issue. Those clients who are more severely depressed are those most likely to require inpatient treatment and medication. Milder depression will be an aspect of many, perhaps even most, of the clients you work with—child or adult. Those with more serious depression will often require more extensive treatment plans, but the inclusive framework of DCT can provide a useful way to think about all types. Later, we will explore how this specific example can be expanded to conceptualize a wide variety of treatment issues.

## DCT's Multiple Orientation to Assessment and Treatment

DCT's four levels provide a systematic framework for organizing treatment strategies for depression. Clients present their depression to therapists and counselors at varying cognitive/emotional levels. Associated with each of the levels or orientations are a variety of voices, narratives, or stories. Research found in Table 6.2 points out that some clients will present their depression tearfully within the sensorimotor orientation, while others will discuss concrete stories of their issues. Still others will be more distant from their emotions and talk about their depression in a reflective/formal operational manner. Very few clients will talk about their depression with awareness of dialectic/system, "self-in-system" issues.

Table 6.2 contains rephrased and summarized comments of actual depressed clients. These examples are portions of stories clients told about themselves as they discussed their depression. In this group of hospitalized depressed patients, 15 percent were identified as predominantly sensorimotor in orientation, 55 percent as concrete, and only 30 percent as predominantly reflective/formal operational (Rigazio-DiGilio & Ivey, 1990). The word *predominantly* is particularly important to notice. Few people and clients solely operate within a single frame. Expect people to talk about one concern within one orientation, then shift level and talk about another issue from a different frame. And most clients will be able to talk about their issues at multiple levels. Again, we should recall research that indicated that those who functioned in a balanced manner at multiple levels showed fewer psychological and physical symptoms than mono-orientation people (Heesacker et al., 1995).

DCT suggests that the first issue is to join the client's language system where she or he "is." This means that individual, family, and cultural empathy is basic and that effective listening skills are needed to learn the client's way of voicing his or her story. It also means that it is highly useful to assess client cognitive/emotion orientation. If the client is voicing issues predominantly within the sensorimotor or concrete orientation, it does little good to attempt analysis at the reflective/formal operation level. Similarly, if the client is highly analytic and abstract, he or she is predominantly reflective/formal. In the early stages, the reflective client may resist or be unable to reframe and discuss the depression with specific examples (concrete) and may be unable to reach deeper sensorimotor dimensions of emotion.

Thus, the first task is to assess the cognitive/emotional level that a client is presenting, and then match your language and early interventions to their way of being. DCT has termed this horizontal development. As the client or patient's story is told, the specific questions of the DCT questioning sequence can be used to mismatch orientation and help the client tell the same story at a different level. For example, a distressed child, adolescent, or adult may be very depressed and sad over the loss of a friend. The first task is usually to join the client within the sensorimotor orientation and allow them to work through the emotion. If the emotion is indeed worked through, then it is time to move to concrete examples and linear stories and later to abstract reflection on the stories. Note that the same story of loss is told emotionally through tears at the sensorimotor level, then it is told again in terms of concrete details, stories, and examples, and, finally retold as the client reflects on patterns of loss and its meaning.

Children and many adolescents and adults will have difficulty in formal reflection unless you adapt your questions and interventions carefully, building on their predominantly concrete skills. Similarly, abstract types, such as professionals and graduate students (even in counseling and therapy master's and doctoral programs) may have difficulty in providing concrete examples and resist the catharsis and direct experiencing associated with the sensorimotor level. Most theories of counseling are predominantly formal and highly abstract with relatively limited attention to the concrete specifics of interview action. Even less attention is given to sensorimotor issues where emotions are experienced most fully. Piagetian scholars estimate that less than half of the populations reach full formal operations.

The discussion thus far has not involved the dialectic/systemic orientation where clients examine themselves in family, group, community, and cultural context. An example of a depressed patient's comment repeated from Table 6.2 follows:

> What I learned when I was growing up has not prepared me for dealing with loss. My parents did everything to protect me and my sister. ... We were never taught to look for problems and try to fix them, or that natural things would occur, and we would have to adjust. This talk is making it clear that I don't know what to do, so I completely pull into myself and become paralyzed.
>
> (Rigazio-DiGilio & Ivey, 1990, p. 474)

Often, depressed patients have internalized anger and loss and blame themselves. DCT would like to broaden work with depression to include social history, family, community, and multicultural issues. Therapy frequently works on the depression by blocking/changing it with medication (sensorimotor). Concrete therapies may include listening to the client's story, thought-stopping, or assertiveness training. Reflective/formal action could include analysis of cognitive patterns or client-centered work on self-esteem. DCT would see all of the above as potentially beneficial, but would also like to see attention given to the dialectic/systemic level where the focus turns to self-in-relation and to self-in-context.

The patient in the above paragraph had already voiced her emotions within the sensorimotor level; she had told concrete stories of depression; and she had reflected on these stories through formal analysis. At the dialectic/systemic level, the client is asked to tell the story again, but this time giving attention to issues such as intergenerational family history, gender, community, and multicultural issues. In the example above, the family of origin had overly protected the child from loss while simultaneously denying serious alcohol abuse. This second child in a family of three had taken the role of the quiet, withdrawn child, which was then extended to marriage and later life. In addition, the case illustrated issues of gender, as males were preferred in her family and ethnic group. The client had very much adapted the North American pattern of cultural individualism and took on more responsibility for her behavior than would be appropriate in other, more relationally oriented cultures.[7]

In summary, DCT states that clients need to talk about their issues at multiple levels. It is helpful to examine our stories from more than one perspective. The field of counseling and therapy is gradually moving away from the "single best" theory and strategy as we move toward a postmodern view of self and psychology. Nonetheless, there is still considerable thought given to finding the "magic" solution, particularly if that magic can be found in a pile. There is argument in the literature on incest survivors on what is the most appropriate treatment. In reviewing this literature, Beaver (1994) found evidence that different findings on therapy effectiveness could be explained by the need to help survivors work through their issues at multiple levels. Different therapeutic methods seem to focus on different orientations.

## Integrating Alternative Theories and Strategies in Treatment Planning

Treatment planning within DCT follows closely the model presented with the developmental sphere (Figure 6.4). That is, specific strategies of counseling and therapy are *predominantly* associated with the varying orientations of the sphere. Medication and massage, for example, are sensorimotor strategies associated with the body. Assertiveness training is a concrete example, while engaging in dream analysis is typically a reflective/formal strategy. The community and family genograms are designed to help clients see self-in-system and thus are representative of the dialectic/systemic orientation. Each of these methods helps clients give voice to their multiple selves and the underlying complexity of any story of narrative.

While one single intervention, such as medication, may provide an important, even vital lever, for therapy with depression, DCT theory suggests that it is important to consider other avenues of treatment as well to prevent recurrence. We should note, however, that effective use of medication will enable clients to tell their concrete stories

---

7   This case illustrates rather clearly that North America—Canada and the United States—indeed has a "culture." Expectations within this large context deeply affect the way men and women react to issues and concerns. DCT states that awareness of self as a cultural being is an important part of counseling and therapy.

more clearly and reflect on them more ably. Again, we see that the word *predominantly* is important.

Dream analysis is considered a predominantly reflective/formal method. However, effective dream analysis requires clients to tell the story of the dream in considerable concrete detail. In the process of the narrative, the client may be moved to tears as they express themselves at the bodily sensorimotor level. If a multicultural therapist used dream analysis with a client, we would expect the dream to consider family, gender, and ethnic/racial issues and images as they might be related in the dream. Furthermore, we can conduct a postmodern analysis of the dream and find an infinite array of meanings and voices.

DCT has organized many of counseling and therapy's strategies into categories that are *predominantly* sensorimotor, concrete, reflective/formal, and dialectic/systemic. DCT terms this categorization the "Epistemology of Counseling and Therapy." For treatment of depression, DCT theory argues that each area needs to be considered as a treatment alternative and that most effective treatment will ensure that clients consider their issues at multiple levels with multiple voices.

Predominantly Sensorimotor Strategies

> Body work
>> Acupuncture
>>
>> Acupressure
>>
>> Massage
>>
>> Yoga
>
> Emotional catharsis
>
> Gestalt hot seat
>
> Imagery
>
> Medication
>
> Meditation
>
> Relaxation training

Predominantly Concrete Strategies

> Automatic thoughts chart (A.T. Beck)
>
> Assertiveness training
>
> Concrete telling of stories and narratives
>
> Crisis intervention

Decisional counseling

Desensitization therapy

Positive asset search for strengths

Rational emotive analysis of a single event

Solution-oriented therapy

Thought stopping

## Predominantly Reflective/Formal Strategies

Client-centered therapy

Cognitive therapy

Dream analysis

Logotherapy treatment of hyper-reflection

Pattern analysis of stories, narratives, or other concrete strategy

Psychodynamic therapies

Malaysian dream analysis

Rational emotive therapy

## Predominantly Dialectic/Systemic

Analysis of projective identification

Analysis of transference

Community genogram

Family genogram

Family dream analysis

Introspective Developmental Counseling

Trauma treatment

## Theories and Strategies That Attempt to Work with Multiple Levels

Cognitive-Behavioral Therapy (Predominantly concrete and reflective/formal)

Developmental Counseling and Therapy

Family therapy

Feminist therapy

Multicultural Counseling and Therapy

Self-help groups (AA, ACOA, bulimia groups, Weight Watchers, etc.)

Stress management

Developmental Counseling and Therapy believes that the most complete resolution of client issues will occur when at least some time is spent working with the client within each developmental orientation. While no form of cognitive/emotional expression is considered "best," the multiple perspectives provided by working through issues at multiple levels is recommended.

However, the issue of cost benefit analysis needs to be considered. DCT theory holds that a change in any part of the whole will result in change throughout. Thus, a mildly depressed client with constantly repeating negative self-statements might profit immensely from the cognitive-behavioral strategy called thought-stopping (Chapter 9) and require no other treatment. Another depressed client might obtain sufficient support from mild medication for a short time or participation in a weekend psychoeducational group on stress management. A full menu of treatment within all developmental levels may not be necessary.

However, most seriously depressed clients will benefit from a more broadly-based treatment plan. Epidemiological studies have demonstrated that childhood abuse is associated with psychiatric disorders in adulthood, such as mood, anxiety, and substance abuse disorders (Norman, Byambaa, Butchart, Scott, & Vos, 2012). Such clients can benefit from early medication that is soon reduced so that underlying issues can be addressed. DCT's typical treatment plans would include an expanded version of the DCT assessment interview (see Practice Exercise 6.1). Here, special attention would be given to the client's development in the family, community, and culture, with special attention to specific images and stories in relation to family—"Could you tell me what occurs for you when you focus on your family?" The family and community genograms would be included to help provide awareness that the depressed individual is a self-in-relation. Special attention would be given to finding positive images of strength in both the family and community, even though both may have contributed heavily to the present depression. DCT has found that clients, even those seriously depressed, who start from a base of strength are more able to focus in and work with difficult issues.

Drawing from the DCT assessment interview, the DCT therapist would co-construct a treatment plan with the depressed client, and this would ideally include therapies chosen from each developmental orientation. Body work (yoga, meditation, relaxation, nutrition, jogging) would be considered fundamental, but the specific choice would be that of the client. If the client had indication of abuse in the family of origin, support groups in the community would be recommended and considerable attention would be paid to dialectic/systemic issues of self-in-relation and community. Cognitive-behavioral therapy (CBT) techniques at the concrete and reflective/formal level would be utilized for working with immediate issues, as research to their effectiveness is clear. However, CBT strategies tend to give relatively less emphasis to the sensorimotor and dialectic/systemic orientations, and thus DCT would emphasize these issues more strongly, particularly with an emphasis on imagery at the sensorimotor level to bring out emotional issues more fully.

The focus thus far has been on conceptualizing a treatment plan for depression, but how does this relate to treatment planning in general?

## Developing a Generalized Plan for Treatment

As you might expect, DCT suggests that assessing client cognitive/emotional orientation and matching skills and strategies to client needs and style is basic to all treatment planning. If you are doing vocational counseling and focusing on a concrete plan for action, the client can also benefit from reflective analysis of her or his own behavior via formal/reflection of patterns in past work experience and client-centered techniques. The vocational client must also look at self-in-system and the nature of the broad job market.

You may be working with a client distressed over an impending divorce; the client presents at the formal operational level and talks in a very analytic fashion. There is need to join the client at this level via cognitive therapy, client-centered techniques, or logotherapy's work on meaning or hyper-reflection. The client may be avoiding emotion. In such cases, drawing out concrete examples of the client's narrative may be helpful and then asking the client to generate single images of difficult or traumatic situations in the marriage. In this way, you may help the client experience emotion that has heretofore been denied. Again, referral to a support group of people recently working through divorce may be highly useful. Multicultural issues of gender, spirituality, and socioeconomic status may need to be considered at the dialectic/systemic level.

## Process/Outcome Research: A Case Example

Fukuhara (1984) employed DCT assessment and treatment in a successful seven-interview series of sessions with a young female university student in Japan. The case is interesting, as it suggests that emotional/cognitive development may be a universal phenomenon, but that it may play itself out differently among men and women and those of varying cultures.

### Client Assessment and Therapeutic Approach

The young woman client in this case was age eighteen at the time of counseling and was self-referred. Early in the first interview (as translated from the Japanese), she introduced her issue as follows:

> This spring, I met this boy … and thought our love would last a long time. However, when I returned from summer vacation, he did not even seem to want to talk to me. This finally made me so angry that

> I became aggressive and we had a fight. Surprisingly, my boyfriend seemed to like being told off. Still, he doesn't ask me out and the only time I see him is at the activity club. … I project into the future and think that if I continue to love him, we would eventually get married. What would my life be then? Would I have to make sacrifices to his will? … Would this eventually destroy my love for him? Should I give up on him now? (p. 1)

The issue this young woman faced seemed to be one of intimacy, but this issue manifests itself differently in Japanese culture—that is, the level of involvement would not typically appear among North American clients. In terms of DCT cognitive-emotional assessment, there is a good deal of sensorimotor emotion, while the client's words are concrete and descriptive.

## Client Cognitive-Emotional Movement through Interventions

The concrete/sensorimotor description of the issue required Fukuhara to use listening skills in a concrete fashion. The client needed to tell her stories, especially her emotional story, in great detail. Fukuhara utilized the skill of reflection of feeling almost exclusively in the first session. The reflections were focused on naming and clarifying specific feelings, and problem solving was avoided. The reflections were concrete ("You felt angry when your friend didn't call you," "We are sad when that happens"). Patterns of emotions associated with formal operations were not explored until later in the interview series ("We seem to feel anger about many situations").

In the first interview, the client's perception of the relationship with her boyfriend was "He is mine; I am his," despite the realities of a relationship that had clearly ended. The client's cognition was "stuck" or immobilized by an unrealistic sensorimotor perception that influenced much of her thinking and behavior and interfered with performance in other areas as well.

The first three sessions focused on person-centered listening, during which the client moved toward a conceptual frame that allowed for more distinctions between herself and her former boyfriend. For example, in session 3, the client was able to express "He should be different from me, but I cannot admit it." The interview plan at this point called for Fukuhara to enter the client's frame as fully as possible. This close relationship between therapist and client allowed the young woman to start the process of truly separating from her "loved one."

From the beginning of the interview series to the conclusion, the client gradually moved from an overly attached, embedded relational orientation to one in where she was appropriately separated and independent. Three external counselors observed the interview series and rated the client's reality testing—that is, how realistic was the client's frame of reference toward the world. The client became more realistic as therapy progressed.

By interview session 4, the client was able to engage in more formal thought and developed a stronger sense of self-in-relation. Fukuhara then returned to the sensorimotor level for more in-depth experiencing of emotion, using Gestalt techniques to "activate" client feeling, thinking and action. Sessions 4 and 5 used some of the concepts of Ellis's rational disputation.

The client at interview 6 was able to separate herself fully: "I am myself; he is himself." The final session focused around plans for the future: "I have to do something for my own good." In these final interviews, the client was able to step back and look at herself in a system of operations. She was able to reflect on herself and her patterns both as a person and as a woman in Japanese society.

## Case Summary

Fukuhara's case is particularly interesting, as it illustrates the cognitive growth and development that can occur in a client in the brief course of counseling and therapy. The client's language at both surface and deep structure levels has clearly changed.

This case illustrates the cross-cultural similarity of a basic male-female issue of love and relationship, separation and attachment. Nonetheless, in different cultures, the script of the interview and the degree of attachment or separation may play out differently. Fukuhara comments that despite cultural differences, "much of counseling theory is basically applicable to individuals whatever their issues or background" (p. 6).

# Theory into Practice

Practice Exercise 6.2 asks you to generate a list of your own present competencies within each of the developmental orientations. What theories, strategies, and skills do you presently have for work at each developmental level? Consider these as you might develop your own list of competencies for working with clients who present with depression and other concerns.

---

**PRACTICE EXERCISE 6.2. Identifying Your Own Personal Style, Present Competencies, and Goals**

None of us can be fully versed in all helping strategies, techniques, and theories. This exercise asks you to examine yourself and your own personal style, your present competencies within each DCT cognitive/emotional orientation, and your goals for developing new expertise in the future.

1. *What is/are your preferred cognitive/emotion orientation(s)?* You have had an introduction to the importance of sensorimotor experience as a foundation, the usefulness of concrete storytelling, the value of a reflective/formal

*(Continued)*

---

**PRACTICE EXERCISE 6.2. Identifying Your Own Personal Style, Present Competencies, and Goals (Continued)**

consciousness, and the significance of balancing all these orientations with self-in-relation and self-in-system, the dialectic/systemic orientation.[8]

Reflect back on your life experience and identify meaningful events or situations that relate to each of the cognitive/emotional orientations. Can you identify a general preferred style? How able are you to operate within each orientation? Are there some levels that are less comfortable for you?

2. *What is your present knowledge and skills in the strategies, techniques, and theories presented on page 26?* In addition, be sure to register other areas of personal expertise not represented in that list. List your areas of at least some competence and classify them for your level of expertise. Rank yourself on a five-point scale (1 as high, 5 as low).

Do your areas of expertise match your own preferred cognitive/emotional style? Most counseling, psychology, and social work students appear to be most comfortable within the reflective/formal orientation and often find themselves impatient with the examples and repetition of stories often associated with clients of a predominantly concrete orientation. How effective will you be with clients who are different from you?

3. *What are your goals for the future in terms of developing further expertise?* Again, review the list on page 26. What areas do you see yourself as needing further development as you work through this text and as you plan your professional career?

---

The DCT framework brings a special challenge to the therapist or counselor, as it demands expertise in multiple theories and interventions. Very few of us can be equally expert in all modes of helping. A partial answer to this issue is that working with a team of intervention specialists may be often more effective than you attempting to do all the work yourself. DCT also stresses the use of support groups in the community, such as AA, cancer support groups, Wounded Warriors, and Parents Without Partners. Only the rare counselor or therapist can be equally effective individual, family, and community intervention specialists.

The DCT framework is one of the newest of the theories described in this book. While early clinical and research findings have been promising, clearly much study and experience will be needed to verify the framework more fully. Fortunately, DCT

---

8   Self-assessment instruments are available for this exercise and are included in the Instructor's Manual.

was designed as an open system and, as such, is constantly subject to change and modification over time. Furthermore, DCT is only one integrated approach to counseling and therapy. Lazarus's multimodal therapy (1976; 1981; 1986) and Assagioli's (1976; 2010) psychosynthesis are other important metatheoretical models.

DCT does not reject any form of therapy. Rather, it seeks to find what is best in each therapy, and more than that, how each therapy might be beneficial to some individual client or family. The community and multicultural orientation is vital to effective practice of Developmental Counseling and Therapy.

DCT also offers a theoretical framework for integrating seemingly diverse approaches to the field. The development roots in Piagetian thinking led to a focus on client cognition and emotion. This, in turn, is an attempt to move away from imposing an external frame of reference on the client and to move to a more egalitarian co-constructive relationship. As mentioned before, DCT hopes that the counselor and therapist will work "with the client" rather than "on the client."

# References

American Psychiatric Association. (2013). *Diagnostic and statistical manual of mental disorders* (5th ed.). Washington, DC: Author.

Assagioli, R. (1976). *Psychosynthesis*. New York, NY: Penguin.

Assagioli, R., & Firman, D.T. (2010). *The act of will*. Amherst, MA: Synthesis Center Incorporated.

Beaver, A. (1994). A review of the research literature on incest survivors. Unpublished comprehensive paper, University of Massachusetts, Amherst, School and Counseling Psychology Program.

Beck, A.T. (1967). *Depression: Clinical, experimental and theoretical aspects*. New York, NY: Harper & Row.

Beck, A.T., & Haigh, E.A.P. (2014). Advances in cognitive theory and therapy: The generic cognitive model. *Annual Review of Clinical Psychology, 10*, 1–24. doi.org/10.1146/annurev-clinpsy-032813-153734.

Beck, J.S. (2011). *Cognitive behavior therapy*. New York, NY: Guilford.

Brentano, F. (1984). *Psychologie vom empirischen Standpunkt*. Vienna, Austria (3rd ed. Leipzig, Germany, 1925). Cited in R. Chisholm, "Intentionality." In P. Edward (Ed.), *The encyclopedia of philosophy*. New York, NY: Macmillan, 4, 201–204.

Brown, G., & Harris, T. (1978). *Social origins of depression*. London, UK: Tavistock.

Chatwal. J., & Lane, R. (2016). A cognitive-developmental model of emotional awareness and its application to the practice of psychotherapy. *Psychodynamic Psychiatry, 44*, 305–26.

Cheek, D. (1976). *Assertive Black … puzzled White*. San Luis Obispo, CA: Impact.

Chung, R.C.Y., & Bemak, F. (2012). *Social justice counseling: The next steps beyond multiculturalism*. Thousand Oaks, CA: Sage Publications.

Ellis, A. (1982). *Reason and emotion in psychotherapy*. New York, NY: Lyle Stuart.

Erikson, E. H. (Ed.) (1963). *Youth: Change and challenge*. New York, NY: Basic books.

Fry, P., Knopf, G., & Coe, K. (1980). Effects of counselor and client racial similarity on the counselor's response patterns and skills. *Journal of Counseling Psychology, 27*, 130–137.

Fukuhara, M. (1984). *Is love universal?—From the viewpoint of counseling adolescents.* Paper presented at the forty-second annual conference of the International Association of Psychologists, Mexico City.

Geiger, P. (2018). *Intentional intervention in counseling and therapy.* New York, NY: Routledge.

Gilligan, C. (1982). *In a different voice.* Cambridge, MA: Harvard University.

Haley, J. (1980). *Leaving home: The therapy of disturbed young people.* New York, NY: McGraw-Hill.

Heidegger, M. (1926). *Being and time.* New York: Harper and Row.

Heesacker, M., Pritchard, S., Rigazio-DiGilio, S., & Ivey, A. (1995). *Development of a paper-and-pencil measure of cognitive-developmental level.* Unpublished paper, University of Florida, Gainesville, Department of Psychology.

Ivey, A. (1986/2000). *Developmental therapy: Theory into practice.* San Francisco, CA: Jossey-Bass.

Ivey, A. (1991). *Developmental strategies for helpers: Individual, family and network interventions.* Pacific Grove, CA: Brooks/Cole.

Ivey, A.E., & Rigazio-DiGilio, S.A. (1990). *The standard cognitive-developmental classification system.* In A.E. Ivey, *Developmental strategies for helpers: Individual, family and network interventions* (pp. 301–306). Pacific Grove, CA: Brooks/Cole.

Ivey, A., & Zalaquett, C.P. (2011). Neuroscience and counseling: Central issue for social justice. *Journal for Social Action in Counseling and Psychology, 3,* 103–116.

Ivey, A., Ivey, M.B., & Zalaquett, C.P. (2018). *Intentional interviewing and counseling: Facilitating client development in a multicultural society* (9th ed.). Belmont, CA: Cengage Learning.

Ivey, A.E., Ivey, M.B., Myers, J.E., & Sweeney, T.J. (2005). *Developmental counseling and therapy: Promoting wellness over the lifespan.* New York, NY: Houghton-Mifflin/Lahaska.

Jackson, B. (1975). Black identity development. *Journal of Educational Diversity and Innovation, 2,* 19–25.

Kessler, R.M., Hutson, P.H., Herman, B.K., & Potenza, M.N. (2016). The neurobiological basis of binge-eating disorder. *Neuroscience and Biobehavioral Reviews, 63,* 223–238. doi.org/10.1016/j.neubiorev.2016.01.013.

Lacan, J. (1966/1977). *Écrits: A selection.* New York, NY: Norton.

Lane, R.D. (2008). Neural substrates of implicit and explicit emotional processes: A unifying framework for psychosomatic medicine. *Psychosomatic Medicine, 70,* 213–230.

Lane, R., & Schwartz, G. (1987). Levels of emotional awareness: A cognitive-developmental theory and its application to psychopathology. *American Journal of Psychiatry, 144,* 133–143.

Lazarus, A. (1976). Multimodal assessment. In A. Lazarus (Ed.), *Multimodal behavior therapy.* New York, NY: Springer.

Lazarus, A. (1981). *The practice of multimodal therapy.* New York, NY: McGraw-Hill.

Lazarus, A. (1986). Multimodal therapy. In J. Norcross (Ed.), *Handbook of eclectic psychotherapy* (pp. 65–93). New York, NY: Brunner/Mazel.

Lewinsohn, P.M., Olino, T.M., & Klein, D.N. (2005). Psychosocial impairment in offspring of depressed parents. *Psychological Medicine, 35,* 1493–1503. doi.org/10.1017/S0033291705005350.

Mailler, W. (1991). *Preparing students for the workplace: Personal growth and organizational change.* Presentation at the North Atlantic Regional Association for Counselor Education and Supervision. Albany, New York, October.

McLean, S.A., Paxton, S.J., Massey, R., Hay, P.J., Mond, J.M., & Rodgers, B. (2014). Stigmatizing attitudes and beliefs about bulimia nervosa: Gender, age, education and income variability in a community sample. *International Journal of Eating Disorders, 47,* 353–361. doi:10.1002/eat.22227.

Meara, N., Pepinsky, H., Shannon, J., & Murray, W. (1981). Semantic communication and expectations for counseling across three theoretical orientations. *Journal of Counseling Psychology, 28,* 110–118.

Meara, N., Shannon, J., & Pepinsky, H. (1979). Comparisons of stylistic complexity of the language of counselor and client across three theoretical orientations. *Journal of Counseling Psychology, 26,* 181–189.

Noonan, L. (2010). *It's sensational! The never-ending list of sensations.* Retrieved from http://larisanoonan.com/sensations-list/.

Norman, R.E., Byambaa, M., De, R., Butchart, A., Scott, J., & Vos, T. (2012). The long-term health consequences of child physical abuse, emotional abuse, and neglect: A systematic review and meta-analysis. *PLoS Medicine, 9*(11), e1001349. doi.org/10.1371/journal.pmed.1001349.

Piaget, J. (1926/1963). *The origins of intelligence in children.* New York, NY: Norton.

Piaget, J. (1985). *The equilibration of cognitive structures.* Chicago, IL: University of Chicago.

Praszkier, R. (2016). Empathy, mirror neurons and SYNC. *Mind & Society, 15,* 1–25.

Reas, D.L. (2017). Public and healthcare professionals' knowledge and attitudes toward binge eating disorder: A narrative review. *Nutrients, 9,* 1267.

Rigazio-DiGilio, S.A., & Ivey, A.E. (1990). Developmental therapy and depressive disorders: Measuring cognitive levels through patient natural language. *Professional Psychology: Research & Practice, 21,* 470–475.

Schaumberg, K., Welch, E., Breithaupt, L., Hübel, C., Baker, J.H., Munn-Chernoff, M.A., ... Bulik, C. M. (2017). The science behind the academy for eating disorders' nine truths about eating disorders. *European Eating Disorders Review, 25,* 432–450. doi: 10.1002/erv.2553.

Seligman, M. (1975). *Helplessness.* San Francisco, CA: Freeman.

Seligman, M. (2011). *Flourish. A visionary new understanding of happiness and well-being.* New York, NY: Free Press.

Shostrum, E. (1966, producer). *Three Approaches to Psychotherapy.* Santa Ana, CA: Psychological Films. (Film).

Singh, M.K., & Gotlib, I.H. (2014). The neuroscience of depression: Implications for assessment and intervention. *Behaviour Research and Therapy, 62,* 60–73.

Sue, D.W., & Sue, D. (2016). *Counseling the culturally diverse: Theory and practice* (7th ed.). Hoboken, NJ: Wiley.

Thapar, A., Collishaw, S., Pine, D.S., & Thapar, A.K. (2012). Depression in adolescence. *Lancet, 379,* 1056–1067. doi.org/10.1016/S0140-6736(11)60871-4.

Zalaquett, C., Chatters, S., & Ivey, A. (2013). Psychotherapy integration: Using a diversity-sensitive developmental model in the initial interview. *Journal of Contemporary Psychotherapy, 43,* 53–62.

# Credits

# PART II

# Historical Theories of Counseling and Psychotherapy

## The First, Second, Third, and Fourth Forces

Major historical theoretical trends mark the field of counseling and psychotherapy. These major theories are often called "forces," in that the ideas have had such an immense impact on the field. Although somewhere between five hundred and one thousand theories of change can be identified, psychodynamic, behavioral, existential-humanistic, multicultural, and cognitive theories remain the most influential. There is general agreement regarding the first four forces, however, a fifth force, was presented in the previous section Part I: multicultural counseling and therapy (MCT).

The First Force—psychodynamic theory—is primarily associated with its founder, Sigmund Freud. Freud, who was medically trained in neurology, developed a theory of personality that made the assumption that human motivation was propelled by conflicts between instinctual, mostly unconscious, psychological forces. He called these intrapsychic elements the id, ego, and superego. Although Freudian theory remains influential, derivatives of this theory have the most immediate impact on practice today. At this time, the work of John Bowlby, as supported by the researcher Mary Ainsworth, on attachment theory is especially important. Understanding the basic concepts of attachment theory presented here will give you a solid foundation for object relations theory, ego psychology, and the many permutations of psychoanalytic thought.

Other psychodynamic theories arose, like those of Carl Jung and Alfred Adler, Karen Horney, Margaret Mahler, and famous developmentalists like Jean Piaget and Erik Erikson, but all these theories made the same basic assumption: There is a dynamic mind, conscious and unconscious, that influences the behavior of humans. Elements of the unconscious psyche interact to produce motives for behavior and thought processes.

The Second Force—behavioral theory—has long been associated with B.F. Skinner. Again, the concepts have been extended and modified. Skinner clearly identified himself as a behaviorist. He considered the antecedents and the consequences of actions to be more important than constructs like the "mind" and "cognition" to explain behavior.

In an attempt to bring the scientific method to bear on the understanding of human behavior, John B. Watson, using ideas he had gleaned from the likes of Ivan Pavlov and others, decided to declare that psychology should only concern itself with observable behavior. A science of behavior was built on only observable behavior. Assumptions about underlying psychological causes of behavior were not admitted. The unconscious was declared fictitious and its study a waste of time. Serious psychology would focus on observable, controllable, behavior. The behavioral perspective gained great momentum in the twentieth century because it was a powerful tool in training, education, and industry. John B. Watson and others conducted a thorough explication of Classical Conditioning, and B.F. Skinner explained and expertly defended the processes of Operant Conditioning.

Despite being considered separate from cognitive and cognitive-behavioral theory, the techniques and strategies of the behavioral approach are now embedded in both.

The Third Force—existential-humanistic theory—has its origins in European philosophy but achieved its maximum influence in counseling and therapy through the seminal work of Carl Rogers. The work of Viktor Frankl and of Frederick (Fritz) Perls is presented in detail as representing two important extensions of the third-force orientation. They include active attempts to engage clients in experiencing and awareness-increasing activities. The existential-humanistic-experiential conception has deeply influenced the way all other theories are practiced.

The humanistic perspective arose in reaction to the deterministic and pessimistic psychoanalytic view and the mechanistic behavioral perspective to support more optimistic views that humans are motivated by their potential to be creative and productive in response to their social and environmental conditions. The existential part of the humanist view recognizes the reality of being in a world and the opportunity that we have to choose a path for ourselves. Humanism is hopeful, focuses on subjective, conscious experience, tries to solve human concerns and emphasizes the human potential to grow in a positive manner. The humanist philosophy respects diversity and confronts reality as it is, both the painful and pleasurable, the good and the bad. Humanism assumes that people have choices about their behavior and possess free will to act and also must assume responsibility for choices and consequences. The humanist perspective differs from the biological perspective in that the assumptions about causes for behavior lie in human self-efficacy, choice, and free will as opposed to the determinism of biological causes. Humanist and existential philosophies emphasize free will and responsibility as central to the nature of being.

The fourth force, cognitive theory, or cognitive-behavioral theory, includes such authorities as Albert Ellis, Aaron Beck, William Glasser, and Donald Meichenbaum. They demonstrated the importance of "mind" as well as behavior. The cognitive-behavioral tradition is currently the most frequently practiced of all orientations. In response to the empty organism theory of behaviorism, the cognitive perspective developed explanations for human behavior that suggest that human behavior is thoughtful—behavior is guided by thought processes. Indeed, the cognitive perspective suggests that much of human behavior is mediated by thought processes like memory and attention, belief systems, attitudes, and language. Cognitivists believe that humans bring significant conscious processes into the mix and that much of human behavior is mediated by conscious processes. Belief systems, value systems, thought processes, reason, and intelligence have a significant impact on why we do the things we do and act the way we act. The cognitive perspective suggests that much of human behavior is significantly influenced by cognitive processes and is thus amenable to our thoughtful control.

More recent work in this area, however, has realized that it also relies on Skinner and others as a foundation. In addition, CBT has modernized with a new awareness of mindfulness, yoga, the body, biofeedback, and the neurosciences.

The Fifth Force—multicultural counseling and therapy (MCT) relates to these historical theories and for that reason was presented in Part I. MCT recognizes that traditional theories of helping developed in a predominantly Northern European and North American context. As such, these traditional theories are relevant for working with clients from those cultures but have some limitations with clients of other cultures. For example, most historical theories of helping have been generated by European American White males and, as such, tend to have gender and cultural limitations. Moreover, there was relatively little consideration of family issues in the first-, second-, third-, and fourth force orientations.

The multicultural counseling and therapy approach may be described as unifying in that it seeks to respect multiple perspectives and use different approaches in individual and culturally appropriate treatment. MCT draws heavily on first-, second-, third-, and fourth-force theory in its actual practice but constantly adapts new constructs to meet the diverse needs of clients. As culturally diverse nations, the United States and Canada increasingly are finding it necessary to find new ways to think about delivery of counseling and therapy services. In this process, MCT recognizes the value of traditional approaches. In addition to integrating and utilizing these historical theories of counseling and psychotherapy, MCT is generating its own conceptions, as illustrated in Chapter 5.

The following five chapters, then, focus on description of psychodynamic, behavioral, cognitive, existential, and humanistic approaches. At the same time, effort is made to recognize innovations that extend the value and influence of these basic theories of counseling and psychotherapy.

### CHAPTER 7

# Psychodynamic Counseling and Therapy
## Conception and Theory

## CHAPTER GOALS

Sigmund Freud, the father of psychoanalysis, was the first to fully provide an organized way to explain human behavior. He offered a novel theory to explain human mental activity and behavior that before had seemed unknowable and almost mystical. His conceptualization identified specific emotional forces underlying human activity. While discussions of his legacy sometimes bring more heat than light, there can be no disputing his importance in the development of Western psychological thought. Figures that followed Freud, such as Carl Jung, Alfred Adler, and Karen Horney, built new psychodynamic frameworks based on Freud.

## SPECIFIC GOALS OF THIS CHAPTER:

1. Summarize the worldview of psychoanalytic and psychodynamic theory and illustrate that it is far from a single orthodox framework.

2. Give special attention to multicultural issues and the psychodynamic frame of reference.

3. Present some central theoretical constructs, giving special attention to the Object Relations developmental framework and focusing on the work of Bowlby and Ainsworth.

4. Introduce Interpersonal Therapy (IPT), a validated and time-limited psychotherapy focusing on interpersonal issues that maintain distress and contribute to mental disorders.

5. Extend this framework through consideration of Taub-Bynum's view of the family unconscious, a theory and practice that help relate psychodynamic theory to current multicultural trends.

6. Realize the value of psychodynamic theory for case conceptualization.

7. Learn some central techniques from this theory through practice exercises.

8. Engage in a beginning psychodynamic interview using the five stages of counseling and establish some guidelines for a more multiculturally oriented psychodynamic practice.

9. Review research and neuroscience support for the psychodynamic therapies.

10. Bring theory into practice by engaging in exercises designed to master free association and interviewing.

# The Psychodynamic Frame of Reference

Freud's extensive writings organize human functioning and conceptualize the emotional and irrational feelings underlying behavior. His many disciples provide a constant impetus for change in psychotherapy through addition to and modification of his concepts. Those who started from a Freudian orientation include close followers like Ernest Jones and revisionists and neo-Freudians, such as Alfred Adler, Erik Erikson, Karen Horney, Melanie Klein, and Harry Stack Sullivan. When names such as Fritz Perls (Gestalt therapy), Alexander Lowen (bioenergetics), and Eric Berne (transactional analysis) are added, it is easy to see how profound Freud's influence remains.

The psychodynamic frame of reference presented in this chapter starts with Freud but then moves to the more multiculturally relevant attachment theory of John Bowlby that was supported by the work of Mary Ainsworth. Following from that is Object Relations theory with its focus on individuals' need to form relationships, especially with family caregivers such as the mother. Interpersonal Therapy (IPT) is briefly discussed to illustrate the power of interpersonal relationships and social roles. IPT is one of the few psychosocial interventions psychiatry residents in the United States are mandated to be trained for professional practice. Pioneering research of Bruce Taub-Bynum is then presented as it shows how family and multicultural influences can be made more explicit in the psychodynamic model. Examples of psychodynamic concepts in action complete the chapter.

# The Psychodynamic Worldview

"If Freud's discovery had to be summed up in a single word, that word would without a doubt have to be 'unconscious,'" wrote Laplanche and Pontalis (1973, p. 474). The word unconscious means the portion of our mind that is not accessible to the conscious mind, but nonetheless affects behavior, thought, and feeling. There is a lot going on in the client's mind that neither of them knows. More broadly, it also means everything that we are not aware of at a given moment—both biological and psychological. Individuals are unaware (unconscious) of what is impelling and motivating them toward action.

Psychodynamic theory needs to be contrasted with psychoanalytic theory. As used here, the term psychoanalytic refers specifically to Freud's theory and orientation. Psychodynamic theory is a broader set of constructs that includes psychoanalytic theory as an important foundation. Some key aspects of the definition of psychodynamic theory used in this chapter are presented in Table 7.1.

---

**Table 7.1. Key Aspects of the Psychodynamic View (Note that these central dimensions remain important in all modern variations, including Interpersonal Psychotherapy and the Multiculture work of Taub Bynum**

1. *Client developmental history is important and needs to be considered for full client understanding.* Freud is often considered the first developmental psychologist. Basic to his orientation and the psychodynamic frame of reference is the importance of childhood experiences in determining how we act and behave in the present.

2. *Important in our developmental history are the key people we have related with over time—our object relations.* In psychodynamic language, object relations is the term given to relationships with people in our life. We develop in relationship to people—our family, friends, and peers.

3. *We are unaware (unconscious) of the impact of biological needs, of past developmental object relations, and of cultural determinants on our present behavior.* The unconscious is the reservoir of our memories and biological drives, most of these we are unaware of.

4. *We constantly act out in our daily lives our developmental history and our unconscious biological drives.* From the psychodynamic frame of reference, we are heavily ruled, sometimes even completely determined, by forces outside our awareness. However, some psychodynamic theories claim biology is central in unconscious development, whereas others focus more on life-span developmental issues. Increasingly, the influence of multicultural factors in unconscious development is being recognized.

5. *The task of counseling and therapy is to help the client discover the unconscious roots of present behavior.* Through psychodynamic techniques and concepts, such as free association, interpretation, and analysis of transference, we can help the client discover and understand the background of present behaviors, thoughts, and feelings.

## REFLECTION EXERCISE

What do you think about the psychodynamic concepts presented in Table 7.1?

What is the main idea underlying all the concepts?

Do you believe these concepts are central to every psychoanalytical or psychodynamic position?

Each of the points presented in Table 7.1 would be modified greatly if one were to assume any of a variety of alternative views of the psychodynamic approach. Nonetheless, all in the field agree on the central importance of the unconscious. The position emphasized in this chapter is basically that of Bowlby's (1958, 1969, 1973, 1988) attachment theory, a variation of the object-relations orientation.[1] Attachment theory takes an ecological person-environment approach to psychodynamic thought and is currently rapidly increasing in influence. Ainsworth has conducted the basic research supporting the theory.

The chapter will close with consideration of Taub-Bynum's psychodynamically oriented work (1984, 1992), which builds on Jungian theory and shows how family and multicultural forces are in action at the conscious and unconscious levels.

# The History of Multicultural Issues and the Psychodynamic Tradition

Psychodynamic theory has received a great deal of criticism, much of it from women and minority groups. Historically, psychoanalytic theory tends to be seen as male and elitist in origin. Many still think of psychoanalytic theory as a monolith, with orthodox interpretations based on libido theory and unconscious sexuality. With sexist concepts such as penis envy, a highly verbal intellectualized orientation, and a reputation for long periods of treatment, psychodynamic theory has been viewed by many as therapy only for the wealthy.

# Integrating Multicultural and Feminist Issues with a Psychodynamic Approach

Comas-Diaz and Minrath (1985) were early to demand that issues of ethnicity and race become part of the psychodynamic treatment process. Rather than separate multicultural issues from therapy, the modern psychodynamic approach encourages you as a counselor to use these issues as part of therapy. If there is some form of prejudice in your background, it will show in countertransferential form in the interview. If you have done work on multicultural issues, you may be able to use multicultural factors as part of the free association and insight processes, which are effective psychodynamic therapy.

Taub-Bynum (1984, 1992) makes the above general points more explicit. He points out that we learn about ourselves and our culture in the family and proposes, in his

---

1   Shortly before John Bowlby's death, Allen was fortunate to have a two-hour interview with him where his research and attachment theory were reviewed. At the end of the session, Allen asked "So, Dr. Bowlby, how do you conduct therapy." He smiled and said, "Essentially you would view a traditional psychoanalytic session, with free association and interpretation as the central strategies, but attachment theory would serve as the basis for underlying theory leading to the associations and interpretations."

complex extension of the psychodynamic model, that we need to focus on the *family unconscious*. From the family unconscious perspective, each individual is a specific focus of experience in the family and culture, but much of that experience is also shared with others. Family experience is implicated in the inner landscape of each person who shares the same family, both unconsciously and consciously.

Jean Baker Miller's classic feminist book *Toward a New Psychology of Women* (1976, 1991) criticized the psychodynamic perspective from a woman's perspective (Hartling, 2008). A woman's sense of self has been generated in a family and cultural context, and Baker Miller argues that many women "do good" while "feeling bad." Society has placed conscious and unconscious roles on women that restrict their ability to cope with conflict. In terms of therapeutic work with women, Baker Miller would point out that the psychodynamic techniques are dangerous unless issues of gender are considered.

# Psychodynamic Theory and Insight

Psychodynamic approaches are oriented to understanding and insight. Sue and Sue (2016) comment

> We need to realize that insight is not highly valued by many culturally different clients. There are also major class differences as well. People from lower socioeconomic classes frequently do not perceive insight as appropriate to their life situations and circumstances. ... Insight assumes that one has time to sit back, to reflect and contemplate about motivation and behavior ...
>
> Likewise, many cultural groups do not value insight. In traditional Chinese society, psychology is not well understood. ... Many Asian elders believe that thinking too much about something can cause problems. ... "Think about the family and not about yourself" is advice given to many Asians as a way of dealing with negative affective elements. *This is totally contradictory to Western notions of mental health—that it is best to get things out in the open in order to deal with them.* (p. 227) (Emphasis added)

Psychodynamic approaches are indeed focused on insight. The required self-disclosure and interpersonal openness are sometimes seen as immaturity by Asian cultures. Many African Americans, Native Americans, and other minority members would strongly endorse variations of these statements. Sue and Sue's comments should give us all reason to pause as we review some central constructs of psychodynamic theory.

# Central Constructs of Traditional Psychodynamic Theory

Psychodynamic methods have been described as an "uncovering therapy," in that the goals of therapy are focused on discovering the unconscious processes governing behavior—unconscious functioning. Once these unconscious processes are discovered in their full complexity, the individual is believed able to reconstruct the personality.

# Id, Ego, Superego, and the Role of Anxiety

## The Id

The three main components of human personality are the id, the ego, and the superego. Understanding how they work is essential to uncovering unconscious functioning. The id constitutes the instinctual aspect of the personality; its contents are unconscious. Part of the id is hereditary and innate; part is acquired and repressed. The id is almost totally unconscious and may be either playful and creative or destructive.

## The Superego

By way of contrast, the superego is totally learned as the child matures in the family and society. Conscience, ideals, and values are within the realm of the superego. Whereas the id is uncontrolled, the superego may seek to control.

In the superego may be found internalized rules of the family and cultural history. It is in superego functioning that issues of gender roles, attitudes toward one's affectional orientation, and other multicultural issues are most relevantly explored. For example, the homeless, the Gulf war veteran suffering from post-traumatic stress disorder, or the gay male afraid to "come out of the closet" may have incorporated society's discriminatory attitudes at an unconscious level and blame themselves for their difficulties.

## The Ego

The ego serves as a mediator between the superego (conscious rules from family and society) and the id (unconscious rebellion or playful storehouse). In traditional Freudian theory, the ego is sometimes seen as being at the mercy of these two competing forces. Modern ego psychology theorists, such as Erikson (1963) and Kernberg (2016), talk about increasing ego functioning and giving the person more power to control her or his own life.

Encouraging client development of ego strength and personal agency is a major goal. This may be increased through assisting the client to understand the interplay of ego with id and superego. The ego operates at conscious, preconscious, and unconscious levels of experience, although it is primarily manifested in counseling at the conscious level. Freud formulated the outcome of psychoanalysis in the slogan "where id was there ego shall be" (Freud, 1933, p. 80).

### REFLECTION EXERCISE

Imagine that you are at a coffee shop and have just seen someone drop a 50-dollar bill on their way out of that place. Nobody else is around, and you are particularly hungry. What would your id tell you to do? Remember that the id is driven by the pleasure principle and seeks to have physical needs met immediately—with little regard for consequences. What would your ego and superego tell you to do? What kind of dialogue would they have? What do you think you will do in this situation? What do you think other persons will do? What would that say about their personality functioning?

## Balancing Id, Ego, and Superego

If you work psychodynamically, you will need to take a position on the respective roles and importance of id, ego, and superego dimensions. If you place the id as central in importance, you will find orthodox, traditional analytic theory most helpful to you in uncovering the roots of anxiety. If you take an id or drive-oriented position, you may be more interested in and supportive of medication. If you place the ego as central to your theory, you will find ego theorists such as Erikson or Hartmann most helpful.

The position stressed in this chapter is that of Bowlby and Taub-Bynum, who recognize the importance of id and ego functioning are more oriented to the superego and environmental/contextual issues. This balance of person and environment is more in accord with the multicultural counseling and therapy approach.

## The Ego Defense Mechanisms

What is the ego defending itself from? Generally speaking, the answer is anxiety. But where does the anxiety come from? It tends to come from conflicts between internal biological drives and wishes (id) and demands of the environment (superego). For practical purposes, think of what your clients feel inside when they face serious conflict, either consciously or at an unconscious level. Thus, ego defense mechanisms are oriented to protecting and strengthening the ego, which somehow has to balance these competing demands.

# How Defense Mechanisms Arise

The specific role of defense mechanisms is well illustrated through Bowlby's (1940, 1951, 1988) observations of British children separated from their parents during World War II. The children were taken from their homes in London to protect them from the intense German bombing and placed in homes in the countryside. Needless to say, this was a high anxiety-provoking time for the children.

Bowlby observed that the young children who were separated from their parents became depressed and morose but gradually learned to cope and to behave more "normally." When their parents visited them, most children did not greet them enthusiastically; rather, they edged toward their parents carefully. Some might display anger and even seek to hurt their parents.

Bowlby points out that the anxiety associated with the loss of the caregiver was so intense that the children *defended* themselves against another loss. *Avoidant behavior* and *acting-out* behavior are two types of defense mechanisms that protect not only children but also adults from deeper internal conflicts and the experience of anxiety. Bowlby noted that it was functional for the children to defend themselves against further anxiety—specifically, a re-experience of loss when the parents returned to London. The defense mechanisms worked effectively to protect against emotional pain.

Bowlby may be considered a *developmental ecologist* in that he recognizes that each unique individual develops in relationship to the environment. Bowlby takes biology as a given but provides clear evidence that environmental factors shape the nature of individual uniqueness.

A family and multicultural view would extend the concepts of defense mechanism, maintaining that varying family backgrounds and varying cultural issues will have relevance to the type of defense mechanism selected (Taub-Bynum, 1992). For example, an older child taken from London might use the more positive defense mechanism of sublimation (discussed in Table 7.2) and survive the emotional trauma by taking care of and supporting other younger children. This child may have learned such behavior and thinking patterns in the family of origin. Family-of-origin patterns, then, are transferred as survival defense mechanisms in later life.

Imagine you are a therapist working with one of these children years later. As an adult, the individual may be suffering from deep anxiety that may play itself out in many ways (defense mechanisms and an array of pathologies such as depression, phobias, and so on). The client may talk to you about "not caring about the loss of parental support and nurturing" years ago. One of your therapeutic tasks, according to psychodynamic theory, is to *uncover the historic roots* of present anxiety, depression, or other ineffective current behavior.

# The Antisocial Personality as a Defensive Structure

Nowhere is the importance of underlying mechanisms of defense more key than in your understanding of the antisocial personality. This diagnostic classification is often considered the most difficult to treat. Following from Bowlby, it is important to think of such behavior as a set of defense mechanisms used to protect the individual from harm.

Underlying the antisocial client's bravado and manipulation is a person whose dependency needs were never met. Although there is evidence that some antisocial behavior has a genetic foundation, family environments of antisocial individuals frequently are full of neglect and abuse (Krastins, Francis, Field, & Carr, 2014). When you do establish a relationship with an antisocial client, he or she unconsciously fears the loss of this relationship and thus strives to avoid or to destroy it. The child diagnosed with conduct disorder often reappears in later life as the antisocial personality. You can safely assume many children who are difficult to manage experience abusive and assaultive home lives. The conduct disorder and/or antisocial client has learned that the "best defense is a good offense." Thus, when you work with difficult clients, recall that you are working with defensive structures (their offensive behavior) that cover up underlying issues.

# The Existence of Multiple Defense Mechanisms

The antisocial client's attempts to leave a healthy therapy relationship can be considered a defense mechanism, which might be termed a reaction formation (doing the opposite of the desired) to the client's own underlying dependency needs. When you confront such clients, they will often use denial as a major way to protect themselves. Their repressed behavior is a continuation of past issues.

Your difficult task as a psychodynamic therapist is to break through the defensive structure and work for understanding of how the present situation was influenced by past history. More than one defense mechanism may be represented by a single episode of behavior, feeling, or thought. Table 7.2 lists examples of defense mechanisms.

Counselors and therapists tend to think about defense mechanisms as abstract ideas. In truth, clients indicate again and again in very concrete ways their defensive style. Bowlby's attachment theory provides some very concrete ways showing how you can use defense mechanisms to assist in understanding clients and in helping them break out of ineffective patterns of thinking, feeling, and behaving. These defense mechanisms are learned through our developmental history in the culture.

**Table 7.2. Examples of Defense Mechanisms**

Following are examples of defense mechanisms, how these might be used by different types of clients, and possible positive benefits of each (interpretations derived from Laplanche & Pontalis, 1988).

1. *Repression and continuation.* An underemphasized generic concept of the defense mechanism is that our behavior, thoughts, and actions are repressed from the past. Winnicott (1990) maintains that all defense mechanisms are methods the child (and adult) uses to repress pain. These mechanisms stem either from denial of internal drives (id wishes) or hurts from external reality (superego pressures).

   Therefore, in a broad sense, defense mechanisms are all repressed continuations of past biological and environmental issues and stressors. Many, perhaps even most, of your clients will be continuing old behavior, thoughts, and emotions in some form from their developmental past.

   The remainder of the defense mechanisms are elaborations of this basic point. Your task as a therapist, as Winnicott and Bowlby imply, is to find the underlying structure of the anxiety and the purpose of particular defense mechanisms used by the client.

2. *Denial.* This is the most difficult and troublesome defense mechanism. Many of your clients will refuse to recognize their traumatic and troublesome past. War veterans often deny the origins of their distress in combat; the antisocial client will deny needs for dependency and attachment; and the survivor of abuse or rape may unconsciously forget (deny) that he or she was abused.

   At the same time, denial can be healthy. If we allow ourselves to be in touch with our past and present pain all the time, we can only become depressed.

3. *Projection.* When a client refuses to recognize behavior or thoughts in the self and sees, or projects, this behavior onto someone else, the defense mechanism of projection is likely to be in operation. One is most often troubled by behavior in others that is similar to one's own behavior.

   At an extreme level, you will find projection in the paranoid client. The person with a paranoid style often has a history of real persecution in the family of origin or developmental past. He or she has learned to project onto others anticipated persecution. As it happens, persecution often results in a self-fulfilling prophecy. However, there can be positives to paranoia. For example, when buying a used car, it might help to be a bit paranoid.

   Similarly, one of the most important helping skills may be related to projection. In empathy, we try to see the world as others see it and project ourselves into the client's worldview. Some of us become so empathetic and entwined with others that we literally project ourselves into the client and fail to see the client.

4. Displacement. This defense mechanism is a variety of transference in that the client's feelings or thoughts are transferred or directed toward a person other than the originating source. The worker who has a bad day on the job and then treats her or his spouse badly is a common symptom of displacement. When your antisocial client acts out against you for no apparent reason, he or she is likely to be displacing anger and aggression around past maltreatment onto you.

   You may notice that each of the defense mechanisms relates to others. In a sense, displacement is behavior repressed and continued from the past. Displacement denies what it is really happening and often projects onto others the events of the day or the past. The displacement may enact itself in an opposite form of the conscious—that is, reaction-formation. These defense mechanisms are not clearly distinct entities. Rather, defense mechanisms are simply alternative constructions of the same continued event from the past.

   You will find that one defense mechanism construction is more useful at times, and that another mechanism, at first seemingly totally different, is useful at others.

*(Continued)*

**Table 7.2. Examples of Defense Mechanisms** *(Continued)*

**5.** Sublimation. A more positive defense mechanism, sublimation takes repressed instinctual energy and unconscious continuation from the past and channels them to constructive work, such as artistic, physical, or intellectual endeavors. A person who is frustrated sexually or is a survivor of abuse may turn to movie making, athletics, or creative writing and be rewarded well by society for these efforts.

Sublimation, however, may fail in the long term as repressed anger and hurt may show up in surprising places. Many survivors of child abuse sublimate past hurt and become counselors and therapists (see Miller, 1981). The danger here is that wounded helpers who have denied or sublimated their own history of abuse may unconsciously prevent clients who have been abused from looking at their own past history.

**6.** Other mechanisms. The five mechanisms presented here represent only a beginning. Other mechanisms include: fixation (being immobilized at an earlier level of development); rationalization (the making up of rational reasons for irrational or inconsistent behavior); regression (returning to an early childhood behavior when faced with a life event somehow resembling an old traumatic injury); conversion (translating unconscious mental functioning into physical symptoms such as headaches); identification (acting and behaving like someone else); and reaction-formation (doing the opposite of unconscious wishes), among other mechanisms.

## Sex Role Development

The Oedipal period (four to seven years) is the time that the child learns to understand the sex role he or she is to undertake. (Many now would consider this a bit naïve.) As can be seen in the oral and anal periods, the child has already received considerable training in sex roles through the holding environment and how the control issues of the anal period been have been handled by the culture. What is distinctive about the Oedipal period is that the child develops awareness of the meaning and importance of sex roles themselves and brings together all previous learnings in a total Gestalt.

# John Bowlby and Developmental Ecology

John Bowlby (1958, 1969, 1973, 1988) presents one of the clearest expositions of object-relations theory. According to Schwartz (2015), Bowlby's attachment theory represents a central part of the history of psychoanalysis, although he did not follow the traditional individualistic points of view. Bowlby (personal communication, January 1987) describes his ideas as having developed in opposition to Melanie Klein, the first major object-relations theorist. Bowlby is also interested in information-processing theory, social ecology, and psychological science.

He may be construed as a developmental ecologist, as he stresses the importance of the child developing in relation to context and environment. A brief summary of attachment theory and research is presented in Table 7.3.

# Attachment Theory

Bowlby's concepts are often described as attachment theory. The primary task in the mother-child relationship is for the child to learn how to become securely attached. If the child can become attached, it has a secure base for exploring. Using an attachment framework clarifies the developmental tasks specified in Freud's oral stage.

As a developmental ecologist, Bowlby emphasizes the joint construction of the mother-child relationship: the child is not only affected by the environment, but the child also impacts that same environmental context. For example, some children seem to be neurologically equipped for closer relationships than others. Moreover, Bowlby points out that the child's natural biological endowment develops in relationship with the mother. Child and caregiver grow (or deteriorate) in an ecological process of mutual social influence.

Bowlby points out that three major patterns of attachment exist: securely attached, anxious resistant (generated by an ambivalent and alternating accepting-and-rejecting mother-child relationship), and anxious avoidant (generated by a rejecting and impoverished relationship). Original research by Ainsworth and others (Ainsworth, 1985; Ainsworth & Bowlby, 1991), has verified these attachment patterns and its centrality in understanding human development. Furthermore, current research continues to validate this system, identify neural basis of attachment, offer practical applications to the field of education, counseling and psychotherapy, and suggest future areas of research (Bush et al., 2017; Cassidy, Jones, & Shaver, 2013). Table 7.3 reviews basic attachment research. Most important in supporting Bowlby's theories, however, is longitudinal research that shows that children's pattern of attachment assessed in the early months is highly predictive of later adjustment.

# Separation

There is also a second task related to attachment, that of separation (Polat, 2017). A securely attached child is able to separate and individuate. The task of separation may be considered roughly analogous to the sense of autonomy and personal control associated with Freud's anal period. Bowlby recognizes the importance of these concepts but stresses attachment and a stable base in the family as critical for human development.

You will find that your clients demonstrate Bowlby's theories right in front of your eyes. In the relationship they have with you, their attachment patterns are often repeated. You will discover how childhood attachment patterns of secure, ambivalent, and anxious avoidance manifest themselves in the relationship and in past history and current behavior.

In summary, Bowlby's ecological/ethological position contrasts rather markedly with that of Freud but does not deny the validity of Freud's biological determinism. It can be argued that Freud did not give adequate attention to the fact that the child develops in a person-environment social context that affect children's growth and development.

## Practical Implications

The practical implications for the counselor and therapist from Bowlby's work include:

1. Helping us become aware of the importance of early child relationships for later development;

2. Suggesting that psychoeducational interventions in terms of family education are critically important;

3. Indicating the importance of infant child care (including extended family, babysitters, and infant school) as important areas of counseling intervention;

4. Enabling us to identify likely early childhood experiences of our clients, thus underlining the importance of varying our style of therapeutic interaction and relationship according to the developmental history of our client. (For example, an adult who was insufficiently attached as a child may need more support and empathy from us, whereas an adult who was overly attached now may need encouragement to individuate and separate.)

---

**Table 7.3. Attachment Research**

John Bowlby's theory has had immense influence. However, it was Mary Ainsworth who has verified Bowlby's work in a variety of cultural situations, including Africa (1967) and Europe (1977). Essentially, Ainsworth confirmed that children need secure attachments with the caregiver if they are to develop and eventually become separate human beings in accord with cultural expectations.

The Ainsworth Strange Situation Procedure (Ainsworth, Blehar, Waters, & Wall, 1978) provides a laboratory situation for testing the nature of a child's attachment. The child is videotaped with toys in situations in which the mother is first present and then absent. The focus is on how the child responds when the mother returns. Securely attached children tend to smile and hug the returning mother. Anxious, resistant children tend to show angry resistance on the mother's return. Anxious/avoidant attached children ignore or even back away from the mother and may show as much interest in a stranger as they do their own mothers. (These patterns of child interaction are similar to those observed by Bowlby in his work with children during World War II and discussed earlier in this chapter.)

Current research focusing on the client-therapist relationship as an attachment (e.g., Mallinckrodt, 2010; Wallin, 2007) shows a significant positive association between security in the client-therapist relationship and depth of therapeutic exploration (Janzen, Fitzpatrick, & Drapeau, 2008). Clients with insecure attachment styles are less likely to form strong therapeutic alliances, and therapists may need to work harder to establish secure attachments with such clients (Diener & Monroe, 2011). Levy, Ellison, Scott, and Bernecker's (2011) recent review of three meta-analysis studies with a total of 1,467 clients indicates that participants with secure attachments are likely to have better therapeutic outcomes than those with attachment anxiety.

This introduction to the complex world of object relations is but a beginning. Although focused on a self-in-relation to other context and of demonstrated cultural relevance, Bowlby's framework may still give insufficient attention to multicultural issues. The following discussion adds a family and multicultural focus to understanding and treatment from a psychodynamic perspective.

## Object-Relations Theory

Object Relations theory leads to a new precision invaluable to all counselors and therapists in understanding the key word relationship. Object relations could be translated as "people relations." Object- relations theory is concerned with examining the relations between and among people and how the history of interpersonal relationships is transferred from the past to present behavior. The major object or person in a client's history is the caregiver, most often the mother. However, depending on social, economic, and cultural considerations, the caregiver can be the father, a couple, or a grandmother.

In traditional rural Puerto Rican culture, the caregiver is really the entire extended family. In Africa and Aboriginal Australia, the primary caregiver may be anyone in the extended family or the whole community. Issues of single parenthood, adoption, and same-sex parents further change the concept of caregiver. Some would argue that day-care workers need to be considered part of the caregiver complex. Regardless of terminology, all are important objects in the development of the child.

## Interpersonal Psychotherapy (IPT)

Interpersonal Psychotherapy is a dynamically-informed, time-limited form of treatment developed by Gerald L. Klerman and Myrna M. Weissman (1987). The focus of IPT is interpersonal issues. The basic premise of IPT is that social and interpersonal distress exacerbates the onset and relapse of psychological disorders (Markowitz & Weissman, 2012). IPT's theory incorporates Sullivan's and Meyer's observations of the importance of interpersonal context and environment in the course of psychological disorders, and Bowlby's understanding of emotional attachment and the consequences of interpersonal loss and separation (Bowlby, 1998).

The following summarizes the basic psychosocial knowledge underlying IPT (Markowitz & Weissman, 2012):

- Social supports protect against psychopathology;
- Whatever the 'cause' of a depressive episode, it always occurs in an interpersonal context and usually involves disruption of significant attachments and social roles;
- Death of a significant other (grief), antagonistic relationships (role disputes), life disruptions or losses (role transitions), and isolative lack of social support (inter-

personal deficits) are negative life events or circumstances that place vulnerable individuals at risk for a depressive episode; and

- It is useful to work on change in social functioning in the 'here and now' to improve symptoms (p. 3).

Psychological disorders are frequently trigger by an interpersonal crisis. Interpersonal issues fall into one of four categories: (a) grief—a complicated bereavement reaction following the death of a loved one; (b) role transition—an unsettling major life change such as illness or retirement; (c) role dispute—a conflict with an important person such as parent, spouse, or boss; or (d) interpersonal deficits—difficulties to establish relations or social isolation. The client and therapist identify the central interpersonal crisis or predicament. This critical issue becomes the primary focus of treatment.

IPT has three phases: 1. Initial phase, usually sessions 1–3, includes: a) evaluation: diagnosis, identification of any comorbid disorder, and application of the interpersonal inventory to review current and past relationships; b) case formulation: definition of diagnosis and its relationship with the key interpersonal issue; and, c) treatment plan: description of intervention with clear focus on interpersonal issue and set of action steps to achieve change. 2. Middle phase, usually sessions 4–9, comprises the main work of resolving the interpersonal issue and reduce symptoms. Key techniques used during this phase includes Clarification, Communication analysis, Interpersonal incidents, Use of affect, Role playing, Problem solving, and Homework. 3. Final phase, sessions 10–12, includes discussion of termination, reviews improvement, consolidates gains, and anticipates future issues. Typically, resolving the interpersonal issue reduces interpersonal stress, enhances interpersonal skills, and improves social support.

Empirical research supports the use of IPT for a variety of affective disorders, anxiety disorders, eating disorders, combat stress, addictions, and living with HIV; and for a wide range of national and international clients; and from children and adolescents to older adults. IPT is typically used in individual therapy but group applications are effective and are used by the World Health Organization (World Health Organization and Columbia University, 2016).

# Family Unconscious and Multicultural Psychodynamic Theory

Taub-Bynum (1984) talks about three interrelated levels of unconscious functioning—the individual, the family, and the collective, or multicultural unconscious. The individual unconscious is similar to that described in earlier portions of this chapter and is characteristic of most individualistic, Eurocentric approaches to psychodynamic thought.

## The Family and the Multicultural Unconscious

According to Taub-Bynum (1984), "The Family Unconscious is composed of extremely powerful affective (emotional) energies from the earliest life of the individual" (p. 11). This statement is in accord with object relations theory but reframes and extends these concepts. Essentially, our life experience in our family of origin enters our being in both positive and negative ways. Experience *in the family* (as contrasted with experience solely with a single caregiver) is transmitted to the child and becomes very much a part of the child's being (and later, of course, the adolescent and adult being).

Thus, the construction, development, and recognition of the family of origin becomes essential for understanding the individual's development. Many of the social and environmental constructions of reality the individual absorbs come from the family, which itself is located in a cultural context.

Taub-Bynum draws from Jungian psychology for his concept of the multicultural or collective unconscious (see Jung, 1935). Jung talks of the collective unconscious as drawing on all the thought and behavior patterns over time. Much of the collective unconscious is the repository of client experience in the family. As indicated in Chapter 3, when you work with an individual, the family and the culture are also present. From this frame of reference, this construct of the collective unconscious becomes closely allied with issues of multicultural empathy and understanding.

## Family and Culture

The family is where we first experience and learn the culture. The family unit is the culture bearer—and we need to recall that the nature of the family and its functions vary widely among cultures. Taub-Bynum speaks of the "powerful affective energies" we experience in the family. The interplay between individual and family affective experience is the formative dialectic of culture. It is not really possible to separate individuals, families, and culture, for their interplay is so powerful and persistent.

## Therapeutic Implications of the Family and Multicultural Unconscious

You as counselor or therapist can assume that the client is in some way acting out the family and multicultural unconscious. In some cases, the client will present a unique personal construction of the issue or concern, but in others, family or cultural influences are more powerful and important than are individual forces. Practice Exercise 7.1 will help you understand ways to help focus a client's exploration and how to bring the multicultural unconscious into the session.

**PRACTICE EXERCISE 7.1. Focusing Questions**

The following focusing questions are designed to illustrate the interrelationship of the individual, the family, and the cultural context. Read these examples, think of a particular client or interview, and practice specific questions and clarifications appropriate to the context of that interview.

Think about the microskill of focus as a simple introduction to a very complex issue. If a client presents an issue and you focus on the issue by emphasizing personal pronouns ("You seem to feel …") and "I" statements, the client will talk about the issue on an individual basis. If you focus on the family in connection with the individual, the process of therapy changes ("How did you learn that in your family?" "How does that experience relate to your family of origin?"), and the client will talk about issues from a family orientation.

At the multicultural level, the focus changes to the impact of the context and culture on the client's development and present worldview ("How does the Irish experience of Yankee oppression in Boston relate to how your family generated its ideas in the world, and how does that play itself out in you?" "What does being African American (or other minority group) have to do with your family experience and your own view of yourself?").

# Generation of Family Symptoms over Time

At a more complex level, Taub-Bynum talks about the intergenerational transmission of symptoms in a family. If you construct a family history/genogram of an alcoholic client, you often find several alcoholics in the family over the generations. Family theory (see Chapter 12) gives central attention to this dynamic.

The story of Kunta Kinta in Alex Haley's book *Roots* (1977) illustrates the above point. Kunta Kinta, taken into slavery from Africa, provided his family with an image that played itself out over the generations, right to the time when Haley wrote his famous book. Family members acted out this story over the generations in differing ways, but much of their thinking and behavior could be traced to this ancestor. For example, an upstanding member of the family might be acting out the positive intergenerational family script, whereas another family member might be in trouble with the law and acting out the negative family script. Each of these family members could be said to be engaging in a set of defense mechanisms that could be explained by tracing individual, family, and cultural history.

# Free Association: The Past Repeats in the Present

Free association is the basic technique and strategy of the psychodynamic approach. Free association is the method according to which, without exception, voice must be given to all thoughts that enter the mind (Barratt, 2017). Those thoughts can be based on a specific element (word, number, dream image, or any kind of idea at all) or can be produced spontaneously. However, you will find that free assocation, much as described here can be a useful adjunct to virtually all interviews at key points.

The following exercise (7.2) uses focused free association. By engaging in the exercise, the material and concepts of this chapter will be more useful and understandable.

---

**PRACTICE EXERCISE 7.2. Free Association**

Consider each item presented below and think about it before moving on to the next. While this is a psychodynamic strategy, you will find it useful in counseling and therapy with many clients, even though you may adhere to another theory such as cognitive-behavioral therapy. Note that the links found between the association and the original conversation represents a change in cognition.

- Focus now on a current concern or issue for yourself. Take time and consider it fully. (It sometimes helps to visualize an image of the issue. What do you see, hear, and, especially, feel as you think about the issue?)

5. What emotions do you have around that issue? Focus now on your feelings. Locate that feeling physically in your body and really focus on it.

6. Allow your mind to drift to an earlier time in your life (the earlier the better) associated with that feeling. What comes to your mind? You may experience visual images, fragments of feelings, or remember a specific situation. Allow yourself to experience those old thoughts and feelings once again.

7. How do you connect your present concern with the past? How are the two similar? Does the association between them give you some new thoughts about the meaning of the present concern?

8. Think about your gender, family of origin, and cultural/ethnic identification. How do these factors relate to your experience?

This simple, but often very powerful, exercise encapsulates both the theory and practice of the psychodynamic approach to counseling and therapy. Psychodynamic theory holds that the technique of free association is important in the belief that whatever comes to mind from the past IS significant and somehow IS connected to current life issues. The sequence in this exercise started with an issue of concern for you. Then, using imagining and sensorimotor experiencing techniques, you were asked to locate the feeling physically in the body. Free association can often be much more powerful and understandable if conducted in a sensorimotor fashion and images are used.

The concrete description of both present issues and past free association is important in making connections between the two or discovering patterns from the two. The making of connections or formal operational patterns is vital to psychodynamic thought and requires that one be able to engage in verbal work of this type. It also requires a highly trusting relationship between therapist and client.

From a multicultural frame, psychodynamic thought has been roundly criticized as overlooking issues of social justice and as "alien" to cultures that may not wish to disclose personal feelings and issues (Casas, Suzuki, Alexander, & Jackson, 2016). The fifth point in the above exercise, although not usually associated with psychodynamic theory, leads the client to talk at the level of systems in which the individual developed and therefore can add a multicultural dimension to the psychodynamic approach.

# Using Psychodynamic Theory for Case Conceptualization

When asked how he worked with clients in therapy, Bowlby (personal communication, January 1987) replied clearly and directly: "Clients treat us as they were treated—this is our guide for treatment." What Bowlby is saying is that you can expect clients to repeat their developmental history with you. Their developmental history in their family of origin is particularly important, and you can anticipate that many client behaviors with you in the here and now of the interview may be traced back to past experience.

For example, if the client is narcissistic and attention seeking, you can anticipate that somehow this behavior relates to what happened in the family. Most likely, as children, narcissistic clients were rewarded by parents for certain types of behavior. In therapy, this client will likely seek the same type of admiration from you, even though you and many others in the client's life find such behavior undesirable. Moreover, the narcissistic client often has a developmental history wherein he or she was only rewarded by parents and others for certain types of achievement; the child's very real need for admiration and support for just being a child was not met.

Miller (1981) talks about the importance of meeting the healthy narcissistic needs of the child. If these needs are met, the child will have a secure, attached base as described by Bowlby and Ainsworth in this chapter. Developing a working alliance with your clients is similar. However, many children become instruments of their parents' desire. Avoid projecting your needs on the client. Narcissistic, obsessive-compulsive, and many other types of clients are often in varying ways trying to meet unmet needs from the past, as can be seen in the following discussion of a dependent client.

# The Dependent Client: A Case Conceptualization

In the interview, you can expect the client with dependency issues to treat you in a dependent fashion. Expect dependent clients to ask your opinion and advice, attempt to please you, be very demanding of your time, and when especially needy, appear on your doorstep asking for special help. Think about your own experience of dependent and needy people. What are your own thoughts and feelings toward this type of individual? Take a moment and write down some of these thoughts and feelings.

Dependent clients treat you as they were treated in their family of origin. Psychodynamic theory (and Bowlby, in particular), suggest that clients repeat their developmental history again and again. When clients respond in a dependent, needy way in the interview, you can anticipate that somehow this behavior can be traced back to the past and their family of origin. How do you imagine dependent clients might have been treated in their families? Allow yourself a moment to think about the possible developmental antecedents in the family of origin for the dependent client.

Dependent clients can come from a variety of family backgrounds, but certain typical patterns may be anticipated. Many have had parents who modeled dependency. If the client is female, most likely, due to cultural conditioning and stereotypes, the client had a mother who modeled dependency and a father who dominated and made all the decisions. The dependent client was often not allowed to make decisions but rather learned it was safer to do what one is told.

## Listening to Developmental History

In the here and now of the therapeutic relationship, you learn about the past relationships of the client. Needless to say, your dependent client will not always follow the stereotyped pattern described above, but if you use good listening and observation skills and ask questions about the family of origin, you can discover the unique historical developmental path of the client.

## Anticipating Current Issues or Challenges

You can also anticipate what some of the dependent client's present difficulties are likely to be. For example, in their current relationships, dependent clients can be expected to play out their dependency in self-destructive ways. Whether male or female, dependent clients tend to attach to people who are stronger than they are and who will make their decisions for them. The stronger person initially enjoys the feelings of adulation and power the dependent person gives them, but later finds the neediness too much and starts rejecting the dependent individual.

When dependent persons feel themselves rejected in a relationship, they tend to try harder, complain, or otherwise exaggerate their dependent style. Women who have relationships with males who have the need to dominate (for example, antisocial or narcissistic personality styles) are in danger of abuse. In many dependent cases, expect a history of family abuse that will tend to be repeated in the current relationship—that is, female dependent clients are especially subject to abuse. The antisocial client, by way of contrast, often acts out past history of abuse by abusing others. Imagine the difficulties likely to occur when the antisocial male establishes a relationship with a dependent female.

Vocationally, expect the personality style to repeat on the job. The dependent person may constantly ask the boss for directions. Clearly, vocational counseling could profit by more attention to personality style or disorder.

## Summary

When conceptualizing a case, first note how the client is treating you in the here and now of the interview. The ways clients treat you provide clues to (1) developmental history in their family of origin; (2) the nature of their current interpersonal relationships; and (3) likely functioning in their work environment. This information gives you some indication of the future life of the client and concerns that may be anticipated in relationships, work, and childrearing. Keep in mind, however, that most clients are mixtures of varying personality styles/disorders. In a single interview, various pieces of developmental history will be manifested in the ways the client treats you.

## Basic Interviewing and Treatment: Techniques of Psychodynamic Therapy

As we have seen, the developmental history of the client is reflected in the here and now of the interview as the client repeats what happened in the past with the counselor/therapist. Although behavior in the session represents a continuation of the past, defense mechanisms cloud the picture, and you will need to sort through with clients the more precise nature and underlying meaning of their surface behavior. In this section, we consider some specifics of interviewing and treatment planning based on the psychodynamic frame of reference (Ivey, 1991).

A basic rule of thumb in psychodynamic therapy is *to treat clients differently than they were treated in the past*. The most obvious and elementary point is that if clients are treating us as they were treated in the past, our task is to treat them differently in the interview, even though they may try our patience and understanding and perhaps even threaten us personally. For example, a conduct disorder child or an antisocial adult is particularly difficult for many in the helping field. Professional helpers are usually "nice" people and find it difflcult to work with those who aren't nice.

As noted earlier, conduct disorder children and antisocial personality clients tend to be anxious-ambivalent and have serious histories of abuse, and therefore these clients will often treat you in some sort of an abusive fashion. If you react to these clients as others in their history have, you can expect them to continue their behavior. If you react differently—specifically, if you treat them differently than they were treated in the past—there is some possibility that they will develop a useful relationship with you that can make a difference in their lives.

In short, to help clients, you must react to client maltreatment of you with patience, firmness, a clear sense of boundaries, and evidence of caring, as displayed in the Rogerian relationship, but with a difference. It is your task to think quickly on your feet and not allow yourself to be taken in by the client's presentation. Simply seeing antisocial clients' world solely as they present it to you is likely to fail, since they can use your empathy and understanding to manipulate you.

Another important rule to remember is to treat the dependent, insecurely attached client differently. With dependent clients, you must offer a solid relationship. Do not run from dependent clients' demands, but remember to maintain your boundaries. In the beginning stages, allow some dependent behavior and then gradually lead clients toward more independence or interdependence. Encourage clients to share their feelings and thoughts toward you. Providing these clients with accurate, nonjudgmental feedback on the nature of the relationship can be helpful.

These therapeutic efforts are designed to move dependent clients away from a hierarchical relationship. The dependent client has been at the low end of a relationship hierarchy for a long time, and moving them toward an egalitarian orientation where plans for change are co-constructed can be extremely beneficial. Multicultural, feminist therapy, and developmental counseling and therapy all place special emphasis on the egalitarian relationship as basic to change processes.

From a psychodynamic frame of reference, the relationship you establish with the client is of crucial importance. Your understanding of your own developmental history plays a vital role. If you do not understand and accept your own relationship history, you are more likely to find yourself "triggered" by difficult clients and reacting to them ineffectively.

The following subsections discuss some specific techniques drawn from psychoanalytic theory that can be used in the therapeutic relationship to clarify how the past is repeating in the present.

# The Skill of Interpretation

Psychodynamic counseling approaches are interpretive, and interpretation is its main tool (Ungar, 2015). Interpretation is a sophisticated and complex skill when intellectual knowledge of psychodynamic theory is integrated with clinical data of the client. In Chapter 4, we defined the microskill of interpretation as the renaming of client experience from an alternative frame of reference or worldview. Applied specifically to psychodynamic approaches, the skill of interpretation comes from the worldview of psychoanalysis and seeks to identify wishes, needs, and patterns from the unconscious world of the client.

Some specific guidelines for interpretation may be suggested. First, the counselor needs to use attending skills carefully so the data for an interpretation are clear. Next, the interpretation should be stated and the client given time to react. The helper may check out the client by asking "How do you react to that?" or "Does that ring a bell?" or "Does that make sense?" The check-out encourages the client to think through and assimilate or reject the interpretation.

Intentional psychodynamic therapists produce clients who can make their own interpretations. When clients interpret their own story in new words, they will realize an insight. *Insight* may be described as the ability to look at old information from new perspectives, and thus is directly related to intentionality and creative responding. The person who is able to interpret life experience in new ways through insight is able to generate new "sentences" to describe the world.

However, it is also important to note that these new descriptions are almost invariably verbal. A verbal insight, or new sentence, is most valuable if the client is able to take the new information out of the session and use it in daily life. A major criticism of some psychodynamic approaches is their constant emphasis on insight, which produces a client who is searching diligently in the past while continuing to have difficulties coping with present-day living.

Interpretations have traditionally been made from an individualistic, ego psychology frame of reference that puts the core of the issue and decision making in the individual. There is, however, an increased awareness of how the psychodynamic model can be extended through interpretations made from a family or multicultural frame of reference. Consider the following example with a client suffering from depression, as frequently occurs with the dependent personality style:

> Client: I'm really depressed; it's been taking a long time for me to understand myself, but I can only be happy if I do something for others—but they always seem to want more. I feel I'm never liked for myself.
>
> Individualistic interpretation: Your pattern seems to be to try to do things for others and pay little attention to yourself. That would seem

to go back to the way you solved problems as a child. You didn't feel adequate, so you tried to please others. Here, we see you continuing that behavior now.

Family interpretation: Your place in your family was as a placater. Everyone else was arguing, and you took on that role—and then they kept you in it and still do even today. You're very good at keeping your new family flowing smoothly.

Multicultural interpretation (gender oriented): Women in North American culture are expected to take the caring role. We've learned to define ourselves through relationships with others. It's natural, but the question is, What do you want?

Multicultural interpretation (ethnic/racially oriented): Puerto Rican women are expected to put the family interests ahead of their own— it's in our tradition of Marianismo: How can we respect that tradition and find our place in this US society?

Each of the interpretations above can be helpful. In fact, each approach can be useful with the same client at various points in the interview or treatment series.

# Free Association

Just as the word unconscious can be used to summarize Freud's theory, so can the technique of free association be used to summarize psychodynamic methodology. At an elemental level, free association simply encourages the client and the counselor to say anything that comes to mind (Barratt, 2017).

Freud developed free association in his early work with hysterics, encouraging these patients to search for underlying unconscious factors. He refined the technique in his own self-analysis, particularly in his work with dreams. It was out of dream analysis, in particular, that Freud discovered the "royal road to the unconscious." If one is allowed to say anything at all that comes to mind (no matter how seemingly irrelevant), there is a pattern that frequently emerges to explain the meaning of a behavior, a dream, or a seemingly random thought.

There are some practical, common questions that most therapists and counselors use at some point in the interviews. These questions relate to the concept of free association. When you ask a client "What comes to your mind?" "What do you think of next?" or even "What is the last thing that comes to mind?" you are using questions closely related to free association.

The exercise at the beginning of this chapter introduced you to this technique. Free association techniques can be used in the classic open way of psychoanalysis or in a more focused way to precisely encourage discussion of family and multicultural issues.

Free association is an invaluable technique, regardless of the theoretical technique you select. Because free association focuses on the client's construction of issues, it provides you with access to inner dialogues, thoughts, and feelings that you might miss from other frames of reference. Furthermore, free association gives you and the client access to often surprising and valuable information, sometimes even pointing out possible abusive history where other eliciting techniques failed to do so. Practice Exercise 7.3 lists a number of free association exercises and techniques.

---

**PRACTICE EXERCISE 7.3. Free-Association Exercises and Techniques**

A useful practice exercise is to guide a volunteer "client" through the four cognitive/emotional developmental orientations. Begin your exercise by informing your client what you are planning to do and share the following list of questions with her or him. Once you and your client have selected a topic for discussion, ask the first question and assess the client's cognitive/emotional developmental orientation (or multiple levels) on this specific issue.

The purpose of these exercises is to illustrate some basic and practical aspects of psychodynamic functioning. The person who moves through each exercise carefully will have a more complete sense of the importance of free association and its potential implementations in the counseling interview. Yet, these exercises are only a beginning to an incredibly complex theory.

1. *The symbols of everyday life.*

   Much of Freudian and psychodynamic thought is based on sexuality and sexual symbolism. A good way to understand symbols and their meanings is to go through few basic free association/creativity exercises. Take a separate sheet of paper and brainstorm as many as you can think of when you hear the word penis. Make this list as long as you can. Now, take the word *vagina* and make as extensive a list as you can.

   Now, having made the two lists, expand them further. What objects in everyday life remind you of the penis and the vagina? What about types of people, the universe, things in your own living room? Make that list as long and extensive as you can. It can be suggested that brainstorming and creativity are closely allied to the processes of free association. Having completed your list, you may find it helpful to turn to the tenth lecture in Freud's A *General Introduction to Psychoanalysis* (1920/1966), widely available in paperback form. You will find that many of the words and symbols you generated are listed in that chapter. It was in similar, but structured, fashion that Freud slowly constructed his entire theory of personality.

*(Continued)*

**PRACTICE EXERCISE 7.3. Free-Association Exercises and Techniques** *(Continued)*

As time and interest permit, take the words intercourse, *death, love, hate, breast, masturbation, birth, body*, and other specific words of interest to you. In each case, brainstorming a list of words will reveal a general pattern of the symbols that represent that idea or concept in everyday life.

2. *The Freudian slip.* Slips of the tongue are often small windows on the unconscious. A student once walked into our office and asked if we gave "objectionable" tests. It takes but a very quick free association to understand this student's unconscious feelings. Not all such slips are as easily understood. But if one allows oneself to free associate, it is often possible to find the meaning of the error in speech. Think back on your own speech errors or those of your friends, then free associate their meanings.

   The process of examining the psychology of errors may be studied in more detail in Freud's second, third, and fourth lectures (1920/1966). Errors also show in our forgetting appointments, dropping things at crucial times, behavior that seems to repeat itself unnecessarily, and in many other ways. Again, free association is a route toward understanding the meaning of these errors.

3. *Dream analysis.* Recall and write down a dream you have had. Then sit back, relax, and focus on one aspect of that dream. Letting your free associations lead you, open your mind to whatever comes. Afterward, see if any patterns or new ideas emerge that help you understand the dream.

   As an alternative, keep the whole dream in mind and relax. This time, free associate back to an early childhood experience. Then follow that experience and go back to an even earlier childhood experience. In some cases, a third experience association may be helpful. Return to your dream and determine if the dream is related to your associations.

   The preceding processes are similar to those employed in analysis of dreams. An examination of Freud's lectures five through fifteen will reveal that you have anticipated some of his constructs and ideas. It is possible, using free association techniques, to realize intuitively many of Freud's concepts before you read them. This direct experiencing of free association should help you to understand the intellective aspects of his theory more fully.

*(Continued)*

**PRACTICE EXERCISE 7.3.** **Free-Association Exercises and Techniques** *(Continued)*

4. *Analysis of resistance.* Resistance is the name given to "everything in the words and actions of the client that obstructs his gaining access to his unconscious" (Laplanche & Pontalis, 1973). Most likely, in one of the preceding exercises, you "blocked" at some point and couldn't think of a word. Your free associations stopped for a moment. These blockages are mini examples of resistance and illustrate the operation of the general defense mechanism of repression. To recover the lost association that was blocked, it is important that one first focus on the block itself. The following example may prove helpful.

    Let us assume you want to understand your feelings toward your parents or some other important person in your life in more depth. One route to this is free associating a list of words that come to your mind in relation to this individual. For example, suppose that one free associates to one's lover the following:

    *warmth, love, that hike to Lake Supreme, bed, touching, sexuality,* (block), *tenderness, an argument over my looking at another person, anger, frustration,* (block). First, one can get a general picture of feelings and important thoughts via this free association exercise. It is next appropriate to turn to the block and to use one of the following techniques to understand the block (or resistance): (1) free associate, using the block as a starting point (a clue may come via this route); (2) sing a song, let it come to your mind as you relax, then free associate from that song; (3) draw a picture, and once again free associate; (4) go to the bookshelf and select a book, or go to a dictionary and select a word, and free associate from what you select (sometimes the answer will be there immediately).

    This small set of exercises does not explain resistance in its full complexity. If you have entered into it fully and flexibly, you may have broken through one of your own blocks or resistances and developed a slightly better understanding of yourself. An examination of Freud's nineteenth lecture will amplify these concepts and perhaps suggest additional exercises for you.

5. *Analysis of transference.* We sometimes find people we immediately dislike. Psychodynamic theory suggests that we have transferred past feelings related to someone from our past onto this new individual. Select someone you have difficulties with and try some of the free association exercises already suggested. Later, examine Freud's twenty-seventh lecture and compare what you anticipated with what he said.

# Dream Analysis

Dream analysis is another important technique of psychodynamic approaches (Sandford, 2017). Dream analysis can be conducted at a surface level by examining the manifest or observed content of the dream. Underlying the conscious parts of the dream is the latent content containing deeper structures of meaning. Free association can be used by psychodynamic counselors in the analysis of dreams at both levels. It is also important to note that these techniques can be applied directly in work with children if used sensitively with concrete language.

When conducting a dream analysis for the first time, it is helpful to use the five-stage structure of the interview. Practice Exercise 7.5 provides an exercise in psychodynamic interviewing that can focus on a dream. The same structure provided in this exercise can be useful when working with a variety of other issues as well.

# Adapting Interviewing to Work with Current Real Issues

Although dream analysis is often a good place to start practicing psychodynamic interviewing, a more effective approach is to use the five-stage structure with special emphasis on focused free association with any important client topic. We believe that although dreams may be "the royal road to the unconscious," free association is too useful a technique to be reserved only for dreams.

For example, you may be working with an adult child of an alcoholic (ACOA). Many ACOAs have split off and forgotten painful childhood experiences. Once you have developed a trusting relationship with the ACOA client, the focused free association techniques can be very useful in helping these clients recover their lost childhood experiences. In the following brief example, which has been abbreviated for clarity, note that the repetition of key words, as in Gestalt therapy, intensifies the experience for the client:

> Client (a nondrinker going through a second divorce from a second alcoholic wife): Yes, I tried so hard to please Joanie, but she continued to drink no matter what I did. Everyone at the office says I'm good at getting along with people, but I simply could never please her.
>
> Counselor (using nonverbal observation): I notice that when you said you "could never please her" that you seemed to almost cringe at that moment. Could you go back and visualize an image of Joanie and say "I could never please her."
>
> Client: I can see her. "I could never please her."
>
> Counselor: Again.
>
> Client (more weakly): "I could never please her."

Counselor: Again.

Client (almost inaudible and near tears): "I could never please her."

Counselor: What are you feeling in your body right now?

Client: My head aches. It hurts.

Counselor: Could you get with that feeling in your head? (pause) What comes to your mind as you think about your childhood in an alcoholic family? Can you get an image of yourself in your family?

Client (pause): I see myself cringing in my bedroom. Mom is standing over me. She's drunk and she's going to hit me. I never could please her either.

A common pattern among children of alcoholics is to repeat the family structure they grew up with. In the example above, the client has played the peacemaking or placating role in the family of origin and repeats this pattern once again in relationships. The counselor in the case above noted that the client was trying to please the counselor again and again in the interview. As with the dependent personality presented earlier, ACOA clients will repeat with you in the interview how they themselves were treated in the past. The free association technique leads to an understanding of the parallels between the past and the future.

# Analysis of Resistance

Another important theoretical and methodological issue in psychodynamic approaches is analysis of resistance. Resistance includes everything in the words and behaviors of the client that prevents access to unconscious material. The temptation in many approaches to helping is to ignore resistance and find another, easier route toward client verbalization. The effective psychodynamic counselor or therapist, by contrast, often gives primary attention to areas of client resistance. Well managed, working through resistance may be key to the relationship and to change. It can be an opportunity rather than a problem.

In the process of counseling, a client will sometimes fail to hear an important statement from the counselor. The client may say, "What?" and a puzzled look may appear on her or his face. Alternatively, the client may hear the therapist but forget what was said within a minute or two. Other types of resistance occur when the client blocks on something he or she is trying to say, leaves out a key part of a dream, comes late to an interview, or refuses to free associate.

The German word Freud used for resistance—Widerstand—is actually better translated as a rheostat that controls the amount of electricity available. Freud was telling us that resistance is the amount of unconscious psychic energy the client can allow out at a particular time. Unfortunately, resistance, the English translation, implies working against the therapist, a serious conceptual error in much of today's counseling and therapy practice. What many consider resistance is actually the client's best effort to communicate with you, not against you.

One approach to analysis of resistance is to label or interpret the resistance and then encourage the client to free associate to the facts and feelings associated with the resistance. The exercises in Practice Exercise 7.3 provide some specifics for using client resistance in a more positive fashion

Tables 7.4 and 7.5 present relevant research and neuroscience information related to psychodynamic therapy.

---

**Table 7.4. Evidence Base of Brief and Long-term Psychodynamic Therapy**

Research provides evidence that psychodynamic psychotherapy is an effective treatment of specific mental disorders (Shedler, 2010; Leichsenring, Hiller, Weissberg, & Leibing, 2006; Leichsenring, Leweke, Klein, & Steinert, 2015). A meta-analysis of twenty-six studies of brief dynamic psychotherapy has yielded effect sizes comparable to other approaches, and it may be slightly superior to some other psychotherapies at long-term follow-up (Fonagy, 2003). The strongest evidence supports relatively long-term psychodynamic treatment of some personality disorders, such as borderline personality disorder (Fonagy, 2015).

The following lists various disorders helped by psychodynamic psychotherapy: Anorexia nervosa (Dare, Eisler, Russell, Treasure, & Dodge, 2001); borderline personality disorder (Bateman & Fonagy, 2001; Clarkin, Levy, Lenzenweger, & Kernberg, 2004a, b; Yeomans, Clarkin, Kernberg, 2015; Kernberg, 2016); depressive disorders (Leichsenring, 2001; Maina, Forner, & Bogetto, 2005); DSM-IV Cluster C personality disorders (e.g., avoidant or obsessive-compulsive personality disorder) (Svartberg, Stiles, & Seltzer, 2004); generalized anxiety disorder (Crits-Christoph, Connolly Gibbons, Narducci, Schamberger, & Gallop, 2005); panic disorder (Milrod et al., 2007); social anxiety disorder (Bögels, Wijts, Oort, & Sallaerts, 2014); and somatoform disorders (Hamilton et al., 2000; Monsen & Monsen, 2000).

Current evidence supports the use of psychodynamic therapies in the treatment of depression (Fonagy, 2015). Driessen et al. (2015) reviewed 54 studies (33 randomized clinical trials) totaling 3,946 subjects and reported that short-term psychodynamic psychotherapy was significantly more effective than control conditions at post-treatment on depression, general psychopathology, and quality-of life-measures.

Larger randomized trials focusing on borderline personality disorder treatment supported to a great extent transference-focused psychotherapy (TFP) (Fonagy, 2015; Yeomans et al., 2015; Kernberg, 2016). Recently, a randomized controlled study comparing psychoanalytic-interactional therapy (PIT), a transdiagnostic treatment for severe personality disorders, nonmanualized pychodynamic therapy by experts in personality disorders (E-PDT), and control groups in the treatment of patients with DSM-5 Cluster B personality disorders showed a significant effect of both PIT and E-PDT on all measures of change (level of personality organization, overall psychological distress, depression, anxiety and interpersonal difficulties). Both treatments achieved similar outcome improvements. No significant improvements were observed in the control groups (Leichsenring et al., 2016).

A rigorous meta-analysis on the treatment of depression and anxiety using randomized controlled studies, manual-guided treatments, and reliable outcome measures showed that psychodynamic psychotherapy therapeutic effects were significantly larger than treatment-as-usual groups and no-treatment groups. Moreover, psychodynamic psychotherapy was as effective as other forms of psychotherapy (Leichsenring et al., 2006).

**Table 7.5. Neuroscience and Psychodynamic Therapy**

Study of brain changes using neuroimaging have shown psychodynamic psychotherapy normalizes specific abnormalities and reduces symptoms observed before treatment (Abbass, Nowoweiski, Bernier, Tarzwell, & Beutel (2014). A massive analysis of extant studies undertaken by Abbass et al. (2014) revealed normalization of synaptic or metabolic activity in limbic, midbrain, and prefrontal regions. These normalizations occurred in association with improved clinical outcomes on a total of 210 people (94 healthy controls; 116 patients) and various mental disorders (mood, panic, somatoform, and borderline personality disorders).

For example, a study of changes of brain activation pre– and post–short-term psychodynamic inpatient psychotherapy in clients suffering from panic disorders showed that fronto-limbic circuit activation patterns normalized and panic-related symptoms improved significantly (Beutel, Stark, Pan, Silbersweig, & Dietrich 2010).

The discovery of the mirror neurons system, the system of brain neurons that get activated when we observe other people's experience, have become an important part of psychodynamic theorizing. Mirror neurons help understand the high empathy the therapist may feel for the client and reveal the intense interpenetration achieved when they are in personal contact (Olds, 2006). Based on this system, the analyst can access and feel the client's state and intent. According to Gallese, Eagle, and Migone (2007), mirror neurons allow the therapist to grasp the client's internal experience and sense of their actions. They applied this process to the understanding of the therapist's countertransference reactions and interpersonal relation with the client.

# Theory into Practice

Practice Exercise 7.4 presents an exercise in free association and imagery that includes gender-related, religious, or cultural symbols. This exercise, if presented well and timed carefully, can be highly useful in an interview situation. Most of us can recall key images from the past that can help us think about issues from new perspectives. If used sensitively, such imaging techniques, combined with free association, can be extremely helpful.

PRACTICE EXERCISE 7.4. **Focused Free Association and Guided Imagery Using Gender, Religious, and Cultural Symbols, Competencies, and Goals**

The following exercise is designed to help clients recognize and use strengths from their gender, religion, and cultural background. When employed carefully, using concrete language, the exercise also can be effective with children.

1. Inform your client as to your process and intent. Rather than surprise the client, tell her or him what is about to happen and why it is potentially helpful. Specifically, let the client know that all of us carry images that can be personally helpful and supportive in stressful situations.

*(Continued)*

---

**PRACTICE EXERCISE 7.4. Focused Free Association and Guided Imagery Using Gender, Religious, and Cultural Symbols, Competencies, and Goals** *(Continued)*

2. Generate an image. Ask your client to relax and then to generate a positive image that can be a resource. Suggest that the image be related to religion or cultural background. It is possible that a single image may encompass all three dimensions. A Franco-American woman, for example, might focus on Joan of Arc. Alternatively, a Jewish Canadian client might focus on the Star of David; a Navajo on a mountain or religious symbol; a Mexican American on the Christian cross or the pyramids near Mexico City.

3. Focus on the image. Using developmental counseling and therapy techniques, ask your client to see the image in her or his mind. What does she or he see, hear, feel? Ask the client to locate positive feelings in the body. Then, identify that image and feeling as a positive resource always available to the client.

4. Take the image to the issue or concern. Using relaxation and free-association techniques, guide the client to the issue that has previously been discussed or to any issue the client chooses. Suggest to the client that he or she use the positive resource image to help work with the client issue. It is important to stress to the client that the image may or may not solve the issue. If the issue is too large, the image should be used to work on a small part of the issue rather than to solve it.

---

The purpose of the next exercise is to illustrate how the skills and concepts explored in this text may be used to conduct a basic interview from a psychodynamic perspective. Analysis of a dream or a client's reaction to an authority figure works well in the following framework.

Alternatively, you may have identified a repeating life pattern when you note that the client tends to have a certain style of response, thought, feeling, or behavior in several situations.

If you wish, you could go through the stages by yourself, thinking to yourself about one of your own dreams, your reactions to authority, or your own repeating patterns.

**PRACTICE EXERCISE 7.5. An Exercise in Psychodynamic Interviewing**

The framework presented here will provide you with an introduction to how psychodynamically oriented counseling and therapy may be conducted.

*Stage 1: Empathic relationship.*

Develop rapport with the client in your own natural way. Inform the client that you will work through some basic psychodynamic understandings about a dream, a relationship with authority, or a life pattern. Decide the issue to be worked on mutually.

*Stage 2: Story and strengths.*

Use the basic listening sequence (BLS) of questioning, encouraging, paraphrasing, and reflection of feeling to bring out the issue in detail. If a dream, be sure that you bring out the facts of the dream, the feelings in the dream, and the client's organization of the dream. If you are working with an authority issue, draw out a concrete situation and obtain the facts, feelings, and organization of the issue. In the case of repeating patterns, draw out several concrete examples of the pattern. Once you have heard the issue presented thoroughly, summarize it using the client's main words; check it out to ensure that you have understood the client correctly.

At this point, it is often wise to stop for a moment and use the positive asset search. Specifically, use the BLS to draw out the facts, feelings, and organization of something positive in the client's life. This may or may not be related to the dream or authority figure. Clients tend to move and talk more freely from a base of security.

*Stage 3: Goals.*

Setting up a specific goal of understanding may be useful. A general goal may be to find earlier life experiences related to the dream, authority issue, or repeating life pattern. Use the BLS to specify what the client would like to gain from this interview.

*Stage 4: Restory.*

Depending on your purpose and your relationship with this client, there are three major alternatives for analyzing the client's issue that may be useful.

Alternative 1: Summarize the dream, authority issue, or pattern, and summarize the desired outcome of the session. Ask your client "What comes to

*(Continued)*

---

**PRACTICE EXERCISE 7.5. An Exercise in Psychodynamic Interviewing *(Continued)***

mind as a possible explanation?" If you have communicated the fact that you have been listening, you will often find that clients generate new ideas and interpretations on their own. The structure provided by the interview and listening are often sufficient to help clients analyze and understand their own issues and concerns.

Alternative 2: Summarize the issue, and then reflect the central emotion you may have noted in the conflict or ask the client what one single emotion stands out from the first part of the interview. Ask the client to focus on that emotion and stay with that feeling. Through the use of the focused free-association exercise, direct the client to concentrate on that emotion and then to free associate back to an earlier life experience—the earlier the better. (Free associations are more valuable if made from an emotional state rather than from a state of clear cognitive awareness.) Most clients' first association is with some experience in their teenage years, whereas others associate to a recent event. In either case, draw out the association using the basic listening sequence.

You now should have the facts, feelings, and organization of the dream, reaction to authority, or pattern and the facts, feelings, and organization of the first association. Based on a clear summary of these two, you and the client should be able to find some consistent pattern of meaning. The discovery and notation of these patterns are an example of a basic psychodynamic interpretation.

You will often find repeating key words in both the association and the original dream or issue. Deeper understandings may come from continuing the exercise as below.

Alternative 3: Continue as in Alternative 2 above, but ask your client to free associate to even earlier life experience. Again, use the focused free-association technique. Draw out these earlier free associations with the BLS. You may assemble over time a group of recollections, and you will find several patterns in the associations that repeat themselves in general daily life.

At this point, the client may make her or his own interpretations of meaning, or you may add your own interpretations. Generally speaking, interpretations generated by the client are the longer lasting.

*Stage 5: Action.*

Psychodynamic therapy is not typically oriented to the transfer of learnings from the interview to daily life. However, it may be helpful to ask the client

*(Continued)*

to summarize the interview. What did the client summarize as the main facts, feelings, and organization of the interview? As appropriate, you may want to add to the client's perspective and work toward some action.

*Comment*

It may be observed that the structure of the interview plus the microskills discussed earlier are most basic to structuring a successful psychodynamically oriented interview. However, cultural and individual empathy, client observation skills (both of verbal and nonverbal behavior, incongruities, pacing, and leading), and the positive asset search are all critical dimensions in a successful session. What psychodynamic theory adds to the process is a content, a specific direction and purpose to enable use of the skills—the uncovering of life patterns and relating them back to earlier life experiences with specific theoretical interpretations.

Psychoanalysis contributes important concepts and techniques to the field of counseling and psychotherapy. The concept that transference occurs in the therapeutic relationship represents one of such contributions. It is highly likely your clients will transfer their past history of interpersonal relationships into the interview. Before your eyes, you will find clients repeating with you their past relationships with significant others. If you are working with a client facing a divorce, you may find that client reacting to you personally in the here and now as he or she did with the spouse. Whether or not you choose to work on these issues, awareness of this transferential pattern is nonetheless essential, regardless of your theoretical orientation.

The repetition of your own life patterns in your relationship with the client and/or the client's transference to you is equally possible. This is countertransference. Certain clients "push a button" with us as therapists. These clients may represent, through their words and behaviors, issues in our own lives that we have not worked through. Dealing with the complex issues of transference and countertransference can be difficult, and it is here that supervision and consultation with colleagues and supervisors may be most helpful to you and your clients.

The best way to deal with your own countertransference toward the client is to openly acknowledge its possible existence. The psychodynamic approach can be very useful for understanding clients and why they behave as they do. At the same time, the very real complexity of the client may mean that highly sophisticated psychodynamic therapists may spend so much time on endless analysis that the patient's behavior never changes. Thus, although psychodynamic theory can be considered a useful frame of reference for conceptualizing clients and for helping clients think about themselves in new and more positive ways, the approach may be most effective when used in concert with other theories, particularly multicultural and cognitive-behavioral interventions, so that behavioral—as well as intellectual—change is actually ensured.

# References

Abbass, A.A., Nowoweiski, S.J., Bernier, D., Tarzwell, R., & Beutel, M.E. (2014). Review of psychodynamic psychotherapy neuroimaging studies. *Psychotherapy and Psychosomatics, 83*, 142–147. doi:http://dx.doi.org.ezaccess.libraries.psu.edu/10.1159/000358841.

Ainsworth, M. (1985). I. Patterns of infant-mother attachment. In Attachments across the life-span. *Bulletin of the New York Academy of Medicine, 61*, 771–812.

Ainsworth, M., Blehar, M., Waters, E., & Wall, S. (1978). *Patterns of attachment*. Hillsdale, NJ: Erlbaum.

Ainsworth, M., & Bowlby, J. (1991). An ethological approach to personality development. *American Psychologist, 46*, 333–341.

Barratt, B.B. (2017). Opening to the otherwise: The discipline of listening and the necessity of free-association for psychoanalytic praxis. *International Journal of Psychoanalysis, 98*, 39–53. doi:10.1111/1745-8315.12563.

Bateman, A., & Fonagy, P. (2001). Treatment of borderline personality disorder with psychoanalytically oriented partial hospitalization: An 18-month follow-up. *American Journal of Psychiatry, 158*, 36–42.

Beutel, M.E., Stark, R., Pan, H., Silbersweig, D., & Dietrich, S. (2010). Changes of brain activation pre-post short-term psychodynamic inpatient psychotherapy: An fMRI study of panic disorder patients. *Psychiatry Research: Neuroimaging, 184*, 96–104. doi:10.1016/j.pscychresns.2010.06.005.

Bögels, S.M., Wijts, P., Oort, F.J., & Sallaerts, S.J. (2014). Psychodynamic psychotherapy versus cognitive behavior therapy for social anxiety disorder: An efficacy and partial effectiveness trial. *Depression and Anxiety, 31*, 363–373. doi:10.1002/da.22246.

Bowlby, J. (1940). The influence of early environment in the development of neurosis and neurotic character. *International Journal of Psychoanalysis, 21*, 154–78.

Bowlby, J. (1951). *Maternal care and mental health*. Geneva, Switzerland: World Health Organization.

Bowlby, J. (1958). The nature of a child's tie to his mother. *International Journal of Psychoanalysis, 39*, 350–373.

Bowlby, J. (1969). *Attachment*. New York, NY: Basic Books.

Bowlby, J. (1973). *Separation*. New York, NY: Basic Books.

Bowlby, J. (1988). *A secure base*. New York, NY: Basic Books.

Bush, N., Jones-Mason, K., Coccia, M., Caron, Z., Alkon, A., Thomas, M., … Epel, E. (2017). Effects of pre- and postnatal maternal stress on infant temperament and autonomic nervous system reactivity and regulation in a diverse, low-income population. *Development and Psychopathology, 29*, 1553-1571. doi:10.1017/S0954579417001237.

Casas, J.M., Suzuki, L.A., Alexander, C.M., & Jackson, M.A. (2016). *Handbook of multicultural counseling*. Thousand Oaks, CA: Sage.

Cassidy, J., Jones, J.D., & Shaver, P.R. (2013). Contributions of attachment theory and research: A framework for future research, translation, and policy. *Developmental Psychobiology, 25*, 1415–1434. doi:10.1017/s0954579413000692.

Clarkin, J.F., Levy, K.N., Lenzenweger, M.F., & Kernberg, O.F. (2004a). The Personality Disorders Institute/Borderline Personality Disorder Research Foundation randomized control trial for borderline personality disorder: Progress report. Paper presented at the Annual Meeting of the Society of Psychotherapy Research, Rome, Italy.

Clarkin, J.F., Levy, K.N., Lenzenweger, M.F., & Kernberg, O.F. (2004b). The Personality Disorders Institute/Borderline Personality Disorder Research Foundation randomized control trial for borderline personality disorder: Rationale, methods, and patient characteristics. *Journal of Personality, 18*, 52–72.

Comas-Diaz, L., & Minrath, M. (1985). Psychotherapy with ethnic minority borderline clients. *Psychotherapy, 22*, 418–26.

Crits-Christoph, P., Connolly Gibbons, M.B., Narducci, J., Schamberger, M., & Gallop, R. (2005). Interpersonal problems and the outcome of interpersonally oriented psychodynamic treatment of GAD. *Psychotherapy: Theory/Research/Practice/Training, 42*, 211–224.

Dare, C., Eisler, L., Russell, G., Treasure, J., & Dodge, L. (2001). Psychological therapies for adults with anorexia nervosa. Randomised controlled trial of out-patient treatments. *British Journal of Psychiatry, 178*, 216–221.

Diener, M.J., & Monroe, J.M. (2011). The relationship between adult attachment style and therapeutic alliance in individual psychotherapy: A meta-analytic review. *Psychotherapy, 48*, 237–248. doi:10.1037/10022425.

Driessen, E., Hegelmaier, L.M., Abbass, A.A., Barber, J.P., Dekker, J.J., Van, H.L., … Cuijpers, P. (2015). The efficacy of short-term Psychodynamic Psychotherapy for depression: A meta-analysis update. *Clinical Psychology Review, 42*, 1–15.

Erikson, E. (1963). *Childhood and society* (2nd ed.). New York, NY: Norton. (Original work published 1950).

Fonagy, P. (2003). Psychoanalysis today. *World Psychiatry, 2*(2), 73–80.

Fonagy, P. (2015). The effectiveness of psychodynamic psychotherapies: An update. *World Psychiatry, 14*, 137–150. doi:10.1002/wps.20235.

Freud, S. (1933). *New introductory lectures on psycho-analysis.* Standard Edition. New York, NY: Norton.

Freud, S. (1964). Negation. In S. Freud, *On metapsychology* (pp. 435–442). London, UK: Penguin. (Original work published 1925).

Freud, S. (1966). *A general introduction to psychoanalysis.* New York, NY: Norton. (Original work published 1920).

Gallese, V., Eagle, M.N., & Migone, P. (2007). Intentional attunement: Mirror neurons and the neural underpinnings of interpersonal relations. *Journal of the American Psychoanalytic Association, 55*, 131–176.

Gurevich, H. (2016). Orpha, orphic functions, and the orphic analyst: Winnicott's "regression to dependence" in the language of Ferenczi. *American Journal of Psychoanalysis, 76*, 322–340. doi:10.1057/s11231-016-9049-2.

Haley, A. (1977). *Roots: Saga of an American family.* New York, NY: Doubleday.

Hamilton, J., Guthrie, E., Creed, F., Thompson, D., Tomenson, B., Bennett, R., … Liston, R. (2000). A randomized controlled trial of psychotherapy in patients with chronic functional dyspepsia. *Gastroenterology, 119*, 661–669.

Hartling, L.M. (2008). Jean Baker Miller: Living in connection. *Feminism & Psychology, 18*, 326–335. doi:10.1177/0959353508092085.

Ivey, A. (1991). *Developmental strategies for helpers: Individual, family, and network interventions.* Pacific Grove, CA: Brooks/Cole.

Janzen, J., Fitzpatrick, M., & Drapeau, M. (2008). Processes involved in client-nominated relationship building incidents: Client attachment, attachment to therapist, and session impact. *Psychotherapy: Theory, Research, Practice and Training, 45*, 377–390. doi.org/10.1037/a0013310.

Jung, C. (1935). The personal and collective unconscious. In C. Jung, *Collected works* (Vol. 7, pp. 87–110).

Kernberg, O.F. (2016). New developments in transference focused psychotherapy. *International Journal of Psychoanalysis, 97*, 385–407. doi:10.1111/1745-8315.12289.

Klerman, G.L., Weissman, M.M., Rounsaville, B.J., & Chevron, E.S. (1987). *Interpersonal psychotherapy of depression*. New York: Basic Books.

Krastins, A., Francis, A.J.P., Field, A.M., & Carr, S.N. (2014). Childhood predictors of adulthood antisocial personality disorder symptomatology. *Australian Psychologist, 49*, 142–150. doi:10.1111/ap.12048.

Laplanche, J., & Pontalis, J.B. (1973/1988). *The language of psychoanalysis*. London, UK: Hogarth.

Leichsenring, F. (2001). Comparative effects of short-term psychodynamic psychotherapy and cognitive-behavioral therapy in depression. A meta-analytic approach. *Clinical Psychology Review, 21*, 401–419.

Leichsenring, F., Hiller, W., Weissberg, M., & Leibing, E. (2006). Cognitive-behavioral therapy and psychodynamic psychotherapy: Techniques, efficacy, and indications. *American Journal of Psychotherapy, 60*, 233–259.

Leichsenring, F., Leweke, F., Klein, S., & Steinert, C. (2015). The empirical status of psychodynamic psychotherapy—an update: Bambi's alive and kicking. *Psychotherapy and Psychosomatics, 84*, 129–148. doi.org/10.1159/000376584.

Leichsenring, F., Masuhr, O., Jaeger, U., Rabung, S., Dally, A., Dümpelmann, M., ... Streeck, U. (2016). Psychoanalytic-interactional therapy versus psychodynamic therapy by experts for personality disorders: A randomized controlled efficacy-effectiveness study in Cluster B personality disorders. *Psychotherapy and Psychosomatics, 85*, 71–80.

Levy, K.N., Ellison, W.D., Scott, L.N., & Bernecker, S.L. (2011). Attachment style. *Journal of Clinical Psychology, 67*, 193–203.

Maina, G., Forner, F., & Bogetto, F. (2005). Randomized controlled trial comparing brief dynamic and supportive therapy with waiting list condition in minor depressive disorders. *Psychotherapy and Psychosomatics, 74*, 43–50.

Mallinckrodt, B. (2010). The psychotherapy relationship as attachment: Evidence and implications. *Journal of Social and Personal Relationships, 27*, 262–270. doi:10.1177/0265407509360905.

Markowitz, J. C., & Weissman, M.M. (2012). Interpersonal psychotherapy: Past, present and future. *Clinical Psychology & Psychotherapy, 19*, 99–105. doi.org/10.1002/cpp.1774.

Miller, A. (1981). *The drama of the gifted child*. New York, NY: Basic Books.

Miller, J. B. (1976). *Toward a new psychology of women*. Boston, MA: Beacon.

Miller, J. B. (1991). The development of women's sense of self. In J. Jordan, A. Kaplan, J. Miller, I. Stiver, & J. Surry (Eds.), *Women's growth in connection* (pp. 11–26). New York, NY: Guilford.

Milrod, B., Leon, A.C., Busch, F., Rudden, M., Schwalberg, M., Clarkin, J., Aronson, A., ... Shear, M.K. (2007). A randomized controlled clinical trial of psychoanalytic psychotherapy for panic disorder. *American Journal of Psychiatry, 164*, 265–272.

Monsen, K., & Monsen, T.J. (2000). Chronic pain and psychodynamic body therapy. *Psychotherapy, 37*, 257–269.

Olds, D.D. (2006). Interdisciplinary studies and our practice. *Journal of the American Psychoanalytic Association, 54*, 857–876.

Polat, B. (2017). Before attachment theory: Separation research at the Tavistock clinic, 1948–1956. *Journal of the History of the Behavioral Sciences, 53*, 48–70. doi:10.1002/jhbs.21834.

Rigazio-Digilio, S., & Ivey, A. (1990). Developmental therapy and depressive disorders: Measuring cognitive levels through patient natural language. *Professional Psychology: Research and Practice, 21*, 470–75.

Rizzolo, G.S. (2016). The critique of regression. *Journal of the American Psychoanalytic Association, 64*, 1097–1131. doi:10.1177/0003065116679111.

Sandford, S. (2017). Freud, Bion and Kant: Epistemology and anthropology in *The Interpretation of Dreams*. *International Journal of Psychoanalysis, 98*, 91–110. doi:10.1111/1745-8315.12564.

Schwartz, J. (2015). The unacknowledged history of John Bowlby's attachment theory. *British Journal of Psychotherapy, 31*, 251–266. doi:10.1111/bjp.12149.

Shedler, J. (2010). The efficacy of psychodynamic psychotherapy. *American Psychologist, 65*, 98–109. doi:http://dx.doi.org.ezaccess.libraries.psu.edu/10.1037/a0018378.

Svartberg, M., Stiles, T., & Seltzer, M.H. (2004). Randomized, controlled trial of the effectiveness of short-term dynamic psychotherapy and cognitive therapy for Cluster C personality disorders. *American Journal of Psychiatry, 161*, 810–817.

Sue, D.W., & Sue, D. (2016). *Counseling the culturally diverse: Theory and practice* (7th ed.). Hoboken, NJ: Wiley.

Taub-Bynum, E.B. (1980). The use of dreams in family therapy. *Psychotherapy: Theory, Research, and Practice, 17*, 227–31.

Taub-Bynum, E.B. (1984). *The family unconscious*. Wheaton, IL: Quest.

Taub-Bynum, E.B. (1992). *Family dreams: The intimate web*. Ithaca, NY: Haworth Press.

Ungar, V. (2015). The toolbox of the analyst's trade: Interpretation revisited. *International Journal of Psychoanalysis, 96*, 595–610. doi:10.1111/1745-8315.12346.

Yeomans, F.E., Clarkin, J.F., & Kernberg, O.F. (2015). *Transference focused psychotherapy for borderline personality disorder: A clinical guide*. Washington, DC: American Psychiatric.

Wallin, D. (2007). *Attachment in psychotherapy*. New York, NY: Guilford.

Winnicott, D.W. (1990). *Human nature*. New York, NY: Brunner/Mazel.

World Health Organization and Columbia University. (2016). *Group interpersonal therapy (IPT) for depression* (WHO generic field-trial version 1.0). Geneva, Switzerland: WHO.

# CHAPTER 8

# Behavioral Therapy and Counseling
## Behavioral Foundations of Change

Insight is not action. Understanding the underlying causes or unconscious motivations of individual difficulties does not necessarily change one's everyday life. Behavioral therapy and counseling is centrally concerned with concrete change and actions.

## SPECIFIC GOALS OF THIS CHAPTER:

1. Describe the evolving view of Behavior Therapy, which has moved from an emphasis on observable behavior and action to include the inner world of cognitions.

2. Point out some multicultural implications of Behavior Therapy and its practice.

3. Present central constructs of Behavior Therapy, such as applied behavioral analysis, that are basic to behavioral interventions.

4. Present some key behavioral techniques, including relaxation training, systematic desensitization, social skills training, and acceptance and commitment.

5. Provide you with an opportunity to assemble Behavior Therapy ideas in a model assertiveness training interview that will give you a practical introduction to behavioral counseling and therapy.

6. Learn some central techniques from this theory through practice exercises.

7. Bring theory into practice by engaging in exercises designed to master relapse prevention and assertiveness training.

# The Behavioral Frame of Reference

Historically, counseling and therapy texts have separated behavioral and cognitive theory and methods. During the past decades, however, those interested in behavioral change have developed a more cognitive orientation. Simultaneously, the more cognitive theorists have integrated behavioral techniques as part of a broader treatment approach. For educational purposes, we will follow the historical development, as behaviorism was considered the second force in psychology. The conceptions of the cognitive-behavioral theorists Albert Ellis, Aaron Beck, and Donald Meichenbaum will be featured in the following chapter. All three use many of the techniques and ideas discussed in both this chapter and Chapter 9.

# The Power of Reinforcement: A Case Example

Historically, behavioral therapy is rooted in the work of the behaviorists John Watson, Ivan Pavlov, and B.F. Skinner. In Skinner's view, our behavior is determined by what happens to us as a result of our behavior. If we are reinforced for what we do, then likely we will continue to engage in that behavior. If we are ignored or punished, the behavior is likely to cease. In its purest form, behavioral therapy seeks to help control the consequences of our behavior, thus leading us to change our actions.

Consider the following true scenario, as outlined in Ivey and Hinkle (1968), and its implications:

> *The cast*: (a) A professor noted for the quality of his knowledge of subject matter. He understands that he will make a presentation and be video-recorded but is unaware of the purpose of the session. (b) Six students trained in "attending behavior" and who know "how to pay attention" to the professor.
>
> *Outline of plot*: The students are told to engage in "typical" classroom behavior for the first portion of the lecture. Then, at a signal, they are to "attend" to the professor physically through eye contact and manifestations of physical interest. At another signal, they are to return to typical student nonattending behavior.
>
> *The question*: What happens to the professor? And the students?
>
> *The play in synopsis form*: The professor enters the room carrying his notes. He looks up at the camera peering into the room, then at his notes. He does not look at the assembled students. There is a thirty-second pause, and he begins. The lecture is heavily laden with references to "exciting" research and clearly shows extensive preparation. Occasionally, the professor looks up from his notes and observes

the students engaging in typical classroom behavior of notetaking. He then returns to his paper and continues on. For ten minutes, his hands remain motionless and do not rise above the seminar table.

The signal comes and the students are alerted. They are now focusing all attention on the professor. He, however, is deeply in his notes and does not look up for thirty seconds. When he does, it is only briefly, but he apparently notes a student attending and gazing at him. Shortly, he looks up again briefly at the same student and is again reinforced. Again, he looks up for a longer time and sees the student following him closely. He next raises his head and looks around to the rest of the class. They, too, are attending to him. Immediately, he becomes animated; he gestures for the first time. His verbal rate increases, his physical involvement through gestures and other characteristics is obvious. The students raise a few questions, and the professor continues his discussion without notes. The quality of his knowledge of the material is still apparent as the flow of content is constant, but with less reference to specific research. However, a new classroom scene emerges. He is involved, and the students are involved.

At another signal, the students stop attending and return to their notepads. The professor continues his talk uninterrupted. He does not stop, but he noticeably slows down. He looks to the students for further support and reinforcement, which is not forthcoming. His verbalization slows down further. Resignedly, he returns to his notes and continues through the rest of his lecture, once again resting his presentation on others' knowledge instead of his own.

*(Allen Ivey and John E. Hinkle, Reach, pp. 1, 4, 6. Copyright © 1968 by Allen Ivey and John E. Hinkle. Reprinted with permission.)*

The students comment later that it was difficult to stop attending and return to typical student behavior, as they had found the material most stimulating. The students state they had enjoyed his presentation while they had attended and felt they had deserted the professor who needed them as they needed and wanted him.

This is nothing but a simple exercise in what psychologists call the "Greenspoon effect," after the late Dr. Joel Greenspoon, a behaviorist who showed that speakers will increase the frequency of use of certain words when reinforced by listeners making gestures of assent (Colman, 2015). Psychology classes have for years reinforced their professors by alternately smiling (reinforcing) or ignoring (non-reinforcing) their professors. Typically, the students have used this as a game to get a professor to stand in a certain place in the classroom or perhaps get him walking back and forth in front of the class.

> **REFLECTION EXERCISE**
>
> What do you think about the Greenspoon effect?
>
> Can you remember a situation when you reinforced the conversation of another person using nods, smiles, or expressions of approval such as "mmm-hmm?"
>
> Would you be amenable to try it in future conversations?
>
> What other examples of effective reinforcement changing behavior comes to your mind?

The power of such shaping techniques and positive reinforcement can never be forgotten. If you work with your clients, these concepts can be invaluable. Innumerable concepts and programs for modifying the behavior of children, prisoners, couples, athletes, overeaters, smokers, alcoholics, drug addicts, and many others have been based on the elementary ideas of positive reinforcement and reward.

# Collaboration as Basic to Behavioral Therapy

The above description is not fully representative of behavioral therapy today. After considerable theorizing, political struggle and infighting, research, and careful evaluation of clinical results, behavioral counseling and therapy now focus on personal choice and the value of collaboration. Furthermore, with the evolution of what is now termed cognitive-behavioral therapy and counseling (CBT), the role of cognition and thought (internal speech) has become important in the practice of most behavioral clinicians. Emotion has gained a new center stage, and CBT has become a major force in counseling and psychotherapy.

# The Evolving Behavioral Worldview

Behavioral therapy is related to the concept of modernity (a.k.a. modernism), a philosophic approach that emphasizes the impact of science. Modernism and behaviorism value rationality and objectivity, and both are rooted in the ideal of progress—the faith that science can solve human challenges—and in a devaluation of the past (Nickles, 2017). The worldview of behaviorism may be described as antithetical to the psychodynamic approaches, which emphasize the idea that history drives and directs the present.

Behaviorism developed primarily in the United States and is very typically American in that it is scientific, forward moving, optimistic, and concerned with "what works." The worldview presented by B.F. Skinner suggests that we humans can have the closest approximation to "freedom" through recognizing that we can control and shape behavior in our culture and our families if we choose. We can choose what behavior to reinforce. The question is, of course, who decides?

# An Evolving Behavioral Humanism

Albert Bandura, one of the most prominent psychologists, helped move the field to an evolving "behavioral humanism" by emphasizing that the client should be deeply involved in the choice and direction of treatment. Behavioral theorists now acknowledges individual rights and collaboration in the treatment process.

Bandura's work on self-efficacy (1982, 1989, 1997), a concept very similar to intentionality, stresses that individuals grow best when they feel they are in control of their own destiny.

# The Move Toward Cognition

In the classical Skinnerian view, internal mental processes and cognitions are given little attention; the focus has been instead on direct, observable behavior. Bandura's work was key in the shift to a more cognitive orientation. Cheek (2010) presents an important early statement of the cognitive-behavioral framework, and Meichenbaum (1991) is perhaps most prominent in solidifying what has become a major change in behavioral psychology.

Meichenbaum (1991) emphasizes person-environment interaction. He believes behavior to be reciprocally influenced by thoughts, feelings, physiological process, and the consequences of behavior. This approach may be contrasted with the behavioral tradition that placed the locus of control in the external environment. Clients assume a much more important role in this newer tradition.

Currently, CBT does not hold that there is "one reality" or that the task for the therapist is to educate or correct clients' misperceptions (errors in thinking, irrational thoughts). Rather, CBT holds that there are "multiple realities," and a collaborative task for clients and CB therapists is to help clients appreciate how they create such realities and how it affects the way they feel and behave.

# A Feminist Critique of Behaviorism

Kantrowitz and Ballou (1992) applauded the shift of behavioral theory from a strict individual orientation to awareness of how the social context affects development. For example, if a woman has a behavioral difficulty, no longer can we find "fault" with the person. Therapists can more accurately see how environmental interactions affect behavior and internal thought.

However, Kantrowitz and Ballou point out that "individuals are expected to improve their adaptive capacities to meet the environmental conditions that serve to reinforce the dominant (male) social standards" (p. 79). Assertiveness training is insufficient help for a woman suffering harassment in the workplace. Kantrowitz and

Ballou state that action in the community and challenging standard social norms must be considered part of the therapeutic process. This view is strongly supported by the new multicultural competencies for counselors, with their emphases in multicultural, advocacy, and social justice skills and practices (Ratts, Singh, Nassar-McMillan, Butler, & McCullough, 2016).

How a person develops in the culture, particularly around issues of gender, are given relatively little attention in Behavioral theory. In short, despite its many positive qualities, Kantrowitz and Ballou maintain that behavior therapy needs to be used with caution and sensitivity. Cheek's (1976; 2010) early work, discussed below, and Meichenbaum's new construction of CBT are important in addressing these issues.

# The Multicultural Approach and Behavioral Issues

The origins of behavioral psychology obviously lie in concrete behavior, with minimal attention given to philosophic constructs. Thus, behavioral counseling and therapy has presented somewhat of a puzzle to those committed to a multicultural approach.

Behavioral techniques tend to be successful in producing change and, owing to their clarity of direction and purpose, are often understandable and acceptable to minority populations. At the same time, the behavioral approach can run into difficulties in multicultural situations over the issue of control. Early ventures in behavioral psychology often gave the therapist, counselor, or teacher almost complete power, and decisions sometimes focused on controlling the client rather than helping the client control him- or herself. Behavioral psychology has been forced to overcome some of these early issues and the resultant fears among minority clients and their advocates.

# Making Behavioral Counseling and Therapy Culturally Relevant

Probably no one person has done more to make behavioral counseling and therapy multiculturally relevant than Donald Cheek, whose pioneering book *Assertive Black ... Puzzled White* (2010) shows how to use assertiveness training in a culturally relevant way with African American clients. In an imaginary introductory dialogue, Cheek speaks directly to some of the issues underlying assertive behavior (comments from the authors in italics):

> Me [*Cheek*]: ... A Black person has got to know when to be assertive and when to kiss ass.

[*Knowing is a cognitive act. Cheek focused not just on assertive behavior, but also on the thinking, cognition, and emotion that guides that behavior. Cheek's 2010 book can now be read as one of the clearest early presentations of cognitive-behavioral counseling.*]

*You:* But so does everybody.

*Me:* I mean it in terms of survival baby—survival—I mean whether or not the man even lets you live. Ain't that many Whites who got to worry about being killed because they want to be assertive enough to vote. ...

You see the authors on assertiveness have not sufficiently considered the social conditions within which its live—and have lived. That blind spot in many ways alters or changes the manner that assertiveness is applied ... Current assertive authors have a great approach—it's an approach that can really aid Black folks, in fact they need it—but at the time these authors are unable to translate assertiveness training into the examples, language and caution that fit the realities of a Black lifestyle. (pp. 10–11)

Cheek calls his approach to assertiveness and behavioral methods didactic assertiveness training. He points out that assertive behavior varies between African American and White cultures and that both groups need to understand the frame of reference of the other. He also points out that the passive nonviolent stance of the Black freedom movement represented a particularly powerful type of Black assertiveness. Assertiveness is not aggression; rather, it is culturally relevant behavior and thinking teaching and encouraging people or groups stand up for their rights. Recent studies also confirmed cultural and gender differences in assertive behavior. A study by Parham, Lewis, Fretwell, Irwin, and Schrimsher (2015), on a sample of 231 undergraduate students majoring in business at one of four academic institutions, found White males and African American females to be the most assertive.

# Central Constructs of Behavioral Therapy and Counseling

The following section focuses on constructs that are foundational to behavioral approaches.

## Applied Behavioral Analysis

Behavioral counseling rests on applied behavioral analysis, a systematic method of collaboratively examining the client and the client's environment, and jointly developing specific interventions to alter the client's life conditions. Successful applied behavioral analysis rests on four foundations:

1. The relationship between the counselor and the client;
2. The definition of the issue through operationalization of behavior;
3. The understanding of the full context of the issue through functional analysis; and
4. The establishment of socially important goals for the client.

## Client-Counselor Relationship

It was once thought that those who engaged in behavioral approaches were cold, distant, and mechanical. A classic research study in 1975 by Sloane and others forever changed this view. This research examined expert therapists from a variety of theoretical orientations and found that behavioral therapists exhibited higher levels of empathy, self-congruence, and interpersonal contact than other therapists, while levels of warmth and regard were approximately the same. Behavioral therapists may be expected to be as interested in rapport and human growth as those working from any other orientation. If one is to help clients develop, one must be a reinforcing person.

Behavioral therapists have very specific methodologies and goals. In addition to working toward rapport, behavioral therapists engage in careful structuring of the interview. They are willing to share their plans collaboratively with the client in the expectation that the client will share with them in the therapy process.

Relationship variables have differing meanings, according to individual and cultural background. It is important that eye contact, body language, vocal tone, and verbal following be culturally appropriate. Too many reflective listening skills can result in mistrust unless culturally appropriate sharing is included. A relationship can develop slowly or quickly.

For instance, working with urban Aboriginals in Australia or with the Inuit or Dene in the Arctic, the professional helper may take half an interview or more, simply to become acquainted, learn the family system, share personal anecdotes, and so on before trying to find out what the client wants to talk about. At the other extreme, a relationship can develop quickly with many urban White professionals who can be fully intimate and open with a therapist immediately on entering the room. If you have some skill in observation and listening, some beginning knowledge of multicultural differences in style, and a willingness to share at least part of yourself, you have the basics to establish yourself as a helper in multicultural settings.

## Operationalization of Behavior

Clients often bring to the therapist clouded, confused, and abstract descriptions of their issues. You can help clients become much clearer if you focus on concreteness and specifics of behavior. The temptation for many formal operational counselors is to think and talk abstractly. Operationalization of behavior will help you and the client "get down to cases" and discover what is really happening. Table 8.1 exemplifies a way to achieve behavioral operationalization.

---

**Table 8.1. A Behavioral Example**

Let us assume that you have a client who is depressed and talks about feeling sad. In psychodynamic therapy, you might seek to discover the roots of the sadness, whereas in cognitive or humanistic therapies, you might want to help the client alter the way he or she thinks about the world. However, in behavioral therapy, particularly with applied behavioral analysis, the task is to determine what the patient does specifically and concretely when he or she feels depressed. The following dialogue illustrates this:

*Counselor:* You say you feel depressed. Could you tell me some of the specific things you do when you are depressed?

*Client:* Well, I cry a lot. Some days I can't get out of bed. I feel sad most of the time.

*Counselor:* How does your body feel?

[Contrary to some stereotypes, behaviorally oriented therapists are very oriented to emotions and stress the importance of emotional issues. Many therapists would settle for "sad," but here, special effort is taken to make the emotion based more in actual sensorimotor experience.]

*Client:* It feels tense and drawn all over, almost like little hammers are beating me from inside. It gets so bad sometimes that I can't sleep.

The counselor's two questions have made the behaviors related to the general construct of depression far more obvious. Crying, failure to get out of bed, feelings of bodily tension, and inability to go to sleep are operational behaviors that can be seen, measured, and even counted. The feelings of sadness, however, are still somewhat vague, and further operationalization of the sentence "I feel sad most of the time" might result in the following, more specific, description of behaviors:

*Counselor:* A short time ago you said you feel sad much of the time. Could you elaborate a little more on that?

*Client:* Well, I cry a lot, and I can hardly get moving. My wife says all I do is whine and complain.

*Counselor:* So, sadness means crying and difficulty in getting moving … and you complain a lot. You also said you felt tense and drawn inside … it feels like hammers.

Here, the counselor ties in the vague feelings of sadness with the more concrete operational behaviors mentioned by the client and locates them more specifically in sensorimotor space.

# Making the Behavior Concrete and Observable

The objective of operationalization of behavior, then, is the concretizing of vague words into objective, observable actions. Virtually all behavioral counselors will seek this specificity at some point in the interview, believing it is more possible to work with objective behavior than with vague, nonspecific concepts, such as depression and sadness.

A simple but basic clue when engaging in operationalization of behavior is to ask, "Can I see, feel, hear, or touch the words the client is using?" The client may speak of a desire for a "better relationship" with a partner. Since the behavioral therapist cannot see, feel, hear, or touch *better relationship*, he or she would seek to have this concept operationalized in terms of touching, vocal tone, or certain verbal statements (for instance, "I wish my partner would touch me more and say more good things about me").

Again, it is important to note that making vague terms as specific as possible can be useful to you in other theoretical orientations. The clarity that comes with a careful behavioral analysis often provides a basic understanding for truly appreciating the client's worldview and environmental situation.

# Functional Analysis

*The ABCs of Behavior*. An individual's behavior is directly related to events and stimuli in the environment. Another task of the behavioral therapist is to discover how client behaviors occur in the "natural environment." Behavioral counselors and behavioral therapists talk about the A-B-Cs of functional analysis—that is, the study of antecedent events, the resultant behavior, and the consequence(s) of that behavior (Table 8.1 illustrates this approach). The behavioral counselor is interested in knowing what happened just prior to a specific behavior, what the specific behavior or event was, and what the result or consequence of that behavior was on the client and the environment.

**Figure 8.1. Out-of-Seat Behavior**

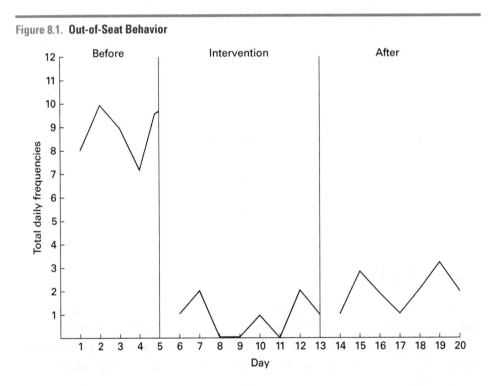

The next chapter will focus primarily on cognition and explores parallel A-B-Cs for inner thoughts and feelings.

In the following examination of functional cause-and-effect relationship, the counselor comes to understand the sequence of events underlying the overt behavior of a client. Out of such functional patterns, it is possible to design behavioral programs to change the pattern of events.

*Counselor*: So far, I've heard that you are generally depressed, that you get these feelings of tiredness and tension. Now, could you give me a specific example of a situation when you felt this way? I want to know what happened just before the depression came upon you, what happened as you got those feelings and thoughts, and what resulted after. First, tell me about the last time you had these feelings.

*Client*: Well, it happened yesterday (sigh). I came home from work and was feeling pretty good. But when I came in the house, Bonnie wasn't there, so I sat down and started to read—

*Counselor* (interrupting): What was your reaction when your wife wasn't home?

*Client*: I was a little disappointed, but not much, I just sat down.

*Counselor*: Go ahead.

*Client*: After about half an hour, she came in and just walked by me … I said hello, but she was angry at me still from last night when we had that argument. Funny, I always feel relieved and free after we have an argument … almost like I get it out of my system.

*Counselor*: Then what happened?

*Client*: Well, I tried to get her to talk, but she ignored me. After about ten minutes, I got really sad and depressed. I went to my room and lay down until supper. But just before supper, she came in and said she was sorry, but I just felt more depressed.

*Counselor*: Let's see if I can put that sequence of events together. You were feeling pretty good, but your wife wasn't home and then didn't respond to you because she was angry. You tried to get her to respond and she wouldn't (antecedents). Then you got depressed and felt bad and went to your room and lay down (resultant behavior). She ignored you for a while, but finally came to you and you ignored her (consequences). The pattern seems to be similar to what you've told me about before: (1) you try something; (2) she doesn't respond; (3) you get discouraged, have depressed feelings and tensions, sometimes even crying; and (4) she comes back to you and apologizes, but you reject her.

From a cognitive-developmental frame, the counselor summarized concrete cause-and-effect sequence through the A-B-C analysis. This awareness of sequence is characteristic of late concrete operations. Then, the counselor used the word *pattern*, thereby helping the client see that this one concrete example is representative of repeating behavior. If the client is not cognitively able to think in patterns (formal operations), it is preferable to stay with a single example and work on that specific situation.

# Reinforcers and Reinforcement Patterns

Important in performing functional analysis is being aware of how behavior develops and maintains itself through a system of rewards of reinforcers and punishments. At the simplest level, we can state that whatever follows a particular piece of behavior will influence the probability of that behavior happening again. In the above case, the husband gained no attention from his wife until he became depressed. At this point—and at this point only—she came to him. Therefore, the wife's behavior heavily influences the probability of his becoming depressed. On this subject, Skinner (2014) notes:

> Several important generalized reinforcers arise when behavior is reinforced by other people. A simple case is attention. The child who misbehaves "just to get attention" is familiar. The attention of people is reinforcing because it is a necessary condition for other reinforcements from them. In general, only people who are attending to us reinforce our behavior ... Attention is often not enough. Another person is likely to reinforce only that part of one's behavior he approves of, and any sign of his approval becomes reinforcing in its own right. (p. 78)

Patterns of attention are particularly important in understanding human relationships. In the above case, the husband gets attention only when he becomes depressed, and his wife's attention at that time only reinforces further feelings of depression and hopelessness. If she were to attend to him when he initiated behavior, it is possible—even likely—that certain portions of his pattern of depression would be alleviated. However, neither does the husband attend to (reinforce) his wife's coming to him in the bedroom. He ignores her and thereby continues the pattern of mutual lack of reinforcement. Either individual could break the self-defeating pattern of antecedents, behavior, and consequences. Any meaningful functional analysis must examine the reinforcement patterns maintaining the system of an individual or couple. The word *pattern* is formal, and with many clients it will be necessary to work only with one single situation and examine in detail the concrete ABC sequence. Once several single situations have been mastered by the client, it may then be possible to examine formal patterns of behavior.

The social reinforcers of *attention* and *approval* are particularly potent and vital in human relationships. However, other reinforcers (money, grades, or other tangibles, as well as social rewards, such as smiles, affection, and recognition) must be considered in any functional analysis. In many cases, negative attention (punishment) is often preferred to being ignored. Ignoring a human being can be a very painful punishment; just think about relational school bullying involving social exclusion (Elpus & Carter, 2016; Lehman, 2015).

## REFLECTION EXERCISE

Elpus & Carter (2016) analyzed five periods (2005–2013) of the biannual School Crime Supplement to the National Crime Victimization Survey. Their findings revealed that music ensemble and theater students were significantly more likely to be targets of in-person bullying than non-arts students. One of the bullying types observed in their analysis was relational bullying. This type of bullying includes socially isolating a victim.

From a behavioral point of view, why is this form of bullying so powerful?

What behavioral principles are involved?

Have you or any of your classmates ever experienced this type of bullying? If so, find out what made it so powerful.

# Establishing Behavior Change Goals

If a counselor is to help a client, the intended behavior change must be relevant to the client (Bruni et al., 2017; Zoder-Martell, Dieringer, & Dufrene, 2016). As Sulzer-Azaroff and Mayer (1977) point out early on:

> Applied behavioral analysis programs assist clients to improve behaviors that will promote their own personal and social development. Consequently, prior to its implementation, a program must clearly communicate and justify how it will assist the client to function more effectively in society, both in the near and distant future. It also must show how any changes that accompany the behavior change of focus will not interfere. It does not deal with the client's or the community's short- and long-range goals … Nor should it serve individuals or agencies whose goals are to the detriment of either clients or their immediate and broader societies. (p. 7)

*Making the Goals Concrete*. During the goal-setting phase of the interview, the counselor works with the client to find highly specific and relevant goals (Sulzer-Azaroff, 1985). Rather than setting a generalized goal such as "My goal is not to be depressed anymore," the behavioral counselor will work toward detailed specific plans. One early goal might be as basic as going to a movie or learning to dance. Later goals might be to join a community club, start jogging, and find a job. Applied behavioral analysis breaks the abstract idea of depression down into manageable behavioral units and teaches clients how to live their lives more happily and effectively. One can do something about specifics; as concrete goals are achieved, the depression lifts.

Throughout applied behavioral analysis, there is an emphasis on concrete doing and action. The individual must do something that can be seen, heard, and felt. Thoughts are less important, but these become central in behavioral psychology's offshoot: cognitive-behavioral psychology (discussed in the next chapter). Interestingly, behavioral psychotherapy often tends to be especially effective with depressed clients, as its emphasis on doing and acting rather than on self-reflection gets the client moving. The emphasis on movement, action, and doing, again, tends to be typically North American and pragmatic in orientation.

Behavioral activation is a third-generation behavior therapy for treating depression. It is based on a Skinnerian psychological model of behavior change, generally referred to as applied behavior analysis. After a meta-analysis of 34 studies, including 2,055 participants, the therapy was considered an effective alternative treatment of depression in adults (Mazzucchelli, Kane, & Rees, 2009).

Behavioral psychology is concerned with doing. Functional analysis will have a more lasting meaning for you if you actually practice it. The exercises in Practice Exercise 8.1 provide you an opportunity to do so.

---

### PRACTICE EXERCISE 8.1. Applied Behavioral Analysis

The following exercises have been chosen as basic to successful behavioral and cognitive-behavioral practice.

*Operationalization of Behavior*
The following are vague statements a client might present in interview:

"I'm depressed."

"I'm the best."

"I'm no good as a parent."

"He argues all the time."

"I'm unhappy."

"She doesn't love me anymore."

"The boss doesn't like me."

"The boss harassed me."

*(Continued)*

When clients give you vague statements such as the above, your task is to help them become more concrete and specific.

For example, if the client says, "The boss harassed me," your task would be to obtain the concrete specifics of "harassment." You can obtain these concrete specifics by asking:

"Could you give me a specific example of what the boss did?"

"What do you mean, 'all the time?'"

"What happened, specifically?"

"What words does he use?"

"How loudly does he talk?"

"Where did he touch you?"

"What is the situational/environmental context?"

"Who holds the power?"

"What's the boss's behavior toward other men/women/minorities?"

*Interview a friend or colleague.* When you hear a vague statement such as those described above, using the above guidelines, ask open questions until you get the concrete specifics of the behavior.

At times, you will want to concretize a sequence. In the example below, the focus is on making an argument specific. You can do this simply by asking:

"What happened in the argument?"

"What did she or he say?"

"What did you say?" (to concretize the event or behavior)

"What happened before?" (to obtain antecedents)

"What happened afterward?" (to obtain consequences)

To ensure you have heard the client correctly, use the microskill of summarization to lay out the sequence of events, followed by a check-out to ensure your understanding is similar to the client's. Also, be aware of the social context of your analysis. You are seeking to help an individual, but your efforts will often be most effective if conducted with contextual awareness and action.

Again, with your friend or colleague, using these ideas, draw out the sequence of events.

*(Continued)*

**PRACTICE EXERCISE 8.1. Applied Behavioral Analysis *(Continued)***

*Functional Analysis*

A functional analysis is a systematic and sequential operationalization of behavior. The questioning techniques above are basic to a functional analysis. In conducting a functional analysis, think about the ABCs of behavior. In the following examples, note the importance of the word *do*, which focuses on action, so characteristic of behavioral counseling and therapy.

*A—Antecedent events*

You may examine antecedent events as well as feelings and emotions:

"What happened just before the argument?"

"What were you doing?"

"What were they doing?"

"Could you just step back and describe the event step by step—give me lots of details."

"What did you feel beforehand?"

"How did the other person seem to feel?"

It may also be useful to explore the environment:

"Where did this occur?"

"What else was going on?"

"Who else was there?"

You may think of the newspaper sequence of *who, what, when, where, why,* and *how* questions to enrich the background.

A critical check-out question that should be asked at each segment of any careful functional analysis is "Have we missed anything important?"

Summarize the antecedents to ensure that you have heard them correctly.

*B—Behavior that occurred (resultant behavior)*

Here, you focus on the immediate argument and important sequence of events or interaction during the critical period.

Use the questions suggested for functional analysis above, and pay attention to feelings and emotions that accompanied the behavior.

Again, summarize the behavior and check to see if you missed something important.

*(Continued)*

**PRACTICE EXERCISE 8.1.** **Applied Behavioral Analysis** *(Continued)*

*C—Consequences*

The essential here is what specifically happened as a result of all the above. Some possible helpful questions here include:

"What was the upshot of the whole event?"

"Could you explore what happened for you as a result and what happened for the other person?"

"How did you feel when it was over?"

"Are there situational or environmental checks on you or others that may have power and influence over the total situation?"

Again, summarize the behavior and check to see if you missed something important.

This completes the ABC analysis of behavior, and this will give you a good conception of what occurred for the client or clients in many varying types of difficult situations. It can be useful regardless of the theory or system you are using.

*Establishing Behavior Change Goals*

Once you have completed a functional analysis, the task is to establish, with the client's participation, specific goals for behavioral change.

Many clients can participate very effectively in analyzing behavioral sequences, but when you ask them "What is your goal for change?" they often will return to vague, nonspecific concepts.

Clients who have just been depressed, suffered sexual harassment, or experienced an argument may say "I want things to be better," which is too abstract for any real action. Your task as a therapist is once again to help them become more specific about their goals for change.

Some helpful types of questions follow. This information provides you with data revealing that change can be sought in the areas of antecedents, the behavior itself, the consequences, or some combination of these three.

"Given that we have discussed your parental argument (your depression, the issue of harassment) and conflict in detail, what, specifically, would you like to change?"

"We could change how you behave before the argument occurs, how you talk and behave when one does occur, or what you do after an inevitable argument happens."

*(Continued)*

This example is likely to be too complex for most clients, and thus the following types of questions may be more useful.

"Ideally, what one single thing would you most like to change?"

"Let's explore that in more detail. What would you have to do differently?"

It is helpful to use a fantasy directive, such as "fantasize an ideal solution if everything were exactly like you'd wish it to be."

A situational question such as "What can we do to help change the system where this happened?" will help add a multicultural focus.

Again, practice. Take a friend or colleague through the specifics of operationalizing behavior, defining the A-B-C sequence, and establish clear, measurable goals for behavioral change.

Regardless of whatever behavioral technique or strategy you chose to use from the several included in this chapter, your interventions will be most effective if they include a carefully constructed functional analysis and operationalization of behavior. Including situational/environmental issues in your functional analysis will help keep you aware of possible multicultural and social justice–related issues.

# Behavioral Treatment Techniques

Intentional Behavioral Treatment often starts with carefully applied behavioral analysis. The central constructs and exercises presented earlier are essential assessment prerequisites for the treatment techniques discussed here.

An important task of the behavioral counselor is to select from among the many possibilities now existing the most appropriate behavioral change procedure for the individual client. Some key behavioral change procedures follow.

## Positive Reinforcement

Perhaps the most direct behavioral technique is the provision of rewards for desired behavior. The systematic application of positive reinforcement to human beings began with an important experiment by Greenspoon (1955), who demonstrated that it was possible to condition people to "emit" more plural nouns whenever the "counselor" smiled or nodded his head. In the context of what appeared to be a normal interview, Greenspoon conducted a typical interview, with the exception that whenever the client uttered a plural noun, the interviewer smiled and nodded. Very soon the client was providing him with many plural nouns.

Smiles, nods, and the attention of others are particularly reinforcing events. Also, several techniques based on reinforcement exists, such as extinction (removal of reinforcement), satiation (repeated presentation of the desired stimulus to reduce its attractiveness and effect on behavior), negative reinforcement (strengthening a behavior by removing or stopping a negative or aversive stimulus), response cost (removing reinforcement after an undesirable or disruptive behavior is emitted), and time out (temporarily removing a person from an environment where unacceptable behavior occurred) (Lovitt, 2011).

We all seek reinforcement and reward. Those who provide us with these rewards tend to be our friends; those who do not we tend to ignore or avoid. Money is another powerful positive reinforcer. It may be said that we work because we are rewarded or reinforced with money. In any applied behavioral analysis that is fully effective, the counselor will be able to note the positive reinforcers and rewards that maintain the behavior.

The search for the ABCs of behavioral sequences will often unravel seemingly complex and mystical behavior. When learning theory concepts, such as extinction, shaping, and intermittent reinforcement, are joined together, extremely powerful and effective programs of human change can be developed. At the most sophisticated level, elaborate economies have been developed in prisons, psychiatric hospitals, schools, and other settings where tangible reinforcers in the form of tokens are given for desired acts immediately after they have been performed. At a later point, the tokens may be exchanged for candy, books, or privileges. Important to the success of positive reinforcement and token economies is the clear identification, by the client, of the desired behavior and the reward. Too long a delay in reinforcement dulls its effectiveness in changing behavior. Current research shows that token economy procedures are equally effective for increasing on-task behavior during group and individual instruction (Jowett Hirst, Dozier, & Payne, 2016).

Current virtual classroom management programs to implement a token economy reinforcement system exist (see Robacker, Rivera, & Warren, 2016). They are easy to implement to help modify student behavior, provide relevant data to monitor student progress, and establish a communication system with students and parents. This new software can be operated on a desktop, tablet, or iPad.

# Relaxation Training

Physical body tension is characteristic of many clients who enter counseling or therapy. This tension may show itself in a variety of ways, including statements of fear or tension in social situations; direct complaints of sore, constantly tense muscles; impotence and frigidity; difficulties with sleep; and high blood pressure. There is clinical evidence that high-anxiety clients will reduce the tension (Chen, Huang, Chien, & Cheng, 2016). Most seriously depressed clients also benefit from relaxation training as part of their treatment regimen (Klainin-Yobas, Oo, Suzanne Yew, & Lau, 2015).

Surprisingly, simply teaching people the mechanics of systematic relaxation techniques has been sufficient to alleviate many seemingly complex issues. Rather than search for the reasons that a client is unable to sleep, for example, behavioral counselors have found it more effective in many cases to teach the client relaxation techniques. The simple procedure of training clients in relaxation can be an important way to bring totally new views of the world to them. Through finding that they can control their bodies, clients can move on to solve many complex personal difficulties.

For this reason, virtually all counselors and therapists today are becoming skilled at training clients in relaxation techniques similar to the exercises presented in Practice Exercise 8.2. A client may learn the rudiments of relaxation training in a fifteen-minute session, but careful planning and training are needed if relaxation techniques are to become part of a client's life.

---

**PRACTICE EXERCISE 8.2. Two Relaxation Exercises**

Most programs of relaxation are based on a tension-relaxation or direct relaxation procedure. The two systems discussed here usually will be found in some form among the many relaxation training programs and exercise audiotapes available in the counseling field. To use the following exercises most effectively, have a friend or family member read them to you slowly, while you go through the procedures yourself.

Then, change roles and help the other person enter the same relaxed state you have just enjoyed. As a final step, adapt the material below into your own relaxation program and place it on an audio file for your own and others' use.

**Tension-Relaxation Contrast**

Many people live at such a high level of tension that they find it difficult to start relaxing. Tension-relaxation contrast shows the beginner in relaxation what tension is and how it may be controlled systematically. As a first step, the person who is to go through relaxation training should be seated comfortably in a chair or be lying on the floor. An easy, casual manner and good rapport are essential for the counselor.

1.  Start the procedure by suggesting that the client close her or his eyes and take a few deep breaths, exhaling slowly each time.

2.  Tell the client, "We are going to engage in a systematic relaxation program. You'll find it's something you'll enjoy, but we must go at your own pace. If you find I'm moving too fast or too slowly, let me know. In general, I'll know how you are doing, as I can watch your response and will time what I'm doing to where you are. First, I'd like you to tighten your right hand—that's right—hold it tight for about five seconds—one, two, three, four, five. Now, let it go, and notice the difference between

*(Continued)*

relaxation and tension. Notice the feeling of ease as you let your hand go. What we'll do is go through your body in much the same fashion, alternately tightening and letting go of each muscle group. Let's begin …

3.  Continue by having the client tighten and loosen the right hand once again. Remember to have the client notice the difference between relaxed and tense body states. Awareness of muscle tension is one key goal of relaxation training. After you have done the right hand for a second time, continue through the rest of the body in the order suggested in number 4 below. Each time, have the client: (1) tighten each muscle group; (2) hold the tension approximately five seconds; (3) let the tension go; and (4) notice the difference between tension and relaxation. As the training progresses, it is not necessary to comment on awareness at each muscle group, but mention awareness of the contrasting feelings from time to time. Occasionally, it is helpful to suggest taking a deep breath, holding it, and then exhaling while noting the contrast between tension and relaxation.

4.  A suggested order for muscle groups follows:

    right hand

    right arm

    left hand

    left arm

    neck and shoulders together

    neck alone

    face and scalp

    neck and shoulders again

    chest, lungs, back

    abdomen-stomach

    entire upper body—chest, back, lungs, abdomen, face, neck, both arms, followed by a deep breath held and then exhaled slowly and gently

    abdomen-stomach again

    buttocks

    thighs

    entire body

5.  Complete the exercise by suggesting that the client continue to sit or lie still, noticing the feelings of relaxation and ease. When he or she wishes, suggest opening the eyes and returning to the world.

*(Continued)*

---

### Direct Relaxation

Many people prefer this form of relaxation if they find the alternate tensing and loosening tiring and/or uninteresting. However, it has been found that the tension-relaxation procedure is often a good place to start with the beginner in relaxation. Eventually, many people will want to shift to some form of direct relaxation.

One form of direct relaxation is to use the above order of muscle groups and go through them one at a time. However, no tension is used, and the client simply lets each muscle group go, one at a time. With practice and experience, the relaxation can be as complete without the practiced tension.

A second form of direct relaxation involves visualization and imagery. Following is one brief example approach for relaxation. As in tension-relaxation contrast, the client may sit or lie down. In this form of relaxation, the relationship between the counselor and client is even more important.

1.  Start the procedure by suggesting that the client close her or his eyes and notice the feelings inside the body. Take some time and suggest that the client notice the breath going in and out, the feeling of the chair or floor on the buttocks and back, and the feeling of the temperature in the room. All this should be done slowly, easily, and comfortably. The effort focuses on bringing the client to a here-and-now awareness of body experience.

2.  Then, suggest that the client freely think about a scene in the past where he or she felt at ease and comfortable and happy. Suggest that the client go to the scene and enjoy the feelings and thoughts that go with that happy time, noticing as many details and facts as possible. The client may wish to notice the feelings in the body at that time, such as movement of the air, temperature, and body movements. Let the client continue with the visualization as long as desired and then become silent, letting him or her determine when to come back.

3.  Alternatively, let the client know that he or she will have some time to enjoy the scene and experience, and that you'll remind them to come back in a while. After about ten minutes, gently say that it is time to return to this room. Suggest that the eyes remain closed and that he or she note once again the feelings in the body connected with this room, as in the first part of the exercise. Suggest that the eyes may open when the client wishes.

## Biofeedback, Neurofeedback, and Self-Regulation

Today, it is possible to use instrumentation to monitor tension in muscles, heartbeat, and blood flow as part of a treatment plan to help clients alleviate tension. Biofeedback combines many of the relaxation procedures of behavioral psychology for analysis and treatment of a variety of client tension patterns.

Biofeedback has become an increasingly popular treatment technique for tension headaches and general stress reactions. It has been used to support behavioral and cognitive behavioral treatment (Lehrer, 2016) and in many cases of pain control (Sielski, Rief, & Glombiewski, 2016). Biofeedback is considered efficacious for the treatment of anxiety, attention deficit hyperactivity disorder, chronic pain, headache, and hypertension; and can be a supplementary treatment of alcoholism/substance abuse, arthritis, diabetes, headache (pediatric), insomnia, and traumatic brain injury (Yucha & Montgomery, 2008).

Common varieties of biofeedback include heart rate (HRV), surface electromyographic (sEMG) recordings of muscle tension in particular sites, and electroencephalographic (EEG) measures from various sites. Neurofeedback, also known as biofeedback for the brain, is rapidly gaining a place in medicine and stress management (Collura, 2014; Sitaram et al., 2017).

Relaxation training, biofeedback, and stress management all can help people relax and ease blood flow, as blood vessels constrict when we are faced with stress. There are some important multicultural issues around stress control. African Americans, for example, suffer from hypertension, with all its resulting complications. Leary (1991) reports that the blood vessels of African Americans who went through a stress test took ten times longer to return to normal levels than did those of Whites. Psychosocial stressors are associated with blood pressure increase and in African Americans (Ford et al., 2016; Armstead, Hébert, Griffin, & Prince, 2013). An ongoing stressor for African Americans (and most likely other minorities as well) is a general environment that is nonsupportive to their cultural differences. These studies clearly suggest that biofeedback, relaxation, and stress management are important programs to facilitate not only mental health, but also physical health for minorities.

## Systematic Desensitization

Systematic desensitization is a useful technique to solve more complex personal issues surrounding anxiety and tension. Many people feel anxious in specific situations or in relation to certain objects, animals, or people—that is, they have phobic difficulties that cause extreme anxiety.

The assessment portion of systematic desensitization is useful in helping you understand the specific nature of a wide variety of client difficulties. The collaborative generation of an anxiety hierarchy will help you identify the client's issues in a very concrete way. This information can be combined with typical behavioral change methods or with psychodynamic, decisional, and other treatment alternatives.

Systematic desensitization consists of three primary steps: (1) training in systematic deep muscle relaxation; (2) construction of anxiety hierarchies; and (3) matching specific objects of anxiety from the hierarchies with relaxation training. It is impossible to be simultaneously relaxed and anxious; thus, the purpose of systematic desensitization is to train an automatic relaxation response in conjunction with a previously feared object. Systematic desensitization has proven effective with anxieties or phobias such as those about snakes, heights, death, sexual difficulties, and examinations.

Examination anxiety is particularly appropriate for desensitization, as the procedure has proven useful with innumerable students in many academic institutions around the world (Rajiah & Saravanan, 2014).

The first steps in systematic desensitization involve training in relaxation and applied behavioral analysis of the antecedents, resultant behavior, and consequences relating to the student's examination issues. A typical situation is the student who, on thinking of a forthcoming examination, experiences mild anxiety, with gradually increasing anxiety and tension until the examination itself occurs; at this point, the student might block facts important in the examination, feel physically ill, or even leave the examination room.

## Constructing an Anxiety Hierarchy

In the construction of an anxiety hierarchy, it is helpful to develop an anxiety scale. Wolpe and Lazarus (1966) suggest: "Think of the worst anxiety you have ever experienced or can imagine experiencing, and assign to this the number 100. Now think of the state of being absolutely calm and call this 0. Now you have a scale. On this scale how do you rate yourself at this moment?" (p. 73).

Two things can be accomplished with this type of scale: (1) the counselor and the client develop a common understanding of how anxious the client was or is at any time in the past or present; and (2) the beginning and end points of an anxiety hierarchy have been established. Then, through questioning and further applied behavioral analysis, it is possible to fill in and rate stress-producing experiences. An example anxiety hierarchy for a student suffering from examination anxiety is presented below:

_____ 0 School is over, and I have no more exams for another year.

_____ 10 On the first day of class, the professor tells us the course plan and mentions examination plans.

_____ 30 About a week before the examination, I realize it is coming.

_____ 50 Two days before the examination, I get particularly nervous and begin to find it hard to concentrate.

_____ 70 The day before the examination, I get sweaty palms and feel I am forgetting things important to me.

_____ 85 The night before the exam, I find I can't sleep and wake up in the middle of the night.

_____ 90 As I walk to the exam, I find myself shaking and feeling almost ill.

_____ 95 As I enter the room, my hands sweat; I fear I am forgetting everything; I want to leave.

_____ 99 When the tests are passed out, I feel totally tense, almost unable to move.

_____ 100 As I look at the examination I see a question or two that I really don't know and I absolutely panic. I leave the room.

The importance and value of this type of individualized, collaborative assessment cannot be overstressed. It is important that you personally take time to practice the construction of anxiety hierarchies. As relapse prevention reminds us, if we do not seek actively to transfer our learnings, the information will be lost.

## Multicultural Implications

A special feature of anxiety hierarchies is that they concretize anxiety very specifically and in smaller units. If you work with a woman or minority who suffers some type of harassment or discrimination in the workplace, you can anticipate considerable stress. Legal action itself causes stress. To help these clients understand and manage the stress, constructing an anxiety hierarchy can be helpful. Similarly, such hierarchies for eating disorders, depression, phobias, and so on can be highly useful in clarifying diagnosis and helping plan more effective treatment.

## Using the Hierarchy for Treatment

Following completion of the anxiety hierarchy, the client is asked to sit with eyes closed and visualize a variety of scenes close to the 0 point of anxiety. These scenes may be of school being over or of an enjoyable activity, such as a picnic or walking in the woods. The therapist asks the student to note the easy feelings of relaxation and then moves gradually up the hierarchy, having the client visualize each scene in the hierarchy. If tension is felt, the client may indicate this by a raised finger. For example, if tension is experienced as the student visualizes the situation two days before the examination, the therapist and student would work to note the tense muscles and relax them while still thinking of the usually tension-producing scene.

Gradually, the client learns to visualize all the scenes in the anxiety hierarchy while relaxed. This type of training may take several interviews, but it has been demonstrated to be effective. When students find themselves in similar tension-producing situations, they are able to generate relaxation behaviors to counteract the feelings of tension.

Similar work with anxiety hierarchies has proven equally effective in many anxiety and phobic situations. Some of the most dramatic demonstrations of desensitization procedures have been with snake phobics who, as a final test, allowed a snake to crawl over them (Bandura, Blanchard, & Ritter, 1969). In fact, exposure-based therapies are especially effective with children (Higa-McMillan, Francis, Rith-Najarian, & Chorpita, 2016).

# Modeling

Seeing is believing, it is said, and behavioral counselors and therapists have found that watching films or videotapes of people engaging in successful behavior is sufficient for clients to learn new ways of coping with difficulties (Weiner & Craighead, 2010). For example, Bandura (1976) found that live modeling of snake handling was even more effective than systematic desensitization in teaching those with snake phobias to cope with their anxieties.

> After observing the therapist interacting closely with the snake, clients were aided through other induction procedures to perform progressively more frightening responses themselves. At each step the therapist ... performed the activities fearlessly and gradually led the clients to touch, stroke, and hold the midsection of the snake's body with gloved and then bare hands for increasing periods ... As clients became more courageous, the therapist gradually reduced [the] level of participation and control over the snake until eventually clients were able to tolerate the squirming snake in their laps without assistance, to let the snake loose in the room and retrieve it, and to let it crawl freely over their bodies. (p. 256)

In a sense, modeling is one of the most simple and obvious ways to teach clients new behaviors. Seeing and hearing directly, either live or via film or videotape, brings home a message much more clearly and directly than direct advice and description. Modeling can be combined with relaxation, assertiveness training, and other behavioral techniques in developing uniquely individualized programs for clients. Modeling is a key ingredient in social skills training. Video modeling, a technique that involves showing the client video footage of successful behavior, has been used successfully with children with Attention Deficit Disorder (ADD), behavioral disorders, autism spectrum disorders, learning disabilities, cognitive disabilities, and various physical disabilities; and it is considered an evidence-based practice for youth with autism spectrum disorders (Axelrod, Bellini, & Markoff, 2014). Furthermore, portable video modeling and recordings of children's own appropriate behaviors facilitate prosocial behavior (Macpherson, Charlop, & Miltenberger, 2015). Self-modeling takes advantage of self-observation to improve our own behavior (Harasym, Langevin, & Kully, 2015).

# Social Skills Training

An increasingly important part of behavioral methods is that of skills training—teaching clients and others specific modes of responding. There is a wide variety of systematic formulations for teaching communication skills, life skills for difficult/delinquent adolescents, marital skills, skills for psychiatric patients, and prosocial skills to children with a variety of diagnoses (Mikami, Jia, & Na, 2014) and intellectual disabilities (O'Handley, Ford, Radley, Helbig, & Wimberly, 2016), among others. Skill training may be considered a theory of psychotherapy and change in its own right. Most often, skill training involves the following cognitive-behavioral components:

1. *Rapport/structuring.* Clients/trainees are prepared cognitively and emotionally for the instruction.

2. *Cognitive presentation and cueing.* Usually, some form of explanation and rationale for the skill is presented. In stress inoculation, Meichenbaum, using Socratic-type questions, helps clients in a collaborative fashion better understand the nature of stress and why it is important to learn stress management.

3. *Modeling.* Role-plays, videotapes, audiotapes, and demonstrations are commonly used so that trainees can see and hear the behaviors of the skill in action. Cognitions from earlier stages are paired with specific observable behaviors.

4. *Practice.* One does not always learn a skill by cognitive understanding and watching. Most skill trainers require their clients/trainees to engage in the skill through role-played practice possibly supplemented by videotape and audiotape feedback. It is important that the skill be mastered to a high level, or it is likely to be lost over time.

5. *Action, generalization.* All skill training emphasizes the decision to take the learning outside and beyond the immediate situation of the training session. In some cases, a full relapse prevention worksheet will be employed. The cognitive-behavioral therapist works with the client (or clients if the treatment is conducted on a group basis) to anticipate possible barriers or obstacles that might interfere with their employing coping skills. In this way, clients become their own therapists.

One key cognitive-behavioral skill training program is that of the microskills framework of Chapter 4. Now it is common to teach listening (attending behavior) and communication skills such as observing behavior, acknowledging feelings, and summarization with in-session microskill roleplays. It has been found that teaching these skills is not only useful for training in counseling and therapy, but also for a wide variety of patient and client groups. The microskills model has been widely used for interviewers, counselors and therapists, as well as peer counseling training throughout the world in multiple languages and cultures.

# Assertiveness Training

Some individuals passively accept whatever fate hands them. You may know someone who acts as a "doormat" and allows friends and family to dominate him or her. This person may allow others to make decisions, let strangers cut in front while standing in line, or accept being ignored by a waiter for an hour. Individuals who may be overly passive in their behavior can benefit from assertiveness training and learn to stand up for their rights.

You may also know someone who is overly aggressive and dominating, who tells others what to do and what to think. This person may interrupt conversations rudely, cut in front of others in line, and yell at waiters. This aggressive individual can also benefit from assertiveness training.

Assertiveness training involves learning to stand up for your rights—but to simultaneously consider the thoughts and feelings of others (Peneva & Mavrodiev, 2013). Assertiveness training is associated with psychological well-being and self-esteem (Sarkova et al., 2013). While emphasizing overt behavior, assertiveness training also focuses on client cognitions. Alberti and Emmons (1970/2017) are recognized as the pioneers of assertiveness training. Bower (1990) and Bower and Bower (1995/2004) have written highly useful statements on the framework. Bower (1976, 1990) and Phelps and Austin (2002) specifically apply the model to women. Cheek (2010) first discussed the multicultural implications of the framework and provided important linkage for more cognitively oriented assertiveness training.

The specifics of assertiveness training are outlined in Practice Exercise 8.3. If you can conduct a basic applied behavioral analysis and can pinpoint behavior with some precision, you should be able to conduct assertiveness training with some understanding and skill. Practice Exercise 8.3 is oriented toward behavioral assertiveness training with minimal attention to internal cognitive states. If you or a depressed, agoraphobic, or normal client does not have some attention paid to their internal states of thinking and feeling, change is much less likely to occur and be maintained. The cognitive dimensions of CBT stressed in Chapter 9 are critical for producing enduring change.

## REFLECTION EXERCISE

Do women get penalized for being "too" assertive?

Have you or any of your classmates ever experienced this type of penalty? If so, find out what made it so powerful.

Williams and Tiedens (2016) responded affirmatively and offered the following findings from their review of 71 studies. On average, women were disparaged more than men for identical assertive behaviors of the verbal type, such as negotiating for a higher salary or asking a neighbor to turn down the music. Women were not penalized for assertiveness that was expressed through nonverbal means (e.g., expansive bodily stances, physical proximity) or for using paraverbal cues (e.g., speaking loudly or interrupting).

What do you think about these findings?

# Multicultural Dimensions

Imagine you are working with a woman or minority who is dealing with discrimination and the associated stress. One important dimension of being able to engage in assertiveness training is feeling good about oneself. Sometimes people who experience discrimination believe that the stressors they suffer are "their fault" and that "if only" they behaved more effectively, their issues would resolve.

Current research studies observed differences in assertiveness by race and ethnicity. In a study by Parham, Lewis, Fretwell, Irwin, and Schrimsher (2015), data showed White American males to be the most assertive, with African American females next. White females ranked third, followed by Vietnamese females, concluding with Vietnamese males.

In addressing these attitudes, cognitive instruction, as discussed in Chapter 9, can be a vital part of assertiveness training. Furthermore, the ideas of multicultural counseling and therapy (Chapter 5) clearly show that the focus of your intervention must often be on changing the environment, not just the individual. In assertiveness training language, there is a need to help individuals change cognitions about themselves and their environments so that they can be more effective and assertive.

Cheek (2010), for example, talks of the importance of "a foundation for the Black perspective." Assertiveness training does not seek to have African Americans behave or think like European Americans nor to have women think like men. Assertiveness training seeks to recognize the perspective and worldview of different multicultural and gender groups. Cheek (2010) notes that the African American cognitive perspective includes the following:

1. Familiarity and experience in both the African American and European American perspectives.

2. A frequent distrust of European Americans, with accompanying emotions such as anger and rage.

3. An emphasis on race and its importance.

4. Internal conflict as to whether to talk in "White" or "Black." African Americans are bidialectical.

5. An ability to "fake it" with European Americans.

The early work of Cheatham (1990), Parham (1990), and White and Parham (1990) addressed many of the same issues, leading to the conclusions that behavioral change is insufficient and that cognitive work on societal issues must be part of any treatment program with minorities. Focusing on the individual solely will often be seen as "blaming the victim." Cheatham argues that techniques such as assertiveness training, although useful, raise the question of causation: Did the issue originate in the client or society? If the latter is the issue, Cheatham advocates action by the counselor in the community or society as the best route toward individual change. Given this, the non–African American therapist or counselor must put behavioral treatment in context. Clearly, the techniques and ideas of this chapter have multicultural relevance, but they can only be accepted as part of the solution.

Similar issues of the meaning of assertiveness training with various groups can be raised. For example, assertiveness training for Latinas needs to be conducted with cultural sensitivity, for women from a Spanish-speaking tradition face different challenges when they act assertively than do most European American women. What is assertive for European American cultures may be considered intrusive and aggressive by those from other cultural groups. This latter point is especially true for those who may come from more sensitive cultures.

European American women usually find assertiveness training helpful, but it is most helpful if combined with issues around being a woman in society. Kantrowitz and Ballou (1992) give special attention to assertiveness training, stating that in a practical setting, assertiveness training should not be used to teach women a man's style of being. Cheek (2010) supports this point, noting that assertiveness training should be oriented to the African American culture and not "make Blacks White."

# Acceptance and Commitment Therapy

Acceptance and Commitment Therapy is a "third wave" behavioral treatment—treatments that contextualize thoughts and behaviors (Eifert & Forsyth, 2005). This therapy, developed by Steven Hayes, does not focus on changing unwanted emotions or thoughts. Human suffering, including anxiety and depression, is considered part of life. Our repeated attempts to make them disappear is what creates distress and mental disorders. Clients can lead meaningful lives in spite of their unwanted experiences. Their attempts to control their thoughts and feelings or "escape" their challenges and issues is counterproductive.

The overall goal of Acceptance and Commitment is to increase psychological flexibility. The specific goals are the acceptance of unwanted thoughts and feelings, and the creation of a life that has personal value for the client. Clients are encouraged to accept that their unwanted thoughts and feelings exist and to embrace them. Clients are empowered to choose what is important to them, what they value, and the direction they want to go in their life. Last, clients are encouraged to take actions and change their behaviors to realize their values.

Six core processes for developing psychological flexibility are described below (Harris, 2006),

1. *Acceptance* is the active embracement of the thoughts and feelings that would otherwise bring distress without attempts to change them.

2. *Cognitive defusion* involves techniques to change the way clients interact with or relate to their thoughts. For example, a negative thought could be repeated out loud until its impact is reduced, or can be treated as an object by giving it a color, shape, and size. The aim of defusion is to weaken the undesirable effects the thoughts have on the client. This allows the thoughts to exist, without giving them undue attention.

3. *Being present* is to have a nonjudgmental contact with current thoughts and inner sensations. It allows clients to have flexibility and control over their actions in a way that is consistent with their values.

4. *Self as context* relates to the view that the language and words that we use have implications for our thoughts and behaviors. It aims to help clients realize that what one thinks of as "self" or "I" is merely a concept. By recognizing this, clients are able to see their own experiences more objectively without attachment to them. This in turn allows clients to see their inner thoughts as different from their consciousness, which makes them less threatening.

5. *Values* include helping clients clarify their values and recognize that these values are purposes that guide their lives.

6. *Committed action* is the development of patterns of action linked to chosen values. Includes concrete goal setting and paths toward reaching those goals. Use techniques such as shaping, exposure, stress management, and skill acquisition.

The United States Substance Abuse and Mental Health Services Administration (SAMHSA) has now listed Acceptance and Commitment Therapy (ACT) as an empirically supported method and part of its National Registry of Evidence-based Programs and Practices (NREPP).

A study by Avdagic, Morrissey, and Boschen (2014) found that Group ACT led to steeper reductions in symptoms and higher levels of worry reduction than Group CBT. Other meta-analyses have found acceptance and commitment to be similar in effect than cognitive behavioral therapy (Hayes, 2004). Overall, this therapy is succeeding in areas where success has not been common in applied psychology (Hayes, Levin, Plumb-Vilardaga, Villatte, & Pistorello, 2013).

# Eye Movement Desensitization and Reprocessing

Eye movement desensitization and reprocessing (EMDR) is a set of strategies developed by Francine Shapiro (2001, 2013) for work with trauma. The complex method has eight phases that integrate many of the cognitive-behavioral techniques. Research results are increasingly promising.

The eight phases of EMDR include client history taking and involving the client very much in the direction of treatment. Part of early preparation is to empower clients and make them aware of how "safety and dysfunctional material from the past is arising internally" (Shapiro, 2001). During these first two phases, the memory is identified.

The third phase of EMDR asks clients to develop an image of their traumatic experience and then make a statement summarizing their thoughts and feelings about the trauma ("I should have done X." "It was my fault." "I'm helpless."). A positive self-statement is generated to replace the negative cognitions, and a scale (similar to the anxiety scale of systematic desensitization) is developed for levels of discomfort. These scales serve as a means to measure the immediate progress of the client and, later, client generalization to the real world.

In the fourth phase—desensitization—clients do three things simultaneously (image, thoughts, and note their physical body sensations) while the therapist moves the index finger in front of the eye. Then, the client empties the image from the mind, focuses on physical sensations and a positive self-statement ("I did the best I could." "It was not preventable." "I'm capable."). The reprocessing continues via an array of variations on the above. For example, the fifth phase focuses on "installation," and here the newer positive cognitions are given more force.

Phase 6 is a body scan where the client holds the negative event in mind and searches for remaining tension. These body feelings are also worked on carefully using similar methods. Phases 7 and 8 work on issues of closure and reevaluation of treatment progress.

There is strong clinical evidence that EMDR is an effective therapy for post-traumatic stress disorder. A review of twenty-four randomized controlled trials showed positive effects of EMDR therapy in the treatment of emotional trauma and other adverse life experiences (Shapiro, 2014). Furthermore, EMDR applied to patients with chronic psychotic disorders and post-traumatic stress disorder reduced trauma symptoms and paranoid thoughts, with many reaching the status of their psychotic disorder in remission (De Bont et al., 2016).

We should note some clear underlying principles in EMDR. First, images and body sensations are focused on, coupled with clear cognitive/emotional self-statements. This is followed by positive experiences and positive self-statements. This structure is, of course, similar to the positive asset search of the empathic conditions and the microskills. It is also similar to the positive use of images in Developmental Counseling and Therapy (DCT). Moreover, many techniques of cognitive-behavior therapy use these principles. Whether the saccadic eye movements are an active ingredient of treatment or not remains a concern (Schubert & Lee, 2009; Jeffries & Davis, 2013). Some researchers have suggested EMDR works because it represents a form of exposure to the dreaded stimulus (Sanderson & Carpenter, 1992). It is possible that the overlaying of positive images and experiences on the negative, particularly with body sensations included, will turn out to be increasingly important in the future.

# Relapse Prevention

Relapse prevention is a set of techniques and strategies developed by Marlatt (1980), and Marlatt and Donovan (2007), that have become foundational to counseling and therapy. It is an axiom of therapy that clients often will lose knowledge, behaviors, and new skills gained from therapy if the counselor does not take specific action to help clients maintain these gains.

In your client sessions, you may see some changes taking place. Then, the client returns to the home or work environment and faces the same issues that led to therapy. For example, an adult suffering from severe alcohol use or a teenager suffering from bulimia must live with the same family and/or job circumstances that likely played an important part in generating the original difficulties. Your task in relapse prevention is to work with clients to help them find workable strategies for the future.

## Helping the Client Cope with the Environment

Environmental realities (family, job, the availability of cigarettes, drugs, and so on) often conspire to make long-term behavioral maintenance almost impossible. To combat the difficulties of the environment, Marx (1982) developed a four-point program to help clients become more prepared to manage the post-counseling environment.

1. *Anticipate difficult situations.* Clients can often predict the circumstances likely to be threatening to their resolve to maintain their behavioral change program. Clients, with the counselor's assistance, can identify high-risk situations that might sabotage new learning and serve as an early-warning system so that they will be on guard against relapse.

2. *Regulate thoughts and feelings.* Emotions can sometimes get out of control and make us feel incompetent, upset, or temporarily irrational. Relapses are less likely to occur if clients expect these temporary responses and then return to a rational approach and learn from their mistakes.

3. *Diagnose necessary support skills.* Although we may help clients change behavior, their old patterns may reemerge when they are in a hurry or when faced with other stressors. Techniques such as assertiveness training, time management, or key cognitive skills may be useful in helping clients avoid eventual relapse.

4. *Regulate consequences.* A key behavioral concern is to provide appropriate conse-quences for behavior. When a client maintains a new behavior, there will be no thunderous applause. That support must come from the client, who must learn how to create meaningful rewards for good actions and behavioral maintenance.

# Theory into Practice

Completing the following exercises will help you practice behavioral counseling. Relapse prevention originated within behavioral therapy, but it is now employed by many other therapeutic approaches. Assertiveness training is a well-researched inter-vention that has been applied to a variety of areas, such as social skills, parent-child issues, physical performance, and self-care. Both are important skills to master.

## Making Relapse Prevention Work for You

Practice Exercise 8.3 summarizes the Relapse Prevention program so you can use it with a real or role-played client. Note that Relapse Prevention is skill specific. For example, a client may want to stop overeating. The task of the therapist is to help the client un-derstand the several strategies that are available for controlling overeating. Once clients have learned the behavioral techniques to slow down the rate of eating (that is, eat only in specified places and times, monitor calories, understand how emotions affect eating, and eliminate discretionary eating), they are ready to begin preparing for the hurdles in the environment once counseling is over and they must manage on their own.

---

PRACTICE EXERCISE 8.3. **Relapse Prevention Worksheet**

Self-Management Strategies for Skill Retention

By Robert Marx

(Go through this worksheet by yourself, perhaps using a behavior you have difficulty in maintaining. Alternatively, use the form to go through the dan-ger of relapse with a real or role-played client.)

**I. Choosing an Appropriate Behavior to Retain**

Describe in detail the behavior you intend to retain:

_____

_____

How often will you use it? _____

*(Continued)*

How will you know when a slip occurs? _____

_____

## II. Relapse Prevention Strategies

A. Strategies to help you anticipate and monitor potential difficulties—regulating stimuli

1. Do you understand the relapse process? What is it?

2. What are the differences between learning the behavioral skill or thought and using it in a difficult situation?

3. Support network? Who can help you maintain the skill?

4. High-risk situations? What kind of people, places, or things will make retention especially difficult?

B. Strategies to increase rational thinking—regulating thoughts and feelings

5. What might be an unreasonable emotional response to a temporary slip or relapse?

6. What can you do to think more effectively in tempting situations or after a relapse?

C. Strategies to diagnose and practice related support skills—regulating behaviors

7. What additional support skills do you need to retain the skill? Assertiveness? Relaxation? Microskills?

D. Strategies to provide appropriate outcomes for behavior—regulating consequences

8. Can you identify some likely outcomes of your succeeding with your new behavior?

9. How can you reward yourself for a job well done? Generate specific rewards and satisfactions.

## Predicting the Circumstance of the First Lapse

Describe the details of how the first lapse might occur, including people, places, times, emotional states.

*SOURCE:* Adapted from R. Marx, University of Massachusetts.

**PRACTICE EXERCISE 8.4. An Applied Behavioral Analysis and Assertiveness Training**

The purpose of this exercise is to integrate the concepts of this chapter in a practical format that you can use to implement assertiveness training in your own counseling practice. With a role-played client who is willing to discuss a specific situation when he or she may have been too passive or too aggressive, work carefully through the following interview:

1.  Empathic Relationship. Remember that data indicate that behaviorally oriented counselors and therapists offer as much or more warmth than other orientations to helping. Establish rapport with your client in your own unique way, and use attending behavior to tune in to the client and client observation skills to note when you have established rapport.

    Give special attention to structuring the interview and telling your client ahead of time what to expect. Behavioral counseling operates on a mutuality between counselor and client.

2.  Story and Strengths. Your goal is to get a clear, behavioral definition of the issue. The basic listening sequence (BLS) will help you draw out the specific behavior. Identify a clear, specific instance when the individual was not sufficiently assertive. Asking for concrete examples will facilitate operationalizing the present overly passive or overly aggressive behavior.

    Use applied behavioral analysis to find out the antecedents of the behavior. What was the context, and what happened before the behavior occurred? Define the negative behavior even more precisely. Finally, what were the consequences after the behavior? In each case use questioning skills to describe the behavior.

    A role-play is a particularly useful way to obtain further behavioral specifics. Once you have a clear picture of antecedent-behavior-consequence, have your client role-play the situation again with you acting as the other person(s). Make the role-play as real and accurate as you can. Finally, draw out positive assets of the client and the situation. What strengths does the client have that will be useful in later issue solution? You may find it necessary to provide your client with positive feedback, as nonassertive clients often have trouble identifying any positives in themselves or the situation.

    Again, one of the best ways to obtain behavioral data for assertiveness training is to assist your client in conducting a role-play with you where the situation is recreated in behavioral specificity.

*(Continued)*

3. Goals. Determining outcomes. Develop clear, specific behavioral goals with your client. You will want to use listening skills and operationalization of behavior methods. Is the goal established by your client clear, specific, and attainable? Will it lead to change?

4. Restory. Generating alternative solutions. At this point, you have the goals of the client that can be contrasted with the issue as defined. In addition, you have some positive assets and strengths of the client. With your client, review the goals and then practice in a role-play the new behaviors represented by those goals.

   Continue practicing with your client until the client demonstrates the ability to engage in the behavior. You may find that relaxation training, charting, modeling, and other behavioral techniques may be useful to supplement and enrich your behavioral program.

5. Action. Generalization. It is easy for a successful therapist to stop at the fourth stage. Here, it is critical that specific behavioral plans be made with your client for generalization of the behavior beyond the session. Use the relapse prevention form offered in this chapter with your client. Be clear and specific with your behavioral goals, and anticipate the likely relapse potential. Behavior that is not reinforced after training is likely to be lost and then lamented two weeks later.

6. Follow-up. One week after the interview, follow up with your client and determine if behavior actually did change. Later follow-ups can be useful to both you and the client. As necessary, use the relapse form to analyze any difficulty with behavioral generalization.

Table 8.2 presents current evidence of behavioral interventions effectiveness. Table 8.3 reviews the neuroscience foundations of behavioral interventions.

Table 8.2. **Research Box: Evidence Base of Behavioral Therapy**

Several Behavior Therapy Interventions enjoy strong empirical support. Exposure therapy, developed from behavioral theories of learning such as Mowrer's (1960) two-factor learning theory, states that fear and avoidance are learned through both classical and instrumental conditioning (Makinson & Young, 2012).

Prolonged Exposure (PE) therapy is a specific form of exposure therapy developed to treat PTSD. This model explains that PTSD's symptoms develop as (a) traumatic experiences become associated with similar neutral stimuli that subsequently acquire the power to cause the same anxiety and (b) the individual's avoidant behaviors become learned responses (negative reinforcement) to that anxiety.

*(Continued)*

**Table 8.2. Research Box: Evidence Base of Behavioral Therapy** *(Continued)*

The manualized PE treatment consists of nine to twelve 90-minute sessions. The initial sessions gather information about the client's stressors, provide psychoeducation about the treatment, and teach relaxation techniques. Remaining sessions are devoted to imaginal exposure to the traumatic events and in vivo exposure homework. Change is achieved through the habituation of anxiety response to cues associated with trauma (Powers, Halpern, Ferenschak, Gillihan, & Foa, 2010). PE have strong research support for its efficacy as a treatment of PTSD. Powers et al. (2010) meta-analyzed 16 randomized controlled trials and found consistent support for the efficacy of PE over control conditions. The Institute of Medicine (2008) systematically reviewed research on treatments of PTSD and found moderate to high evidence to support PE's efficacy as a treatment.

Specific phobias is another set of disorders treated with exposure therapy. Specific phobias are among the most common anxiety disorders in adults and children. A specific phobia is an intense fear that interferes with daily life. The treatment of choice for specific phobias is in vivo exposure (Botella et al., 2016).

Behavioral activation (BA) for depression is a treatment that enhances environmental positive reinforcement for adaptive, nondepressed behavior, and decreases unhealthy behavioral avoidance (Farchione, Boswell, & Wilner, 2017). On the basis of functional analysis and context-dependent strategies, this form of treatment teaches clients the role their environment plays in the maintenance and exacerbation of their depression and trains them to identify and modify those behaviors, increasing clients' self-efficacy and reducing depressive symptoms. BA can be applied to in a wide range of settings and clinical populations (Moshier & Otto, 2017) and its efficacy is comparable with other psychotherapies and medications for depression (Moradveisi, Huibers, Renner, Arasteh, & Arntz, 2013). Current conceptualizations of BA suggest that improvements in client's depression results from increased positive reinforcement of nondepressive and healthy, behaviors and a reduction in avoidance and other behaviors contributing to the depression (Hopko, Ryba, McIndoo, & File, 2015).

Behavioral couples therapy (BCT), a family treatment for substance abuse is as effective or more effective for married or cohabiting substance-abusing clients than traditional individual-based treatments. BCT results in greater reductions of substance use and partner violence, and higher levels of relationship satisfaction and functioning (Klostermannm, Kelley, Mignone, Pusateri, & Wills, 2011).

Also, a host of interventions for children that rely on operant conditioning principles have received empirical support, such as behavioral parent training and behavioral modification-based elementary school–based interventions, including behavioral interventions for managing pediatric ADHD (Antshel, 2015).

In addition, assertiveness training evolved from research by behavior therapists in the 1940's and 1950's as a form of social skills training and behavior therapy for clients with interpersonal difficulties. They conceptualized assertiveness as the result of a set of learned behaviors and communication skills that could be learned (Alberti and Emmons, 2017). Research have provided support for the effectiveness of assertiveness training in the US and abroad. For example, Eslami, Rabiei, Afzali, Hamidizadeh, & Masoudi (2016) found that conducting assertive training in a sample of Iranian high school students decreases their anxiety, stress, and depression. Global studies of assertiveness suggest that the global manager, in order to become more effective, needs to fully understand employee differences as represented by gender, national culture, and ethnicity (Parham, Lewis, Fretwell, Irwin, & Schrimsher, 2015).

Behavior therapy is also an established evidence-based intervention for Tourette's Syndrome and the management of tics characteristic of persistent tic disorder (PTD). Behavior therapy has demonstrated its efficacy across multiple RCTs and produces treatment effects comparable to those observed with antipsychotic medications. Indeed, professional organizations recommend behavior therapy as a first-line intervention for individuals with mild-to-moderate tic severity (McGuire et al., 2015; Murphy et al., 2013). Reviews of behavioral therapies for the treatment of Tourette's Syndrome have shown that habit reversal training (HRT), exposure with response prevention, and self-monitoring, are effective treatments for this disorder (Frank & Cavanna, 2013).

Additional information regarding effectiveness of the third wave of behavioral interventions can be found in the Research Box of Chapter 9.

**Table 8.3. Neuroscience and Behavior Therapy**

Our brains are programed to learn. Behavioral principles of learning are relevant for understanding how the brain learns. Fear and anxiety exemplifies this. Yes, at the genetic level the brain is encoded to learn, but we learn more behaviors than what it is programed at birth. For example, the fear response is innate but we still need to learn what the potential dangers in life are and what the predictors of danger are. Such learnings are based on associative fear memory and serve as the basis for fear, anxiety disorders, and escape/avoidance behavior. Thus, understanding the neurobiological mechanisms that mediate storage and retrieval of fear memories, as well as the underlying processes to weakening these memories are essential for clinical counseling and therapy (Kindt, 2014).

Pavlovian fear conditioning offers a practical model to study associative fear memory and its underlying neural, cellular and molecular mechanisms. Armed with these tools, behavioral neuroscience has begun to unravel the neurobiological foundations of associative fear learning and memory. Furthermore, recent findings on disrupting the reconsolidation of fear memory have open up new ways to provide long-term relief to clients suffering from excessive fears (Kindt, 2014).

Pain is another area of behavioral interest. Behaviorally conditioned cues associated with pain induce cortical responses that enhance our pain experience. Research following patients with acute pain show an emergence of cortical activation of emotion-related regions as the pain becomes more chronic. This highlights the important role of emotional regulation in the evolution of pain from acute to chronic. Furthermore, when negative mood is experimentally induced in pain free individuals, their pain responses to noxious stimulation are enhanced and an increment of activities in broad areas of relevant neural circuits, such as the prefrontal cortex, is observed (Okifuji & Turk, 2010).

The following are two additional observations regarding the relationship between neuroscience and behavior therapy. Clients with blood-injection-injury phobia develop a hypotensive response (feeling queasy) to experiences or even images of blood or injections (different than the usual phobic arousal response). The result is a sudden drop in blood pressure that may lead to feeling of queasiness or fainting. Tailored exposure procedures alleviate or resolve the phobic avoidance syndrome and normalize function (Barlow, 2014).

Unwanted adverse events during drug treatment have been noted on a number of mental health and physical conditions. Research shows that such negative reactions are often determined by behavioral factors rather than just medication. These negative outcomes are powerful enough to abolish the therapeutic efficacy of potent pain medications, in both brain and actual patient behavioral reports. Brain scans reveal that the lack of effect is mediated by higher activity in the hippocampus (Bingel, 2014). A recent study by Kam-Hansen et al. (2014) showed similar effects on a study of migraines.

Advancements in the field of behavioral neuroscience are contributing to the development of novel models of counseling and psychotherapy. Our field is moving toward a behavioral health orientation.

Behavioral techniques work, and clients often benefit from and enjoy the specificity of these techniques. At the same time, some clients will change their behavior but still feel that something is missing. These clients may benefit from the addition of more cognitive methods (Chapter 9) to your treatment plan, or some may want to examine the reasons their behavior developed as it did. In short, you may find that behavioral counseling benefits from association with other helping theories and by the framing in a multicultural and social-justice framework.

# References

Alberti, R., & Emmons, M. (1990/2017). *Your perfect right* (6th ed.). San Luis Obispo, CA: Impact. (Original work published in 1970).

American Psychiatric Association. (2013). *Diagnostic and statistical manual of mental disorders* (5th ed.). Washington, DC: Author.

Antshel, K.M. (2015). Psychosocial interventions in Attention-Deficit/Hyperactivity Disorder. *Child and Adolescent Psychiatric Clinics of North America, 24* (1), 79–97.

Armstead, C.A., Hébert, J.R., Griffin, E.K., & Prince, G.M. (2013). A question of color. *Journal of Black Psychology, 40*, 424–450. doi:10.1177/0095798413494404.

Avdagic, E., Morrissey, S., & Boschen, M. (2014). A randomised controlled trial of acceptance and commitment therapy and cognitive-behaviour therapy for generalized anxiety disorder. *Behaviour Change, 31*, 110–130.

Axelrod, M.I., Bellini, S., & Markoff, K. (2014). Video self-modeling. *Behavior Modification, 38*, 567–586. doi:10.1177/0145445514521232.

Bandura, A. (1976). Effecting change through participant modeling. In J. Krumboltz & C. Thoresen (Eds.), *Counseling methods* (pp. 248–264). Troy, MO: Holt, Rinehart & Winston.

Bandura, A. (1982). Self-efficacy: Mechanism in human agency. *American Psychologist, 37*, 122–147.

Bandura, A. (1989). Human agency in social cognitive theory. *American Psychologist, 44*, 1175–1185.

Bandura, A. (1997). *Self-efficacy: The exercise of control*. New York, NY: Worth.

Bandura, A., Blanchard, E., & Ritter, B. (1969). The relative efficacy of desensitization and modeling approaches. *Journal of Personality and Social Psychology, 13*, 173–199.

Barlow, D.H. (2014). The neuroscience of psychological treatments. *Behaviour Research and Therapy, 62*, 143–145. doi.org/10.1016/j.brat.2014.09.003.

Bingel, U. (2014). Avoiding nocebo effects to optimize treatment outcome. *Journal of the American Medical Association, 312*, 693–694.

Botella, C., M Ángeles, P., Bretón-López, J., Quero, S., García-Palacios, A., & Rosa María Baños. (2016). In vivo versus augmented reality exposure in the treatment of small animal phobia: A randomized controlled trial. *PLoS One, 11*(2).

Bower, S. (1976). Assertiveness training for women. In J. Krumboltz & C. Thoresen (Eds.), *Counseling methods* (pp. 467–474). Troy, MO: Holt, Rinehart & Winston.

Bower, S. (1990). *Painless public speaking*. Northamptonshire, UK: Thorsons.

Bower, S., & Bower, G. (1985/2004). *Asserting yourself*. Reading, MA: Perseus Books.

Bruni, T.P., Drevon, D., Hixson, M., Wyse, R., Corcoran, S., & Fursa, S. (2017). The effect of functional behavior assessment on school-based interventions: A meta-analysis of single-case research. *Psychology in Schools, 54*, 351–369. doi:10.1002/pits.22007.

Cheatham, H. (1990). Empowering Black families. In H. Cheatham & J. Stewart (Eds.), *Black families* (pp. 373–393). New Brunswick, NJ: Transaction.

Cheek, D. (1976/2010). Assertive Black … puzzled White. San Luis Obispo, CA: Impact.

Chen, Y.-F., Huang, X.-Y., Chien, C.-H., & Cheng, J.-F. (2016). The effectiveness of diaphragmatic breathing relaxation training for reducing anxiety. *Perspectives in Psychiatric Care*. doi:10.1111/ppc.12184.

Collura, T. (2014). *Technical foundations of neurofeedback*. New York, NY: Taylor & Francis.

Colman, A.M. (2015). *A dictionary of psychology* (4th ed.). New York, NY: Oxford University Press. doi:10.1093/acref/9780199534067.001.0001.

De Bont, P.A., Van den Berg, D.P., Van der Vleugel, B.M., De Roos, C., De Jongh, A., Van der Gaag, M., & Van Minnen, A.M. (2016). Prolonged exposure and EMDR for PTSD v. a PTSD waiting-list condition: Effects on symptoms of psychosis, depression and social functioning in patients with chronic psychotic disorders. *Psychological Medicine, 46*, 2411–2421. doi:10.1017/S0033291716001094.

Eifert, G., & Forsyth, J. (2005). *Acceptance & commitment therapy for anxiety disorders: A practitioner's treatment guide to using mindfulness, acceptance, and values-based behavior change strategies.* Oakland, CA: New Harbinger Publications.

Elpus, K., & Carter, B.A. (2016). Bullying victimization among music ensemble and theatre students in the United States. *Journal of Research in Music Education, 64*, 322–343. doi:10.1177/0022429416658642.

Eslami, A.A., Rabiei, L., Afzali, S.M., Hamidizadeh, S., & Masoudi, R. (2016). The effectiveness of assertiveness training on the levels of stress, anxiety, and depression of high school students. *Iranian Red Crescent Medical Journal, 18*(1), e21096.

Farchione, T.J., Boswell, J.F., & Wilner, J.G. (2017). Behavioral activation strategies for major depression in transdiagnostic cognitive-behavioral therapy: An evidence-based case study. *Psychotherapy, 54*, 225-230. doi: 10.1037/pst0000121.

Ford, C.D., Sims, M., Higginbotham, J.C., Crowther, M.R., Wyatt, S.B., Musani, S.K., … Parton, J.M. (2016). Psychosocial factors are associated with blood pressure progression among African Americans in the Jackson Heart Study. *American Journal of Hypertension, 29*, 913–924. doi:10.1093/ajh/hpw013.

Frank, M., & Cavanna, A.E. (2013). Behavioural treatments for Tourette Syndrome: An evidence-based review. *Behavioural Neurology, 27*, 105-117. doi:10.3233/BEN-120309.

Greenspoon, J. (1955). The reinforcing effect of two spoken sounds on the frequency of two responses. *American Journal of Psychology, 68*, 409–416.

Harasym, J., Langevin, M., & Kully, D. (2015). Video self-modeling as a post-treatment fluency recovery strategy for adults. *Journal of Fluency Disorders, 44*, 32–45. doi.org/10.1016/j.jfludis.2015.01.003.

Harris, R. (2006). Embracing your demons: An overview of acceptance and commitment therapy. *Psychotherapy in Australia, 12* (4), 1–8.

Hayes, S. (2004). Acceptance and commitment therapy, relational frame theory, and the third wave of behavioral and cognitive therapies. *Behavior Therapy, 35*, 639–665.

Hayes, S., Levin, M., Plumb-Vilardaga, J., Villatte, J., & Pistorello, J. (2013). Acceptance and commitment therapy and contextual behavioral science: Examining the progress of a distinctive model of behavioral and cognitive therapy. *Behavior Therapy, 44*, 180–198.

Hendershot, C.S., Witkiewitz, K., George, W.H., & Marlatt, G.A. (2011). Relapse prevention for addictive behaviors. *Substance Abuse Treatment, Prevention, and Policy, 6*, 17. doi.org/10.1186/1747-597X-6-17.

Higa-McMillan, C.K., Francis, S.E., Rith-Najarian, L., & Chorpita, B.F. (2016). Evidence base update: 50 years of research on treatment for child and adolescent anxiety. *Journal of Clinical Child & Adolescent Psychology, 45*, 91–113. doi:10.1080/15374416.2015.1046177.

Hopko, D.R., Ryba, M.M., McIndoo, C., & File, A. (2015). Behavioral Activation. In C.M. Nezu & A.M. Nezu (Eds.), *The Oxford Handbook of Cognitive And Behavioral Therapies* (pp. 229–258). New York, NY: Oxford University Press.

Institute of Medicine. (2008). *Treatment of posttraumatic stress disorder: An assessment of the evidence.* Washington, DC: The National Academies Press.

Ivey, A., & Hinkle, J. (1968). Students, the major untapped resource in higher education. *Reach* (a publication of the Colorado State University Collegian), *6*, 1, 4.

Jeffries, F.W., & Davis, P. (2013). What is the role of eye movements in eye movement desensitization and reprocessing (EMDR) for post-traumatic stress disorder (PTSD)? A review. *Behavioural and Cognitive Psychotherapy, 41*, 290–300. doi:10.1017/S1352465812000793.

Jowett Hirst, E.S., Dozier, C.L., & Payne, S.W. (2016). Efficacy of and preference for reinforcement and response cost in token economies. *Journal of Applied Behavioral Analysis, 49*, 329–345. doi:10.1002/jaba.294.

Kam-Hansen, S., Jakubowski, M., Kelley, J.M., Kirsch, I., Hoaglin, D.C., Kaptchuk, T.J., & Burstein R. (2014). Altered placebo and drug labeling changes the outcome of episodic migraine attacks. *Science Translational Medicine, 6*, 218ra5–218ra5.

Kantrowitz, R., & Ballou, M. (1992). A feminist critique of cognitive-behavioral therapy. In L. Brown & M. Ballou (Eds.), *Theories of personality and psychopathology: Feminist reappraisals* (pp. 70–87). New York, NY: Guilford.

Kindt, M. (2014). A behavioural neuroscience perspective on the aetiology and treatment of anxiety disorders. *Behaviour Research and Therapy, 62*, 24-36. doi.org/10.1016/j.brat.2014.08.012.

Klainin-Yobas, P., Oo, W.N., Suzanne Yew, P.Y., & Lau, Y. (2015). Effects of relaxation interventions on depression and anxiety among older adults: A systematic review. *Aging & Mental Health, 12*, 1–13. doi:10.1080/13607863.2014.997191.

Klostermannm, K., Kelley, M.L., Mignone, T., Pusateri, L., & Wills, K. (2011). Behavioral couples therapy for substance abusers: Where do we go from here? *Substance Use & Misuse, 46*, 1502–1509.

Leary, W. (1991, October 22). Black hypertension may reflect other ills. *New York Times*, p.52.

Lehman, B. (2015). Physical and nonphysical bullying victimization of academically oriented students: The role of gender and school type. *American Journal of Education, 122*, 133–159. doi:10.1086/683294.

Lehrer, P. (2016). Biofeedback. *Policy Insights from the Behavioral and Brain Sciences, 4*, 57–63. doi:10.1177/2372732216683709.

Lovitt, T.C. (2011). Applied behavior analysis. *Intervention in School and Clinic, 47*, 252–256. doi:10.1177/1053451211424598.

Macpherson, K., Charlop, M.H., & Miltenberger, C.A. (2015). Using portable video modeling technology to increase the compliment behaviors of children with autism during athletic group play. *Journal of Autism and Developmental Disorders, 45*, 3836–3845. doi:10.1007/s10803-014-2072-3.

Makinson, R.A., & Young, J.S. (2012). Cognitive behavioral therapy and the treatment of posttraumatic stress disorder: Where counseling and neuroscience meet. Journal of Counseling and Development, *90*, 131–141.

Marlatt, G. (1980, March). *Relapse prevention: A self-control program for the treatment of addictive behaviors*. Invited address presented at the International Conference on Behavior Modification, Banff, Alberta, Canada.

Marlatt, G., & Donovan, D. (2007). *Relapse prevention: Maintenance strategies in the treatment of addictive behaviors* (2nd ed.). New York, NY: Guilford.

Marx, R.D. (1982). Relapse prevention for managerial training: A model for maintenance of behavior change. *Academy of Management Review, 7*, 433–441.

Mazzucchelli, T., Kane, R., & Rees, C. (2009). Behavioral activation treatments for depression in adults: A meta-analysis and review. *Clinical Psychology: Science and Practice, 16*, 383–411. doi:10.1111/j.1468-2850.2009.01178.x.

Meichenbaum, D. (1985). *Stress inoculation training*. New York, NY: Pergamon Press.

Meichenbaum, D. (1991). Evolution of cognitive behavior therapy. In J. Zeig (Ed.), *The evolution of psychotherapy*, II. New York, NY: Brunner/Mazel.

Meichenbaum, D. (2007). Stress inoculation training: A preventative and treatment approach. In P.M. Lehrer, R.L. Woolfolk, & W.E. Sime (Eds.), *Principles and practice of stress management* (3rd ed.) (pp. 497–516). New York, NY: Guilford Press.

Mikami, A.Y., Jia, M., & Na, J.J. (2014). Social skills training. *Child and Adolescent Psychiatric Clinics of North America, 23*, 775–788. doi:10.1016/j.chc.2014.05.007.

Moradveisi, L., Huibers, M.J., Renner, F., Arasteh, M., & Arntz, A. (2013). Behavioural activation v. antidepressant medication for treating depression in Iran: Randomised trial. *The British Journal of Psychiatry, 202*, 204–211. doi.org/10.1192/bjp.bp.112.113696.

Moshier, S.J., & Otto, M.W. (2017). Behavioral activation treatment for major depression: A randomized trial of the efficacy of augmentation with cognitive control training. *Journal of Affective Disorders, 210*, 265–268. doi.org/10.1016/j.jad.2017.01.003.

Mowrer, O.H. (1960). *Learning theory and behavior*. New York, NY: Wiley.

Murphy, T.K, Lewin, A.B., & Storch, E.A. (2013). Practice parameter for the assessment and treatment of children and adolescents with tic disorders. *Journal of the American Academy of Child Adolescent Psychiatry, 52,* 1341–1359.

Nickles, T. (2017). Historicist theories of scientific rationality. In E.N. Zalta, (Ed.), *The Stanford Encyclopedia of Philosophy*. Retrieved https://plato.stanford.edu/archives/sum2017/entries/rationality-historicist/.

O'Handley, R.D., Ford, W.B., Radley, K.C., Helbig, K.A., & Wimberly, J.K. (2016). Social skills training for adolescents with intellectual disabilities. *Behavior Modification, 40*, 541–567. doi:10.1177/0145445516629938.

Okifuji, A., & Turk, D.C. (2015). Behavioral and cognitive–behavioral approaches to treating patients with chronic pain: Thinking outside the pill box. *Journal of Rational-Emotive Cognitive-Behavioral Therapy, 33*, 218–238. doi 10.1007/s10942-015-0215-x.

Parham, J.B., Lewis, C.C., Fretwell, C.E., Irwin, J.G., & Schrimsher, M.R. (2015). Influences on assertiveness: Gender, national culture, and ethnicity. *Journal of Management Development, 34*, 421–439.

Parham, T. (1990). Do the right thing: Racial discussion in counseling psychology. Paper presented at the American Psychological Association Convention, Boston, Massachusetts.

Parham, J.B., Lewis, C.C., Fretwell, C.E., Irwin, J.G., & Schrimsher, M.R. (2015). Influences on assertiveness: Gender, national culture, and ethnicity. *The Journal of Management Development, 34*, 421–439. doi 10.1108/JMD-09-2013-0113.

Peneva, I., & Mavrodiev, S. (2013). A historical approach to assertiveness. *Psychological Thought, 6*, 3–26.

Phelps, S., & Austin, N. (2002). *The assertive woman*. San Luis Obispo, CA: Impact.

Powers, M.B., Halpern, J.M., Ferenschak, M.P., Gillihan, S.J., & Foa, E.B. (2010). A meta-analytic review of prolonged exposure for posttraumatic stress disorder. *Clinical Psychology Review, 30*, 635–641.

Rajiah, K., & Saravanan, C. (2014). The effectiveness of psychoeducation and systematic desensitization to reduce test anxiety among first-year pharmacy students. *American Journal of Pharmaceutical Education, 78*, 163–169.

Ratts, M.J., Singh, A.A., Nassar-McMillan, S., Butler, S.K., & McCullough, J.R. (2016). Multicultural and social justice counseling competencies: Guidelines for the counseling profession. *Journal of Multicultural Counseling and Development, 44*, 28–48. doi:10.1002/jmcd.12035.

Robacker, C.M., Rivera, C.J., & Warren, S.H. (2016). A token economy made easy through Classdojo. *Intervention in School and Clinic, 52*, 39–43. doi:10.1177/1053451216630279.

Sanderson, A., & Carpenter, R. (1992). Eye movement desensitization versus image confrontation: A single-session crossover study of 58 phobic subjects. *Journal of Behavior Therapy and Experimental Psychiatry, 23,* 269–275.

Sarkova, M., Bacikova-Sleskova, M., Orosova, O., Madarasova Geckova, A., Katreniakova, Z., Klein, D., … Van Dijk, J.P. (2013). Associations between assertiveness, psychological well-being, and self-esteem in adolescents. *Journal of Applied Social Psychology, 43,* 147–154. doi:10.1111/j.1559-1816.2012.00988.x.

Schubert, S., & Lee, C.W. (2009). Adult PTSD and its treatment with EMDR: A review of controversies, evidence, and theoretical knowledge. *Journal of EMDR Practice and Research, 3,* 117–132.

Shapiro, F. (2001). *Eye movement desensitization and reprocessing (EMDR): Basic principles, protocols, and procedures* (2nd ed.). New York, NY: Guilford.

Shapiro, F. (2013). *Getting past your past: Take control of your life with self-help techniques from EMDR Therapy.* New York, NY: Rodale.

Shapiro, F. (2014). The role of eye movement desensitization and reprocessing (EMDR) therapy in medicine: Addressing the psychological and physical symptoms stemming from adverse life experiences. *Permanente Journal, 18,* 71–77. http://doi.org/10.7812/TPP/13-098.

Sielski, R., Rief, W., & Glombiewski J.A. (2016). Efficacy of biofeedback in chronic back pain: A meta-analysis. *International Journal of Behavioral Medicine, 24,* 25–41. doi:10.1007/s12529-016-9572-9.

Sitaram, R., Ros, T., Stoeckel, L., Haller, S., Scharnowski, F., Lewis-Peacock, J. … Sulzer, J. (2017). Closed-loop brain training: The science of neurofeedback. *Nature Reviews Neuroscience, 18,* 86–100. doi:10.1038/nrn.2016.164.

Skinner, B.F. (2014). Science and human behavior. The B.F. Skinner Foundation. Retrieved from http://www.bfskinner.org/newtestsite/wp-content/uploads/2014/02/ScienceHumanBehavior.pdf.

Sloane, B., Staples, F., Cristol, A., Yorkston, N., & Whipple, K. (1975). *Psychotherapy versus behavior therapy.* Cambridge, MA: Harvard University Press.

Sulzer-Azaroff, B. (1985). *Achieving educational success.* Troy, MO: Holt, Rinehart & Winston.

Sulzer-Azaroff, B., & Mayer, G. (1977). *Applying behavior-analysis procedures with children and youth.* Troy, MO: Holt, Rinehart & Winston.

Weiner, I.B., & Craighead, W.E. (2010). *The Corsini encyclopedia of psychology*, Vol. 1. Hoboken, NJ: Wiley.

White, J., & Parham, T. (1990). *The psychology of Blacks.* Englewood Cliffs, NJ: Prentice-Hall.

Williams, M.J., & Tiedens, L.Z. (2016). The subtle suspension of backlash: A meta-analysis of penalties for women's implicit and explicit dominance behavior. *Psychological Bulletin, 142,* 165–197. doi.org/10.1037/bul0000039.

Wolpe, J., & Lazarus, A. (1966). *Behavior therapy techniques.* Elmsford, NY: Pergamon Press.

Yucha, C., & Montgomery, D. (2008). *Evidence-based practice in biofeedback and neurofeedback.* Wheat Ridge, CO: Association for Applied Psychophysiology and Biofeedback.

Zoder-Martell, K.A., Dieringer, S.T., & Dufrene, B.A. (2016). Introduction to the special issue: The use of applied behavioral analysis to address student academic referral concerns. *Psychology in the Schools, 53,* 5–7. doi:10.1002/pits.21882.

### CHAPTER 9

# Cognitive-Behavioral Therapy and Counseling
## Cognitive Foundations of Change

Integration of thought, action, and emotions is the task of cognitive-behavioral therapy and counseling (CBT). The previous chapter accented behavior but reported that Behavior Therapy has moved from an emphasis on observable behavior and action to include the inner world of cognitions, experiencing, and context (Brown, Gaudiano, & Miller, 2011; Dimidjian et al., 2016).

The focus of this chapter is on the work of the therapists whose writing emphasizes cognition. It is critical to recall that thought without accompanying action (cognition without accompanying behavior) is considered empty by Ellis, Beck, Meichenbaum, and Glasser.

## SPECIFIC GOALS OF THIS CHAPTER:

1. To present the worldview provided by the cognitive-behavioral tradition.

2. To relate the cognitive orientation to multicultural counseling and therapy.

3. To describe the key ideas of four important cognitive-behavioral theorists—Ellis, Beck, Meichenbaum, and Glasser—and to illustrate some of their work with case examples.

4. To bring theory into action by encouraging you to test out the ideas of this theoretical orientation through practice exercises.

5. To review some of the evidence base and neuroscientific base of cognitive-behavioral therapy.

6. To introduce the third wave of cognitive and behavioral therapies.

# The Cognitive-Behavioral Frame of Reference

All cognitive behavioral therapies share a mediational proposition that affirms the existence of a thinking process and evaluation of external and internal events that affect an individual's responses to those events (Dobson & Dobson, 2016). *Cognitive processing* and *appraisal* are the terms used to designate these processes. Because negative symptoms, emotions, and behaviors are cognitively mediated, they can be modified by changing dysfunctional thinking and beliefs (Beck, Davis, & Freeman, 2015; Bennett-Levy, Thwaites, Haarhoff, & Perry, 2015). Table 9.1 explains the fundamental propositions of cognitive-behavior therapy.

Dysfunctional thinking is common to all psychological disturbances and affects clients' feelings and behavior. When clients learn to examine and evaluate their thinking in a more adaptive way, they improve their mood and their behavior (Beck, 2011).

---

**Table 9.1. CBT Basic Propositions**

According to Dobson (Dobson & Dozois, 2001; Dobson & Dobson, 2016) all cognitive-behavioral approaches share four foundational propositions or hypotheses:

1. The access hypothesis: The content and process of our thinking is knowable and, with appropriate training and attention, we can become aware of our own thinking.

2. The mediation hypothesis: There is cognitive mediation between events and our typical responses to them. The way we think about or interpret our experiences affects how we feel about our experiences. Our thoughts and beliefs strongly influence the way we behave. Our thinking can be monitored, assessed, and measured.

3. The change hypothesis: Intentionally modifying our thoughts can change the way we feel and behave in any given situation. Cognitive-based strategies are designed to make our responses more functional and adaptive.

4. The realist hypothesis: We live in a real world. An objective reality exists and the more accurate our appraisal of this reality, the higher our chances to adapt successfully to it and maintain a good mental health. Conversely, misperceptions of this reality would lead us to experience negative emotions and interpersonal outcomes.

---

## REFLECTION EXERCISE

What do you think about the idea that your own thoughts affect the way you feel and act?

What role do you give to your relationships in the way you feel and behave?

How does your culture influence the way you feel and act?

# The Move Toward Cognition

Initially, behavior counselors and therapists gave little attention to internal mental processes and thoughts. Instead, their focus was on direct, observable behavior. Albert Bandura's work was key in the shift to a more cognitive orientation. Bandura emphasizes that the client should be deeply involved in the choice and direction of treatment. His work on self-efficacy (1982, 1989, 1997) stresses that individuals grow best when they feel they are in control of their own destiny. Meichenbaum (1991) stresses person-environment interaction. Both believe behavior to be reciprocally influenced by thoughts, feelings, physiological process, and the consequences of behavior. Clients assumed a much more important role in the production of their own behavior. Within this view, the goal of the collaborative task for clients and therapists was to help clients appreciate how they create such realities.

In different ways, three additional figures—Albert Ellis, Aaron Beck, and William Glasser—have been leaders in this therapy. All three stress the importance of two goals in counseling and therapy: (1) to examine how clients think about themselves and their world and, if necessary, to help them change these cognitions; and (2) to ensure that clients act on those cognitions through behavior in their daily life—thus the term *cognitive-behavioral*.

Consequently, cognitive-behavioral theory has some useful elements to assist you in developing your own conceptualization (cognitions) about the therapeutic process and some techniques and actions (behaviors) that are useful in helping you decide the nature of your own work in the field.

How a person develops in the culture, particularly around issues of gender, was given virtually no attention until recently, as the primary focus of this theory has been on individual thinking. However, the wide national and international popularity of this approach has led to its effective adaptation to clients from different cultural backgrounds (Diaz-Martinez, Interian, & Waters, 2010; Guo & Hanley, 2015; Shattell, Quinlan-Colwell, Villalba, Ivers, & Marina, 2010).

Diaz-Martinez and colleagues (2010) combined cognitive-behavioral therapy with cultural values such as *familismo* (value of the family), *marianismo* (selfless sacrificing for the family), and *respeto* (respect) to understand and resolve psychological distress experienced by a Venezuelan woman. The culturally sensitive adaptation helped the counselor make sense of the Latina client's automatic thoughts and negative core beliefs. It also facilitated client conceptualization, treatment formulation, and application of coping strategies and cognitive change to improve the client's mental health and well-being.

# Multicultural Issues in Cognitive Therapy

Multiculturalism and the concept of worldview has been stressed throughout this book. A worldview is a way of organizing and construing our experience. You come to the study of counseling and therapy with a worldview that has been molded by your unique personal background, your family, and your cultural history. Kantrowitz and Ballou (1992) were among the first to seriously critique and challenge the cognitive-behavioral frame of reference:

> Challenging beliefs and thoughts may not fit well with many cultural and gender socialization patterns ... Asians, for example, have been taught to create emotional harmony and avoid conflict in accord with their cultural norms. Traditionally, women's perceptions, views and thoughts, have been minimized and misunderstood. (p. 81)

> There is nothing in the theory that enhances sensitivity to gender, race, and class issues ... The lack of careful consideration of gender, class, race, and ethnic factors as well as contextual information, specific antecedents, and consequences of specific beliefs and behaviors is a problem in cognitive-behavioral conceptualizations of pathology. Also problematic is their attribution of responsibility, implied by their goal of changing the individual client. (Also see Ballou, West, & Hill, 2008)

The last point is of particular importance. Multicultural counseling and therapy focuses on the importance of working with the client on issues of oppression and of seeking to change environmental context. One of the great cognitive shifts of this century has been the self-awareness movement of African Americans, Hispanic/Latinas/os, women, gay men and lesbians, those who face physical issues and disabilities, the older adults, and others. It can be argued that the changes in consciousness brought about by the Black identity movement have done more for African American mental health than all counseling theories combined.

# Cheek and Integrative Theory

Although the consciousness-raising movement has resulted in the development of multicultural theories of helping, its relationship to cognitive theories discussed here and in the preceding chapter should be mentioned. Cheek (2010), in his pioneering work on assertiveness training (see previous chapter), gave equal attention to the way African American clients viewed themselves and their condition as he did to assertiveness training techniques themselves. He is very likely the first person in the CBT movement who included multicultural cognitive issues as an explicit part of the treatment process.

# Cognitive Theory and the Multicultural Challenge

All four theorists discussed in this chapter—Donald Meichenbaum, Albert Ellis, Aaron Beck, and William Glasser—have used their techniques successfully with culturally different clients. Part of what is involved in surmounting discrimination, prejudice, and unfairness is generating a new cognitive view of self and the ability to change situations. Achieving such goals requires multicultural, social justice, and advocacy skills on the part of the therapist (Ratts, Singh, Nassar-McMillan, Butler, & McCullough, 2015).

In the chapter's first case example illustrating multicultural and social justice intervention, Albert Ellis helps a young gay male come to terms with his lifestyle orientation. In another example, a rational emotive behavior therapy group intervention program for African American adolescents was developed by Piotrowski and Franklin (1990). The program identified issues the youths had in their daily lives and then analyzed these issues through the lens of REBT method and theory. In this way, the adolescents were able to use cognitive change techniques on themselves, balancing issues of personal responsibility with injustice in the environment. The program concluded with role-playing and assertiveness training exercises to help the youths generalize their cognitive learning to actual behavior outside the group.

Cognitive techniques have potential and value in multicultural counseling. However, as Kantrowitz and Ballou (1992) indicated years ago, the emphasis in the approaches of Meichenbaum, Ellis, Beck, and Glasser is very much on individual change, with minimal attention given to consciousness raising of broader systemic issues, such as diversity and social justice.

# Meichenbaum's Construction of Cognitive-Behavioral Therapy

Donald Meichenbaum (1991, 2007) views cognitive-behavioral therapy as concerned with helping the client define issues and concerns cognitively as well as behaviorally and with promoting cognitive, emotional, and behavioral change and preventing relapse (see Chapter 8).

Meichenbaum's conception of cognitive-behavioral therapy summarizes many of the ideas of this book: Our task as therapists is to define the issues (and goals) with our clients; we then apply a wide variety of techniques to produce cognitive, emotional, and/or behavioral change. Finally, we must act if we are to ensure that behavioral change is to be maintained in the environment of the real world. Whether we commit ourselves to psychodynamic, behavioral, existential/humanistic, or some other orientation, meeting the criteria of this brief outline should be useful.

# Meichenbaum's Central Constructs

Meichenbaum (1991, 2007) outlines ten central tenets of cognitive-behavioral therapy. As you read the following, note how his modern view, based on traditions of behaviorism, expands our conception of the helping process. The following ten points are abstracted and paraphrased from Meichenbaum's presentation to the Evolution of Psychotherapy Conference (1991).

1. *Behavior is reciprocally determined by the "client's thoughts, feelings, physiological processes, and resultant consequences"* (p. 5). No one of these elements is necessarily most important. Thus, the therapist can intervene in the interacting system by focusing on thoughts or feelings, using medication, or changing consequences. Meichenbaum points out that with clients suffering from depression, the amount of criticism coming from the spouse (resultant consequences in the environment) is the most important predictor of relapse.

2. *Cognitions do not cause emotional difficulties, rather, they are part of a complex interactive process.* A particularly important part of the cognitive process is "metacognitions," where and when clients learn to comment internally on their own thinking patterns and thereby act as their own mentor or therapist. "Moreover, cognitive-behavioral therapists insure that clients take credit (for) behavioral changes they implement" (p. 7).

The cognitive structures we use to organize experience are our *personal schemas*. We learned these constructions from past experience, and changing ineffective schemas is an important part of therapy (p. 7). For example, clients who are diagnosed with anxiety disorders have particular concerns about issues of loss of personal control and physical well-being. Depressed individuals are prone to be concerned about issues of loss, rejection, and abandonment. Individuals who are particularly concerned about the issues of equity, fairness, and justice are prone to have issues with anger.

Meichenbaum and Gilmore (1984) describe the case of a lawyer who was the only son of an immigrant father. The lawyer, who evidenced difficulties with controlling his anger and experienced accompanying hypertension, marital discord, and depression, reported that he would "never allow anyone to take advantage of [me] like people who took advantage of [my father]. Got that!" The lawyer carried with him a personal schema concerning the issues of fairness and equity that colored the way he appraised events. This personal schema not only contributed to his short fuse and anger issue, but it also played a role in his altruistic behavior, as reflected in his being active in such movements as Amnesty International, a world agency for protecting human rights.

The cognitive-behavioral therapist helped this lawyer appreciate how he viewed the world and the impact of his personal schema (issues about fairness) on how he appraised events. Over the course of therapy, the client came to see the price he paid, the toll taken—both interpersonally and intrapersonally—for his particular way of viewing the world and himself. Collaboratively with the therapist, the lawyer came to better understand and alter his way of thinking and to cope with personal concerns.

3. *"A central task for the CBT therapist is to help clients come to understand how they construct and construe reality"* (p. 7). In this statement, Kelly's (1963) personal construct theory has been joined with the behavioral tradition. Meichenbaum stresses that clients and counselors can work collaboratively to explore cognitions and desired changes.

4. *"CBT takes issue with those psychotherapeutic approaches that adopt a rationalist or objectivist position"* (p. 8). This is an important and radical position that challenges the concepts of Ellis. Meichenbaum's approach is more existential-humanistic in nature and is interested in how clients subjectively experience the world. He stresses the importance of reflecting key words and phrases of clients and of mirroring their feelings back to them "in an inquiring tone" (the microskills of encouraging and reflection of feeling). By mirroring, Meichenbaum seeks to help clients understand how they have constructed reality.

5. *"A critical feature of CBT is the emphasis on collaboration and on the discovery processes"* (p. 8). Meichenbaum talks about the importance of having clients make their own discoveries. He recommends using a variety of behavioral techniques, such as those presented in this and the previous chapter, to facilitate the discovery process.

6. *Relapse prevention is a central dimension of cognitive-behavioral therapy.* Marlatt and Donovan's (2007) model (Chapter 8) has become central to the thinking of many different approaches to counseling and therapy (Hendershot, Witkiewitz, George, & Marlatt, 2011).

7. *"CBT holds that the relationship that develops between the client and the therapist is critical to the change process"* (p. 10). Empathy and listening skills (Chapters 3 and 4) are critical, as well as the important relationship dimensions stressed by Rogers (Chapter 11) and those presented in the last chapter (see Table 13.1).

8. *"Emotions play a critical role in CBT"* (p. 11). Much like psychodynamic theory, Meichenbaum's view of CBT suggests that clients bring into the therapy session the emotional experiences they have had with others. Past life experiences are seen as affecting how clients react with you in the session, and emotions are the route toward understanding the nature of the relationship.

9. *"CBT therapists are now recognizing the benefits of conducting CBT with couples and families"* (p. 12). In this sense, CBT is moving toward the network treatment constructions of marriage and family counselors and therapists.

10. *CBT can be extended beyond the clinic setting for both prevention and treatment.* Meichenbaum points out that CBT techniques have been used in probation offices, schools, hospitals, the military, and infant home visitations. It is becoming clearer that psychoeducational work is an important part of preventing drug and alcohol abuse and that it can be a useful part of any treatment program.

In summary, it can be seen that cognitive-behavioral therapy and counseling build on a behavioral foundation and provide an integrating framework for many differing and seemingly oppositional forms of therapy and counseling.

# Stress Inoculation and Stress Management

A useful technique is that of teaching clients how to deal effectively with stress (Meichenbaum, 2007). This training program involves three distinct phases: (1) helping clients develop a cognitive understanding of the role stress plays in their lives; (2) teaching specific coping skills so they can deal with stress effectively; and (3) working with thoughts and feelings about the stressful situation so they will be motivated to do something about stress. Meichenbaum makes the important point that cognitive awareness of stress is not enough to produce change, nor are learning skills. One must actually decide to do something.

## An Example

A professional couple may be faced with difficulties in their lives and may very frequently argue with each other. Their issues could be defined as a "marital difficulty," or it could be defined as a difficulty in coping with stress. The couple both may work and have two children and be active in the community. There simply isn't time to "do it all" effectively, and this becomes a major stressor in itself. The first task in stress inoculation is to help the couple define the issue as one of stress. This in itself can be useful, as the couple no longer has to blame each other for their difficulties and now can see the impact of their environment on the marriage.

Second, it is possible to teach stress reduction procedures, such as relaxation training and decision making (so that the couple does fewer things more systematically), and social skills (often via a form of assertiveness training) so that they might learn alternatives to constant work. These behavioral skills can lead to important changes and will likely involve techniques of modeling, role-play, and direct instruction. Finally, knowing one has difficulties with stress and having some skills are not enough. Will the couple decide for action? At the point of generalization, their emotional and cognitive world may again become stress engendering, and maladaptive thinking (and the accompanying dysfunctional emotions) will prevent them from a decision to act. The relapse prevention may be employed to ensure action. The therapist may follow up with this couple to ensure that they actually do implement the systematic plan of behavioral change that has been pinpointed.

# Developing a Stress Management Program

Most therapists and counselors today find themselves required to do some sort of stress inoculation or stress management training. Stress management combines many of the behavioral techniques described in the previous chapter, plus important cognitive techniques of this chapter. Assertiveness training is often an important part of stress inoculation. A model group stress management program includes, but need not be restricted to, the following:

1.  Establishing rapport and program goals. Usually, there is a special topic or need the group shares. For example, your group might be teenagers, adult children of alcoholics, women dealing with job stress, or an inpatient group diagnosed as borderline.

    Your task at this stage is to establish rapport, share your program goals, and learn the individual needs of your members. Modify your program to meet their wishes and needs.

2.  Cognitive instruction. Following the collaborative model, draw out from your group their ideas of the origins of stress and what it does. Help them organize their ideas and then provide additional information through handouts, lecture, or media, as appropriate.

3.  Stress management training. Usually, this takes the form of relaxation training, sharing of coping mechanisms, and social skills and assertiveness training (see Chapter 8). Many workshops include training in listening skills such as those presented in Chapter 4. Cognitive instruction following from the concepts in this chapter are also useful parts of the program.

    You will want to tailor your stress management program to the special needs of your group.

4. Homework. Relapse prevention techniques, such as those summarized in Chapter 8, are an important part of a stress management program. Unless your trainees are encouraged to take home what they have learned, the experience with you will likely be soon forgotten. Different types of homework can be assigned to reinforce learning from the stress management program (e.g., practice relaxation daily, use a time-management scheduler).

# Extensions of Stress Management Training

The concepts of stress management and stress inoculation now have been expanded to include specific suggestions as to how to work with victims of trauma (rape, abuse, and even victims of school violence and terrorist attacks). These techniques are increasingly vital as a treatment framework in its own right. Meichenbaum (2007) presents his innovative ideas with many suggested clinical interventions.

A nine-session stress inoculation was used with rape survivors by Foa et al. (1991). The program was found to be more effective than supportive counseling, and long-term follow-up revealed significant improvement in post-traumatic stress disorder. The overall content of the sessions was similar to the general concepts presented in this chapter. Foa et al. (1999) reported that the comparison of exposure therapy, stress inoculation training, and their combination for reducing post-traumatic stress disorder in 99 female assault victims, showed that all treatments reduced severity of PTSD and depression, compared with a waitlist control group. A group of 107 working individuals with above-average levels of distress participated in acceptance and commitment therapy ($n = 37$), stress inoculation training ($n = 37$), or a waitlist control group ($n = 33$). The group interventions were delivered in two half-day training sessions and were equally effective in reducing stress, compared to a waitlist control (Flaxman & Bond, 2010).

# Albert Ellis and Rational Emotive Behavior Therapy

Albert Ellis's rational emotive behavior therapy (REBT) originated in the mid-1950s as he became increasingly aware of the ineffectiveness of psychoanalysis to produce change in his patients. He found himself in an extremely successful private practice of psychoanalysis, yet was dissatisfied with the results he was obtaining. Gradually, he found himself taking a more active role in therapy, attacking the client's logic, and even prescribing behavioral activities for patients to follow after they left the counseling session (Ellis, 1983a). The result of this change has come to be known as rational emotive behavior therapy, a pioneering method of cognitive-behavioral therapy (Ellis & Joffe Ellis, 2011).

*Role of Emotion.* Emotion is central in rational emotive behavior theory. Unless the *E* in REBT is present, change is unlikely to occur. A rationalist position is not enough. Ellis himself is often seen personally as a highly rational and logical person. Yet, awareness of others' emotions and constructions of reality is central to his approach. For example, Weinrach (1990) provides a personal anecdote in that he describes his first observations of Ellis in action as he supervises a beginning helper:

> One of the students played a tape that reflected virtually no mastery of the REBT concepts of techniques, had been exhaustively taught and demonstrated over the previous three days … As the tape played, other group members and I expected Al to show some understandable frustration or exasperation. To the contrary, Al proved to be the ever-patient, tender, and gentle master teacher. He started at the very beginning and taught this student the basics of REBT, step-by-step. That experience forced me to reconcile the discrepancy between Al's public and private personae. (p. 108)

*Broad Basis.* Ellis's rational emotive behavior therapy, as with other cognitive-behavioral theories, is broad and eclectic. Ellis does not hesitate to use techniques from many differing theoretical orientations, according to the unique needs of the client. With a client having a sexual difficulty, Ellis may use his own cognitive strategies, but he will also use Masters and Johnson's (1970) sensate-focusing techniques and the behavioral techniques of progressive relaxation and modeling (Ellis, 1983b).

*Importance of Acceptance.* Ellis unconditionally accepts all manner of clients, just as does Rogers. And, like Perls, Ellis is searching for authenticity. Ellis encourages clients to think rationally and be in touch with their emotions. He may use bibliotherapy and ask clients to write journals to increase their understanding. He may use humor or sarcasm, as appropriate, with the client. He constantly stresses "homework" as important to the change process, seeking to have clients generalize ideas from the interview to their daily lives. It could be argued that his emphasis on what happens outside the interview was the precursor to relapse prevention described in Chapter 8.

We will first consider Ellis's approach to therapy in action and then examine the constructs and systems underlying his interviewing style.

## Case Presentation: Am I Gay?

Ellis's pioneering work in sexuality and sexual counseling is particularly noteworthy (Ellis, 1958). He was one of the first to recognize that being a gay male or a lesbian is an alternative lifestyle rather than a "clinical problem." Ellis may or may not have spent time developing rapport. He has a unique personal style and is known for starting the interview with a direct, rather confrontative challenge. Ellis is nonjudgmental about lifestyle issues. But he would urge that the individual make a decision based on personal preference rather than absolute musts and learn to live with that decision comfortably.

The following transcript illustrates how Ellis (1971) rapidly moves into direct action with the client, with the goal of eventually helping the client decide how he wants to live with the idea of being gay. Ellis's work on this case is typical of much of his thinking—and very advanced for his time. If the same client were treated today with rational emotive behavior therapy, we would expect that attention must also be paid to the issue of discrimination against gay men and lesbians.

1.  *Therapist*: What's the main thing that's bothering you? [Open question]

2.  *Client*: I have a fear of that I'm gay—a real fear of it!

3.  *Therapist*: A fear of becoming a gay? [Encourager]

4.  *Client*: Yeah.

5.  *Therapist*: Because "*if I were gay— what*?" [Open question, oriented to helping the client think in terms of logical consequences, a skill basic to REBT work. Note that Ellis here focuses on thoughts or cognitions about being gay rather than on behavior. "*It is not things, but how we view things*" that is most important.]

6.  *Client*: I don't know. It really gets me down. It gets me to a point where I'm doubting every day. I do doubt everything, anyway.

7.  *Therapist*: Yes. But let's get back to—answer the question: "If I were gay, what would that make me?" [Directive, open question]

8.  *Client* (pause): I don't know.

9.  *Therapist*: Yes, you do! Now, I can give you the answer to the question. But let's see if you can get it. [Opinion, directive]

10. *Client* (pause): Less than a person?

11. *Therapist*: Yes. Quite obviously, you're saying: "I'm *bad* enough. But if I were gay, that would make me a total shit!" [Interpretation, logical consequences. This particular interpretation also focuses on the logical consequences of the client's thinking. Note that A = the possible facts, B = the beliefs about the facts at A, and C = the emotional consequence. Ellis is particularly skilled at drawing out the cognitive thought patterns or sequences in client thinking and emotion.]

    [Ellis often uses language to shock, and in this process, the client realizes that even if the "worst" is said, the client still survives and is respected by Ellis. Underneath the "tough" demanding exterior, Ellis demonstrates immense positive regard for the strengths within each individual.]

12. *Client*: That's right.

13. *Therapist*: Now, why did you just say you don't know? [Open question]

14. *Client*: Just taking a guess at it, that's all. It's—it's just that the fear really gets me down! I don't know why.

15. *Therapist* (laughing): Well, you just gave the reason why! Suppose you were saying the same thing about—we'll just say—stealing. You hadn't stolen anything, but you thought of stealing something, and you said, "If I stole, I would be a thorough shit!" Just suppose that. Then, how much would you then start thinking about stealing? [Psychoeducation—sharing information/instruction, closed question]

16. *Client*: (silence)

17. *Therapist*: If you believed that: "If I stole it, I would be a thorough shit!"— would you think of it often? Occasionally? [Closed question]

18. *Client*: I'd think of it often.

19. *Therapist*: That's right! As soon as you say, "If so-and-so happens, I would be a thorough shit!" you'll get obsessed with so-and-so. And the reason you're getting obsessed with being gay is this nutty belief, "If I were gay, I would be a total shit!" Now, look at that belief for a moment. And let's admit that if you were a gay, it would have real disadvantages. Let's assume that. But why would you be a thorough shit if you were gay? Let's suppose you gave up girls completely, and you just screwed guys. Now, why would you be a thorough shit? [Encourager; interpretation, directive, open question. Here, we see the more inclusive microskill of logical consequences, as discussed in Chapter 4, used in its fullest sense.]

20. *Client*: (mumbles incoherently; is obviously having trouble finding an answer)

21. *Therapist*: Think about it for a moment. [Directive]

*(Albert Ellis, Growth Through Reason: Verbatim Cases in Rational-Emotive Therapy, pp. 102–103. Copyright © 1971 by Wilshire Book Company.)*

In later stages of the interview, Ellis seeks to have the client decide what he wants to do for logical reasons that are satisfactory emotionally—hence the term rational emotive. The individual must think and feel a decision is correct. This interviewing style may be most appropriate for Ellis, as it is congruent with his personality. It is not wise that you be as forceful and direct if this style is not personally authentic for you. His wife, Debbie Joffe Ellis is as skilled as he, and much more gentle.

Some confuse Ellis's personal style with his theory. It is possible to use the theory of rational emotive behavior therapy in a fashion that is authentic to you (Ellis and Joffe Ellis, 2011).

*Integrating Theory and Action.* The goal of the client and therapist in this session was to change cognitions about the idea of being gay (cognitive), to make decisions about how one wants to live (cognitive-existential), and to then act/behave according to those decisions (behavioral).

When encouraging the client to act on his cognitions, Ellis is likely to use role-plays similar to those of social learning theory (modeling; Bandura, 2012; Pratt et al., 2010) or Kelly's (1963) fixed-role therapy. He almost certainly would recommend "homework" in the final stages of the interview to ensure that the client does something different as a result of the session. In the follow-up interview, Ellis would likely check carefully on whether or not the client had done anything differently in the time between sessions.

Current therapeutic work with clients debating sexual orientation would possibly include homework assignments to help build awareness of the gay pride movement and examine the role of media in stereotyping, and bibliotherapy. Ellis has a long history of tolerance for difference. He would support a gay male or lesbian client in activities oriented toward helping the community become more aware of the group's special needs. While working with a client, Ellis would continue to challenge the basic assumptions and logical structure of the client's thinking. He would not hesitate to challenge any client whose thoughts and emotional patterns are self- or socially defeating.

## Central Theoretical Constructs and Techniques of REBT

Ellis and the REBT approach focus more on dysfunctional thoughts than do other therapies, although the importance of emotional foundations is also stressed. The REBT view is that people often make themselves emotional victims by their own distorted, unrealistic, and irrational thinking patterns. Ellis takes an essentially optimistic view of people, but criticizes some humanistic approaches as being too soft at times and failing to address the fact that people can virtually "self-destruct" through irrational and muddled thinking. The task of the REBT therapist is to correct clients' thought patterns and minimize irrational ideas while simultaneously helping them change their dysfunctional feelings and behaviors.

However, one cannot change irrational and ineffective thinking unless one first can identify such statements in the interview. Let us look at this most basic skill.

## Identifying Irrational Statements

In the interview, clients will frequently use such irrational statements as "If I don't pass this course, it is the end of the world"; "Because my parents have been cruel to me as a child, there is nothing I can do now to help myself"; "As the economy is lacking jobs, there is no meaning to my life"; "If I can't get that scholarship, all is ended"; and "The reason I have nothing is that the rich have taken it all." All of these statements represent "helpless" thinking, a common result of irrational thought.

For example, the gay client presented in the foregoing transcript began with an irrational statement that Ellis helped extend and clarify. For example, "Therapist 11: Yes. Quite obviously you're saying: 'I'm bad enough. But if I were gay, that would make me a total shit.'" Here, Ellis identifies a key irrational statement that will be the focus of the ensuing interview and treatment series.

There are many irrational or dysfunctional ideas. Following are five particularly common ones identified by Ellis (1967) in his early work. In these statements, you will also find an underlying demand for perfection accompanied by a denial of the impossibility of that perfectionistic demand. Read these examples carefully, and think about those that might apply to you:

1. It is a *necessity* to be loved and approved of by *all* important people around us. "If he (or she) doesn't love me, it is awful."

2. It is *required* that one be *thoroughly* competent, adequate, and achieving if one is to be worthwhile. "If I don't make the goal, it's all my fault."

3. Some people are bad and *should* be punished for it. "He (or she) did that to me and I'm going to get even."

4. It is better to *avoid* difficulties and responsibilities. "It won't make any difference if I don't do that. People won't care."

5. It is *awful* or *catastrophic* if things are not the way they are supposed to be. "Isn't it terrible that the house isn't picked up?" (p. 84)

This list can be amplified, but more at issue is your ability to recognize irrational thinking in whatever form it takes. Listen carefully to those around you, and you'll discover that the world is full of irrational ideas and thoughts. Particularly, search the above statements for "all-or-none" thinking—irrational thinking that helps the client avoid the complexity of life. The words *should*, *ought*, and *must* are useful indicators of irrational thinking.

The basic therapeutic maneuver is always to be on the alert for irrational thinking, and when it is observed, to work on it directly, concretely, and immediately. REBT counselors vary in their use of microskills, but Ellis uses a large number of open and closed questions, directives, interpretation, psychoeducation, and opinion. The listening skills of paraphrasing and reflection of feeling play a less prominent role in his therapy. Table 9.2 presents a current categorization of irrational beliefs.

An abbreviated REBT self-help form is presented in Table 9.3. This form may be helpful in aiding you to identify your own and your clients' faulty thought patterns. In addition, the table summarizes the A-B-C/D-E-F patterns discussed in the following subsection.

## The A-B-Cs of Cognition

Perhaps Ellis's most important contribution is his A-B-C theory of personality that can be summarized as follows:

A—the "objective" facts, events, behaviors that an individual encounters.
B—the person's beliefs about A.
C—the emotional consequences, or how a person feels and acts about A.

People tend to consider that A causes C, or that facts cause consequences. Ellis challenges this equation as naive, pointing out that it is what people think about an event that determines how they feel. Applying the A-B-C framework to the preceding interview with the gay client, we see that:

A—The "objective fact" is the possibility of being gay.
B—The client believes being gay is bad and self-denigrating.
C—Therefore, as an emotional consequence, the client experiences guilt, fear, and negative self-thoughts.

In this case, the client has short-circuited B, concluding that "if I am a gay, I am bad." Thus, Ellis's goal is to dispute this belief system. What the client thinks about being gay is causing his anxiety and difficulties, not the objective facts of the situation. There are obviously numerous people—gay, lesbian, and heterosexual—who believe that alternative lifestyles are valid and who do not come to the same conclusion at C that this client does.

Ellis's approach in this case, then, was to *challenge* the client's logic: "If I were gay, I would be a total shit." He points out the A-causes-C conclusion and challenges the irrationality of this "logic." Again, it can be seen that it is not the specific beliefs that are challenged, but rather the unfoundedness of those beliefs, that leads to illogical conclusions.

Ellis does not challenge the client's goals and values (that he doesn't want to be gay) but instead attacks his absolute demands about achieving these values (that under no conditions must he be gay; that he would be a worthless "shit" if he were gay). The emphasis of the therapy is on changing the way the client thinks about the behavior, rather than on changing the behavior itself.

The A-B-C framework is really the nugget of Ellis's theory. It is not the event that really troubles us, but instead the way we think about the event. Ellis's theory is closely akin to humanistic therapies that focus on meaning and the importance of how a person interprets the world. Frankl (Chapter 11), for example, survived the horrors of a Nazi concentration camp. He comments on how his survival depended on his ability to believe certain things about the events around him and to find something positive on which to depend. Beliefs were more important to survival than objective facts.

**Table 9.2. Current REBT Categories of Irrational Beliefs**

Current categories of irrational beliefs articulate the following four belief processes—inferences about an event: demandingness, catastrophizing/awfulizing, low frustration tolerance (LFT), and a global evaluation or self-downing.

1. Demandingness: Also known as absolutisms; inflexible requirements expressed in terms of *musts, should, have to,* and *oughts* (e.g., "I should not be in pain"; "I should experience no stress in life.").

2. Catastrophizing: Evaluating of negative events as worse than they could be (e.g., "This is 110 percent terrible!" "It is horrible that I failed this important quiz!").

3. Low Frustration Tolerance (LFT): The evaluation that certain situations are unbearable (e.g., "I can't stand this!" "I can't deal with these difficulties.").

4. Global Evaluation or Self-downing: Defensive self-critical belief related to situations when achievements are not experienced as satisfactory. It is the tendency to be excessively critical and to make global negative evaluations of oneself (e.g., "The world is worthless"; "I am useless if I have difficulties.").

(Adapted from Ellis and Joffe Ellis, 2011, and Suso-Ribera et al., 2016).

# The D-E-Fs of Promoting and Maintaining Change

*D* stands for disputing irrational beliefs and thinking. It is at this point that Ellis's work first became controversial. When the logic of the client's A-B-C thought patterns is ineffective, Ellis becomes directly challenging and confrontative: "But why would you be a thorough shit if you were a gay? Let's suppose you gave up girls completely, and you just screwed guys. Now, why would you be a thorough shit?" This language and style offended many people in the 1950s and 1960s, a time when Rogerian listening and respect were at their greatest influence. Furthermore, Ellis's tolerance and openness to cultural difference were ahead of his time.

It is now widely recognized that disputing and challenging clients' logical systems is an effective mode of intervention and that rational disputation is an important therapeutic strategy. In the later sections of this chapter, you will see that Beck and Glasser both use disputation, but in a gentler manner than that associated with Ellis.

*E* is the effect that disputation (or other interventions) have on the client. At this point, the client generates a more effective belief system or philosophy about the situation. In the above example, the fact of being gay has not been changed, but the client generates a new way of thinking about himself: "It's OK to come out of the closet and be a gay man—if I wish to take that direction."

*F* stands for new feelings. The client has new emotions associated with the situation: "I'm gay and I'm proud and I feel good about myself." REBT emphasizes emotional change as foundational. Although much of REBT work focuses on logical thinking, unless logic is ultimately integrated with emotion, change will be unlikely to last. Emotional change is basic if we are to prevent relapse into old ways of thinking and feeling. Use the form on Table 9.3 to gain a personal understanding of the ABCDEF model.

## Debbie Joffe Ellis: A Personal Description of Ellis' Work

I worked with Al (Albert Ellis) in every aspect of our work lives in the years we were together—the final decade of his life, including teaching and co-leading groups. Al would frequently demonstrate compassion and acceptance when people were experiencing painful emotions, reminding them of their human fallibility, and encouraging them to embrace a balanced perspective of their adversities. He would incorporate humor when he assessed that might help group members and clients, and when he assessed that it could be helpful he would express in outlandish and colorful ways to help shift any of their rigid adherence to self-defeating thinking.

Albert Ellis and the methods of REBT are not one size fit all. The effective REBT practitioner is willing to be flexible and adjust his or her tone and manner to facilitate rapport and to encourage clients openness towards learning how to help themselves not only feel better, but GET better!

During a presentation that I co-led with Al, a member of the audience, a practicing psychologist, said that she was always pressuring herself to write one more paper, and shared that this was causing extreme stress that was affecting her sleep, health, and wellbeing. She shared later that she was bracing herself for Al to reprimand her and strongly tell her to get off her backside and just do it-but instead Al was able to pick up on her perfectionistic tendencies and compulsive need to do things perfectly well, and her lack of self-acceptance. She was making herself feel inadequate and worthless in addition to stressing herself out.

With humor—telling her that there are thousands more papers she could write—not only one more as she described, and with a tender manner, he suggested that if she didn't tell herself that she needed to do papers perfectly well, she might get more done and minimize stress. He disclosed that he—at the age of 92 at that time—was working on 5 new books and scores of articles, and if he thought that he should do all perfectly well—he might not get anything done! He continued to tell her that through making effort to do good rather than perfect work he got much work done, and it still helped many people.

This woman shared later that Al's words, his humor and his conveyance of unconditional acceptance of her despite and including her flaws and self-defeating perfectionism, led to her feeling immense relief, and calm, and she intended to continue to work on reducing her perfectionistic tendencies and changing her lack of unconditional self-acceptance.

## Ellis and Multicultural Issues

Ellis's general attitude toward multicultural issues is one of respect for clients' particular values. He does not seek to change these values unless they are self-defeating and overly rigid. Ellis (1991) presents a case example that illustrates this approach:

> I am seeing a woman right now who is a Mormon, semi devout, but she is also pregnant and has a lover who is an Orthodox Jew whom

she might well decide not to marry. So her problem is whether to get an abortion, because if she does, her church and her Mormon family will probably excommunicate her. So I deal with her differently than I would with somebody who comes from a less rigid family and religion. I know that she is going to have a hard time with her cultural group if she does get an abortion, and therefore, in her particular case, it might even be better to have the child and see another man who might want to marry her and become a Mormon.

So when people have strong religious and cultural values, I accept their values but also show them how they may be defeating themselves in terms of their own standards. They can, using REBT, choose to stick with their cultural values or decide to change them without damning themselves. Thus, if my Mormon client did decide to go through with an abortion, I would help her to accept herself, in spite of her "wrong" act, and then to plan on becoming pregnant again after she marries. So there are some "samenesses" about REBT theory and practice for most people and most cultures. But clients can also keep their cultural values and then not needlessly upset themselves when they lead to frustration and/or are not perfectly followed. (p. 16)

---

**Table 9.3. REBT Self-Help Form**

This form can be used for examining yourself. It also can be used with equal effectiveness in the interview with your clients and/or as a homework assignment for them.

A. *Objective fact, event, or behavior.* List and describe the activating events, thoughts, or feelings that happened just before you felt emotionally disturbed or acted in some self-defeating way.

B. *Identify the irrational beliefs.* Look at the description of events, thoughts, or feelings above and examine them for irrational thinking.

C. *Emotional consequences.* How did you feel after the fact, event, or behavior? What did you do to produce it? How would you like to change?

   Write A and C on a separate piece of paper.

A. *Activating Event* describe in the more precise way what happen that made you feel emotionally distressed and act in a self-defeating way.

B. *Irrational Beliefs* Circle all those that apply or add additional beliefs.

   1. I MUST do well or very well.
   2. I am a BAD or WORTHLESS PERSON when I act weakly or stupidly.
   3. I MUST be approved or accepted by people whom I find important.
   4. I NEED IMMEDIATE GRATIFICATION for my needs.
   5. Other people MUST live up to my expectations or it is TERRIBLE.
   6. It's AWFUL or HORRIBLE when major things don't go my way.
   7. I CAN'T STAND IT when life is really unfair.
   8. Additional irrational beliefs

*(Continued)*

**Table 9.3. REBT Self-Help Form (Continued)**

C. *Disputes* Look at the irrational belief and then challenge it. Examples:

"Why MUST I do so very well?" "Where is it written that I am a BAD PERSON?" "Where is the evidence that I MUST be approved or accepted?"

D. *Effective Rational Beliefs*

These can replace irrational beliefs. Examples: "I would prefer to do well, but I don't HAVE TO BE that perfect." "I am a person who acted badly, but not a BAD PERSON." "There is no evidence that I HAVE TO BE approved, although I would like to be."

E. *More positive and rational feelings and behaviors.* Finally, place here the feelings, behaviors, and thoughts you are experiencing after challenging and working on your irrational beliefs.

Can you make the following commitment? "I will work hard to repeat my effective rational beliefs forcefully to myself on many occasions so that I can make myself less disturbed now and act less self-defeatingly in the future."

*SOURCE:* This form is summarized from a longer form authored by Joyce Sichel and Albert Ellis (1984) copyrighted by and available from the Institute for Rational-Emotive Therapy, 45 East 65th Street, New York, N.Y. 10021.

## Extending REBT

At times, Ellis moves to what could best be considered an instructional model in that he actively teaches clients how to think. This instructional model is supplemented by homework assignments where clients are encouraged to try out newly learned behaviors and to report back on their success. Ellis often has his clients take audio recordings of the interview home with them so that they can review the session during the week.

If the task of the REBT counselor is to free the client from irrational thinking, a parallel and more positive goal is to equip the client with beliefs that are satisfactory and functional for everyday life. For example, it is not enough to help free the gay client from irrational thoughts and fears about being gay. It is also necessary to provide an opportunity for this client to explore a new set of beliefs and actions and to test their rationality and workability.

## Summary

The following puts the basic tenets of REBT into brief list form:

1. Expect your clients (and yourself, your family, and your friends) frequently to make impossible, perfectionistic statements about themselves and others.

2. The basic treatment rule is to dispute the rationality of the perfectionistic cognition and to teach clients how to do their own realistic, open-minded disputation.

3.  In therapy, it may be useful to work through several irrational statements in a step-by-step A-B-C process and search for repeating patterns of thought and emotion.

4.  Agreed-on homework can help your clients take their new knowledge into the real world.

5.  Do not hesitate to add Gestalt, behavioral, or other techniques to the REBT structure if you feel it helps you and your client reach your joint goals.

# Aaron Beck and Cognitive Therapy

Aaron Beck, a leading cognitive-behavioral therapist, first became known for his success in treating depression. The personal strength and warmth of Beck are perhaps best illustrated by a case from his well-known book *Cognitive Therapy and the Emotional Disorders* (1976). He describes a depressed patient who had failed to leave his bedside for a considerable period of time. Beck asked him if he could walk to the door of his room. The man said he would collapse. Beck said, "I'll catch you." Through successive steps and longer walks, the man was shortly able to walk all over the hospital and in one month was discharged.

*Relationship as Central to Change.* How are such "miracles" accomplished? First, Beck is a powerful and caring individual who himself believes that change is possible. He is willing to provide himself as a support agent for the client and has specific goals and behaviors in mind for the client. In this case, he sought to change the way the depressed person thought about himself. Through slow, successive approximations, from shorter to longer walks with Beck's help, the client was able to change his behavior.

This case illustrates the importance of relationship and behavior as well as cognitive change. In Beck's framework, we would call the basic cognitive change a move from "I can't" to "I can." Basically to much of behavioral work is taking small steps toward success. Somewhere along the continuum of change, clients will likely realize that they can do something to help themselves. It is this attitude of "I can" that is basic to generalizing learned behavior and ways of thinking from the therapy hour to real life.

Beck has outlined important principles for working with many types of patients. Since his early work with depression, he has demonstrated that his concepts are equally effective with anxiety disorders (Clark & Beck, 2010a), personality disorders (Beck, Davis, & Freeman, 2015), and many other issues. The following transcript reveals some of the characteristics of Beck's interviewing style.

## Case Presentation: Depression

In the following session, Beck uses a relatively direct interviewing style. When the client says, "Now I'm all alone!" Beck probes this statement for underlying meaning and logic. In this search for meaning, there are clear parallels to the approach of Frankl's logotherapy. By implicitly questioning the logic underlying the client's overgeneralization or automatic thought, Beck attempts to produce change in cognitive processes similar to Ellis's attack of irrational thought patterns.

In theory and practice, Beck focuses on identifying automatic thoughts, internal self-statements that help clients organize their thinking patterns. This is a critical difference from the approach of Ellis. Beck does not focus on unconscious motivation; nonetheless, his psychodynamic roots still influence his work to some extent. For example, he considers automatic thoughts to be rooted in early parent-child interactions and to repeat in adulthood. Many of our long-term schemas (core schemas) are acquired during childhood (Young, Klosko, & Weishaar, 2003).

In the following vignette (Diffily, 1984), Beck uses many questions to encourage clients to explore themselves and their situations.

> Strain grips the face of the young woman on the television monitor. Hers would be a pretty face were it not for the puffy, reddened eyes, and the glistening tear-tracks splotched on her cheeks.
>
> "My husband wants to leave me," Linda is saying to someone out of camera range. "He wants to go for an unspecified length of time. Then maybe he'll come back. He says it's non-negotiable; he wants no more commitment." She has difficulty controlling her voice; breathy sobs punctuate her recitation.
>
> "I've gotten more and more depressed," Linda continues. "It felt like I had a guillotine over me, or like I had cancer. I told him maybe he'd better leave. And now—(she begins sobbing in earnest)—now I'm all alone!"
>
> The camera draws back, bringing into view a man seated at the table with Linda. His most striking feature is a thatch of thick white hair smoothed back from his face. Behind his glasses the psychiatrist's eyes are at once gentle and probing. He regards Linda calmly. "What do you mean, all alone?" asks Beck.
>
> [This is the first step toward searching for automatic thoughts. By asking "What do you mean, all alone?" Beck is moving beneath the surface structure sentence to find the underlying thinking patterns.]
>
> "I don't have Richard!" she gasps, mopping at her eyes with a tissue from the box on the table. "Life wouldn't mean anything without him. I love him so much."

[Here we see A—the objective facts, "I don't have C"—the emotional consequence, a classic Ellis irrational thought pattern. Beck, however, if searching for the automatic thought patterns underlying the depression.]

"What do you love about him?" Beck asks.

"I don't know," Linda says, shaking her head, confused. "I guess I live for him. He's so rotten. But I remember the good stuff."

[In this exchange, the client begins to examine her own faulty automatic thoughts.]

CLICK. In the darkened viewing room, Beck pushes a switch and freezes the images of Linda and himself on the monitor. He turns to a visitor and explains his strategy for this emergency therapy session. "First, you always summarize the patient's thoughts to her. This gives clarity and reassures her that you understand. Second, you have to figure out where you're going to move in. It's very difficult in a crisis situation. You have to think on your feet." Beck explains that according to his theory of depression, the patient will underestimate herself and exaggerate her degree of loss and a negative view of the future. "You have to explore these channels and work it through."

CLICK. The video images move and talk. On the screen, Beck summarizes for Linda his first therapy session with her six weeks earlier, reminding her that Richard had made certain promises and commitments regarding their marriage. "What happened between then and now?"

[Highly characteristic of the cognitive-behavioral approach is the search for sequence. Much like the antecedents, behaviors, and consequences of functional analysis explored in Chapter 8, CBT is concerned with ordering of events but gives much more stress to internalized thoughts and feelings than do behavioral methods.]

"I don't know. I really think he lied to me." She begins to sob again. "This is like a bad dream."

"Richard deceived you?"

"He did. I feel like a fool," Linda cries, "for believing him."

CLICK. To his visitor, Beck says, "This is aggravating the problem; she is feeling deceived, feeling foolish. Which angle am I going to explore—her actual loss, or the hurt to her pride? You have to make a split-second decision."

CLICK. On the screen, Beck is talking quietly to Linda. "What have you lost?" He is going for the loss angle first.

"I lost my best friend, someone to talk to." She pauses and adds rue-fully, "Even though he didn't want to listen to me." What else? "I've lost the father of my children. Financial support, security."

[Note the "all-or-none" thinking on the part of the client. The CBT therapist will recognize the very real hurt, but will not accept that all is lost. Common to irrational ideas and automatic thoughts is over-generalization of negatives and deletion of possible positives.]

"What hurts you most?" Beck wonders. "The money?"

"No—losing him. I've lost all my hopes." What hopes? "That things would work out for us."

Aren't there other hopes? Beck asks.

Linda looks doubtful. "I guess I'm not letting them come in. But who would want me? He rejected me. I'm not lovable."

[The above is a good example of rational disputation. The client's faulty thinking patterns are challenged by the therapist. Note below how humor can be used to challenge patterns of thinking.]

"Do you really believe that? Is Richard the supreme arbiter of that?" Beck says. "Should we trust his judgment?"

Laughter. Linda, incredibly, is laughing. "Don't make me laugh when I'm crying!" she is saying through a mixture of giggles and sobs.

A brief smile plays across Beck's face; he continues pressing his point. "Richard broke promises to you on and off for months. And you feel terrible that a guy like that doesn't love you? Why should his problem be reflected in your self-image?"

Beck asks Linda to list her husband's good and bad qualities. He re-cords them on a long sheet of lined paper divided into two columns. When Linda finishes her list, the "bad" column is twice as long as the "good" column.

[This may be recognized as a form of decisional balance sheet. Problem-solving techniques are often used in CBT.]

"Is this the kind of man you'd want for a mate?" the psychiatrist asks.

"It really sounds dumb when you write it out," she admits.

Eventually, Beck elicits another admission from Linda: Even though she is suffering from dire emotional stress and pain, she can endure it and even adopt a more positive view of her future. "I guess I've been standing it so far," Linda says, "so I can stand it now."

[The faulty automatic thoughts about her husband have been adequately challenged, and Linda can now revise her personal constructions of herself, her ex-mate, and her situation.]

CLICK. Beck's visitor, moved by the emotions and the glimpse of hope she has viewed on videotape, has a question for him.

"Didn't you want to hug Linda, to comfort her, instead of just asking questions?"

"Empathy and understanding," the psychiatrist answers, "are not enough in therapy. As in any branch of medicine, you tend to empathize with the patient. But most reassuring to the patient is your understanding of her problem, and your ability to give her a mastery of the situation." In no way, Beck emphasizes, was Linda's depression "cured" by this one session; she had to come back for therapy on a regular basis for a while. But using his therapeutic approach—one that has inspired considerable interest and excitement among mental health professionals worldwide—a therapist can "snap people out of a severe depression very quickly" and help them start coping with their problems in a constructive, rewarding way.

(Selection from Anne Hinman Diffily, "Aaron Beck: A Profile," Brown Alumni Monthly, pp. 39–46. Copyright © 1984 by Brown University. Reprinted with permission.)

## Beck's Central Theoretical Constructs and Techniques

Beck gives central attention to the cognitive process. He points out that there is a constant stream of thoughts going through our minds, not all can we listen to. These thoughts move so rapidly that Beck calls them "automatic thoughts" and points out that it is difficult to stop them. In the case of the woman described in the transcript, she automatically thought her life would be "over" and she would be "alone" without her husband. Beck is concerned with stopping such harmful automatic thoughts and having the person examine his or her mode of thinking and eventually develop new forms of cognition.

## Changing Faulty Thought Patterns

Beck uses a collaborative working approach. A sort of meeting of the experts, where the counselor is an expert on the theory and interventions and the client is an expert on him- or herself. In Beck's model, the therapist seeks to change the clients' thinking patterns and way of constructing their worldviews. This requires the following steps, all of these may be identified in the case example above:

1. *Recognizing maladaptive thinking and ideation.* The woman in the case example above felt that "all was lost" because of her husband leaving.

2. *Noting repeating patterns of ideation that tend to be ineffective.* Beck terms such repeating patterns automatic thoughts. You may, for example, have been frightened by a dog and now all dogs are scary for you. You "automatically" think all dogs are dangerous. The therapeutic task is to break down the illogical thinking patterns to help you realize the distinctions between safe and unsafe dogs. With the depressed woman, the task becomes to help her recognize that her present difficulties do not mean that she needs to be totally depressed.

3. *Distancing and decentering help clients remove themselves from the immediate fear, thought, or troublesome situation so they can think about it from a distance.* This results in obsessive thinking becoming less of a "center" in the person's life. When Beck asked, "Do you really believe that? Is Richard the supreme arbiter of that?" and the client laughed, she was clearly decentering her thoughts about the issue.

4. *Changing the rules.* This is important in working with faulty thinking and automatic thoughts. The therapist talks with the client about the logic of the situation. For example, you may rethink your dog phobia through realizing that the chances of being bitten by a dog are at best one in a thousand. When Beck had his client fill out an elementary problem-solving balance sheet of the pros and cons of her husband, he helped her change the rules of her thinking.

Beck's system has proven particularly effective with depressed clients whose worldview is full of pessimistic automatic thoughts that forcefully affect their behavior. Beck has a list of "faulty reasoning" that in many ways is similar to Ellis's conceptualizations of irrational ideas. Beck's list (see Table 9.4) includes such concepts as dichotomous reasoning (assuming things are either all good or all bad—"I'm either perfect or I'm no good.") and overgeneralization ("If my husband leaves me, I'm totally alone.").

---

**Table 9.4. Cognitive Distortions**

1. *Catastrophizing.* Thinking that the worst outcome in a situation will happen and that will be overwhelming and unbearable. Other possible outcomes are not considered. Examples: "Losing my partner will be the end of my life." "I would not be able to feed my family if I lose my job."

2. *Emotional reasoning (emotionalizing).* Feelings are perceived as facts. Assuming that something is true because you feel strongly about it. Feelings guide the interpretation of reality. Examples: "I feel very anxious about this, so I know it is a bad situation." "I have the feeling that my supervisor does not value my work anymore."

*(Continued)*

**Table 9.4. Cognitive Distortions *(Continued)***

**3.** *Polarization (all-or-nothing, dichotomic thought):* Events are perceived in absolute terms, with only two categories (e.g., right or wrong duality) available. The range of options between these poles are overlooked. Examples: "This meeting was a flat-out failure." "This person is either an expert or a fake."

**4.** *Selective abstraction (tunnel vision, mental filter, negative filter):* Attention is given to only one aspect of a complex situation, typically a negative aspect. Other aspects are overlooked. Examples: "That one typo ruined the whole paper." "Cannot believe that participant; it was the only negative comment, and now I will need to restructure how I teach the workshop."

**5.** *Mental reading (mind reading):* Knowing what others are thinking. Assuming without any evidence that you know what is in the other person's mind, without considering other possible options. Examples: "He does not like me and will not invite me to another date." "She is thinking that I am a nerd."

**6.** *Labeling:* Placing a rigid label on oneself, a person, or a situation instead of labeling the specific situation or behavior. Examples: "I'm stupid." "She is incompetent." "This is an insensitive guy."

**7.** *Minimization and maximization:* Positive experiences or situations are minimized, while negative aspects are magnified. Examples: "My supervisor is great, but so are all the other supervisors." "I got a good grade, but others scored even better."

**8.** *Imperatives ("I should have" and "I have to"):* Events are interpreted in terms of how things should have been rather than how things are. Absolute demands or assertions are used to self-motivate or modify your behavior. Examples: "I have to be perfect in all I do." "Nobody should be able to push my buttons."

(Adapted from Knapp and Beck, 2008.)

Clients will manifest a multitude of variations on perfectionism. Automatic thoughts and irrational ideas tend to be obsessive in nature, as they are repeated over and over again. An underlying structure of obsessive behavior and thought is often perfectionism. However, what makes ideas irrational are their unattainability, over-generalization (one must reach 100 percent of everything), or significant distortion of occurrences.

Beck's cognitive therapy assumes that clients can examine themselves. Many patients, particularly the depressed, are embedded in their own construction of the world. Beck recognizes that their particularly self-centered worldview may indeed be accurate, but if one thinks about alternatives, these alternatives may be even more useful and certainly more growth producing. In this area, important parallels to Kelly's (1963) personal construct theory should be noted. The depressed individual has a set of ineffective personal constructs, which are hypotheses this person uses to frame the world. The next reflection exercise asks you to think about Beck's cognitive triad of depression. The task of the therapist is to change the client's constructs in the expectation that if the way one views the world is changed, the way one acts in the world will also change. Practice Exercise 9.1 provides an exercise for taking the cognitive-behavioral approach into practice.

REFLECTION EXERCISE

The cognitive triad (a.k.a. the negative triad): Depressed clients usually exhibit a cognitive triad that involves automatic, spontaneous negative thoughts about the self, the world or environment (including others), and the future.

Examples of this negative thinking include:

The self: "I'm worthless" or "I am spoiled goods."
The world: "The world is a dangerous place" or "No one cares about me."
The future: "Nothing will ever change" or "Things can only get worse!"

Review Linda's case. Can you identify any evidence of the cognitive triad? What were her thoughts about the future?

Think about people you know. Is there anybody who seems to engage in the kind of thoughts that form the cognitive triad?

## The Daily Record of Automatic Thoughts

As indicated in the case example above, negative automatic thoughts often take time to alleviate and change. One technique Beck recommends is the use of the daily record of automatic thoughts. Table 9.5 depicts a portion of the record of the automatic thoughts of a male who was diagnosed as having an obsessive-compulsive personality disorder. Using the daily record method can help the client learn how to identify thinking patterns.

Experience has shown that automatic thoughts often reappear unless closely monitored for a period of time outside of the interview. The client is instructed to mark on the daily record each time an automatic thought intrudes and the client feels uncomfortable. Just the act of recording by itself reinforces and promotes change.

It is crucial that the therapist monitor this form and encourage clients to continue using the form for a sufficient time period to ensure that automatic thoughts do not relapse. If the daily record is discontinued too soon, the client will likely relapse into old patterns of automatic thoughts. Table 9.5 reveals that the obsessive-compulsive client was able to monitor emotions and thoughts in two situations and change the outcome to a more positive one. For example, his record notes he was in tears at the movie. Many obsessive-compulsive types, contrary to popular stereotype, cry easily yet feel uncomfortable about it. The data gained from the daily record provide the counselor with new information for further cognitive-behavioral treatment. At this point, the cognitive therapist can focus on a variety of techniques to understand the meaning of the tears, such as the use of images at the sensorimotor level.

**PRACTICE EXERCISE 9.1. An Exercise in Cognitive-Behavioral Therapy**

The diverse content of cognitive-behavioral theory can be organized into a systematic interview using the following structure. It is suggested that you find a volunteer client who is willing to work through the several stages. A suggested topic for the session is some form of irrational idea or faulty thinking. Perhaps the most common and useful topic for this session is the frequent desire many of us have for being "perfect."

1.  *Empathic relationship.* As before, develop a rapport in your own way, and inform your client that you would like to work on some aspect of his or her desire for perfection.

2.  *Story and strengths.* Using the basic listening sequence, draw out the facts, feelings, and organization of the client's desire for perfection. Try to enter the client's meaning system and reflect the underlying meaning you observe. Point out something positive in the client's meaning system as part of the exploration. Search for irrational ideas or faulty reasoning.

3.  *Goals.* Determine outcomes. Pinpoint very specific goals for your client. They should be cognitively and behaviorally specific and measurable: As one rule, can you and your client "see, hear, and feel" concrete change?

    The concept of concreteness involves specifics, not vague generalizations ("Could you give me a specific example of a better resolution of your drive for perfection?"). Here, you may find your client resisting and retreating once again to faulty, irrational thinking in defining goals.

4.  *Restory.* Generate alternative solutions. Here, many options are open for you, and you will have to decide your route toward action. You may wish to attack the faulty, irrational thinking using the Beck or Ellis model, or you may decide to use stress inoculation, skills training, or assertiveness training.

5.  *Action.* Cognitive-behavioral approaches emphasize the importance of taking behavior back home. Several alternatives for ensuring generalization have been made through this text. You may wish to have your client fill out a relapse prevention form, or you may simply assign homework and follow-up during the week with a phone call to see if cognitive and behavioral change is indeed occurring.

**Table 9.5. An Obsessive-Compulsive Personality's Daily Record**

| Date | Situation (Describe Briefly) | Emotions | Automatic Thoughts | Rational Response | Outcome |
|---|---|---|---|---|---|
| 5/12 | Office | Anxiety, fear | If I don't do the report perfectly, I'll get fired. | Do the best you can. Nobody's perfect. | Felt better. Boss liked report. |
| | Dinner | Anger | Why doesn't my wife have things ready on time? | I'm lucky she cooks at all. I need to help her more. | I helped with meal. |
| | Movie | Tears, sadness | Why am I doing this? It always happens in sad places. | Just enjoy the movie. It's OK to cry. | More tears? Why? |

The daily record can also provide the counselor or therapist specifics of client behavior and thinking for further diagnosis and assessment. This is an important technique and one highly useful in counseling and therapy from many theoretical orientations. It is recommended that you use this format in several practice exercises so that you can master this important part of cognitive theory.

*Adding Family/Multicultural Dimensions.* The chart of automatic thoughts tends to put the responsibility for most change within the client. As such, multicultural theory would point out that this method fails to consider contextual issues. Gender and multicultural dimensions can be added to the automatic thoughts chart by adding a column focusing on context. In the above example, the obsessive-compulsive male could review the entire record as an example of sex-role stereotyping learned in the family of origin. In this case, cognitive consciousness raising about the oppressiveness of male roles may be beneficial.

For many individuals, reviewing automatic thought patterns from a gender, family, or multicultural perspective can be very helpful. Women and minorities, for example, may sometimes blame themselves for lack of job advancement. If the record of automatic thoughts is reviewed for examples of sexism or racism, this may change the meaning and the cognitions of the client. At the same time, it is important to balance internal and external responsibility for change. Information gained from such analysis may require you as counselor or therapist to take action in the environment.

We must never forget that many—perhaps most—of our clients are in some way harmed by context. To place internal responsibility for change on one person is sometimes highly naive.

# Other Techniques and the Issues of Trauma and Veterans

Much like rational emotive behavior therapy, Beck's cognitive therapy does not hesitate to draw on techniques and concepts from other theories. Relaxation training, role-plays, and skills training are all part of the cognitive therapist's potential repertoire.

Many clients will likely have serious histories of abuse, neglect, and trauma. Veterans will present higher ratios of trauma and depression. In a study including face-to-face interviews with 36,309 adults during the 2012–2013 National Epidemiologic Survey on Alcohol and Related Conditions-III, past-year and lifetime prevalence were 4.7 percent and 6.1 percent, respectively. Substance use, mood, anxiety, personality disorders, and past-month disability were significant in these groups. Among respondents with lifetime PTSD, 59.4 percent sought treatment, but it took an average of 4.5 years between the onset of the disorder and their first treatment (Goldstein et al., 2016). The researchers concluded that *DSM-5* PTSD is a prevalent, highly comorbid, and disabling disorder and is associated with delayed help seeking. Table 9.6 offers a list of current treatments for PTSD.

---

**Table 9.6. Cognitive-Behavioral Treatments for PTSD**

According to the Veterans Administration, Department of Defense's National Center for PTSD, Exposure Therapies, Cognitive-Cognitive Therapy, and Eye Movement Desensitization Reprocessing, have strong evidence base and are considered first-line treatments for PTSD (U.S. Department of Veteran Affairs, 2017; Zalaquett, 2013).

*Exposure-based therapies* (ET) emphasize in-vivo, imaginal, and narrative (oral and/or written) exposure, but also generally include elements of cognitive restructuring (e.g., evaluating the accuracy of beliefs about danger), as well as relaxation techniques and self-monitoring of anxiety. Examples of therapies that include a focus on exposure include Prolonged Exposure Therapy, Brief Eclectic Psychotherapy, Narrative Therapy, written exposure therapies, and many of the cognitive therapy packages that also incorporate in-vivo and imaginal/narrative exposure.

*Cognitive-based therapies* (CT) emphasize cognitive restructuring (challenging automatic or acquired beliefs connected to the traumatic event, such as beliefs about safety or trust), but also include relaxation techniques and discussion or narration of the traumatic event orally, through writing, or both. Examples include Cognitive Processing Therapy and various cognitive therapy packages tested in RCTs.

*Stress Inoculation Training* (SIT) places more emphasis on breathing retraining and muscle relaxation, but also includes cognitive elements (self-dialogue, thought stopping, role playing) and, often, exposure techniques (in-vivo exposure, narration of traumatic event).

*Eye Movement Desensitization and Reprocessing* (EMDR) (extensively studied in a large number of RCTs) closely resembles other CBT modalities in that there is an exposure component (e.g., talking about the traumatic event and/or holding distressing traumatic memories in mind without verbalizing them). This is complemented with a cognitive component (e.g., identifying a negative cognition, an alternative positive cognition, and assessing the validity of the cognition). A major part of this is relaxation/self-monitoring techniques (e.g., breathing, "body scan").

Alternating eye movements are part of the classic EMDR technique (and the name of this type of treatment); however, comparable effect sizes have been achieved with or without eye movements or other forms of distraction or body stimulation. Although the mechanisms of effectiveness in EMDR have yet to be determined, it is likely that they are similar to other trauma-focused exposure and cognitive-based therapies.

# William Glasser and Reality Therapy

If Albert Ellis's rational emotive behavior therapy could be summarized as "Be rational and think about things logically," William Glasser's reality therapy could be summarized by saying, "Take responsibility and control of your own life and face the consequences of your actions." Clients can learn that they are not victims, that they can control their own behaviors, that they have options available to them, and that they have hope for a better present and future (Wubbolding, 2017). Although research on reality therapy is limited, it is a frequent treatment of choice if one works with difficult clients, particularly acting-out or delinquent youth or adults.

Especially in the early stages of therapy, some younger clients, particularly those who are acting out or delinquent, will not "stand still" for the approaches of Ellis and Beck. However, after you establish a working alliance with such clients, perhaps through reality therapy, you can return successfully to cognitive-behavioral techniques.

Glasser's reality therapy can be considered a cognitive-behavioral therapy, but one that focuses very much on realism and how to treat difficult clients. We will first examine a case study and then return to theoretical constructs.

## Case Presentation: Probation Client

Counseling sessions within reality therapy can range from a regularly scheduled fifty-minute hour to brief personal encounters in the dining room, classroom, or other setting. Many clients do not want to come to the office for the highly verbal and sophisticated treatments that we as therapists might prefer to offer. Reality therapy offers a viable alternative that you can use as a basis for working with difficult clients and later incorporate other forms of helping within it.

The following interview shows the second phase of reality therapy. The client is an eighteen-year-old young man on probation for repeated offenses of a minor nature, including selling alcohol to minors, assault, and petty theft. The counselor in this case is a county probation officer, and the meeting occurs in the community half-way house. They are just finishing a game of ping-pong.

1. *Counselor*: Got ya! 21 to 18. Took me three games, but I finally got one.
2. *Client*: Yeah, you pulled it off finally. Man, I'm pooped. [They sit down and have a cup of coffee.]
3. *Counselor*: So, how have things been going? (Open question)
4. *Client*: Well, I looked for jobs hard last week. But nothing looked any good. The bastards seem to know I'm coming and pull the help wanted sign down just as I come walking in.
5. *Counselor*: So, you've been looking hard. How many places did you visit? [Paraphrase, closed question; note search for concrete behavior]

6. *Client*: Oh lots. Nobody will give me a chance.

7. *Counselor*: Maybe I can help. Tell me some of the places you've been. [Directive, with continued emphasis on concreteness. Where Beck and Ellis often move clients to formal operational thought, the Glasser approach focuses on specifics—one of its values for the many concrete operational clients you will encounter.]

8. *Client*: I tried the gas station down the street. They gave me a bad time. Nobody wants me. It's really tough.

9. *Counselor*: Where else did you go? [Closed question]

10. *Client*: I tried a couple other stations too. Nobody wants to look at me. They don't pay too good anyway. Nuts to them!

11. *Counselor*: So you haven't really done too much looking. Sounds like you want it served on a silver plate, Joe. Do you think looking at a couple of gas stations is really going to get you a job? [Paraphrase, interpretation, logical consequences. Here we see a lead, particularly typical of reality therapy that places considerable emphasis on the consequences of actions. The point is similar to applied behavioral analysis, but the way of reaching consequences is quite different.]

12. *Client*: I suppose not. Nobody wants to hire me anyway.

13. *Counselor*: Let's take another look at that. The economy is pretty rocky right now. Everyone is having trouble getting work. You seem to think "they" are after you. Yet, I've got a friend about your age who had to go to thirty-five places before he got a job. How does that square with you looking at three places and then giving up? Who's responsible—you, the service station owners, or the economy? [Directive, information giving, open question; note confrontation and emphasis on the word *responsible*. Responsible action is the formal operational concept toward which most of reality therapy aspires.]

14. *Client*: Yeh, but, there's not much I can do about it. I tried.

15. *Counselor*: Yeh, at three places. Who's responsible for you not getting a job when you only go to three places? At a time like this you've really got to scramble. Come on, Joe! [Interpretation plus logical consequences]

The interview continues to explore Joe's lack of action, with an emphasis on responsibility. At points where a Rogerian counselor might have paraphrased or reflected feelings and attitudes (such as at Client: 4, 8, and 10), the reality therapist opted for more behavioral specifics through questions and interpretation. The process of examining Joe's behavior is closely akin to that of the behavioral counselor using applied behavioral analysis. However, the use of the behavioral data is quite different in reality therapy. Instead of seeking to change behavior, the reality therapist works on changing awareness of responsibility. Once the focus of responsibility has been acknowledged and owned by the client, it is possible to start planning a more effective job search. Later in the interview, the process of planning evolves.

51. *Counselor*: So, Joe, sounds like you feel you made a decision this past week not to really look for a job ... almost as if you took responsibility for not getting work. [Reflection of meaning, interpretation. Note that placing the locus of decision in the client can be a helpful strategy in any approach to helping. It is here that reality therapy truly becomes cognitive-behavioral. At the same time, this is a clear example of moving away from a societal, contextual focus.]

52. *Client*: Yeh, I don't like to look at it that way, but I guess I did decide not to do too much.

53. *Counselor*: And what about next week?

54. *Client*: I suppose I ought to look again, but I really don't like it.

The reality therapist at this point moved to a realistic analysis of what the client might expect during the coming week on the job market, constantly emphasizing the importance of the client, Joe, taking action and responsibility for his life. A practice role-played job interview was held, and several alternatives for generating a more effective job search were considered. Joe tried to escape responsibility at several points ("I couldn't do that"), but the counselor confronted him and allowed no excuses or ambivalence.

A reality therapist will use skills and ideas of other theoretical orientations when they serve the purpose of assisting the client to confront reality more effectively. More likely, the reality therapist will be her or his natural self and use humor, sarcasm, and confrontation in very personal ways to assist the client in understanding behavioral patterns and developing new action approaches. Role-playing, systematic planning, and instruction in intentional living are important tools in reality therapy.

Although many who practice reality therapy approaches may be in power situations (guards, principals, rehabilitation counselors), they still tend to be themselves and to use reality therapy as an extension of themselves; this adds a tone of genuineness and authenticity to the process at a more significant level than would be possible with other approaches. For example, a prison guard trained in reality therapy can simply state his position realistically as one of power and control. Then, with the role relationships clearly established, the process of involvement, teaching of responsibility, and relearning can occur.

## Central Theoretical Constructs of Reality Therapy

In describing the basic tenets of reality therapy, Glasser (1965) states that all clients have been unsuccessful in meeting their needs and that in attempts to meet their needs, they often tend to select ineffective behaviors that virtually assure their failure. Further,

All patients have a common characteristic: they all deny the reality of the world around them. Some break the law, denying the rules of society; some claim their neighbors are plotting against them, denying the improbability of such behavior. Some are afraid of crowded places, close quarters, airplanes, or elevators, yet they freely admit the irrationality of their fears. Millions drink to blot out the inadequacy they feel but that need not exist if they could learn to be different; and far too many people choose suicide rather than face the reality that they could solve their problems by more responsible behavior. Whether it is a partial denial or the total blotting out of all reality of the chronic backward patient in the state hospital, the denial of some or all of reality is common to all patients, Therapy will be successful when they are able to give up denying the world and recognize that reality not only exists but that they must fulfill their needs within its framework.

A therapy that leads all patients toward reality, toward grappling successfully with the tangible and intangible aspects of the real world, might accurately be called a therapy toward reality, or simply Reality Therapy. (p. 6)

Reality therapy can best be described as a commonsense approach to counseling. What Glasser advocates is finding out what people want and need, examining their failures and their present assets, and considering factors in the environment that must be met if the needs are to be satisfied. One cannot meet needs except in a real world; people must face a world that is imperfect and not built to their specifications and must act positively in this world. The worldview of reality therapy is that people can do something about their fate if they will consider themselves and their environment realistically.

## The Importance of Responsibility

As might be anticipated, reality therapy focuses on conscious, planned behavior and gives relatively little attention to underlying dimensions of transference, unconscious thought process, and the like. The goal is to consider the past as being past and done with; the present and the future are what are important. Yet, reality therapy does not emphasize applied behavioral analysis or the detailed plans of assertiveness training or systematic desensitization. Rather, almost like rational emotive behavior therapy, reality therapy focuses on responsibility and choice. What is central is that clients examine their lives to see how specific behavior is destructive. The more important step, however, is to take responsibility that Glasser (1965) defines as "the ability to fulfill one's needs and to do so in a way that does not deprive others of the ability to fulfill their needs" (p. 13). Learning responsibility is a lifelong process.

Given the population that reality therapy often serves (clients of street clinics; prison inmates; schoolchildren; and others in institutional settings), it is clear that relationship and trust are particularly important. The institutions that children and prisoners must cope do not easily build the almost automatic trust relationship that seems to be a given in a traditional client-therapist setting. The personhood of the reality therapist becomes especially important. The qualities of warmth, respect and caring for others, positive regard, and interpersonal openness are crucial.

Reality therapy is much more likely to be practiced in settings other than the counseling office, although this method is also used in the standard clinical setting. The individual practicing reality therapy may be a classroom teacher or perhaps work as a prison guard. The possible multiplicity of relationships requires a special type of person to maintain consistency. This challenge provides an opportunity for the reality therapist to serve as a continuing model of personal responsibility to the client outside the counseling environment.

## Cognitive Trends in Reality Therapy

A critical part of reality therapy is client awareness of consequences of actions: "If you do X, then what is the consequence?" Reality therapy, in a highly nonjudgmental fashion, attempts to help individuals learn what they can expect when they act in certain ways. In this sense, you may again note a similarity and a difference from rational emotive behavior therapy. In REBT, the consequences are those inside the person (feeling depressed, and so forth), whereas in reality therapy, the consequences may indeed be inside, but the emphasis *is* on what happens in the outside world when the client fails to face reality and be responsible.

Glasser continually expanded his thinking but remained true to the basic constructs of the method and theory described above. In his 1981 book, *Stations of the Mind*, he builds a comprehensive picture of the workings of the "internal world" of the mind. Glasser notes that the "internal reality" of the mind (cognitions) must be able to understand how the individual relates to external reality.

## Control Theory

Control is an important aspect of Glasser's theory. "We Always Have Control Over What We Do" is a chapter heading in Glasser's book for the general market, *Take Effective Control of Your Life* (1984). At issue is how the individual exercises that control. One can choose misery as a way of life because it is an excuse from trying harder and may win help or pity from others, and so on. Psychosomatic illness is considered a specific type of internal control to help individuals avoid reality. A "headaching" person may benefit because this is the only time he or she is able to lie down and rest. Drugs and alcohol are still other ways people exert control to avoid facing reality.

His theory of control provides an important additional tool to the therapist working with an individual client. The therapist insists that the client "own" thoughts, behavior, and feelings and be responsible for them. The logic is that if one can exert control toward seemingly unsatisfactory ends, such as drugs, headaches, stealing, and interpersonal conflict, then one can reframe control more positively.

Glasser talks about "positive addictions," which range from spending time with friends to jogging to movies to meditation—anything through which an individual can use to obtain a "high" in a more satisfactory and healthy way. The world offers us the opportunity for negative addiction or for positive addiction. We choose our addictions and our fate. We can choose headaches, or we can choose joy. *The choice is ours. We are in control.*

Glasser's emphasis on control implicates a more immediate, confrontational, and cognitive point of view. With certain clients, reality therapists may use more direct and forceful confrontations of thought patterns, active teaching of alternative perceptions of reality, and an emphasis more on internal states and thoughts.

The following Tables 9.7 and 9.8 briefly review the evidence base of CBT and its neuroscientific foundation.

---

**Table 9.7. Research Box: Evidence Base of Cognitive Behavioral Therapy**

In general, the CBT evidence base is very strong. Hofmann and colleagues (2012) reviewed a sample of 106 meta-analyses examining CBT treatment for various disorders. CBT received the strongest support for the treatment of anxiety disorders, somatoform disorders, bulimia, anger control issues, and general stress. In eleven studies comparing CBT with other treatments, CBT showed higher response rates in seven of the studies.

Supplementing the strong support above are the following:

1. Analysis of 26 studies, including 1,981 participants, found that CBT was superior to alternative therapies among patients with anxiety or depressive disorders (Tolin, 2010).

2. CBT was demonstrated as effective with adult anxiety in randomized controlled trials in two meta-analytic studies (Olatunji, Cisler, & Deacon, 2010; Otte, 2011).

CBT efficacy to reduce symptoms of adult ADHD was shown in a review of nine published randomized controlled trials (RCTs). CBT was superior to waiting list and active control groups, with a small-to-moderate effect size (SMD = 0.43, 95% CI [0.14, 0.71], $p = .004$) (Young, Moghaddam, & Tickle, 2016).

Other meta-analyses reported that CBT is an efficacious treatment for uncontrolled and excessive worry in older adults with generalized anxiety disorder (Hall, Kellett, Berrios, Bains, & Shonagh, 2016); helps manage pediatric migraine (Ng, Venkatanarayanan, & Kumar, 2017); and is effective for the treatment of depression in children age thirteen years old or younger (Yang et al., 2017).

Unfortunately, no meta-analytic studies of CBT have been reported on ethnic minorities and low-income samples in the United States (Hofmann, Asnaani, Vonk, Sawyer, & Fang, 2012). This, of course, has been a common criticism of CBT and its general failure to consider systemic and contextual issues.

**Table 9.8. Neuroscience and Cognitive Behavior Therapy**

Neuroscience research has expanded our knowledge about neurobiological correlates of mental processes and changes occurring in the brain due to CBT interventions. Studies based on brain imaging techniques (e.g., positron emission tomography [PET], functional magnetic resonance imaging [fMRI]) have shown that cognitive activity contributes to dysfunctional behavior and emotional experience through selective perception, poor memory and recall, and cognitive distortions.

Studies have also shown that such activity can be changed using metacognitive and mindfulness techniques. Neurobiological changes occur after CBT in patients with spider phobia (arachnophobia), obsessive-compulsive disorder, panic disorder, social phobia, major depressive disorder, and chronic fatigue syndrome (Jokić-Begić, 2010).

Comparisons of brain activity pre- and post-CBT interventions for depression have identified changes localized to specific frontal, cingulate, and limbic areas (Collerton, 2013). There is decreased activity in the limbic system, especially the amygdala, with the dorsolateral prefrontal cortex becoming relatively more active and orbitomedial and cingulate cortex less active after treatment. This balancing of cognitive and affective processing is a major goal of all counseling and psychotherapy. These changes are consistent with what is known about the processing of emotional stimuli (Beck, 2008). Furthermore, pretreatment levels of cingulate's emotional activity can even predict response to CBT with some reliability (Siegle et al., 2012).

Similar changes in those brain areas are seen after CBT treatments for anxiety, schizophrenia, and eating disorders. This suggests that CBT may be associated with a decrease in emotionality (calming and less limbic activity) and an increase in thoughtfulness (increased dorsolateral frontal activity), a change expected from CBT theory (Clark & Beck, 2010b).

Furthermore, neuroscientific findings indicate that the way we think about our own thoughts (metacognition) produces changes in the brain (Collerton, 2013). Studies on effective mindfulness CBT reveal that the intervention increases electrical activity on the left-sided anterior section of the brain (Davidson et al., 2003).

A recent study by Mason and colleagues (2017) showed that CBT strengthens specific connections in the brains of patients diagnosed with psychosis. Furthermore, the stronger connections were associated with long-term reduction in symptoms and recovery eight years later. The researchers evaluated and followed up twenty-two participants before and after receiving CBT. The investigation showed that long-term psychotic symptoms were predicted by changes in prefrontal connections during prosocial facial affective processing, and long-term affective symptoms were predicted by threat-related amygdalo-inferior parietal lobule connectivity. In addition, greater increases in dorsolateral prefrontal cortex connectivity with the amygdala after CBT predicted higher subjective ratings of recovery after eight years. The findings suggest that neural level reorganization after CBT predicts the subsequent recovery path of people with psychosis across eight years.

As Paquette and colleagues indicate, by changing the mind, we change the brain (2003).

# Third-Wave Behavioral and Cognitive Therapies

We have reviewed traditional cognitive behavior therapy, which seeks to eliminate negative thoughts and long-held schemas, or question their credibility and replace them with more adaptive thoughts. Third-wave cognitive behavior counseling and therapy does not encourage direct intervention on negative thought, nor does it engage in the elimination of these (Barraca, 2012). Techniques such as thought stopping or cognitive restructuring are not promoted. The third wave of behavioral therapies is characterized by themes such as metacognition, cognitive fusion, emotions, acceptance, mindfulness, dialectics, spirituality, and therapeutic relationship.

Third-wave therapies, such as Behavioral Activation (BA), Acceptance and Commitment Therapy (ACT), Mindfulness-Based Cognitive Therapy (MBCT), and Dialectic Behavior Therapy (DBT), propose alternative interventions for intrusive thoughts, painful memories, unpleasant daydreams, or ruminative depressive narratives. Each of these treatments has been supported by numerous efficacy studies, which overall attest to at least moderate-to-large effect sizes for between-group comparisons, using primarily wait list (WL) or treatment as usual (TAU) conditions, or within group comparisons (Dimidjian, Arch, Schneider, Desormeau, Felder, & Segal, 2016).

Table 9.9 provides a brief summary of current third-wave therapies.

---

**Table 9.9.** Third-Wave Cognitive Behavior Therapies (Kahl, Winter, & Schweiger, 2012)

**Acceptance and Commitment Treatment**

Acceptance and commitment therapy (ACT) is a method of behavioral therapy that is based on functional contextualism and the relational frame theory. It posits the following psychopathological processes as central to mental disorders: (1) cognitive fusion; (2) experiential avoidance; (3) attachment to a verbally conceptualized self and a verbally conceptualized past; (4) lack of values or confusion of goals with values; and (5) absence of committed behavior that moves in the direction of chosen values. The treatment contains psychoeducation about key mechanisms, exercises in mindfulness, and cognitive defusion. The value orientation of the patient is elicited and discussed, and patients are supported in value-driven behavior, in contrast to behavior driven by emotional or experiential avoidance.

**Behavioral Activation**

Behavioral activation is a third-wave method for treating depression and other mental disorders. It emerged from studies analyzing the necessary components of classical cognitive therapy. These studies showed that behavioral activation is a stand-alone component that has a similar or superior efficacy compared with cognitive therapy. Behavioral activation has evolved from a long behavioral tradition seeking to increase positive reinforcement by scheduling appropriate patient behaviors and thus achieving antidepressant action. Important changes compared with earlier versions are a shift from "pleasant" activities to value-driven activities, a shift strongly influenced by ACT and the adoption of the concept of "opposite action" from dialectical behavioral therapy (DBT). The goal is to bring the patient into contact with diverse, stable, and valued sources of positive reinforcement. Behavioral activation encompasses psychoeducation, activity monitoring, scheduling of antidepressant activities, and troubleshooting.

**Cognitive Behavioral Analysis System of Psychotherapy**

The cognitive behavioral analysis system of psychotherapy (CBASP) was specifically developed for the treatment of patients with chronic depression. CBASP assumes that skills deficits in the area of operational thinking lead to a failure of interpersonal behavior and subsequent depression. The method comprises three therapeutic techniques: situational analysis, interpersonal discrimination exercise, and consequating (how they will reward and punish their own behaviors) strategies, all with the aim of teaching operational thinking and interpersonal behavior driven by empathy and personal values.

The fundamental assumption of a preoperative cognitive style in chronic depressed patients is supported by one study, demonstrating that preoperative thinking is more pronounced in patients with chronic depression than in patients with episodic depression and healthy volunteers.

*(Continued)*

**Table 9.9.** Third-Wave Cognitive Behavior Therapies (Kahl, Winter, & Schweiger, 2012) *(Continued)*

**Dialectical Behavioral Therapy**

Dialectical behavioral therapy was originally developed for parasuicidal patients with borderline personality disorder (BPD). Modifications have now been developed for substance abuse and eating disorders. DBT assumes that skills deficits in the area of emotion regulation are at the center of these disorders. Accordingly, DBT teaches a broad spectrum of skills in the areas of mindfulness, distress tolerance, emotion regulation, and interpersonal effectiveness.

The skills deficit model underlying DBT was supported in a study showing that the extent of skills use mediated the effects of DBT and led to decreased suicidal behavior, decreased depression, and better anger control. DBT has been shown to result in a positive therapeutic relationship and to impact substantially intrapsychic and personality factors, not merely reducing symptoms.

**Metacognitive Therapy**

Metacognitive therapy (MCT) evolved from classical cognitive therapy. Metacognition is the aspect of cognition that controls mental processes and thinking. Knowledge about metacognition originated in research on learning and decision making in children. MCT posits that the cognitive attentional syndrome, a psychopathological state consisting of repetitive cognitive processes, such as worrying, rumination, dysfunctional threat monitoring, and dysfunctional cognitive and behavioral copying, is at the core of depressive and anxiety disorders. MCT abstains from content-oriented interventions, uses attention training techniques to develop skills in cognitive flexibility, teaches a special form of mindfulness (detached mindfulness) and guides cognitive and behavioral experiments to change metacognition.

The underlying concept of MCT is that metacognitions must change in order for psychological treatment to be effective. This assumption was supported by a study showing that change in metacognitions was a better predictor of outcome than change in cognitions in patients with obsessive-compulsive disorder treated with exposure or response prevention techniques.

**Mindfulness-based Cognitive Therapy**

Mindfulness-based cognitive therapy (MBCT) arose from experiences in the application of Buddhist meditation techniques in medicine. It was specifically developed to reduce the number of relapses in patients with major depression. MBCT uses psychoeducation and encourages the patients to practice mindfulness meditation. A core goal is to develop metacognitive awareness, which is the ability to experience cognitions and emotions as mental events that pass through the mind and may or may not be related to external reality. The focus is not to change "dysfunctional" thoughts but to learn to experience them as internal events separated from the self.

# Practicing CBT Therapy

All the cognitive-behavioral approaches discussed in this chapter, including the third-wave cognitive behavioral therapies, represent vibrant and research-supported interventions. Each one emphasizes the role of cognitions in wellness, stress, and mental disorders. Also, each one tends to put the issue or concern "in the client." This, of course, is true for most individualistically oriented helping theories. Reality therapy, for example, stresses the need for the client to adapt to necessary environmental contingencies. Sometimes clients come from oppressive families, neighborhoods, and cultural histories. Although it is important that the client adapt to reality, such adaptation can result in clients returning to oppressive systems with the idea that the "fault" is in them rather than in the environment. Rational emotive behavior therapy and Beck's cognitive approach also can fall prey to what some call "blaming the victim" and to a focus on curing the "ills" of the client, when family and society are also responsible.

Nonetheless, each of these therapeutic systems is open to cultural and family perspectives and cultural difference. Guidelines for using cognitive-behavioral methods in multicultural settings are not extensive, however. When practicing cognitive-behavioral counseling and therapy, it is incumbent on you as the therapist to be culturally aware. In this sense, a review of Cheek's early work on assertiveness training with African American clients described in the previous chapter can be particularly helpful. His work provides a model for balancing individual and cultural issues in the therapy and counseling situation.

The major focus of work in cognitive approaches is at the concrete and formal operational levels of cognition. Relatively little attention is given to systemic, gender, and multicultural issues that affect client cognitions. For the most part, responsibility for change is placed in the individual.

# References

Ballou, M., West, C., & Hill, M. (2008). (Eds.). *Feminist therapy theory and practice; Current perspective*. New York, NY: Springer.

Bandura, A. (1982). Self-efficacy mechanism in human agency. *American Psychologist, 37*, 122–147.

Bandura, A. (1989). Regulation of cognitive processes through perceived self-efficacy. *Developmental Psychology, 25*, 729–735.

Bandura, A. (1997). *Self-efficacy: The exercise of control*. New York, NY: Freeman.

Bandura, A. (2012). On the functional properties of perceived self-efficacy revisited. *Journal of Management, 38*, 9–44.

Barraca, J. (2012). Mental control from a third-wave behavior therapy perspective. *International Journal of Clinical Health & Psychology, 12*, 109–121.

Beck, A. (1976). *Cognitive therapy and the emotional disorders*. New York, NY: International Universities Press.

Beck, A., Davis, D.D., & Freeman, A. (2015). *Cognitive therapy of personality disorders* (2nd ed.). New York, NY: Guilford.

Beck, A.T. (2008). The evolution of the cognitive model of depression and its neurobiological correlates. *American Journal of Psychiatry, 165*, 969–977.

Beck, J.S. (2011). *Cognitive behavior therapy: Basics and beyond* (2nd ed). New York, NY: Guilford.

Bennett-Levy, J., Thwaites, R., Haarhoff, B., & Perry, H. (2015). *Experiencing CBT from the inside out: A self-practice/self-reflection CBT workbook for therapists*. New York, NY: Guilford.

Brown, L.A., Gaudiano, B.A., & Miller, I.W. (2011). Investigating the similarities and differences between practitioners of second and third wave cognitive-behavioral therapies. *Behavior Modification 35*, 187–200.

Cheek, D. (1976/2010). *Assertive Black ... puzzled White*. San Luis Obispo, CA: Impact.

Clark, D.A., & Beck, A.T. (2010a). *Cognitive therapy of anxiety disorders: Science and practice*. New York, NY: Guilford Press.

Clark, D.A., & Beck, A.T. (2010b). Cognitive theory and therapy of anxiety and depression: Convergence with neurobiological findings. *Trends in Cognitive Sciences, 14*, 418–424.

Collerton, D. (2013). Psychotherapy and brain plasticity. *Frontiers in Psychology, 4*, 548, 1. doi:10.3389/fpsyg.2013.00548.

Davidson, R.J., Kabat-Zinn, J., Schumacher, J., Rosenkranz, M., Muller, D., & Santorelli, S.F. (2003). Alterations in brain and immune function produced by mindfulness meditation. *Psychosomatic Medicine, 65*, 564–570.

Diaz-Martinez, A.M., Interian, A., & Waters, D.M. (2010). The integration of CBT, multicultural and feminist psychotherapies with Latinas. *Journal of Psychotherapy Integration, 20*, 312–326. doi:10.1037/a0020819.

Diffily, A. (1984). Aaron Beck: A profile. *Brown Alumni Monthly*. Providence, RI, pp. 39–46.

Dimidjian, S., Arch, J.J., Schneider, R., Desormeau, P., Felder, J.N., & Segal, Z.V. (2016). Considering meta-analysis, meaning, and metaphor: A systematic review and critical examination of "third wave" cognitive and behavioral therapies. *Behavior Therapy, 47*, 886–905. doi.org/10.1016/j.beth.2016.07.002.

Dobson, D., & Dobson, K.S. (2016). *Evidence-based practice of cognitive-behavioral therapy* (2nd ed.). New York, NY: Guilford Press.

Dobson, K., & Dozois, D. (2001). Historical and philosophical basis of cognitive-behavioral therapy. In K. Dobson (Ed.), *Handbook of cognitive-behavioral therapies* (pp. 3–39). New York, NY: Guilford.

Ellis, A. (1958). *Sex without guilt*. Secaucus, NJ: Lyle Stuart.

Ellis, A. (1967). *Rational-emotive psychotherapy*. In D. Arbuckel (Ed.), *Counseling and psychotherapy*. New York, NY: McGraw-Hill.

Ellis, A. (1971). *Growth through reason*. Palo Alto, CA: Science and Behavior Books.

Ellis, A. (1983a). *The origins of rational-emotive therapy (RET)*. *Voices, 18*, 29–33.

Ellis, A. (1983b). The use of rational-emotive therapy (RET) in working for a sexually sane society. In G. Albee, S. Gordon, & H. Leitenberg, (Eds.), *Promoting sexual responsibility and preventing sexual problems*. Hanover, VT: University Press of New England.

Ellis, A. (1991). Using RET effectively: Reflections and interview. In M. Bernard (Ed.), *Using rational-emotive therapy effectively* (pp. 1–33). New York, NY: Plenum.

Ellis, A., & Joffe Ellis, D. (2011). *Rational emotive behavior therapy*. Washington, DC: American Psychological Association.

Flaxman, P.E., & Bond, F.W. (2010). A randomised worksite comparison of acceptance commitment therapy and stress inoculation training. *Behaviour Research and Therapy, 48*, 816–820.

Foa, E., Rothbaum, B., Riggs, D., & Murdock, T. (1991). Treatment of post-traumatic stress disorder in rape victims: A comparison between cognitive-behavior procedures and counseling. *Journal of Clinical and Consulting Psychology, 99*, 715–23.

Foa, E.B., Dancu, C.V., Hembree, E.A., Jaycox, L.H., Meadows, E.A., & Street, G.P. (1999). A comparison of exposure therapy, stress inoculation training, and their combination for reducing posttraumatic stress disorder in female assault victims. Journal of *Consulting and Clinical Psychology, 67*, 194–200. doi.org/10.1037/0022-006X.67.2.194.

Glasser, W. (1965). *Reality therapy*. New York: HarperCollins.

Glasser, W. (1981). *Stations of the mind*. New York, NY: HarperCollins.

Glasser, W. (1984). *Take effective control of your life*. New York, NY: HarperCollins.

Goldstein, R.B., Smith, S.M., Chou, S.P., Saha, T.D., Jung, J., Zhang, H., … Grant, B.F. (2016). The epidemiology of DSM-5 posttraumatic stress disorder in the United States: Results from the National Epidemiologic Survey on Alcohol and Related Conditions-III. *Social Psychiatry and Psychiatric Epidemiology, 51*, 1137–1148. doi:10.1007/s00127-016-1208-5.

Guo, F., & Hanley, T. (2015). Adapting cognitive behavioral therapy to meet the needs of Chinese clients: Opportunities and challenges. *PsyCh Journal, 4,* 55–65. doi:10.1002/pchj.75.

Hall, J., Kellett, S., Berrios, R., Bains, K.U., & Shonagh, S. (2016). Efficacy of cognitive behavioral therapy for generalized anxiety disorder in older adults: Systematic review, meta-analysis, and meta-regression. *American Journal of Geriatric Psychiatry, 24,* 1063–1073.

Hendershot, C.S., Witkiewitz, K., George, W.H., & Marlatt, G.A. (2011). Relapse prevention for addictive behaviors. *Substance Abuse Treatment, Prevention, and Policy, 6,* 17. doi.org/10.1186/1747-597X-6-17.

Hofmann, S.G., Asnaani, A., Vonk, I.J.J., Sawyer, A.T., & Fang, A. (2012). The efficacy of cognitive behavioral therapy: A review of meta-analyses. *Cognitive Therapy and Research, 36,* 427–440. doi.org/10.1007/s10608-012-9476-1.

Jokić-Begić, N. (2010). Cognitive-behavioral therapy and neuroscience: Towards closer integration. *Psychological Topics, 19,* 235–254.

Kantrowitz, R., & Ballou, M. (1992). A feminist critique of cognitive-behavioral therapy. In L. Brown & M. Ballou (Eds.), *Theories of personality and psychopathology: Feminist reappraisals* (pp. 70–87). New York, NY: Guilford.

Kahl, K.G., Winter, L., & Schweiger, U. (2012). The third wave of cognitive behavioural therapies: What is new and what is effective? *Current Opinion in Psychiatry, 25,* 522–528.

Kelly, G. (1955/1963). *The psychology of personal constructs* (Vols. 1 and 2). New York, NY: W. W. Norton.

Knapp, P., & Beck, A.T. (2008), Cognitive therapy: Foundations, conceptual models, applications and research. *Revista Brasileira de Psiquiatria, 30,* S54–S64.

Mason, L., Peters, E., Williams, S.C., & Kumari, V. (2017). Brain connectivity changes occurring following cognitive behavioural therapy for psychosis predict long-term recovery. *Translational Psychiatry.* Published online January 17. doi:10.1038/tp.2016.263.

Masters, W., & Johnson, V. (1970). *Human sexual inadequacy.* Boston, MA: Little, Brown.

Meichenbaum, D. (1991). Evolution of cognitive behavior therapy. In J. Zeig (Ed.), *The evolution of psychotherapy, II.* New York, NY: Brunner/Mazel.

Meichenbaum, D. (2007). Stress inoculation training: A preventative and treatment approach. In P.M. Lehrer, R.L. Woolfolk, & W.E. Sime (Eds.), *Principles and practice of stress management* (3rd ed.) (pp. 497–516). New York, NY: Guilford Press.

Meichenbaum, D., & Gilmore, J. (1984). The nature of unconscious processes: A cognitive-behavioral perspective. In K. Bowers & D. Meichenbaum (Eds.), *The unconscious reconsidered.* New York, NY: John Wiley.

Ng, Q.X., Venkatanarayanan, N., & Kumar, L. (2017). A systematic review and meta-analysis of the efficacy of cognitive behavioral therapy for the management of pediatric migraine. *Headache: The Journal of Head and Face Pain, 57,* 349–362. doi:10.1111/head.13016.

Olatunji, B.O., Cisler, J.M., & Deacon, B.J. (2010). Efficacy of cognitive behavioral therapy for anxiety disorders: A review of meta-analytic findings. *Psychiatric Clinics of North America, 33,* 557–577.

Otte, C. (2011). Cognitive behavioral therapy in anxiety disorders: Current state of the evidence. *Dialogues in Clinical Neuroscience, 13,* 413–421.

Paquette, V., Levesque, J., Mensour, B., Leroux, J.M., Beaudoin, G., & Bourgouin, P. (2003). Change the mind and you change the brain: Effects of cognitive-behavioral therapy on the neural correlates of spider phobia. *Neuroimage, 18,* 401–409.

Piotrowski, C., & Franklin, G. (1990). A rational-emotive approach to problems of Black adolescents. *Journal of Training and Practice in Professional Psychology, 4,* 44–51.

Pratt, T.C., Cullen, F.T., Sellers, C.S., Winfree, L.T., Madensen, T.D., Daigle, L.E., ... Gau, J.M. (2010). The empirical status of social learning theory: A meta-analysis. *Justice Quarterly, 27,* 765–802. doi:10.1080/07418820903379610.

Ratts, M.J., Singh, A.A., Nassar-McMillan, S., Butler, S.K., & McCullough, J.R. (2015). Multicultural and social justice counseling competencies. Retrieved from http://www.counseling.org/docs/default-source/competencies/multicultural-and-social-justice-counseling-competencies.pdf?sfvrsn=20.

Shattell, M.M., Quinlan-Colwell, A., Villalba, J., Ivers, N.N., & Marina, M. (2010). A cognitive-behavioural group therapy intervention with depressed Spanish-speaking Mexican women living in an emerging immigration community in the United States. *Advances in Nursing Science, 33,* 158–169. doi:10.1097/ANS.0b013e3181dbc63d.

Siegle, G.J., Thompson, W.K., Collier, A., Berman, S.R., Feldmiller, J., Thase, M.E., & Friedman, E.S. (2012). Toward clinically useful neuroimaging in depression treatment prognostic utility of sub-genual cingulate activity for determining depression outcome in cognitive therapy across studies, scanners, and patient characteristic scanners and cognitive therapy outcome. *Archives of General Psychiatry 69,* 913–924. doi:10.1001/archgenpsychiatry.2012.65.

Suso-Ribera, C., Jornet-Gibert, M., Ribera Canudas, M.V., McCracken, L.M., Maydeu-Olivares, A., & Gallardo-Pujol, D. (2016). There's more than catastrophizing in chronic pain: Low frustration tolerance and self-downing also predict mental health in chronic pain patients. *Journal of Clinical Psychology in Medical Settings, 23,* 192–206. doi:10.1007/s10880-016-9454-y.

Tolin, D.F. (2010). Is cognitive-behavioral therapy more effective than other therapies? A meta-analytic review. *Clinical Psychology Review, 30,* 710–720.

U.S. Department of Veteran Affairs. (2017). National center for PTSD: Treatment overview. Retrieved from https://www.ptsd.va.gov/professional/treatment/overview/index.asp.

Wubbolding, R.B. (2017). *Reality therapy and self-evaluation: The key to client change.* Alexandria, VA: American Counseling Association.

Weinrach, S. (1990). Anecdotes. In D. DiMattia & L. Lega (Eds.), *Will the real Albert Ellis please stand up?* (pp. 42–43, 108–109, 124–125). New York, NY: Institute for Rational Emotive Therapy.

Yang, L., Zhou, X., Zhou, C., Zhang, Y., Pu, J., Liu, L., Gong, X., & Xie, P. (2017). Efficacy and acceptability of cognitive behavioral therapy for depression in children: A systematic review and meta-analysis. *Academic Pediatrics, 17,* 9–16. doi.org/10.1016/j.acap.2016.08.002.

Young, J.E., Klosko, Janet S., & Weishaar, M.E. (2003). *Schema therapy: A practitioner's guide.* New York, NY: Guilford Press.

Young, Z., Moghaddam, N., & Tickle, A. (2016). The efficacy of cognitive behavioral therapy for adults with ADHD. *Journal of Attention Disorders,* 1–14. doi:10.1177/1087054716664413.

Zalaquett, C. (2013). *Post-traumatic stress disorder. Practice briefs.* Alexandria, VA: American Counseling Association. Knowledge Center.

### CHAPTER 10

# The Existential-Humanistic Tradition and the Impact of Carl Rogers

The existential-humanistic view focuses on men and women as people who are empowered to act on the world and determine their own destiny. The locus of control and decision lies within the individual, rather than in past history or in environmental determinants. At the same time, the humanistic aspect of this tradition focuses on people-in-relationship one to another. It is this combination of individual respect and the importance of relationship that gives this framework its long-lasting strength.

## SPECIFIC GOALS OF THIS CHAPTER:

1. Describe the general worldview of existential-humanistic theory. The worldview of this orientation greatly influences the practice of counseling and therapy, even though the practitioner may follow another theoretical direction.

2. Examine person-centered theory and its possible relevance for work with multicultural populations.

3. Present central theoretical and practical constructs from the work of Rogers over three main periods of his development.

4. Provide you with an opportunity to practice person-centered therapeutic techniques.

5. Present Motivational Interviewing therapy and its basic principles.

6. Review some of the evidence base and neuroscientific bases of the theories presented in the chapter.

# The Existential-Humanistic Frame of Reference

The roots of the existential-humanistic tradition lie in philosophy, but Carl Rogers and his person-centered counseling have been most influential in popularizing the existential-humanistic point of view and making it accessible and relevant to clinical and counseling practice. Rogers's approach is designed to help you enter the worldview of the client and then to facilitate the client finding his or her own new direction and frame of thinking.

The existential-humanistic tradition does not have all the answers for helping victims and survivors, but its deep tradition of caring and of individual free choice is an important part of any treatment you might chose. As such it has had an influence on all major theories. The philosophic aspects of this theoretical approach are well received in virtually all cultures, and its major theorists have had wide impact and acceptance throughout the world.

*The Existential-Humanistic Worldview*: Existentialism is rooted in the work of philosophers such as Kierkegaard (1813–1855); Sartre (1946, 1956); Camus (1942, 1958); Heidegger (1962); Laing (1967); Husserl (1931); and Tillich (1961). Rollo May (1958, 1961, 1969) brought existential thought to the awareness of counselors and psychologists in the United States. Binswanger (1958, 1963) and Boss (1958, 1963) were particularly relevant in organizing the many threads of existentialism for the practice of counseling and therapy.

However, today there is one influential therapist carrying the existential torch—Irving Yalom (1980, 2017). His books and presentations carry considerable weight and you may view his presentations on YouTube by inserting his name in your browser. Existentialism is best experienced, rather than just read about. A useful short summary of the existential movement will be found in Flynn's 2006 book *Existentialism: A Very Short Introduction*.

*Being-in-the-world* has been defined as the most fundamental concept of existentialism: we are in the world and acting on that world while it simultaneously acts on us. Any attempt to separate ourselves from the world alienates us and establishes a false and arbitrary distinction. Alienation results either from separateness from others and the world or from our inability to choose and act in relationship. The central task of therapy and counseling, then, is to enable the alienated client to see him- or herself in relationship to the world and to choose and act in accordance with what he or she sees. Racism, sexism, homophobia, and the failure to understand difference lead to alienation by producing separation from others, a main cause of existential anxiety and aloneness.

To facilitate analysis, existentialists often think of the individual in terms of the *Eigenwelt* (the person and her or his body), the *Mitwelt* (other people in the world), and the *Umwelt* (the biological and physical world). Alienation can be experienced in one or more areas—that is, the person may be alienated from her or his own self and body, from others, or from the world. A general process of existential analysis is to enable the person to study what the world (both Mitwelt and Umwelt) and her or his relationship to that world are like. Then, having examined the world, the person is assumed free to act, rather than only to be acted upon. The issue of action, however, brings with it the possibility of existential anxiety.

Although existential anxiety may result from alienation, it may also result from failure to make decisions and to act in the world. Choices and decisions are often difficult; any time we choose, we must accept the fact that by choosing, we deny other alternatives and possibilities. Although choice may be painful, it is likely to be less so than the anxiety created by not choosing.

# Existential Commitment, Intentionality, and the I-Thou Relationship

Existential commitment is the decision to choose and to act; such action can be expected to alleviate anxiety. Yet, because of our being-in-the-world, we must constantly make choices that reactivates anxiety. This circle of choice and anxiety causes some existentialists (such as Sartre and Kierkegaard) to become pessimistic and dubious. Others (such as Buber and Tillich) regard the issue of choice as opportunity rather than as difficulty. As used throughout this book, intentionality is a key existential construct that holds that people can be forward moving and act on their world, yet must remain keenly aware that the world acts on them as well.

The existential-humanistic tradition recognizes the infinite variety of life experience and being-in-the-world as an opportunity rather than as a difficulty. Basic to this philosophy is assuming responsibility for choice and acting intentionally in the world.

The person who adopts the existential-humanistic position has made an intentional commitment toward what is positive and possible in human relations. Buber (1970) talks of the importance of "I-Thou" relations between people—that is, a relationship where others are seen as people rather than as objects. The intentional individual seeks I-Thou relationships as opposed to it-it relationships when people are seen as things. Buber's concept of I-Thou relationships speaks directly to multicultural concerns: How can we learn to stand in relationship to those different from ourselves?

# Summary

The existential-humanistic point of view is an attitude toward the counseling interview and the meaning of life. The main points of this mode of counseling can be summarized as follows:

1. We are in the world; our task is to understand what this means. It is clear that the meanings we generate vary from culture to culture.

2. We know ourselves through our relationship with the world, and in particular through our relationships with other people.

3. Anxiety can result from lack of relationship (with ourselves, with others, or with the world at large) or from a failure to act and choose.

4. We are responsible for our own construction of the world. Even though we know the world only as it interacts on us, it is we who decide what the world means and who must provide organization for that world.

5. The task of the existential-humanistic therapist or counselor is to understand the client's world as fully as possible and ultimately to encourage her or him to be responsible for making decisions. However, existential counselors will also share themselves and their worldviews with clients as is appropriate.

6. A special issue is that the world is not necessarily meaningful. Existentialists like Sartre and Kierkegaard often develop a negative and hopeless view of what they observe to be the absurdity and cruelty of life. However, humanistic existentialists, such as Buber and May, suggest that the very confusion and disorder in the world are an opportunity for growth and beauty.

7. The distinction between existential and existential-humanistic positions can be defined as one of philosophy or faith. If a person sees the many possibilities in the world as a problem, he or she has a problem. If a person sees the array of possibilities as infinite opportunity, she or he will choose to act.

## REFLECTION EXERCISE

### Six Months to Live

Imagine that your physician told you today that you had six months to live:

What experiences would you want to have in the time ahead?

What have you always wanted to do but did not because you were too busy?

What things would you start doing?

Who would you want to spend time with?

What friends would you reach out to that you haven't seen or talked to in a while?

What would you immediately stop doing?

Who brings you down that you should stop spending time with?

What would you want your legacy to be?

We hope this exercise serves as a reminder that you have free will and you can use it to choose the life you want to live. The choice is yours.

# Multicultural Issues and the Existential-Humanistic Tradition

The positive view of human nature and the desire for an egalitarian approach make existential-humanistic theory and practice appealing to women and other multicultural groups. At the same time, a multicultural approach raises some issues about this tradition. The intense preoccupation with the individual and free choice is at times incompatible with a more environmentally oriented approach.

For example, the work of Rogers and Frankl has been immensely popular in Japan. But Japanese culture places more importance with the group and the individual-in-relation than do these European-North American theories. Techniques of listening and focusing on individual decisions may at times be inappropriate with African American, Native American, and Hispanic/Latina/o cultures that focus on the person-in-relationship.

Ballou and Gabalac (2002) note that women and other oppressed groups do not have the necessary conditions for growth. The third force incorrectly places the total responsibility and obligation on the individual for her growth and development. The authors comment that person-centered theory and other humanistic approaches often submerge the Umwelt and Eigenwelt of existential theory into an individualistic "I-centered" theory. When this happens, Buber's elegant statement of "I and Thou" is lost, as is the awareness of our connectedness to the world at large—the Umwelt. Neither women nor any other group construct their own reality without external influences. External forces are really influential.

# The Rogerian Revolution

The word *self-actualization* is now a basic part of North American culture and can be traced to Rogers's influence, as can be seen in the following comments of Rogers and Wallen (1946):

> Counseling ... [is] a way of helping the individual help [the] self. The function of the counselor is to make it possible for the client to gain emotional release in relation to ... problems and, as a consequence, to think more clearly and more deeply about ... self and ... situation. It is the counselor's function to provide an atmosphere in which the client, through ... exploration of the situation, comes to see ... more clearly and to accept (personal) attitudes more fully. On the basis of this insight [the client] is able to meet ... life problems more adequately, more independently, more responsibly than before. (pp. 5–6)

This worldview, now commonplace in counseling and therapy and in Western society as a whole, represented a radical departure following World War II. Whereas psychodynamic and behavioral counseling and therapy viewed humankind as the often-unknowing pawn of unconscious forces and environmental contingencies, existential-humanistic psychology, particularly as interpreted by Rogers, stresses that the individual could "take charge" of life, make decisions, and act on the world.

Undergirding this worldview is a faith that people are positive, forward moving, basically good, and ultimately self-actualizing. Self-actualization, or mental and emotional health, may ultimately be defined as experiencing one's fullest humanity.

Self-actualizing people enjoy life thoroughly in all its aspects, not only in occasional moments of triumph. The task of the counselor is to assist the person in attaining the intentionality and the health that are natural to each individual. When a person becomes truly in touch with the inner self, that individual will move to positive action and fulfillment. Maslow's hierarchy of needs is presented in Figure 10.1.

## Adding Multicultural Dimensions to Self-Actualization Theory

The concept of self-actualization as described above has been criticized from a multicultural frame of reference (see Rigney, 1981; Lerner, 1992). If carried too far, self-actualization can become self-centeredness. In North America, the emphasis on self-actualization at times obscures the idea of the person-in-relationship to others.

Different cultures and social classes place different emphasis on Eigenwelt (the person and her or his body), Mitwelt (other people in the world), and Umwelt (the biological and physical world). Some upper- and middle-class clients have learned to believe that the Eigenwelt is perhaps the only desirable mode of being. This focus has led to some alienation of women and others from counseling and therapy.

The microskill of focus is a simple, but effective, way to balance Eigenwelt, Mitwelt, and Umwelt. Assume the following lesbian client is oriented to relationship as well as self-actualization. Note the variation in responses as the therapist focuses on different dimensions.

> *Client*: The professor just doesn't understand. He keeps talking about self-actualization and finding one's own way. I can't find my own way. My lover, Jenny, and I are very close. I don't want to be separate from her—we are as one. Right now she's sick and how can I find my own way if she's not OK? I don't even feel able to go out and work right now.
>
> *Therapist* (focusing on Eigenwelt): *You're* feeling overwhelmed, and *you* don't quite know what to do. What can *you* do to work through *your* present difficulties?
>
> [The italics highlight *you* as representative of a possible Eigenwelt response that may lead the client to self-actualization].

**Figure 10.1. Maslow's Hierarchy of Needs**

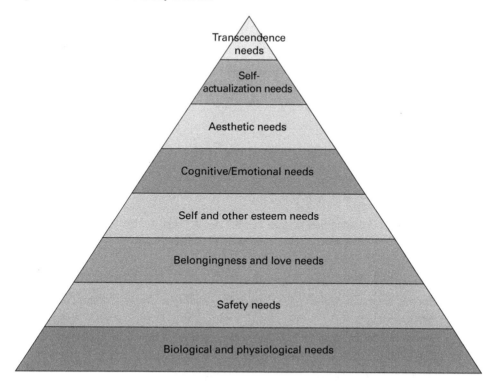

*Therapist* (focusing on Eigenwelt and Umwelt): *Jenny's* terribly important to *you.* The *relationship* sounds like the most important thing in *your* life right now. The question is how the *two of you* can survive this difficult time. *You're both* worried and upset and feel lost.

*Therapist* (focusing on Umwelt): The possibility of losing your *job* sounds very worrisome. You are wondering if issues of discrimination aren't part of the picture as well. Tell me some more about what's going on *at work.*

Each of the above listening responses can be useful and can be used in the Rogerian existential approach. Rogers constantly sought to help people work together. In some ways, the very terms *person-centered* and *client-centered*, attractive though they may be, can obscure the theoretical and practical value of Rogerian theory for non–middle-class and non–European-North American clients.

## The Influence of Rogers

The humanistic philosophy remains important in all counseling and therapy and has been supported by research over the years (see Table 10.1). Most practitioners who have adopted other theories or taken an eclectic or meta-theoretical approach still employ Rogers's interviewing skills and humanistic attitudes.

It should be noted that Rogers was never content with the status quo. He constantly changed, shaped, and adapted his ideas over the years, increasingly emphasizing in his later years the importance of awareness and action on issues. The next section presents three views of Rogers: nondirective, client-centered, and person-centered.

Although his methods changed at each stage of his development, his underlying faith in humanity and the individual-in-relationship remains constant. Table 10.1 shows Rogers's conditions for counseling and therapeutic change.

## REFLECTION EXERCISE

Rogers believed the following were necessary conditions for change. Furthermore, he suggested that these conditions were sufficient for constructive personal change to occur:

1. Two persons are in psychological contact.
2. The first, whom we shall term the client, is in a state of incongruence, being vulnerable or anxious.
3. The second person, whom we shall term the therapist, is congruent or integrated in the relationship.
4. The therapist experiences unconditional positive regard for the client.
5. The therapist experiences an empathic understanding of the client's internal frame of reference and endeavors to communicate this experience to the client.
6. The communication to the client of the therapist's empathic understanding and unconditional positive regard is to a minimal degree achieved.

What do you think? Are these conditions enough for change to occur? Can you think of other therapeutic factors that may facilitate change?

Adapted from Rogers, C. (1957). The necessary and sufficient conditions of therapeutic personality change. *Journal of Consulting Psychology, 21*, 95–103.

Table 10.1. **Research Box: Evidence Base of Person-Centered Therapy**

Rogers's methods have deeply influenced other approaches to helping. A landmark series of very early studies by Fiedler (1950a, b, 1951) sought to define the therapeutic relationship and studied psychoanalytic, Rogerian, and Adlerian persuasions. Fiedler found that expert therapists of these various persuasions appeared more similar to each other than they did to inexperienced therapists within the same theoretical orientation. An equally important study was conducted by Barrett-Lenard (1962), who found higher levels of facilitative conditions among experienced therapists.

*(Continued)*

**Table 10.1.  Research Box: Evidence Base of Person-Centered Therapy *(Continued)***

*Relationship as Central in Many Theories*

The above-mentioned studies prompted an avalanche of research of the Rogerian qualitative dimensions during the ensuing years. Results highlight the importance of the therapeutic relationship. "The counseling relationship has consistently been found to contribute to the success of the therapeutic process" (Orlinsky & Howard, 1986, p. 7). The success of the therapeutic intervention depends on the participants establishing an open, trusting, collaborative relationship or alliance. Failure to form such an alliance is associated with client noncompliance with treatment plans, early termination, and poor outcome.

*Research Findings*

The Rogerian tradition permeates our field. His influence is even larger than most admit. As you review this research history, recall that much of therapy was sterile until Rogers showed us that relationship is critical. And, of course, attending and listening are essential. The very words "reflection of feeling" are those of Carl Rogers. Consider the following research history as a clarification and extension of Carl Rogers contribution.

In a comprehensive review of psychotherapy research, Strupp (1989) comments: "The first and foremost task for the therapist is to create an accepting and empathic context" (p. 718). The Psychotherapy Research Project of the Menninger Foundation compared different types of therapy, and found that "supportive mechanisms infiltrated all therapies, psychoanalysis included, and accounted for more of the achieved outcomes (including structural changes) than anticipated" (Wallerstein, 1989, p. 195). According to Lambert and Barley (2001), the common factors most frequently studied have been the person-centered facilitative conditions of empathy, warmth, congruence, and the therapeutic relationship. Decades of research indicate that counseling and therapy is an interpersonal process.

Coming nearly seventy years after the Fiedler studies, the consistency of research on the dimensions of the Rogerian model is notable. The common factors are recognized as the major contributors to therapy outcome (Norcross & Wampold, 2011a; Wampold, 2015). Elliott and Freire (2008) reviewed more than 180 scientific outcome studies and found that Person-Centered/Experiential (PCE) therapies led large pre-post client change and these gains are maintained over time. Furthermore, PCE therapies were clinically and statistically equivalent to other therapies and better than control conditions (waitlist).

Angus, Watson, Elliott, Schneider, and Timulak (2015) examined research studies published between 1990 and 2015 and concluded that humanistic psychotherapy is an evidence-based practice for depression, interpersonal difficulties, coping with psychosis, self-damaging behaviors, and chronic medical conditions and should be included in current clinical practice guidelines.

Two new interesting areas of research relate to movement synchrony (In-Sync model) and inter-brain coupling between patient and therapist (Koole & Tschacher, 2016). This research would advance our understanding of movement synchrony and inter-brain coupling, and how could we use them to improve the therapeutic relationship and facilitate emotion regulation and change.

*Matching Therapeutic Style to Client Needs*

Rogers pointed out in 1975 that many therapists fall short of offering empathic conditions, and that therapy and counseling can be for better or worse. Strupp and Hadley (1976) and Strupp (1989) have illustrated this point. They reviewed a large number of studies indicating possible deterioration as an effect of the psycho-therapeutic process and pointed out the importance of a solid relationship appropriate to the need level of the client. Strupp (1977) caught the essence of this argument, saying that "the art of psychotherapy may largely consist of judicious and sensitive applications of a given technique, delicate decisions of when to press a point, when to be patient, when to be warm and understanding, and when to be remote" (p. 11). Strupp suggests that simple application of a few empathic qualities is not enough. These qualities also must be in synchrony with the client—at the moment—in the interviewing process. Norcross and Wampold (2011b) and Wampold (2015) confirmed the importance of adapting counseling and psychotherapy to the client's characteristics. Four patient characteristics (reactance/resistance, preferences, culture, religion/spirituality) are effective in adapting psychotherapy and two (stages of change, coping style) are probably effective.

## Case Examples from Three Periods of Rogers's Work

Rogers believed in and acted on his theories. His life was a personal demonstration of intentionality and self-actualization, as he constantly changed and grew. Three main stages of his process have been identified, as follows:

Stage 1: Nondirective (1940–1950). This stage emphasizes the acceptance of the client, the establishment of a positive nonjudgmental climate, trust in the client's wisdom, and permissiveness. It uses clarification of the client's world as the main technique. Rogers's writings give a central emphasis to skills in the counseling process.

Stage 2: Client-centered (1950–1961). This stage centers on reflecting the feelings of the client, incorporates resolving incongruities between the ideal self and real self, avoids personally threatening situations for the client, and uses reflection as the main technique. Skills are not emphasized; rather, a major emphasis on the counselor as a person is evolving.

Stage 3: Person-centered (1961–1987). This stage is characterized by increased personal involvement, with more stress on relational issues. While maintaining consistency with all past work, Rogers moved increasingly to emphasizing present-tense experience, a more active and self-disclosing role for the counselor, group as well as individual counseling, and consideration of broader issues in society, such as cultural differences and the use of power. The emphasis on skills has remained minimal, with an emphasis instead on counselor attitudes. Coupled with this is an extensive emphasis on experiencing oneself as a person-in-relation to others. A review of Rogers's transcripts, however, reveals a more interpretive helping style.

In the following pages, brief examples of each of the three major phases of Rogers's growth and development will be explored through the presentation and analysis of brief excerpts from interview sessions typical of each period.

## The Nondirective Period

A special gift made by Rogers to the counseling profession was a new openness to what was happening in the interview process. Through detailed notes and discussion and through the new medium of audio-recording, Rogers shared in great detail what he actually did in the counseling interview. Up to that time, the primary mode of training counselors and therapists had been in formal classrooms and one-to-one discussion of what the therapist remembered from an interview.

A classic research study by Blocksma and Porter (1947) revealed that what therapists say they do in an interview and what they actually do are two different things. Rogers's ability to share what he was doing, coupled with the work of Blocksma and Porter, have forever changed the nature of counseling and therapy training. There remains, however, strong resistance to this openness, particularly among some psycho-analytic therapists, who often prefer more abstract discussions of underlying unconscious conflicts to what actually happens in the session.

## Interview Example

The following transcript is taken from Rogers's nondirective phase when he was trying explicitly to draw out the client and impose as little of the counselor's orientation as possible (Rogers & Wallen, 1946). His belief was that interference from the counselor would only slow natural client growth. The microskills used in this interview are all attending skills and are extremely apparent. As a useful practice exercise, fill in the blank space to the left of the counselor response with the microskill(s) being used. (A listing of the microskills used can be found at the end of the chapter.)

1. *Client:* I wish I knew how to pray.
\_\_\_\_\_2. *Counselor:* Do you want to tell me some more about that?
3. *Client:* I'm all in a mess. I can't sleep. Last night I walked the streets most of the night in a pouring rain. I haven't been able to sleep all the time I've been on leave. I was home for a while, and I couldn't even talk to my folks there. You see, my buddy was killed, and I just can't get over it.
\_\_\_\_\_4. *Counselor:* That's been a pretty upsetting blow to you.
5. *Client:* Well it has. You see, my buddy was my only real friend—I don't make friends easily, never have had very many—and he and I always stuck together. [Tells how they met and some of the things they had been through.] We worked on the same gun crew, and we knew each other so well we never had to tell each other what to do. We could just signal by the way we looked. In this particular scrap the enemy planes were coming over plenty. It was pretty hot. The ammunition box was getting empty, and I just glanced at my buddy. He knew what I meant, and he went to get another box. While he was doing that a shell exploded right near him and killed him. (pause) I just can't get over it. I feel—I feel as though I caused his death.
\_\_\_\_\_6. *Counselor:* You feel that somehow you are to blame for the fact that he was killed.
7. *Client:* Yes I do. I don't see why, well, there's one thing I haven't mentioned. Maybe that has something to do with it. My buddy and I, we got along swell. We hardly ever quarreled, but just the day before this all happened we had quite an argument. (He relates the details of the argument.) We really got sore at each other. I wouldn't even speak to him for several hours afterwards. You know, I think that does have something to do with it. I guess that quarrel makes me feel that I am to blame for what happened.
\_\_\_\_\_8. *Counselor:* You feel that your being angry at him in some way was responsible for killing him.

9. *Client*: You know, I think that's it. I haven't thought that through before. Maybe I was scared to think it through. Somehow it helps to talk about things like this. You see, I didn't usually quarrel with my buddy, and I guess it hit me hard to think that we had an argument just the day before he was killed. It doesn't seem so bad when you tell about it. He was really a great guy. (He goes on to tell at some length about his buddy and his buddy's accomplishments and the good relationship they had together. The conversation then turns into other channels, and he talks about his own family and again mentions the fact that he had been very upset while home on leave.) I don't know what you've done sir, but this has sure helped me a lot. I don't see why I felt so much to blame as I did.

____10. *Counselor*: It seems to have helped to get it off your chest. Is that it?

11. *Client*: It sure has. I wonder, sir, if it would be too much if I could write to you if I ever feel this way again. I'm probably shipping out pretty quick so I don't think I'll have a chance to see you again, but maybe I could write you a letter.

____12. *Counselor*: I'd be delighted to get a letter from you even if you're not feeling upset. I hope you will write to me.

13. *Client*: Well, thanks a lot for talking with me. I've got to go now but you may be hearing from me. (pp. 120–121)

Rogers provides an interesting personal analysis of this interview. He points out that the counselor does not direct the depth of the interview, but rather attempts to establish conditions so that the client can determine how far or deep to go. Whereas many counselors might have wanted more concreteness and specifics about the situation, the worker in this case accepts the sailor's definition of what happened however he wants to talk about it. A psychodynamic counselor might object to the failure to consider unconscious thought processes underlying the relatively simple surface structure sentences of the sailor; other theorists might have different objections.

## Rogers's Response to Critics

Rogers tended to reply in a particularly disarming fashion to those who criticized his work. He suggested that each therapist must find her or his own way of being authentic with another person, and that those whose views differed from his would select counseling theories that worked best for them. Thus, Rogers exhibited unusual congruence within himself. He emphasized and respected clients' right to determine what was right for themselves, but he also respected his critics' ability to determine what was right for themselves.

Missing from the above transcript is Carl Rogers, the person. Rogers had an unusual ability to communicate warmth and authenticity nonverbally. Those who adopt the client-centered approach would stress that your personhood and ability to be with the client in the session are as important as—or even more important than—the specific words you say. It is this philosophic and humane dimension of the theory that has perhaps had the most effect on the practice of all counseling and therapy.

## Nondirective Listening

Rogers's nondirective style has continuing relevance. When clients are truly into their own experience, it is important to focus totally on them. Clients need to be heard, and we as counselors and therapists need to learn their construction of the world.

Through empathy and by using the listening skills, we provide clients with a chance to learn what they themselves think. Table 10.1 shows research supporting the positive effect of the relationship and the Rogerian conditions.

A pure listening approach as represented in the foregoing transcript is not always appropriate. At times, the nondirective style can bring about difficulties in multicultural counseling. For example, African American clients working with a European American therapist sometimes mistrust the Rogerian mirroring response. They might want to know who you are as a person, and they might reject a helping approach that is solely focused on mirroring back what is said. Sue and Sue (2016) found that some traditional Asian American clients often prefer a more directive approach and will not respect a counselor who cannot and will not give advice and direction.

Consequently, although listening is considered a central skill in counseling and therapy, it is one of many techniques that form the overall strategy of professional helping. During the client-centered period, Rogers was increasingly willing to interpret and influence clients.

## The Client-Centered Period

Most excerpts from Rogers's work from this period are highly verbal and would require a client deeply interested in introspection. As such there may be less of value in this period for multicultural counseling than in his other periods. The client-centered style of helping is currently used relatively infrequently.

### Interview Example

The following interview segment illustrates the work of the second period of Rogers (1961, pp. 84–85). The client, Mrs. Oak, talks about how hard it is for her to accept any help or positive reactions from others. The complexity of the counselor's sentences has greatly increased compared with those in the nondirective period interview.

Although the emphasis is still very much on the client and the client's perceptions, there is also an interpretive dimension in that the counselor seems to lead the client at times.

*Client*: I have a feeling … that you have to do it pretty much yourself, but that somehow you ought to be able to do that with other people. [She mentions that there
have been "countless" times when she might have accepted personal warmth and
kindliness from others.] I get the feeling that I just was afraid I would be devastat-
ed. [She returns to talking about the counseling itself and her feeling toward it.]
I mean there's been this tearing through the thing myself. Almost to—I mean, I
felt it—I mean I tried to verbalize it on occasion—a kind of—at times almost not
wanting you to restate, not wanting you to reflect, the thing is mine. Course all
right, I can say it's resistance. But that doesn't mean a damn thing to me now …
The—I think in—in relationship to this particular thing, I mean, the—probably
at times, the strongest feeling was, it's mine, it's mine. I've got to cut it down
myself. See?

*Counselor*: It's an experience that's awfully hard to put down accurately into words,
and yet I get a sense of difference here in this relationship, that from the feeling
that "this is mine," "I've got to do it," "I am doing it," and so on, to a somewhat
different feeling that "I could let you in."

[The counselor's reflection of meaning catches the main points of Mrs. Oak's statement
in brief form, thus feeding back to her what her inner world is truly like. In addition,
the basic incongruity between real and ideal self is reflected back to the client; Mrs.
Oak's statement has a vagueness that would prompt many other counselors to search
for more concreteness and to ask for specifics. A psychodynamic therapist might observe the sexual symbolism in the words "I've got to cut it down myself" and the therapist's response "I could let you in."]

*Client*: Yeah. Now I mean, that's—that it's—well, it's sort of, shall we say, volume two.
It's— it's a—well, sort of, well, I'm still in the thing alone, but I'm not—see—

*Counselor*: M-hm. Yes, that paradox sort of sums it up, doesn't it.

*Client*: Yeah.

*Counselor*: In all of this, there is a feeling, it's still—every aspect of my experience is
mine and that's kind of inevitable and necessary and so on. And yet that isn't the
whole picture either. Somehow it can be shared or another's interest can come in
and in some ways it is new.

[There is an interpretive flavor to the last two therapist statements as new meanings are
put on old experience. Yet, as they very much come from the client's worldview, these
leads are a reflection of meaning but close to a paraphrase. The increased involvement of
the therapist since Rogers's first period is apparent. Note also that the therapist goes so far
as to use "I" when talking about the client rather than "you"; this could be considered a
sign of strong empathy in that the counselor can see the world through the client's eyes.]

*Client*: Yeah. And it's— it's as though, that's how it should be. I mean, that's how it—
has to be. There's a—there's a feeling, "and this is good." I mean, it expresses, it
clarifies it for me. There's a feeling—in this caring, as though—you were sort of

standing back—standing off, and if I want to sort of cut through to the thing, it's a—a slashing of—oh, tall weeds, that I can do it, and you can—I mean you're not going to be disturbed by having to walk through it, too. I don't know. And it doesn't make sense. I mean—

*Counselor*: Except there's a very real sense of rightness about this feeling that you have, hm?

*Client*: M-hm.

(*Carl R. Rogers, Client-Centered Therapy, pp. 84–85. Copyright © 1951 by Houghton Mifflin Harcourt.*)

[It is particularly important to note the emphasis in the paraphrase. The therapist has selectively attended to the positive aspects of the client's message ("this is good") and simultaneously ignored negative aspects ("it doesn't make sense"). Behavioral counselors have often pointed out that Rogerian counseling involves selective attention and that a complete verbal "shaping" process occurs in this mode of counseling than in more systematic behavioral approaches. Regardless of whether this view is accepted or not, the selective attention to positive, forward-moving aspects of the client is an example of the positive emphasis of this theory.]

Rogers goes on to comment that this was a turning point for Mrs. Oak, who learned that it was all right to accept others and to discover positive things in herself. This acceptance is, of course, crucial in the development of a positive self-actualizing personality.

## A Multicultural Critique of the Client-Centered Period

The focus in the foregoing interview is still very much on the individual and her construction of events. Very little attention is paid to how others might view the same events. The goal of the interchange seems to focus on Mrs. Oak finding her own "space." Rogerian theory holds that after Mrs. Oak has found herself, she will be better able to relate with others. A feminist or multicultural critique might be that Mrs. Oak could find herself even more rapidly given a more immediate focus on relationships and the role of women in society, with a secondary focus on her own perceptions. The emphasis in the first two periods of Rogers's work was on individual counseling and therapy.

If Mrs. Oak was a Lakota Sioux, the individual-focused approach of the interview likely would be inappropriate. Although it would be important to listen to her individual constructions (as in the nondirective period), the focus of counseling interventions would probably emphasize the Mitwelt, the family, extended family, and community. For a Lakota Sioux, an individual issue remains unresolved until it is considered in the broader network of relationships. In addition, it would be important for you as therapist to present yourself in the interview as a real person with real thoughts and feelings. In multicultural settings, the boundaries between therapist and counselor change, which presents a very real challenge to the practice of traditional counseling and therapy.

Rogers moved toward multicultural emphasis and understanding in his final, person-centered period.

## The Person-Centered Period

Stage 3 of Rogers's development reflects a vastly increased involvement and activity on the part of the counselor. Rogers became interested in encounter groups and broadened his view of helping. To the traditional skills of reflection of feeling and paraphrasing, he added new skills of self-disclosure, feedback, and questions.

### Interview Example

In the following interview, Rogers (1970) acts as facilitator for an encounter group:

*Art*: When the shell's on it's, uh

*Lois*: It's on!

*Art*: Yeah, it's on tight.

*Susan*: Are you always so closed in when you're in your shell?

*Art*: No, I'm so darn used to living with the shell, it doesn't even bother me. I don't even know the real me. I think I've, well, I've pushed the shell away more here. When I'm out of my shell—only twice—once just a few minutes ago—I'm really me, I guess. But then I just sort of pull in a cord after me when I'm in my shell, and that's almost all the time. And I leave the front standing outside when I'm back in the shell.

*Facilitator*: And nobody's back in there with you?

[Art is the focus of group interaction at the moment. He describes his feelings of being shut off from people in a vivid metaphor of life in a shell. Art as a group member is using effective self-disclosure skills. Lois and Susan, through completion of Art's sentence and the focused closed questions, show that more people than group leaders and counselors can be helpful. The facilitator's interpretation is critical because it brings past and present experience together in one existential moment. Art is experiencing being alone in the shell at this moment as he has in the past in other situations. Yet, paradoxically, he is alone with a supportive facilitator and group. This integration of past and present experience in "moments of truth" appears in most theories of helping and is particularly important.]

*Art* (crying): Nobody else is in there with me, just me. I just pull everything into the shell and roll the shell up and shove it in my pocket. I take the shell, and the real me, and put it in my pocket where it's safe. I guess that's really the way I do it—I go into my shell and turn off the real world. And here—that's what I want to do here in this group, you know—come out of my shell and actually throw it away.

*Lois*: You're making progress already. At least you can talk about it.

*Facilitator*: Yeah. The thing that's going to be the hardest is to stay out of the shell.

*Art* (still crying): Well, yeah, if I can keep talking about it I can come out and stay out, but I'm going to have to, y'know, protect me. It hurts. It's actually hurting to talk about it. (p. 26)

[Lois provides a good example of a feedback statement, and the facilitator expresses his opinion and reaction. Together, the two support Art in the immediate moment and help him clarify his own experience.]

Rogers was personally deeply affected by his learnings in group work, and during this period, he also developed an interest in couples counseling (1972), personal power (1977), the learning process (1969), and world peace (Gendlin, 1988). Despite these diverse interests that continued to grow and expand until his death at the age of eighty-five in 1987, Rogers maintained his consistent respect for the individual, stressed the importance of research, and constantly emphasized the ability of the person to find his or her own direction—but always in relationship to another human being.

## Central Theoretical Constructs and Techniques

The central issue in Rogerian and existential-humanistic counseling lies in how the individual perceives the world. "Experience is reality" is a statement that implies both explicitly and implicitly that what one thinks is happening in the world is indeed happening. There are an infinite number of ways where we and our clients can view the world, an infinite number of ways of interpreting that world, and an infinite number of ways of acting on that world.

## A Person-Centered Theory

Rogers's best-known book is entitled *On Becoming a Person* (1961), and that title is a reflection of the theory and the man. In the Rogerian view, there seems to be no definable end to counseling work; this emphasis on process toward possible futures is particularly illustrative of the existential-humanistic orientation, which stresses individual choice.

At the same time, there is a potential issue in the term *person-centered*, in that counselors and therapists have sometimes limited the scope of what Rogers meant by the concepts of Eigenwelt, Mitwelt, and Umwelt. Although Rogers did not use the language of German existentialism, he was very concerned that persons extend their view beyond themselves to others and to the world at large. Rogers would endorse expanding his and others' humanistic concepts to issues beyond the individual.

Practice Exercise 10.1 provides you an opportunity to construct, using only listening skills, an interview in Rogers's person-centered mode. You may be surprised to find that you can conduct a complete and effective session using only the skills of the basic listening sequence. This exercise does not introduce you to the full range of Rogerian response possibilities, but it does illustrate what is possible if one is willing to enter the world of the client and truly attempt to see the world as the other perceives it.

---

**PRACTICE EXERCISE 10.1.  An Exercise in Person-Centered Therapy**

A person-centered theorist might argue that our world is too full of advice giving and people telling other people what to do. Your goal in this exercise is to enter the frame of reference of the client and use only listening skills represented by the basic listening sequence and perhaps reflection of meaning. No advice, suggestions, or interpretation is allowed! To make the task somewhat easier, you may use questions, but aim each question toward the frame of reference of the client. A good topic for a real or role-played "client" may be the act of procrastination, putting off something until later. However, any of a variety of topics may be used for the practice session.

*Empathic Relationship*

Begin the interview by establishing rapport, until you and the client are comfortable. Remember that rapport is particularly important throughout the session. Structure the interview honestly by saying that you want to understand and listen and not give advice. You might initiate the session by saying, "You want to talk about ..."

*Story and Strengths*

Use primarily the reflective listening skills of encouraging, paraphrasing, and reflection of feeling. Periodically summarize what the "client" says so the session has a continuous structure. After you have heard the concern fairly clearly, you may wish to paraphrase or reflect positive meanings or actions inherent in what the client has been saying. This is a specific way to manifest positive regard and demonstrate the positive asset search.

*Goals*

Determine agreed-upon outcomes. Your client very likely has implied how he or she would like things to be. As you begin to understand the client's issues, paraphrase or summarize how the client would like things to be.

*(Continued)*

**PRACTICE EXERCISE 10.1.  An Exercise in Person-Centered Therapy** *(Continued)*

Here, you will likely find it necessary to ask a question related in some form to the following: "How would you like things to be?" You have heard the "real self" and the issue during data gathering, and this is the opportunity to draw out the "ideal self" or the ideal solution.

*Restory*

Generate alternative solutions. Important in person-centered theory is the distinction between the real and ideal. Summarize this incongruence of real and ideal with the confrontation statement "On the one hand, your issue is ..., but on the other hand, your ideal solution is ... Now, what comes to your mind as a possible resolution?" Alternatively, you may wish to talk about how the person views him- or herself and how he or she would like to view him- or herself. Again, the question may not be necessary, as the clear summary of the real and ideal often enables clients to start generating their own solutions out of their own personal constructs.

*Action*

Use the basic listening sequence and reflection of meaning to understand and listen to what the client generates. This may be considered the action phase of the interview in which the client generates a new view on the issue from his or her own internal frame of reference.

You may wish to summarize what the client has generated as alternative solutions and see if the client is interested in actually doing something about her or his situation. As Rogerian theory does not emphasize this phase of helping, you may find it worthwhile to consider action and generalization techniques from relapse prevention, or you may simply ask the client "What one thing will you do or think differently this coming day because of our discussion?"

Simply being heard accurately frees many people for creative, intentional responding. This exercise is taken from the nondirective period of Rogerian theory but may be adapted to include other skills (self-disclosure, feedback) added in later Rogerian periods. If you have mastered the constructs presented in preceding chapters, you can rather rapidly enter into a relatively effective person-centered interview.

## Seeing the World from the Client's Perspective

Given the infinite possibilities in life, each person's experience and perceptions will be at least somewhat different from anyone else's. A central task of the counselor is to understand and empathize with the unique experiential world of the client.

Perhaps more than anyone else, Rogers was able to listen empathically and carefully to other human beings. As he understood them and their perceptions, he consistently found positive, self-actualizing forces in them. Those committed to the humanistic counseling approach are almost always able to find positive elements in even the most troubled individual.

The following story provides a beginning point for exploring the complexity of human interactions and the Rogerian positive approach:

> A child attempts to string beads onto a shoelace. The plastic end of the lace has been torn off, and the tip is frayed badly. The child sits quietly and determinedly for fifteen minutes, attempting an impossible task. Then, with a sudden shout of frustration, the shoes are thrown about the room. At that moment the child's father comes over and strikes the child for "lack of patience."

In this case, the child is obviously forward-moving and purposeful. But the perception of reality is unrealistic, in that the task is impossible, given the frayed string and the age of the child. Viewing the child from an objective perspective, it is easy to see that the child's expression of anger is a normal reaction to growing frustration. But what about the father's reaction?

The father's behavior appears reprehensible and irrational. Such behavior cannot represent forward-moving self-actualized personhood. In such a real-life case, the counselor would first consider the situation for possible danger to the child and would take specific action to ensure that the child was safe from abuse.

Assuming that abuse is not an ongoing issue, how would the Rogerian therapist deal with this situation? In counseling, the father would be encouraged to talk about the situation in considerable detail. There would be an emphasis on the emotional underpinnings of the incident, and quite likely, the father would share other incidents where he lost his temper. At this point referral for behavioral anger management may be wise.

This example illustrates an important point: *Human interactions are often more complex than they seem at a surface level.* As the complex father/child interaction is explored in depth over a series of sessions, the counselor might uncover the fact that the father has tried very hard to find work but has been unsuccessful, that the father is a single parent, and that he himself was abused as a child. The person-centered counselor would tend to focus more on the experience and emotion of the father and pay relatively less attention to the facts of the incident. The counselor would reflect the positive elements of the father's behavior (trying to make it to do the "right thing") and understand and accept the negative behavior. The counselor's strong positive regard would come through, and the father's striking of the child could be viewed as a natural reaction to frustration similar to the child's natural reaction to frustration.

The above interpretation, however, would not be made explicit. Rather, the counselor would communicate her or his faith that the father could become more intentional and self-actualized if he so chose. At issue here, however, is that children and those who experience abuse may not have time to wait for the perpetrator to heal. Abuse and assault must not be allowed to happen again. In such situations, it is important to use a balanced approach: the counselor acts to stop the abusive situations and protect the child and then applies Rogerian concepts as part of a broader treatment plan.

# The Real Self and the Ideal Self: Multicultural Implications

A critical issue in Rogerian counseling (presently the most popular existential-humanistic view) is the discrepancy that often occurs between the real self and the ideal self. An individual needs to see her- or himself as worthy. Often, an individual loses sight of what he or she really is in an effort to attain an idealized image. This discrepancy between thought and reality, between self-perception and others' perceptions, or between self and experience leads to incongruities. These incongruities in turn result in areas and times where the person is not truly her- or himself. The father who strikes the child lacks congruence. The objective of therapy with this client is to resolve the discrepancies between ideal and real self, thus eliminating the tension and substituting forward-moving self-actualization.

From a multicultural frame of reference, the emphasis in Rogerian theory on ideal self and real self tends to obscure relational and broader environmental issues. As such, you may find it helpful to add a broader focus when working with many clients.

For example, it would be within the Rogerian tradition to help clients focus on real relationships and ideal relationships. Such a focus would help individuals think of themselves as persons-in-relation to significant others. This focus would entail a change in the style of counseling and therapy usually associated with Rogers. But when one considers Rogers's life development, one would suspect that these concepts are not too distant from where he was heading at the end of his life. Clearly, Rogers was focusing on a more ideal world as contrasted with the real world (Umwelt).

Furthermore, theorists of a more psychodynamic orientation have argued that Rogers's emphasis on the self as a central construct goes back to his own roots in a strict German family. His self-psychology from this frame of reference represents an unconscious rebellion against and an attempt to cope with family and cultural controls. Rogers, who once studied for the ministry, constantly stressed the importance of a natural relationship among human beings. This data seems to support the idea that Rogers was not as free of past developmental history as he stated in his theories.

# Motivational Interviewing

Clients commonly discuss change with counselors and therapists. Improving mental adjustment to demanding situations, coping with stress, or improving wellness are among the most frequent areas of change sought by clients. Clients often are ambivalent or unmotivated to seek the change they want or need, and counselors and therapists typically advise them to change, using a directing and sometimes confrontational style of communication. Clients in turn respond in a passive or resistant way to this style (Rollnick, Butler, Kinnersley, Gregory, & Mash, 2010).

Motivational interviewing is a person-centered, goal-oriented therapeutic approach developed by Miller and Rollnick to help clients explore and resolve ambivalence toward their mental and behavioral concerns (Miller, 1983; Miller & Rollnick, 1991, 2013). Motivational interviewing (MI) builds on Carl Rogers's view that change can be achieved through the process of self-actualization and includes most of his core concepts (Crisp, 2015). MI uses a supportive, empathetic, reflective, nonjudgmental, and collaborative style to reduce ambivalence, enhance motivation for positive change, and reinforce client's change talk related to achieving their goal (Miller & Rollnick, 2013).

As you read the following discussion of MI, you may want to refer frequently to Chapter 4, which discusses microskills and solution-oriented therapy. Microskills are built on listening and empathic understanding, while the influencing skills (as you will recall) focus on developing and resolving discrepancies and inconsistencies through respectful and supportive confrontation. The five stages of the interview are a useful model to enhance MI. Solution-oriented therapy (SOT), like MI microskills, and, of course, Carl Rogers, all seek to focus on the client and the client's goal setting.

However, a special strength of MI is its emphasis on motivation and the client's desire for real change. SOT and microskills also emphasize change, particularly with their emphasis on the action stages of the interview and using behavioral psychology's relapse prevention. Mastery of MI, microskills, and SOT by themselves provide a powerful counseling and therapy set of tools. In addition, you will note that since their beginning, microskills consciously have included a major focus on multicultural issues and social justice. Thus far, like many other theories discussed in this book, MI has given only minimal attention to these issues.

Motivational Enhancement Therapy (MET) represents a newer adaptation of MI. MET is a manualized, four-session program, well supported by research (National Registry of Evidence-based Programs and Practice [NREPP], 2017). Both MI and MET work on facilitating and engaging intrinsic motivation within the client in order to change target behavior.

Motivational interviewing is based on the following assumptions:

- Ambivalence about change is normal and constitutes a motivational obstacle in changing.
- Ambivalence can be resolved by working with the client's intrinsic motivations and values.
- An empathic, supportive, yet directive counseling style provides conditions under which change can occur.
- Direct persuasion, advice, lecturing, and aggressive confrontation does not help reduce ambivalence. Direct persuasion increases client defensiveness and reduces likelihood of change.
- Motivation to change is elicited from within the client and is not imposed from outside forces.
- The counselor's task is to work collaboratively with the client and offer guidance.
- The client's task is to articulate and resolve their ambivalence.

## REDS: The Basic Principles

The practice of MI is guided by four principles: Resistance, Empathy, Discrepancy, and Self-Efficacy (Miller & Rollnick, 1999/2013; Motivational Interviewing Network of Trainers, 2014):

**R:** Roll with resistance: Confrontation builds resistance; therefore avoid argumentation.

**E:** Express empathy: Allow client to let you know you understand (even if you don't agree).

**D:** Develop Discrepancy: Help client to see difference between their current negative behavior and desired change behaviors.

**S:** Support Self-Efficacy: Empower your clients for change.

*Roll with Resistance.* Clients are usually ambivalent about change. When clients perceive conflicts between their views of their issues and those of the counselor, resistance takes over. Sometimes, a client's discrepant views trigger a "righting reflex" on the counselor—a tendency born from concern, to ensure that the client understands and agrees with the need to change and to solve the problem for the client (Rollnick, Miller, & Butler, 2007, p. 7). Instead of confronting resistance, MI counselors "roll with it." They do not challenge any statements or behaviors that signal resistance; they let the client define their concerns and issues and suggest possible solutions. During this process, the counselor invites the client to explore new perspectives or possibilities. For example, instead of talking about why binge drinking is bad, in a nonjudgmental way the counselor encourages the client to talk about why they binge-drink and what are the effects. The effort is not on imposing goals or strategies, but on encouraging the client to consider alternative perspectives on the issue. Even if clients dispute the need for change, the intention is to transfer the responsibility for arguing for change to the client via *change talk*—overt verbalizations that demonstrate recognition of the need for change, concern for their current position, intention to change, or the belief that change is possible.

*Express Empathy*. Empathy involves seeing the world as the client sees it. Accurate empathic responses communicate that you understand what the client feels. When clients feel heard and understood, they tend to share their experiences in more depth. Client openness facilitates counseling. For example, if a client feels you understand his or her experience, the more likely they will be to talk about issues, such as alcohol addiction or compulsive eating, and about the reasons why they cannot stop. This in turn will allow more opportunities to engage change talk.

*Develop Discrepancy*. Motivation for change occurs when clients perceive a mismatch between where they are and where they would like to be. This involves exploring the pros and cons of his or her current behaviors, as well as of changes to current behaviors, to raise or intensify an awareness of the discrepancy between the client's current behaviors and their future goals or values. For example, during the counseling interview, a student may realize that his current binge-drinking behavior may jeopardize his or her future goal of becoming a police officer. Developing such discrepancy will elicit movement toward consistency between the client's behaviors and his or her goal. When clients realize that their current behaviors are in conflict with their goals, motivation for change increases. Ultimately, it is the client who should present the arguments for change.

*Support Self-Efficacy*: MI counselors believe clients have within themselves the capacity to change. They believe in self-actualization. However, clients have often tried and failed previous attempts to change their behaviors. Their new efforts to stop excessive drinking or eating are filled with doubts about their ability to achieve their goals. MI counselors use a strengths-based approach to support clients' self-efficacy. They focus on previous successes and highlight skills the client already has to encourage change. Desired change will not materialize unless the client believes that he or she has the competencies and resources to overcome challenges and barriers to successfully implement new behaviors. If a client believes that he or she has the ability to change, the possibility of changing is greatly improved.

## MI Techniques

The practice of MI involves the skillful use of certain techniques for guiding the process toward eliciting client change talk and commitment for action (change). Change talk involves communication indicating the client may be considering the possibility of change. MI uses several of the microskills presented in Chapter 4. The mnemonic

OARS helps facilitate remembering the skills: **O**pen-ended Questions, **A**ffirmations, **R**eflections, and **S**ummaries. Whether expressed in a verbal or nonverbal way, these communication skills need to be adapted to be culturally sensitive and appropriate to the client you are working with.

The following table (10.2) reviews MI's evidence-base. Table 10.3 summarizes MI's neuroscience foundation.

---

**Table 10.2. Research Box: Evidence Base of Motivational Interviewing Therapy**

Motivational Interviewing has been cited in more than 25,000 articles, including over 200 randomized clinical trials examining MI interviewing processes and outcomes (Miller & Rollnick, 2013).

The National Registry of Evidence-based Programs and Practice rates MI as an effective therapy for the treatment of alcohol use, alcohol-related injuries, cocaine and opiate use, and retention in treatment. Motivational Enhancement Therapy (MET), the MI adaptation that includes assessment feedback to clients, is an effective treatment for substance use, alcohol consumption, drinking intensity, and marijuana use (NREPP, 2017).

Recent meta-analyses studies provide further support. A meta-analysis of 119 studies showed that MI increased clients' engagement in treatment and their intention to change (two variables linked to motivation to change). The results also show that MI was effective for both individuals with high levels and low levels of distress, affected by a variety of disorders. Furthermore, MI was more effective than no treatment, waitlist in the treatment of a variety of disorders, and was as effective as other well-established therapies (Lundahl, Kunz, Brownell, Tollefson, & Burke, 2010). A meta-analysis of 25 randomized controlled studies has support for Motivational Enhancement Therapy as an intervention for treating substance use (Lenz, Rosenbaum, & Sheperis, 2016). In addition, the program has been shown to be effective in enhancing the treatment of anxiety disorders and in reducing anxiety sensitivity (Korte & Schmidt, 2013).

---

**Table 10.3. Neuroscience and Client-Centered Therapy**

Carl Rogers brought empathy to centrality in the helping field. Neuroscience's fMRI studies of the brain take us to a new level in our understanding of the meaning and value of empathy. The brain's mirror neurons and mirror system gives us an understanding of the place of empathy in the communication process (Spunt, 2013). Skin conductance, also provides a physiological demonstration of the importance of empathy in the counseling relationship (Marci, Ham, Moran, & Orr, 2007). Client and therapist seem to match their levels of skin conductance during the counseling session, a process called "neural coupling." This match disappears when client and therapist do not understand one another. Neurophysiology is showing that empathy is indeed a necessary (and sometimes sufficient) condition for the relationship, which can enable the client to change by him- or herself.

Neuroscience research confirms that empathy is essential in navigating our social environment and developing intellectual and emotional understanding (Ivey & Daniels, 2016; Ivey, Daniels, Zalaquett, & Ivey, 2017; Ivey, Ivey, and Zalaquett, 2018). A meta-analysis conducted by Fan et al. (2011) across 40 fMRI studies showed that *affective empathy* is associated with increased activity in the insula, while the right supramarginal gyrus recognizes a lack of empathy (Engen & Singer, 2013). *Cognitive empathy* is associated with higher activity in the midcingulate cortex and the dorsomedial prefrontal cortex (MCC/dmPFC). All these studies are useful in that we now realize that empathy is more complex than originally described by Rogers. Furthermore, paraphrasing (cognitive empathy) and reflection of feeling (emotional empathy) distinctions are clarified.

*(Continued)*

**Table 10.3. Neuroscience and Client-Centered Therapy *(Continued)***

Neuroimaging studies by Lamm, Decety, and Singer (2011) also show that emotional components are shared vicariously. When we experience direct pain ourselves (firsthand sensation), the somatosensory motor cortex, insula, and anterior cingulate cortex (ACC) are activated. When we watch others experience pain (secondhand pain), the insula and ACC are activated, but not the somatosensory cortex. The insula integrates visceral and autonomic information with salient stimuli, acting as an infrastructure for the representation of subjective bodily feelings of positive and negative emotions. Eres et al. (2015) found greater gray matter density in these places.

We think of Rogerian positive regard, authenticity, and being with the client as key aspects of listening. Counselors activate key brain structures when they listen. The ventral striatum becomes active when encountering abstract positive communication. The microcounseling approach identified the concrete behaviors of listening in 1966 and developed the term "attending behavior," followed by specific behavior dimensions of paraphrasing and reflection of feeling. The importance of culturally appropriate eye contact, body language, vocal tone, and verbal following has since become a basic standard counseling practice. Rogerian microskills of attending behavior, paraphrasing, reflecting feelings, and summarizing were studied in Japan by Kawamichi and colleagues (2014). They found those who listen lights up the brain of the other, while not listening metaphorically turns the light off.

Listening makes a difference in all cultures.

# Theory Practice

The beauty and strength of the existential-humanistic tradition lie in its strong faith in humankind, opportunity for personal growth, and the infinite possibility of experience. As with psychodynamic theory, the existential-humanistic approach tends to be highly verbal. Concerned with the meaning of life and individual satisfaction, the therapy can be verbose. As such, it appeals mainly to middle- and upper-class individuals. The positive philosophy of Rogers appears to be particularly applauded by those of a multicultural orientation, but Rogerian methods of slow reflection, lack of action, and failure to consider immediate problem solving seem inappropriate for these groups. The tendency for existential-humanistic counseling to ignore person-environment transactions in daily practice is a major limitation with some clients. The intense preoccupation with the individual and free choice is at times incompatible with a more environmentally oriented and contextually aware approach.

However, the existential-humanistic philosophic tradition does speak to multicultural concerns in that it, perhaps more than any other set of theories, focuses on *human relationship*. If we supplement the basic ideas of Rogers with more focused emphasis on the Mitwelt and Umwelt, perhaps we are doing as he would wish.

Given its concerns and drawbacks, what does the existential-humanistic movement offer the beginning counselor or therapist that is immediately useful? Perhaps the major contribution of Rogers has been his emphasis on empathic and accurate listening and his willingness to open the interview to inspection and research through audiotape and films. The attending skills explored in Chapter 4 rest heavily on Rogers's classifications and discussion in his early work. The qualitative conditions of warmth, respect, and concreteness are derived from his seminal thinking.

Motivational interviewing represents the next stage of person-centered therapy. Deeply rooted in the Rogerian approach, MI infuses a directive emphasis to help clients resolve their ambivalence toward change. The goal is not to impose therapists' values on clients' lives, but to guide them toward change talk. The counseling and psychotherapy theories presented in the next chapter also belong to the humanistic tradition but are distinguished by a strong focus on experiencing.

# References

Angus, L., Watson, J.C., Elliott, R., Schneider, K., & Timulak, L. (2015). Humanistic psychotherapy research 1990–2015: From methodological innovation to evidence-supported treatment outcomes and beyond. *Psychotherapy Research, 25,* 330–347. doi.org/10.1080/10503307.2014.989290.

Ballou, M., & Gabalac, N. (2002). *Rethinking mental health and disorder: Feminist perspectives.* New York, NY: Guilford.

Barrett-Lennard, G. (1962). Dimensions of therapist response as causal factors in therapeutic change. *Psychological Monographs, 76,* 43. (Ms. No. 562).

Binswanger, L. (1958). The existential analysis school of thought. In R. May, E. Angel, & H. Ellenberger (Eds.), *Existence* (pp. 191–213). New York, NY: Basic Books.

Binswanger, L. (1963). *Being-in-the-world: Selected papers of Ludwig Binswanger.* New York, NY: Basic Books.

Blocksma. D.D., & Porter, E.H. (1947). A short-term training program in client-centered counseling. *Journal of Consulting Psychology, 11,* 55–60.

Boss, M. (1958). *The analysis of dreams.* New York, NY: Philosophical Library.

Boss, M. (1963). *Psychoanalysis and Dasein analysis.* New York, NY: Basic Books.

Buber, M. (1970). *I and thou.* New York, NY: Scribner's.

Camus, A. (1942). *The stranger.* New York, NY: Random House.

Camus, A. (1958). *The myth of Sisyphus.* New York, NY: Knopf.

Crisp, R. (2015). Can motivational interviewing be truly integrated with person-centered counselling? *The Australian Journal of Rehabilitation Counselling, 21,* 77-87. doi.org/10.1017/jrc.2015.3.

Elliott, R., & Freire, E. (2008). *Person-centred/experiential therapies are highly effective: Summary of the 2008 meta-analysis.* Retrieved from https://www.pce-world.org/images/stories/meta-analysis_effectiveness_of_pce_therapies.pdf.

Engen, H.G., & Singer, T. (2013). Empathy circuits. *Current Opinion in Neurobiology, 23,* 275–282. doi:10.1016/j.conb.2012.11.003.

Eres, R., Decety, J., & Molenberghs, P. (2015). Individual differences in local gray matter density are associated with differences in affective and cognitive empathy. *NeuroImage, 117,* 305–310.

Fan, Y., Duncan, N., De Greck, M., & Northoff, G. (2011). Is there a core neural network in empathy? An fMRI based quantitative meta-analysis. *Neuroscience and Biobehavioral Reviews, 35,* 903–911.

Fiedler, F. (1951). Factor analysis of psychoanalytic, nondirective, and Adlerian therapeutic relationships. *Journal of Consulting Psychology, 15,* 32–38.

Fiedler, F.E. (1950a). A comparison of therapeutic relationships in psychoanalytic, nondirective, and Adlerian therapy. *Journal of Consulting Psychology, 14*, 435–436.

Fiedler, F.E. (1950b). The concept of an ideal therapeutic relationship. *Journal of Consulting Psychology, 14*, 239–245.

Flynn, T. (2006). *Existentialism: A very short introduction*. Oxford, England: Oxford University Press.

Framboise, T., & Iow, K. (1989). American Indian adolescents. In J. Gibbs & L. Hwang (Eds.), *Children of color* (pp. 114–147). San Francisco: Jossey-Bass.

Gendlin, E. (1988). *Carl Rogers. American Psychologist, 43*, 127–128.

Heidegger, M. (1962). *Being and time*. New York, NY: HarperCollins.

Husserl, E. (1931). *Ideas: General introduction to pure phenomenology*. London, UK: Allen & Unwin.

Ivey, A., & Daniels, T. (2016). Systematic interviewing microskills: Developing bridges between the fields of communication and counseling psychology. *International Journal of Communication, 10*, 1–21.

Ivey, A., Ivey, M.B., & Zalaquett, C.P. (2018). *Intentional interviewing and counseling: Facilitating client development in a multicultural society* (9th ed.). Belmont, CA: Cengage Learning.

Ivey, A.E., Daniels, T., Zalaquett, C.P., & Ivey, M. (2017). Neuroscience of attention: Empathy and counseling skills. In T. Daniels, L.K. Jones, & L.A. Russell-Chapin (Eds.), *Neurocounseling: Brain-based clinical approaches*. Alexandria, VA: American Counseling Association. doi:10.1002/9781119375487.ch5.

Kawamichi, H., Yoshihara, K., Sasaki, A.T., Sugawara, S.K., Tanabe, H.C., Shinohara, R., ... Sadato, N. (2015). Perceiving active listening activates the reward system and improves the impression of relevant experiences. *Social Neuroscience, 10*, 16–26. doi:10.1080/17470919.2014.954732.

Koole, S.L., & Tschacher, W. (2016). Synchrony in psychotherapy: A review and an integrative framework for the therapeutic alliance. *Frontiers in Psychology, 7*, 862. doi.org/10.3389/fpsyg.2016.00862.

Korte, K.J., & Schmidt, N.B. (2013). Motivational enhancement therapy reduces anxiety sensitivity. *Cognitive Therapy and Research, 37*, 1140–1150.

Laing, R. (1967). *The politics of experience*. New York, NY: Ballantine.

Lambert, M.J., & Barley, D.E. (2001). Research summary on the therapeutic relationship and psychotherapy outcome. *Psychotherapy: Theory, Research, Practice, Training, 38*, 357–361.

Lamm, C., Decety, J., & Singer, T. (2011). Meta-analytic evidence for common and distinct neural networks associated with directly experienced pain and empathy for pain. *NeuroImage, 54*, 2492–2502.

Lenz, A.S., Rosenbaum, L., & Sheperis, D. (2016). Meta-analysis of randomized controlled trials of motivational enhancement therapy for reducing substance use. *Journal of Addictions & Offender Counseling, 37*, 66–86. doi:10.1002/jaoc.12017.

Lerner, H. (1992). The limits of phenomenology: A feminist critique of the humanistic personality theories. In L. Brown & M. Ballou (Eds.), *Theories of personality and psychopathology* (pp. 8–19). New York, NY: Guilford.

Lundahl, B.W., Kunz, C., Brownell, C., Tollefson, D., & Burke, B.L. (2010). A meta-analysis of motivational interviewing: Twenty-five years of empirical studies. *Research on Social Work Practice, 20*, 137–160. doi:10.1177/1049731509347850.

Marci, C.D., Ham, J., Moran, E., & Orr, S.P. (2007). Physiologic correlates of perceived therapist empathy and social-emotional process during psychotherapy. *Journal of Nervous and Mental Disease, 195*, 103–111. doi:10.1097/01.nmd.0000253731.71025.fc.

May, R. (1958). The origins and significance of the existential movement in psychology. In R. May, E.A. Angel, & H. Ellenberger (Eds.), *Existence* (pp. 3–36). New York, NY: Basic Books.

May, R. (Ed.). (1961). *Existential psychology*. New York, NY: Random House.

May, R. (1969). *Love and will*. New York, NY: W.W. Norton.

Miller, W.R. (1983). Motivational interviewing with problem drinkers. *Behavioural Psychotherapy, 11*, 147–172.

Miller, W.R., & Rollnick, S. (1991/2013). *Motivational interviewing: Preparing people to change addictive behavior*. New York, NY: Guilford Press.

Motivational Interviewing Network of Trainers. (2014). *Motivational interviewing: Resources for trainers*. Retrieved from http://www.motivationalinterviewing.org/sites/default/files/tnt_manual_2014_d10_20150205.pdf.

National Registry of Evidence-based Programs and Practice. (2017). Motivational enhancement. Retrieved from https://nrepp.samhsa.gov/AdvancedSearch.aspx.

Norcross, J.C., & Wampold, B.E. (2011a). Evidence-based therapy relationships: Research conclusions and clinical practices. *Psychotherapy, 48*, Mar., 98–102. doi.org/10.1037/a0022161.

Norcross, J.C., & Wampold, B.E. (2011b). What works for whom: Tailoring psychotherapy to the person. *Journal of Clinical Psychology, 67*, 127–132. doi:10.1002/jclp.20764.

Orlinsky, D.E., & Howard, K.I. (1986). Process and outcome in psychotherapy. In S.L. Garfield & A.E. Gergin (eds.), *Handbook of psychotherapy and behavior change* (3rd ed., pp. 311–381). New York, NY: Wiley.

Rigney, M. (1981, April). A critique of Maslow's self-actualization theory: The "highest good" for the aboriginal is relationship (Videotape). Adelaide, Australia: Aboriginal Open College, Adelaide, Australia.

Rogers, C. (1957). The necessary and sufficient conditions of therapeutic personality change. *Journal of Consulting Psychology, 21*, 95–103. doi:10.1037/h0045357.

Rogers, C. (1961). *On becoming a person*. Boston, MA: Houghton-Mifflin.

Rogers, C. (1969). *Freedom to learn*. Columbus, OH: Merrill.

Rogers, C. (1970). *On encounter groups*. New York, NY: HarperCollins.

Rogers, C. (1972). *Becoming partners*. New York, NY: Delta.

Rogers, C. (1977). *On personal power*. New York, NY: Delacourt.

Rogers, C., & Wallen, J. (1946). *Counseling with returned servicemen*. New York, NY: McGraw-Hill.

Rollnick, S., Butler, C.C., Kinnersley, P., Gregory, J., & Mash, B. (2010). Motivational interviewing, BMJ, 340:c1900. Retrieved from http://www.bmj.com.ezaccess.libraries.psu.edu/content/340/bmj.c1900.

Rollnick, S., Miller, W.R., & Butler, C.C. (2007). *Motivational interviewing in health care: Helping patients change behavior (applications of motivational interviewing)*. New York, NY: Guilford Press.

Sartre, J. (1946). *No exit*. New York, NY: Knopf.

Sartre, J. (1956). *Being and nothingness*. London, UK: Methuen.

Spunt, R. (2013). Mirroring, mentalizing, and the social neuroscience of listening. *International Journal of Listening, 27*, 61–72. doi:10.1080/10904018.2012.756331.

Strupp, H. (1977). A reformulation of the dynamics of the therapist's contribution. In A. Gurman & A. Razin (Eds.), *Effective psychotherapy* (pp. 1–22). Elmsford, NY: Pergamon Press.

Strupp, H. (1989). Psychotherapy: Can the practitioner learn from the researcher? *American Psychologist, 44*, 717–724.

Strupp, H., & Hadley, S. (1976). Contemporary view on negative effects in psychotherapy. *Archives of General Psychiatry, 33*, 1291–1302.

Sue, D.W., & Sue, D. (2016). *Counseling the culturally diverse: Theory and practice* (7th ed.). Hoboken, NJ: Wiley.

Tillich, P. (1961). Existentialism and psychotherapy. *Review of Existential Psychology and Psychiatry, 1*, 8–16.

Wallerstein, R. (1989). The psychotherapy research project of the Menninger Foundation: An overview. *Journal of Consulting and Clinical Psychology, 57*, 195–205.

Wampold, B.E. (2015). How important are the common factors in psychotherapy? An update. *World Psychiatry, 14*, 270–277.

Yalom, I. (1980). *Existential psychotherapy*. New York, NY: Basic Books.

Yalom, I. (2017). *The gift of therapy: An open letter to a new generation of therapists and their patients.* New York, NY: HarperCollins.

### CHAPTER 11

# The Humanistic-Experiential Tradition

## The Experiential Foundations of Change

# The Experiential Tradition

Experiential counseling and therapy is rooted in the humanistic, existential, and phenomenological traditions. They believe we are sensing organisms that construct our own realities. Focusing on our subjective constructions in the here-and-now of the session provides the key to change and growth.

As a counselor or therapist, you will likely work with individuals who have suffered severe life difficulties and trauma. You may conduct counseling and therapy with survivors of physical, sexual, and emotional child abuse, rape, or extreme racism or discrimination. One of the most difficult situations you may face will be working with individuals who find that they carry the HIV virus or actually have AIDS. Each of these clients has suffered major personal assaults. How can you then make any sense of what has happened?

*Logotherapy* was Viktor Frankl's personal answer to the major life crisis he faced. You may find his courageous answer to the most complex issues of life beneficial not only to your clients, but also to you. When concrete actions fail, and life seems to have no positive meaning, Frankl's logotherapy can be invaluable. Fritz Perls, introduced below, takes a very different direction from Rogers and Frankl and also offers an important humanistic view of the individual. You will find that his techniques are very active and directive. Whereas Rogers would listen, Perls would be active and on the spot in directing the change process.

Frankl provides a balancing force between Rogers and Perls. Rogers might be described as an attending or listening therapist and Perls as an influencing therapist. Frankl appears to use both attending and listening skills according to the varied needs of the client. All three individuals offer much of practical value to the practice of counseling and therapy.

# Viktor Frankl and Logotherapy

Logotherapy holds that the critical issue for humankind is not what happens, but how one views or thinks about what happens. Thus, Frankl stresses the importance of cognitive change. But logotherapy is also concerned with action; it emphasizes changing behavior in the real world. Frankl was a forerunner to the cognitive-behavioral movement (Mahoney & Freeman, 2004; Frankl, 2004a), and his position provides an important bridge between existential-humanistic and cognitive-behavioral theories.

Frankl is a theorist with a humanistic-experiential message of faith and hope. His logotherapy is concerned with the search for meaning in life. Frankl was able to reframe his life situation in the concentration camp and find positive reasons for living in the midst of negatives. He faced the existential dilemma of the meaning of life under the most extreme conditions. Through finding positive meaning in suffering, Frankl has given us all new hope.

The following quotations from Frankl's writings represent the best case study.

# Case Example: Frankl's Search for Meaning

Frankl's positive view of the human condition reflects a lifetime of struggle to find the positives in humankind. In his book *Man's Search for Meaning* (2006), Frankl relates his experiences in German concentration camps during World War II. Although Frankl describes the horrors of the concentration camp, the book is more a testimony to the power of the human spirit and its capability of survival under the most inhuman of conditions.

Note how, in spite of the dehumanizing environment, Frankl finds something meaningful that enables him and others to survive. He believed that even in the most painful and inhumane situation, life has potential meaning (Frankl, 2004, 2006, 2014).

In the narrative below, we have highlighted the positives in the negative situation by using italics. In many cases, Frankl focused his attention away from the immediate situation and toward positive relationships with the world—an action that helped him survive.

> We stumbled on in the darkness, over big stones and through large puddles, along the one road leading from the camp. The accompanying guards kept shouting at us and driving us with the butts of their rifles. Anyone with very sore feet supported himself on his neighbor's arm. Hardly a word was spoken; the icy wind did not encourage talk.
>
> Hiding his mouth behind his upturned collar, the man marching next to me whispered suddenly: "If our wives could see us now! I do hope they are better off in their camps and don't know what is happening to us."
>
> *That brought thoughts of my own wife to mind.* And as we stumbled on for miles, slipping on icy spots, supporting each other time and again, dragging one another up and onward, nothing was said, but we both knew: *each of us was thinking of his wife.*
>
> Occasionally I looked at the sky, where the stars were fading and the pink light of the morning was beginning to spread behind a dark bank of clouds. *But my mind clung to my wife's image, imagining it with an uncanny acuteness, I heard her answering me, saw her smile, her frank and encouraging look. Real or not, her look was then more luminous than the sun which was beginning to rise.*

*A thought transfixed me: for the first time in my life I saw the truth as it is set into song by so many poets, proclaimed as the final wisdom by so many thinkers. The truth—that love is the ultimate and the highest goal to which man can aspire. Then I grasped the meaning of the greatest secret that human poetry and human thought and belief have to impart: The salvation of man is through love and in love. I understood how a man who has nothing left in this world still may know bliss, be it only for a brief moment, in the contemplation of his beloved.* In a position of utter desolation, when man cannot express himself in positive action, when his only achievement may consist in enduring his sufferings in the right way—an honorable way—in such a position man can, through loving contemplation of the image he carries of his beloved, achieve fulfillment. For the first time in my life I was able to understand the meaning of the words, "The angels are lost in perpetual contemplation of an infinite glory."

In front of me a man stumbled and those following him fell on top of him. The guard rushed over and used his whip on them all. Thus my thoughts were interrupted for a few minutes. *But soon my soul found its way back from the prisoner's existence to another world, and I resumed talk with my loved one: I asked her questions and she answered; she questioned me in return, and I answered.* (pp. 58–60)

In the winter and spring of 1945 there was an outbreak of typhus which infected nearly all the prisoners. The mortality was great among the weak, who had to keep on with their hard work as long as they possibly could. The quarters for the sick were most inadequate, there were practically no medicines or attendants. Some of the symptoms of the disease were extremely disagreeable: an irrepressible aversion to even a scrap of food (which was an additional danger to life) and terrible attacks of delirium. The worst case of delirium was suffered by a friend of mine who thought that he was dying and wanted to pray. In his delirium he could not find the words to do so. *To avoid these attacks of delirium, I tried, as did many of the others, to keep awake for most of the night. For hours I composed speeches in my mind. Eventually I began to reconstruct the manuscript which I had lost in the disinfection chamber of Auschwitz, and scribbled the key words in shorthand on tiny scraps of paper.*

(Viktor E. Frankl, *Man's Search for Meaning*, p. 55. Copyright © 2006 by Beacon Press.)

These quotes show how Frankl shifted attention from the immediate horror of the here and now to other issues. Particularly, he thought of his wife and his relationship with her. His was a sane response in an insane situation. At a more basic level, Frankl found meaning outside the horror of the immediate situation, which gave him strength to cope with life's difficult reality.

There are times when issues cannot be solved—the rape has occurred, the HIV infection proven by a medical test, an automobile accident prevents the client from returning to previous employment. In such cases, how we think about what happened and the meaning of our lives—our cognitions—are as important as or more important than any concrete behavioral change we can make.

# Central Theoretical Constructs and Techniques of Logotherapy

The task for the logotherapist is to help the client find meaning and purpose in life— *and then to act on those meanings.* Logotherapists are interested in carefully learning how the client constructs a worldview. Once they have this understanding, they are willing and ready to move actively to promote client change.

# Cognitive Change and Finding Positive Meanings

Many war veterans will raise issues of the meaning of life in therapy, as will an African American or a Hispanic Latina/o youth who have experienced discrimination and feels beaten. Almost all clients of any cultural background will bring issues or concerns relating to meaning. Since the definition of meaning sometimes depends on the religious, ethnic, and cultural background of your client, you need to be prepared to deal with a variety of meaning and belief systems, ranging from Christian and Jewish to Mormon to Muslim. Being a gay male or lesbian, physically challenged, economically disadvantaged, or from a particular ethnic/racial group will also challenge and change the structure of the meaning system.

*Helping Clients Find Meaning in Difficult Life Situations.* The route toward intentionality and meaning is through carefully listening to the client's construction of meaning of the world. Then, if necessary, the logotherapist will intervene directly and actively to facilitate change in the client's construct or meaning system, but in accord with the cultural tradition of the client. Frankl is keenly aware that meaning is constructed not only in the individual, but also from the cultural tradition of the client.

*Cultural Issues Are Important in Meaning Making.* Cultural and family traditions are often keys to meaning change in clients. This change in meaning may be represented in thought or played out in direct action. It is important that you be aware of many differing types of constructed meaning systems among individuals of varying cultural backgrounds.

The listening aspect of Frankl's logotherapy seems close to that of Rogers, and the influencing aspect is almost as powerful and direct as that of Perls. Yet, logotherapy extends existential and humanistic-experiential thinking and practice in its awareness of cultural traditions as part of meaning making.

*Searching for Positive Meanings.* To help clients find personal meaning and to make more sense of their lives, Frankl offers a positive philosophy, as exemplified by his life and by his influential writings. Talking with or listening to Frankl personally is an exercise in life itself—a sermon in motion—and in this sense, Frankl is very similar to Rogers. The person you are in the interview is as important as or more important than your therapeutic skills. *In addition, you must find the person in your client and what is meaningful to that child, adolescent, man, or woman before you.*

Many clients suffer from day-to-day issues of meaning. How does one make sense of a meaningless job, learn to cope with a less-than-satisfactory personal relationship, or relate to difficult parents or in-laws? Frankl provides a basic philosophy that helps us to focus on meaning and may enable us to search with our clients as they find their unique meanings—perhaps differently constructed meanings from ours, but nonetheless workable for them.

# Taking Meaning into Behavioral Action

Frankl (2006, 2014) has framed a theory and a method of helping that have gained increasing prominence (see also Mahoney & Freeman, 2004). The techniques he developed—dereflection, paradoxical intention, and change of attitudes—are popular methods with some research support (Frankl, 2006, 2014; Lukas, 2014, 2015). Frankl's conceptions around change of attitudes and dereflection may be found in varying forms in cognitive-behavior modification, rational emotive therapy, and the structural/systemic family theories. Paradoxical intention is one of the key methods that can be used to produce rapid change, used by Frankl as early as 1929.

Lukas (2014, 2015) is a major logotherapy theorist and practitioner. She has outlined four main logotherapy techniques that therapists can use to facilitate client growth and movement toward meaningful living: modification of attitudes, paradoxical intention, dereflection, and the appealing technique.

# Modification of Attitudes

Clients can hold negative attitudes toward themselves despite overtly positive life situations. For example, an extremely attractive and personable client may see him- or herself quite negatively. Alternatively, clients may have really serious difficulties and be unable to do anything about them. In each case, the logotherapeutic task is to change the way the person thinks about the situation—a goal similar to that of the cognitive approach. Modification of attitudes is most often conducted directly through sharing opinions, arguing (as in Ellis's rational emotive therapy), or offering positive suggestions with the client. At issue is assisting the client to take a new view of the situation.

*Reframing Attitudes.* The positive asset search or positive reframe (Chapter 4) is one technique in logotherapy for modification of attitudes. However, it is of crucial importance to first listen carefully to clients' negative meanings and constructions. Clients need first to tell their stories fully and completely and to feel heard. If you use the techniques of positive reframing or the positive asset search too early, the client may likely turn away from you. An important guideline is: Do not try to modify attitudes or cognitions until the client feels thoroughly and respectfully heard.

The following brief example from one of Allen's videotaped interviews illustrates the specifics of finding positive meanings in negative situations:

*Counselor* (after listening to the client's deepest fears and hearing how he thought himself close to death in quicksand—the client had talked about feelings of guilt about survival—"Why me?"): Is there anything positive? I know it sounds like a totally negative experience. Was there anything you could see that was positive about what happened?
[This short counselor comment catches the essence of the search for positive meanings. It is a simple point, so direct that its importance is sometimes lost in professional jargon and theorizing.]

*Client*: Well, it sure felt good when they saved me. I was scared, I felt guilty, but at least they came and got me.
*Counselor*: So you felt that help was there even though you were afraid.
*Client*: And you know what, one of the guys who helped get me out I thought didn't like me before. But he asked me to work for him the following week. I never thought of that before.

The ultimate existential issue is survival and finding something positive in the simple act of being-in-the-world. Those who have experienced war, child abuse, rape, AIDS or other terminal illness, or other trauma have all survived. Mere survival for some will be sufficient to satisfy existential needs, but the issue will be more complex for others. Resources for understanding the worldview and specific needs of trauma victims can be found in the work of Rauch, Eftekhari, and Ruzek (2012) on veterans; Katz et al. (2015) on female veterans' survival of sexual trauma; Bovin, Wolf, and Resick (2017) on survivors of rape; Gutermann et al. (2016) on child abuse; and Sue and Sue (2016) on racial discrimination.

*Deciding for the Future.* Although what is past is past, one can modify and change the way one thinks about it. Thinking of the past negatively is making a "decision for the past." By questioning the client's past interpretations, the therapist can help the client make a decision for the future. Those who suffer trauma often make decisions for the past—and for very good reason, since it is difficult not to focus on the negatives of trauma. The modification of attitudes, as demonstrated in the foregoing interview, undergirds much more complex survivor issues. Combining an understanding of the specific needs of trauma survivors with the basic approaches of Frankl or Lukas will give you a good foundation for helping your clients live and cope with the effects of trauma.

> Frankl (1979) reminds us that some people must live with impossible situations and impossible memories:

> This was the lesson I had to learn in three years spent in Auschwitz and Dachau: those most apt to survive the camps were those oriented toward the future, toward a meaning to be fulfilled by them in the future ... But meaning and purpose were only a necessary condition of survival, not a sufficient condition. Millions had to die in spite of their vision of meaning and purpose. Their belief could not save their lives, but it did enable them to meet death with heads held high. (p. 37)

Modification of attitudes cannot change the past, but it can help people live with the past and the present more intentionally. The point is to find something positive, something to live for out of and beyond the trauma experience. As a therapist or counselor, you will need a good deal of patience, strength, belief, knowledge, and power to help your clients modify their attitudes toward these impossible traumatic situations.

*Paradoxical Intention*

Frankl was the first therapist to use the concept of paradox. In 1929, Frankl had a phobic client who was suffering from severe agoraphobia. Analysis and other methods were not working. Improvising, Frankl suggested that instead of being afraid of fainting on the street, the patient should deliberately try to collapse. Frankl (2004) unequivocally defines his paradoxical intention technique as "encouraging the patient to do, or wish to happen, the very things (she or) he fears—albeit with tongue in cheek." The next week, the patient was cured. Frankl did not recall what he had advised, so the patient told him, "I just followed your advice, Doctor. I tried hard to faint but the more I tried, the less I could, and consequently—the fear of fainting disappeared!" Thus, the technique was born.

Paradoxical intention has become an important therapeutic skill. Shoham-Salomon and Rosenthal's (1987) meta-analysis of twelve studies revealed the technique is as effective as other interventions for similar disorders. Paradoxical intention for insomnia has strong research for the treatment of insomnia (American Psychological Association, 2017; Morin et al., 2006).

However, Frankl (2004) warns of confusing paradoxical intention with so-called symptom prescription. In symptom prescription, the patient is told to exaggerate the symptom, say, a fear. In paradoxical intention, however, the patient is encouraged to wish to happen what he or she fears to happen. In other words, the fear itself is not dealt with, but rather the object of fear.

# Dereflection

Dereflection, according to Lukas (2015), uses our ability to "forget ourselves" and brings about a therapeutic reordering of attention—turning it from the issue of concern toward other more positive contents of our thinking. Many of us "hyper-reflect" on our issues and our negative feelings and experiences. The objective of dereflection is systematically to change the focus of our attention. Put in its most simple and direct terms, the task of the therapist is to encourage the client to think about something else other than the concerning issue.

*Refocusing Attention.* Techniques of dereflection may be as simple as encouraging a person who has lost a limb to start thinking about a new career, helping a cancer patient focus on helping others rather than on self, or encouraging a retired person to find an interesting hobby. It is true that the facts of the situation cannot be changed and that it is difficult to reframe issues of illness, age, and loneliness as having positive components. However, it is possible to find something else on which to focus one's attention.

*Changing the "Meaning Core" of One's Life.* Instead of being depressed about the loss of a limb, the handicapped person, through refocusing of attention, can work toward a new goal; the cancer patient can think about others; and the aging individual may make new friends in the process of enjoying a new hobby. The concept of refocusing has many important variations that are clearly described by Frankl (2006) in a chapter on dereflection, in which he also devotes special attention to issues of sexual functioning. Lukas (2014, 2015) is another useful source for ideas about this concept.

*Dereflection and Sexual Dysfunction.* Dereflection may be especially useful in therapy for those with sexual dysfunction. For example, impotence can be caused when the man focuses excessive attention on whether or not he will have an erection. He is hyper-reflecting on himself and his fear, which in turn causes more impotence.

The logotherapist would help this client dereflect and possibly focus attention on the wife or on sexual stimuli. When one focuses attention on another, it is difficult to think about oneself; at such a time, natural autonomic functions start working effectively.

A similar approach may be used with a person suffering from insomnia. Instead of trying to fall asleep, the individual may decide to use this time to study or for an enjoyable activity. After a relatively short period of time, many clients will naturally get tired and fall asleep. This simple technique is partly born of logic and of common sense. However, it takes considerable creativity and expertise to find what each individual client needs to avoid hyper-reflecting on the negative. Furthermore, changing patterns of attention may require you to use modification of attitudes as well as some form of paradoxical intention.

# The Appealing Technique

The appealing technique Lukas (2014) suggests may be effective for clients experiencing drug or alcohol detoxification or for those clients you cannot reach via other methods. The appealing technique is reminiscent of the concepts used by Alcoholics Anonymous (AA) and some drug therapy groups. In this approach, one simply appeals to the client to do better and to change. The counselor takes the position that the client's situation is not hopeless and directly attempts to bring the client to a similar awareness. For example, the drug-abusing client may be asked to state out loud, "I am not helpless. I can control and direct my fate."

In some situations, with an understanding and supportive counselor or therapist, the appealing technique can work. It is clearly different from the "sophisticated" techniques of psychoanalysis or behavior therapy. Some helpers find themselves embarrassed by this approach. Some feel it does not have sufficient theoretical implications. However, if you as a helper believe, you will find that some clients will respond to this exhortative approach, which appeals to the human spirit. Witness the effectiveness of AA and some drug treatment programs that use similar techniques to the appealing process.

*Maintaining Flexibility of Approach.* Logotherapy in the application of technique is an intentional approach to change. There are theoretical and practical reasons for trying to help a client change in a certain direction, but if the first technique does not work, logotherapy does not hesitate to "mix and match" and change the approach to meet the unique human needs of the client.

Practice Exercise 11.1 offers a practice exercise in some dimensions of logotherapy that you may find beneficial in your own work in counseling and psychotherapy.

---

**PRACTICE EXERCISE 11.1. An Exercise in Logotherapy**

Viktor Frankl and his colleague, Elisabeth Lukas, give almost as much attention to hearing and understanding the worldview of the client as does Carl Rogers and person-centered therapy. Thus, you can easily adapt Practice Exercise 10.1, an exercise in person-centered therapy, to logotherapy.

Particularly good topics for this exercise include procrastination, a difficulty with a colleague or housemate, boredom, or concern over illness or the

*(Continued)*

**PRACTICE EXERCISE 11.1. An Exercise in Logotherapy *(Continued)***

loss of someone important. Indicate to your real or role-playing client that you are going to be talking about what the issue or concern means to her or him and that solving the issue will be secondary.

*Stages 1, 2, and 3. Empathic Relationship, Story and Strengths, Goals.*

Use the first three stages of the interview here. Basically, use listening skills and the basic listening sequence to draw out the issue. However, add one central dimension: Ask yourself and your client, "What does this mean to you?" "What does this say about your deeper values?" "Why is this important?" Ask these meaning-oriented questions after you have heard the issue defined clearly. And as you reach the third stage of the interview and the goal is established, ask what the goal means to the client and why the client values that goal. In the process of asking questions about meaning, you will find that a new depth is added to the interview and that clients frequently start talking about their lives, whereas before they were talking about concerns.

In this process, you will want to add the skill of reflection of meaning. A reflection of meaning is similar to the paraphrase, but focuses more on deeper issues underlying the surface structure sentence.

*Stage 4. Restory.*

Generate alternative solutions. Once having heard the client and the client's meaning, you have two central alternatives:

You may summarize the issue and its meaning to the client and contrast it with a summary of the ideal goal and its meaning. Through the summary, you will have pointed out possible discrepancies and mixed messages in the client's meaning system. Then, through listening skills and reflection of meaning, you can encourage further self-exploration. The goal here is to discover the underlying, more deeply felt meanings guiding the client's action.

If the client wishes to act on meaning, select one of the four major techniques of logotherapeutic action (change of attitudes, paradoxical intention, dereflection, or the appealing technique). If the first technique does not work, try another. Logotherapy does not hesitate to try several approaches in an attempt to meet the unique needs of your client.

*(Continued)*

---

**PRACTICE EXERCISE 11.1. An Exercise in Logotherapy *(Continued)***

Out of this portion of the interview, your goal is to facilitate client examination of meaning and through the influencing approach to help your client change and act on her or his meanings system.

*Stage 5. Action.*

As with other existential-humanistic and humanistic-experiential orientations, logotherapy does not give extensive attention to generalization and maintenance of behavioral change. You may ask your client to think about the interview over the next few days and talk with you personally or by phone. If it seems relevant, ask your client to try one thing differently during the time period before you have the follow-up talk.

# Multicultural Implications of Logotherapy

Logotherapy grew out of cultural oppression—the German treatment of Jews during the Holocaust. Frankl's powerful humanistic-experiential approach appeals to the human spirit and thus is particularly adaptable to multicultural counseling and therapy. Many culturally diverse groups may find Frankl's philosophy and specific methods particularly applicable because they represent a response to personal and cultural oppression.

The listening style of Rogers is particularly compatible with Frankl's ideas, and it is easy to integrate the views of humankind put forth by Rogers and Frankl. Each was an admirer of the other's work. Such mutual respect is rare in the sometimes highly competitive world of psychological theory and practice.

*Adapting Logotherapy to Multicultural Practice.* Logotherapy leaves considerable room for you to generate your own culturally relevant integration of theory and practice. Frankl would endorse drawing from traditional and meaningful helping techniques from each culture. Perhaps more than any other single theory of helping, logotherapy is represented throughout the world with commitment and passion from its adherents. Logotherapy appears to be highly adaptable to multicultural and to gender differences. It is interesting that Frankl, a male theoretician, is represented internationally by a woman, Elisabeth Lukas.

*Spirituality and Psychotherapy as Reconciliation.* The title of an early paper by Lukas (1989) is "From Self-Actualization to Global Responsibility." In this paper, she talks about "education toward responsibility" and maintains that individual self-examination is a limited way to view therapy and counseling:

> We must be concerned about a *future worthy of human beings*. …
> This concern deserves the trouble to look up from our navels and
> focus our feelings on something beyond our Ego—feelings which in
> turn could release energies for the spiritual renaissance of our gener-
> ation. (p. 5.) (Emphasis added)

Lukas argues for three sensitivities: the feeling for the sacred, the feeling for the necessary, and the feeling for otherliness. The sacred is spiritual being—our relationship with transcendence and Nature. The necessary represents our ability to deal with challenging situations—for example, trauma, oppressive situations, or physical disfigurement. Life, as Frankl discovered in the Nazi concentration camp, is not all positive. We must do all we can to cope with the impossible.

The feeling for otherliness speaks to our relations with friends, family, and strangers. "The Otherliness of the other person is not something just to be tolerated; it is, instead, something to behold, something that in fact enriches the beholder" (p. 15). Lukas stresses that we must learn to accept and appreciate the Other—"The I and the very different. You can be integrated in a common We." Lukas describes logotherapy as an *agent of reconciliation*. Logotherapy seeks to reconcile us to God and Nature, to the most difficult of challenges we face, and to each other.

# Fritz Perls and Gestalt Therapy

Frederick (Fritz) Perls devised Gestalt theory to fill the theoretical gaps of psychoanalysis, and he came to be regarded as a "guru" of existentialism and experiencing in the 1960s. "Doing your own thing" captures the essence of Perls and his approach.

Perls deeply believed that individuals who became aware of themselves and their experience in the immediacy of the here and now could become more authentic and purposeful human beings. Many of his techniques were directed to helping individual clients and groups become aware of who they were and what they really wanted.

Perls saw human nature as holistic, consisting of many varied parts that make a unique individual. We start life more or less "together," but as we grow and develop, we encounter experiences, feelings, and fears in life that cause us to lose parts of ourselves. These "splits" from the whole, or the Gestalt, must be reintegrated if we are to live intentional, self-actualized lives. Thus, Gestalt therapy is centrally concerned with integrating or reintegrating our split-off parts into a whole person.

The Gestalt worldview is that people can be responsible for their actions in the world and, further, that the world is so complex that very little can be understood at any given moment. Thus, Gestalt therapy tends to focus extensively on the present-tense, immediate, here-and-now experience of the client.

## Case Example: Gestalt Dreamwork

The following excerpt is typical of the work of Perls (1969a). In this case, he was working with a client's dream. In Gestalt dreamwork, each part of the dream is believed to represent a part of the dreamer. The task of the Gestalt therapist is to find how the parts relate together as a unity. Note particularly the consistent present-tense immediacy in the session and the willingness to direct client action. It is astounding that these techniques, now almost fifty years old, still catch our interest and astonish us with their power.

1.  *Meg*: In my dream, I'm sitting on a platform, and there's somebody else with me, a man, and maybe another person, and—ah—a couple of rattlesnakes. And one's up on the platform, now, all coiled up, and I'm frightened. And his head's up, but he doesn't seem like he's gonna strike me. He's just sitting there and I'm frightened, and this other person says to me—uh—just, just don't disturb the snake and he won't bother you. And the other snake, the other snake's down below, and there's a dog down there.

2.  *Fritz*: What is there? [Open question]

3.  *Meg*: A dog, and the other snake.

4.  *Fritz*: So, up here is one rattlesnake and down below is another rattlesnake and the dog. [Paraphrase; note how Perls works in the present tense. The emphasis is on immediate sensorimotor and concrete experience rather than formal operational analysis.]

5.  *Meg*: And the dog is sort of sniffing at the rattlesnake. He's—ah—getting very close to the rattlesnake, sort of playing with it, and I wanna stop—stop him from doing that.

6.  *Fritz*: Tell him. [Directive]

7.  *Meg*: Dog, stop! / *Fritz*: Louder. / *Meg*: Stop! / *Fritz*: Louder. / *Meg* (shouts): STOP! / *Fritz*: Louder. / *Meg*: (screams) STOP! [This example is particularly representative of Gestalt repetition exercises. Repeating words again and again often leads to deeper, more emotional experience.]

8.  *Fritz*: Does the dog stop? [Closed question]

9.  *Meg*: He's looking at me. Now he's gone back to the snake. Now—now, the snake's sort of coiling up around the dog, and the dog's lying down, and—and the snake's coiling around the dog, and the dog looks very happy.

10. *Fritz*: Ah! Now have an encounter between the dog and the rattlesnake. [Directive]

11. *Meg*: You want me to play them?

12. *Fritz*: Both. Sure. This is your dream. Every part is a part of yourself. [Directive, interpretation]

13. *Meg*: I'm the dog. (hesitantly) Huh. Hello, rattlesnake. It sort of feels good with you wrapped around me.

14. *Fritz*: Look at the audience. Say this to somebody in the audience. [Directive]

15. *Meg* (laughs gently): Hello, snake. It feels good to have you wrapped around me.

16. *Fritz*: Close your eyes. Enter your body. What do you experience physically? [Directive. This type of sensorimotor body technique is particularly emblematic of Perls and Gestalt therapy. Emotions are to be experienced immediately rather than reflected on abstractly. As such, Gestalt exercises should be used with care with children and many less verbal clients.]

17. *Meg*: I'm trembling. Tensing.

18. *Fritz*: Let this develop. Allow yourself to tremble and get your feelings (whole body begins to move a little). Yah. Let it happen. Can you dance it? Get up and dance it. Let your eyes open, just so that you stay in touch with your body, with what you want to express physically … Yah … (she walks, trembling and jerkily, almost staggering). Now dance rattlesnake … (she moves slowly and sinuously graceful) … How does it feel to be a rattlesnake now? [Directive, open question. The building and magnification of sensorimotor experience are considered basic to Gestalt work.]

19. *Meg*: It's—sort of—slowly—quite—quite aware, of anything getting too close.

20. *Fritz*: Hm? (Encourager)

21. *Meg*: Quite aware of not letting anything get too close, ready to strike.

22. Fritz: Say this to us. "If you come too close, I____" [Directive]

23. *Meg*: If you come too close, I'll strike back!

24. *Fritz*: I don't hear you. I don't believe you, yet. [Feedback]

25. *Meg*: If you come too close, I will strike back!

26. *Fritz*: Say this to each one, here. [Directive]

27. *Meg*: If you come too close, I will strike back!

28. *Fritz*: Say this with your whole body. [Directive]

29. *Meg*: If you come too close, I will strike back!

30. *Fritz*: How are your legs? I experience you as being somewhat wobbly. [Open question, feedback. Perls was often concerned about clients' bodies being physically grounded on the earth.]

31. *Meg*: Yeah.

32. *Fritz*: That you don't really take a stand. [Interpretation]

33.  Meg: Yes, I feel I'm ... kind of, in between being very strong and—if I let go, they're going to turn to rubber.

34.  *Fritz*: Okay, let them turn to rubber (her knees bend and wobble). Again. ... Now try out how strong they are. Try out—hit the floor. Do anything (she stamps several times with one foot). Yah, now the other (stamps other foot). Now let them turn to rubber again (she lets knees bend again). More difficult now, isn't it? [Directive, closed question]

35.  *Meg*: Yeah.

36.  *Fritz*: Now say again the sentence, "If you come too close _____" ... (she makes an effort) ... (laughter) ... [Directive]

37.  *Meg*: If—if you ...

38.  *Fritz*: Okeh, change. Say "Come close." (laughter) [Directive]

39.  *Meg*: Come close.

40.  *Fritz*: How do you feel now? [Open question]

41.  *Meg*: Warm.

42.  *Fritz*: You feel somewhat more real? [Interpretation]

43.  *Meg*: Yeah.

44.  *Fritz*: Okeh. ... So what we did is we took away some of the fear of being in touch. So, from now on, she'll be a bit more in touch. (pp. 162–164) [Interpretation and the beginning of formal reflection on the experience.]

It is useful to compare Perls and Rogers on their use of microskills. In Rogerian counseling, attending and listening skills are primary, whereas Perls predominantly uses the influencing skills of directives, feedback, and interpretation. While Rogers emphasizes empathy and warmth and positive regard, Perls is somewhat personally distant and remote during the session. His respect for others shows only when they become truly themselves. Although both Rogers and Perls sought genuine encounters with others, Rogers tended to wait patiently for them, whereas Perls demanded that authentic relationships develop quickly and strongly.

# Central Theoretical Constructs and Techniques

Gestalt can be described as centrally concerned with the totality of the individual's being-in-the-world. The complexity and possibility of the world can be dealt with, according to humanistic-experiential thought, in a wide variety of ways. Perls chooses to emphasize here-and-now present-tense experiencing as a way to integrate people in relation to themselves, others, and the world. There is thus a corresponding decrease in emphasis on past or future.

Perls (1969a) writes: "Whenever you leave the sure basis of the now and become preoccupied with the future, you experience anxiety" (p. 30). Perls suggests that the mode of being-in-the-world is to center on oneself and get in touch with one's own existential experience; this makes for a very "I-centered" individualistic view of therapy.

# The Role of Relationship

The focus of Perls on individuals making decisions alone—"doing their own thing"—is similar to the emphasis of Rogers on self-actualization, but Perls carries the idea considerably further. In terms of actual practice, Perls does not give much attention to the individual-in-relationship. Yet, when his clients truly were able to find themselves, to identify themselves as authentically in real relationship to others, Perls would often embrace them with joy.

Thus, although Perls's system does not focus on relationships, it should be stressed that *real and authentic relationships* were important to him. In the final stages of his life, he established a Gestalt community on Vancouver Island, British Columbia. The idea of the community was to extend Gestalt ideas of the "whole" to group and community interaction. Unfortunately, Perls died before his ideas could be tested. Clearly, in his last works, he was moving toward environmental and interpersonal interaction and action.

Lerman's (1991) critique of Perls is gentler than her commentary on Rogers. She recognizes that Gestalt therapy is more concerned with environmental reality than with person-centered theory. However, she feels that Perls gave insufficient attention to the role of trauma in therapy and that he uncritically accepted a Maslow (1971) type of need hierarchy. In her view, the emphasis on self-actualization misses the importance of self-in-relation.

*Gender and Multicultural Issues.* Enns (1987) gives special attention to Gestalt therapy's implications for women. She suggests that Gestalt exercises can be helpful for women in three ways: (1) helping women become aware of themselves as distinct individuals having their own power (particularly in that "I" statements are used); (2) facilitating the expression of anger through any of a variety of Gestalt exercises; and (3) enabling more choice. Gestalt therapy is highly concerned that individuals make their own choices and, as such, can be very helpful to women who have been culturally discouraged from making their own choices.

These same three choices above, however, may be less beneficial for individuals of various cultural groups. The direct personal affirmations of individual choice suggested by Perls can come into serious conflict with the cultural values of Asian Americans and Native Americans, who may tend to believe that decision making is made in context rather than as a purely individual matter. The word *Gestalt* implies that the individual is a whole in a context of family and community. It seems clear that clients of many cultures can and will respond to Gestalt interventions, if used with cultural sensitivity and an egalitarian, nonhierarchical approach. The culturally sensitive use of Gestalt therapy requires that you be sure that your client is ready and understands why you are using these particular interventions.

# Gestalt Techniques

Perls was a charismatic, dynamic therapist who was trained in classical psychoanalysis but profoundly aware of its limitations. He brought his formal knowledge and a formidable clinical talent to the counseling interview. He and his coworkers have been able to document both Gestalt therapy theory and technique in a rather complete form (see Perls, Hefferline, & Goodman, 1951; Fagan & Shepherd, 1970; Perls, 1969a, 1969b; Roubal, 2016; Stevens, 1971/2007; Yontef & Simkin, 2014). However, the most effective way to understand Gestalt therapy is to experience it.

Although Gestalt theory can be discussed in considerable detail, the primary purpose of this section is to examine some techniques for enhancing awareness of interpersonal experiencing developed by Perls and his coworkers. It can be argued that Perls's major contribution is methodological rather than theoretical. Over the years, he developed a wide range of techniques that vitalize existential experiencing.

The following techniques should always be used in a working relationship and with a full sense of ethics. Reading about them will be of no value unless you practice them experientially. These methods are easily integrated into interviews, regardless of theoretical orientation.

1. *Here-and-now experiencing.* Most techniques of Gestalt therapy are centered on helping the client experience the world now rather than in the past or future. What is done is done, and what will be will be. Although past experiences, dreams, or future thoughts may be discussed, the constant emphasis is on relating them to immediate present-tense experience. In the transcript, Perls again and again directs the client to awareness of the here and now.

2. *Directives.* Gestalt therapists constantly tell their clients what to do in the interview, although decisions for their own later action are the clients' own. For example, Meg (number 5) talks in the past tense about her dream. Perls, through the simple directive "Tell him," brings the past to the present. Throughout this session, Perls constantly directs the movement of the client. Feedback (number 24), questions relating to feelings (number 30), and interpretations (number 32) give additional strength to the directives.

3. *Language changes.* Gestalt clients are encouraged to change questions to statements in the belief that most questions are simply hidden statements about oneself. For example, "Do you like me?" may actually be the statement "I am

not sure that you like me." The therapist suggests that the client change questions to "I" statements. Clients are also often asked or told to change vague statements about some subject to "I" statements, thus increasing the personal identification and concreteness in the interview.

The client is frequently directed to talk in the present tense ("Be in the here and now"), as this also adds power and focus to the issue or concern. Gestalt therapists point out that the counselor can see and understand only what is before him or her. Talking about issues is considered less effective than experiencing them directly. Although questions are generally discouraged, "how" and "what" questions are considered more acceptable than "why" questions, which often lead to intellectualization.

4. *The empty-chair technique.* Perhaps the best-known and most powerful of the many Gestalt techniques, the empty-chair technique, is also one of the easiest to use in counseling practice. When a client expresses a conflict with another person, the client is directed to imagine that the other person is sitting in an empty chair and then to talk to that person. After the client has said a few words, the counselor directs the client to change chairs and answer as if he or she were the other person. The counselor directs a dialogue between the client and the imaginary other person by constantly suggesting chair changes at critical points. Through this exercise, the client learns to experience and understand feelings more fully. The client also often learns that he or she was projecting many thoughts onto the other person.

5. *Talking to parts of oneself.* A variation of the empty-chair technique is to point out client splits, immobility, or impasses to the client. The two sides of an issue, or conflicting parts within the person, are drawn out. Sometimes the therapist seeks details for clarity; at other times, the counselor moves immediately to the exercise. The two sides of the person then engage in a dialogue, using the empty-chair technique. By discussing the conflicted issues reflected by the split, the person often spontaneously generates a new solution or answer.

A variation on the foregoing often occurs when the counselor notes incongruities or mixed messages in client body language or between client body language and words. In such cases, the Gestalt therapist may have the tense right hand talk to the loose left hand or the jiggling right leg talk to the upset stomach. Through such imaginative games of body dialogue, quick and important breakthroughs in understanding often occur.

6. *Top dog and underdog.* Gestalt therapists constantly search for the authoritarian and demanding "top dog," which is full of "shoulds" and "oughts." In contrast, the "underdog" is more passive, apologetic, and guilt ridden. When these two dimensions are observed, the empty-chair technique or a dialogue often helps the client to understand and experience them more fully.

7. *Staying with the feeling.* When a key emotion is noted in the interview, particularly through a nonverbal movement, the Gestalt therapist will often immediately give attention to the feeling and its meaning. Perls's suggestion (number 18) to Meg to let her trembling develop exemplifies the use of this technique. This is a simple technique, but it can be invaluable whether you are a Rogerian, psychodynamic, or a feminist counselor.

8. *Dreamwork.* In dreamwork, the Gestalt approach most closely resembles its psychoanalytic foundation. Yet, unlike psychoanalysis, Gestalt does not use dreams to understand past conflicts, but rather as metaphors to understand present-day, here-and-now living. The dreamwork with Meg, above, provides a good illustration. The parts of a dream are considered as aspects of the client. Any piece (person, object, scene, or thing) of a dream is a projection of the client's experiential work. Through acting out the dream, the client can integrate the split pieces into a whole person.

Each of these techniques can be used in multicultural settings, providing there is a base of sufficient understanding and trust between client and therapist. For example, Gestalt dreamwork can be expanded to include the multicultural family and dream concepts mentioned in the psychodynamic chapter. When combined with Gestalt interventions, such dreamwork can be very powerful and emotional. For other examples, the empty-chair technique can be used to increase a woman's or gay male's understanding of how another person may have maltreated them. The top dog/underdog technique is made to order for discussion of oppression.

Through these and other powerful techniques, Perls made an impressive impact on the practice of counseling and psychotherapy. More than any other therapist, he has been able to show that clients can rapidly be moved to deep understanding of themselves and their conditions. Although his theoretical foundations have been criticized and there is little empirical evidence validating his approach, there is no question that the work and life of Perls are an important expression of the humanistic-experiential tradition.

Current evidence supporting the counseling therapies presented in this chapter are found in Table 11.1.

**Table 11.1. Research Box: Evidence Base of Logotherapy and Gestalt Therapy**

The effectiveness of humanistic, existential, and experiential therapies has been supported by research. Elliott's (2002) meta-analysis of 86 studies on the effectiveness of humanistic therapies showed significant changes and stable posttreatment gains on clients treated with this modality. Randomized clinical trials showed significant gains over untreated clients. These gains were similar to the amounts of change observed in other therapies (e.g., cognitive-behavioral therapy).

*(Continued)*

**Table 11.1. Research Box: Evidence Base of Logotherapy and Gestalt Therapy *(Continued)***

Hollon and Ponniah (2010) reviewed 125 studies of counseling therapies for mood disorders in adults. They found that behavior therapy (BT), cognitive-behavior therapy (CBT), and interpersonal psychotherapy (IPT) are efficacious and specific, and brief dynamic therapy (BDT) and emotion-focused therapy (EFT, commonly associated with Gestalt therapy) are possibly efficacious in the treatment of major depressive disorder (MDD).

Several studies support the effectiveness of logotherapy for the treatment of mental disorders, such as depression, especially in clients with chronic illnesses. Vos, Craig, and Cooper (2015) found clear support for structured interventions like logotherapy. Clients benefited more from therapeutic groups focused on meaning than social support groups, treatment as usual, or waiting list. Clients found greater meaning or purpose in life. Also, clients' level of psychopathology decreased, and their self-efficacy increased. Existential therapy seemed very helpful to address meaning-orientated and existential concerns in clients affected by physical illnesses. The sense of meaningless interferes with the rehabilitation process of individuals who are paralyzed due to a medical illness. Julom and De Guzmán (2013) developed and tested a logotherapy program for the 16 randomly selected, paralyzed patients in a rehabilitation center in the Philippines. All of the patients receiving the logotherapy intervention increased their life meaning, whereas the patients in the control group remained at the same meaninglessness level.

A comparison of the effectiveness of group cognitive-behavioral therapy and logotherapy in reducing depression and increasing life expectancy in clients affected with drug addiction showed both therapies are equally effective in reducing depression (Khaledian, 2016). Robatmili and colleagues (2015) used a randomized controlled trial to investigate the effectiveness of group logotherapy in reducing depression in college students in Iran. The experimental group depression score was significantly lower than the control group after participating in ten sessions of group logotherapy.

Gestalt therapy was evaluated in a three-year research project in the United Kingdom (Stevens, Stringfellow, Wakelin, & Waring, 2011). The results were compared with the CORE (Clinical Outcomes in Routine Evaluation) system, which is the most widely used approach to evaluate counseling and psychotherapy in that country. The results showed that Gestalt therapists are as effective as other therapists working in treatment centers and in primary care settings. Gestalt therapists showed reliable and clinically significant results (56.3%), similar to those of the benchmark studies (53%, 58.3%, and 61.0%).

A review conducted by Hender (2001) identified two randomized controlled trials, one pseudo-randomized controlled study and four comparative studies with control groups that compared Gestalt therapy to another therapy or waitlist. Gestalt therapy increased in some positive outcomes when compared against other therapies like CBT. Wagner-Moore (2004) reports that the two-chair technique is superior to other counseling interventions for specific psychological dilemmas, such as conflict splits, decisional conflict, marital conflict, and unfinished business.

# Perls and Rogers

Like many other orientations to helping, Gestalt therapy has been influenced by the Rogerian tradition. For example, in a recent discussion of the present state of Gestalt theory, Yontef and Simkin (2014) place a greater emphasis on the relationship of client and therapist and argue for more softness, as compared with the "hardball" approach of Perls. Unfortunately, research studies comparing Rogerian and Gestalt methods are virtually nonexistent. However, opinion is that Gestalt therapy facilitates change faster than do Rogerian methods, but that it also has the potential for more destructive impact on the client if the therapist moves too fast. The Gestalt therapist is often seen by the client as a "guru," which means that the therapist has even more power. Strupp and Hadley (1976) and Linden and Schermuly-Haupt (2014) have documented thoroughly the dangers of the charismatic therapist for fragile clients.

It seems wise, particularly for beginning counselors and therapists, to use these powerful techniques with a real sensitivity to the worldview and experience of the client. Negative effects of therapy are possible (Rozental et al., 2016). Be advised to seek specific training and supervision before implementing these techniques.

# Practical Implications of the Humanistic-Experiential Tradition

As a humanistic-experiential theorist, Frankl's work sometimes tends to be verbal, reflective, and formally operational in nature. Perls's direct sensorimotor approach may be inappropriate for clients who are not ready, and if Gestalt exercises are used too soon, they may even be personally and culturally offensive.

As stressed throughout this book, manipulative and insensitive therapists are the greatest danger in the field. Theories may not always be personally and culturally sensitive, but if you are aware and growing, you can almost always adapt theory to meet the needs of the client.

The powerful Gestalt activation exercises described in this chapter have become an important part of the techniques of many effective therapists of varying orientations, from cognitive-behavioral to psychodynamic and even those with a specific multicultural orientation.

Current theory and practice may lead one to conclude that the balanced listening and influencing approach of Frankl may gradually come to center stage as the most prominent humanistic-experiential theory. This approach deals openly and honestly with issues of pain and how to surmount these difficulties through personal action with the support of the therapist or counselor.

# References

American Psychological Association. (2017). Paradoxical intention for insomnia. Society of Clinical Psychology. Retrieved from https://www.div12.org/psychological-treatments/treatments/paradoxical-intention-for-insomnia/.

Bovin, M.J., Wolf, E.J., & Resick, P.A. (2017). Longitudinal associations between posttraumatic stress disorder severity and personality disorder features among female rape survivors. *Frontiers in Psychiatry, 8*, 6. doi:10.3389/fpsyt.2017.00006.

Elliott, R. (2002). The effectiveness of humanistic therapies: A meta-analysis. In D.J. Cain, (Ed.), *Humanistic psychotherapies: Handbook of research and practice* (pp. 57–81). Washington, DC: American Psychological Association. doi:10.1037/10439-002.

Enns, C. (1987). Gestalt therapy and feminist therapy: A proposed integration. *Journal of Counseling and Development, 66,* 93–95.

Fagan, J., & Shepherd, I. (1970). *Gestalt therapy now.* Palo Alto, CA: Science and Behavior Books.

Frankl, V.E. (2004a). Logos, paradox, and the search for meaning. In M.J. Mahoney & A. Freeman (Eds.), *Cognition and psychotherapy* (pp. 83–100). New York, NY: Plenum.

Frankl, V.E. (2004b). *The doctor and the soul.* London, UK: Souvenir Press. (Original work published 1946).

Frankl, V.E. (2006). *Man's search for meaning.* Boston, MA: Beacon. (Original work published 1946).

Frankl, V.E. (2014). *The will to meaning: Foundations and applications of Logotherapy.* New York, NY: Plume.

Gutermann, J., Schreiber, F., Matulis, S., Schwartzkopff, L., Deppe, J., & Steil, R. (2016). Psychological treatments for symptoms of posttraumatic stress disorder in children, adolescents, and young adults: A meta-analysis. *Clinical Child and Family Psychology Review, 19,* 77–93. doi:10.1007/s10567-016-0202-5.

Hender, K. (2001) Is Gestalt therapy more effective than other therapeutic approaches? Centre for Clinical Effectiveness, Monash University, Victoria, Australia. Retrieved from http://www.gestaltbodymind.co.uk/Gestalt%20therapy%20effeectiveness%20comparisons.pdf.

Hollon, S.D., & Ponniah, K. (2010). A review of empirically supported psychological therapies for mood disorders in adults. *Depression and Anxiety, 27,* 891–932. doi:10.1002/da.20741.

Julom, A.M., & De Guzmán, R. (2013). The effectiveness of logotherapy program in alleviating the sense of meaninglessness of paralyzed in-patients. *International Journal of Psychology and Psychological Therapy, 13,* 357–371.

Katz, L.S., Cojucar, G., Hoff, R.A., Lindl, C., Huffman, C., & Drew, T. (2015). Longitudinal outcomes of women veterans enrolled in the Renew sexual trauma treatment program. *Journal of Contemporary Psychotherapy, 45,* 143–150. doi:10.1007/s10879-014-9289-5.

Khaledian, M.M. (2016). On the effectiveness of group cognitive-behavioral therapy and logotherapy in reducing depression and increasing life expectancy in drug addicts. *Research on Addiction, 9,* 63–80.

Lerman, H. (1991). The limits of phenomenology: A feminist critique of the humanistic personality theories. In L. Brown & M. Ballou (Eds.), *Personality and psychopathology* (pp. 8–19). New York, NY: Guilford.

Linden, M., & Schermuly-Haupt, M.L. (2014). Definition, assessment and rate of psychotherapy side effects. *World Psychiatry, 13,* 306–309. http://doi.org/10.1002/wps.20153.

Lukas, E. (1984). *Meaningful living: Logotherapeutic guide to health.* Cambridge, MA: Schenkman.

Lukas, E. (1989, June). *From self-actualization to global responsibility.* Paper presented at the Seventh World Congress of Logotherapy, Kansas City, MO.

Lukas, E. (2014). *Meaning in suffering: Comfort in crisis through logotherapy.* New York, NY: Purpose Research.

Lukas, E. (2015). *The therapist and the soul: From fate to freedom.* New York, NY: Purpose Research.

Mahoney, M., & Freeman, A. (Eds.). (2004). *Cognition and psychotherapy.* New York, NY: Springer.

Maslow, A. (1971). *The farther reaches of human nature.* New York, NY: Viking.

Morin, C., Bootzin, R., Buysse, D., Edinger, J., Espie, C., & Lichstein, K. (2006). Psychological and behavioral treatment of insomnia: Update of the recent evidence (1998–2004). *Sleep, 29,* 1398–1414.

Perls, F. (1969a). *Gestalt therapy verbatim*. Moab, UT: Real People Press.

Perls, F. (1969b). *In and out of the garbage pail*. Moab, UT: Real People Press.

Perls, F., Hefferline, R., & Goodman, P. (1951). *Gestalt therapy: Excitement and growth in human personality*. New York, NY: Dell.

Rauch, S.A.M., Eftekhari, A., & Ruzek, J.I. (2012). Review of exposure therapy: A gold standard for PTSD treatment. *Journal of Rehabilitation Research and Development, 49*, 679–687.

Robatmili, S., Sohrabi, F., Shahrak, M.A., Talepasand, S., Nokani, M., & Hasani, M. (2015). The effect of group logotherapy on meaning in life and depression levels of Iranian students. *International Journal for the Advancement of Counselling, 37*, 54–62. doi:10.1007/s10447-014-9225-0.

Roubal, J. (Ed.) (2016). *Towards a research tradition in gestalt therapy*. Newcastle, UK: Cambridge Scholars.

Rozental, A., Kottorp, A., Boettcher, J., Andersson, G., & Carlbring, P. (2016). Negative effects of psychological treatments: An exploratory factor analysis of the negative effects questionnaire for monitoring and reporting adverse and unwanted events. *PLoS ONE, 11*(6), e0157503. http://doi.org/10.1371/journal.pone.0157503.

Shoham-Salomon, V., & Rosenthal, R. (1987). Paradoxical interventions: A meta-analysis. *Journal of Consulting and Clinical Psychology, 55, 1*, 22–28.

Stevens, C., Stringfellow, J., Wakelin, K., & Waring, J. (2011). The UK gestalt therapy CORE research project: Findings. *British Gestalt Journal, 20*(2), 22–27.

Stevens, J. (1971/2007). *Awareness: Exploring, experimenting, experiencing*. Gouldsboro, ME: Gestalt Journal Press.

Strupp, H., & Hadley, S. (1976). Contemporary view on negative effects in psychotherapy. *Archives of General Psychiatry, 33*, 1291–1302.

Sue, D., & Sue, D. (2016). *Counseling the culturally diverse: Theory and practice* (7th ed.). New York, NY: Wiley.

Vos, J., Craig, M., & Cooper, M. (2015). Existential therapies: A meta-analysis of their effects on psychological outcomes. *Journal of Consulting and Clinical Psychology, 83*, 115–128. doi:10.1037/a0037167.

Wagner-Moore, L.E. (2004). Gestalt therapy: Past, present, theory, and research. *Psychotherapy: Theory, Research, Practice, Training, 41*, 180–189. doi:10.1037/0033-3204.41.2.180.

Yontef, G., & Simkin, J. (2014). Gestalt therapy. In D. Wedding & R. J. Corsini (Eds.), *Current psychotherapies* (10th ed.) (pp. 299–338). Itasca, IL: Peacock.

# PART III

# Systems and Family Counseling and Therapy and Theoretical Integration

**H**umans are born into an intricate set of systems and subsystems. Central to individual development is the family and the cultural context. Although the primary emphasis in this book is on individual counseling and therapy, there is also a consistent emphasis on family and multicultural considerations. An attempt has been made to demonstrate that it is possible to use both family and multicultural theories and methods in the individual interview.

## The Importance of Systems and Family Theory

It is now time to consider system and family counseling and therapy theory as part of the mainstream in individual work. Practicing individual counseling without awareness of the main constructs of systems and family therapy will leave you with a constricted and somewhat limited awareness of the human condition.

Chapter 12 presents the essential concept of systems and describes a biopsychosocial model to understand contextual influences in human behavior. The basics of family theory and a list of current theories follows. Commonly used family therapy techniques are presented afterward. All of the techniques can be adapted and integrated in the counseling of clients and with other theories of this book. As such, they have special multicultural relevance, as the family of origin is where the client's culture manifests most clearly.

Multicultural issues are important in family therapy, and family theorists may have discovered the importance of this area before individually oriented theorists. Examples of multicultural contributions to family therapy theory are featured in the chapter.

Advocacy and social justice are central to our professions. Counselors and therapists are called to promote the well-being of individuals, groups, and their own professions within the systems and organizations they are immersed in. When appropriate, we advocate at individual, group, institutional, and societal levels with the specific goal of promoting equity for all people and groups. Removing barriers and obstacles that prevent access, growth, or development of clients aim to end oppression and injustice, and to create a more just society.

# Integrating Theory and Practice

Chapter 13 invites you to take stock of what you have learned, identify key aspects that could increase your effectiveness as a counselor and therapist, and start generating your own views of counseling and psychotherapy. Carlos happened to talk to a graduate student now practicing counseling and therapy. The student was asked, "Which theoretical orientation in your courses do you find more helpful now that you are really working with clients?"

The graduate responded:

> "Well, at the time I finished the counseling program, I could discuss and write about the various theories fairly easily and directly. I knew how they were similar and how they differed. Now that I work with real clients, I find that I've integrated theory in such a way that I seldom think of it anymore. I'd be hard pressed to know which theory is my favorite, but I do know "what works" with various people I see. Psychodynamic theory helps me conceptualize clients and their developmental history. I never think of Rogers anymore, but somehow I know he is with me. I find that cognitive-behavioral techniques work, and I wish I had learned more of them when I had the chance. But my clients are increasingly culturally different now, and I feel less able to work with people whose background is different from my own. Some workshops I've completed on family therapy concepts have been especially helpful."

As part of this chapter, you will be asked to summarize key theoretical constructs in a brief fashion and generate your own ideas about counseling and psychotherapy. While you do this, be aware that the field is changing and growing. You will be a part of that growth. With your help and participation, the field will continue to evolve and adapt to the needs of its clients for years to come.

### CHAPTER 12

# Systems and Family Counseling and Therapy

## The Holistic Approach to Change

The counseling and psychotherapy theories presented in previous chapters tend to focus on individual treatment. Clients tend to look for individual counseling for their anxiety, depression, and other behavioral disorders. Nevertheless, each person belongs to a variety of systems and subsystems, such as family, work environment, and society that significantly influence their behavior in positive or negative ways.

The focus of systems and family therapy is on the family or system as a whole. Systems, marriage, and family therapists treat the whole system or family to successfully achieve desired changes. These counselors and therapists believe the client is part of a system that functions by maintaining all of its members. Changes in one member of the system trigger actions by the remainder of its members to restore the system to its original balance, a state known as homeostasis. They assert that if change will happen and remain over time, the whole needs to be involved in the treatment.

## SPECIFIC GOALS OF THIS CHAPTER:

1. Define and present the basics of systems.
2. Describe the worldview that undergirds systems therapy and family therapy.
3. Present the central constructs of family therapy, along with a description the family life cycle.
4. Stress the importance of a multicultural perspective when providing counseling and psychotherapy to families.
5. Report the evidence base of family therapy.
6. Demonstrate the theory in action with a case illustration.

> *The whole is more than the sum of its parts.*
>
> —**Aristotle**, *Metaphysics*

# A Word about Systems

A system is a network of mutually dependent parts (components, elements, entities, factors, individuals, pieces, etc.) comprising a unified whole. Systems are larger than the sum of their parts. They are organized and purposeful. They continually influence their interrelated parts. All this occur for the purpose of maintain the system (Bertalanffy, 2015).

A neuron, a software, a person, a family, and an organization, are examples of systems. All systems share the following characteristics: have inputs, outputs, and feedback mechanisms; maintain an internal homeostasis (a stable status) within the changing external environment; display properties that are different from those of the individual elements; and have boundaries (Bertalanffy, 2015). Each system includes subsystems, and these are embedded within larger systems.

A component or part of a system can be almost anything. It can be an organ in a person (the brain is a part of your body), a member in a family, or a group in a society. The interaction between the different parts in the system and between the system and its environment can be beneficial (they promote the growth and progress of the system) or harmful (they stall progress or deteriorate the system).

## REFLECTION EXERCISE

Think about the systems you are part of—your family, your school, your group of friends, your society. How do these systems influence you? Do they facilitate or limit what you do?

You and several other members form your family with its own unique properties. The members function (consciously or unconsciously) synergistically to give the family a life of its own that is greater than the sum of its parts. Well-functioning families encourage full development of all members. In other cases, survival of the family system mean that some family members suffer, while others gain. In extreme cases, families fall apart. Reflect on your own family from a system perspective.

What are some key characteristics of the interpersonal interaction within your family?

How is your family different from other families in your neighborhood?

What do you think might be the interactions of families from different ethnic or cultural backgrounds?

Because the members of families are interconnected, the behavior of each individual is shaped by feedback they receive from their family. A mixture of positive and critical feedback promotes growth and change in the family as a whole.

What kind of feedback did you get from your family? How this feedback helped you become the person you are now?

All families exist in a socio-cultural context that includes school, religious, medical, government, and other systems.

Which of these systems and others impacted your family and your own personal development?

If you think of the power of systems on your own life, you can see why we recommend systems and family thinking be part of your one-on-one interviewing practice.

# The Systems Worldview

The systems worldview is an interdisciplinary theory about every system in nature, in society, and in many scientific domains. It is also a framework that enables us to investigate phenomena from a holistic approach (Capra & Luisi, 2015). Similar to Aristotle, the systems worldview focuses its attention on the whole. The system as a whole determines, in significant ways, how the parts behave (Bertalanffy, 2015). Ecosystems include all aspects of the environment (e.g., microorganisms, humans, geography, climate), and everything within an ecosystem is interconnected. Because everything is interconnected, a change in any component of an ecosystem will create a ripple effect in all other parts of the ecosystem; those effects will in turn affect everything else, including the original change agent. This interconnectivity and interactional causality is the hallmark of the ecological approach (McMahon, Mason, Daluga-Guenther, & Ruiz, 2014).

*Systems worldview in counseling and therapy.* If we want to understand stress, trauma, or any mental disorder, we will do better by considering the relationships between individual clients and their interactions with the other system constituents such as family, friends, community, school, etc. By doing this, we will find that the elements of this system are interconnected toward a shared purpose and those that conflict. Table 12.1 showcases the importance of focusing on systems or families.

---

Table 12.1. **The Client Who Wanted to Stop Drinking**

A client with a serious alcohol abuse was referred to an addictions counselor with a known record of effectiveness. The therapist worked with the client for more than six months, seeing him three times a week, using motivational interviewing, which is an evidence-based practice for the treatment of addictions. Initially, the client began to reduce his alcohol consumption and started to improve his demeanor. He was also successful in coping with cravings. The counselor focused each session on the cognitive biases and negative self-talk of the client. Daily thought records were used to monitor internal dialogue between sessions, and cognitive restructuring served to change negative internal dialogues within each session. Relevant homework helped advance treatment goals. Progress was good until mid-semester.

By the end of the third month, the client began to drink more heavily again. He stopped completing daily records and homework by the fifth month. He also requested seeing the counselor only once a week, arguing work-related demands. At the end of the sixth month, the client was back to his earlier heavy drinking levels.

*(Continued)*

**Table 12.1. The Client Who Wanted to Stop Drinking *(Continued)***

The concerned counselor began to suspect that there was more going on in the client's life than he was disclosing in counseling and asked for any important changes occurring since he began treatment. Initially, the client could not recall anything of importance but soon thereafter reported sharing with his family and coworkers that he was attending counseling and gaining great control over his drinking.

It became clear that the client faced high amounts of pressure from family and coworkers to resume his drinking. He was the soul of the party, the guy who got everybody entertained, and the lead of the group. Quitting alcohol was perceived as a threat. Relatives and coworkers wanted him to drink heavily again as a way to ensure he kept his leading role.

Shifting from individual counseling to family and systems counseling helped achieve the client's goals. The counselor involved the family and coworkers in treatment and helped the client learn additional social skills to maintain his leading role without the use of alcohol.

The systemic view asserts that we cannot fully understand a phenomenon simply by studying or observing the specific components or parts. We need to apply a holistic vision to uncover its function and purpose (Bertalanffy, 2015). The example presented in Table 12.1 illustrates this idea. We can begin from the analysis of the specific client but to fully understand their issues, we need to use a systemic perspective.

# The Bioecological Model

The bioecological model represents a contemporary application of systems theory to the understanding of clients' issues (Bronfenbrenner, 1981). Urie Bronfenbrenner emphasizes the importance of understanding that human behavior is influenced by six systems that includes the individual and his or her surrounding environment: the microsystem, the mesosystem, the exosystem, the macrosystem, and the chronosystem. Table 12.2 briefly describes these systems. Figure 12.1 illustrates the application of the bioecological model to the client who wanted to stop drinking.

**Table 12.2. Urie Bronfenbrenner's Bioecological Model**

- *The individual:* The individual and his or her personal characteristics actively influence social interactions and their individual development (e.g., age, sex, physical or mental health).

- *Microsystem:* Refers to all the settings that influence a person's interactions. These are the settings that most immediately and directly impact the person's development (e.g., family, peers, school, religious institutions).

- *Mesosystem:* Refers to those situations or events where two microsystems come together in some respect (e.g., relationship between the person and his or her friend's family; interactions between the family and teachers).

*(Continued)*

**Table 12.2. Urie Bronfenbrenner's Bioecological Model** *(Continued)*

- *Exosystem:* Refers to environmental elements that have a profound but indirect influence on a person's development (e.g., family social networks, neighborhood context, local politics).

- *Macrosystem:* Refers to the broad culture in which individuals live. Cultural contexts include socioeconomic status, poverty, ethnicity, developing and industrialized countries.

- *Chronosystem:* Refers to the environmental events and transitions that occur throughout an individual's life, as well as his or her sociohistorical circumstances (e.g., life transition, such as moving to another state or divorce; historical events, such as a presidential election; or engagement in war conflict).

**Figure 12.1. A Representation of the Bioecological Model of Human Development to the Client Who Wanted to Stop Drinking**

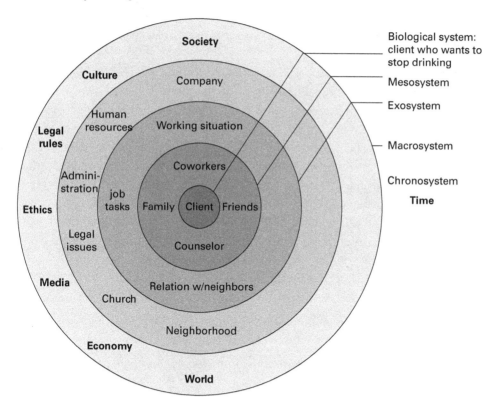

The work of Lau and Ng (2014) and McMahon and colleagues (2014) represent two practical examples of the application of ecological theory to counselors' work. The first uses a bioecological model to conceptualize and improve counselor-in-training practices with a systemic focus. The latter provides an intentional model of ecological school counseling based on the bioecological model.

# Ecological Counseling

Nobody lives in a vacuum. We all are influenced by the systems in which we live. *Ecological counseling* integrates personal and environmental factors through focusing on their interaction to explain clients' issues. True to its systemic roots, the model asserts that the person is inextricably situated within specific and interdependent ecological systems. They define counseling as "contextualized help-giving that is dependent on the meaning clients derive from their environmental interactions" (Conyne & Cook, 2004, p. 6).

Ecological counselors expand individual counseling and therapy by adopting a worldview that includes psychosocial assessments and interventions applicable across ecological systems, including peer groups, families, institutions, and communities. They cover the complexities of the person-environment relationships in order to understand the client's challenges or concerns and develop intervention strategies. Their strategies range from increasing positive fit between their clients and their environment, remove barriers to clients' success, and engage in social change efforts to create a more just environment.

Each individual carries particular capacities, preferences, and history through the varying environmental settings in which he or she grows and lives (Cook, 2012). The interactions between the person and environment result in the construction of the individual ecological niches. These niches are what we experience as our world. Ecological counselors and therapists aim to understand the client's ecological niches to assist them to live a satisfying life. Successful counseling is accomplished by helping clients improve their interactional quality through interventions directed at both the personal and environmental systems (Cook & Coaston, 2012).

Cook and Coaston (2012) offer a set of specific questions to begin to develop an ecological analysis. The following is just a small sample to illustrate their approach:

> How is the issue or concern situated within the client's ecology (who, what, when, where)? And what does it mean to the client?
>
> Where does the client live out his or her life physically and interpersonally (where is the client's ecological niche)?
>
> What are the client's important interactions with people? Groups? Community or neighborhood? Larger systems? How do these interactions influence the client's life? (p. 136)

Questions like these would help the counselor understand the client's daily experiences and gain a larger perspective of each client within their own circumstances. Empowered with this holistic representation, counselors can offer interventions, such as learning new skills, use available resources, or encourage advocacy skills learning to assist clients engage in effective ways to accomplish their desired changes.

Also important is to conceptualize the client and the therapy from a systemic view. Table 12.3 introduces Breunlin, Pinsof, and Russell's (2011) systemic way to think about client and therapy.

---

Table 12.3. **The Client System and the Therapy System**

We can think of counseling and therapy as the encounter of two systems (Breunlin, Pinsof, and Russell (2011). The client system comprises all the people relating to and resolving the client's presenting issue. The client system in the case of the individual who wanted to stop drinking (see Table 12.1) included his immediate family, social network, and job-related network. This system is unique to this particular client.

Clients are always embedded in a network of systems, even if members of some of these systems are not present in the counseling room (Breunlin et al., 2011). We need to consider all of the people directly involved in counseling at any given time, and also all members of the client system not directly involved in the counseling process. Those that are not immediately present as part of the family system may be the most important for change.

The therapist system includes all of the persons involved in providing counseling for the client system. Even though the therapist is commonly the only member of the therapist system, many clients require the participation of co-therapists or adjunctive therapies involving additional providers. Sometimes this system includes counselor's supervisors and consultants, as well as counselors providing therapy to other members of the client system.

# What Is a Family?

*Each family system is in a constant state of change.*

—Allen Ivey

Available statistics do not support the traditional definition of family as father, mother, and biological children. Today many children are raised by unmarried couples; gay and lesbian couples; single women without a male partner; people living together without getting married; mothers of young children working outside the home; people of different races married or cohabitating together; and combinations of relatives and friends (Morin, 2011). Also, family definition and meaning vary across different cultures. Many Hispanic/Latinos/as consider friends as part of their families and assign them responsibilities similar to those assigned to kinship.

To capture this diversity, family is defined currently as a group of people affiliated by kinship, affinity, or co-residence (Crossno, 2011, p. 60). This definition of family accommodates a variety of accepted patterns of relation, such as cohabitation, blended families, single-parent and two- and three-generation families, and same-sex marriages.

## REFLECTION EXERCISE

How do you define family?

Do you ascribe to the traditional portrayal of family as a unit comprised of a married mother and father and their biological children living together under one roof?

In most societies, family represents the essential group where individual development takes place. Here is where individuals experience the strongest emotional interactions and long-lasting experiences foundational to self-concept and self-esteem. Yet, the characteristics of the family as a whole are different from the total sum of its members. The family has a history, function, and purpose of its own, all of these different from those of the specific member. This is the reason why families are thought of as interactive systems where component members continually interact.

The family is in a dynamic equilibrium, fluctuating between periods of stability and disequilibrium. Stability among the members helps the family system remain stable. Members bound together by mutual support, expectations, social roles, and long-lasting love ties and bundles of experiences. But members do not remain the same over time. Members grow, take new roles, add new members, move, or die due to age, accidents, or illnesses. Changes in one of the members affect the whole family system. Yet, families are constantly attempting to maintain equilibrium or family homeostasis, a process when the system uses feedback in response to major changes to restore or reach a new level of equilibrium. Transition points during the family's life cycle greatly exemplify the homeostatic process (see Table 12.4).

**Table 12.4. Family Life Cycle Stages**

| Family Life Cycle Stage | Important Emotional Process of Transition |
| --- | --- |
| Independence stage: single young adult | Leaving home, assuming emotional, social, and financial responsibility for self |
| Coupling stage: Joining other | Commitment to this new system and joined families |
| Parenting stage I: young children | Accepting new members into the family system |
| Parenting stage I: adolescents | Increasing flexibility of family system's boundary, accepting children's dependence and grandparents' frailties |
| Launching stage: children exit | Changes in the nest, accepting exits (grown children; own parents) from and entries (grandchildren) into the family system, refocusing on marital dyad |
| Families in later life | Accepting the shifting of generational roles and diminishing capacities due to aging, dealing with loss of spouse, and other |

# Family Therapy

Family therapy—also referred to as couple and family therapy, marriage and family therapy, family systems therapy, and family counseling—is a form of systemic psychotherapy. This form of therapy is both a specific way of thinking about human behavior and a set of therapeutic techniques for treating families. Family therapists emphasize family relationships as an important factor in psychological health and they work with families and couples to improve the quality of their relationships, cope with challenges, adapt to transitions, and improve mental health disorders. The American Association for Marriage and Family Therapists (2018) asserts that family patterns of behavior influence clients and therefore may need to be a part of a treatment plan.

Studies of families and mental disorders have progressed positively over time and are recognized as an evidence-based treatment for several disorders (Lebow, 2016; Heatherington et al., 2015). Long past is the view that the family is the primary causal agent in clients' psychological disorders and that the identified client was a "scapegoat" for all of the family's hidden dysfunctions. Blaming of the parents for causing their sons' or daughters' schizophrenia via poor parenting and "double-bind messages" (Bateson, Jackson, Haley, & Weakland, 1956) or via daily interactions with a "schizophrenogenic" mother (Fromm-Reichmann, 1948) have been dismissed (Miklowitz, 2004).

Current family therapy approaches focus on the family's way of reacting to and organizing itself around one of its members' psychological issues and how these reactions protect against or contribute to the risk of recurrence.

Family therapists are aware that clients exist in a web of relationships. The family interaction is basic to human change and this is where we can treat a wide range of relationship difficulties and mental disorders. These include marital distress, child– parent conflicts, anxiety, depression, and even individual psychological issues. For family therapists, context is everything, much as Urie Bronfenbrenner suggests.

Multicultural considerations when working with a family are presented in Table 12.5.

**Table 12.5.** **Multicultural Family Worldview**

The current definition of the family as a system with specified relationships, roles, and rules applies to a wide variety of family types (gay and lesbian, single-parent, blended, and nuclear). African American, Hispanic/Latina/o, and Native American cultures many times include an extended network of relatives and friends as part of their family. These members are perceived as active components of the family systems, and many times, they take over the parental roles in the event of an illness or death of the biological or adoptive parents.

Cultural definitions of family carry a variety of expectations with them. Individualistic cultures emphasize personal success in school, sport, and work. Cooperative cultures accent the value of success via cooperative work in school, sports, and work. The case of Jorge (see Table 12.9) highlights the importance of family values, expectations, and experiences.

*(Continued)*

**Table 12.5. Multicultural Family Worldview** *(Continued)*

Culturally sensitive family therapists spend time learning about the worldviews of their clients before attempting to help the family. They integrate in the therapeutic session family traditions and ways of doing things. They integrate the cultural concepts, values, and metaphors of the family they are working with. They adapt their theoretical models to the cultural characteristics of the specific family. They respect and honor the family worldview when implementing selected interventions to promote change.

## REFLECTION EXERCISE

Severe, recurrent psychiatric disorders—notably schizophrenia and bipolar disorder—dramatically affect the life of an individual, his or her family, and their larger contexts. Schizophrenia leads to more hospitalizations than any other mental disorder and with bipolar disorder is one of the major causes of disability. Both produce major family and societal costs. Pharmacological treatments have improved significantly, but even with medications, most clients present severe impairments in work and social functioning, and their relapse rates and suicide risks are very high. These observations suggest that the concept of brain disease (e.g., "illnesses are produced by chemical imbalances in the brain") may not be accurate.

Current evidence suggests that genetic, biological, psychological, and social variables interact at the onset and continuity of the mental disorders. Furthermore, psychosocial variables affect the structure and function of the brain and the timing of gene expression.

Based on what we have learned about systems and family theory, we suggest that comprehensive models focusing on the dynamic processes in the family environment and social systems, and psychological and biological vulnerabilities of the client, are likely to have greater capacity for success than models that place emphasis on only one of these components.

What do you think, and why?

Google "better prognosis hypothesis" for schizophrenia to learn about the different international studies researching why outcomes for schizophrenia are better in developing countries compared with developed countries. Most of these studies attempt to assess the effect of family and social systems in the recovery from schizophrenia.

# Family: Positive and Negative Effects

Families impact in positive and negative ways the mental and physical health of their members (Anderson, 2014). A caring family provides emotional, economic, and other forms of support that increases the overall health and wellbeing of its members.

Conflictive and stressful families negatively affect the lives of their members. For example, family distortion of information, the accumulation of errors as information passes through a family network, can lead to family conflict and deterioration. Family denial—the refusal to recognize or accept facts when they conflict with existing family beliefs—is another source of family conflicts. Think about the Somali Minnesotan families who believed anti-vaccination leaders and prevented their children from this protective method. They end up with forty-eight confirmed cases of children under the age of ten infected with the highly contagious and potentially deadly measles virus (Forliti, 2017).

Competition between different members of the family may lead some of them to do whatever they feel is necessary for their own survival (for example, a younger member may take money from parents to bring attention to him- or herself, upset for the larger attention given to an older sibling). This competition for attention between the members is damaging, but it represents a reaction to the interactions of the family as a whole. The younger child's behavior does not derive from his or her individual characteristics, as he or she may be considered a conscientious child within other systems, such as school or neighborhood. The family interactions compel family members to do things that they may not do outside of the family.

## REFLECTION EXERCISE

What are some examples of distortion of information, denial, and counterproductive competition observed in your own family as you grew up?

What was their effect on you and your family?

How did these characteristics influence how you now behave?

## Individual or Family Treatments

Individual and family therapies are typically used in behavioral health agencies and community settings serving youth and adults. Both forms of treatment show high levels of success. For example, treated children using individual or family therapy function better than 75 percent of the children in the control groups. What is surprising is the fact that only between 5 to 10 percent of children and their families make use of these outpatient child-based therapy services (Weisz, Sandler, Durlak, & Anton, 2006; Weisz, Weiss, Han, Granger, & Morton, 1995).

The following section presents family therapy theories.

## Current Theories of Family Therapy

There are many theories of family therapy and many different classifications available. You are encouraged to seek further knowledge, as an extensive review of each would take a whole book and more! Different classifications of family theories have been proposed (e.g., Kaslow, Bhaju, & Celano, 2011). We have chosen the classification offered by Nelson and her students. Table 12.6 presents brief descriptions of the major theories of family therapy and their leaders.

**Table 12.6.  Major Theories of Family Therapy**

| Major Marriage and Family Therapy Theories | Leaders | Central Conceptualization |
|---|---|---|
| Structural Family Therapy | Salvador Minuchin; Charles Fishman | Family issues arise from within the family structure. Goal of therapy is to restructure the family system by establishing boundaries and avoiding enmeshment. |
| | | Role of the therapist is to perturb the system if the structure is too rigid (disorganized or closed) or too diffuse (enmeshed) to reorganize the family structure. |
| Strategic Therapy | Mental Research Institute; John Weakland; Don Jackson; Paul Watzlawick; Richard Fisch<br><br>Family Therapy Institute; Jay Haley; Cloé Madanes<br><br>Milan Family Therapy; Mara Selvini Palazzoli; Luigi Boscolo; Gianfranco Cecchin; Giuliana Prata | Family members often engage in patterns of communication that perpetuate their issues. Attempts to implement their own solutions maintain or escalate (augment) their issues.<br><br>Goal of therapy is to help family define clear and reachable goals and break the maladaptive pattern of communication. |
| Solution-Focused Brief Therapy | Steve de Shazer; Insoo Kim Berg; Yvonne Dolan; Eve Lipchik | The goal is to help client think or do things differently in order to increase their satisfaction with their lives.<br><br>Counselor works to shift client's goals, focusing on what they want to achieve in the future and engage in solution talk. |
| Psychodynamically Informed Family Therapy | Sigmund Freud; Erik Erikson; Nathan Ackerman; David Scharff & Jill Savege Scharff (object relations); John Bowlby (attachment theory) | Sexual and aggression drives are intrinsic to human nature. Internalized objects, as well as early experiences, affect later relationships, as these are projected onto new relationships, enabling the repetition of old patterns of interaction.<br><br>Goal of therapy is to free the family members from their past constraints and focus on healthy ways to interact with others. |
| Experiential and Humanistic Family Therapy | Carl Whitaker; Virginia Satir; Richard Schwartz (Internal Family Systems Therapy) | Goal of therapy is to focus on the experiences that promote growth and change in the present. Facilitate freedom of expression and genuine ways of relating with others.<br><br>Providing a warm and accepting counseling atmosphere will facilitate personal growth, love, interest, attention, acceptance, and understanding among the family members. |

*(Continued)*

**Table 12.6. Major Theories of Family Therapy** *(Continued)*

| | | |
|---|---|---|
| Cognitive Behavioral Family Therapies | Ivan Pavlov; John Watson; Edward Thorndike; B.F. Skinner; Albert Bandura; Frank Dattilio | Family relationships, cognitions, emotions, and behavior mutually influence one another.<br><br>Goal of therapy is to modify specific negative or dysfunctional patterns of thinking and/or behavior to alleviate the presenting symptom. |
| Narrative Family Therapy | Michael White; David Epston; Jill Freedman; Gene Combs | Goal of therapy is to change the way the clients view themselves and assist them in reauthoring their story in a positive way light.<br><br>Counselors help clients find a different story that is not saturated with their negative concerns. |
| Contextual Family Therapy | Ivan Boszormenyi-Nagy | Goal of therapy is to work with the values and ethics transmitted across generations to increase trustworthiness in family member relationships and reduce negative or destructive interactions. The aim is to change ways that are destructive to individuals and relationships and posterity (e.g., revolving slate, destructive entitlement). |
| Bowen Family Therapy | Murray Bowen; Edwin Friedman | Goal is to increase differentiation of self (thoughts/emotions/self/others), intermediate detriangulation, lowering anxiety to respond instead of react. Decrease emotional reactivity, increase intimacy one on one with important others. |
| Emotionally Focused Therapy | Les Greenberg; Susan Johnson | Emotion is a target and agent of change. Primary emotions, such as sadness or joy, draw partners closer. Secondary emotions like rage or hate push partners away.<br><br>Goal of therapy is to facilitate new experiences to reduce the expression of secondary emotions and focus on primary ones. This new corrective emotional experience helps clients change. |
| Gottman Method Couple Therapy | John Gottman; Julie Gottman | Therapy is primarily dyadic; and couples need to be in emotional state to learn how to cope with their issues and change.<br><br>Therapy attempts to be a positive affective experience, facilitate positive sentiments in the couple, and encourage good communication to promote change. |

The following section describes a variety of creative family therapy techniques.

## Techniques of Marriage and Family Counseling and Therapy

Marriage and family counselors and therapists are not limited to the techniques espoused by the specific models they embrace. Today's practitioners use many of the basic techniques presented here to gain a better understanding about the family system and to promote change. Ethical practice and sensible use of these techniques are required, as they are not a solution but a way to activate movement in the family. Each of the techniques below can be used to facilitate engagement of family members and gain their perspective on the family system and ecology.

## Family Genogram

The family genogram is a technique used early in family therapy to gain a graphic representation of the family structure, demographics, and history (Ivey, Ivey, & Zalaquett, 2018). Table 12.7 offers guidance for developing a family genogram. Instructions on how to develop a community genogram can be found in Chapter 2. The family genogram provides a significant amount of data for the therapist and family members. Typically, symbols are used to depict three or more generations. The transgenerational information helps in understanding how the family's past shapes the present and their future. Review Chapters 2 and 5 for information regarding family and community genograms. Community genograms provide an additional understanding of the diversity and availability of community resources, and they are frequently used in conjunction with a family genogram to capture a larger picture of the client's bioecological systems (Harris & White, 2014).

## Ecomap

The ecomap is a diagrammatic representation of the informal and formal systems in the client's life and ecology. Also, it can be used with families and organizations (Bennett & Grant, 2016). The ecomap helps counselors assess the adequacy of resources and support systems available to the client. Circles are used to represent different systems affecting the client. Distance between the circles and the client indicates the extent of the influence. The ecomap can also identify the exosystems, or those systems that affect other family members but do not have a direct impact on the client. The client builds the ecomap by identifying all the current factors that have some impact on his or her life. The visual representation of the client's current situation increases understanding and informs of possible avenues for achieving desired goals.

## Social Network Mapping

A social network map helps clients identify and define their social supports (Price, 2011). Social supports are important for the client's well-being, as they provide opportunities for social integration, nurturance, sense of worthiness, and practical assistance to resolve difficult or challenging situations. Concentric circles, with the client in the innermost ring, are used to identify and place social supports. Placement in relationship to the innermost ring helps gauge the client's perceived amount of support received. Closeness to the center indicates strong perceived support. Research with children has used social network maps with three concentric ring zones: closest, close, and remote; divided into three sectors: family, relatives, and other important people (e.g., friends, teachers) (Pirskanen, Jokinen, Kallinen, Harju-Veijola, & Rautakorpi, 2015).

## Reframing

Reframing is a technique used by family counselors and psychotherapists to change the client's view of a particular issue, event, or person. An extended description is offered in Chapter 4, under *Microskills*. The therapist redefines a situation or a behavior, modifying the initial meaning offered by the client. When the client is able to view that situation from another perspective, the meaning of that situation changes (Reynaert & Janne, 2011). Typically, the technique is used to change the negative value ascribed to a situation. For example, being stopped from driving by peers after an all-night party may be perceived as an upsetting event by the client, but his perception may change into a positive one once the event is described as an intentional action to prevent him from hurting himself and others while driving under the influence of alcohol. Through reframing, the negative situation was reframed into a positive event.

## Tracking

Tracking is a process used by family therapists to clearly identify sequences of events leading to specific outcomes (Minuchin & Fishman, 1981). The therapist listens carefully to family stories and records specific events and their sequence. This process allows the therapist to identify the sequence of events operating in a system to keep it the way it is. Interventions can be designed to provide information that determine what happens between points A and D to create E, the result.

## Communication Skill-building Techniques

All theories require effective communication; consequently, the structure of the interview and teaching of the microskills presented in Chapter 4 are fundamental. All the attending microskills presented in Chapter 4 are useful for effective family communication. Furthermore, all theories use microskills in varying degrees (Ivey et al., 2018). Faulty communication styles are usually involved in family conflicts. These communication styles often disrupt or prevent healthy family functioning. Effective communication skill building between a couple or between family members can have positive effects on their functioning and resolution of issues. In terms of coping, partners or family members can support each other if they are able to communicate about their own stress, identify stress in their partners, and figure out what kind of support will be helpful (Falconier, 2015). Listening techniques, including restatement of content, reflection of feelings, taking turns expressing feelings, and nonjudgmental discussions, are some of the methods employed in communication skill building.

## Family Sculpting

Family sculpting physically re-creates the family system and represents family members' relationships to one another at a specific point in time. Sculpting visually portrays the roles of each family member and heightens family members' awareness of each other's actions. Furthermore, the family sculpture may bring to the surface previously undetected relational dynamics between family members (Faddis & Cobb, 2016). Family sculpting serves as an assessment tool and provides insights for the development and implementation of specific therapeutic interventions.

## Family Photos

The family photos technique has the potential to provide a wealth of information about past and present functioning. One use of family photos is to go through the family album together. Verbal and nonverbal responses to pictures and events are often quite revealing. Adaptations of this method include asking members to bring in significant family photos and discuss reasons for bringing them, and locating pictures that represent past generations. Through discussion of photos, the therapist often more clearly sees family relationships, rituals, structure, roles, and communication patterns.

## Special Days, Mini-vacations, Special Outings

Couples and families that are stuck frequently exhibit predictable behavior cycles. Boredom is present, and family members take little time with each other. In such cases, family members feel unappreciated and taken for granted. "Caring Days" can be set aside when couples are asked to show caring for each other. Specific times for caring can be arranged with certain actions in mind (Stuart, 1980).

## The Empty Chair

The empty-chair technique, most often used by Gestalt therapists (Perls, Hefferline, & Goodman, 1994; Yontef & Simkin, 2014), has been adapted to family therapy. In one scenario, a partner may express his or her feelings to a spouse (empty chair), then play the role of the spouse and carry on a dialogue. Expressions to absent family, parents, and children can be arranged through employing this technique.

## Family Choreography

In family choreography, arrangements go beyond initial sculpting; family members are asked to position themselves as to how they see the family and then to show how they would like the family situation to be. Family members may be asked to reenact a family scene and possibly resculpt it to a preferred scenario. This technique can help a stuck family and create a lively situation.

## Family Council Meetings

Family council meetings are organized to provide specific times for the family to meet and share with one another. The therapist might prescribe council meetings as homework, where one case at a time is set and rules are outlined. The council encompass the entire family, and any absent members have to abide by decisions. The agenda may include any concerns of the family. Rules may suggest one member speaks at a time and may prohibit attacking others. Family council meetings help provide structure for the family, encourage full family participation, and facilitate communication.

## Strategic Alliances

This technique, often used by strategic family therapists, involves meeting with one member of the family as a supportive means of helping that person change. Individual change is expected to affect the entire family system. The individual is often asked to behave or respond in a different manner. This technique attempts to disrupt a circular system or behavior pattern.

## Prescribing Indecision

The stress level of couples and families often is exacerbated by a faulty decision-making process. Decisions not made in these cases become troubling in themselves. When straightforward interventions fail, paradoxical interventions often can produce change or relieve symptoms of stress. Such is the case with prescribing indecision. The indecisive behavior is reframed as an example of caring or taking appropriate time on important matters affecting the family. A directive is given to not rush into anything or make hasty decisions.

## Putting the Client in Control of the Symptom

This technique, widely used by strategic family therapists, attempts to place control in the hands of the individual or system. The therapist may recommend, for example, the continuation of a symptom such as anxiety or worry. Specific directives are given as to when, where, and with whom, and for what amount of time one should do these things. As the client follows this paradoxical directive, a sense of control over the symptom often develops, resulting in subsequent change.

The techniques presented above are used by family therapists in their practices. They apply them having the best interest of the client in mind and with respect to their uniqueness and cultural characteristics. Personalization and customization of application are a must. Table 12.8 summarizes research evidence that supports family therapy.

---

**Table 12.7. The Family Genogram**

The family genogram is one of the most fascinating techniques you can use to learn about our clients' family histories. Armed with symbols and conventions, some of these are described below, clients and counselors can create a comprehensive map of a client's history, relationships, diversity, resources, and losses, just to mention a few. Furthermore, by reflecting on the contents observed in the genogram, clients can reach newer insights of family structure, rules, values, important relationships, and other important aspects of their family. Clients' reflections may focus on current, past, or future aspects of their relationship with their families. In fact, you and your client can learn much about how family history affects the client. By learning about their history you may be able to assess what aspects the client perceives as positive or negative and their emotional, cognitive, and behavioral consequences.

The family genogram may help your client remember important family stories that are passed down through the generations. These family stories may be sources of pride and can be central in identifying family strengths (such as a story about a revered uncle who saved several neighbors from a raging fire). These stories are wonderful resources that enable clients and help them recognize personal strengths.

The use of a family tree is a wonderful adaptation to help a child develop a family genogram. Children typically enjoy drawing a tree and putting their family members on the branches, wherever they wish.

The following summary will provide you with the basics to begin using the family genogram technique. You may want to try the following steps using your own family before you focus on somebody else's family. These steps were provided by Ivey, Ivey, and Zalaquett (2018). You can supplement them with the steps offered to develop a community genogram (see Chapter 2).

1. List the names of family members for at least three generations (four is preferred) with age and dates of birth and death. List occupations, significant illnesses, and dates of death, as appropriate. Note any issue with alcoholism or drugs.
2. List important cultural/environmental/contextual issues. These may include ethnic identity, religion, economic, and social class considerations. In addition, pay special attention to significant life events, such as trauma or environmental issues (e.g., divorce, economic depression, major illness).
3. Basic relationship symbols for a genogram and an example of a genogram can be found below.
4. As you develop the genogram with a client, use the basic listening sequence to draw out information, thoughts, and feelings. You will find that considerable insight into one's personal life issues may be generated in this way.

*(Continued)*

**Table 12.7. The Family Genogram** *(Continued)*

Developing a genogram with your client and learning some of the main facts of family developmental history will often help you understand the context of individual issues. Let's use the example provided in Table 12.9, "Will Jorge Go to College?" What might be going on at home that results in Jorge's academic failure in school? Note that this would be one of the first questions a counselor using a family genogram would ask. Using this technique may have changed the focus onto the family and saved about three months of resolution time. Other questions may include "How might intergenerational issues be affecting Jorge?" "What are the implications of the ethnic background of this family?" The migrant farmworker families are affected by both their immigrant status and their Mexican origin. How are these factors impacting Jorge and his family? What else occurs to you?

You will find the books *Community Genograms: Using Individual, Family and Cultural Narratives with Clients* (Rigazio-DiGilio, Ivey, Kunkler-Peck, & Grady, 2005) and *Ethnicity and Family Therapy* (McGoldrick, Giordano, & Garcia-Preto, 2005) valuable and enjoyable resources to help you sharpen your genogram-building skills and expand your awareness of racial/ethnic issues.

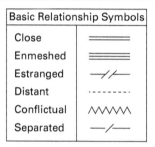

Jorge's Family Genogram

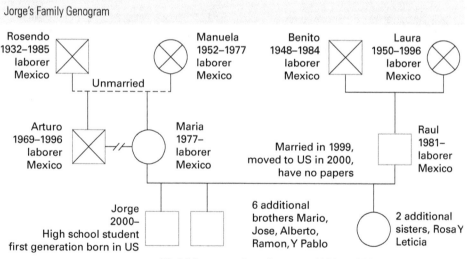

**Table 12.8. Research Box: Evidence Base of Family Therapy**

Research shows that marriage and family therapy is as effective, and in some cases more effective, than individual treatments for many mental health disorders such as adult schizophrenia, depressive disorders, adult alcoholism and drug abuse, children's conduct disorders, adolescent drug abuse, anorexia in young adult women, childhood autism, chronic physical illness in adults and children, and marital distress and conflict (American Association for Marriage and Family Therapists, 2018).

Lebow (2016) reports that there is a wide number of well-validated treatments ready for dissemination and use by couple and family therapists internationally. He cites the work of McFarlane (2016) and Miklowitz and Chung (2016) with schizophrenia as unique treatments leading to significantly lower rates of recidivism than other psychosocial and psychopharmacological treatments. Family treatments are now used to treat a wide array of issues, suggesting the value of couple and family therapy for both family and individual issues.

Fischer, Baucom, and Cohen (2016) reviewed the evidence base of cognitive-behavioral couple therapy (CBCT) and behavioral couple therapy (BCT), and reported that several meta-analyses have confirmed the efficacy of BCT and CBCT across trials in the United States, Europe, and Australia. Furthermore, they indicate that cognitive-behavioral couple-based interventions adapted to individual therapy are at least as effective as individual cognitive-behavioral therapy (CBT) across a variety of psychological disorders, and its effectiveness increases when partners participate in the treatment.

McFarlane (2016) indicates that family psychoeducation therapists have abandoned the earlier assumptions that family pathology caused relapse and deterioration in schizophrenic clients. Family psychoeducation therapists engage the family members as partners who complement the therapist's interventions. They report that this approach produces a 50 to 60 percent reduction in relapses compared with treatment as usual. More than 100 studies support this significant outcome. International and ethnic adaptations increase treatment efficacy.

Jewell and colleagues (2016) reviewed evidence from nine RCTs studying eating disorder–focused family therapy and concluded that this modality of treatment is the strongest evidence-based treatment for adolescent anorexia nervosa. Three additional RCTs indicate eating disorder–focused family therapy is an effective treatment for adolescent bulimia nervosa.

# Theories in Action

The following case, presented in Table 12.9, illustrates the power of using a family therapy approach in counseling.

**Table 12.9. Will Jorge Go to College?**

Jorge was a sixteen-year-old Mexican American high school student involved in the College Assistance Migrant Program (CAMP) of his school. CAMP is a unique federally funded educational support and scholarship program that helps students from migrant and seasonal farm-working backgrounds to reach and succeed in college. Both of Jorge's parents have emigrated from Mexico to work in the fields throughout the United States. Jorge was academically successful in school and demonstrated a capacity to attend college. His goal was to pursue a career in education.

*(Continued)*

**Table 12.9. Will Jorge Go to College?** *(Continued)*

Jorge was progressing well in the program and in his school. He secured a good job, was responsible, participated in CAMP activities, got in a relationship with a girl, and maintained a 4.0 grade point average. Soon after the beginning of 12th grade, he broke up with his girlfriend, started missing the CAMP meetings, and got low grades for the first time. This created a major concern for his teachers and CAMP workers. Worried about Jorge, they approached him, only to find out that he was sad but could not pinpoint any probable cause.

Because of the break-up and the perception that moodiness is a normal stage for adolescents, everybody backed up and left him alone, only to note that Jorge did not improve at all over the following month. Then, they sent him to an evaluation that produced a diagnostic of major depression and further treatment. The counselor found that Jorge was the oldest of eight brothers, with one more on the way. His pregnant mother could no longer endure working on the farms, and there was a dire need to make up for the lost income to feed the whole family. Jorge was the first generation in his family to be close to graduating from high school and to have a chance to go to college. But he was pressured by his parents to quit school and his part-time job so he could work on the farm full time. Three months of individual therapy produced no change. The counselor changed to a family therapy approach and involved the parents in the counseling sessions.

Soon, the counselor learned that both Jorge's father and mother went to work in the fields at the age of fourteen, and they believed that that was their son's destiny, too. Their belief was reinforced by the pressing need for additional income and the fact that Jorge was the eldest son, which in Hispanic/Latino families carries the demand to assume responsibility for their younger siblings and assume a parental role in the father's absence. All of this carried a much larger weight than completing high school or attending college. Jorge understood and accepted his family's traditions, rules, and needs. Realizing that his fate was sealed, he got depressed and lost interest in his relationship and schoolwork. Furthermore, he could not see any way to help with this complex situation, other than going to work in the fields. His dreams were shattered, and there was nothing he could do about it. This was his destiny, and he needed to accept it (fatalism, the belief that all events are predetermined and therefore inevitable is found among many Hispanic/Latino families).

Through the counseling work with the family, ways to find food sources, supplement their income, and pay for Jorge's college tuition were found. Furthermore, using many of the techniques listed in this chapter with sensitivity to their Mexican worldview, traditions and values were discussed, and alternative solutions were entertained. The final outcome included viable ways for the family to sustain themselves with the help of different programs for low-income families and a path for Jorge to complete high school and attend college. Soon thereafter, Jorge's mood improved. He worked with the school to redo poorly completed homework and regained his previous grades. He graduated with honors and a few years later received his teaching diploma. He still continues to support his brothers and sisters and both ailing parents.

This case demonstrates the importance of context in a person's situation. The systems Jorge belongs to clearly influenced him. Assuming that his depression was within him, not understanding the interplay of familial values on Jorge's situation would have extended an unsuccessful individual treatment. His individual goals in high school were at variance with the family forces acting on him. These forces were dictating a different path. This example raises the importance of understanding family relationships and cultural values.

# References

American Association for Marriage and Family Therapists. (2018). *About marriage and family therapists.* Retrieved from http://www.aamft.org/iMIS15/AAMFT/Content/About_AAMFT/About_Marriage_and_Family_Therapists.aspx.

Anderson, J. (2014). The impact of family structure on the health of children: Effects of divorce. *The Linacre Quarterly, 81*(4), 378–387. doi.org/10.1179/0024363914Z.00000000087.

Bateson, G., Jackson, D., Haley, J., & Weakland, J. (1956). Toward a theory of schizophrenia. *Behavioural science, 1,* 251–254.

Bennett, J., & Grant, N.S. (2016). Using an ecomap as a tool for qualitative data collection in organizations. *New Horizons in Adult Education and Human Resource Development, 28,* 1–13. doi:10.1002/nha3.20134.

Bertalanffy, L. von (2015). *General system theory: Foundations, development, applications.* New York, NY: George Brazziler.

Breunlin, D.C., Pinsof, W., & Russell, W.P. (2011). Integrative problem-centered meta-frameworks therapy I: Core concepts and hypothesizing. *Family Process, 50,* 293–313. doi:10.1111/j.1545-5300.2011.01362.x.

Bronfenbrenner, U. (1981). *The ecology of human development: Experiments by nature and design.* Cambridge, MA: Harvard University Press.

Capra, F., & Luisi, P.L. (2015). *The systems view of life: A unifying vision.* Cambridge, UK: Cambridge University Press.

Conyne, R.K., & Cook, E.P. (2004). Understanding persons within environments: An introduction to ecological counseling. In R.K. Conyne & E.P. Cook (Eds.), *Ecological counseling: An innovative approach to conceptualizing person-environment interaction* (pp. 3–36). Alexandria, VA: American Counseling Association.

Cook, E.P. (Ed.). (2012). *Understanding people in context: The ecological perspective in counseling.* Alexandria, VA: American Counseling Association.

Cook, E.P., & Coaston, S.C. (2012). Behavior is changeable. In E.P. Cook (Ed.), *Understanding people in context: The ecological perspective in counseling* (pp. 129–160). Alexandria, VA: American Counseling Association.

Crossno, M.A. (2011). Bowen family systems theory. In L. Metcalf (Ed.), *Marriage and family therapy: A practice-oriented approach* (pp. 39–64). New York, NY: Springer.

Faddis, T.J., & Cobb, K.F. (2016). Family therapy techniques in residential settings: Family sculptures and reflecting teams. *Contemporary Family Therapy, 3,* 43–51.

Falconier, M.K. (2015). TOGETHER—A couples' program to improve communication, coping, and financial management skills: Development and initial pilot-testing. *Journal of Marital and Family Therapy, 41,* 236–250. doi:10.1111/jmft.12052.

Fischer, M.S., Baucom, D.H., & Cohen, M.J. (2016). Cognitive-behavioral couple therapies: Review of the evidence for the treatment of relationship distress, psychopathology, and chronic health conditions. *Family Process, 55,* 423–442. doi:10.1111/famp.12227.

Forliti, A. (2017, May 3). *Measles outbreak sickens dozens of Minnesota Somalis. Washington Post.* Retrieved from https://www.washingtonpost.com/national/health-science/measles-outbreak-sickens-dozens-of-minnesota-somalis/2017/05/03/6b3be752-3029-11e7-a335-fa0ae1940305_story.html.

Fromm-Reichmann, F. (1948). Notes on the development of treatment of schizophrenics by psycho-analytic psychotherapy. *Psychiatry, 11*(3), 263–273.

Harris, J., & White, V. (2014). *A dictionary of social work and social care.* New York, NY: Oxford University Press.

Heatherington, L., Friedlander, M.L., Diamond, G.M., Escudero, V., & Pinsof, W.M. (2015). *25 Years of systemic therapies research: Progress and promise. Psychotherapy Research, 25,* 348–364. doi:10.1080/10503307.2014.983208.

Ivey, A., Ivey, M.B., & Zalaquett, C. (2018). *Intentional interviewing and counseling: Facilitating client development in a multicultural society* (9th ed.). Belmont, CA: Cengage Learning.

Jewell, T., Blessitt, E., Stewart, C., Simic, M., & Eisler, I. (2016). Family therapy for child and adolescent eating disorders: A critical review. *Family Process, 55,* 577–594. doi:10.1111/famp.12242.

Kaslow, J.K., Bhaju, J., & Celano, M.P. (2011). Family therapies. In S. Messer & A. Gurman (Eds.), *Essential psychotherapies: Theory and practice* (3rd ed.) (pp. 297–344). New York: Guildford Press.

Lau, J., & Ng, K. (2014). Conceptualizing the counseling training environment using Bronfenbrenner's ecological theory. *International Journal for the Advancement of Counseling, 36,* 423–439. doi:10.1007/s10447-014-9220-5.

Lebow, J.L. (2016). Editorial: Empirically supported treatments in couple and family therapy. *Family Processes, 55,* 385–389. doi:10.1111/famp.12240.

McFarlane, W.R. (2016). Family interventions for schizophrenia and the psychoses: A review. *Family Process, 55,* 460–482.

McGoldrick, M., Giordano, J., & Garcia-Preto, N. (Eds.) (2005). *Ethnicity and family therapy* (3rd ed.). New York, NY: Guilford Press.

McMahon, H.G., Mason, E.C.M., Daluga-Guenther, N., & Ruiz, A. (2014). An ecological model of professional school counseling. *Journal of Counseling & Development, 92,* 459–471. doi:10.1002/j.1556-6676.2014.00172.x.

Miklowitz, D.J. (2004). The role of family systems in severe and recurrent psychiatric disorders: A developmental psychopathology view. *Development and Psychopathology, 16,* 667–688.

Miklowitz, D.J., & Chung, B. (2016). Family-focused therapy for bipolar disorder: Reflections on 30 years of research. *Family Process, 55,* 483–499. doi:10.1111/famp.12237.

Minuchin, S., & Fishman, H.C. (1981). *Family therapy techniques.* Cambridge, MA: Harvard University Press.

Morin, R. (2011). The public renders a split verdict on changes in family structure. *The Pew Research Center.* Retrieved from http://www.pewsocialtrends.org/files/2011/02/Pew-Social-Trends-Changes-In-Family-Structure.pdf.

Perls, F., Hefferline, R., & Goodman, P. (1994). *Gestalt therapy: Excitement and growth in the human personality.* Gouldsboro, ME: Gestalt Journal Press.

Pirskanen, H., Jokinen, K., Kallinen, K., Harju-Veijola, M., & Rautakorpi, S. (2015). Researching children's multiple family relations: Social network maps and life-lines as methods. *Qualitative Sociology Review, 11,* 50–69.

Price, B. (2011). How to map a patient's social support network. *Nursing Older People (through 2013), 23*(2), 28–35.

Reynaert, C., & Janne, P. (2011). Reframing "reframing": Another look at "reframing" inspired by a sonnet by Charles Baudelaire. *American Journal of Family Therapy, 39,* 419–430. doi:10.1080/01926187.2010.537239.

Rigazio-DiGilio, S.A., Ivey, A.E., Kunkler-Peck, K.P., & Grady, L.T. (2005). *Community genograms: Using individual, family and cultural narratives with clients.* New York, NY: Teacher's College Press, Columbia University.

Stuart, R. (1989). *Helping couples change.* New York, NY: Guildford Press.

Weisz, J.R., Sandler, I.N., Durlak, J.A., & Anton, B.S. (2006). A proposal to unite two different worlds of children's mental health. *American Psychologist, 61,* 644–645.

Weisz, J.R., Weiss, B., Han, S.S., Granger, D.A., & Morton, T. (1995). Effects of psychotherapy with children and adolescents revised: A meta-analysis of treatment outcome studies. *Psychological Bulletin, 117*, 450–468.

Yontef, G., & Simkin, J. (2014). Gestalt therapy. In D. Wedding & R.J. Corsini (Eds.), *Current psychotherapies* (10th ed.) (pp. 299–338). Itasca, IL: Peacock.

### CHAPTER 13

# Toward an Integrated Counseling and Psychotherapy

## Becoming a Good Counselor or Psychotherapist

We were mesmerized observing a young counselor providing services to a deeply depressed client. We had been observing the counseling interaction from behind the one-way mirror, listening intensely to the verbal exchanges with the client, and noticing the nonverbals demonstrated during this fifty-minute session. After the counseling session ended, we complimented the counselor for her wonderful ability to establish a working relationship and her masterful application of advanced counseling skills.

The young counselor responds with a smile, appreciating the feedback and asking for detailed criticism and suggestions. She is not afraid of receiving feedback. Finally, she openly express her desire to learn additional theories and techniques and to improve her therapeutic effectiveness. There is so much to learn, she adds.

We believe she is on her way to becoming an effective counselor. She loves what she does and celebrates the progress made in the treatment of depression symptoms. Yet, she is excited about the possibilities of what she might accomplish in the future. And, yes, there is so much to learn. There are so many theories and techniques available. There is so much diversity in clients' individual, group, and cultural characteristics. There are multiple reasons for consultation, as well as possibilities for treatment. The young counselor can do a lot to advance her expertise, not only in theories, techniques, and models of intervention, but also in building effective client-therapist relationships, or any other dimensions of counseling she sets her mind to learn.

The question is how to become and stay effective. The intentional counselor sees potential, is eager to learn more, and seeks feedback from others.

The first step in becoming an intentional counselor is to maintain a beginner's attitude. Your awareness, knowledge, skills, and actions—even those you have known for a long time—can be further developed or sharpened.

An intervention that we have used for months or years can be improved by eliminating unnecessary steps. These thoughts that we have when working with a difficult client perhaps can be changed by altering our cognitive approach. The concerning emotions we experience when working with a client or family that are different from ourselves may change if we learn more about their particular background and cultural worldview. The way we engage the client into action during the time between this and the next session can be improved by inviting them to participate in the design of the recommended activity. Effective therapists maintain a beginner's attitude, and then they practice.

The second step is intentional, deliberate practice. A large amount of work does not translate into larger expertise. Instead, you may end up tired or exhausted. Smart, intentional practice involves breaking down the skill into smaller components and practicing to fine-tune each of the skills, one at a time. Effective counselors engage in deliberate practice. The intentional practice is followed by feedback.

The third step is to seek feedback. We are very biased in the way we evaluate our progress and mastering of the skills. Effective counselors look for supervisors, colleagues, and experts on the skills they want to improve for further education and evaluation. Furthermore, they seek feedback from their clients regarding the quality of the therapeutic relationship, impact of the interventions, and progress regarding their reason for consultation. Then, they use this feedback to engage in deliberate practice to further advance their competencies.

Good counselors and therapists are made, not born (Miller, Hubble, & Duncan, 2008, Geiger, 2018). They work intentionally and continuously seek feedback regarding their performance (Chow, Miller, Seidel, Kane, Thornton, & Andrews, 2015). When they consistently use a measure of the alliance with a standardized outcome scale, their clients deteriorate less, stay longer, and achieve clinically significant changes at a rate that is double the rates of therapists who do not use this type of feedback (Boswell, Kraus, Miller, & Lambert, 2015).

Recent randomized clinical trials confirmed that the use of formal assessment and discussion with the client about their experiences of the process and outcome of counseling doubles the rate of clinically significant outcomes, decreases dropout rates by about half, and diminishes deterioration rates by one-third (Miller, Bargmann, Chow, Seidel, & Maeschalck, 2016). Unfortunately, the use of this type of feedback is low, in spite of the many brief instruments available (Seidel, Andrews, Owen, Miller, & Buccino, 2017).

This book contains many skills, concepts, and theories—all can help you become even more accomplished as a counselor or therapist. And there are many more—it is said that more than a thousand approaches and interventions now exist! The rehearsal and practice of the basics can build a new and increasing understanding, which later becomes integrated into your own natural style. Listening, of course, is the most vital, regardless of what you are doing. And hearing client stories and the client's way of experiencing the world enables you to bring your own theoretical approach to them with sensitivity and expertise. You are becoming an increasingly good counselor/therapist.

# Evidence-based Relationships

Evidence-based treatments are studied and applied within a relationship between counselor and client. Research has consistently shown the importance of the relationship, which is the largest contributor to client change. Using variables of the relationship known to work can significantly improve your effectiveness.

The American Psychological Association's Task Force on Evidence-Based Therapy Relationships offers the following practice recommendations for counselors and therapists (Norcross, 2011).

1.  Make the creation and cultivation of a therapy relationship and working alliance, characterized by elements found to be demonstrably effective, a primary aim in the treatment of clients. Recall that this relationship is based on empathic listening and understanding.

2.  Adapt or tailor psychotherapy to the specific client characteristics using what is known to work (e.g., adapt to client's culture, preferences, level of defiance-compliance, place on the stages of change).

3. Routinely monitor clients' responses to the therapy relationship and how they react to ongoing treatment. Such monitoring leads to increased opportunities to reestablish collaboration, improve the working alliance, modify technical strategies, and avoid premature termination.

4. Use evidence-based therapy relationships and evidence-based treatments adapted to the client to generate the best outcomes.

The effectiveness of counseling and psychotherapy is well established (American Psychological Association, 2012). Furthermore research on the contributors to therapeutic change identify the relationship with the therapist as the largest contributor. *Being with the client is more essential than focusing on your usual theory of practice.*

# The Search for the "Best" Theory

*If Sigmund Freud was alive today, he'd be turning over in his grave.*

—**Yogi Berra**

In many ways, it was simpler during much of Freud's lifetime. There was really only one major theory, and all one had to do was learn it. Behavioral therapy, cognitive-behavioral theory and existential-humanistic concepts complicated the issue, but still one only had to decide what the "best" theory was. The task for new counselors and therapists remained simply deciding on a single theoretical commitment. That single decision is no longer an effective option. As mentioned in Chapter 1, the number of current theories is much, much larger.

Historically, the field tends to talk about First, Second, Third, Fourth, and Fifth Force theories of helping, as these terms describe the major theories in the historical order when they appeared. Psychodynamic theory is considered First Force, due to Sigmund Freud's vast influence at the beginning. New ideas from object-relations theory, self-theory, and attachment theory have brought new life to Freud's constructs.

Behaviorism is considered Second Force due to the work of early behavioral theorists such as John Watson and B.F. Skinner. Carl Rogers's person-centered therapy brought a new, more humanistic view to the field—the Third Force. It is his work and that of Abraham Maslow that focused an entire generation of therapists on the importance of the person and relationship in therapy. The ideas of Rogers, Frankl, and Perls are now part of the understanding and practice of most counselors and therapists, even if they state adherence to another theoretical orientation. Furthermore, the centrality of the therapeutic relationship has been confirmed by multiple randomized clinical trials.

The Fourth force, Cognitive Therapy or Cognitive Behavioral Therapy builds on the contributions of Beck, Ellis, Meichenbaum, and Glasser.

Multicultural Counseling and Therapy (MCT) has become recognized as a distinct Fifth Force in the field. The traditional theories gave minimal attention to the cultural base of helping until MCT appeared on the horizon. This theoretical orientation has reshaped the field. MCT is also different from the other four forces, as it does not discount the importance of any theoretical orientation. Rather, MCT recognizes, adapts, and supports all approaches to therapy so long as they are developing increased awareness and sensitivity to multicultural issues. Now, social justice skills and advocacy skills have been added, creating the multicultural competencies and social justice skills. MCT is becoming the central meta-theory of helping due to its recognition that all helping stems from a cultural base.

# The Foundational Theories

The first six chapters explored concepts that can be useful in understanding the five major theoretical orientations above: cultural intentionality and community; empathy and family understanding; the microskills and solution-oriented therapy; and Developmental Counseling and Therapy (DCT). If you are skilled in these concepts, you have a solid foundation for mastering the many complexities of theory and practice in counseling and psychotherapy.

The empathic conditions, particularly as they integrate community and family concepts, have been presented as important in all theoretical orientations. Positive regard and the positive asset search of the microskills have been stressed throughout this book—helping your client build on strengths is increasingly recognized as a basic foundation for change and growth in counseling and therapy.

The Basic Listening Sequence of the microskills framework is used by virtually all theories to draw out client stories and narratives. The five-stage structure of the interview is useful to structure your work in existential-humanistic, cognitive-behavioral, and other theoretical frames of reference.

The DCT model is an integrative framework itself that focuses on entering the meaning-making world of the client. DCT argues that helping theory must start with the client. Once we make sense of how the client organizes the world, we can then select theory and strategies systematically and with a theoretical rationale for our actions. Geiger, (2018) provides a clear and practical update of DCT.

*Postmodernism and Narrative therapy.* Postmodernism is a philosophical theory that asserts that the act of knowing is subjective or interpretive. The knower is unable to acquire direct or objective knowledge (Phipps & Vorster, 2015). Narrative therapy is based on the concept that humans, unable to comprehend events objectively, produce narratives or stories about these events.

This argument is supported by postmodern theorists. Without a direct capacity to access "reality," humans create stories to represent what it is known, a process delimited by our own historical and cultural views. Their postmodern philosophical development has had a significant impact on the field of counseling and therapy. The modern ideas of the previous century took the real world for granted. It was just easily accessible. Treatments needed to focus on challenging irrational beliefs and replacing them for rational ones. But rational definitions were built on the idea of an objective world.

For postmodernism, reality is a function of the constructs of the observer. All perceptions, all knowledge are subjective or interpretive. What it is important now is the role of the subjective experience of the client. His or her stories are what they know and what influences their psychological well-being, relationships, and dealings with society.

According to narrative therapy, humans story their experience. They do this to make sense of their lives, to assign meaning to those experiences. The role of the counselor or therapist is to decipher how the client is storying his or her world, the meanings he or she is ascribing to these stories, the impact of these stories on the client's life. And, if the story leads to negative feelings, thoughts, or behaviors, help clients reauthor a more satisfying and open-ended story (White & Epston, 1990).

# Common Factors

Accumulated evidence identifies the qualities and actions of intentional and effective therapists. Based on the best available evidence, Wampold (2015) offers a list of fourteen qualities and actions of effective counselors and psychotherapists. These qualities and actions, presented in Table 13.1, can be used to guide therapists to continue improving and sharpening their competencies. Of course, different therapists conducting a variety of treatments in different contexts may rely on some more than others.

**Table 13.1. Fourteen Qualities and Actions of Effective Counselors and Psychotherapists**

Effective therapists maintain systemic awareness of the client's characteristics and context. Characteristics of the client refer to the culture, race, ethnicity, spirituality, sexual orientation, age, physical health, motivation for change, and so forth. The context involves available resources; e.g., SES (socioeconomic status), family and support networks, vocational status, cultural milieu, and concurrent services; e.g., psychiatric, case management, etc. Otherwise, even the best therapist may lose clients—or worse, damage them.

Effective therapists have a sophisticated set of interpersonal skills, including

a. Verbal fluency

b. Interpersonal perception

c. Affective modulation and expressiveness

*(Continued)*

**Table 13.1. Fourteen Qualities and Actions of Effective Counselors and Psychotherapists (Continued)**

**d.** Warmth and acceptance

**e.** Empathy

**f.** Focus on other

Clients of effective therapists feel understood, trust the therapist, and believe the therapist can help him or her. The therapist creates these conditions in the first moments of the interaction through verbal and importantly nonverbal behavior.

Effective therapists are able to form a working alliance with a broad range of clients. The working alliance is described as collaborative, purposeful work on the part of the client and the therapist. It involves agreement about the goals of therapy. If the relationship is not working, two things need to be considered. First, thoughtful referral that maintains client safety. Second, look at yourself. What do you still need to learn? Seek supervision so that this seldom happens in the future, but accept that no one is appropriate for all clients.

Effective therapists provide an acceptable and adaptive explanation for the client's distress. Clients want an explanation for their symptoms or problems. The explanation must be consistent with healing practice and be compatible with their attitudes, values, culture, and worldview, which means treatments are adapted for clients.

The effective therapist provides a treatment plan that is consistent with the explanation provided to the client and the individual goals that are most important.

The effective therapist is influential, persuasive, and convincing. The therapist presents the explanation and the treatment plan in a way that convinces the client that the explanation is correct and that compliance with the treatment will benefit the client. This process leads to client optimism and hopefulness, increased expectancy for mastery, and enactment of healthy actions.

The effective therapist continually monitors client progress. Therapists are particularly attentive to evidence that their clients are deteriorating.

The effective therapist is flexible and will adjust therapy if resistance to the treatment is apparent or the client is not making adequate progress. The effective therapist takes in new information, tests hypotheses about the client, and is willing to be wrong and adjust treatment when necessary by using a different theoretical approach, referral to another therapist, or use of adjunctive services (meditation, acupuncture, etc.).

The effective therapist does not avoid difficult material in therapy and uses such difficulties therapeutically. It is not unusual that the client will avoid material that is challenging. When the difficult material involves the relationship with the client, the effective therapist addresses the interpersonal process in a therapeutic way. Observation of nonverbal behavior both in yourself and the client is an important clue that may be missed.

The effective therapist communicates hope and optimism. Those with severe and/or chronic problems typically experience relapses, lack of consistent progress, or other difficulties. Effective therapists mobilize client strengths and resources to facilitate the client's ability to solve his or her own problems.

The effective therapist is aware of his or her own psychological process and does not inject his or her own material into the therapy process unless such actions are deliberate and therapeutic.

The effective therapist is aware of the best research evidence related to the particular client in terms of treatment, problems, social context, and so forth.

The effective therapist seeks to continually improve. Many, perhaps most, stop reading research new methods once they are established. Consider supervision and group supervision as a life-long practice. This will help remove the danger of burn-out.

# Searching for Theoretical Integration

*"What treatment, by whom, is most effective for this individual with that specific problem, and under which set of circumstances?"* Gordon Paul made this classic statement in 1967, and drawing from the best of all theories became respectable. Nonetheless, eclecticism has still been criticized for lack of a central theoretical rationale for therapeutic action.

Over time, research and clinical practice have revealed that traditional theories have considerable value. A key issue has been how they can be integrated in a meaningful fashion. Eclecticism as a systematic frame lacks a rationale for changing theories or methods with clients other than the intuitive preference and clinical experience of the practitioner.

Lazarus's multimodal therapy (1981, 1986) was a major attempt to organize therapy theory, primarily from a behavioral frame of reference. He divides treatment into seven parts, the "BASIC-ID" (**B**ehavior, **A**ffective response, **S**ensations, **I**mages, **C**ognitions, **I**nterpersonal relationships, and **D**rugs). At issue is drawing from each dimension for a holistic treatment plan. Lazarus was one of the first to organize eclecticism into a more coherent and organized way of thinking.

Integrative theories are currently becoming more numerous and influential. You will note that Meichenbaum's discussion of cognitive-behavioral theory in Chapter 9 brings diverse theories together in a coherent fashion and thus is becoming broader in scope than traditional behavioral frames of reference. Developmental Counseling and Therapy (DCT) integrates theory and practice in a different format (Chapter 6). It provides an overall rationale from moving from sensory methods to behavioral to cognitive to systemic approaches. DCT, perhaps more than other theories, emphasizes sensorimotor and systemic/cultural foundations of experience, arguing that network treatment is essential if change is to be maintained over time.

You will be asked in this chapter to generalize your own integrated view of counseling and psychotherapy. You have been exposed to many alternatives that have stood the test of time or, if new, show some promise of influencing future change. As a professional, you will be part of the process of moving the field toward a new view. How can you continually add new dimensions while retaining the best of the past?

# Multicultural Counseling and Therapy as the Theoretical Fifth Force

Multicultural counseling and therapy (MCT) does not dismiss traditional methods of helping and recognizes their value, *so long as they are employed in a culturally meaningful and culturally sensitive fashion.* Furthermore, MCT starts from a different place than traditional theory. MCT asks you to start with client assessment of individual, family, and cultural experience. Rather than impose a theory on a client, MCT seeks to find how the client constructs and makes meaning in the world. MCT stresses an egalitarian, nonhierarchical therapist/client relationship. Then, MCT suggests that counselor and client together can draw from other theories in an integrated fashion to meet individual, family, and cultural needs.

In effect, the multicultural orientation works to turn the history of counseling and therapy on its head and seeks a major new direction. The issue is not imposing a theory on a client, but rather working *with* the client in a culturally sensitive fashion to find a technique, strategy, theory, or set of theories that meet the client's needs. *Self-in-relation* becomes the focus rather than individually oriented self-actualization.

MCT stresses the importance of using traditional First, Second, Third, and Fourth Force theory. Toward what cultural and individually appropriate goal are the client and his or her therapist oriented? Does a European American seek self-understanding? Then, perhaps a Rogerian or psychodynamic approach may be appropriate. However, if the goal turns out to be feeling less anxious in social situations, the method may be cognitive-behavioral. If the client is a woman, feminist therapy or gender-aware CBT assertiveness training may be called for. And if the client is Latina, then culturally sensitive assertiveness training is required, which acknowledges the complexities of changing a woman's role and actions. We live immersed in systems and any clear understanding of the client situation should include a family therapy or systems perspective.

MCT might expand Gordon Paul's earlier statement with the following additional specifics:

> What set of treatments, by whom, is most effective for this individual or family with what specific issue, with what specific culturally and individually appropriate goal, under which set of circumstances, and how can relapse of treatment be prevented? Moreover, how can we involve this client (and family) in treatment planning in an egalitarian culturally sensitive fashion?

How might you rephrase the above comments? How will you personally organize this exciting—but extremely complex—field? What sense do you make of the integrative approaches, such as those of Meichenbaum, Lazarus, and Ivey's, and of Developmental Counseling and Therapy? Would you place multicultural issues at the core of your theory, or will they be more peripheral? These are important questions that will define you as a professional. Not only will you be making these decisions; you will be asked to define the rationale for what you decide. You will be working with some very important people—interviewees, clients, and clients; using one or more of the following modalities of interventions:

1. Individual Interventions

   Counseling and therapy (drawing from First, Second, Third, Fourth and Fifth Forces or other major theoretical orientations)

   Helping clients fill basic needs for money, shelter, clothing

   Advocating and crisis intervention

   Medication

2. Family Interventions

   Family therapy and counseling

   Family education in parenting skills

   Marital counseling

   Divorce, legal issues

   Mediation

   Family support groups

3. Group Interventions

   Group counseling and encounter groups

   Multicultural consciousness-raising groups (women, African Americans, Vietnam vets)

   Self-esteem groups

   AA, ACOA, and other self-help groups

   Psychoeducational and skills training groups

   Peer counseling

4. Community Interventions

   Systems therapy

   Social justice initiatives

   Racism/oppression training

   Community action (organizing local government, church, and school groups)

   State and federal action and advocacy

Advocacy and social justice are important at all the levels of interventions listed above. Counselors and therapists strive to help the individual and its context (groups, community, society). They empower individuals, couples and groups to actively confront unfair situations, inequality, and injustice. They also advocate for equal access to resources and opportunities for all members of society as they understand the importance of fairness for health and wellbeing (Ratts & Pedersen, 2018). Factors such as barriers to access, racism, discrimination, and microaggressions are detrimental to the physical health and mental health of clients. All of these and other forms of oppression affect the individual clients and the bioecological systems they live in. Whether intentional or unintentional, oppression negatively affect the mental health of marginalized individuals and communities (Zalaquett & Chambers, 2017; Ratts & Pedersen, 2014).

Advocacy requires counselors and therapists to act at the individual (micro), community (meso), and public policy (macro) levels as outlined in the Advocacy Competencies document (Decker, Manis, & Paylo, 2016; Lewis, Arnold, House, & Toporek, 2002). Central to the Multicultural and Social Justice Counseling Competencies (MSJCC) is multicultural and social justice praxis (Ratts et al., 2016). Counselors and psychotherapists are called to integrate multiculturalism and social justice into their practices. Effectively balancing individual counseling with social justice advocacy is key to addressing the issues and challenges that individuals from marginalized populations bring to counseling. Work with your client to learn about their multicultural and social justice issues. Doing so will allow you to determine best level of intervention: individual level, community-wide level, or both.

The following summary of major theories presented in Table 13.2 is designed to help you work toward your own integration of counseling and psychotherapy theories.

**Table 13.2. Overview of Five Major Forces in Counseling and Psychotherapy Theory**

| Theoretical System and Relationship to Foundational Theories and Family Theory | Worldview | Major Concepts and Techniques |
| --- | --- | --- |
| *Multicultural Counseling and Therapy (The Fifth Force)* | | |
| Foundational theories (relational dimensions, microskills, decisional counseling, developmental counseling and therapy) explicitly and implicitly utilized as part of overall theoretical conception, but modified with cultural frames of reference. Systems and family therapy concepts considered essential. Bioecological models are central ingredients. | Counseling and therapy have been culturally encapsulated. The individual and family are based in the culture. The counselor or therapist needs to approach counseling with multicultural awareness. Many authors stress issues of development in the family and society. Seeks to integrate first-, second-, third-, and fourth force theories as part of worldview of counseling and therapy theory and case conceptualization. | As a major theoretical group, the main point of agreement is that issues of culture, gender, and other multicultural issues need to take a central place in the helping process. Collaboration and contextual treatment planning are essential. Consciousness raising about ethnicity/race and gender issues often critical in the helping process. Emphasis on self-awareness, knowledge, skills, and intentional action. |
| *Psychodynamic (The First Force)* | | |

*(Continued)*

**Table 13.2. Overview of Five Major Forces in Counseling and Psychotherapy Theory** *(Continued)*

| | | |
|---|---|---|
| Foundational theories not explicitly considered, but post-hoc examination shows that these concepts help explain the value of these orientations and makes their implementation more explicit. | The past is prelude to the present, and much of the past is held in the unconscious. Individuals are deeply influenced by the past, and we must understand this past if we are to facilitate individual growth. | These are the most complex set of theories available. The development of the person rests on early life experience. The interaction of person and environment is largely played out in the unconscious. |
| Family concepts not prominent, although attachment theory and the family unconscious are adding this emphasis. | Sigmund Freud is major philosopher. | Traditional Freudian theory emphasizes the Oedipal complex as central to development, whereas object relations and attachment theories focus on early infant and child experience as more important. |
| Historically, minimal attention to gender and multicultural issues. | The pragmatic and optimistic Bowlby stressed that we can facilitate growth through understanding and action. Taub-Bynum focused on family and cultural history playing themselves out in the individual. | Free association, dream analysis, and awareness of transference, countertransference, and projective identification are important. |

*Behavioral Theory Foundations (The Second Force)*

| | | |
|---|---|---|
| Foundational theories often integrated into understanding and planning treatment. Decisional counseling and social skills portion of microskills a standard part of counseling and therapy. Family concepts historically have not been important, but behavioral family approach illustrates how theory can be integrated. | Deeply rooted in the idea of progress and faith in science to solve human challenges. B. F. Skinner often seen as major philosopher.<br><br>More recent constructions such as Acceptance and commitment therapy provide a new integration of behaviorism with other theories. | Through functional analysis, it is possible to understand the antecedents, resultant behavior, and consequences of the behavior. From schedules of rewards, to token economy, to assertiveness training, many highly specific and proven techniques of behavioral change are available. |

*Existential/Humanistic/Experiential Theory Foundations (The Third Force)*

| | | |
|---|---|---|
| The foundational concepts of empathy and the listening portion of microskills have been derived from this orientation. | The human task is to find meaning in a sometimes meaningless world. | Each individual constructs the world uniquely. |
| Family concepts historically have not been important, but are compatible. Has not consciously embraced MCT but is compatible. | Rogers stresses the ability of the person to direct one's own life; Frankl, the importance of positive meanings; and Perls that people are wholes, not parts, and can take direction of their own lives.<br><br>Heidegger, Husserl, Binswanger, and Boss have been most influential at a basic philosophical level.<br><br>Rogers's person-centered theory.<br><br>Frankl's logotherapy.<br><br>Perls's Gestalt therapy. | Rogers stresses the importance of self-actualization and careful listening to the client.<br><br>Frankl emphasizes spirituality and a variety of specific techniques to facilitate the growth of meaning.<br><br>Perls, with his many powerful techniques, may be described as the action therapist. |

*(Continued)*

**Table 13.2. Overview of Five Major Forces in Counseling and Psychotherapy Theory** *(Continued)*

*Cognitive Theory Foundations (The Fourth Force)*

| | | |
|---|---|---|
| Foundational theories tend to be implicit rather than explicit. Cognitive aspects of developmental counseling and therapy may help integrate this framework more closely with MCT, particularly action at the sensorimotor and systemic level, which is often missing in CBT.<br><br>Family concepts historically have not been important, but are compatible. | Roots lie in stoic philosopher Epictetus—"We are disturbed not by events, but by the views we take of them.<br><br>Attempt to integrate ideas about the world with action in the world. Ellis's rational-emotive therapy. Beck's cognitive therapy. Meichenbaum's construction provides a new integration of behaviorism with other theories. He works on social skills training, stress inoculation, and anger management therapy.<br><br>Glasser's work is similar, but focuses very effectively on schools and youth in institutions.<br><br>Cheek supplies a culturally-relevant view. | Currently a popular theoretical orientation, as the system allows integration of many ideas from seemingly competing theories.<br><br>Major focus is on thinking patterns and their modification, but maintains a constant emphasis on homework and taking new ideas out into the world and acting on them. |

# Relapse Prevention

Change gained through therapy often disappears in the complexities of life after therapy unless change is planned. Although we may help clients feel less anxious via Rogerian therapy or by implementing assertiveness training, both techniques may fail if there is no plan for follow-up and treatment generalization. At this time, it may be useful to return to Chapter 8 and review the steps of relapse prevention.

Relapse prevention is a multidimensional, multimodal approach to maintaining human change. If we want to avoid relapse and therapeutic failure, we may have to work with families, schools, and other systems as well.

# Constructing Your Own View or Theory of Counseling and Psychotherapy

In preparation for therapeutic practice, it is important that you think through your own view of the helping process. This book has suggested you be familiar with multiple theoretical approaches and the skills and techniques of many orientations.

Despite this recommendation, we recognize that no one individual can do it all. However, a network of cooperating helping professionals indeed can do it all. Thus, it is also crucial that you define your own place in a network of counselors and therapists and assess how you can collaborate with these other professionals for the benefit of clients. In the following pages, you are asked to think about yourself and your own personal reactions to the many ideas presented in this book.

# Importance of Worldview

The construction you make of the helping process is derived from your worldview. Chapter 1 defines worldview as how you think the world works. A worldview is a theory about the nature of things. In turn, a theory may be described as a framework where you organize facts and their relationship one to another. Identifying your own worldview is critical to your role as a professional and your own integration of the helping field.

Narrative therapy challenges the traditional "objective" approach implicit in much of our traditional theory, maintaining that who you are determines your use of theory (Denborough, 2014; White & Epston, 1990). The objective approach means that we "objectively" select a theory, much as Paul (1967) suggests, and then apply it correctly to the client. Ahia (1991, 2005) argues for intersubjectivity, which may be defined as the awareness that we make our choices from often unconscious family and multicultural experience. Neuroscience names this a function of the default mode network (Ramirez, 2015). Intersubjectivity also implies that the therapist is sensitive to both his and her own and the client's family and multicultural selves.

The following exercises will help start the process of generating your own integrated approach. Personal Theory-building Exercise 13.1 provides questions that will help you evaluate yourself, your worldview, and your intersubjective thoughts and feelings about clients and yourself.

---

Thoery Personal Theory-building Exercise 13.1. **What Is Your Counseling and Therapy Worldview?**

The purpose of this concluding exercise is to ask you to consider your own construction of counseling and therapy.

What is important to you? Where do you stand? Where are you heading? How does your family and cultural history relate to these issues?

1. How do you view the goals of counseling and therapy?

   Client-centered theory focuses on self-actualization; behavioral theory, on behavioral change; psychodynamic theory, on awareness of unconscious forces; family theory, on an adequate family organization; feminist theory, an awareness of one's gender; multicultural theory, on becoming aware of how individual and family have been shaped and affected by the environment and history; and narrative therapy on the stories or narratives you create to make sense of your experiences.

   These are only a few of the types of goals offered by different theoretical orientations. Consider these and other personal goals and values of your own. What do you want to have happen for your clients in your work as a counselor and therapist? Write a statement of your values and convictions regarding the key goals and values you have for the helping process.

*(Continued)*

**Thoery Personal Theory-building Exercise 13.1.** **What Is Your Counseling and Therapy Worldview?** *(Continued)*

**2.** Where do your values and convictions come from? How were they derived? Do they come from reading this book? Or are they influenced by your own lifespan developmental process? How does your family, gender, and multicultural background affect your values?

  The key constructs in your worldview are generated in a gender, family, and multicultural context. Write a statement and discuss how your own lifespan development relates to your selection of worldview and goals.

**3.** Where might your worldview be limited with some of your clients? Given the vast array of multicultural experience you will encounter, what types of groups do you need to learn more about? What types of values and behaviors might give you difficulty?

  None of us can relate equally well with all clients. Write a statement describing areas where you need to learn more, and indicate some specific steps you plan to take to reach an expanded awareness.

**4.** What additional questions would you ask of yourself and others? The questions here are only the beginning of serious questioning on the nature of counseling and psychotherapy practice.

# You as an Integrative Theorist in a Multicultural World

Some might argue that it is impossible not to have a theory. But many of us need to look at ourselves, our values, and our competencies so we can make our implicit theories more explicit and understandable both to ourselves and others. This book argues that the task of the professional counselor and therapist is to know as many theories and techniques as possible—their similarities and differences—and to select from each theory concepts that are most helpful to the client.

Theories from your frame of reference, however, may not be enough. It is also important to enter and understand the client's world in a nonhierarchical, egalitarian fashion. We have suggested that rather than imposing a theory of your choice on clients, you may engage your clients as co-participants in this process, as more and more theorists and researchers suggest. Furthermore, it is your task to learn how your client constructs and makes sense of the world—to consider the nature of their meaning-making systems and the narratives they produce.

The theories in this book are only views—constructions of the world. Chapter 1 began with the Escher print *Relativity* that shows that there is no "right side up." By turning the print, you can gain a new view, a new way of thinking. There are many ways to view the print and to view "reality."

Similarly, we must recall that theory is simply description, a way to examine reality, a set of constructs. They are our maps, our stories about the world. If we become enmeshed in the belief that our theory of counseling and therapy is reality, then we enter an illusion. An illusory view of the world may be functional for you, but not for everyone.

You will likely encounter some people engaged in the practice of counseling and therapy who believe they have found the "truth," the "final answer," "the way" to conduct counseling and therapy. We suggest they are persons who have found stories that work for them and their clients. Of course, there are those who are like false prophets. However, as the authors of this book have learned over time, even false prophets sometimes present important, albeit partial, truths. Consequently, it is important to listen and learn and be willing to consider alternative perspectives of the world and of new theories.

For example, there was a time in the field when meditation was considered irrelevant and outside the range of counseling and psychotherapy practice. Meditation is now a standard technique in many stress management programs. Furthermore, mindful meditation is an effective practice for wellbeing, stress reduction, and the treatment of several psychological disorders. Similarly, issues of women's development and multicultural understanding were once considered to be peripheral and unimportant "fringe areas" of study. However, these areas have become central to our field. The lesson to be learned is: Beware of prophets proclaiming a new truth—they just may be right!

Personal Theory-building Exercise 13.2 provides a final exercise that asks you to review your own thinking about this book and organize its meaning in your own way.

---

**Personal Theory-building Exercise 13.2. Twelve Questions to Ask Yourself About Your Own Construction of the Counseling and Psychotherapy Process**

1. What is your overall worldview, and how does it relate to multicultural issues? Have you carefully elaborated your worldview and its implications for your future practice?

2. What are the central dimensions of your definition of ethical practice?

3. As you think about each of the empathic concepts, what is your personal construction of their meaning? What sense do you make of them?

4. With which microskills and concepts do you feel particularly comfortable and competent? Which have you already mastered, and do you need further work so they can actually be used in the interview?

5. How do you make sense of the focusing concept? How might you choose to focus your interventions? Can you focus on individuals, family context, and the multicultural surround?

6. What will be your position on research and keeping up with new ideas? How does learning about evidence-based practices fit here?

7. The relationship does matter. How are you going to implement what is known works in establishing and maintaining a positive relationship with your clients? Tailoring your approach to the uniqueness of the client with whom you are working increases effectiveness. So does Rogers's approach.

8. What is your understanding and integration of the challenge of multicultural counseling and therapy? What place will this Fifth Force of helping have in your mind and in your practice?

9. What theories of counseling and therapy appeal to you? What type of integration of these diverse theories are you moving toward? The book has attempted to stress that all theories are potentially valuable to some clients, but you are not expected to be immediately skilled in all.

   Learning theories in more depth is a life-long practice. Where do you personally plan to start, and what type of professional curriculum for further learning do you see for yourself in the future?

(Continued)

**Table 13.4. Twelve Questions to Ask Yourself About Your Own Construction of the Counseling and Psychotherapy Process (Continued)**

**10.** How are you planning to learn more about the neuroscience of counseling and therapy? How are you going to infuse this learning into your practices? Neuroscience and basic biological processes offer validation to what we do, but also help us learn about ways our interventions work. Lifestyle, health-related behaviors, mental and physical stress, and mental disorders can be alleviated more expeditiously if you understand the brain, body, and mind benefits of improvements in these systems.

**11.** How many of the practical counseling/clinical exercises presented in this book have you completed, and with what level of mastery? If you have engaged in practice exercises examining yourself and specific counseling skills, and in the practice of interviewing style using alternative theoretical approaches, you may have established a beginning "counseling portfolio" on which you can build in the future.

If you have approached this book from an experiential practice frame of reference, you have a more solid understanding than those who have chosen to read and think. Taking theory into practice and seeing if it "works" is where one truly integrates theory and skills and makes them part of one's being.

**12.** Have you examined how your personal developmental history in family and culture affects your answers to the above questions? It is critical that you constantly be able to reflect on yourself and how your personal history and present life issues affect your performance as a counselor or therapist.

The general or meta-theoretical position requires that each counselor or therapist develop her or his own conception of the counseling process and remain constantly open to change and examination. A student working through the draft of this book commented, "I think I've got the point. I find myself rewriting the book in my own way. I use some of it, but ultimately the book I am rewriting in my head is mine, my own general theory that is similar in some ways to the book, but in other ways very different."

We hope that you will rewrite this book and use it authentically in your own way.

At the same time, we hope that you will extend that same privilege to your clients.

How might they seek to help you rewrite and reconstrue your constructions of counseling and therapy? Counseling and therapy are very much about listening and learning—for all of us as therapists and for our clients as well.

# References

Ahia, C.E. (1991, October). *Enhanced therapeutic skills: Family and ethnic dynamics, Part I.* Paper presented at the North Atlantic Association for Counselor Education and Supervision, Albany, NY.

Ahia, C.E. (2005). A cultural framework for counseling African-Americans. In C. Lee et al., *Multicultural issues in counseling: New approaches to diversity* (3rd edition). ACA Press (Chapter 5).

American Psychological Association. (2012). *Recognition of psychotherapy effectiveness.* Retrieved from http://www.apa.org/about/policy/resolution-psychotherapy.aspx.

Boswell, J.F., Kraus, D.R., Miller, S.D., & Lambert, M.J. (2015). Implementing routine outcome monitoring in clinical practice: Benefits, challenges, and solutions. *Psychotherapy Research, 25,* 6–19. doi:10.1080/10503307.2013.817696.

Chow, D.L., Miller, S.D., Seidel, J.A., Kane, R.T., Thornton, J.A., & Andrews, W.P. (2015). The role of deliberate practice in the development of highly effective psychotherapists. *Psychotherapy, 52,* 337–345. doi:10.1037/pst0000015.

Cummings, N. (1988). Emergence of the mental health complex: Adaptive and maladaptive responses. *Professional Psychology, 19,* 308–315.

Decker, K.M., Manis, A.A., & Paylo, M.J. (2016). Infusing social justice advocacy into counselor education: strategies and recommendations. *The Journal of Counselor Preparation and Supervision, 8*(3). http://dx.doi.org/10.7729/83.1092.

Denborough, D. (2014). *Retelling the stories of our lives: Everyday narrative therapy to draw inspiration and transform experience.* New York, NY: Norton.

Lazarus, A. (1981). *The practice of multimodal psychotherapy.* New York, NY: McGraw-Hill.

Lazarus, A. (1986). Multimodal therapy. In J. Norcross (Ed.), *Handbook of eclectic psychotherapy.* New York, NY: Brunner/Mazel.

Lewis, J., Arnold, M.S., House, R., & Toporek, R.L. (2002). *Advocacy competencies: Task Force on Advocacy Competencies.* Alexandria, VA: American Counseling Association.

Miller, S., Hubble, M., & Duncan, B. (2008). Supershrinks: What is the secret of their success? *Psychotherapy in Australia, 14* (4), 14–22.

Miller, S., Bargmann, S., Chow, D., Seidel, J., & Maeschalck, C. (2016). Feedback-informed treatment (FIT): Improving the outcome of psychotherapy one person at a time. In W. O'Donohue & A. Maragakis (Eds.), *Quality improvement in behavioral health* (pp. 247–262). Switzerland: Springer International.

Norcross, J.C. (2011). *Conclusions and recommendations of the interdivisional (APA divisions 12 & 29) task force on evidence-based therapy relationships.* Retrieved from http://societyforpsychotherapy.org/evidence-based-therapy-relationships/.

Paul, G. (1967). Strategy of outcome research in psychotherapy. *Journal of Consulting Psychology, 31,* 109–118.

Phipps, W. D., & Vorster, C. (2015). Refiguring family therapy: Narrative therapy and beyond. *The Family Journal, 23*(3), 254-261.

Ramirez, D. (2015). *Default mode network (DMN): Structural connectivity, impairments and role in daily activities.* New York, NY: Nova Science Publishers.

Ratts, M.J., & Pedersen, P.B. (2014). *Counseling for multiculturalism and social justice.* Alexandria, VA: American Counseling Association.

Ratts, M.J., Singh, A.A., Nassar-McMillan, S., Butler, S.K., & McCullough, J.R. (2016). Multicultural and social justice counseling competencies: Guidelines for the counseling profession. *Journal of Multicultural Counseling and Development, 44,* 28–48. doi:10.1002/jmcd.12035.

Seidel, J.A., Andrews, W.P., Owen, J., Miller, S.D., & Buccino, D.L. (2017). Preliminary validation of the rating of outcome scale and equivalence of ultra-brief measures of well-being. *Psychological Assessment, 29,* 65–75. doi:10.1037/pas000031.

Wampold, B.E. (2015). How important are the common factors in psychotherapy? An update. *World Psychiatry, 14,* 270–277.

White M., & Epston, D. (1990). *Narrative means to therapeutic ends.* New York, NY: W.W. Norton.

Zalaquett, C.P., & Chambers, A.L. (2017). Introduction to the special issue: Counseling individuals living in poverty. *Journal of Multicultural Counseling and Development, 45,* 152–161. doi:10.1002/jmcd.12071.

# Credits

Tab. 13.1: Bruce E. Wampold, "Fourteen Qualities and Actions of Effective Counselors and Psychotherapists," https://www.apa.org/education/ce/effective-therapists.pdf. Copyright © by Bruce E. Wampold. Reprinted with permission.

# INDEX

CPSIA information can be obtained
at www.ICGtesting.com
Printed in the USA
FSHW022040120121
77632FS